THE COMPLETE
OUTSIDER

THE COMPLETE
OUTSIDER

ALWAYS ALMOST:
NEVER QUITE

BRIAN SEWELL

QUARTET BOOKS

Outsider was first published in 2011 by Quartet Books Limited
Outsider II was first published in 2012 by Quartet Books Limited
A member of the Namara Group
27 Goodge Street, London, W1T 2LD

This paperback edition published in 2019 by Quartet Books Limited

A catalogue record for this book is available from the British Library

ISBN 9780704374645

Offset by Tetragon, London
Printed and bound in Great Britain by TJ International Ltd, Padstow, Cornwall

Contents

FOREWORD BY NAIM ATTALLAH   VII

OUTSIDER

ACKNOWLEDGEMENTS   XIII

PRELUDE   XV

1   *Mother*   I

2   *Father*   17

3   *Stepfather*   24

4   *School*   36

5   *Intermezzo*   57

6   *National Service as a Squaddie*   71

7   *National Service as a Subaltern*   91

8   *The Courtauld Institute*   108

9   *Student Life*   123

10   *A Second Intermezzo: 1957–1958*   159

11   *Christie's in 1958*   197

12   *Further Misgivings at Christie's*   225

13   *Abandoning God*   256

14   *Christie's in the Doldrums*   267

15   *Dénouement*   304

   Coda   337

OUTSIDER II

ACKNOWLEDGEMENTS   343

1 *Introduction*   345

2 *Scratching a Living*   350

3 *Return to Kensington*   380

4 *Salvador Dali in Cadaques*   394

5 *Joseph McCrindle*   411

6 *The Seventies*   421

7 *Turkey*   437

8 *The Blunt Affair*   461

9 *The Aftermath of the Affair*   492

10 *The Evening Standard*   523

11 *The Venomous Critic*   547

12 *Mother*   561

13 *Heart Attacks*   576

14 *Television*   583

15 *Loose Ends*   595

16 *Death*   614

INDEX   621

Foreword

'Of course I'm resigned to oblivion. The great book on Michelangelo is not written. It won't be on anybody's shelf. That is the only afterlife I should have liked, to have written that book, and I now know I shan't. I suspect I shall die in harness with the *Evening Standard*, scribbling ephemera. And the book won't be there.'

These words,[1] the last comments printed in my interview with Brian Sewell conducted back in the last century, were not entirely destined to be accurate. True, there was no book on a great Renaissance hero, but there were two classic volumes of autobiography, which deserve to be ranked alongside the finest memoirs of recent times and reprinted here as one volume.

I learnt about the project first from a mention in 'The Londoner's Diary' in the then *Evening Standard* by Sebastian Shakespeare, saying publishers had been rejecting Brian's first volume of memoirs, doing the rounds from his literary agent, the mightily respected Toby Eady. Shakespeare could not understand why there was any problem in publishing them. Nor could I, and immediately telephoned Brian at his Wimbledon house requesting I arrange for an immediate collection of the manuscript. I read it that weekend and we had arranged to publish it with Quartet by the following Monday.

That Christmas, it was a bestseller, garlanding impressive reviews and Brian willingly attending signing sessions in Hatchard's, appearances at literary festivals and much else in the hurly-burly which is now considered legitimate book promotion – and all with a minimum of fuss. Evening events might need a minicab home, but

---

1 The interview with Brian Sewell is reprinted in *No Longer With Us: Encounters with Naim Attallah* (Quartet Books, 2018)

afternoon or morning activities were usually got to by buses from Wimbledon – a transport hub with seemingly endless possibilities. He began work on his second volume immediately and delivered an almost perfect manuscript six months after the publication of the first volume. It was published with equal success.

He had a certain reputation: waspish, disrespectful of women artists, highly critical of many successful modern painters and always could be relied upon to make caustic remarks at will on radio programmes or in newspaper interviews. Yet I was to find him the most gentle, kind and considerate of men, quite the opposite of his public persona. We were to become close friends. He even told me he thought of Quartet as his family. And we were honoured to publish other work; a book about his beloved dogs, a charming fable about a fragile donkey, a definitive anthology of his critical writings on modern British artists, even a collection of his more radical political pieces – he was, after all, a recipient of the prestigious Orwell Prize.

One incident must suffice to indicate just what an exceptional person Brian was. A time came when his considerable earnings from royalties were causing us horrendous cash-flow problems. I went to see him – his cancer was beginning to bite – to tell him I needed his banking details as I intended to pay him in monthly stages as and when Quartet's finances allowed. He refused and insisted I must pay him when I could. I objected, demanding his payment details. His imperious rejection, though warmly given, was followed by a letter from him confirming his wishes. Even though, a few months later, Quartet was able to honour the debt, he checked to see if we really could afford it.

It's become a cliché to recall those who pass on as wonderful, unique or truly missed, but in the absence of Brian, I cannot think of any words more truthful.

NAIM ATTALLAH

OUTSIDER

For Gillon Aitken, without whose
persistent persuasion for twenty
years, this book would not, at last,
have been written.

Acknowledgements

Grudgingly I must confess my dependence on my mother's diaries as well as my own. She was so indefatigable a recorder of our lives against the larger background of events that I know, for example, and knew at the time, that as we were walking from Whitstable to Seasalter on 3 October 1935, Mussolini's armies were pouring over the border from Eritrea into Abyssinia; how many other small boys had the name Haile Selassie on their lips that day, I wonder. She also kept letters – my stepfather's, from which I was to learn how extended and warm his wooing was, and mine when in the Army or away exploring Europe, have lent accuracy to recollection. As I have outlived most of my contemporaries and all my early friends, her diligence and hoarding have been invaluable. So too have been the corrections proffered by Keith Cheyney, the archivist of Haberdashers – the more generous for knowing how much I loathed the school. At Christie's another archivist, Lynda McCleod, seems always to have been amused by my requests for help, as though uncovering ancient history is fun; and Noël Annesley too, doffing his importance there, has generously reverted to his earliest role as my assistant. From below stairs, as it were, Ray Perman and John White remembered things appalling and hilarious of which, at the time I did not know, and our tripartite conversations brought a little helpless laughter into John's life as cancer inexorably shortened it; Ray, I hope, will one day write an unofficial history of the underbelly of the firm. I have also had vital, enthusiastic and unstinting assistance from Malcolm Rudland, musician extraordinary and Secretary of the Peter Warlock Society.

Prelude

Michelangelo's autobiography, dictated to his pupil and amanuensis Ascanio Condivi, is not a work of fiction, but of adjustment and correction, a rebuke, as it were, to Giorgio Vasari, his admirer and first biographer, who had in a number of small things offended him – with, for example, suggestions of arrogance, avarice and homosexuality. When, in my last years at school, I read Condivi's account, I took it to be the truth, but as a student at the Courtauld Institute learned that it was not – at least not quite, but was instead as Michelangelo wished the truth to be. This was a warning to be sceptical with the texts of all who write of their own lives.

The nagging to write of mine began some ten years after the Blunt Affair of 1979. 'You must write your autobiography,' said strangers – but these were strangers who had a vested interest in that event and thought that there were facts still to be revealed and spies and quislings still to be unmasked. When friends joined the chorus of demand it was because they thought my recollections of a decade or so in the employ of Christie's, that historic saleroom of the arts, too amusing to be lost and already at risk after a heart attack that had all but killed me and left the organ damaged and erratic. On Anthony Blunt, the friend who had guided so much of my life and even whose last full day was spent giving me a tutorial, so to speak, on drawings by Nicholas Poussin and his imitators, I felt unready to say more; on Christie's I felt that I could not yet tell the truth of my love-hate relationship with the firm without bruising the heels of those who were once my enemies there; and there were, moreover, other matters on which I felt unable to be open, yet if I did not tell the whole truth it would not be truth at all.

On these last, approaching my eightieth year and old enough to be neither embarrassed nor ashamed, I no longer feel the need for reticence. I was the victim of circumstances that used to matter much, but now much less or not at all; they mattered in the Thirties into which I was born and in the Fifties when I was a young man – then I was constrained by the sensibilities of others and governed by the discreet conventions of the day, but in all but one their mattering faded as I grew older and society less hidebound. The exception was the elusive identity, character and temperament of my father which, as my mother, the only living person who knew the truth, grew older, became for me an obsession, the need to know a torment. I am now wholeheartedly in sympathy with those who, adopted, seek their biological parents, and am convinced that nothing should be allowed to impede them. To the question 'Who is my father?' his name and whereabouts must be the immediate answer. I knew only that mine was dead. Now that I know a great deal more of him I am amused by the coincidences of our natures and abilities. If this book was written for anyone, it was for the handful of readers who have shared the anguish and longing of the rootless child.

Writing it has not been easy. I have been both analyst and patient. Decades too late the analyst has at last realised the reasons for so much that happened to the fool – too trusting, too naive, too influenced by his mother's instructions that he should never shake the tree but wait till the ripe fruit falls. If only she had taught him to be pushy, to dissemble, to tell only the considered truth, his life might have been more successful, whether as art historian or scribbler; but she brought him up in the arms of the Roman Catholic church and taught him to be frank (too frank too often) and truthful. Well into the second decade after her death she is still my principal demon, the only one who still affects my life; for much of her legacy I am grateful; at the rest of it I shudder. I have dug deep into indiscretion and some may say that I have dug deeper into prurience; perhaps I have, but again it is for the benefit of readers who are troubled by their private natures and feel that they alone are driven so.

Prelude

I have no doubt that many who admire me – my 'doting elderlies,' as an old woman friend once dubbed them – will be disgusted. So be it – truth is nothing if not whole. From that friend, Mary Debbane, with whom for many years I walked my dogs early every morning, I had no secrets and she was never shocked; the guardian of my sanity in the worst moments of my later life, she is now dead, but she heard it all before she went.

CHAPTER I

Mother

My earliest recollection of my mother is of my looking down on her and recognising fear. I have no memory of looking up at her, of seeing the bodyless head in which analysts who bother themselves with the earliest artistic impulses of the child would have us believe, the great smiling face of the adult looming over the cradle or the pram, but looking down from the not inconsiderable height of an overhanging branch has stayed with me all my life, not because of the adventure of climbing there – that I remember not at all – but for the startling clarity of a powerful emotion that I had never seen before and did not comprehend. The tree still stands in the garden of Cefn Bryntalch, an unlovely Victorian house in Powys recently described by agents selling it as 'innovative for its use of Neo-Georgian style which is worked into the expressive forms of brick vernacular revival' (house agents rival art critics in the meaningless jargon of their propaganda). The stout trunk of the tree bifurcates at ground level, the lesser part leaning at a shallow angle, forty-five degrees or so, over a slope; nothing could have been easier for a toddling infant to climb – and it is so still – but within a few feet, because of the slope below, the drop is perilous. Because I did not understand my mother's fear I could not share it, and was quite content to be where I was when she left me to fetch the gardener, who climbed a ladder, slung me over his shoulder and put me down in safety.

My other early memory of her is the day when, standing in the bath, waiting to be lifted from it and wrapped in a towel, there was a long, long, pause, and then she said, quite ruminatively, 'Just think, you might have been a little Indian boy.' And so I might, I suppose, for she had had an affair with the Maharajah of Kutch and had tales to tell of that benighted Indian province, its windblown heat, its barren sandy wastes and its Great Rann, a salt morass into which its rivers squander rains so rare that they betray the seasons. 'The poorest Maharajah in India,' she said of him, describing the palace in Mandvi, 'but very beautiful.' Was he really the Maharajah, I wonder now, or just a member of the princely family? She could not endure the heat and wind, she said, and less still the other women, and after some months returned to England. In 1994 a television company that specialised in travel programmes asked me if there was anywhere off the beaten track that I would like to go. 'Kutch,' I replied at once, surprising them with my immediacy, 'to the Great Rann, the desert, the inland mountains and the palace at Mandvi, if it still stands.' The researchers, however, typical of all who work in television, misinterpreting a relief atlas in which borders were not distinguished by political colours, took Kutch to be in Pakistan and set about getting permits and visas to film in that country instead of India; too late they discovered their error and we went to the North-West Frontier and thereabouts instead.

My mother had other adventures. She had been to Sarawak at the invitation of some member of the Brooke family, perhaps Charles Vyner Brooke, the last of the so-called White Rajas of the territory, for she maintained a sparse correspondence with him until his death in 1963. She had been engaged to an army officer stationed in the Malay States, as the federated provinces of the Malay Peninsula were then called, but, on finding the climate there intolerable, she broke it off. She had had a more romantic, more emotionally lasting affair with a young man from an Anglo–Chilean family named Bushell in Santiago (I think without going there) who died of tuberculosis, but with whose mother she remained in touch until the outbreak of war in 1939. And she spent enough time in Paris to know it as least as well as she knew London.

Though born in Dublin in 1900, most of her girlhood had been spent in Hampstead, where her father, who had made something of a fortune in developing cinemas, had a house in Fitzjohn's Avenue. Educated at home, with no thought that she might one day have to support herself, she learned to play the violin and cello, later passing her violin to me but continuing with the cello until arthritis crippled her fingers – both instruments, particularly the cello, were very good. She also had some talent in painting and modelling, but her wish to become a student at the Slade School was frustrated by her father, precipitating her first break with him. She joined the workshop of George Frampton, a Royal Academician described in his day as 'Highly accomplished and firmly based on the true principles of his art', and claimed to have played some small part in his marble and granite memorial to Edith Cavell in St Martin's Place – but it must have been very small indeed, for she was only twenty when it was erected and she can never have had the muscles or the technical skill to work in stone. I suspect that she merely coincided with, rather than worked on, what is at best a very dull monument, but being there, perhaps only making tea, was enough to engender her belief that she had contributed to its making. I know only that, holding her hand as a small boy, it was the sculpture at which I was compelled to gaze more frequently than any other.

She then served some sort of apprenticeship with a now forgotten painter of portraits, William Bruce Ellis Ranken (1881–1941), of whose work I have inherited a trophy dated 1923, a large drawing of a nude; it is not, alas, of my mother. This I think came to a disagreeable end, probably sexual if I can judge from her angry response to my probing. She was then taken on by Kate Ruskin Coughtrie, a painter and sculptor so obscure as to be omitted from all works of reference, but who taught her to paint moderately well and to model figures in terracotta – which my mother continued to do late into her life, vaguely in the manners of Rodin and Dalou. Of her early attempts nothing survives – only the ghost of it in the Elfin Oak in Kensington Gardens. This, the stump of an ancient oak in Richmond Park, was first carved with animals and fairy-tale figures by Ivor Inness (another forgotten sculptor) in 1911; by the late Twenties it had fallen into disrepair because the painted figures were as much modelled in Barbola paste as carved, and Barbola, though inherently resistant to water, nevertheless deteriorated if not painted and the paint renewed every five years or so. When, in 1930, the Oak was removed to Kensington Gardens, it was my mother who assisted Innes with the essential repairs, remodelling the deteriorated figures, again in Barbola, one entirely her invention; there was a second restoration after the war, but the next period of neglect was so long – half a century or so – that when they were at last restored again, at the whim of Spike Milligan in 1997, Barbola was no longer in production and the very damaged figures were fully-carved for the first time by craftsmen who knew nothing of their earlier history.

It was through Coughtrie that my mother encountered Sickert, whom she described as an unkempt and smelly old man with a sharp wit. 'Do come again when you need not stay so long,' she thought a fine thing to say to an unwanted visitor, and used it herself until her dying day. Fitzjohn's Avenue is not much more than spitting distance from Camden Town and Mornington Crescent, and I suspect that my post-war boyhood memories of the area, of Bowman's – a furniture shop with aspirations akin to those of Heal's to lead their clientele into the world of Modernism – and to the Bedford Theatre to see Wolfit playing Lear in a Shakespeare season and, later, his astonishingly ham interpretation of Mathias in The Bells, were inspired by her wish to give me, by proxy, a share in events and an atmosphere that she had years before enjoyed.

Through Coughtrie too, there was some contact with relics of Roger Fry's collapsed Omega Workshops, one of whom, a Miss Quayle (known only as Quaylie), had continued the ragged end of the business from a couple of first floor rooms in Dover Street; she was later to prove a stout friend, offering my mother occasional employment in the miserable post-Depression days of the earlier 1930s.

If any of this suggests a young woman of high seriousness, then that is a grave error. My mother had an allowance from her father, and one dress that survived until her death – probably because, as a very short flapper-cum-charleston dress in heavy silver thread, it could not be re-fashioned – was made by Worth and fetched £3,000 at Christie's, suggesting that the allowance had been generous. With boy friends equally comfortably off, she knew the Café Royal, the Café de Paris, snorted cocaine, learned to drive on some young man's Lanchester and had, I think, as much sexual restraint as an alley cat. Put very simply, the Twenties were a decade in which she wantonly enjoyed herself – until she met my father and became pregnant.

For a devout Roman Catholic girl in 1930 – or rather woman, for she was always as old as the twentieth century – this was an appalling problem. My father's solution was to pay for an abortion, as he had in other brief and casual affairs, but this my mother could not accept. She had by then quarrelled so often with her father that she would not turn to him for help, nor to her mother whom she knew would do exactly as she was told; an aunt in Dublin, after whom she had been named, came to her rescue in some small way, and so too did my father's mother, a doughty woman of considerable wealth who, in the first two or three years of my life, let us spend time in her house in Wales (hence the tree-climbing episode that is my earliest memory) and later gave my mother a very small allowance. For this there were several conditions: that the sum, in cash, was to be collected monthly from her solicitor's offices at 5, Norfolk Street, just off the Strand, that I was always to accompany my mother, and that the identity of my father was never to be disclosed to me. The allowance ceased when my mother married my stepfather in 1942 and my grandmother then made a new will in which no further provision of any kind was made for me. In effect, I was wiped from the family's history.

As soon as I was old enough to ask questions, our visits to Cefn

Bryntalch ceased. My grandmother had a grandson, Nigel, born in July 1917, fourteen years my senior and legitimate – though only by the skin of teeth, for the immature and unstable marriage of his parents took place after he was born. He had hardly ever seen his father and as his mother had deserted them, his grandmother had become responsible for his welfare and education and these took precedence over any needs that I, illegitimate, might have. It must be difficult now, well into the next century, for anyone to understand how sullying was the stigma of illegitimacy to both mother and child in 1931, the year of my birth. The blood relationships of the child were far less important than his legitimacy, and if this was not established by marriage, preferably before the event, then the child might well be taken from his mother's arms and despatched to those of adoptive parents or to the anonymity of the orphanage. The unmarried mother was without status; she dropped to the bottom of society's heap and her child might, for ever, be similarly marked for life with a birth certificate that betrayed him, denied him education, profession and, certainly, inheritance.

My grandmother, enough of a socialite to appear in the auto-biography of Kenneth Clark – he of *Civilisation* – would never have wanted any of her friends and peers to know of an illegitimate grandchild. She had, as it were, adopted my half-brother Nigel because my immature and irresponsible father had, almost six months after his birth, married his mother – a girl to whom he was soon referring as a vampire. Delayed it may have been, but it was legitimacy enough for our grandmother to settle on him a private income within months of the marriage and his abandonment by both parents. The difference between us was that by the time I was born, my father had committed suicide and there was thus no possibility of my being made legitimate by a *post partum* marriage.

In 1934 my mother's mother and Aunt Jessica both died, my mother's father having refused all reconciliation to the point of not informing her of either death, and there remained no hope of support, emotional, familial or financial other than the tiny monthly stipend from my father's mother, whom we never saw or communicated with again. We lived in ill-furnished rooms in basements and attics, a few weeks here, a few more there, some of which we left in the middle of the night, whisper quiet, tip-toe treading, wearing as much of our clothing as we could, not bundled against the cold, but for easier carrying, the rent unpaid. We lived – the word suggests some continuity, but this was true only in the wider sense of staying in more or less the same area for years – at worst in Shepherd's Bush, at best, from my point of view because both were so near the Gardens, in middle Kensington and Notting Hill. These, in the 1930s, hard hit by the Great Depression, were more run down than we can now imagine, the houses rarely painted and even the most respectable rarely without lodgers; spare rooms in Eldon Road, where I was eventually to buy a house and live for thirty years, were before and after the Second World War much occupied by the lesser curators of departments at the Victoria and Albert Museum.

My mother may have been something of a prostitute. This is putting it too baldly, but it is the only way in which I can explain why, throughout years of pinching penury, she kept her evening dresses in repair, often undertaking considerable alterations to keep them fashionable, dismantling them to recut the pattern and sewing them together again on a hand-turned Singer sewing machine. She kept her looks too. In her thirties, slim on her near-starvation diet, tall but small-boned, with a fine skin and an exquisitely pale complexion enhanced by rich brown hair, although she always affected a tragic air, subtly shadowing the sockets of her large dark eyes, she looked a decade younger; on the street, with her long legs and stride, men turned their heads for her. When she wore her evening dresses, she looked wonderful.

Always on these occasions Tilly came to stay – Tilly, who never removed her black cloche hat, Tilly who, when bathing me, would never wash me 'down there' (a working-class inhibition, I suppose), but soaped the flannel and then threw it at my stomach with an exultant 'There's a slap in the belly with a wet fish!' Tilly took me to Shepherd's Bush Market to see, standing on wooden crates to give them height amidst the stalls of fruit and vegetables, hucksters selling remedies for almost every common illness of the belly and the skin, constipation, diarrhoea, duodenal ulcers, afflictions of the liver, kidneys and urinary systems, shingles and eczema – this last the most dramatic, for it involved painting the skin in patches of brilliant gentian violet as frightening as any of the disfiguring strawberry birthmarks that were then a common sight. Most haunting of all, wandering among the stalls but selling nothing, was a man in a flat cap that, though ordinary enough in front, was hugely enlarged at the back to contain a monstrous growth on his skull and neck. He was, said Tilly, living on the money paid him in advance by the local hospital in exchange for his body when he died – but then she paid him a penny to doff the cap and show me the pale blue-veined monstrosity that lay beneath.

It was there too that I first heard the word 'bugger' and, some-how instinctively knowing that it was taboo, treasured it until my mother took me to have tea with an old Russian woman who lived in the gloomy basement of a house in Redcliffe Gardens – a White Russian, said my mother, lending a mysterious gloss to the exotic business of being Russian as she outlined the history of the Revolution as though it were a saga or romance. Paris, I then learned, had been full of wonderful White Russians when she lived there in the Twenties. Mrs Frangopoulo, having married a Greek merchant, had been fortunate enough to escape from Leningrad with more than her skin. She had a samovar and entertained me with small black velvet bags from which, having loosened the double-drawstrings, she withdrew her toys, wrapped in scraps of silk, chamois, or crumpled tissue paper – dumpy little animals, smooth and glistening in chalcedony, obsidian and agate (I was enchanted by these names), and a tiny vase of precious jewelled flowers that profoundly disappointed me, when, having been told that these delicate trifles would tremble if I breathed on them, I found that they did so only if given something of a thump. Even now I view the treasures of Carl Fabergé with scepticism rather than delight.

How did my mother know Mrs Frangopoulo? Perhaps through some White Russian contact in Paris. How did she know Paul Nash, with whom one early summer in my life, at four or five, I walked along Lulworth Cove and was given a stone with a hole through it that he found on the beach; how did she know Eric Ravilious and why did she choose, in the 1950s, to buy a house in the village, Castle Hedingham, in which he had lived twenty years before; and how did she know William Coldstream well enough to send me to him for tuition and assessment when I thought that I wanted to become a painter? These three and other artists she could easily have encountered in her years on the fringe of Fitz-rovia, as it were, but what possible reason could there be for her knowing Magda Lypescu, first the mistress and then the morganatic wife of Carol II of Rumania? They were in Paris concurrently between 1928 and 1930 and must have established something of an acquaintance then. King Carol was in London on a state visit in 1938, and while the streets of London on a cold and damp November day were lined with crowds entertained to see two kings in an open carriage, my mother and I were having tea in Madame Lypescu's suite in, I think, the Savoy. Again my mother had to explain matters – the word morganatic (wonderful to a boy of seven, with all its implications), and the fact that while Carol was in Buckingham Palace, his mistress was not far away if he wished to come and see her. It was not all that she explained. Madame Lypescu was a heavy woman wearing an ankle-length dress, the colour an intense dark emerald, the material silk, a heavy lustrous taffeta slippery to the touch – and touch it I did, for at one point she bade me climb onto her lap (not an activity that I much cared for, thinking myself too old for such toddler nonsense), and over the slippery cliffs of her thighs the climbing was not easy; I preferred to stand beside her and let her run her fingers through my curls. It was then that I became aware of a confusing smell, both enthralling and repellant. My mother's response to my question, later, was that King Carol forbade Madame Lypescu to bathe too often and that what had so intrigued me was the combination of expensive perfumes with her natural body odour. Once in a while over many years since, when required to squeeze the obstructed anal glands of a beloved bitch, I have been overwhelmingly reminded of tea in the Savoy.

The one element of stability in my haphazard childhood was the cottage in Whitstable to which we often retreated for months on end. Much altered now, its front door then opened onto the narrow street leading to the harbour, along which, in the middle of the day, walked a woman with a basket covered by a white napkin, crying 'Hot pies, hot pies!' Never once did we buy one. Within the front door was the living room; to the left lay the small bedroom, and beyond lay a steep step down into the kitchen in an open plan of sorts, through the rear window of which I could clamber straight onto the shingle beach; there was no bathroom and the lavatory was at the end of a short passage open to the skies. In summer, that it had no bathroom hardly mattered, for we had the sea – my mother swam like a fish and I was so much accustomed to it that my skin glistened with salt; in winter, a zinc bath that hung in the passage to the loo had to be hauled in and filled with water boiled in saucepans and kettles. My mother bathed in my stale water. I learned to wash her back. I became accustomed to her nakedness. It was a useful preparation for the privations of the war.

How we lived – in the sense of paying bills – I do not know. There was enough money to buy bottles of the cherry brandy with which my mother occasionally drugged me to sleep before leaving the cottage for purposes I never knew, and at some point we acquired Prince, a tall white dog with long black ears, whose job it was to guard me. I was sometimes sent to the harbour when the fishing boats came in, to see if, with the sixpence in my hand, I could buy enough fish for dinner and sometimes the fishermen gave me fish too small to sell. I do not remember being hungry, as I do in the periods of intense rationing during and immediately after the war, but nor can I recall anything resembling a birthday treat or Christmas feast, and I suspect that my taste for scrag ends and hocks, for offal, necks and the heads of animals was founded then.

In the winter, facing north, Whitstable could be bitterly cold, and once in a while the sea was silenced by the ice that stilled it, the familiar beach then eerie; then we lived all day in the tiny kitchen, dressed and undressed there, and going to the bedroom was an arctic adventure. The kitchen table was the centre of our lives; on it we both drew and painted and I constructed cardboard castles and stage sets for the tales we read. And the tales? – tales re-told for a child from the Old Testament and the New, from Greek mythology, from Shakespeare and the Arthurian legends, from jiggety Longfellow's Hiawatha and the Wayside Inn, and tales of the origins of stars; what could be more magical than lying flat on our backs on the deserted beach, staring at the night sky, listening to my mother speak of the ancient origins of the Great Bear and the Milky Way? I did not know at the time, and nor did she, that so much of this tale-telling would prove to be a sure foundation for me as an art historian.

Winter and summer we walked to Tankerton and Swale Cliff in one direction and in the other to Seasalter – which I much preferred, for in one of the meadows that we crossed was a discarded, wheel-less, railway carriage in which an old man lived, almost always leaning from one of the windows that were raised and dropped by a broad leather strap, hoping to offer tea to any passer-by who might spend five minutes gossiping. That snug carriage with its smoking stove, worn rugs and collapsing furniture, its smell of coal, tobacco and bacon, was nearer the lives of Mole, Ratty and Badger in the *Wind in the Willows* than to the chill realities of Whitstable, and it was my first experience of envy.

All my memories of Whitstable are fragmentary and disordered, but still sharp. A boy with whom I occasionally played, who lived in a nearby house with a balcony that overhung the beach, jumped from it to show how impossible it was to hurt oneself on shingle – we had just been jumping from breakwaters – and broke a leg; his scream, the shattered limb – his left foot had landed on a sawn-off post beneath the shingle – and the never seeing him again have stayed with me. At the end of the High Street there was a horse trough in which a drunken, old and (as I was later to know) very bad local landscape painter, Dan Sherrin, occasionally chose to lie on hot summer afternoons until sober enough to walk home. Red-sailed barges plying close to the steeply shelving beach at high tide were a constant excitement, and once a year the summer regattas at West Beach were the great event, for in these there were races for six-oared gigs (the rowing boats towed by sailing vessels), for yachts and yawls, and the three-man randan in which the middle rower pulls a pair of sculls and the rowers fore and aft a single oar. Of the swimming races the most thrilling was the greasy pole to which young men swam, then to climb it for the prize of a leg of mutton presented – at least for the regatta of 1938 – by Mr Hadler, the butcher in Harbour Street. The circus too was a summer event, Lord John Sanger's great tent erected on Whitstable Salts, a meadow just to the west of the town, where, among the giant sea-lions and midget ponies, horse-riding monkeys and untameable lions, the star turn in 1937 was Jumbo 'the Elephant Goal-Getter', who challenged the champion goal-kicker of the Whitstable Football Club.

Beyond the town there were jaunts by bus to Faversham and Canterbury. Faversham in winter was extraordinarily bleak; facing north across the Swale to the Isle of Sheppey, the flat land barely above sea level, there was nothing in the view, but my mother made me look at it and see something in its straight horizontal lines, the drab greys and drabber browns, the wide leaden skies and the expanse of white when snow had fallen. 'It's like Siberia,' she said, and told me a little more of Russian history; and ever since, Siberia – to which neither of us ever travelled, though Omsk,

Tomsk and Irkutsk were then engraved on my brain – has for me been Faversham, extended, expanded, magnified. Canterbury and its cathedral, on the other hand, made no lasting impression.

It was on one of these jaunts that we saw pickers harvesting hops and got off the bus to look at them. In retrospect I am sure that this must have been at my insistence, for to have done so seems entirely alien to my mother's nature. In those hopfields we glimpsed a world of poverty and privation of which I knew nothing, and yet I envied these Eastenders down from the slums of London for an annual holiday, the fathers paid a pittance to climb tall ladders and strip the vines of hops, the women cooking over open fires, the children running wild, and all of them living and sleeping in the ramshackle lean-to shelters that they constructed from tarpaulin sheets and timber props. They seemed not to mind, perhaps not even to realise, that a small boy, probably in a silk shirt (silk shirts were to play a part throughout my life) saw them as something between strange creatures in a menagerie and the illustrations of a fairy-tale; my mother, possibly also in silk and almost certainly in unsuitable court shoes, felt compelled to accept a cup of tea – this I recall only for her determination not to let it touch her lips, but somehow to pour it away discreetly without the giver seeing. The impression that this episode made on me, ideal and enviable in the beginning, changed at the outbreak of war when the Evacuation of 1939 and the Blitz of 1940 revealed so much more of the lives of those who lived in the East End. It was, I suspect, the first foundation of the uncomfortable political position, moderately Conservative, profoundly in favour of the Welfare State, that has all my adult life disenfranchised me.

Where was my education in this random and haphazard life? In every conventional sense there was no education, yet I cannot remember a time when I could not read and was not having my curiosity aroused. I know that reading began with the many tales of Beatrix Potter and that my morality and manners were as much formed by the Tailor of Gloucester, Ginger and Pickles and Squirrel

Nutkin as any other early influence, but I was early beyond such children's books and when I was still small enough to perch on the foot of my mother's crossed leg I could read a newspaper propped against her knee. In winter we went often to the little cinemas in Notting Hill, spending whole afternoons in the darkness, sitting through the featured film twice – though as much for warmth as education. It was thus that I saw Disney cartoons when they were still black and white, Popeye and Olive Oil, Mickey Mouse and his entourage, and such more profoundly influential films as Charles Laughton's *Henry VIII*, *Rembrandt*, *Captain Bligh* and *Quasimodo*, and Elisabeth Bergner in *As You Like It*, establishing for me, even at that early age (it was 1936), a canon of blond beauty that I was later to apply to boys.

Shakespeare we encountered too at the Regent's Park Open Air Theatre, but the only production there that I recall with any clarity was the more than faintly ridiculous *Lady Precious Stream*, supposedly a traditional Chinese tale handed down by word of mouth for at least two thousand years, and only then recently translated into English by S. I. Hsiung. This 'Chinese Cinderella', as it was dubbed, had a peculiarly stilted, puppet-like quality, at the same time tippy-toed and shuffle-shod, as dramatic as my Godmother's Willow Pattern china.

Far more exciting for the infant aesthete was the appearance of Ram Gopal, then only nineteen and exquisitely ambiguous, with his Hindu dancers and musicians, at the Vaudeville Theatre in the winter of 1939, soon after war had been declared. What did I make of him? What were the feelings that he aroused? Seventy years later I can offer no answer other than the certainty that some indefinable longing was the consequence. Russian Ballet, seen a month later, in January 1940, left no impression of any kind, but the pantomimes did – those grand, luxurious productions at the Lyceum, the Stoll and the Coliseum, with their revolving stages, flying ballets, synchronised ranks of Tiller Girls, Grand Finales and full orchestras, their rough and tumble sowing in me an undying ambition, never fulfilled, to play the Widow Twanky in Aladdin. In the programme for Cinderella at the Coliseum in December 1939 there was a list of Air Raid Shelters in the vicinity, but in the 1941 programme there was nothing of the kind – by then most Londoners had become quite fatalistic about the Blitz and we took our chances.

That I can document this early exposure to the theatre is largely due to my mother's notes on programmes – 'Brian and Mamma', with the date and the ticket stubs, some of which are for a few shillings, but most are for front stalls at up to half a guinea. How could she afford such extravagance? Half a guinea may well have been more than she spent on rent and certainly more than we ever spent on a week's food. She may, occasionally, have sold a water-colour or a drawing, and equally occasionally she may have played her cello in some small professional capacity, but again and again I am compelled to wonder if there was some less virtuous source of income. Has my headstrong sexual nature been inherited from her? By 1938 the man who was to become my stepfather was much in evidence and taking us to theatres, but before then . . . ?

Other aspects of my education were as precocious. By the time the war began in September 1939 there was not a major museum or art gallery in London that I did not know, and the National Gallery was above all my favourite. We went there always on Connoisseurs' Day when an admission charge of sixpence was imposed to deter the hoi polloi; of this the consequence was that the gallery was all but empty and our conversations bothered no one. My mother's instruction, given in different rooms, was to find the painting that I most liked, decide why I liked it, then to seek her out and return to it to explain my conclusions. It was a simple but effective ruse to make me look and think. My thoughts were puerile. I liked Baldovinetti's portrait of a lady for her Borzoi profile, wiry fair hair and startling blue background; I liked Murillo's *Two Trinities* for its soft colours and its comforting Catholic familiarity; and I was entranced by Botticelli's *Mars and Venus*, somehow knowing that it meant far more than I could see – it was also a painting that gave me much difficulty in explaining my interest to my mother – this at an age when I had not the slightest knowledge of matters sexual and yet was aware of something that I could not define.

When the war intervened and the National Gallery was emptied of its permanent collection, it continued to function with the Picture of the Month, a series of exhibitions that did not shirk the risk to masterpieces by bringing back to Trafalgar Square only unimportant old masters from the safety of the Manod Slate Quarry in Wales, but brought Rembrandt's *Margaretha de Geer*, Hobbema's *Avenue*, Renoir's *Umbrellas* and, above all, Velazquez's *Rokeby Venus*, which was seen by nearly 37,000 visitors. There were also exhibitions of work by such contemporary artists as Sickert and Augustus John, and of War Pictures by Sutherland, Kennington, Ginner, Ravilious, Nash and others of their generation – thus was my interest in pictures broadened. How much did I understand? How certain was I, if at all, that I would at some future point, be able to understand what was beyond me then? To what extent was I beginning to reach beyond my mother's teaching?

CHAPTER 2

Father

Well into my adult life my father was a shadowy figure. That he died before I was born was the answer to my very earliest enquiry, and it now seems odd that I was for so long content with that, but as I had no friendship with other children of any age or parentage until I was eleven, perhaps it was not odd at all. In my young manhood, that is in my twenties, my mother was occasionally careless enough to let slip snippets of information, unguarded in other contexts, and into these I was able to weave recollections of other such morsels and even earlier events, the significance of which I had been unable to fathom at the time. At fourteen, in the summer of 1945, for example, I told her that I had been to Eynsford and was quite bewildered by the incomprehensible fierceness of her reaction − it was as though I had trespassed on some private property exclusively hers, and sullied Eden. My school set up a harvest camp that year − and following years − near Sevenoaks; the war in Europe over, rationing was suddenly even more severe than during it and, as the armed forces had not yet begun to demobilise, volunteers were desperately needed to bring in a harvest more precious that year than ever before, schoolboys an obvious pool of labour. I and another boy were sent to a farm near Eynsford. There, among many more serious activities, we drank cider in the village pub and got mildly drunk. How could so innocent a prank cause such a baffling reaction from my mother? By then, however, I had learned when not to enquire and, as with so many other small mysteries, set the matter aside.

Twenty years later, stricken by the breakdown of my first long homosexual relationship, a breakdown of which my mother's subconscious jealous behaviour had been the principal cause, I determined to tell her of my sexuality and did so in a letter, knowing that this she would read, but that any face to face confession would be so interrupted that I might not finish it, or worse, that the rising tension would lead to a row. She returned my letter with no expression of warmth or understanding, but with only the words 'You are just like your father.' This I could not set aside. I pressed repeatedly for more. She still would not give me his name but the anger of prompted recollection drove her on: she told me that my father had for some years lived in Eynsford with another man who satisfied his taste for being sodomised while fucking his women friends, one of whom she had been. That, I observed to myself, scarcely made me 'just like' him. If she disliked being in bed with two men, she disliked even more being one of two women with one man, which was often the alternative. His response had been to take a lease for her on the tiny cottage in Whitstable that had been the scene of so much of my childhood, discovered by chance when he had fallen into a drunken sleep on the train from London to Eynsford and been carried so much further on, and fuck her there.

Was it in any way a love affair. What did he see in her? She was beautiful; she was undoubtedly random and enthusiastic in her sexual responses; and in her ability to play the violin and cello she may have been professionally useful, for he was something of a composer. What did she see in him? By many accounts his looks were suave – Augustus John described him as tall, blond, pale and handsome, his expression constantly derisive, but their mutual friend Ottoline Morell put him down as 'soft and degenerate'. Was she attracted to him as a man who was sexually insatiable, a man incapable of emotional and sexual fidelity combined? – I doubt if in any way she shared his barely concealed interest in sexual sadism. Or was it that the unsuccess of this melancholy genius, frustrating his career and driving him into a state of dejection from which there could be no recovery, triggered a profound sympathy? One thing is certain – that their sexual interest in each other outlasted his Eynsford years, for these ended in late November 1928 and the conjugation of which I was the consequence must have taken place in mid-October 1930 and probably in his flat in the basement of what is now 12A Tite Street, Chelsea.

I was well into my fifties when, still not identifying him, she confessed the most significant information – that finding herself two months pregnant in December 1930 she had demanded of him some permanent and exclusive relationship, preferably marriage, although at that time he seemed settled with a woman named Barbara Peache, who passed for his wife. He offered to pay for an abortion, £5 the going rate as he well knew, his having paid that sum often enough for other women friends. She, a Catholic, refused, and the next thing she knew was that he was dead, poisoned by gas in the Tite Street flat. She was, I am certain, convinced that she had precipitated his suicide with her demand and bore that guilt for the rest of her life; it coloured her relationship with me and tainted her relationship with my stepfather. Suicide was not the verdict at the inquest. Suicide in 1930 was a criminal act subject to so severe a moral condemnation in all branches of Christianity that no one who had committed it could be buried in sacred ground; in recognising that there was no absolute proof of it in this case, the jury and the Coroner, who recorded an open verdict, performed a great kindness to my grandmother, whose anguish was pitiable, though she put on a brave performance at the inquest. Nigel, my father's earlier (and perhaps earliest) son (there could easily be more of us), remembered her back at Cefn Bryntalch saying that she felt as though she had killed him; seven years later she was still wearing black.

Have I inherited anything from my father? A great deal is known about his life and my impression from the mass of letters and other documentation is that he was obsessed with women and had no interest in sex with men, or between men, other than as an amused spectator. My mother's recollection of his being buggered by Hal

Collins, his friend and factotum in Eynsford, is unique, but I do not doubt it, for it is not the sort of thing she could have imagined; it may well have been Hal's initiative and not my father's, drunk – as both so often were – or not. Who can know? – I observe in passing that in my long life I have encountered many heterosexual men who do not care a damn what kind of sex they have as long as they have it. That he knew how abandoned sodomy can be, there is evidence enough in the obscene, though not very funny, rhymes and limericks in which he pilloried his enemies and occasionally his friends; they suggest a not wholly unsympathetic and far from condemnatory view of the proceedings, as in

> You'll love to meet the buggered bull,
> Whose little arse-hole's always full.
> He never seems to tire a bit,
> In fact, he simply thrives on it.
> He doesn't stop to pick and choose,
> The customers line up in queues,
> And as from east and west they come,
> He eagerly presents his bum.

If my father was in some sense sexually sadistic – the evidence for flagellation comes from other sources than my mother – then in this I am not his heir. Kenneth Clark described him as of a 'combative amorality which made him legendary in the early Twenties,' and in this too I do not reflect him. If there is such a thing as an aesthetic gene and it is possible to inherit it, then my intense response to music may be his gift to me, but it could as easily have come from my mother, who was entirely responsible for my hopeless ambitions as a violinist. The one thing that really intrigues me is that his uncle, John Postle Heseltine, a trustee of the National Gallery and founder member of the Art Fund, was a passionate and important collector of drawings by old masters and that, decades before I knew this, I had, as a schoolboy with ten shillings weekly pocket money, begun to trawl the Saturday markets of Portobello Road and Faringdon in search of them, and within days of my fifteenth birthday had bought my first 'parcel' of them at Christie's for 3 guineas – more than fifty drawings at a blow. That drawings were, within weeks of my graduating at the Courtauld Institute, to become my field of professional expertise, was mere coincidence, no doubt.

In July 1986, in Ankara, lying in a bath of cold water, eating strawberries, I came to a conclusion. Petter Kolrud, an old friend and my companion on many Turkish explorations, was with me, sitting on the end of the bath, and we were talking, the subject my misery at not knowing the identity of my father. How could it be that a man of fifty-five could still be so disturbed by such a matter? We were on our way to north eastern Turkey to make an inventory of Armenian churches there; we had spent the day in the city's great archaeological museum and should have been bubbling with excitement; but there we were, in the pale green bathroom of a shoddy hotel, he calming my rage at the cussedness of my mother a thousand miles away. Absurd though it may seem, this was a defining moment. We were to be away for at least six weeks – nearer eight in the event – but throughout them I clung to my new resolve to confront my mother, already in the early stages of dementia. It was the most trying thing that I have ever done, wearing, exhausting, disagreeable and bullying; she prevaricated, dissembled, lied and pretended not to understand. Her defiance astonished me and she held to it to the very end, for it was not to me that she eventually divulged the name – Philip Heseltine, alias Peter Warlock – but to a friend shrewd enough to ally himself with her and agree that I had been heartless and unfeeling.

Once knowing who my father was, an enervating nausea has affected me whenever I have attempted to put flesh on the small bones bequeathed me by my mother. There was first an early memoir by his friend, Cecil Gray, *Peter Warlock*, 1934, given me by his daughter, Pauline. In 1992 his son, Nigel Heseltine, published *Capriol for Mother*, another memoir, ending on a reproachful, even slightly hysterical note in which he seems to discard the two most probable causes of Warlock's death, suicide or a faulty gas tap, in favour of murder by Bernard van Dieren, a slightly sinister older friend and even more forgotten composer, who was not only the last man to see Warlock alive, but was the sole beneficiary of his will, made as long before as January 1920. Barry Smith, a musicologist, contributed a scrupulous biography with *Peter Warlock*, in 1994; more detached and measured in both pace and mood, indefatigably researched, this is likely to remain for ever the authoritative life, though I dare say that the enthusiastic zealots of The Peter Warlock Society, to whom I am deeply indebted, will add bells and whistles when they can.

If I have any opinion on the cause of Warlock's death it is that his putting out the cat – no more than a kitten – with food, at 6.40 in the morning (heard by the woman who lived in the flat above), suggests the suicidal intention of turning on the gas. That in the midst of what must have been a terrible emotional crisis, he cared that much for the animal, I find endearing and perhaps the only thing I understand about the man.

At his death he had no money and seems to have been dependent on the contribution made to the household by Barbara Peache – £200 a year. He had no prospect of work in music publishing, criticism or musicology. His sound but merciless criticisms of composers, performers and writers had dented friendships and made enemies. His assessment of himself as a writer of remembered songs and forgotten choral compositions was, two years before his death, that he had been in error in seeing himself as in any way creative, and as 'having drifted, more or less by chance, into a milieu where I do not belong and can never really belong . . . but how hard it would be to get out of such a groove after being in it for years . . .' And so it proved – a self-inflicted death the only way, 'that fatal hour,' as Augustus John put it, 'when he put the cat out, locked the door, and turned on the gas'. I was more fortunate and in one way and another realised early that I too had been in error in seeing myself as creative; the only groove from which I have not been able to escape has been writing art criticism for a newspaper.

In the merrier mood of the Eynsford years Warlock wrote a not unsuitable epitaph for himself –

> Here lies Warlock, the composer,
> Who lived next door to Munn the grocer,
> He died of drink and copulation,
> A great discredit to the nation.

Peter Warlock or Philip Heseltine? He began his life as the latter and ended it as the former, 'resolved finally to abandon all further use of the family name'. On his gravestone in the old Nightingale Road Cemetery in Godalming the inscription is intriguingly confused with PHILIP PETER WARLOCK written in equally large letters, and below, in smaller capitals, SON OF COVIE AND ARNOLD HESELTINE, whose grave it also is. It is as Peter Warlock that he is remembered as a composer, as Warlock that he is to be found in reference books. I cannot bear to hear his music, but in my mother's papers, on her death in 1996, I found sheets and sheets of it and, far odder, a catalogue of the North Italian drawings that once belonged to John Postle Heseltine – by Titian, Bellini, Mantegna, Carpaccio, Tintoretto et al – and another, of his thirty-one drawings by Rembrandt.

CHAPTER 3

Stepfather

Of the ceremony and witnesses at my parents' wedding I remember nothing other than the handsome staircase and heavily patterned carpet of the registry office, but my suicidal rage against the event is as clear now as it was then. I could think of no more immediate remedy for what I saw as a monstrous intervention in our lives than, careless of the consequences, throwing myself down the stairs, the more broken bones the better. This plan, however, was defeated by the carpet, thick and soft; no bones snapped, no intolerable pains shot through my small frame, not a scrape or scratch was to be seen – hurt lay only in the ignominy of being set on my feet by the very man for whom I had developed such envious hatred and who, moments earlier, had become my step-father, or rather, my father.

I, who had for so long been contentedly fatherless, even to the extent of not knowing my surname, now had a father whom I did not want. He was not a stranger – indeed, I had been aware of him for years and had been accustomed to calling him Uncle Robert, a role in which I liked him well enough. We first met on Wimbledon Common, an occasional treat in wilder country than Kensington Gardens, when I was six or seven, an encounter engineered by my mother, I suspect, to see how we got on, for clearly she already knew him. I was lying on my back in long grass that had run to seed, examining the bowed heads above me with some intensity, for they were red against the sky, not green. Was this some optical effect, or were they really red? All these decades later, now living near the Common, walking dogs, I still look for red-headed grasses in late summer; they are never as red as I remember. Suddenly, there he was. He wore tweedy-brown plus-fours and had a dog to match, Flossie, smooth and cuddly, the first dog in my life, though never in any sense mine. Over some years he reappeared from time to time, often in evening dress, and I'd hear my mother return very late or even in the morning. Sometimes he took us both to the theatre; whether he thought it good for me or because the dependable Tilly could not babysit, I do not know, but it contributed to the foundation of a habit that was to flourish in my later schooldays. What, I wonder now, was a boy of seven expected to make of Dodie Smith's *Dear Octopus* in 1938? – whatever it was it lay dormant for nearly seventy years until, in 2004, I saw *Festen*, by David Eldridge, another family drama with undercurrents exposed.

Late in August 1939, the month's very last day, I think, the Second World War imminent, Robert drove down to our cottage in Whitstable and removed us to the safety of his cousin's house near Hitchin. This led to some of the happiest and most educative months of my life, but these were preceded by an immediate tragedy – the death of my dog, Prince. Robert shot him and left his body on the beach for the tide to sweep away. Packed among the suitcases in the car I saw Prince led toward the sea and heard the shot. I did not cry, as I would now, but a cold, hard, vengeful aversion lodged in my memory. There was a brief explanation about war – to me a meaningless concept but not to him, with long experience of the First World War, not only in France but in three of its intriguing peripheral campaigns, Mesopotamia, the Balkans (the Gardeners of Salonica) and the taking of Jerusalem by Allenby. In these he had seen what war could do to civilian populations and, convinced that the Germans might invade at once, Whitstable virtually in the front line, he was determined to see that we were safe. Poor Prince was an impediment; he lived on, however, as a rod with which to beat my father's back, for with every 'What do you want?' for birthday or Christmas, the answer was always 'A dog'. To this his response was that I could have a dog 'when the war is over' – and on the 8th of May 1945, when the war came to an end in Europe, I bought a puppy for half a crown, as white and black as Prince had been, but a mongrel terrier bitch entirely lacking his long-legged pointerish nobility.

In Hitchin we saw much more of Uncle Robert; he came down from London every Friday night, slept with my mother, and returned on Sunday evening. During the week I too slept with my mother – as I had always done – and resented, deeply, my being lifted from her bed late in these weekend evenings and removed to a smaller bed, warmed with stone hot water bottles clad in buttoned flannel jackets, in a distant room. Though I tried to stay awake so that I could object to it, I always failed. To my 'Why can't *he* sleep in the little room?' the answer was another question, shifting guilt – 'Surely you can't be so selfish as to begrudge him the comfort of a bigger bed?'

There was then a long hiatus. In December 1939 we returned to London and for some months there was no Uncle Robert. Nor was there any war. With snow and ice it was a savage winter, but there was food and coal enough and it was no more uncomfortable than any previous winter; in any other year we would have enjoyed its severities in Whitstable, but the town was barricaded behind defences and we were not allowed to go to it. I learned to sing 'The last time I saw Paris' – a silly sentimental song to an unsuitably jaunty tune – and my mother talked of the wonders of the Louvre. In the high summer of 1940, however, the bombing of London began, peripherally and tentatively at first, but in earnest and more accurately by early September. My mother walked with me from Kensington to Kennington, where my godmother lived in an enviable mansion flat decorated in strong blues and yellows, furnished as though it were a farmhouse in Normandy – 'This is where you must come if anything happens to me,' her instruction impressively urgent. When a nearby house was hit by an unexploded bomb we fled, not with clothes or other sensible belongings, but she lugging her cello and me her violin, and when half London was on fire we somehow made our way to Saffron Walden and the house of an old dame to whose son my mother had at some time been engaged. It was from her rooftop (the house had a tower and a winding staircase) that at night we watched the orange glow of London in flames forty miles away.

Back in London, numbed by the persistent bombing, there was a sense that this was how life must be and fatalism replaced fear. In the middle of a summer day, hand-in-hand in Kensington High Street, we were blown by bomb blast through the window of a shop that sold skeins of knitting wool, its window shattered a split second earlier, and there we lay, laughing, among the shards of glass and unravelled miles of wool. One morning we went to early Mass at the Carmelites in Church Street and found it bombed; the Catholic church on the south side of the High Street was bombed too, a great crucifix wedged at an angle across the entrance, seeming to bar entry to the roofless shell. We stopped going to Mass. And then Uncle Robert reappeared. Early in 1942 he married my mother without sacramental ceremony, legally adopted me and changed my name to his. We were an instant family and Uncle had become my father.

My mother and he expected me to believe this. He treated me then as I now treat a rescued dog that must learn an unfamiliar name; as I in my time have said over and over again in a dog's ear 'Your name is Titian,' or Schubert, or Nusch, so he said that my name was Brian Sewell and made me write it in my books. For the first time in my life I was made to realise the importance of a surname; for the first time I had a piece of paper with my name on it, an address and, I think, a number, and the important-seeming words Identity Card. My many protests were dismissed. My mother explained the long hiatus with the excuse that my new father had been working on some secret enterprise in Edinburgh, which may well have been true, but this was a man of whom I had been aware for years as Uncle and I believed neither his metamorphosis into father nor the Edinburgh tale. I was offended that they thought me dim-witted enough to accept these fictions when this was the man who had shot my dog, lifted me from my mother's bed and replaced me there. Never having had a father I had no concept of what a father should be, but I knew in my bones that I was being tricked and taken for a fool.

After my mother's death more than half a century later, I read his letters to her; they revealed an honest and continuing passion of which I never saw evidence in their daily behaviour to each other, a passion so intense that from his offices in Chancery Lane he often scribbled notes expressing it; these, if he caught the 3.00 pm collection, were delivered home later that same afternoon. Others, earlier and longer, suggest that my mother bargained with him on my account, for they contained his promises to see to my education and adopt me so that we all bore the same name, to love me as though I were his son and to ask for no other children. In all this I sense what I sensed at the time – that my mother had nothing more than fondness for him (and perhaps not even that) and that the marriage was the only means by which, at the age of 42 (he was ten years older), in the middle of an exhausting war, she could engineer some security for us both.

I do not know how they managed the sexual side of their marriage; I do not know if my mother was still anything of the sexual animal that I am convinced she had been in her twenties; I know only that in the more comfortable circumstances of Robert's flat, after a tantrum about being given a room to myself far from their bedroom, he agreed that I should have a bed in the small room off it that he used as a dressing room. It was little more than a cupboard containing a lofty mahogany wardrobe and the enormous chest-of-drawers between which and the wall a narrow divan was squeezed; this gave me the sense of being hidden away in a corner, the child's craving for the aedicula perfectly satisfied. But then there were the nights when Robert came into the room and masturbated, an urgent, private, silent, business that had nothing to do with me in my dark corner supposedly fast asleep, but was of intense interest; his technique informed my own.

I had long since clumsily indulged in that solitary pleasure, accidentally discovered when I was six or so, but not disclosed to my mother; how is that young children know when something should be secret? But at eight she found me at it in an unlocked bathroom and uttered the formidable threat 'If you do that, you'll never go to a university.' No more was said then or ever again, and as I had no concept of what a university might be, the threat had no specific meaning and could not be assessed; dire though I thought it must be, it did not affect the practice but confirmed the secrecy; when, eventually, a university seemed well within reach, the threat, though always remembered, I knew to be as false as all the others uttered by schoolmasters, priests and non-conformist busybodies. Robert would have been appalled had he known that he had unwittingly demonstrated the simplest and easiest way to masturbate and, that in doing so, he had encouraged me to outgrow my need to be within reassuring distance of my mother, abandon the bed in the dressing room and develop the parallel world of my own room along the corridor.

There was, I am all but certain, an abortion. A doom-laden atmosphere lay heavy in the flat, my mother in bed, depressed, angry and unfriendly (a very rare thing), Robert pacing about in an equally angry sulk, the bathroom out of bounds. A strange doctor came, grim, unsmiling and, to me, unspeaking. And, indeed, the bathroom was occupied for hours, the moans and cries distressing. For days afterwards, it seemed, Robert and my mother hardly spoke, and then she went away – 'Not well . . . in need of country air . . . ' Later, occasionally, some thoughtless or selfish action on my part was rewarded with the reproach 'You will never know how much I've done for you' – and I associated it with the day the unfamiliar doctor came. There was also, once, a wistful response to my expressing a wish that I had had an older brother – 'Well, you might have had a little sister . . . '

Robert Sewell was a good man, but this for all my boyhood years I failed to recognise. He deserved a son of his own and not a second-hand recalcitrant. Early in his days as my father he came into the bathroom to see me bathe, and enquired if I retracted my foreskin and washed there, telling me of the campaign in Mesopotamia in which he had fought and the importance of genital hygiene in the desert, even if no more than a mug of water could be spared for it – wiser than washing your face, he thought. When three years or so later, I was in the throes of puberty, he asked the simple question 'Is there anything you want to know?' I knew exactly what he meant and answered 'No.' There was, as it happened, a great deal, for the schoolboy confusions of my peers at school, and the dissemblings, cautions and prohibitions of those who dipped their toes in the waters of sexual education were scarcely to be believed, but I did not want to be told the truth by him. I did not want to be touched by him, physically or emotionally, and shrank away from his rare attempts to hug or kiss me.

He tried very hard to be my father. His first gift was a kilt. With the Cameron clan in his recent ancestry and the Cameron High-landers his regiment, it must have seemed to him a useful instrument of bonding. He did not just buy one – that was probably not possible in the third year of the war – but took me to a tailor to be measured and fitted, and I hated him for it. The kilt was never worn and it disappeared from my wardrobe. His second gift was cricket gear. Insofar as he could be fanatical about anything, cricket was his mania, and somewhere in London he found an outfitter who still had a cream flannel shirt, a pullover in cable stitch, white kid boots and enough heavy cream flannel cloth to make trousers for a boy. Though better dressed for it than any other boy at Haberdashers', I had no talent for the foolish game and such perfect clothes for it made me feel an idiot.

Haberdashers' was a gift of a different kind. I was nearer eleven than ten when I became Robert's son, a child of absolutely no formal education and much too much that was informal and pre-cocious. He might have persuaded his old school to accept me – certainly he thought that I should be a boarder somewhere safely away from London – but since my birth my mother had never been separated from me even for a day, and she was appalled by the idea. It is usually the son who does not want to be parted from his mother, but in my case I was attracted by the proposal and would willingly have gone; instead, Robert approached school after school in London and took me to be interviewed, but none would have me without a grasp of any form of mathematics, without the formalities of English grammar – what did I know of algebra, they asked, and could I parse a sentence? Haberdashers' was the last of several possibilities, and there Robert was offered hope; it was by then May 1942 and the entrance examination was to be on the 13th of July – if I went to an approved preparatory school for two months it might just be possible to cram my brain with the essentials of mathematics and grammar.

That I passed the examination in any conventional sense I now do not believe. The cramming took place in a shoddy little dame school where I was mercilessly bullied by two older and bigger boys, the brothers Summerfield, and I am still sickened by recall of their punches to my stomach – one restrained me while the other struck; I had had no experience of boys, knew nothing of fighting, and had never, until then, been hurt. I was utterly bewildered by algebra, geometry, parsing and syntax, and I am sure that Haberdashers' let me in only because it was by then a very run-down school of no reputation and uncertain future, its catchment area largely lower middle-class (more Cricklewood than Hampstead), its pupils the sons of small independent shopkeepers and bank managers with social ambitions, and it needed the fees of every pupil it could get.

Robert let Haberdashers' do its worst. At crucial moments but to no effect he paid for extra maths lessons in both the lower and the upper schools, and he argued my case when the headmaster put me into the Remove and would have had me gone. His own contribution to my education lay in steering me away from the Catholicism early instilled by my mother and into the Church of

England traditions of which he was, largely through his love of English choral music, an uncritical supporter. He looked after the financial affairs of several composers and performers, Benjamin Britten one of them, and took me to the first performance of Peter Grimes in 1945 – an occasion of which I ought to remember more than the Adam's apple and excruciating vibrato of Joan Cross; I hated it. It was his interest in organ music that generated mine and pushed me literally into the arms of Alan Harverson, a young rising star of these great instruments in the 1940s, who taught me all I know of them and also took me to his bed. I cannot imagine, had Robert known of this, what he would have done, if anything, but – though we had never spoken of what schoolboys might do together – I knew of his views on homosexuality from the disgust he expressed when cases of importuning were reported in the *Daily Telegraph*. A little later, when his friend Ian Horobin, Warden of Mansfield House University Settlement in the East End, was tried for homosexual offences – it seems that he urged bigger boys to bugger younger while he looked on and masturbated – Robert seethed with a sense of betrayal by a man whom he had known so long and yet been duped by his dissembling.

With my precocious smoking Robert dealt elegantly and effectively. His view was that I should smoke well or not at all; my smuggled Woodbines he discarded with disdain and we set off for an eminent tobacconist in St James's with whom I am certain he had entered into conspiracy. I was persuaded to choose a pipe and a very mild tobacco called Baby's Bottom was suggested, together with a waxed wallet in which to keep it, and all sorts of pipe-smoker's impedimenta, the expense considerable. At home, with some ceremony, all this was put to use and, encouraged to inhale deeply, I was within moments miserably sick. With permission to smoke whenever I wished, the wish abruptly withered. On discovering my wayward sexuality he could hardly have employed a kindred stratagem; besides, I was determined that he should never know; nor should my mother.

Stepfather

As I grew older, Robert played less and less of a role in my life. He did not share my interest in the visual arts and never once went to a gallery or exhibition with me, but to the Saturday morning jaunts that, as a schoolboy, I made in and out of the then many art dealers' premises in Bond Street and thereabouts, he gave a tacit blessing in that he occasionally met me for lunch, sometimes in a Chinese Restaurant in Wardour Street, more often in Manzi's in Leicester Street because, as he told me, the original Manzi had been one of Lord Leighton's models.[1] He saw to it that I went to the theatre, introduced me to the plays of Anouilh, Fry and Rattigan, and encouraged me into the habit of cycling from school into the West End, there to pay four shillings or so for a numbered stool that secured a place in the queue for seats in the pit or gallery when the theatre opened in the evening – and on it, in St Martin's Lane or Shaftesbury Avenue, I sat and wrote a homework essay.

Robert's passion for my mother cooled after five years or so of marriage and they quarrelled mightily. I broke in on them one evening – I was fifteen – and said something like 'For God's sake, why don't you two get divorced?' – to which the answer came, almost in unison, 'We stay together for your sake.' How like them, I thought, to blame me for their misery. Robert took to politics (perhaps persuaded by Ian Horobin who had been a Nationalist MP in the 1930s and was to represent the Conservatives as an MP before his disgrace) and as a distant cousin of Bonar Law (Britain's shortest-lived Prime Minister) had quite a happy time on the fringes of the Conservative Party in its darkest post-war days. My mother developed a number of pseudo-asthmatic ailments that could only be relieved by weeks in the sea air at Eastbourne or sniffing the mud at Westcliff (then believed to be a sovereign cure

1   The dates do not appear to support this: Leighton died in 1896 and the first Manzi premises were established in 1902; it is, nevertheless, possible that a member of the Manzi family had been in London earlier, paving the way. Robert was never a man for tittle-tattle and I am inclined to think that there must have been some authority for his assertion.

for respiratory problems), and it was evident that their lives were falling apart.

There was one cruel event that no one explained adequately at the time and I cannot explain now. Robert took me to the Law Courts one morning and a hearing took place at which I understood that I had the opportunity to reject his adoption and his name. I know that it was painful for him, for before it began he had to tell me himself that he was not my father, and was put out by my response – 'I know. I've always known.' The judge, if that is what he was, put me under extreme pressure with a review of all that Robert had generously done for me, urging me to do 'the decent thing,' ending with the suggestion that as all my schoolfriends knew me as Brian Sewell, that was the name by which I should continue to be known if I wished to stay in touch with them. For a moment my real identity was within my grasp, my real name, my real father, and the gnawing curiosity could end. But I funked it. Exactly as the judge had suggested, rejection of Robert's name seemed too cruel a blow to a man who, to all intents, purposes and onlookers, was indeed my father, but had I known what I was to know later, I would not have hesitated. The anger is with me still.

With an abbreviated birth certificate that gave no indication that I was adopted and sound advice on what I might expect in the army, Robert saw me into National Service – though seeming offended that I had refused his help to get into the Cameron Highlanders. Not a Scot, never seduced by the romantic nonsenses of Scottish history, literature or song, loathing the wail of bagpipes and remembering the rejected kilt, why should I want to join his swaggering regiment? It was at this point that my mother decided that she no longer wished to live in London. He bought her a house in Castle Hedingham and let her go, while he settled down with an air hostess from British European Airways.

Achieved without animosity, this seemed a satisfactory arrangement until he began to die of cancer. Operation after operation, seven in all, weakened him to the point at which nothing more could be done, there was no hope of recovery or even remission, and he was sent to Hedingham to die. He lasted six months and the nursing nearly killed my mother. I was with him for the last few days, with him, indeed, when he died, listening to his apnoea, ready with a soft silk scarf with which to tie his jaw in place when the moment came. Shortly after midnight he opened his eyes for a moment, looked at me intently, and said two words – 'Poor Brian.' An hour or so later he was dead.

'Poor Brian' puzzled me, but before we could bury him I knew why he had said it. A termagant of a woman arrived at the door, demanded entry and said 'All this is mine.' She had with her a rather younger woman and a solicitor with evidence that the one was Robert's wife and the other his daughter. They had seen the notice in the *Telegraph* – a notice intended for his friends, his clients and his regiment, not this – and they had come post haste. She was indeed his wife; she had not seen him for more than thirty years, but there had been no divorce and he had constantly supported her, had paid for the education of his daughter, and had left a will in her favour made many years before. His marriage to my mother had been bigamous and he left her penniless, though as the deeds were in her name, she remained in possession of the Hedingham house, her only asset. Robert's adoption of me, though with the best of intentions, was fraudulent – and my mother knew it.

In his wardrobe I found three live hand grenades from World War I and the pistol with which he shot Prince.

CHAPTER 4

School

Haberdashers' Aske's Hampstead School was housed in a gaunt red brick building designed for it in the last years of the nineteenth century, to which a less aggressively ugly Science Block had been added in 1931. As an institution it had some ancient history in that the medieval haberdashers of London, dealers in beads and buttons, needles and thread, had, having been granted armorial bearings, formed a guild in 1448, late in the reign of Henry VI; Aske, Robert of that ilk, a late seventeenth-century Master of the Haberdashers' Company, in bequeathing money for the education of twenty haberdashers' sons of 'proven poverty,' was responsible for the foundation of the school. By the late nineteenth century, however, poverty had no part to play in the choice of boys to attend, fees had to be paid and entrance examinations passed, and the school was something of a stepping-stone to Oxford and Cambridge for the shop-keeping classes, but Hoxton, the site of the original school, had become a run-down area of slums and shop-keepers were fewer than they might have been – hence the move to Hampstead. This was not, alas, to the jolly Hampstead of the Heath, the fairs, the artists' colony, but to the gloomy northernmost point of West Hampstead, recently developed as a middle class alternative to the new slums of Cricklewood and Kilburn, the local street names Gondar, Menelik and Somali bearing witness to Napier's Abyssinian Campaign of 1868, and Agamemnon, Achilles and Ulysses to a developer with a classical education.

The northern perimeter of the school indeed formed the border with a Cricklewood council estate from which rude boys emerged to mock us for our straw boaters, and access to the school was primarily from the bus and trolleybus routes that intersected at Cricklewood Broadway. Thus it was, in the 1940s, a decade of war and punishing austerity, that Cricklewood was on my map. It was then a nesting-place for European Jews and it was Issy Bonn, an engaging Yiddish humourist on the BBC's Home Service, who dubbed it Cricklevitch and adopted the persona of a local Kosher shopkeeper suffering the hazards of the Blitz. Its most prominent building was a dance hall that seemed to function every hour of the day and we schoolboys in short trousers, already prurient, and more prurient still in trousers long, speculated much over the conjugation of blond factory girls in snoods with the spivs and black GIs who lay in wait outside – wicked stuff for Burra watercolours. The marshalling yards and sidings of the old Midland Railway attracted the Luftwaffe to Cricklewood to drop more than the area's fair share of incendiary and high explosive bombs, and we collected shrapnel on our way to school, a currency to be exchanged for conkers and other treasures to be found in the pockets of small boys – I once swapped what I swore was a piece of fuselage (how could I know?) for a whole doughnut.

I knew haberdashery to be the ground-floor departments of such shops as Barker's, Derry and Toms, and Ponting's in Kensington High Street, associated it with knicker elastic and hat ribbons, and thought it a ridiculous name for a boys' school – not a good beginning. I suspect that some of the masters too thought it an uncomfortable name for a great educational institution, for we were too often reminded that its origin lay with a medieval guild. The school's motto, Serve and Obey, I loathed, thinking it perfect for the tired old things who stood behind haberdashery counters measuring elastic at a penny three-farthings for a yard, but not for a boy who had been taught to think.

In September 1942, on the first day of term, Mr J. F. Cooper, deputy headmaster of the Lower School, despatched me to Form 2B, of which the form master was a mistress, Irene Johnson – we were three full years into World War II and young masters were elsewhere. For me she was the perfect introduction to formal education – that is, largely careless of academic rules and casual with the syllabus. History and English were her subjects, but she had a sister who could sing and with a piano in the room we were occasionally treated to song recitals instead; Irene, it was, who planted an undying love of Schubert in my soul. If she taught us anything of the dynasties of English medieval history, I cannot recall it, but she inspired in me such an interest in weaponry, siege machines and castles, that I was once able to remember the progress of English dominion and decline in France largely through the fate of the castles that were constructed there. As for her conjuring the Crusades, her evocation of Le Crac des Chevaliers in Syria (another castle) was as powerful as her images of Richard the Lion Heart, his Queen Berengaria, and his probable lover, the itinerant lutanist Blondel. Can we imagine any teacher now imprinting images of Le Crac on the eyes and minds of a class of eleven year old boys, or hinting at the particular relationships of men?

She did not stay long at Haberdashers' for the school was no place for free spirits; in the sense that she was both driven and diverted by her enthusiasms she was perhaps very like my mother and I wish now that I had realised earlier just how exceptional she was. I wish too that I had been able to thank her for taking so easily in her stride my odd precocities; on the very first day she put us at our ease by asking each in turn what books we had just read, William and Biggles high among the responses, but when, late in the hour (for we sat in alphabetical order), I rattled off novels by Warwick Deeping, Jeffrey Farnol, Joseph Farjeon and Dornford Yates (whose snooty characters were initially responsible for my passionate interest in beautiful cars), no eyebrow rose and she treated the list as though it were to be expected. These were my mother's borrowings from the local library, and I read them too, avidly engrossed, though having recently re-read both Deeping and Yates, I wonder now what on earth I saw in them – but that is also my response to Trollope, all of whose novels, even the *Golden Lion of Granpere*, I read for pleasure in my later teens.

Irene Johnson also persuaded us to speak, to give short talks on favourite things, a pet or holiday, and again she did not curse me when I chose to go beyond these limits. With Puccini there was a simple life to tell – an unhappy marriage, an almost fatal accident with a car, cancer of the throat, death and a great unfinished work – but with Wagner and the Leitmotiv rage and ignominy were the consequence, for the boy who had agreed to demonstrate on the piano rebelled when I demanded that he find his way through my mother's miniature score of *The Ring*. We read Shakespeare too, performing *Macbeth* text in hand in the shallow empty space before the class, and thus the following year, in the Third Form, were at twelve and thirteen not the least abashed at mounting a full performance of it in the School Hall.

Three things were the cause of abject misery. In English Grammar we were compelled to parse sentences – that is to deconstruct them and name their parts and tenses; but I already spoke and wrote grammatically the English of my elders, instinct and rote my guides, and the exercises merely confused me and, though more often than not my answers were right, they were not based on reason. Even now, earning my living as a scribbler, I still cannot parse and yet I lock horns with editors, propensity and personal precedent the rocks on which I base my argument. But I learned wonderful new things – metonymy, synecdoche, hyperbole and metaphor – and have been in love with English ever since. With mathematics, however, there were no such consolations.

Double Maths, an unbroken hour and a half of it, was the most dreaded entry on the charts of lessons that we were given on the first day of term. Double maths meant ninety minutes of blind incomprehension, of futile struggle with an unintelligible discipline, the letters and language of algebra and geometry impenetrably abstruse, the arithmetical problems absurd – with water leaking at twenty gallons a minute, how many boys must stick their fingers in the dyke if one finger reduces the flow by five eighths of a pint in nine seconds? I could visualise the dyke, the boys, the wind and weather, I could indeed have drawn the problem, but I could not solve it. As for sines, secants and tangents, logarithms and equations, pi and Pythagoras, of these the immediate consequence was the physical shutting-down of my mind and I sat at my desk a hapless idiot, my only achievement – one still with me – the ability to shut my eyes and precisely count against the clock the sixty seconds of a minute. Of the eight years I spent at school at least two, if we string all the hours together, were utterly wasted in lessons on maths, chemistry and physics; my brain was simply not attuned to them.

My stepfather, who could solve finger-in-the-dyke problems as though they were the simplest mental arithmetic, decided that I should have extra maths lessons after school and consulted Cooper, who agreed to teach me twice a week for five shillings an hour, which meant travelling home by bus in the evening rush and in the darkness of the blackout, a small boy often allowed to stand on the upper deck – a privilege forbidden to adults – in the heady atmosphere there of Virginia tobacco, damp cosmetics, sodden rubberised mackintoshes and stale body odours. It was the most extraordinary combination, a smell ranking high above roasting coffee, stinking fish and other street smells of my childhood, seductive and repellant. Extra maths continued until the end of my first term when poor Cooper had to admit that I had shown not the slightest improvement. I had, nevertheless, enjoyed the lessons, for Cooper, a neatly constructed little man, had sat close, his left arm about my shoulders, though often wandering lower; he seemed warm and affectionate in a way that my stepfather was not, and I liked it. I liked the hand on my bare knee and I liked too Cooper's standing behind me, close, after some errand that had taken him from the desk. There was nothing overtly sexual about these contacts, but they were, in today's jargon, inappropriate.

I did not betray Cooper. His moustache bothered me a bit, but to a boy who was at the beastly school only because a newly-acquired and dour stepfather compelled it, Cooper's warm touch was appealing. I sensed – as children do, for they have surprising canniness – that what he did put us both in peril, and said nothing, and it was only my continuing failure to raise the level of my marks in maths that brought an end to our association. The contact did me no harm – I was, I am certain, already queer – but I am convinced that had I told my homophobic stepfather, the consequences would have been appalling, with me, no doubt, consenting to words put in my mouth, the consequence an abiding sense of guilt about sex, my sexuality and my betrayal of a man who gently taught me something about the pleasures of my body, lasting to this day.

Nor did I betray Horace a year later. For a man as hostile to homosexuality as my stepfather to put me into the care of a professional footballer too old to be in the army, was an act of astonishing naivety. I was twelve and showing neither interest in, nor aptitude for, the abominable game of soccer that was com-pulsory in winter in the Lower School, and I spent most games afternoons either in goal where I froze with inattention and the weather, or enraging the little know-alls in my team by invariably being off-side. Where the hell, I wondered, was on-side, and why was it never where I chanced to be? I was always among the last to be chosen for these ad hoc teams, and the games began with ignominy. School reports betrayed me and my step's response was the same for soccer as for maths – extra tuition. Having found a maths master with embracing arms, he now found a footballer with wandering hands, all too willing to explain some unexpected rules and show me how to play a different game.

This was at a stage in the war when Londoners had become blasé about air raids, were hungry and ill-clad, and our motor cars were all standing on piles of bricks in locked garages, their essential parts removed so that, in the event of a German invasion, they would be useless to the enemy. Horace, however, a red-haired and wiry player for Spurs, collected me every Saturday morning in a

Ford Ten Tourer of 1934, for professional footballers, it seems, were among the very few non-combatants allowed a petrol ration. The Ford was a blandishment quite irresistible to a small boy; never mind the privilege of sitting on the touchline (if that is the term in soccer), and of witnessing the manly mysteries of jockstraps, communal bathing, massaging and horseplay after the games – it was the journeys to and fro that I enjoyed, for the Ford's flapping hood was almost always down, and to rattle windblown from pitch to pitch through the bleak environs of London in that puny little car was exquisitely seductive, even thrilling, for I had to play a part in driving it – without a roof it was subject to extreme flexing over bumps and the potholes that were many and deep as a consequence of the Blitz, and I had always to be ready to grab the passenger door and slam it shut; this, in turn, gave Horace an excuse for grabbing me.

I do not know what happened to Horace after that winter. I dare say that school reports indicated no improvement in the game and that my step thought his pound notes better spent elsewhere. I dare say that Horace became disenchanted with 'my little toff', as he invariably introduced me to his mates, their ribald responses beyond my comprehension; perhaps he found a boy less toffee-nosed and innocent, happier to make mutual the pleasures that he offered – I missed his car more than I missed him. In a subsequent winter Haberdashers' introduced me to the ecstatic pleasures of rugger, a game then mercifully unencumbered by obscure and restrictive rules, fast, furious and indelicately physical.

If other boys had such contacts with adults, they did not speak of them, but in my second year at the school, in the Third Form there was an abiding atmosphere of, at first latent, and then active sexuality, curiosity urged on by changes in our bodies, but cruelly ill-informed by feeble and evasive attempts to instruct us. We were urged to keep ourselves pure for the day when we got married and, above all things, to eschew self-abuse, for the consequences of this evil were blindness, debility and early death, to say nothing of moral turpitude. If one boy knew that the erect penis must enter the vagina to make babies, then swiftly all boys knew – but then what? Adler, the boy who told us this, could only suppose that we then had to pee; we were appalled by the thought. Harry Claff, a handsome curly-haired Jewish boy, nearer thirteen than most of us, was the first to ejaculate and solve the mystery of what really happens when men and women conjugate, for spunk – then the word for it – had never been mentioned in lessons that dwelt on the role of bees in the pollination of plants. Harry could demonstrate several times a day until other boys caught up with him and curiosity in his oddly purple penis waned; then he gained supremacy again by bringing to school the first – and in my day, only – pornographic paperback, from which I recall the mystifying phrase 'the love juices streaming down her thighs'. From then on it seemed that almost every boy was obsessed with the idea and practice of mutual masturbation in the air raid shelters (from which we used to remove the light bulbs), behind the fives courts, in the loft above the school hall, in the swimming-bath cubicles (though they had no doors), in the communal bath after rugger or cross-country running, and at the summer harvest camps some boys knew enough to take matters a great deal further, shading into sexual sadism and bondage, even genital bondage, all of which seemed to come about by instinct rather than instruction.

I am convinced that nothing of this did harm and that if any of us in adult life identified ourselves as homosexual, the many happenings at school were not to blame. When, to celebrate the twenty-fifth anniversary of our leaving school an old boy invited me to dine with a dozen or so of my contemporaries, they were all contented married fathers, whose prinked, perfumed and appalling wives spoke of nothing but their university ambitions for their brats, most of them at Haberdashers'. When conversation turned, by chance, to homosexuality, the condemnations of the husbands were as shrill and vituperative as those of their wives, and, the hypocrisy intolerable, in one of those hushed moments when mutual outrage has exhausted company, I heard myself say, my voice perhaps rather too intentionally audible, 'There is not a man at this table with whom I did not have sex when we were boys,' and left the house. It has always puzzled me that heterosexual men have the ability to haul down the shutters on their adolescent sexual experiences and utterly deny them; to me they were unforgettable adventures in revelation, instruction and self-knowledge, too important ever to be denied.

I spent the long summer break of 1944 away from London, sent thirty miles or so north-west to escape the flying bombs of which almost seven thousand were to fall on London and the near south-east between mid-June and early September, when I had to return to school. Leaked intelligence had suggested that some fifty thousand of these first *Vergeltungswaffen* (retaliation weapons) might be despatched, and when the House of Commons heard, three weeks after the engine of the very first cut out, that almost all were falling on London — as most Haberdashers already knew from the long hours spent in the school's air raid shelters — my stepfather explained with some gravity his decision that, for my safety, I should spend the summer in a pub he knew near Mentmore where there was a family of boys. Off I went to learn their country ways. They were far more advanced than young Haberdashers. In the wooded hills above a nearby airfield, watching the movement of planes was varied at the wish of the eldest, at seventeen, waiting to go into the Navy; at will, he buggered his brother of fifteen who, in turn, buggered the next, of fourteen, but that poor boy was allowed only to eye his brother of eleven and mutter 'See what you'll get when the time comes.' I was allowed, indeed encouraged, to watch, but absolutely forbidden to touch or be touched, for this was family business. Do they remember this, I wonder, as they mingle with their sons and grandsons? Newly knowing what could be, intrigued and fascinated by my knowledge, back I went to school, knowing too about scrumping apples, putting my ear to a railway line to tell if a train was coming, and what could be written and drawn in a pub lavatory.

There was one aesthetic adventure. Alone and on a bicycle I rode the long avenue to Mentmore, of which my step had spoken; no one was about, or so I thought until caught peering through slightly parted curtains. It was not quite a twisted ear moment and I must have been coherent in my excuse for trespassing, for I was taken into the kitchen and given tea and cake, and then allowed to peep into a ground floor room or two and see a dust sheet pulled away from furniture, a light switched on near a painting. It was my first experience of a great country house and when, in 1978, I drove Anthony Blunt and Neil MacGregor to Mentmore to view the sale that marked its disposal and dispersal, I realised how sharp my visual memory can be.

In the Upper School I learned to play rugger, though I never quite understood the rules, discovered an unexpected love of cross-country running – it is the loneliness, the self-dependence that is so seductive – and was a reasonable all-rounder at athletics. Confessing to my mother one sports day when my house was weak, that I felt I had to do too much, she pressed a tiny hip flask into my hand with instructions to swig from it if I felt myself flagging. I did, and it made things infinitely worse, legless indeed; I learned later that she had filled it with neat gin. At cricket, the one summer pastime that really seemed to matter at Haberdashers', I was hopeless, never put in to bat or bowl and always condemned to field as long-stop – which at least allowed me to read most of the time. It was Mr Dudderidge, the PT supremo and an Olympic canoeist in the 1936 Games, who at last realised that extreme long sight prevented me from seeing the ball once it left the bowler's hand. Academically I was dogged by failure in maths and science; science I could eventually drop, but maths remained an obstacle. My step resorted to the old business of extra maths tuition when I failed it in the School Certificate exam that was then the equivalent of GCSE, this time by a master more amused by caning than fondling – but still to no effect. Caning I considered the most acceptable of punishments, over and done within minutes and the slate wiped clean; I did not enjoy it but I did not care if the masters did and it had not the slightest effect on my sexual development.

Failing maths, a compulsory subject, meant failing the whole School Certificate exam in spite of distinctions in English and History, and I was put in Form 5R, the Remove as we knew it then, though the current regime at the school (an institution now wholly removed from its Hampstead incarnation) prefers the expression 'Fifth Form Repeaters'. This was the form in which the ineducable were dumped until they left, in which I was both destined for oblivion and bullied. It was a form almost without discipline. One young master, demobbed early for medical reasons, we were told, but of which there was no physical evidence, the boys simply would not allow to teach – uproar greeted the wretched man when he came through the door and drove him out again; after a day on which he wept, we saw no more of him, but as no other master came to take his lessons, we realised that he must have told no one of the state of play, and mayhem was the consequence. Miss Amali Dittrich, a petite and pretty middle-aged Czech who was supposed to teach us French, got much the same treatment: on one occasion I was de-bagged, that is stripped of my trousers and pants – a common jape – and roped to the seat of my desk, helpless to open a book or write a word; as I could not explain what was amiss, she came to see, and discovering my nakedness, let out a little scream and left the room, never to return, more tuitionless periods the consequence.

Dickie, a big and amiable boy, was the ringleader in most of these pranks and it must have been he who decided to go further with the horseplay that had rid us of Miss Dittrich. Off came my trousers and pants again and this time I was tied to the master's wooden chair. Where, I wonder now, did Dickie get so much rope and where had he concealed it? It was stout stuff: it had to be, for the next step was to lower me out of the window to dangle at the level of the Headmaster's room immediately below, that is from the second floor to the first. The odd thing is that I do not remember being terrified, swinging at an awkward angle thirty or forty feet above the tarmac down below, only a determination not to wriggle, unbalance the load and slip from the chair. I suppose the boys did not, mid-morning, expect the Headmaster to be at his desk, but he was and I shall never forget the horror on his face as, alerted by my shadow, he saw me. To give him his due, he thought at lightning speed, put his finger to his lips to silence me and did nothing to alarm the boys above. Not until I had been safely hauled back into the room did he enter it. There were no punishments – it was the last day of term, a common day for tomfoolery, and most of the boys were leaving. Their bullying had been wearying in its frequency, but never as spiteful as the treatment meted out the year before by Murray, who had left. That had been vicious. Murray, older by two years or so, was short, tough, muscular and merciless. He went about with two larger henchmen whose duty it was to secure a victim for Murray's use as a punchbag; first cornered, then dragged in front of him and braced erect to take the blows, I was as often as not that victim and I lived in fear of his repeated punches to my stomach. It was the Summerfield brothers again, but infinitely worse.

There was nothing sexual in Murray's bullying, just the exercise of power and the conscious cold infliction of fear and pain, the exploitation of his stupid henchmen an intriguing gloss. There should be a gentler word than bullying for the behaviour of the older boys in 5R; it was often sexual but there was neither hurt nor harm to it, though the frequency of it was a serious interruption to my attempt to hold on to my hope of eventual academic success. Mutual masturbation had at first been entirely random, urgently performed with any boy or boys willing to join in, but soon selection began to limit it as we became aware of the particular attraction of this boy or that. For some terms Davidson, my closest friend, and I made a common list of desirable partners and, sworn to honesty, compared our respective tallies on the last day to see which of us had had whom and how many times. The third phase was when fierce affections beyond our understanding began to develop, as well as more sophisticated practices. A German-Jewish boy – there were several in my age group who had escaped the Nazis in the later Thirties – for whom I wrote essays and poems in exchange for help with maths, astonished me with an unhesitatingly unsqueamish demonstration of fellatio when we were both fourteen. A year later I was jealously in love with Michael Jessett, a tall athletic boy, and on the night of my sixteenth birthday learned a bitter lesson when he buggered me. My willing-ness to please him, my romantic wanting it to happen, did little to ease the pain of my inexperience and his urgent clumsiness, but what really hurt – and permanently – was what immediately followed; I was lying on my belly, he withdrew, lit a cigarette, patted my bottom and said 'Gosh that was good – if you were a girl I'd do it again.' It was the end of our friendship. Love, if that is what I felt for Michael, froze; later that summer, at harvest camp, when other boys were holding him down and boot-blacking his scrotum for some perceived offence, I could have helped him, but I simply stood and watched. As mawkish as the silly girl he wished I'd been, I had given him the last remaining shred of my virginity and he had thought it a poor alternative. A successful musician, he married early and had children – what we had enjoyed, almost monogamously, for many months, had not the slightest effect on his adult sexuality.

For me, however, this was a turning-point. I knew that I was irrevocably queer, and so did other boys for whom our common sexual activities had been nothing but a step on the way to hetero-sexual maturity; I had friends at Highgate, UCS and St Paul's, and these too, once all willing partners, were changing, drifting steadily in an adult sexual direction that had nothing to do with boys or men. Occasionally they might oblige, but there was little joy in their grudging consent to these comfort wanks for past time's sake.

From academic oblivion I was saved by the decency of two masters in English and History who saw me through a repeated nightmare of School Certificate and Matriculation examinations taken internally and externally over the next two years, summer and winter, the set texts and periods changing in my favourite subjects, adding to the labour. I was then in the Sixth Form, on a two year course of study for the Higher School Certificate and Intermediate BA that pretty well guaranteed entry to a university, but this was an exam that I could not properly sit without first passing the lower School Certificate. Always in maths, a compulsory subject, I failed, and failed, and failed . . . but after the seventh sitting received a slip of paper with the words 'The examiners have decided to grant you a pass in the subsidiary subject Arithmetic. You may now sit higher examinations'.

The unstinting support of these two masters manipulating the indifference of a school that didn't care a damn as long as fees were paid, together with the patience of a stepfather who never let me see his despair, got me through these most difficult years of my school life, still with no clear notion of how I might want to earn my living. A careers adviser, interviewing me when in the Remove, ignored my interests in art and music and suggested that I might sit the Civil Service exam – 'You won't get into the Foreign Office or the Treasury, but you might just scrape into the Ministry of Ag and Fish.' Had I been at a state school, I would have sunk without trace, yet all these decades later it is into precisely my position, apart from fees, that the state education system, with maths still a compulsory subject, puts thousands of gifted children, wasting their time, obstructing their progress, perhaps wrecking their lives.

I must argue that all children are not equal and are not able to respond in equal measure to equal opportunities. I blame no one for my failure in maths, for I had no aptitude for it, but I do blame those who failed to see that, with figures, I was halted by a mental bloc so solid that I felt it physically. Not even for seconds can I retain a telephone number, the time of a train, the A or B number of a road. I know just enough of pounds and pence, euros and cents, miles and kilometres, to find my way about, and that is all I need – I have no wish to calculate the age of the universe or our distance from the Dog Star, and when Global Warming strikes, the men of Lincolnshire must work out for themselves how many fingers they must poke into how many dykes. My two years of hours wasted in *not* learning maths would have been far better spent on languages, motor-cycle maintenance or the history of art.

I hated most of my schoolmasters. Lewin, the sympathetic English master in the Upper School, I almost loved, and years later told him so. Locke, the senior History master who propped my progress through the Sixth Form, I enthusiastically respected; grave and dry, my quotations from *Alice in Wonderland* at the head of every essay on English constitutional history seemed to amuse him, but he could be cutting – 'A parlourmaid in Ponders End has better syntax,' he remarked of an essay on the *Eikon Basilike* written by another boy. Both men broadened my mind and with Lewin I could be frank about my miseries – though not my homosexuality; of Locke I still have a memento, a characteristic note advising me to read *Mémoires de Louis XIV pour L'Instruction du Dauphin*, but without telling me where or how to find a copy. Keevil, the art master, was friendly but indifferent, useless as a teacher, useless even as a basic instructor, but he let me into the art room without question whenever I was bunking off from maths or science – which, with increasing frequency, I did. Often, when I was in the sixths, he left me in charge of younger classes while he disappeared to tinker with his car, a troublesome Morris Ten of the earlier Thirties to which he had fitted an unsuitably lively Hotchkiss engine.

Payne, a mean-minded little man in polished brogues with steel tips (Blakeys) to heel and toe, failed utterly to teach me physics and was much given to twisting my ears in spite, though he occasionally gave me a small mark for a decent diagram. Through some divine malevolence he was appointed my invigilator when I sat, alone in the school hall, the Higher Schools Certificate examination in Art History – a subject self-taught, not in Haberdashers' syllabus, and

therefore examined very much against the wishes of the Headmaster, who was convinced that I would fail, though he gave in to
my stepfather's pleading. So there we were, the two of us, old
enemies, and Payne walked relentlessly up and down, the Blakeys
on his shoes clicking hard against the timber floor, the regularity
quite maddening. Even so, I was given a distinction by the
examiners.

Knight, after bullying me for years, at last tired of the unfair
game and pretended that I was absent; this, when he gathered us
round his high demonstration desk in the chemistry lecture theatre,
gave me unhindered opportunity to fumble in the trousers of other
boys and they in mine. There were two masters called Small, the
younger a post-war addition to the staff who could be reduced to
helpless laughter by the merest whiff of masturbation, but was a
friendly soul, inclined to give boys lifts in his pre-war open version
of the first Ford Prefect. The other Small, elderly, with rimless
spectacles, was an even more spiteful ear-twister than Payne, much
given to patrolling between desks hitting boys painfully hard with
the flat of a ruler on their bowed heads and necks; to have him
behind me was to abandon all concentration on the subject in
hand, bracing myself for the blow. And then there was Barling, the
rugger-playing Wesleyan Welshman who prevailed on the Head
(equally low church) to let him give us religious instruction instead
of French; a conscientious objector, he was mistrusted by the boys
who, all too often, had to bow their heads in honour of an Old
Haberdasher killed or missing in the war. In my day most boys at
the school were low church Christians, if anything, and a headmaster who was a non-conformist suited their parents' religious
views well enough, but Barling's idea of religious instruction was a
vituperative rant against Roman Catholicism and masturbation. He
drove me into furious defence of the Immaculate Conception and
belief in the Transubstantiation of the Host, even into refusal to be
taught by him, but when I walked out of the room there was no
punishment – even he must have realised that his rabid prejudice

was to be shared with converts in his native valleys and could not be regurgitated as religious education.

Worst of all was Callan. It was in the Third Form, when I was twelve that I spent a miserable year under Nat Callan, an English master whom I unreservedly detested. English was a subject in which I was strong – very well read for my age and sustained by an instinctive grasp of grammar – but Callan, nicknamed Nat for reasons now forgotten, though he introduced us to the sonnet and to Keats, pilloried me for my speech in almost every lesson. God knows I had a tough enough time with other boys over the way I spoke – 'You've had elocution lessons,' they mocked, when I did not even know the meaning of the word – tougher by far than any German-Jewish boy with something of Dennis the Dachshund about his English, but to be mocked for it by my English master was incomprehensible. It was Callan's custom to make me read aloud while he stood by my desk, half facing me, his head cocked to one side. Every so often he stopped me and, turning to the class, picked on my pronunciation of a word. 'Sewell says *appreciate* sounding the *c* not as *sh*, but as though it were an *s*. Who else does that?' Not one boy, it seemed – or none was foolish enough to admit it – whereupon Callan, after accusing me of prissiness and affectation, asked 'How then do you pronounce *appreciation?*' And inevitably I was ridiculed for illogic in not sounding the *t* as a *t* instead of *sh*.

These bouts were always humiliating and I always lost. The obvious remedy was to learn to speak as other boys did, but I had little ear for the difference (and still do not, unless it is extreme), and no capacity for mimicry, though I knew and know when I am being mimicked. Besides, there was the problem of betrayal. I spoke as I spoke because it was the way my immediate elders spoke, and to adopt a form of oral camouflage because Callan was so bloody-minded did indeed seem a form of cowardly betrayal. I could not do it. I did not want to do it. I began to skip Callan's classes, spending the hour behind the fives courts or, much riskier, in the lavatories when it was cold or wet; without a watch, this brought other difficulties and air raids occasionally complicated matters. As I could not altogether avoid Callan, I had always to be ready with excuses for absence and having done no prep, and was surprised when, as they grew more and more improbable, he accepted them without question.

I sank from the top to the bottom of the class, but did not care – did not care, that is, until the end of term report in which Callan had written none of the conventions about trying harder, only the brief note 'Is a plausible liar'. I thought I had been implausible. I cannot recall my explanation to my stepfather.

*   *   *

In the Sixth Form I led a small rebellion against compulsory membership of the Cadet Force and the weekly opportunity it offered to a certain type of master and boy to strut and bully. My only support came from my strict Jewish peers who had to be home by nightfall on Friday, the day on which the Force paraded and pretended. Though much my age, they seemed older, wiser and always more adult. Jewish boys were envied for having pubic hair when we had none, for ejaculating when our climaxes were dry, for having jockstraps first, for often being rather good at boxing and rugger, and for being academically brighter. They were not plagued with threats of palsied blindness for their masturbation; they were sceptical, questioning and worldly-wise, and the older boys who looked after the religious needs of the younger every morning, were respected for their gravity. It was these who had the courage to refuse to play the silly war games of the Corps. We were pilloried and punished. One whole day was spent at Bosham in canoes (Dudderidge's idea, no doubt), not canoeing from point to point, but held in a basin where, over and over again, we were compelled to perform the safety exercise of righting a canoe when it has turned turtle – to do that we had to turn it turtle first; the contemporary torture, waterboarding, cannot be much worse. We were also sent off alone on our bicycles for rides of a hundred miles or so, from post office to post office in the Chilterns to collect a note of the next destination; in my case this was once varied to my having to draw churches and other village buildings, including Medmenham Abbey, the artificial ruin in which the Hellfire Club conducted its obscenities – whose wry humour lay behind that instruction, I wonder? How we did these things on the paltry rations of the day I do not know, but we had been schooled in hunger and endurance by five full years of wartime shortage and the harsh austerity that followed it.

My final year at Haberdashers' was wasted, I was exhausted by the business of getting, at long last, my subsidiary pass in arithmetic concurrently with my Higher School Certificate, for which I had neglected Latin, then an essential for University entrance, and I had given no thought, nor been given any advice by the school, as to which university I should try for and what to read when there. There were too the vague ambitions vested in my painting and my neglected violin. I struggled to catch up in Latin, daily spent hours with my violin, played rugger and took rather too strenuously to religion as a cure for my homosexuality – to join the priesthood and be celibate and chaste held strong attractions. Nevertheless I was hopelessly in love with a younger boy, and had been with another, who had left school suddenly; to neither of them did I show my hand though it was obvious enough to boys of my own age, two of whom, Trask and Gaskell, mean-minded twits affecting an attitude *de haut en bas*, mocked me for it publicly and with sickening frequency, 're-fuelling' their euphemism for my supposed sodomy – re-fuelling aircraft in flight, was one of the technical achievements of the day, and in photographs it looked remarkably sexual to those who chose to see it so. It was also a pun identifying the younger boy. I knew, however, as well as they, that I had not 'grown out of it' – the only reassurance ever offered in our rare instructions on matters sexual – knew that it was not a 'phase,' and knew that I could never control it (unless with the help of God), yet, at eighteen, I vowed that I would never again have sex with a boy.

The school gave me what were called Sixth Form Privileges, but this exalted state brought only the responsibility of tolling the school bell every morning to urge laggards walking from Cricklewood to put on pace, and the bellringer had to be hauling on his rope some twenty minutes before assembly. Finding this irksome, I climbed into the belfry roof, found that a slim cord linked the rope to the bell and severed it at both ends (most boys then carried a clasp-knife) leaving no trace; the rope then slithered five storeys to the ground. I was never accused of the offence, but nor did my name again appear on the bellringing rota.

I am inclined to say that the school gave me nothing; certainly it gave me no prizes, not even the prize that I deserved for my Distinction in Art and the History of Art, and at my last Speech Day I watched with growing bitterness as others collected their prize books for similar prowess in less recherché subjects. On the last day of my last term I procured a small revenge on the Headmaster who, though rumoured to have fathered five daughters, drove a Fiat Topolino, that tiny two-seat work of automotive genius. The Upper School lavatories were attached to the building in a lean-to shack, its wide doors swinging open like those of a garage, facing the recreation field; open, they were only inches wider than the Fiat's length and I persuaded other boys to help me lift it sideways in, leaving its nose in one bank of urinals and its tail in the other. I then went to the school hall and removed the smallest pipe from the organ that occupied the rear wall. I have it still, in a cabinet of curiosities with dogs' teeth, a silver glove stretcher and other memorabilia.

But the school did give me something – rugger, cross-country running, confidence in my body and a dawning awareness that whatever I was to do or become would be determined by my own actions, that on my last day at school I was as alone as on my first. A frustrated act of kindness by my Latin master encapsulated all my years at Haberdashers'; he suggested that I should paint a mural for the Classics Room, above the picture rail, and, inspired by the paintings of John Craxton, I began an idealised strip cartoon of the Odyssey but had not quite finished by my leaving day; when I returned to it, late in the summer break, before the boys commenced the autumn term, I found it obliterated with a coat of distemper. Thus had the school wiped me from its memory.

CHAPTER 5

Intermezzo

As the first of several definitions, the Oxford Dictionary has inter-mezzo as 'a musical entertainment interpolated between sections of more serious fare'. Music had begun to dominate my life in my last year at school and in the following two years proved to be a cuckoo in the nest of all other possible ambitions. These were to read History at Oxford, to become a painter and be elected to the Royal Academy, and to play the violin (as a soloist, of course). The violin tutor to whom my mother sent me was Max Rostal, of whose eminence I was unaware. Austrian, Jewish, small, neat, formal and ascetic-seeming, his voice of memorable timbre, he had settled in England in 1934 and was about to become, as player and grey eminence, a profound influence on the performance of chamber music here. I dare say that in the austere years after the war he was glad of whatever fees my mother paid him – they cannot have been much – but in retrospect I wish that he had refused them and not encouraged me (and her). An uncompromising disciplinarian, he forbade me to ride a bicycle with my violin slung over my shoulder and corrected the lazy techniques developed under my mother's tuition, but seemed not interested in soul – either mine or the composer's. Soul was above all things what I wanted to put into my playing, and sometimes I played blind, through tears, moved to them, I hope, less by my playing than by the beauty of the music; I am still moved so, tears welling, shoulders shuddering with silent sobs, breath trapped in my chest. It was my mother's view that a wrong note here or there was of scant importance compared with feeling and emotion, and she gleefully played records of Casals, Thibaud and Cortot to prove her point.

Rostal and I soldiered on for two full years and more and never once did he even hint at what he should – that at best I might play second fiddle in an orchestra and should relegate my playing to the pastime of a competent amateur. My mother could not (or would not) see how weak I was, and nor could I, blinded by dreams, but my stepfather could – yet he said nothing until a few days before I went into the army to do my National Service for two years. Then he put his foot down, asked me to trust his judgement and warned that there could be few things more 'asking for trouble' than for a raw recruit to report to an Aldershot barracks carrying a violin. 'You might just get away with it in a Scottish regiment,' he said, 'but not in a working class mob like the Service Corps.'

Robert was, of course, absolutely right. I tuned the fiddle on short leaves, but there were too many other things to do on 36 or 48 hour passes; I did eventually take it to Aldershot on my first long posting, but when sent on from there, left it at home. After two years of neglect, my need to play it began to seem imaginary and the drive to do so faded. I kept it, tuned it now and then and drew a bow across the strings a little, but never made any serious attempt to revive what skills I may once have had. Now, when I can, at concerts I sit close to the second fiddles and see how expert they are, yet how submissive too, dutiful and unambitious, the soloism beaten out of them. I look at their hands and see delicate fingers with which mine compare as closely as those of an Irish labourer, and curse Rostal for not diverting my ambitions to the trumpet. Within weeks of my mother's death I took my violin to Christie's to be sold. It had been far more her dream than mine.

To become a painter, on the other hand, was more my dream than hers, and without my mother's pushing me into the arms of William Coldstream I might just have achieved it, for as well as my Distinction in Higher School Certificate, I had already had a ghastly picture shown in a mixed bag exhibition at the disreputable Cooling Gallery in Bond Street (a girl feeding a swan, nauseating rubbish long since destroyed), and with a pseudo-Expressionist painting of an *Absinthe Drinker* had won Third Prize in the nationwide School-children's Exhibition that was still an annual event when I began work as a critic. This was noticed by the *Daily Worker*, reproduced and praised as a piece of social comment on a decadent capitalist world, all the more remarkable for coming from a would-be public school. I should have had no difficulty in getting into an art school, but my mother, ever one to exercise influence and pull strings, sent me to Coldstream. What were the strings in this case? Why Coldstream, I have wondered since, now supposing that, though she was older by eight years, they must at some point have tumbled into bed together and that in enlisting his help with me she was forcing him to pay for his casual concupiscence; if this is the case, then it was probably in 1933 when he shared an exhibition, also at the Cooling Galleries, with Henri Enslin du Plessis, an amiable self-taught painter from South Africa, a handful of whose paintings my mother owned and with whom she was still in contact well into the 1970s.

I found Coldstream inscrutable, unsympathetic and seemingly incapable of warm enthusiasm for any other painter's work. Under his tutelage my romantic talent withered. I am not sure that this is true, for precocious ability is often nothing more than mimicry, and adolescent flare can fizzle to ashes in early maturity. True or not, it is what seemed at the time to happen and, within a year or so, Coldstream had convinced me that my technique was meretricious. I liked thick paint; I liked the accidental effects of colours mixed on the canvas rather than the palette; I liked the brave demonstration of the sweeping stroke and sacrificed the accuracy of drawing for the impastose gesture with the loaded brush: Coldstream liked none of these things and sought to tame them, though it now surprises me that he expressed no sympathy for the urban subjects that so often pleased me – the smudged smokey views of London from Parliament Hill, now long lost, and the dark leaden skies and thick yellow sunlight that still combine to lend theatrical magic to the Thames – for he was himself at his most accomplished (least contrived, perhaps) with the metropolitan railway station and the smirch of industry, dubbed 'Squalorscapes' by his friend Graham Bell. My recollection of the chill of our relationship is painful, and I still wonder whether, had Bomberg been my master – I am the same age as Auerbach – I might now be earning my living as a painter instead of a critic; nevertheless, I am convinced that I am a better critic for the experience.

Coldstream could do nothing to a canvas without a haberdasher's tape measure, a ruler and a plumb-line with a weight to chart his unsteady course across it, and he had the mentality of a haberdashery assistant, measuring everything minutely and costing it to the nearest farthing. To remind me of these years I have kept one canvas painted according to his methods, a dry and diligent piece of self-portraiture, pale in tone, tentative in touch and a shrewd imitation of all his mannerisms. As Professor at the Slade School for more than a quarter of a century, 1949–1975, he was to be the most major of major influences on the course of education in art schools throughout the land, on ministers and academics too, and I have no doubt that the long-term consequences of his power as an authoritative committee man have been disastrous – early in his career, the critic Geoffrey Grigson foresaw that this might be so and attacked him as cunning, a racketeer who would take bread from the mouths of better painters, a toady, a snob and with a foot in every camp. He even had a foot in the Courtauld Institute where I became a student concurrently with his later random lessons on the craft of painting – he had known Anthony Blunt, its Director, since at least 1938; I was from time to time grateful for the existence of the back stairs there that enabled me to duck out of his way.

He was rumoured to be extricating himself from an affair with one of the older students, Phoebe Pool, whom I adored. She had been an occasional student with the Euston Road painters in the late Thirties and had fallen in love with him then, but for him it was a thing of inconstancy and liability to which her response was a generally miserable demeanour, her considerable intellectual brilliance dimmed, dulled and disabled by incurable melancholy. To those who chose to speculate they made a strange pair, for Phoebe was a tall but stooping bag of bones, with glasses, a hearing-aid and twin set after twin set, and Coldstream we knew to have been dubbed 'Walking Death'. After almost a decade of struggle with clinical depression Phoebe achieved a brilliant BA in 1957 and followed it with a PhD two years later, her thesis so good that her examiners suggested its publication as a book.

Further bouts of depression delayed this until 1962 and it was achieved only with the persuasion and assistance of Anthony Blunt in writing the captions to the illustrations. The publisher of *Picasso, the Formative Years* then insisted that his name should precede hers on the cover; in his foreword Anthony made it clear that the text was 'entirely hers,' and privately deplored the presentation of the book as primarily his. Nevertheless, without his collaboration the book would never have been finished, for Phoebe was by then so deep in pathological depression that putting in order a pile of photographs and writing lucid notes on them, was quite impossible. Her condition inexorably worsened and, in rational intervals, suicide appealed as a logical end to it: in November 1971 she was killed by a southbound train at Bounds Green station on the Piccadilly line. When told of it, Anthony broke down in tears, and was still in tears when he told me. By 1984 Coldstream was in the grip of senile chorea, and death followed in February 1987. My mother, though by then slipping into the vagaries of senility, cut a notice of his death from the *Daily Telegraph* and tucked it into her diary.

* * *

As for Oxford and History, these were no more than ought-to aspirations inspired by rivalry with other boys at Haberdashers' whose paths through the school had been smoother and more rewarded than mine – the prefects and the prizewinners – but the truth was that I dreaded the prospect, a dread engendered by other boys encountered there competing for a place. I cannot recall which friendly soul sent me the slim pale green prospectus for the Courtauld Institute, but when it reached me one morning in the high summer of 1950 I raced on my bike to Portman Square (where it then was) and, to my surprise, was sent to a tiny office on the second floor overlooking the garden. There I found Charles Clare, the silver-haired, pipe-smoking, warm and kindly Registrar, who said that my Higher School Certificate was enough to let me in and that I could come in October. So ended my unwilling flirtation with Oxford.

Charles, who became a friend and remained so long after his retirement to the Isle of Wight, should not have let me in. It may seem odd, so many years later, for me to have blamed Max Rostal for my wasted years as a would-be violinist and William Coldstream for my failure as a painter, and now to make Charles responsible for what was to be another failure, but this is what it was and he, not I, knew how academically tough the Courtauld had become after a shaky beginning as an unintended finishing school in the 1930s. I was nineteen, but still a boy, absurdly sophisticated in some respects – an habitué of Covent Garden Opera since its reopening in 1948, of Christie's (where I had already bought several parcels of prints and drawings for the minimum bid of 3 guineas – pocket money for six weeks), and of Bond Street art dealers too, none of whom took amiss the regular Saturday morning visits of a curious schoolboy propping a bicycle nearby – yet I was bewildered, overwhelmed indeed, by the sophisticated adult company of the older students among whom I found myself. Most were postgraduates with an Oxford or Cambridge degree in another subject intending to do in two years what I would do in three, and for the men among them, National Service was a thing of the past and some had even been in the real army in the last stages of the war. Among these, the Students' Common Room was no place for an immature and untravelled boy from a school that had in no way prepared him for the complexities of an academic discipline that it did not teach. These older students already knew Rome and

Florence; some had lodgings within walking distance, and for others money seemed never to be in short supply – Delia Dawnay, for example, later to marry Oliver Millar (Blunt's successor as Surveyor of the Queen's Pictures in 1972), flew to Madrid for a long weekend to see the paintings there by Velazquez when he was the required subject of an essay. Michael Jaffé, dapper in even casual clothes and dominant in every conversation, Cecil Gould with KUNSTFORSCHUNGEN writ large on the files he always carried, Francis Hawcroft, John Shearman, John Steer, John Golding, Ronald Alley, Christopher White, Reyner Banham, Jennifer Montagu, Sheila Somers and Michael Kitson (of whom more later) were among the subsequently professorial grandees who overwhelmed not only me but the handful of other school-leavers beginning their first year as undergraduates.

The art history that I had taught myself had been no more than the ability to write essays of some small stylistic elegance, poetic insight and occasionally wry interpretation. These pale reflections of Walter Pater might have served me well as a student of English at Oxford, but as art history they were undisciplined rubbish; they had nothing of Pater's broad intellectual weight and far too much of his literally flowery language – 'powdered all over in the Gothic manner with a quaint conceit of daisies,' he wrote of Botticelli's *Birth of Venus*, and I fell in love with him. That half sentence is the Calais engraved on my heart and I repeat it to myself when now I fall – as occasionally I do – into Dear Reader mode, recalling the schoolmaster who once rebuked me for my purple passages. The first essay required from me by my first tutor, Peter Murray, a dry young stick who could have made a dull business of Michelangelo and Leonardo, was on Filippo Lippi, an ideal painter for the quaint conceit of daisies treatment, and he got it; Anne Hewlett, a fellow new student, reminded me this year, fifty-eight years after the event, of Murray's appalled response – 'Well, that's the first time in my life that a student has written an essay without a single date.'

Art history, I discovered, depends on dates, the *terminus ante quem* and the *terminus post quem*, the dates of death and birth, the dates of commissions and the dates of their completion. It also requires at least a reading knowledge of German, Italian and French, and Dutch and Russian might be useful, as might ancient Greek – Latin was taken for granted. An art historian must be a plain historian too, aware of the whats and whens of Kings, Emperors and Popes; to be confronted with the Guelphs and the Ghibellines of early Italian Renaissance politics when all my history at school had been either English or European as it affected England, was to realise that distant memories of Richard the Lion Heart and Le Crac des Chevaliers were not enough; to be told to read Ludwig Pastor's monumental *History of the Popes* in the original German, was to realise at once what provincial little mice we undergraduates were. There were too the international ramifications of banking and trade and their influence on patronage, the effects of plague, famine and wars of religion might have to be taken into account, and it was often very much a help to be aware of philosophy, medicine, music and literature. Art history, it seemed, opened doors on every aspect of history and culture, for art never stood alone.

And no teenage undergraduate in the first year had ever been anywhere. This was long before the institution of school trips abroad or any form of foreign travel was encouraged, when allowances in foreign currency were restricted to the cost of one night in a decent hotel, when few had cars and European railways were still disrupted by damage inflicted in the war. At home, rationing of all essential foodstuffs was still in force and we none of us had any idea of what might confront us across the Channel. And so we had not crossed it and this put us at a crippling disadvantage.

*   *   *

There was another element of confusion – my attachment to Alan Harverson – and this was indeed the frivolous intermezzo between boyhood and manhood, leading nowhere. With increasing frequency Alan had taken me to his bed in my last years at school – as a man taking the initiative he did not count as one of the boys I had forbidden myself to woo; physically I found him not in the least attractive and enthusiasm cannot have been much in evidence in my cooperation, but in his late teens a boy is carried along by the responses of his body and, in terms of good manners, to have rejected his physical expressions of fondness would have been, I thought, a wretched reward for his countless musical generosities. To a wider audience Alan is, perhaps, still remembered for mastering the organ of the Albert Hall on the last night of the Proms from the late 1940s well into the 1970s, and for a handful of recordings of exquisite performances of music by Mozart and Bach in the 1960s. I remember him most for the musical madness to which he introduced me in the austere post-war years, a schoolboy already in thrall to the range of music to be heard on the BBC's then new Third Programme, suddenly exposed to the glories and subtleties of the organ – Bach, Pachelbel, Widor, Fauré, Reger and Messiaen. Here was a man who with music transported congregations from the dreary sameness of Church of England ritual and made Matins and Evensong glorious occasions, who restored a sense of exaltation to Christmas jollity, to whom the services of Easter were moments of profound belief.

His base was a church in Cricklewood where the parish priest, William Bulman, big, bluff and wonderfully sensible, was an old friend of my stepfather. When I 'got religion,' as they say, Robert saw to it first that I was confirmed in the Church of England in a mass confirmation service at school, for in spite of being a Christadelphian (an American sect that rejects the Trinity and believes every word of the Bible to be inspired and infallible), the Headmaster had appointed a School Chaplain from the bells and whistles department of the C of E, and then made sure that Bill Bulman took me under his unperfumed wing, thus manoeuvring me away from my mother's dormant Catholic influence – how odd that having neglected my soul for some years, and their own souls for that matter, Robert should now engineer this small Protestant victory. Bulman, however, a priest who thought the distinctions between Rome and Canterbury mere matters of semantics, politics and ornament, opined that my baptism as a Roman Catholic and my confirmation in the English church were not incompatible, gave me a Latin Vulgate and suggested that if I was serious about becoming a priest I should think about learning Aramaic (what, I wonder, would my Christadelphian headmaster have said, had I demanded that?), and then decide in which denomination to confine myself, for serving both was, for the moment, quite impossible. When, troubled by uncertainty in the matter of the Transubstantiation of the Host, I bearded him in his study; after some exegesis he summed up his response with 'My boy, you must bring everything to the bar of your own judgement.' This was not helpful: I wanted authority that would either confirm or confound my misgivings about this beautiful and terrible belief, and got instead a gnomic utterance that had no clear meaning for a boy of sixteen. It was, nevertheless, the wisest instruction ever given me. Understanding dawned soon enough and that simple sentence has ever since been my guide in politics and social responsibility; in religion it proved eventually to have been the first insidious blow of scepticism against the received faith that might have been a comfort.

With Bulman's support, Alan formed the St Gabriel's Singers in which, to the accompaniment of organ, harp, cello and fiddle, the fine voices of young professionals sang music then strange and rare. One of them, Heather Harper, then unknown, he let loose on Purcell's *The Blessed Virgin's Expostulation*, a prophetically operatic piece, but the career of another, Dorothy Bond, a protégé of Thomas Beecham and a pretty girl of extraordinary promise remembered now only for having sung the role of Olympia in his 1951 film of *The Tales of Hoffmann*, was cut short by a fatal car crash a year later. There were many more for whom the ad hoc

Singers were a stepping stone for a long professional career, but there were stalwarts too who offered the bright young things the solid backing of experience, among them Primrose Ballard, a formidable contralto, and Mignon Fressard, the harpist, who took me to her bosom and stayed a friend until her death in the 1970s.

Like Dorothy, Mignon was one of many figures who played no important part in my life, made no difference to its progress or direction, and yet enriched it mightily. She was not French, but her husky accent had so long been part of her Piaf reinvention of herself that it rang true. Nor was she Mignon; she was Gladys Adams from Newcastle who long ago had had a French lover whose pillow name for her was Mignon and, ever the northern realist, she knew that as a musician she would go much further with his name than with hers. She played the very largest of harps and seemed waif-like at its strings, for years transporting it in an old Austin Ten with all but the driver's seat removed (there were no hatchbacks then), painted a uniquely bilious yellow so that she could always find it at a glance. In St John's Wood, a stone's throw from Dorothy, she lived in an enviable dead-end mews in which every cottage was occupied by musicians – the cacophony of heaven on a summer's day. She left me her Bechstein, a grand in white lacquer.

Alan not only played organs, he knew about their workings. One midwinter soon after the war, still in his early twenties, he somehow got permission to go to a still very ruined Germany to seek out what baroque instruments had survived in the British Zone, and, close to the Walker family, he persuaded those redoubtable builders of peculiarly British organs to take inspiration from German models of the eighteenth century. He wanted his Bach to sound as it had sounded to Bach himself, crisp and clear, not clouded with rich Victorian confusions, not to be mistaken for Stainer and Stanford, and in designing modern organs – as he did – he had to know how those he most admired were constructed. The immediate consequence of his first German journey was his ingenious specification for the organ at St Gabriel's, rebuilt in 1948–49, an instrument intriguing enough to become almost the property of the BBC so constant was the Corporation's use of it.

With Bill Bulman at the wheel of his ancient Vauxhall 14, priest and organist set off, summer after summer, to explore the cathedrals and organs of France and Italy – this in the days when the travel allowance was only £25, but such a trifle would never have deterred Bill who, a contented comfortable man of substance with an unambitious contempt for bishops and archdeacons, quietly paid for the Singers and the new organ without drawing attention to his generosity. The energy of friendships with other organists formed on these journeys, Fernando Germani of St Peter's and Jeanne Demessieux of Nôtre-Dame among them, resulted in their coming to London, where they not only played the organ at St Gabriel's, but gave spontaneous recitals on every interesting instrument on which they could lay hands. They and Alan played for the sake of playing, experimenting and responding each to the other's challenge, and late one night, in a deserted Westminster Cathedral, Alan and Jeanne had so many stops out that the organ died with the unforgettable groan of a great beast. And my part in this? It was to pull out the stops and turn the pages – my role again in 1954 when, on an organ not designed by Alan, his help was enlisted by the engineers brought in to improve the poor acoustics of the Royal Festival Hall; for days on end we ranged through the pipes and stops from *vox angelica* to *bombarde* – alas, as we all know, to have no remedial affect on that cheap and shoddy building.

A generous teacher and a major player in the spirited revival of interest in organs and organ music after the war, Alan, never pushy, was too soon overtaken by far less able organists, less ingenious and musical, who rarely recognised how much they and their profession owed him. When, in 2006, I was asked to write a brief obituary for the insignificant Lives Remembered column of *The Times*, it was not published, yet thirty-six column inches and a photograph had been devoted to his pupil Lionel Dakers three years earlier – but then he was a Coldstream in the world of organists.

Alan did not usurp my mother as a musical influence – that would have been both unwise and impossible – he simply worked with her. While she opened my eyes to opera at Covent Garden, he took me to concerts and recitals and, of course, exposed me to choral music and the organ – formidable competition for essays on Filippo Lippi, Brueghel and Jan Steen required as a student of art history. At the Courtauld Institute an oddly disturbing episode jogged my sexual relationship with him. Leaving it late one afternoon in May 1951 at precisely the same moment as a man whom I had several times seen leaving both Anthony Blunt's study on the first floor and his chill quarters in the attic, we fell into step and he suggested a drink. I refused, at which he insisted on buying me a milk shake in Baker Street; we sat on high stools at the bar, turned towards each other, drinking something sweet and pink through straws while he went through the performance with which he hoped to fascinate me, while I contemplated the egg on his tie and savoured the tobacco on his breath. A day or two later he waylaid me and invited me to dinner, after which he inflicted the traumatic experience of taking me to his 'club,' which was not in Pall Mall, but in some cellar haunt where I was more or less compelled to dance with him – more food stains and foul breath, and an overwhelming discomfort at the very idea of doing such a thing. I fled. And so did he – within a few days Guy Burgess was headline news in every paper. There cannot have been a student who had not seen him in the Institute; there was not a student who did not suppose the Director to have been in some way involved in his flight with Donald Maclean, yet none of us was dismayed, appalled or outraged at the thought – we simply took it in our strides. This was 1951 and not one single journalist rang the doorbell at 20 Portman Square.

The brush with Burgess did appal me in another sense: were seedy clubs, food droppings and sloppings on my clothes, the empty chatterings of seduction, and mephitic breath, what I in middle age, would inflict on pretty boys? Celibacy seemed ever more attractive.

Espousing the comforts of religion as an instrument of change in what I knew to be my sexual nature, and even that done clumsily as a Catholic born but, for the past decade, not a Catholic bred, I lacked the courage to break with Alan; to do so without hurting his feelings required an external agency beyond our control. One was within reach. Failure haunted me; as though failure as a painter and musician, were not enough, I sensed impending failure as an art historian, the poorest of degrees ahead of me (and what use could that be?); and then Robert, in the summer of 1952 delivered the blow that really broke me, not so much in his admission that he was not my father, but in yet another failure on my part, the failure to grasp the opportunity to demand to know – no matter what the cost to Robert and my mother – who and what I really was. I talked to Charles Clare, suggesting that if I left the Courtauld Institute at once to join the army for my unavoidable two years of National Service, the break would conveniently run from September to September, fitting with university terms; if during these two years I decided that I wanted to return, would the Courtauld accept me and would it allow me to start from scratch, taking the full three year course again? To both questions he answered yes, and then, eyes twinkling, offered me this encouragement – 'You know, you're not as hopeless as you think.' The wasted years of my intermezzo were concluded.

CHAPTER 6

National Service as a Squaddie

In my young days boys were prepared for life by dancing lessons and National Service, and of the two I much preferred the latter. Oh the misery and discomfort, the crippling sense of inadequacy engendered by the hours spent in the compelling arms of a corseted dancing mistress learning the quickstep, the foxtrot and the tango – to these the ingenious bullyings of strutting Warrant Officers and corporals proved infinitely preferable.

What did I learn from National Service? I learned to shoot with a cold accuracy that surprised the men who taught me. I learned to ride a motorcycle and to drive almost everything the Army had on wheels. I learned to pitch a tent and dig a trench and wriggle at a snake's pace on my belly. I learned, if I did not already have them, the habits of neatness and economy. 'Any fool can be uncomfortable,' said one of my instructors, a Captain in the Gloucesters, lately wounded in Korea, and I learned from him to make silk purses from sows' ears. These were practical things that have stood me in good stead, but the less definable things have served me even better. In the intimacy of my platoon it was as though we had sworn the marriage vow to obey, serve, love, honour and keep each other in sickness and in health. We learned lessons in loyalty and interdependence that wove the platoon together; we learned self-reliance and the generous exchange of our modest capabilities; we learned that the strength of a group of men is the strength of the weakest member and that the weakest can be made stronger with forethought and support. With modesty and squeamishness abandoned I learned that compliance is not an easy option, but often the only option in a particular set of circumstances – that one can, and sometimes must, do things about which one has almost overwhelming intellectual and moral reservations, or that are deeply offensive to one's taste. I think I learned – it was never put to the test – that there was nothing that I would not do, that needs must when the Devil drives. I believe this still to be so, though my choices now might be significantly different. I learned too, that separation from my dog was more painful than separation from my parents.

Most of a lifetime later I am so burdened with moral baggage that I have perhaps lost the ruthlessness the Army taught me, but for decades I believed that my two years of National Service had done me far more good than my three as an undergraduate, my eight at school and twenty on my knees in church. National Service revealed depths and darknesses in my soul that I was grudgingly glad to know were there; if I am now capable or making worthwhile moral judgements it is because I was for two brief years a soldier of sorts, not because I am an art historian, a lapsed Conservative, an agnostic Christian.

Only a fool could do two years National Service and resent it as a waste of time. Its benefit to society was formidable. It removed every young man in the land from the unemployment pool for two full years and paid him a mean pittance while training him in essential societary skills, often teaching him a trade that made him readily employable on his return to Civvy Street. It removed him to an almost closed society, monkish in its way, disciplined and orderly, and taught him to manage his indiscipline and disorder, anger and sexuality. Bullying, brutality, intimidation and fear were among its training tools with raw recruits, victimisation too, but even these had their educative purpose and were the stimulus of resources of resilience that had not been tapped before.

The entirely independent decision to enlist was my first indication of maturity. Early in September 1952 I took a specified train to Aldershot. The repeated advertisement for beer along the railway track, 'You are now entering the Strong Country' seemed as weightily portentous as the 'You are now crossing the county boundary' with which Beatrix Potter threatened Pigling Bland. On arrival, my brief experience in the School Corps immediately proved useful – I knew how to clamber into the back of an army truck.

I am not certain that as it swung through the barracks gate I murmured 'All hope abandon, ye who enter here,' but in essence that was the response of all of us. We were puny, skinny boys, half a century ago, a wartime generation brought up on short rations, shorter still in the bleak post-war years, and none of us was over-weight, none of us had a beer belly. We were inclined to be obedient, for we came straight from school, apprenticeships and jobs without much promise. We were not independent and most of us were bound by apron-strings to mothers who had taught us nothing of the 'girly' domestic skills required by the Army, nothing of fending for ourselves. Very few of the lads had regular girlfriends or were married, and the rest of us knew of sex only by proxy or fumbling with other boys – never to be admitted in these circum-stances. But we had neither time nor opportunity for sex, we were imprisoned, or so it seemed, and convinced that the Army cooks put bromide in our tea to undo our sexual appetites; only the regular creaking of an iron bed might indicate that one of us was on the way to orgasm, but most of us were so exhausted that sleep was more important.

We were the Army's property, to use and abuse as its minions thought fit in what was called Basic Training, the weeks of spirit breaking, humiliation and belittlement, degradation and indignity, insult, outrage and affront that seemed to have no connection with courage, heroism and nobility, the great abstract virtues of the military life of which I knew from a French set book at school – Alfred de Vigny's *Servitude et Grandeur Militaires*. We were taught that every moment of the day and night our bodies and souls were not our own but in the common ownership of every officer, commissioned and non-commissioned, from the single stripe of the lance-corporal to the dizzy height of the half-colonel, the loftiest rank that we squaddies would ever encounter. We were to march, drill, run and jump when ordered, sleep, wake and ablute when ordered, and even the emptying of bowels and bladders could be done only when ordered.

Time was not ours – that too was Army property and NCOs were mean with it; things that would have been better done in five minutes had to be done in three, and if done badly, punishment was the consequence. Punishment was always out of all proportion to the misdemeanour; for the merest trace of Brasso polish on the back of a buckle on a gaiter six feet below the sergeant's eye, madness, mayhem and the wanton destruction of hours of scrupulous work preparing kit were immediate. Lance-corporals pretended to be terrified of corporals, corporals of sergeants, sergeants of sergeant-majors, and all used that terror to justify the terrors that they, in turn, on us, inflicted; all had the ability, within a millisecond, to puff to twice their size and turn the rainbow colours of a baboon's backside. To a callow youth who had never suffered worse than six strokes of a cold schoolmaster's cane, and suffered those unseeing, the nose to nose aggression of the purple swollen face, the spray of spittle from the open mouth, the screaming volume of the insults and the orders were a monstrous and terrifying phenomenon – and worst of all was the business of having to shout back, repeatedly – 'louder!' the most dread command – 'I am a prick, a poofter and a pile of shit, dear Corporal!'

There were tears too. Tears broke the tension induced by long hours of irrational discipline, futile punishment, wretched discomfort and the unrelenting exaction of obedience. I saw no one in my intake break into tears before an NCO, but in bed, in darkness, sobs of misery were sometimes audible, the tough little East End bruiser next to me the real surprise; he had strength, stamina and street-vicious responses, but sewing on a button was for him intellectually beyond the gender barrier and not something he could or would do. It had, nevertheless, to be done and he saw it as some sort of self-emasculation. A boy in another section, fastidious, pernickety, uncooperative, gave no help to his mates, got no help from them and probably deserved the blackballing that they, exasperated, gave him; it was cruel – a scrotum boot-blacked raw with new Army brushes is no joke, and with showers permitted only once a week, not much could be done about it. The poor kid fled the barracks to demand sanctuary of the Fathers at Brompton Oratory, but a fat lot of good that did him when they informed the Military Police. We were told that he had been sent to Colchester, to the Army prison there, a Hell beyond the Hell of Dante. It was thus, unconsciously, that we learned to be Stoic philosophers.

Had any of this ill-treatment any point? It did not seem so at the time. It went so far beyond the calculated spite of schoolmasters and prefects that it was beyond comprehension. Why shout when conversational exchange would better do the trick? – but conversation between the high and low is not the Army's way. Why waste time with mindless punishment when more time for a task would have let us do it well? Why bully when explanation would give us understanding? Why exhaust us? Why, worst of all, seem to offer us a moment of conciliation, an inkling that an NCO is not all brute, and then, in some sense, betray us? We were learning when and whom not to trust, yet what surprised me later, after Basic Training – and in isolated cases, during it – was how reasonable senior NCOs could be when not in the Army's public eye. We learned immediate obedience, though some of us had qualms that obedience to the idiocies of barracks NCOs might kill us in Korea, Malaya, Aden and the other theatres of war to which we might be sent. And eventually we realised that Basic Training was exactly what the Army claimed for it – the business of breaking us down in order to build us up again as more self-reliant mentally and stronger physically than we could ever have been without it.

Swiftly it dawned on the sensible among us that we must play the Army's game. If we were told that heaps of coal must be painted white with blanco, then white we painted them; with razor blades we scraped the crystalline deposits from urinals, and with Brasso we polished the heads of nails in floorboards, for this was the off-with-his-head world of Alice in Wonderland. My own particular intellectual crisis came with bayonet practice – the blood-curdling yell and then the plunge into the belly, never the ribs because it might be difficult to withdraw. Could I do this to another boy? That question was impossible to answer, and this was not the moment for debate: all that was required of me was pretence, the pretence of stabbing a sack of straw hanging from a gibbet, a charade that was not, in itself the moral dilemma; that I would deal with if and when it confronted me on a bleak hillside in Korea or the steaming forests of Malaya; only then would I know the answer in an adrenal rush of fear or in the cold logic of survival that I was beginning to discern in myself.

Army life was regulated by the ten minute smoking break every two hours or so. 'Who doesn't smoke?' asked the corporal in charge of our first attempts at rifle drill, and on finding me the only squaddie in the platoon without nicotine-stained fingers, stood me at ease and then instructed the other twenty boys to prop their rifles against me while they smoked or dashed away to pee – this in a chill October morning. Next day I produced Woodbines and matches bought in the NAAFI overnight as evidence that I had joined the smokers. 'You're learning,' said the corporal, and chose another boy to be the prop. I took to reading in these breaks, swiftly transported to saner worlds for a few moments, but these were not to last: a recruit was supposed to have nothing in his pockets other than the customary essentials and, in his left breast pocket, his pay-book, the slim passport-like record of his identity, next-of-kin and pay, but I also had the Penguin edition of a novel by Evelyn Waugh in the opposite pocket of my battledress – unwise on a day when the first parade was to be taken by a Warrant Officer, a senior NCO of the most impressive kind. Inspecting the length of our hair, our shaving skills, our boots and uniforms, when he reached me he tapped the Penguin pocket with his pace-stick – a hefty thing of timber and brass resembling an enormous pair of dividers, with which, swaggering and dexterous, he measured stride – and so quietly that the boys on either side could not comprehend, said 'Wog, Woof or War – which is it?' 'War, Sir.' 'Don't bring it on parade again.' It was a reproach as effective as any scream of rage and a thousand times more intelligent, for it immediately engaged my respect and would have engaged my loyalty had we ever found ourselves in a situation that required it. From this episode I also learned that I had no privacy, that I had not only been observed reading, but that the observer had been close enough to read the cover of the book and mean enough to report it – a spiteful lance-corporal, no doubt, not literate enough to pronounce Waugh's name, hence Wog and Woof, and intent on getting me into trouble.

Almost every minute of our lives was regulated, but from time to time the frantic pace was disrupted by a medical inspection for athlete's foot and its equivalent in the crotch, by the requirement that we should donate blood, at the sight of which, frothing in the bottles, a surprising number of supposedly tough boys fainted, or an interview with a Personnel Selection Officer. My PSO was as hapless as the careers officer who had interviewed me at school: in the RASC (the Royal Army Service Corps as it then was, almost the very bottom of the army heap, the Shit Corps), the two careers it offered were either as a driver or a clerk, neither of interest to a boy besotted with music and art. He decided that a few minutes with an army psychiatrist might be helpful to us both, and I was ushered into the presence of a captain in a neighbouring office. 'Which of your parents do you love best?' he asked. Surely better, I thought, as I have only two, but answered 'Neither,' sensing danger in both directions and disinclined to disclose my bastardy, my rage against my stepfather, my ignorance of my real father and my determination to cut my mother's apron strings. He did not ask me if I might be queer, the question that I most feared, knowing that to tell the truth would wreck my purpose in serving my two years away from home and London. On his advice the PSO decided that I should become a clerk and the Army then taught me how to type – for which skill I have ever since been grateful; it also tried to teach me rudimentary accounting – as conceptually confusing as trigonometry.

I cannot now recall quite how many weeks we spent in Basic Training – two, perhaps, in coming to terms with the brutality of army discipline in Buller Barracks, and another six in the comparative harmony of Willems. We were given occasional short breaks, often with no warning, of which only those who lived in the South-East could take advantage – and even they were hard-pressed to get home and back within 24 hours. So little time meant only that we had a Sunday free of church parade and could sleep all day if we chose. Resisting surrender to homesickness, I slipped away to nearby Fleet where Alice Denne, a friend of my mother who grew Rhodesian tobacco in her conservatory and rolled her own cigars, fed me as though I were a civilised being and not a ravening animal. She had an almost professional knowledge of seventeenth century Dutch still life painting and part of the seriously important Assheton Bennett collection of such things hung on her walls.

Ten or so years earlier an elderly man had knocked on our door in the hope of selling the small wares in a tray hanging from his neck – matches, boot laces and other necessaries from which street hawkers then made a wretched living, and my mother, sensing something amiss, something gentlemanly in the shabbiness, had hauled him in, fed and watered him, questioned and lectured him, and given him money enough to return to the family home, the prodigal brother returning to his sister, Alice Denne. That was the benign, unselfish, practical side of my mother's nature.

With a 36-hour pass from noon on Saturday to midnight on Sunday, real civilisation became possible. I could be in Waterloo early in the afternoon – but then what? From late November until the beginning of March 1953, the Royal Academy mounted one of its great winter exhibitions devoted to Dutch Painting 1450–1750 – 644 paintings, and the great Gallery III hung with

Rembrandts alternating with Cuyps, perhaps the most memorable hang in all my lifetime; this was where I spent every hour of leave that I got, except for the very first of my passes, shortly before it opened. On that occasion, in heavy boots and prickly uniform because no new recruit was allowed to change into civilian clothes, unappealingly naked of hair about the ears and neck, I walked to Covent Garden and spent a guinea on a seat that evening in the stalls circle – twenty-one shillings of the twenty-four that were a squaddy's weekly pay, gone at a stroke. Then I walked to the National Gallery to kill time with old friends, the last of them the Arnolfini Portrait by Jan Van Eyck, that immaculate description of a medieval reality with its convex mirror (of which David Hockney was one day so mistakenly to make so much) and oriental rug, the dog and the discarded shoes, the shutters and, behind the hinge, the crack through which we see the garden. Engrossed, I was almost unaware of the grand old man in black cloak and fedora, the only other being in the room, until he came near and asked 'Who do you think those two people are?' I gave him the obvious answer 'Giovanni Arnolfini and his wife,' to which a histrionic 'No!' was the retort, 'they are Jan van Eyck and his wife.' Then to my 'You've been reading that silly book,' he responded with a triumphant 'Reading it? I *wrote* it.'

The old man was Maurice Brockwell, a curator and historian of art long before art's history became an academic discipline in Britain, of a generation for whom it was enough to write well of whimsical ideas, the silly book his slim volume *The Pseudo-Arnolfini Portrait*, published that year, 1952.

My confusion and embarrassment were put to rest with his inviting me to lunch at the Athenaeum the following day. I explained that I had to be in boots and battledress, but he would not accept refusal and so it was that I found myself not only in his company but that of two painters too, Alfred Munnings and Stanley Spencer. Munnings questioned me closely on the conditions of the National Serviceman, went through a range of appalled reactions, though he must have seen things far worse during the First World War, and said that he would write to my commanding officer – quite the last thing this squaddie wanted and I had to be, I think, rude, to put him off. Stanley – as I was instructed to call him – a tiny man who had spent most of that same war in the Balkans (one of its most intriguing campaigns) in unrelentingly grim conditions, showed no interest in my misfortunes, nor, indeed, in any of our conversations' drifts, and at one point slipped from his chair, I think onto his knees, until his eyes were level with the tablecloth, and then began to adjust the relative positions of the salt, the pepper and all other permanent occupants of the vast white waste, much as Poussin and Gainsborough must have arranged the miniature landscapes that informed their finished paintings. This, Brockwell and Munnings ignored, while I felt as Alice felt at the Mad Hatter's Tea Party, 'very much confused,' the discussion of art as wayward and inconsequential as the Dormouse's disquisition on drawing.

Maurice became something of a friend until his death in December 1958, though he had little respect for the Courtauld Institute and sorely tried my loyalty to it. He lived in Earls Court, in a mansion flat that had seen much better days and which, after the death of his wife early in 1952, gradually descended into near squalour. It was his wife's death that led him, lonely, to play ancient mariner in the National Gallery, and I wonder how many other young men he waylaid – not that he had any interest in young men other than as an anxious tutor. He had outlived all possibility of income; his long curatorship of the Cook Collection of old masters had ended with the outbreak of war in 1939 when he was just short of seventy, and his indefatigable research into the quibbles of the history of Netherlandish art can never have made money for him, any more than they added weight to his reputation as a scholar. What little he had was depleted by what his Times obituarist described as his 'interest' in horse racing. The Athenaeum quietly 'forgot' his subscription, but his landlords finally forced him out of his flat and his last months were spent in The Charterhouse. Of his lifetime of scholarly research papers – mistaken though so many of his assertions were – not a trace remained for those few of us who, on his death in 1958, thought they might be worth preserving.

*   *   *

Our basic training and our corps training complete, someone somewhere in the hierarchy decided on our fate. Given posting application forms on which we were to list our three preferences, boys who were homesick, or had girlfriends, or were even married, hoped to be sent to units in the British Isles; some suggested the safety of Germany and Egypt, but no one asked for a posting that involved active service; in the event, the whole platoon was posted to Korea where British casualties were known to be heavy and winter conditions terrible. Other platoons were sent en bloc to Egypt. Before we were despatched on embarkation leave we were lectured on the weather, clothes, food, conditions, the state of the campaign, leave (in Japan, for us), the political background and what we would experience in the long confinement on a troopship. For the last of these lectures the whole intake was gathered to hear a Brigadier give us instruction on matters sexual – the horrors of syphilis in particular, the treatment for which had us squirming in our seats – did the Umbrella, I wonder, really exist, or was this instrument, inserted into the urethra, then opened as with the spokes of an umbrella and withdrawn, scoring its inner wall to make it bleed, a myth to make us shy away from penetrative sex? At this and tales of the sores and smells that lurk in a Gippo prostitute's vagina there were vague murmurs of distaste, but a sound far more audible and general was that of in-drawn breath when the lecture ended with an admonition to avoid sex with any natives anywhere, 'but if you *must* have it, take your best mate round the back of the barracks and bugger him.'

For me and a handful of others, however, the someone some-where had second thoughts and decided that we might, perhaps, be what was dubbed 'officer material'. With my school record I had not thought of it myself, but there were boys in my intake who had been to a public school and spent years in a Cadet Force, or who simply had a high opinion of themselves founded on class, all of whom thought they should be officers. I was taken off the Korean draft, for which I had already had a week's embarkation leave, and returned to Willems Barracks to await a War Office Selection Board, or WOSB (always spoken of as a Wosby). For some weeks we were astonishingly well-treated: we were nothing more than raw privates, yet we were paired off in small rooms that gave us more privacy than I ever had as an officer cadet, and our sole duty was to read the daily newspapers with which we were supplied and make ourselves aware of the world and its events. There were odd parades to sharpen our drill and occasionally an officer appeared to tell us something of what to expect at a WOSB and how to pass it but, set apart, as we were, it was a deliciously idle few weeks. Boys were called quite randomly to their WOSBs and, whether they passed or failed, disappeared either to a working unit or to Mons, the great officer training unit for the aspiring middle-class dullards of the RASC and the really well-bred boys who had joined the Cavalry.

I shared a room with Eric Biddle, a grammar school boy from Stoke-on-Trent, short, wiry, tough, quick-thinking and intelligent, politically to the left, and perhaps the one boy in our batch who should have become a subaltern, but did not; I dare say his Potteries brogue let him down and, far too honest to pretend, he may not have shone in the WOSB atmosphere, which was very Junior Common Room, but I have no doubt that in command of men, their respect for him would have been far greater than for any of the strutting coxcombs who became the baby officers of the RASC in my time.

One night, when we were both in our beds, reading, two regular army corporals came stamping into our room with all the authority of those who are on official business. Eric, in pyjamas, but given time to put on boots, was hustled off on some specious errand that we neither of us understood, and the remaining corporal unceremoniously buggered me. Much bigger, much stronger, unrelentingly purposeful and with the authority of rank, he just got on with it, my yelps, if any, muffled by the pillow, his entry eased with the spit I heard him hawk. Done, he did not gloat, did not taunt me with proposals that I had asked for it or enjoyed it, offered no reason for it, but merely warned that if I did anything about it, 'they' would not find him, but they'd make bloody sure that I'd never be an officer.

He was, of course, absolutely right and it had been a shrewdly calculated rape. I had not, wittingly, seen the man before and the only thing I knew about him was that he wore corporal's stripes. What would I say if I reported the matter to the Battalion Guard Room, where I would find only National Service amateurs, and what would be the consequences? There could be no WOSB while the Military Police established the facts, and if any of them were to ask if I were queer or had had homosexual experience, that would certainly put an end to my National Service. And what had I lost? – not my virginity. I went to the loo, excreted the evidence, tidied my bed and pretended to be asleep when Eric returned. His explanation next morning, confused and vague, could have been interpreted as evasive, but if he too was buggered – which I doubted, knowing him to be a fighter – he revealed no more to me than I to him. The episode worried me: did I *look* queer, did my behaviour (the term body language had not then come into use) betray me, did the care I took not to look curiously at other boys indicate to the knowing that I was indeed queer? I wonder now whether there was some kind of buggers' network between barracks through which NCOs could exchange likely lads in perfect safety, for later experiences, out of the army, were to suggest that regular soldiers often had a taste for sodomy, or were tolerant and obliging for a fiver, as long as no one accused them of being queer.

As it happened, within a few days we were deprived of the comforts of this interlude and were posted hither and yon, to

Shorncliffe Camp in my case, near Folkestone, where perhaps a dozen of us, waiting for our WOSBs, were put to some use as RASC clerks – it was then that I learned that in the army, rum, whiskey and stout were medical supplies of which the nearby military hospital's store had constantly to be replenished. The rum we had an immediate chance to try when the great surge of the North Sea swept into the English Channel at the end of January 1953; within a week of transferring from Aldershot we were waist deep in the ice-cold sea at Hythe, shoring the defences there with sandbags, rum reassuring us – or so the sergeant thought as we swigged it from what may have been a demijohn, but few of us had any stomach for it.

Shorncliffe was a wretched posting – a run-down barracks so under-manned that we were compelled to stand guard every three or four nights, snatching only scraps of sleep, and were rarely spared for a week-end pass. What hours we had off duty were mostly spent in bed in our chill barrack room, but once in a while we went into Folkestone where there was a cinema enlightened enough to show foreign films – it was there that I saw Kurosawa's Rashomon and was so enchanted by its revolutionary approach to narrative that I went again, alone, to feast on it. Some trouble with my right foot developed – an enraged toughie (my fault, my words) from the East End had, booted, stamped on it, unshod, in the first few days at Aldershot, and the swelling caused then occasionally flared in later months; the medical officer decided that I should go to hospital and have it X-rayed and drained. As hospital for in-patients was regarded as, technically, a posting to another unit, I had to take with me all my documents in a sealed envelope, and these, easing the envelope open before the clerk's spittle had dried, I read as I limped on my way. They were few, and only one was of interest – the report of the psychiatrist in Aldershot who had asked me the which-do-you-love-best question: his conclusion had been that I was emotionally unstable and on no account should I be sent anywhere near a front line. No document was ever torn into smaller shreds nor thrown to the winds over a larger area. Was it, I wondered, the reason why, while other boys were called to their WOSBs, I had been left to rot in idle postings? There had been a flurry of hope on 15 February 1953 when I had been told to report to a WOSB on the 18th, but it was cancelled two days later, with no reason given.

I had two more months to wait, but at last I reported to a WOSB on 15 April, feeling far from well. That I was in the early stages of mumps may well have contributed to my passing. I remember very little of the tests – car tyres suspended from ropes played some part in one that was performed under my command, and I gave a brief lecture on the absence of sexual imagery from Pre-Columbian Mexican sculpture, inspired by either Roger Fry or Aldous Huxley (or perhaps both), to which the supervising officer responded with 'I can't help feeling I've had my leg pulled, but it makes a change from how to look after a horse.' In spite of the headache and swellings in uncomfortable sites or, as I believe, because of their dulling effect on my behaviour, I was competent enough in the tasks through which the army distinguished the able from the incompetent, and was sent on the home leave that was the bonus for passing. My mother's diary records that at 4.00 pm on the afternoon of 17 April 1953 I returned home from my WOSB with a temperature of 104.2 and collapsed. Mumps was diagnosed. Her entry for the following day reads 'Brian very ill indeed. We must get his temperature down.'

Three weeks later – that is after fifteen wasted weeks attached to Shorncliffe Camp – I reached Mons, dumped my kit and went in search of Keith Fowler, another boy who had endured the Shorncliffe doldrum, who had arrived a fortnight earlier. I found his barrack room and walked towards him with arms outstretched to hug him, only to be rebuffed – he was happy to shake my hand, but not to be embraced. There was nothing sexual in my gesture, nor was there anything sexual in my affection for him, but in parrying my action quite so sternly he suggested that he saw it so and needed to demonstrate to all who might be watching that he wanted nothing of it. It was another lesson in the need for restraint and dissembling, another lesson in the fragility of friendships formed in adversity.

Mons I found a long hard slog. The aftermath of mumps affected my energy and stamina, and, seeming to develop an allergy to dust and pollen, I feared that this might become serious enough for those in charge of me to decide that I was unfit to stay in the army – the very last thing that I wanted. It was infantry training all over again, but with a seriousness that far exceeded our experience as raw recruits, and as we crawled and crept and ran and lay concealed and still on the dry heaths of Aldershot, I wished for the cold and damp of autumn that had made tolerable our first attempts in this pretence of war.

It was tough and unrelenting by day and riven by snobbery at night, for the elite young Cavalrymen rarely mixed with the rag, tag and bobtail of the Corps. We were far from equal – young subalterns of the RASC might command one arm of the support on which the tanks and armoured cars of these unhorsed striplings must depend, but we were scarcely distinguishable from the proletarian masses of our men. We shared taxis into town; they drove in and out of camp in 3-litre Bentleys by the dozen – indeed, I suspect that every example of this car, all 1,600 of them built between 1921 and 1927, was at some point in its life in the hands of an Officer Cadet at Mons, as *de rigeur* as the tweed jackets, tight cavalry twill trousers and flat caps that were their off-duty uniforms. Boastful and braying, few made good companions for boys from grammar schools or the wretched in-betweens like Haberdashers' and we were promptly pigeon-holed by perceived background and speech. Not obviously from the one group or the other, I was very much the odd fish and occasionally made to feel it. I valued greatly the friendship of three boys of one caste, John Peile, with whom I am still in touch, Nigel Hensman and Tegner (Christian name forgotten), with whom I am not; of the other caste I can recall none and nothing.

In adversity we all pulled together well enough. Was Coronation Day an adversity? It seemed so at the time, for officer cadets were destined, with ordinary soldiers, to hold back the crowds. Preparing for it took quite a slice out of our training and humiliatingly returned us to the status of squaddies, bullied on the parade ground by day and in the barrack room by night, to achieve levels of perfection in drill and dress matched only by guardsmen Trooping the Colour. 'You will not faint.' This, above all other instructions for Coronation Day, I recall, not in such simple terms, but at extraordinary volume and quite twice the length when embellished with the sexual threats and swearwords customary in army life. 'You will not faint' – but I had an unaccountable tendency to faint, not yet discovered by army doctors, when standing still too long, and never knew quite how long too long might be; Coronation Day was not the most suitable day on which to reveal this frailty. To avoid the faint we had been taught to shift our weight imperceptibly from heels to toes and back again, to wiggle toes and clench our buttocks and breathe deeply, even to divert our minds and concentrate on sex, booze, leave and other pleasures, without losing our grasp of the matter in hand.

We fell into three categories. The least competent and most fortunate were given five days Coronation Leave and sent home. The rest knew what was expected of them – a day of patient endurance and longsuffering, a day on which there could be no customary ten minute break every two hours so that we could smoke a fag and empty our bladders, a day on which, indeed, if needs must, we were told, we must pee where we stood, within our trousers and down into our boots, a day that would not end until the applauding crowds had cheered the Queen, subsided into anti-climax and gone home. This group was to be unexpectedly divided. The day began the night before, bulling best boots yet again and pressing knife-sharp creases into uniforms that grated raw the skin of inner thighs. An hour or two of wakeful sleep was all we had, and then the sluice of cold water and the scrape of razor blade, the attempted emptying of obstinately unready bowels, the rush of breakfast, soggy bacon swimming in grease, eggs fried crisp as biscuits, tinned tomatoes a luke-warm slop, thick wedges of white bread and quite disgusting tea, laced we thought with bromide to unman us, the bitterness of leaves caught in our teeth cutting through the sweetness of the milk and sugar. And then the rush of detailed dressing, the rush of inspection, the rush of being marshalled hither and yon, the day just dawning.

Many of us did indeed stand in the drizzle and pee in our boots, damp without and sodden within, but for others the day for which they had prepared so diligently and long came to an early and bathetic end – they were superfluous and their day of duty was converted into useless leave, useless because, in best bib and tucker on a day when all London's useful functions had come to a stop, there was nothing to do but return to Aldershot.

*   *   *

'Cushy' is the army's word for the weeks that cadets, having graduated from Mons, spent in an RASC barracks in Aldershot learning specifically to be its subalterns. An inglorious but necessary Corps, its officers were expected to be as much clerks and drivers as their men, and much of the training was fun, for in theory we should, on a motorcycle, have been as nimble as a despatch rider, and at the wheel of an articulated truck (that is one with a universal joint amidships linking it to a trailer that doubles its bulk and capacity), as able as any professional trucker. We learned the lore and practice of the convoy, which could be of thirty vehicles at regular intervals and slow, perfect for devastating attack from the air, or of three, each driver properly briefed and capable of reacting individually to emergencies, much faster and safer. Both were, of course, subject to the ten minute smoking break – not the easiest thing to fix when on the road during a military exercise; later, in the real life of the army, we were to learn that many of our men (still boys in late adolescence) regarded these as breaks for masturbation as much as a cigarette, for they found the rattling, vibration and bucking of the old Austin and Bedford trucks that were their workhorses a source of irresistible prostate stimulation. Of this the blind-eyed army must always have known, but no word of it was ever spoken. We drilled as much as was essential to see us through a passing-out parade without disgrace, and the Senior Under Officer – that is, theoretically, the most promising of us, but in fact the most physically beautiful (and young May was both beautiful and imposingly big) – learned to do things ceremonial with a naked sword.

Like ordinary soldiers we slept, polished our boots and brasses, and had our being in a barrack room – only the SUO had a room to himself and his sword. Our evenings were often free and I sometimes slipped away to see Alice Denne, but more often went to a local pub to learn to drink a pint like a real man (I have loathed draught beer ever since), or just lived the simple life of the barrack room at ease. There was some talk of sex, most of it uncertain, but two of us went into town and found it – or so they said. One, a graceless, pushy lout with heavy spectacles, who was to overturn his Singer Nine (an open tourer) and never be seen again, gave us a blow-by-blow account of orgasm between the breasts of an Aldershot trollop – shocking to boys who knew nothing of the norm, let alone such deviations from it. Another, far the oldest of us, a sometime apprentice in the Austin factories in Birmingham and a heavy smoker of the kind who holds his cigarette within the shelter of his cupped hand, had been ordered to get rid of the ungentlemanly nicotine stain that kippered his palm – and he did, overnight, by, as he told us with the air of one used to such things, fingering the vagina of another trollop to make her juices flow. Astounded, most boys responded with a 'Yuck' or 'Ugh,' but I, having a decade earlier read Harry Claff's filthy paperback, already knew of these juices and was inclined to believe that they might indeed have that peculiar property.

On the evening before our passing-out parade, bulling boots and pressing trousers for the last time (we would soon have batmen for such chores) – a corporal strode in and told me that I was wanted by the Commanding Officer. Another corporal, another rape? But there were a dozen witnesses. He was insistent – my state of dress (I wore nothing but a towel) was of no importance and shirt sleeve order would do – and thus, unkempt, I followed him. With the CO was the Captain from the Gloucesters who had been father and brother to us throughout the later stages of our training to be subalterns, a man who had striven to teach us that there was more to this small authority than strut and swagger, that we had a duty of respect and responsibility to our men, that we were part of something infinitely larger than ourselves, and on the CO's other side sat the psychiatrist whose report I had torn to pieces months before. Of this, the CO explained, a copy had just been brought to his notice. The meeting was entirely informal; they sat at a table and I sat with them in a what-have-you-got-to-say-for-yourself debate. Panic turned to ice-cold calm. I argued that having got to within twelve hours of being commissioned without anyone noticing my supposed emotional instability, I had proved the psychiatrist wrong, that I was a first-class shot with the Bren and every hand-held weapon, that there was no army vehicle that I could not drive and the workings of which I did not understand, and that were I to be returned, sans commission, to my old unit in Shorncliffe, the army would have wasted the considerable cost of training me to be something that only one man had said, on the basis of only a very brief interview at the very start of my National Service, that I should not be. I was then sent out to join the corporal. Minutes later I was recalled to be told that the general consensus was that I should be commissioned the following morning. General consensus? Did that mean that the psychiatrist agreed with this decision? I dared not ask.

CHAPTER 7

National Service as a Subaltern

Shortly before we were commissioned we completed posting applications. Germany would have been best for me, for though still largely in ruins, its museums and galleries were slowly reopening and perfection in the language would have been a very useful accomplishment, but the army had the reputation of being cussed in these matters – better not to ask for what one wanted most, for then there was a better chance of getting it. I ruled two lines diagonally across the form and wrote between them ANYWHERE ABROAD. I should have written ANYWHERE AT HOME, for when my posting came, it was to Aldershot and to the very Willems Barracks where I had my basic training as a clerk. And there I went, though I immediately applied for an alternative posting, this time just anywhere.

At Willems I spent my time sorting out the problems of recruits – the desperate need for leave when learning of a girl friend's pregnancy or of a single mother too ill to care for younger siblings, pleading the good character of a soldier when some civil offence caught up with him, even pleading it before a formidable Court Martial when an inexperienced youth had rashly answered back or refused to perform a degrading punishment. The most difficult case was a contemporary at Haberdashers' who had failed his WOSB and been returned to Willems as a despised dogsbody private, to be mocked for his failed ambition by every junior NCO. He broke down in tears when I told him that I had no power to persuade the Board to reverse its verdict or put him through the tests again. I did not remind him of how lofty he, as a prefect and a cricketer, had been with me at school, and how, though we had often had our hands in each other's trousers, he had later scorned me for my homosexuality, but I dare say that he remembered well enough, may even have sought to exploit part of this recollection, and attributed my refusal to help him to something approaching vengeful malice. It was not so. I knew enough of the army's way to be certain that there was nothing I could do for him, not even put my arm round him for old time's sake in a gesture of hopeless comforting (as was my inclination); nor could I rebuke the NCOs in charge of him without betraying the misery of this interview and thus making things much worse for him.

I had to wait till mid November before my alternative posting came – and then it was nothing more abroad than Blandford Forum, one of the jewels of Dorset, to a training battalion where boys learned to drive and then moved on. I, thank God, was given a working platoon of experienced drivers whose duty it was to provide support for other regiments and we were as often as not out on convoy or playing some ancillary part in exercises on Salisbury Plain, Thus it was that I sometimes found myself joyriding in tanks and other armoured vehicles, or cheek by jowl with the big guns of the Artillery. I am deeply grateful for these experiences, for from them I gained some small insight into the daily life of the soldiers of the front line, know something of the heat, noise and discomfort they endure, the sound and fury, so to speak. Have any of our masters in the House of Commons now, such knowledge?

There were many lighter moments. In the early hours of a bitter cold night exercise, Salisbury Plain made magical by frost and moonlight, my dependable Corporal John drove me away from the hostilities to a refreshment van parked on the A303, and introduced me to the luxury of the bacon sandwich – two slabs of white bread thickly buttered, with long hot rashers projecting inches beyond the crust, held firmly in both hands, to be eaten leaning forward to prevent the melting butter from running down the chin and onto one's uniform. I still try from time to time to replicate the experience, but it is not a thing to do alone and somehow neither the bread nor the bacon ever seems to match the original. Returning from another exercise, driven by my fat sergeant, an indolent and evasive man for whom I did not much care (he boasted of a mistress in Crewkerne to whose bosom he too frequently repaired when on duty – but then, with a wife in married quarters on the camp, only when on duty could he go to her), chased a plump piglet along a winding lane. Fearing for its life, I stopped him, stopped the tilly (the army's pet name for a small flat-bed carry-all truck covered with a canvas tilt), gave chase and caught it. But what should a young subaltern with a muddy piglet wriggling in his arms then do? We found neither farm nor farmhouse, nor any evidence of pigs by sight or smell, and were nearing camp when the sergeant said that he would drop me at the officers' mess and then take the piglet, now deeply asleep on my lap, to the police station in Blandford. I believed him. I thought that rescuing the piglet had been my good deed for the day. By extraordinary coincidence there was suckling-pig for dinner in the sergeants' mess a few days later – the officers' mess, full of envy, wondered how this could be?

For my unreliable fat sergeant, Corporal John, another regular soldier living in married quarters, was more than compensation; knowing, usefully devious (but always on my side), his experience, wisdom and guidance kept me out of trouble with pernickety senior officers and, in always seeming to know what was about to happen, he, I and the platoon were always a jump ahead. The platoon, though entirely of National Servicemen, was almost permanent and when a boy reached the end of his two years his leaving did not disturb our equilibrium. Introducing myself, I told them that I was no more interested than they in the idiocies of army discipline and we struck a bargain, so to speak – that as long as they kept themselves and their barrack room reasonably tidy, that would be enough for me, that I'd even tolerate the Windsor knots they tied in their ties, but when they were to be inspected by the Company Sergeant Major or some other hierarch, they

must not let me down. They never did, and on my last night as a
National Serviceman, they gave me in a local pub a send-off that I
took to be not mere ritual, but an expression of genuine affection.
They were mostly rough and tough, incipient teddy-boys, and yet
their immediate superior, their fellow National Serviceman Lance-
Corporal Organ, contrastingly gentle in manner and softly spoken,
managed them very well. I was very lucky to have the support and
loyalty of John and Organ – other subalterns in the battalion
seemed always to be at odds with their NCOs, the jumped-up
second lieutenants thinking that mere rank gave them superiority,
their war-torn sergeants and corporals knowing every one of them
to be a jackanapes. I was lucky too to have such decent men under
my command; only once did I have misgivings, but they were
premature. Expecting a replacement driver I was notified that a
Private de St Croix was on his way. With such a name, I thought,
he must be of ancient Catholic lineage, his ancestors Crusaders,
Plantagenets, Angevins, even the Norman knights and courtiers of
William the Conqueror; and if that were not enough in the
wretched circumstances of an RASC training camp, with such a
name he is probably a public schoolboy who has failed a WOSB
and now feels as disgraced and shamed as that unhappy boy from
Haberdashers. In the event, Private de St Croix was nothing of the
kind, but a tiny, undernourished and very pretty Cockney boy
from the East End who, on announcing himself as Private Deesty
Croiks, could not understand my laughter at such a d'Urberville
moment.

The months passed easily at Blandford, the winter lightened by
playing rugger again, for the battalion at first and then a little
further up the line, and once in a very rough game against the
Navy. On my first reporting to the Commanding Officer he had
quizzed me to see what sort of new puppy had joined his pack, and
I had given a rather diffident answer about my skill, as a hooker;
two or three weeks later, the battalion's hooker injured, again with
diffidence I volunteered to take his place, and as it was only an

hour before the game began and no better offer had been made, I joined the team. Somehow the chemistry was right, the game flowed wonderfully and equally and both sides shone. Before I could get my boots off a messenger from the CO told me to report to him at once and filthy as I was. 'You told me that you were not much good at rugger. That was not true.' I muttered something about not blowing my own trumpet, but the CO, determined to be disagreeable about my modesty, called in his adjutant and told him to make me duty dog for the next week.

The duty dog – a term new to me – turned out to be the officer responsible for the camp and all its works for every hour of the day. Confined to camp, he had to be up at six in the morning and was rarely in bed more than five hours earlier. It was his duty to inspect the guard, the fire precautions and the kitchens, to check the state of every barrack room, the lavatories and ablutions (as the washrooms were called), to ensure that any prisoners were properly cared for and properly employed (this meant such fatuities as blancoing the stocks of coal and cutting the grass round the sergeants' mess with a pair of nail scissors), and being present in the mess hall to deal with any complaints there might be about the food. The duty dog himself was the only man who might dare to comment adversely on the achievements of a sergeant in the Catering Corps and his assistant cooks – my comments on his boiled cabbage and his tinned tomatoes brought a response just short of mutiny. It was a useful experience and a valuable chore, for it meant that no tap ever dripped for want of a new washer, no lavatory cistern ever malfunctioned for more than the time it took to report it, and no door squeaked. It was not on my watch that a barrack room burst into flames (every building on the camp was made of wood), but because of the system of the duty dog, the blaze was extinguished long before the local fire brigade arrived and not a boy was hurt. Every business and institution in civilian life should have its duty dog – were it so, then faxed messages would not be mislaid by newspaper offices and the lavatories of national museums and galleries would never stink like middens (as they occasionally do).

Apart from rugger, the winter pleasures of the mess had been entirely unknown to me – billiards, snooker, table tennis and forms of poker played with dice as well as cards that always ended with the loser having to swallow whatever concoction of alcoholic drinks the winners could afford, poisonous blends of Benedictine, Calvados, Tia Maria and rum perhaps, stirred into half a pint of warm brown ale, the game halted until the last drop was drunk. There were the hazards of the Mess Night too, the formal occasions when we temporary subalterns wore Service Dress, our best kakhi uniforms, and all the married and other older regular officers at the head of the table donned a dark blue uniform of tunics bedizened with chain mail and tight trousers with a broad red stripe, spurs clinking at their heels – it was the wretched RASC pretending to be heroes of the cavalry reaching back to Rupert of the Rhine. We ate, we drank, we passed the port and toasted with grave formality, but on retirement to the drawing room, off came our jackets and the games began. 'Are you there, Moriarty?' was usually the first, the ice-breaker to let loose the vicious brute, the question asked of one officer by another when both, blindfolded, their left hands clasped in an unbreakable grip, lay on the floor with, in their right hands, hefty clubs of close-rolled newspaper. To the answer 'Yes,' the asker then thwacked his weapon where he thought his adversary's head might be. This response was not necessarily immediate; the asker might wait to hear the sound of breathing or a faint shuffle on the carpet, for these could confirm that the answerer was stretching as far away as he could (though the sane man knew that it paid to be as close as possible, where, though more likely to be hit, the blow must be enfeebled by proximity), and the longer he waited the more certain of accuracy he might be; most, however, gambled on the quickest response. The Adjutant, the CO's right hand man and executioner, big, handsome and, we youngsters thought, far too much of a gentleman and too intelligent to be in the RASC, was strong enough with his left hand to twist the forearm of his opponent, forcing him onto his back and thus able to thwack him across the face rather than the back of the skull, splitting a lip or bloodying his nose. We thought this a punishment for some small episode of recalcitrance or cheek that had not merited an official rebuke or penalty; if it was not – and we could never quite be sure – then it was calculated sadism. Was it coincidence that the winner of each bout was judged by the viciousness of his successful strikes rather than their number?

With the departure of the CO, usually well before midnight, High Cockalorum, the roughest game of all, brought these evenings to a close. Eric Partridge, the High Priest of all enquirers into the vernacular, has it that this began as a schoolboys' game, a nineteenth-century variant of leapfrog in which one team of players presents a chain of backs and bottoms achieved by tucking their heads between the legs of the boy or man in front and gripping his thighs, while the rival team tries to break the chain or collapse it with their accumulated weight, by each member taking a long run from behind, leaping along its length as far as possible and holding his position against all attempts to shake him off. Often rougher than any rugger scrum when played by adult men, minor injuries were common and more serious mishaps not at all unusual; these, in official terms, were passed off as 'sustained by 2nd Lt Dobbin in pursuit of his duties'.

Most young subalterns acquired cars – not the 3-litre Bentleys so common at Mons, but equally old Austin Sevens, a rather distinguished Riley Nine (an exquisite small car in its day), a Vauxhall 14 drop-head coupé from that marque's last years of reputation for fine engineering, and mine a very ordinary Morris Ten of 1934, bought as a reliable runner for £30, my gross pay for six weeks or so. And reliable it was for a while, until early one morning on Salisbury Plain, returning from a stolen evening at Covent Garden, the float chamber of the carburettor stuck, neat petrol poured onto the exhaust system, and when I halted the car it burst into flames. I walked back half a mile or so and thumbed a lift; when my Good Samaritan drove past the car, still burning, he slowed to a stop and we ran back to see if anyone needed help, but there was, of course, no one, just an old car burning, dumped, complained my Samaritan. Corporal John asked if I had removed the number plates and, on learning that I had not, at once drove to the carcass and removed all evidence of ownership. I became the passenger in other subaltern's cars, or took to stealing away alone on an old BSA motorcycle, big, heavy and utterly reliable at a steady mile a minute, bare-headed and shirt open at the neck until I ran into a bumble bee, the impact so hard that it was, I thought, like being shot in the chest – and then the sting began to affect my ability to breathe. It was the discovery of a frightening allergy.

I took no long leaves and few weekend passes once the winter of 1953–54 was at an end, wanting to consolidate the separation from my mother and my new sense of independence and to have some continuing benefit from it in my coming years as a student. I was not alone in this, for other subalterns too saw some benefit in escape from the cloying pleasures of home. One of us chose always to spend his leave at Porton Down as a guinea-pig for a cold cure, a wicked deception thought by most of us to be connected with poison gas or nuclear radiation – this on the grounds of gossip in the camp – but he was a Scot, and as payment was to be had for this, he would not listen (but then he would not listen when we told him that introducing Scottish sword-dancing to the mess would be an utter failure). For the rest of us the sea was within reach at Bournemouth, where we might swim, see a film and end the day with dinner away from the formality of the mess; a little more adventurous, we might scamper south to Lulworth Cove, walk across meadows to the sea, swim and then feast on lobsters cooked by an old fisherman with a hut just off the beach. We explored the Piddle villages in the valley of that river, the Tarrants and the Hintons, and we wandered further to Bath and Wells,

Salisbury and Wilton; it was not quite a posting to Germany, where an early Volkswagen might have borne me to Cologne and Frankfurt, even to Munich and Bavaria, but Blandford was not exactly barren of cultural delights.

Early in September 1954, my two years complete, I left Blandford, but not without regret. There had been a suggestion that I might stay on for a third year, upgraded as a regular, and I was sentimentally tempted to do so, but I knew that National Service had done for me exactly what I hoped – it had cleared my decks of clutter. Now I yearned neither to play my violin nor to paint pictures; I had proved to myself that I could be celibate and, through abstinence, could suppress my homosexuality; and I had learned that I could, with a touch of Jesuitical casuistry, unostentatiously maintain my religious observance in the conflicting quotidian circumstances of army life. To have achieved all this and then imperil my new equilibrium by staying on in the army – for one year, perhaps another, seduced by the temptations of rank – might well clutter my life with other enthusiasms and responsibilities from which it would be even less easy to escape. I felt, moreover, compelled to respond to the overwhelming siren call of the Courtauld Institute, older, wiser and far better read than in my first incarnation there, a man rather than a boy.

I was not completely cut off from the army. Transferred to the Reserve, I had to report to the Duke of York's Barracks on King's Road, Chelsea, on Tuesday evenings and play soldiers for some hours, and for the first two summers there was a fortnight's camp with all the discomforts of army life in the field. This meant renewing acquaintance with the open latrine, sharing a long pole on trestles with any other officer who chose to empty his bowels concurrently, a lugubrious embarrassment, screened by draped sacking from the passer-by; it involved the pretence that an officers' mess in a tent should be almost as formal as in some historic barracks surviving from the eighteenth century; and worst of all, I was deprived of coffee (to which I had long been addicted) – the only alternative the disgusting tea that was brewed at every opportunity, the bucket of water, the quarter pound of tea-leaves, a pint tin of sweetened condensed milk, an extra pound or two of sugar, all brought to the boil over a fire of twigs. These were holidays as active and healthy as any bought now at vast expense and they were wonderful fun (how odd to have such a reaction when, at school, I had hated the annual field days); on one I added to my reputation for overturning things (when running an urgent errand for my CO at Blandford I had rolled his Austin Somerset on an icy corner) by testing too far the limits of a Gipsy, Austin's poor and transitory response to the Land-Rover; on another, a sergeant enthralled us with photographs of a hefty whore with a white mouse emerging from her hirsute vagina.

These jaunts with the Reserve should have continued for at least five years, but Suez intervened. This was the moral moment that I had mistily foreseen when learning to use a bayonet. I and many others in the Reserve were instructed to report for duty. I refused. I thought Eden's handling of the Suez Crisis indefensibly illegal and immoral, doubly so in its concurrence with the Soviet invasion of Hungary, and wrote so in a letter of resignation and refusal to my commanding officer in Chelsea. I delivered it myself and watched him read it. 'You realise that this means a Court Martial?' was his response. He did what he could to persuade me not to be so bloody-minded, so self-destructive and even said that if I allowed him to destroy the letter not another word would be said of it, but I sensed uncertainty in his tired old arguments for loyalty and obedience, hearing in them an echo of the unthinking motto of my school, Serve and Obey no matter what (the perfect admonition for Germans under the Nazis), and I stood my ground. He sent me home to wait. And wait I did, for years suffering repeatedly an absurd but mildly disturbing dream of discovering my army uniform to have been destroyed by moth – as, eventually, it was. I heard nothing until 2006 when, in response to an article written on the half centenary of Suez, I received some two dozen letters from others in the Reserve who had done the same and been sent home to await the consequences. They too had heard no more of it. I assume that up and down the country there were so many rebels that, after the international political disgrace of all involved in the Crisis, the army authorities felt that nothing could be achieved by hauling us all before Courts Martial. Our punishment was to be left in ignorance, knowing only that a Damocletian sword might strike at any time, and to be informally excluded from the Reserve, never knowing quite what our status might be if the Cold War became hot. Never again did I set foot in The Duke of York's Barracks as a soldier (now that they are Charles Saatchi's Gallery they have again become my haunt), never again did I enjoy a field exercise, never again did I wear my uniform. My only memento of army service is not, alas, de Vignyan *canne de jonc*, but the army issue clothes brush that was every squaddie's indestructible friend, stamped 8881, the last four digits of my army number; it is still my friend, for no brush inherited from my fastidious stepfather is one jot as effective in removing the hairs of a blonde bitch from the shoulders of a plain blue overcoat.

In my year as a subaltern my lessons were very different from those learned as a squaddie who had discovered a steely core within himself and knew that if needs must, there was nothing that he would not do. I learned that the officers above us were poor stuff, the best of them Captain Rigby and Captain Macnamara of the REME who knew more about engines than Henry Royce – but both had risen from the ranks and were wry in humour and respect; the worst of them, Captain Le Rougetel, in command of the company of which my platoon was part, was a hapless muddler whom subalterns could reduce to panic, hysteria and, very nearly, tears. Haunted by the prospect of compulsory retirement in early middle age, there was about all these left-overs of World War II, the hang-dog air of the professional soldier at the bottom of the heap, there because that was a fair estimate of their worth. My fellow subalterns could be broadly divided into two groups –

middle class boys who took their tasks to be a serious responsibility and were determined to get more out of National Service by putting more into it, and middle class boys who were, with little reason, uppity, relished the opportunity to swagger, and who were often quite gratuitously unpleasant, even bullying, to the young soldiers in their charge. It was never pretty to witness, in the accents of the grammar school, young 'gentlemen' echoing the caricatural abuse of their sergeants. In the RASC the third category of subaltern was never to be found – those born and bred for sacrifice, valiant, dauntless, unhesitating and expendable, the brave and beautiful always driven to the front by rash notions of duty and example, there to be killed off. Subalterns of that kind we knew only as the cavalry cadets with whom we had, for a few weeks, rubbed shoulders as a commonality at Mons.

Today's society is much poorer without National Service. It was a great force for good in society. Within the divisions of rank it sowed seeds of social cohesion across class barriers and was an instrument of mutual benevolence much more than a class-ridden autocracy, its fundamental philosophy close to that of the welfare state. Society has, alas, so altered in the four decades and more since National Service ceased, that it could never be re-instituted; were we to attempt anything of the kind and make it subject to the same implacable discipline, the political correctitudes would smother it at birth and the young would, *en masse*, refuse to serve. For me it was the most important period of my education and, looking back on it, I see that it gave a firm foundation to my social attitudes and politics. It taught me never to trust those in authority, never to despise those without it. It confirmed William Bulman's injunction that I should bring everything to the bar of my own judgement.

*   *   *

What part did my mother play in these army years? She sent me a parcel of long woolly underwear, Chilprufe the marque, when the first winter came. Hoping for chocolate biscuits, fruit cake or other treats that might be shared with my immediate mates, in a rage I sent it back and broke an apron string. Her diary records every one of my snatched visits to the Royal Academy and Covent Garden, her anxieties over the episodes of mumps and pseudo-asthma, and the gift of a trip with her to Paris confidently arranged to fill the eight full days between my passing-out as a subaltern and my first posting. We flew there. Flying to Paris must now seem unremarkable, but in 1953 it was almost adventurous, particularly as the plane flew low and slow enough to count the cows and cathedrals on the way. At fifty-three, my mother, with not a hint of grey in her chestnut hair, was mistaken for my elder sister and behaved so; wholly in command, in the very street off the Rue de Rivoli, in the very hotel in which she had lived, it was as though Paris was her daily beaten track and quite unchanged in the quarter century or so since that had been the case. It was a marvel of a week – the Louvre, the Opera, Versailles, the lamb chops, *tete de veau*, custard tarts and wine astonishing to those accustomed to the austerities of still-rationed post-war London.

The only mishap was my fainting at the Opera during the first act of Boris Godunov with Boris Christoff in the role – not some genteel fit of the vapours, but a proper, deeply unconscious faint. I recovered in the corridor, breathed the night air in the interval, returned to my seat and fainted again. Back in the corridor, dragged there by far from sympathetic Frenchmen who forebade me to make a third attempt to hear Christoff, we slunk away. I had fainted before – at school, usually after games or swimming, in church and even in the street – but these faints were dismissed as growing pains, or not enough breakfast or too long on my knees; once I fainted at a bus stop in Edgware Road, toppling others in the queue like ninepins, I was told, then to be swept off in an ambulance to spend twenty-four hours in a Paddington hospital, mystifying doctors – and it was not until decades later, after a heart by-pass operation, that the frequent blackouts that followed it were attributed to a vaso-vagal syndrome that had probably been present since my birth.

'Have you a history of fainting?' my cardiologist enquired. I replied that I had not, but when I thought about it, found that I could recall what had seemed unaccountable faints throughout my life, as far afield as New York, Ankara and Rawalpindi.

After our return from Paris – in my case with smuggled books from the Olympia Press, Miller's Tropics, Gide's Corydon and Wilde's Teleney among them, more literary than Harry Claff's seminal paperback and rather less astonishing, and a handful of educative photographs retrieved from the undusted top of the wardrobe in my hotel room – my mother's authority faded again. She had from the very start of my National Service been ready to accompany me to the opera on a stolen evening – these were times when even Callas as Norma did not fill the house and on Saturday 23 June 1953, with tickets bought that afternoon, we saw her with Joan Sutherland and the greatly underrated Giulietta Simionato – but these excitements ended abruptly when the Morris died. By the time my National Service ended my mother had a son who was determined to maintain a not unfriendly distance from her, to be a prop only when necessary and to maintain the financial independence that his small income as a subaltern had given him.

*   *   *

And what of sex these past two years? Celibacy was a partial state for me, and sanity lay in sex with my imagination and my hand – easier as a subaltern than as a squaddie denied privacy. If sex became the subject of conversation it was always ribald or downright filthy enough for all to join in the general laughter – most of us were virgins and we knew it, no matter how bold the pretence to be Don Juan. I kept a condom in my wallet, its outline polished in the pigskin for anyone to recognise, but it was my only lie, for no one ever asked if I was queer. In the army I would never have admitted it. There were boys who almost broke my resolve to be celibate, among them a cavalry cadet at Mons with whom I fell asleep in the back of a truck after an exhausting exercise, an RASC cadet with whom I sensed that there had perhaps been a this-can't-happen moment, and a doe-eyed and hopelessly stupid servant in the mess at Blandford who probably had not the slightest notion of just how pretty he was, but they were few. On one of my days as duty dog, inspecting empty barrack rooms, in one of them I found two squaddies naked on a bed, oblivious; for a moment I thought to slip away without disturbing them and then chose the alternative, for had I been any other officer or NCO, all hell would have been let loose. I have never seen such scared rabbits as when I tweaked the toes of a projecting foot. 'I don't care what you do, only that you don't get caught' – and walked away to check the taps and chains in the ablutions.

In a training battalion sex was not a major problem among trainees – they were, for the most part, too exhausted to do anything more than talk about it – but Blandford was also a working unit with soldiers who might spend the best part of two years there, and for these and those in charge of them there were at least the problems of non-specific urethritis and gonorrhoea. Our Medical Officer, a National Serviceman, gauche, inexperienced and hopelessly lugubrious, kept a store of ET Packets (what, I wonder, did ET stand for?) – condoms with lubricant – that were free Army Issue, but available only on application, and none of my men was prepared to report to the RAMC sergeant and signal his intention to go into town in the hope of a random fuck. When a man in my platoon had NSU or the clap, the MO always told me, and it was then my duty to address him and all his mates on this sensitive matter, informally and casually, as the man of the world that I was not; they knew that I was much given to giggling over matters of high seriousness and, with blank-faced frankness, could reduce my admonitions to farce. Their alternative ploy was to pretend innocence, not knowing the word condom, the slang terms French Letter and Johnnie quite strange to them, their function incomprehensible. In frank mood they argued that condoms deadened the sensation (their word for orgasm), that wearing one they might not achieve orgasm at all, that the business took too long and that they might have to finish it off for themselves. There was, among them, an obscure lower class prejudice against masturbation, based, I think, not on any of the Padre's occasional and always oblique and querulous references on Church Parade to the abomination of self-abuse – keeping oneself pure for one's wedding day the great ideal – but to some notion that it was a halfway measure only suitable for boys, and that real men abstained from it to reinforce their fucking.

The only lecturing the subalterns got was from the wives of regular officers when these charmless harridans were brought in from married quarters for sherry before lunch on Sundays. Their only conversation lay in fierce questions about girl friends and our intentions to get married; it was far safer to invent a girl, to describe her every detail, than to be unattached, though I occasionally found it difficult to recall quite what I had earlier said of my Dulcinea. In the absence of these ghastly women the topic of gossip in the Mess was as often as not the affair of Lord Montagu of Beaulieu and his friends and catamites. This had begun in August 1953 with accusations of buggery with two boy scouts and was mightily reinforced with similar accusations in a second case, this time with a pair of admitting and consenting adult airmen, both having taken place in a beach hut in the Palace grounds. The trial in the first matter fizzled out – one of the scouts, too knowing, told too rich a tale – but early in January 1954 its details were greedily recalled when Edward Montagu, his cousin Michael Pitt-Rivers and his friend Peter Wildeblood were all arrested for sexual offences committed with the airmen well over a year earlier and, significantly, months before the scouts came into play. This second trial, for more than half a century known as The Montagu Trial and notorious as a tipping point in the long slow change in the attitudes of society and the law to homosexuality, ended on 24 March 1954 with all the defendants sent to gaol (the airmen were prosecution witnesses).

As Beaulieu was on our doorstep, so to speak, these matters were of more than national interest, they were intensely local; moreover, Montagu and his friends were scarcely older than the battalion's subalterns and the airmen could as easily have been its soldiers. For three full months we spoke of the second trial and the supposed offences with apprehension, awe and dread; could any of us nurture affections or desires that cut across the barriers of rank so carefully maintained in the army or betray the barriers of class outside it? It was unthinkable – except that I had thought it, and with the pretty private who played servant in our Mess. We subalterns were, on the one hand, dutifully appalled, and on the other as dutifully amused by the cruel and brutal humour of the jokes and riddles with which the Mess was awash – the heterosexual imagination is remarkably filthier when the homosexual is the victim of its jibes. At these we guffawed, and I, ashamed of joining in, felt myself to be a pusillanimous little shit. It was all very well for me to play the celibate, but I knew my nature and knew too how easily my celibacy would have evaporated given a Beaulieu opportunity. The legal and social penalties loaded onto Edward Montagu were the harsh punishments of the day, though had he and his friends been of lower social status they would undoubtedly have been harsher; for me they were a terrifying warning.[2]

2 See Lord Montagu of Beaulieu: *Wheels within Wheels*, Weidenfeld and Nicolson, 2000. Peter Wildeblood: *Against the Law*, 1955, republished 1999.

CHAPTER 8

The Courtauld Institute

In so far as sex can ever be the last thing on a young man's mind, so it was with me when I returned to the Courtauld Institute in October 1954. I was fortunate to have this second chance, for I knew that my first had been utterly wasted through my immaturity, through the many diversions that so frequently interrupted study, and through my failure to recognise, at first, the high seriousness of art history as an academic discipline. In my defence, however, I must argue that when that recognition eventually dawned, it was the most powerful instrument in my decision to cut short and start again. The Institute, physically tiny in its home in Portman Square, was capable of managing a student body of only thirty or forty at a time, which meant a very small annual intake of undergraduates – in 1954 it was a dozen – and on my previous performance its decision-makers would have been perfectly justified in taking the view that, while all other applicants for places might be brilliant, they knew very well that I was not. Why then accept me? Much affected by their decision, I was determined to reward them with, at the very least, hard work and loyalty. In this I was particularly supported by one fellow student.

A very different animal from the callow boy of my first incarnation at the Courtauld – a young man now, confident and capable, the perfect example of one for whom National Service had brought extraordinary benefit – in Jill Rigden I found my perfect match. Much the same age, born in Abadan in April 1932, where her father had been a power in the politics and management of Anglo-Persian arrangements over oil, thus providing a background that lent strength to her natural confidence (some students thought it bossiness, and

later, that is exactly what it became), she came to the Institute after
three fruitless years at St Martin's School of Art. Like me, having
profited from the practice of painting, she had abandoned it. We had
no particular ambition to become art historians in any conventional
sense – that is toilers in museums or teachers on the lower slopes of
Academe – indeed, Jill's plans were completely unformed and mine
were gradually hardening in the notion that I should become a
priest, a vocation in which some serious knowledge of the ancestral
arts might be peripherally useful – but swiftly both of us were
moulded, wholly and completely, by the Institute.

Twenty Portman Square was the perfect ivory tower for a course
of study that, though well established in Germany, Italy and France,
had scarcely been acknowledged in England. Here the history of
art, its criticism and connoisseurship, had always been a field
ploughed by amateurs with literary ambitions anxious to reiterate
their received and conventional opinions in prose often more
suited to light romantic fiction. Built on the north side of the
square for the widowed Countess of Home (pronounced Hume)
in the later 1770s by Robert Adam, it was a great house in small for
the woman nicknamed the Queen of Hell, with seven wonderfully
decorated rooms, the magical staircase at its core ingeniously shifting
its axis from narrower north-south to shallower but wider east-
west between the ground and first floors, making the house seem
larger and lighter as one climbs it. Confined within a cylinder, lit
by a glass lantern in its delicately plastered dome, a straight free-
standing flight of thirteen steps divides at the thirteenth into wings
that cling close to the curved walls; from ground level, perspective
dictates that these appear to rise more steeply than they do, as
though they are the wings of a great bird on the point of taking
flight. I can think of other, grander, staircases that offer as pressing
an invitation to climb, but none for which the words wing and
flight are more precisely and poetically applicable; even on a drab
winter morning the light and lift of this staircase exalted my spirit
after half an hour cycling through the fog. Students in my last year

as an undergraduate, thinking to offer entertainment more amusing than the annual garden party given for the staff, thought to perform the daring obscenities of *Lysistrata* on these stairs, but could neither muster enough heroic women nor find space enough in the hall below to accommodate the audience.

In the years just before Home House became the Courtauld Institute, it had been the private residence of Samuel Courtauld and his family. With other acts of munificent generosity he had transferred his lease to house the fledgling athenaeum and in my first incarnation there it seemed that he and his family were still the occupiers and we were mischievous squatters for the day. This was occasionally reinforced by the appearance of Courtauld's daughter, Sydney, wistfully drifting through the pretty rooms, settling longest in the Blue Room on the second floor, her old bedroom hung with hand-painted Chinese wallpaper. Her husband, R.A. Butler, was rumoured to have seized much of Sam Courtauld's furniture when the takeover took place, but there was still enough of the heavy mahogany to give a flavour of his occupation. To the fury of Anthony Blunt, Butler proved the rumour true in 1959 when, five years after Sydney's death, he married Mollie Montgomerie, the widow of her cousin Augustine Courtauld, and made new (and successful) demands for more of his former father-in-law's furniture. Only once before, when defending me from André Chastel's public vituperation over some point of seventeenth century scholarship, had I seen him trembling with cold rage. When I asked why he had given way to Butler, he simply said that he had to; I have since wondered how much Butler may have known of Anthony's then hidden life.

By 1954 the house seemed less a home with a pervading air of domestic wear and tear. The library had grown (and continued to grow) and the faded grandeurs of Adam's exquisite interiors inexorably disappeared behind racks of iron shelves painted a grim khaki green, the files of glass slides and other evidence of functions essential to an institute of academe. The most prominent of these abuses, in the sense that it was open to all passers-by and adjacent to the Students' Common Room, was the marble bathroom on the second floor, a place of homage to the dreams of Alma-Tadema, but roofed with glass and so cold in winter that the chill oozed from it to cleave the warm air of the antiquated central heating system in the passage outside; in it there was just jostling-room for the mittened secretaries to perform, like animals in a menagerie, the daily drudgeries of a university department. We students wondered how the wealthy Courtaulds could ever have tolerated such extravagant discomfort.

Every inch of the house was occupied by books or people. Blunt held state in the first floor ante-room overlooking Portman Square, his rare and esoteric painting by Antoine Caron, a painter then 'enjoyng a rather exaggerated popularity' – as he put in 1953 – but now again forgotten, over the mantelpiece; on either side of it he kept much of his extraordinary collection of original source books from the seventeenth and eighteenth centuries, and to these we had immediate access during his tutorials on Philibert de l'Orme and François Mansart, the two French architects to whom he was attached emotionally as much as mathematically. Johannes Wilde, his *éminence grise* and deputy director, revealed the mysteries of Titian and Rubens in the Etruscan Room overlooking the garden, an interior of such daring imagination and intense colour that Cézanne's *Card Players* over the mantelpiece seemed dulled to a Sickertian sludge (though the cold north light may have had something to do with that). Immediately next door, Elsa Scheerer, their shared secretary and the dragon who protected them and ordered their lives, chain-smoked and typed and tele-phoned in a tiny octagonal ante-room as prettily decorated as the interior of a Georgian sewing-box.

Margaret Whinney, fondly nick-named Dame Margaret, maid of all work but the third power in this land and the high priestess to whom girl students took their emotional as well as academic troubles, occupied a bleak room above Anthony's, her secretary squeezed into a narrow slot of a space that had been a lavatory (the Queen of Hell had evidently not been prepared, for all her Jamaican sugar millions, to pay Adam to decorate rooms that her admirers would not see). Charles Clare kept his Registrar's notes and accounts on the backs of envelopes in the pantry next to the service lift, and students crowded in what had been the second north-facing bedroom, dominated since his death in 1934, by the collection bequeathed by Roger Fry, the most pontifical, vainglorious, grandiloquent, superficial and, unfortunately, influential of all English art critics. We ate our sandwiches and drank our tea in the company of Sickert, Bonnard and Vanessa Bell, an African fetish figure and a mask, and by the door our touching farewells wore away the patina of a substantial bronze by Renoir. In two glass-fronted cupboards flanking the fireplace were his examples of ancient and ethnic pottery that, for reasons traditional but never understood, the students' President and Secretary were required once a year to wash; I shall never forget the horror of feeling an unglazed pot of Assyrian antiquity dissolve into a muddy sludge slipping from the fingers of my left hand.

Lectures were given in the former ballroom, paintings by Fra Bartolommeo and Camille Pissarro at risk from careless shoulders, illustrated by old-fashioned monochrome glass slides of which thousands were stored in the neighbouring reception room, Cézanne's *Lac d'Annecy* its most glorious embellishment. Only in the basement were students deprived of Sam Courtauld's paintings, but the only reasons for being there were to read bound volumes of *English Homes*, a serious architectural supplement to *Country Life*, use the dedicated loos in the chill and mouldering cubicles under the garden paving, or to be bound on some errand to the Winkles, the caretaker and his wife. Winkle, a heavily-built old sailor with all an old sailor's wiles, stoked a fiery boiler big enough to accommodate Shadrach, Meshach and Abednigo, and occasionally changed a washer, replaced a sash-cord, or refixed a rod on the slippery threadbare carpet of the servants' staircase that the students, the lift forbidden them, were compelled to use (down this I found that, with feet rigid at an angle of 45 degrees or so, I could, as it were, ski at great speed if wearing shoes with well-worn leather soles). He gave the impression that nothing was beyond his skills and yet, with a snail's sense of immediacy, did very little. Mrs Winkle's only evident responsibility was the provision of tea for staff and students every afternoon and for both she baked delicious cakes, though never quite enough. If ever we bumped into her she responded to our greetings with complaints about her feet – and well she might, for within her rumpled stockings and slippers down-at-heel, they were as much distorted by excrescences as any pair of Jerusalem artichokes or roots of ginger. Never throwing away anything that might be useful, the Winkles lived in squirrel squalour beyond imagining until a favoured student was allowed a glimpse.

The Winkles and the discomforts of Home House were the farcical elements in a serene comedy. The house was so beautiful inside and out that chaining my bicycle to its railings seemed an act of worship, an uplifting prelude to the activities within, and to climb the stairs and find my way to my adopted table in the far corner of the music room – the main library – was as improving a ritual as any in *The Magic Flute*. I am convinced that Robert Adam's architecture, mathematically Mozartian (three months apart their deaths) was a significant contribution to the aesthetic sensibility of every Courtauld student and to the rapid establishment of the Institute as briefly the greatest school of art history, not only in England – where it had no competition – but in the post-war world. It was not always so. Its pre-war reputation was as a finishing school for well-to-do girls (the boys were few) and no early survivor is left to deny the belief that the Institute closed for Ascot Week. With staff and director drawn from other academic disciplines, teaching was flawed by the amateurism of their interest in art history, and by 1936, that is within four years, London University, to which it was affiliated, had concluded that its academic standards were embarrassingly poor. The following year, its first Director,

W. G. Constable, resigned to take up a career as Curator of Paintings at the Boston Museum of Fine Arts and gain celebrity as the first blind man to become the world's premier authority on Canaletto. Poor Canaletto: Constable, known worldwide as W. G., even after decades of delving into the differences between prime originals, contemporary copies, variants, versions, later imitations and downright forgeries, still could never tell t'other from which, and J. G. Links, who sought to make sense of the confusions that rendered his two volumes of Catalogue Raisonné almost useless, proved only to be another over-affectionate amateur without the necessary eye. Their combined efforts are of value only to the art dealer happy to gull the collector into believing that he has bought an original backed by the as yet unreplaced expert opinion of Constable and Links. Constable was succeeded as Director by Tom Boase, an Oxford medieval history don who knew even less about the history of art. That the Institute was not closed was due to his shrewd reorganisation of its degree courses and his invitation to scholars from the Warburg Institute to teach them.

How can I describe so wonderful a thing as the Warburg in a single paragraph? Aby Warburg was a German art historian whose interests lay as much in the history of ideas, science and such more popular forms of culture as ritual, folk memory, astrology and magic. In 1926 his formidable private library in Hamburg was converted into a public research institute, Die Kulturwissenschaftliche Bibliotek, but, as Warburg (who died three years later) and most of his assistants there were Jewish, it was moved, lock, stock and barrel, to London in 1933, to settle under Collcutt's Tower in the old Imperial Institute; it was incorporated into London University in 1944, there to become a beacon of scholarship of an arcane kind without precedent in British academe, Ernst Gombrich its most celebrated luminary.[3]

---

3 For a sympathetic evocation of Warburg himself, his scholarship, his madness, his 'Hamlet-like psychology', his manic depression and his genius, one should turn to Bernd Roeck: *Florence 1900, The Quest for Arcadia*, Yale University Press, 2009.

Anthony Blunt, so far self-taught as an art historian, 'never', as he observed at the time to Gertrude Bing (the most undeservedly forgotten of the Warburg's early staff) 'having had any training in *Kunstgeschichte* at all . . . ,' joined it as general editor of its publications and began work there in September 1937; his next step was to offer the Courtauld Institute his services as a teacher, hoping for a permanent post. In March 1939 he was appointed the Deputy Director there, but with the advent of war Home House was closed for two years – and might as well have been closed for six. From the autumn of 1939 all the functions of the Institute fell into the hands of Margaret Whinney; it was at first evacuated to Guildford Technical College, but she and the few remaining students returned to Portman Square late in 1941 and bumbled on into desuetude. In 1940 only two students graduated, only one a year between 1942 and 1944, and fourteen in all before 1947, the first year in which graduates might reflect the influence of Blunt.

In April 1945, the war a month from its conclusion, Anthony was appointed Surveyor of the King's Pictures, succeeding Kenneth Clark; he also set about the task of re-opening the Courtauld and organising an academic year to begin in October. When Tom Boase returned from a posting in the Middle East in August, it was for little more than a year as Director; he resigned his post early in 1947 to become President of Magdalen College, Oxford. Anthony was at once appointed his successor and began the task of transforming the underfunded, academically obscure and scarcely reputable Institute into a school of art history that would rival, equal and surpass all the schools of *Kunstgeschichte* and *Kunstwissenschaft* long established in Germany and central Europe. When he moved into the rambling flat in the attic that was his post's most desirable perquisite, Home House became the place not only where he lived and worked, but had his being, and the house provided the perfect atmosphere for both the man and his academic ideals. Anthony was later to claim that he could not imagine the Institute in any other setting, and I cannot imagine it under any subsequent director – with the exception of Michael Kitson (of whom more later) who was not appointed to that post. It was a Cambridge College in small, utterly civilised, hung with masterpieces, dedicated to the cultivation of aptitude and intellect, ideas and reason, in a field so far from a precise science that most panjandrums of London University could comprehend neither how great a gift the Institute had been nor the great gifts it might bestow – that is with the exception of Lionel Robbins, long a professor at the London School of Economics, already recognised as great and good, whose chairmanship of the Institute's Management Committee was a step on the way to trusteeships of the National and Tate Galleries. Physically as tall as Anthony but twice his weight, with a hint of the working-class bruiser about him, Robbins was unaccountably as besotted with him as the half-dozen aging spinsters of the Institute who unreservedly and unrequitedly adored him; the cynic might mistakenly attribute this to Robbins' undoubted social climbing, but to me it seemed the honest devotion of the dog. With considerable cunning he acted as Anthony's protector from enemies and detractors within the machinery of the University.

Under Anthony's wing the Institute attracted the greatest scholars of the post-war years. Lectures, seminars and tutorials were given by Demus, Grabar, Kurz, Buchthal, Wittkower, Gerson, Van Gelder, Clark, Pope-Hennessy, Ettlinger, Gombrich, Frances Yates, Greta Ring and a host of other international luminaries, many of them drawn to London by some business with the Warburg Institute with which the Courtauld shared a learned journal, the association lending it formidable academic respectability worldwide. For students the atmosphere was as forcing as a gardener's hothouse, as puritanical and conditioning as a monastery (and as chaste), encouraging in most of them minds closed to any career that did not involve the further pursuit of art history.

Over three years the syllabus covered the Renaissance from just before Giotto to just after Michelangelo, a long period of English art that spanned either from the Dark Ages to circa 1550 or from

1550 to the then present day, and a special period that could be Byzantine, Romanesque, Gothic or any post-Renaissance century. With luck the courses fell – as they did for me – in that order, locking together chronologically so that when the special period came in the third year, the student was most experienced and mature; the only flaw was that we were at our least mature when confronted with the Renaissance, the foundation stone of all that followed in western art, and had to make sense of not only Leonardo and Michelangelo, Raphael and Titian, but of Jan van Eyck and Roger van der Weyden, Bosch and Brueghel, Dürer and Holbein, the Schools of the Danube and Cologne. This syllabus provided a sound frame for any independent work the student chose to do – one who had specialised in the seventeenth century had no difficulty in tackling French Impressionism, for he was already aware of at least its bare bones from working on the New English Art Club and the Camden Town painters in his English year, nor in making sense of Neo-Classicism, for its antique sources were the same as those of the Italian Renaissance and the classicising branch of the Baroque.

That these were still the early years of the Institute makes Anthony's performance in his first decade as its Director (1947–57) all the more extraordinary. He was, I am certain, talent-spotting. He could be distant with unpromising students, and enthusiastic, warm and generous with others. Never did I see him be unkind to one, with the exception of an American who, as the Professor of Art History at a very minor far provincial university, had chosen to spend a sabbatical year taking the Courtauld's undergraduate course in seventeenth-century art as a refresher; irredeemably dim-witted, he knew less than any of us, understood nothing and, as he could speak not one word of any continental European language, determinedly employed Churchillian mis-pronunciation. With him, Anthony did indeed lose patience. The professor, nicknamed The Ladykiller for his smarmy response to any woman within reach, lasted less than a term, and, feeling himself to have been gravely insulted during a tutorial on Borromini, left, taking with him the bossiest of the secretaries in the marble bathroom. Anthony was perhaps not displeased when students fell away at or before the end of the first year – of the dozen in mine, only six survived to take finals – for he was interested only in teaching those who might one day, even perhaps very soon, be members of a spreading Courtauld team, as it were, capable of holding every academic, administrative and curatorial post open to the art historian. For all sorts of reasons I was never to be one of them, but within weeks of my graduation he did not hesitate to shunt me off to University College to deliver in his stead a couple of lectures on Poussin, and to the University of Birmingham to unburden myself on the rest of seventeenth-century French painting. John White is a much more serious example of Anthony's fast-tracking a student – working for his PhD when I was in my first incarnation at the Institute, he achieved his doctorate in 1952, was immediately appointed Lecturer and was my first tutor there when I returned in 1954; my recollection is that Anita Brookner lectured us on Greuze while she was still working on her PhD; and Michael Kitson, six years my senior and my fellow BA student in 1950–52, was, between 1954 and 1957, one of the triumvirate of tutors who formed me as an art historian.[4]

Of these the first was Johannes Wilde. It was under his guidance that we were introduced to the greatest figures of the Italian Renaissance, yet he never once expressed impatience with the naivety, stupidity, laziness and incompetence of raw and jejune students so evidently drowning in the deep end of art history; the worst rebuke he ever delivered to any of my contemporaries was to John Acton, speaking nonsense of a Titian in the National Gallery – 'But Mr Acton, have you *seen* the painting?' That it was a

---

4 Of all these fast-tracked students, the most well-known now is Neil MacGregor, whom Anthony is reputed to have described as his most brilliant pupil.

rebuke when he said to me, again in a tutorial on Titian, 'Mr Sewell, you like dogs, I believe?' and then produced from a drawer in his desk photograph after photograph of Titian's dogs, from mastiff to muff-warmer, I was uncertain at the time and am so still, preferring to think of it as an instruction to enjoy the simple pleasure to be found in looking at paintings, or to share the private pleasures of the painter himself.

It was Johannes who taught me that though I must be 'humble before the facts,' art history is not merely the disciplined recounting of dates and documents, but an adventure into the spirit and humanity of man, and if I have any further insights into the work of Leonardo, Titian and Michelangelo, they spring from his profound sensibilities as well as from his immaculate scholarship. Tall and stooping, his hands a-tremble, his quirkily poetic English slow in delivery and heavy with the accents of Budapest and Vienna, his demands of us as first-year students were patiently formidable and, occasionally, gently humorous. He published very little, and the students who loved his gentle presence and infinitely subtle mind have only the texts of his lectures on Michelangelo and Venetian painting to support their fragile recollections.[5] In the course of many moves I have lost every essay and lecture note I wrote as a student and have no record – and scant recollection – of what, in my third year, he taught me in tutorials on Rubens, Rembrandt and Jan Steen; later, immediately after graduation, he was persuasive in his attempt to steer me towards Rubens as a subject for my PhD. As for the one northern artist with whom he dealt in my first year, Pieter Brueghel, extending my knowledge deep into the study of prints and drawings, the loss of these notes I regret more than any other.

'This veritable High Priest of *Kunstgeschichte*', as Peter Kidson, one of his earlier English apostles, put it – brought to the Courtauld

5 Michelangelo: *Six Lectures*, Clarendon Press, Oxford, 1978; *Italian Drawings, Michelangelo and his Studio*, British Museum, 1953; and *Venetian Art from Bellini to Titian*, Clarendon Press, Oxford, 1974.

the traditions, wisdom and practice of art history in German-speaking Europe. When Blunt brought him to the Institute in 1947 and appointed him Deputy Director the following year, he not only introduced the most important factor in the extraordinarily rapid growth of the international esteem in which it was held until Anthony's retirement in 1974, but made amends for the suspicion and mistrust that had led to Wilde's internment and deportation to Canada as an enemy alien during the war.

With Johannes we students felt that we were given the purest distillation of ideas and scholarship, and after his lectures and tutorials I felt much the same as I did after choral Mass, though communion with him was founded on demonstrable fact; in this faith did play a part in that, though Johannes encouraged us to reconsider the received wisdom of authority, we preferred to exempt him from such scepticism and enquiry, to accept his teaching as gospel, and believe.[6] The lectures and tutorials of Kitson and Blunt, the second and third of my triumvirate, were entirely different; both felt hesitantly spontaneous, even spasmodic in the sense of having seen in a photograph or a slide on the screen, something not in their notes but so important that it must immediately be discussed, leaving the remainder of the planned lecture undelivered. Anthony might recover enough to end with the suggestion that he would return to the original theme in the next lecture, but Michael either lapsed into silence after well over-running the declared hour, or mumbled a half-hearted 'Well, I'm sorry not to have finished, but if any of you . . . '

In tutorials, which both of them treated as open-ended – they began at 2.00 pm, paused at 4.00 for Mrs Winkle's tea and cakes, and then drew on until almost 7.00, when the Institute closed – if there was much more to be said, then we continued the following

6 For evidence of the devotion of his students see special editions of the *Burlington Magazine* in his honour, June 1961, and in his memory, March 1971.

day. Tutorial groups were very small – four at the most in the first year and perhaps only one in the third – and it was wonderfully exciting for students to be in lively exchange with such minds. In my last year, in a tutorial on François Mansart (one of Anthony's extreme enthusiasms), I made a casual observation that intrigued him, and within minutes groundplans and elevations had spread from the table to the floor and he was urging me to write a note for publication in the *Burlington Magazine*. I didn't, it wasn't, and I now have not the slightest recollection of what it was that so excited him. Anthony it was, of course, who steered me towards Poussin, the great *peintre-philosophe* who was his abiding love, and then opened my eyes to Vouet, La Hyre and Blanchard, to Georges de la Tour and the brothers Le Nain, and to such comparatively minor figures as Vignon and Stoskopff.

It must seem odd to the outsider that Claude was not one of Anthony's enthusiasms – too romantic, perhaps, and insufficiently philosophical and mathematical – but Michael Kitson had the perfect sensibility to deal with so poetic a painter. Claude, he wrote, 'is not a painter who offers instant sensations, . . . one of the great introverts in the history of art . . . his art is subtle, elusive; . . . subjective, it invites a subjective response.'[7] It is a wry thing that instead of becoming the world's acknowledged expert on the man, he was usurped in this by one of his Courtauld pupils, Marcel Röthlisberger; Michael was far too modest ever to nurture such an ambition and far too sweet-natured to be envious of Röthlisberger's success, but to the onlooker it was evident enough that his laurels had been snatched from him. Perhaps, if he had not been quite so conscientiously burdened with teaching at the Institute, his primacy with Claude might have been maintained. In his address at Michael's memorial service in 1998, Neil MacGregor described

---

7 *The Art of Claude Lorraine*, introduction to the exhibition catalogue, Arts Council 1969, reprinted in Michael Kitson, *The Seeing Eye* (a collection of his criticism), Mnemosyne Press, 2008.

him as 'the outstanding scholar critic of his generation, perhaps indeed of the century . . . a man not just respected, but loved . . . of unfailing courtesy of manner and seemingly inexhaustible generosity of spirit.' I recognise how closely, but far more clumsily, I have unconsciously followed him as a writer, and it is in part to him that I owe the range of interests that have enabled me to be a jobbing critic, for with him I tasted not only the divine elixir of Claude but the small beer of Wilkie and Mulready and the large beer of Turner. With Wilkie, Michael led me to the quotidian art of nineteenth-century Germany and an abiding interest in the Schools of Düsseldorf and Munich to which Picasso was attracted before he thought of Paris – but to open such doors is the way of the intelligent art historian.

CHAPTER 9

Student Life

My friendship with Jill Rigden lasted with much the same intensity – domination on her part, submission on mine – until her death in 1998. We were at once brought together by being put in the same tutorial group under John White whose duty he deemed to be to teach us method. This he did so aggressively and so much to the exclusion of any aesthetic excitement we might have experienced, that Jill dragooned the two other students in our group into supporting a minor rebellion. I, having said nothing of my earlier years at the Institute, when Peter Murray's mantra 'Students are the lowest form of life here' was too often heard, was content to let her lead it. We bearded him in his room where, standing himself, he kept us on our feet while Jill expressed her opinion that method could be taught in twenty minutes and be reinforced as we went along, and that what we wanted and needed more than his forensic examination of every shred of documentary evidence, was expanding familiarity with the works of art themselves in some sort of orderly framework. Warming to her attack, she asserted that we did not want to be bogged down with such obscurities as Tino da Camaino and Arnolfo di Cambio, on whom we had unprofitably wasted two tutorials. John White, tall, elegantly dressed and, I think, aghast at the assault, suddenly flung himself onto the settee behind him, a gesture that reduced us all to laughter, not because it was absurdly dramatic (though it was), but because the ancient bearskin that concealed the settee's rents and exuding stuffing could not stand the sudden strain and exploded into a cloud of loose hair that set us all wheezing and sneezing. No better device could have been conceived to ease the tension and, to give

John his due, subsequent tutorials were infinitely more instructive and enjoyable.

It was probably Jill who proposed that some of us should drive to Italy in the Easter break of 1955, though it could equally well have been the result of conversations in The Gondola, a coffee bar in Wigmore Street to which she and I repaired for a sixpenny cappuccino almost every morning. Soundings among other students whom we thought serious resulted in a party of six, for which Jill's tiny pink Austin A30 was too small and for such a journey my very large but very pre-war Wolseley might not be reliable. To our surprise we found that, so early in the season, we could hire a new Vauxhall Velox for £5 a week, with two bench seats and a gear-change lever on the steering column, and a hefty roof-rack for most of our luggage.

With my mother, who was always anxious to know my where-abouts, I left a sheet of paper pompously headed *The Grand Tour*, listing the main cities on our itinerary with approximate dates between 24 March and 1 May 1955, and the names of the students with whom I was to travel – Jill, Margaret Lake, John Acton, Alton Jenkins and Giles de la Bedoyère, to whose name I added the note 'Lives in Wimbledon with his father, who is editor of *The Catholic Herald*' in the belief that if anything was amiss at home he, of all people, would be able to trace us in Italy. Alton, American and the oldest of us, was far more practical and used American Express offices as places from which to pick up mail – to the rest of us this seemed astonishingly worldly-wise.

We stayed in Youth Hostels and very cheap hotels of a kind that lasted into the early Seventies but can now no longer be found. For emergencies we carried a one-man tent that I had kept from my army days, knowing that by lowering the ridge-poles and stretching the outriggers, the four boys could just squeeze into it, leaving the car's bench seats for the girls. Only once were we enough wretchedly situated to use it; making our way over the hills to Rimini by a very minor road on which our speed was little more than walking pace, darkness overtook us and we camped for the night. We should have reconnoitered, but we simply pulled off on a flat patch under trees, sure that we were in uninhabited territory; but we were not and our awakening in the morning was terrifying – men with shotguns shouting in a dialect none of us could understand (though we recognised the tenor of it) hauled us from the tent, while others hammered on the locked doors of the car. For a minute or two, rape and murder seeming imminent, we were seriously scared, but our repeated apologies (and perhaps the fact that there were six of us, six witnesses to any intended crime) eventually calmed the men and they bundled us and our baggage higgledy-piggledy into the car and sent us on our way.

Within an hour we reached the coast road and turned north, Rimini almost in sight, and were astonished to encounter road-racing cars whistling past us towards the south. Then we were chased by a police car and forced off the road. On its very day we were on the course of the Mille Miglia race, and as all lateral roads had been closed we had to explain how we had got there – down a farm track, it seemed. We were then cautiously conducted into Rimini and spent the rest of the day minutely examining the Tempio Malatestiana, a gothic church dedicated to the poverty and piety of St Francis, reconstructed (but unfinished) as an almost pagan temple commemorating the depraved Sigismondo Malatesta and Isotta, the illicit love of his life.

The first Youth Hostel of the journey, in Rheims, stank every-where of urine, and boys were separated from girls only by filthy blankets hanging from a rope across the room. In Dijon we found lodgings with a family who fed us on bread and lentil soup (it was Friday and in Lent) and then put the four boys in one vast bed in which we were all savaged by bed-bugs. In Switzerland the hostels were clinically clean, but by then we all had lice; the eyebrows of the female pharmacist in Basel to whom we sheepishly explained our trouble – seeing that we were six – could not have risen further. Years later, by then working for Christie's, after a week in

Paris inspecting paintings offered the firm for sale, I caught crabs again and, even more sheepishly, went to the august chemist in St James's Street; there, however, crabs were not a matter for stricture and disgrace, and the response of the man behind the counter when I fumblingly apologised for the nature of my errand was a hearty 'Oh don't you worry,' and, holding up a bottle of white liquid, 'all my gentlemen come to me for this.' Really? – I wondered; all those eminent gentlemen in White's and Boodle's?

That we reached Milan in the early hours of the morning was the consequence of an hilarious confusion over trains through the Simplon Tunnel, for at Brig we put the car on the right one to Domodossola, but, after a drink in the station café, ourselves on another going God knows where. As this added hours to our journey and we were far too late to find our sort of hotel open, Jill decided that in Milan we should spend the rest of the night in the baths of the main railway station. I fell asleep in mine and awoke in tepid water to find a fierce concièrge in a white apron shaking my shoulder, while my companions looked on my nakedness as the sons of Noah did on his. In Florence we stayed in the Piazza Santa Maria Novella where, in the Pensione Santa Lucia, the famiglia Brogi gave the girls a small bedroom and, for the boys, abandoned their living room with its great ceiling beams and frescoed decorations – it was the *gran salone* of a small palazzo – and added four truckle beds to the furniture. It was an act of extraordinary kindness, for it gave all six of us room to sit and read, write, talk and play, at Jill's insistence, Canasta.

We had been advised by older students to stay, in Assisi, at the Convent of the American Nuns; a plump and ruddy nun opened the door and, before I could ask for rooms, welcomed me with 'Gee, if it isn't little Lord Fauntleroy,' followed by a gale of laughter. In Venice too we had good fortune, again advised by older students, in finding an apartment on the Giudecca – then the city's least visited quarter, working class and down at heel – in finding an apartment occupied by a penniless Englishwoman, a lost soul who retreated to her bedroom and let us have the run of the rest of it. In the Fifties, for the benefit of workers, the ferry across the Bacino to the Riva degli Schiavone was free if boarded before eight in the morning, and as we were by then in a penny-pinching state, this was a useful discipline in rising early to get on with our art history studies – though we hardly needed it, for the objective in undertaking the journey was the single-minded business of putting flesh on the bones of what we had seen in poor quality coloured reproductions and the monochrome photographs and slides with which lectures and tutorials were illustrated.

The great benefit of the car was that we could see things invariably missed when travelling by train – thus it was that we saw the quirkily beautiful cathedral at Laon, Claus Sluter's *Well of Moses* in Champmol and his *Weepers* (touching embodiments of grief) in the museum in Dijon, *The Miraculous Draught of Fishes* by Konrad Witz in Geneva and the Holbein drawings in Basel. Jill and I were alone in looking at these last and we became increasingly uneasy with what seemed their lifeless quality – that is until one of the warders, understanding our chatter, haltingly explained that they were facsimiles and took us to a curator; she, enthusiastic soul, opened the solander boxes in which the real things lay. For both of us it was a lesson, partly in essential conservation, but more in the need always to question everything that rouses a misgiving. A mesh of scepticism through which to filter what he sees, is the art historian's first defence against the excitements, delusions, assertions and deceits of his peers, for without informed scepticism, he is their dupe.

There were benefits too in the journeying itself, for the laden Vauxhall with three of us on each bench seat, luggage under our feet and more cases on the roof nullifying the few aerodynamic features known to the designers of its body, was most at ease when lolloping along at less than fifty miles an hour. This let us look at landscape, let us see, for example, what Konrad Witz had seen on the journeys between Basel and Geneva that inspired him to paint a topographically accurate view of the Lake in 1444, that most of us believe to have been the first portrayal of a real landscape in the centuries of the Renaissance. In Italy the physical changes in landscape between the valley of the Po and Tuscany, Tuscany and Umbria, Umbria and the Marches, lent us insight into the political rivalries of the Renaissance, the frequent journeyings of artists between the influential centres of painting, sculpture and architecture, the discovery and development of aerial perspective, and the conscious use of observed landscape as the setting for a martyrdom or crucifixion. At another level there was the thrill of cresting the hill at Fiesole or San Miniato al Monte, thence to look down into the great bowl of land in which the city of Florence lies, or of following the winding road from Arezzo to Borgo San Sepolcro to see Piero della Francesca's *Resurrection* and his *Madonna del Parto* at Monterchi; to see Assisi, Siena, Orvieto and Todi from a distance was to experience beautiful astonishments. In the Fifties, Italian towns and cities were much as they had been for centuries; they had no urban fringes, no crass and jarring new developments outside their ancient city walls, and we drove into them with the insouciance of those who know that they will have no difficulty in parking, for every town square had spaces dedicated to the cars of tourists. We parked within yards of Leonardo's *Last Supper* in Milan, Giotto's Arena Chapel in Padua, the Palazzo Diamante in Ferrara and the great church of San Petronio in Bologna; such feats are now impossible.

Alton, Jill and I did the driving; Giles, the Dormouse of this party, had a license but only once was he allowed to take the wheel, so hideously crunching were his attempts to change the gears. Alton drove like every American, relaxed, angled against the door, one hand on the wheel. Jill accelerated hard and slipped the clutch so much that by the time we reached Milan it had to be relined. By the grace of God there was a General Motors garage in the city and by dint of using Opel parts the work could be done within a morning – and that morning provided me with what remains the most exhilarating drive of my life, though I have since driven much faster. Just as I settled down to read a book for a couple of hours, a mechanic took pity on me: a Gullwing Mercedes 300 SL had just been delivered from Stuttgart and he was required to take this exquisite paradigm of aerodynamics for a test run; would I care to come, he asked. He put a clipboard of data in my hand, saw me into the passenger seat, and off we tore, up the autostrada to Como, ticking off the kilometres in seconds, to chuck it about on the corniche to Bellagio, and then race back to Milan through Monza. For that experience, the two seats snug and low, with no room even for a lapdog, the roar of an engine reaching 6,000 rpm with every single revolution of it communicated to the cabin, a mile a minute reached within a twinkling (in eight seconds I know now) and a speedometer calibrated in too few kilometres to outdo the ambitions of the needle (we beat 200 kilometres an hour, more than twice the Vauxhall's maximum without a load), I have ever since been grateful. When, in the spring of 2005, half a century on, I again witnessed the Mille Miglia, no longer a race but an endurance test for geriatric machinery, no fewer than twenty-four Gullwings were paraded, and they looked as thrilling, beautiful and astonishing as ever.

When the Vauxhall was on the move over a long distance, one of us read aloud from an odd assortment of books on which, to eliminate duplicates, we had agreed. We took pocket editions of Berenson on Italian painting, Blunt on Italian artistic theory, Burckhardt on Italian civilisation and other necessaries; the only outsider book that I can remember was a slim volume of poems by T. S. Eliot brought by John Acton, that, had it included *Old Possum's Practical Cats*, I would have stolen and thrown away, but this he knew by heart and could not be persuaded that a crowded Vauxhall was no place for his thumping, gesturing, booming delivery, much too often repeated. As semi-outsiders I took as many essays as I could find by Aldous Huxley, for among them I knew his subversive interpretations of El Greco, Brueghel, Vermeer and Conxolus, and with these I hoped to sow seeds of sedition. I also took Bocaccio's *Decameron* and this proved a suitable companion for our only languourous day in all the weeks we were away; it was Good Friday, a day on which every museum in Florence was closed and half the citizens were on their knees at Tenebrae, a beautiful melancholy service of Holy Week that had survived unchanged since the Middle Ages but was to be changed after 1955. Had I known that this was its last unmodernised year, I too might have spent the day in church; instead, finding what we could for a picnic, we drove out into the countryside and lay in the sun, quaffing Chianti and listening to unexpurgated tales of love, lust, deception and murder.

From the very beginning of the journey, though in the evening we ate proper dinner, picnic breakfasts and lunches were the order of the day – bread, 200 grams of mortadella and 200 of cheese, fruit, wine and water; looking back, I am astonished that six young adults could be content with so little, but in England we were still accustomed to the frugalities of post-war rationing and seemed unable to take advantage of the casual plenty that was everywhere in Italy. There were occasional extravagances; in Milan, after the episode of the baths, we were tempted by the little dishes of trippa Milanese that stood on the counters of coffee bars; in the shade of an arcade in Bologna we lunched on saltimbocca that we could not sensibly afford and drank Lambrusco; and in Mantua, as a breakfast delicacy with great bowls of milky coffee (an addiction for which, if necessary, I would go hungry) we were given a dish of fritto misto, dredged from the lake, the waiter said, that had in it as many infant newts and frogs as minnows. In Florence, in the shade of Ognissanti, we bought glasses of wine from an old man carrying flasks of red and white Chianti on a yoke, dunking the glasses in a bucket of water, and in this simple thing sensed some direct connection with the Quattrocento, imagining that just such a peasant in a yoke was there when Donatello installed his homage to the handsome boy, *St George*, in one of its several external niches. In Assisi, at the end of a long day trying to make sense of who did what and when in the too extensive decoration of the upper and lower churches – a viral obsession for John White and other students of his generation at the Courtauld, for whom the answers have proved more elusive than the solution of the last theorem of Pierre de Fermat – we came upon a man roasting a whole pig; into generous cornets of rolled paper he sliced slivers of flesh and crackling from it, and then plunged his arm deep into the carcass for a handful of chopped onion and sage – that his hands were filthy mattered not at all as we sat eating on a wall with the sunset plain stretching to the west beneath us. Again we felt the past, felt that we were doing exactly what had been done six centuries before by the painters of the frescoes in the gloomy lower church after a day of mixing plaster and clambering about on scaffolding to illuminate for an illiterate peasantry the life of Christ and the miracles of St Francis. And in Venice, tempted by the warm spring sun as we got off the boat from the Giudecca, Jill and I broke away from the others, sat on the Riva degli Schiavone and drank the viscous hot chocolate that is unique to La Serenissima before taking off for our duties among the city's churches – a small event of which the sentimental recollection years later and after Jill's death, brought me to unquenchable tears.

What were the qualities in Jill that so affected me? At first it was perhaps the sense that at the Courtauld we were both in the same boat, that we had both wasted too much time on ambitions that were will-o'-the-wisps and that this, the Courtauld, was a now or never opportunity to make something of our lives. We were both adults with some sense of financial security in that Jill's rich father gave her an allowance, and I, having spent my army savings on a handsome car – a Wolseley 25 of 1936 – had volunteered it and my services to a nearby chauffeur-driven hire service and thus earned money at weekends as a standby minicab driver, occasionally very well tipped if not well paid. We had, in addition, the grants that were then given to almost every university student. And we both had interests beyond the walls of Academe – though mine, apart from motor cars, were largely connected with the visual arts. Even when I was in the army I had, whenever possible, continued to trawl the art dealers of Bond Street, and I now took Jill with me to share the rich and various experience to be gained there. We went, too, to the auction houses, and in the week of the Rees Jeffreys sale at Christie's in November 1954 – that is very early in our relationship – I dragged her, John Acton and Alton Jenkins to see his *Portrait of Derain* by Matisse, so convinced was I that this beautiful picture would be bought by an American collector or museum, never to be seen again (it was, however, bought by the Tate). Apart from the Winter Exhibitions at the Royal Academy, this was not a period of blockbusters, and as the Tate, the National and National Portrait Galleries were impoverished and somnolent, we depended for enlightenment on the annual exhibitions of the Edinburgh Festival brought south by the Arts Council, on the occasional small shows mounted by the Arts Council in their elegant premises in St James's Square, and on what art dealers were prepared to show us. We depended particularly on Colnaghi's, Agnew's and Matthiessen's, but many smaller dealers, working from rooms on first and second floors, were sources of intriguing backwater knowledge and Jill became almost as voraciously enquiring as I.

The Italian journey cemented our relationship. Of the group, Jill and I were the most greedily determined to see everything, to buy the slim limp catalogues bound in pale blue paper published by the *Ministero della Pubblica Istruzione*, with monochrome illustrations the size of postage stamps crowded four to a page (in 1955 no one had thought of vastly expensive encyclopedic catalogues) and to collect the blurred post cards offered by the churches. We were unflagging. For John Acton cigarettes were the most important things in his life – he never had more than one hand available; Alton was languidly and beautifully at ease with himself and had no sense of urgency; young Giles was far more theologically than art historically interested in what we saw and had the makings of an earnest dilettante constantly diverted by irrelevances; only Margaret shared anything of our imperturbable high seriousness but was too often inclined to drift and dream. On our return Jill and I were as loosely connected with them as before.

One morning early in the Summer Term Jill came to me in the library and, in more peremptory tone than usual, commanded me to accompany her to The Gondola at once – 'I have something to say to you.' Not until we were there would she give me an inkling of what it was and then said, without preamble, 'David proposed to me last night.' I knew of David – David Allibone – an ambitious young solicitor with whom she had been involved for some time, and asked if she had accepted him. 'Well no. I need to know what you intend to do.' I had never thought of Jill in such a sense and wondered what on earth had given her the impression that marriage was even a remote possibility. But for carrying her over my shoulder across a piazza near the university in Padua and dumping her on the roof rack of the Vauxhall – it was after dinner, we were both a little drunk and I was driven on by the applause of students, one of whom began to sing La Donna e mobile – we had had no physical contact of any kind and the only sexual trigger to disturb my celibacy of many months had been no thought of her, but a moment in the youth hostel in Basel when, sleeping on the top bunk, I had looked down to see Alton in the lower, serenely and a-sexually beautiful and had longed to touch so sculptural a face. I fumbled my reply, aware that to blurt that I had never thought of marriage might be insulting, and at the same time unwilling to let slip that I was queer. A day or two later, with carefully prepared delicacy, The Gondola was witness to my telling Jill that I had plans in which marriage and children could play no part, that priesthood was my intention. Within a year or so she married David and was eight months pregnant when we sat our Finals in June 1957.

What was this haunting intention to become a priest? What was the source of it? It was partly a resolution of my theological uncertainty as a boy, a rejection of the low church banalities preached at Haberdashers', a recognition that if I believed any of its infallibilities, myths and miracles, then I must believe all – there must be no Church of England halfway house and I must be a Roman Catholic, reason utterly and comfortably suspended in belief. Such a surrender was an attractive proposition, simple, uncluttered and unquestioning, sans argument. It must also have been a response to my homosexuality, offering the comfort that no one would question the unmarried state of a priest in the camouflage of a cassock, and I was convinced that prayer would protect me from any temptations offered by altar boys, servers or other priests, for I had managed to be abstinent, at least in deed, since the rape in Aldershot – and in that I had been the mute object and in no sense a responsive participant. I attended occasional retreats; at these I observed other young men who, from indications to which I was scarcely attuned – excessive piety and a superstitious response to the slavery of ritual, perhaps – I thought might be similarly troubled; what, I wondered, might be the temptations of the seminary? From a letter received in June 1956, it is clear that I had by then taken official steps to train for the priesthood and been accepted as having a vocation; the writer advised me that, though recognising the need to work for my degree at the Courtauld, I should also make time for close study of the texts of the Bible and Apocrypha, and make a start with elementary Greek and, by extension, Aramaic. I did nothing of the kind. With the year of my special period by then immediately ahead – Rubens, Rembrandt, Velazquez, Caravaggio, Poussin, Claude, Bernini and the vast landscape of the Roman Baroque – how could I turn my mind to a dead Semitic language and give it precedence?

In the summer break of 1955 I immediately had work to do. Frederick P. Bargebuhr, a professor at Iowa State University, was in London to work on a paper to be published in the Journal of the Warburg and Courtauld Institutes and required a research assistant. That he had given me the job I again had Charles Clare to thank, though Charles knew perfectly well that, apart from my command of English, I had not the slightest qualification for helping Bargebuhr, whose subject was eventually whittled down to *The Alhambra Palace of the Eleventh Century*.[8] It is a measure of the man that to an article 45 pages long he appended 22 pages of notes, and that tucked into the offprint that he sent to me 'With much appreciation and a cordial good-bye,' were nine more foolscap pages close-typed with corrigenda and addenda that had escaped publication.

When he returned to America his final version of the paper was at least twice as long. In broad terms the subject was the interaction of Jewish and Arabic cultures in Moorish Spain late in the first millennium, its emphasis primarily on gardens, water, fountains, sculptured lions and poetry, but as Bargebuhr was a scholar who could never jettison a notion, no matter how peripheral, on all these matters he was likely to leap as far back as the Chaldeans for a precedent, or forward to demonstrate the continuing influence of Arabic culture in Spain in the eighteenth century – the last of his published footnotes is, absurdly, a quotation from Théophile Gautier.

It was on the poetry that he wished me to concentrate. In Arabic and Hebrew, Bargebuhr was as accomplished as in his native German, but his English was profoundly flawed. After tidying the main text to make it less excruciatingly unreadable, the tedium of re-typing it with all Near Eastern accents added by hand quite maddening, it was my duty to render the poetry into rhyming verse. Whether or not the verses rhymed in Arabic and Hebrew, I could not tell, but he was determined that they should in English. He translated them into German; I then translated the German into English and wrestled it into forms that not even William McGonagall could excel, but he had neither ear nor eye for scansion and was happy when it rhymed. Much of this was done in the Warburg Institute, within earshot of Joseph Trapp, later its Director,

8 *Journal of the Warburg and Courtauld Institutes*, Vol. XIX 1956, Nos. 3–4.

trying his renowned good humour to such a degree that he found a lightless cupboard in which to sequester us. When the paper was at last published I wondered if he, as one of the Journal's six editors, had taken revenge by slashing the length of Bargebuhr's prolix text and abandoning my rhymes in favour of direct translation.

In the early Sixties when I had Rubens on my mind and still nursed the faint hope of academic scholarship, I was, I felt, the only visitor to the Warburg to be greeted by Trapp with a scowl. If I learned not to be noisy in libraries – a thing I already knew – the more useful lesson was the importance of diligence in copy editing and proof reading, though I did not realise it at the time; I also learned not to be disappointed when not thanked in print for working as a dogsbody – such acknowledgements are of great value to those at the bottom of the heap.

My second year at the Courtauld, the year devoted to English art, passed in an unrewarding blur; apart from Hawksmoor and Vanbrugh I could raise little enthusiasm for English architecture and none at all for the tombstone stuff of English sculpture; in English painting, only Reynolds and Gainsborough, Constable and Turner, really raised their heads above the Waters of Oblivion, though, cussedly perhaps, I developed affections for John Singer Sargent, Wilson Steer and Sickert, Gilman, Gore and Ginner, academically sound enough to find, immediately on graduation a year later, employment as a lecturer on these painters at the Tate Gallery. In many ways this English year proved to be the most useful preparation for working in Christie's too, for with 1550 as its *terminus post quem* and the then present day as *terminus ante*, it covered every kind of English painting and watercolour that most frequently appeared at auction. It dealt with Van Dyck, his predecessors, imitators and influence, and concluded with Bomberg who was then still alive. The most tedious subject on which I was compelled to write an essay was English portraiture between Kneller and Reynolds (the one was born in the year that the other died, 1723), but a nodding acquaintance with Knapton, Dandridge,

Pond and Hudson, despairing though I was in making it, proved invaluable three years later – invaluable too because my tutor was Ellis Waterhouse, whose encyclopedic capacity for facts, visual memory and extraordinary range of scholarship (it began with El Greco in 1930 and ended in 1981 with a comprehensive *Dictionary of British Painters*) ensured that he taught us of these pygmy face-painters with a mischievous sense of proportion. It was the beginning of a slightly *de haut en bas* friendship for which I was devotedly grateful when arguing the rights and wrongs of attributions rashly made by directors of Christie's who could hardly distinguish a Gainsborough from a Sawrey Gilpin. When cataloguing in Christie's vaults I put all sorts of things aside for his almost weekly visits and his question 'Anything for me to see?' – and was constantly astonished by how many dull obscurities he had already seen, often decades earlier; his notes on anything he thought should interest me he sent on post cards from Birmingham written as soon as he reached home, his handwriting so small that I could never read it without a magnifying glass – so short-sighted was he that he removed his spectacles to read and held books and papers only squinting inches from his eyes.

Our other guide through the long tedium of English art was Margaret Whinney, determined to ensure that we thought Inigo Jones a match for Palladio and Wren the equal of Bernini; she was a dry and diligent teacher, rarely able to infect us with her enthusiasms for Nollekens, Colley Cibber and their ilk, but her knowledge of English architecture and sculpture was profound; only Vanburgh and Hawksmoor, however, survived her teaching to become my enthusiasms too. We suspected that when the three-year syllabus was devised, all that was left when the male grandees had secured their roles was what none of them wanted, and the drudgery fell to her. One other field was left, fifteenth century Netherlandish painting, and this too she taught ploddingly in annual lectures; only in one small particular did she ever communicate excitement and that was the tale of her sitting with

Jan van Eyck's *Ince Hall Madonna* on her knee and what a thrill it was to have this exquisite tiny masterpiece in her hands before it was exported to Australia; but when it was lent to an exhibition in Bruges in 1956, there to be damned as at best a poor copy and at worst a fake, this pretty nonsense had to be dropped from her narrative. Some of us thought her severe and humourless – and I still cringe when I recall the crushing severity of her rebuke when I duped John Acton, writing an essay on Wren's City Churches, with St Bridget's, Bun Street, the great architect's only use of the Tuscan Order in conjunction with a circular groundplan. John, always late for tutorials, was very late that day, and blurted out as his excuse, his fruitless search for any trace of it. In truth she had our interests at heart, and her warmth could always be glimpsed behind the severity of her gaze over the top of her horn-rimmed spectacles if one looked hard enough. Generous with her scholarship, which was unrivalled in the backwaters to which she was committed (John Summerson, her friend, colleague and Director of the Soane Museum, dared to describe her English sculpture as a daunting subject, inconveniently scattered and not of an inspiring kind),[9] she had no vanity.

The solid grounding that she provided in so many aspects of English art was enlivened by tutorials given by Oliver Millar and Michael Kitson. For Van Dyck and his contemporaries we went to Oliver's offices in St James's Palace where, as Deputy to Anthony Blunt as Keeper of the Queen's Pictures, he did much of the donkey work and was the perfect courtier. Over tea and biscuits he painted Van Dyck as a romantic and Lely as a lecher, but the most daring thing he did was to point us toward the Earl of Rochester as representative of an aspect of court culture usually ignored by art historians. Dame Margaret would never have done that. Michael Kitson thrilled us with his insights when cramming the armatures

9 John Summerson, *Obituary of Margaret Whinney*, Burlington Magazine, 1975, p. 732.

of Turner and Constable into our minds, and an example of the scrupulous discipline with which he constructed these is the chronological study of Constable in the years 1810–1816 published in the Warburg Institute in 1957, on which he must have been working when teaching us.[10] The other Constable, the truth to nature painter turning into one whose deliberately dramatic and restless landscapes are as much the consequence of his experience as a professional painter as of his, at first, aesthetically uncluttered seeing eye, ran side-by-side with his chronology, but did not appear in print until 1976.[11]

With Jill this English year had forced a parting of the ways, for she had chosen to study the centuries before 1550 to ensure a firm grounding for the Gothic art and architecture that was to be her special period. Of the others on the Italian journey, Alton had returned to America, never to be seen again, Margaret had completed the diploma course that lasted only a year, and Giles had disappeared to take up a monastic life as a schoolmaster and the writer of appalling doggerel; only John remained, dreadfully addicted to his cigarettes, much diverted by the cinema and other frivolities of popular culture, and notorious for unhelpfully never completing an essay until almost too late. Willy-nilly this meant closer contact with other students formerly in other tutorial groups and with some in their third year compelled to share tutorials in English art with us because their numbers too were reduced by premature departures. This was the regular pattern. For the third year students there was some advantage in that they spent only two terms on English art, the third a period of concentrated revision, but a more serious disadvantage in that, though they had had in their second year three full terms on their special period (as I and

---

10 *Journal of the Warburg and Courtauld Institutes*, XX, No 3/4 1957, reprinted in Kitson, *The Seeing Eye*, 2008, p. 130 .

11 Kitson: *The Inspiration of John Constable*, Journal of the Royal Society of Arts, CXXIV, November 1976, reprinted in *The Seeing Eye*, 2008, p. 152

my peers would not), they were then not yet at their peak. On first year students we, in our second year, gazed with mature amusement – so many of them seemed so young, as indeed many of them were, school leavers as naive and hapless as I had been in my first incarnation, yet among the girls were Juliet Bareau, soon to become an (and perhaps the) authority on Goya, and Wendy Dimson who, as Wendy Baron, became unarguably the authority on Sickert, and among the boys there was Robin Chanter, later Librarian at the British Institute in Florence.

Hearts stopped when Robin first walked into the Students' Common Room. Tall, slim and languid, at twenty-six he astonished us with his beauty and unconscious elegance, the immaculate suit of fine greenish tweed marred only by the urine drippings of a man wearing boxer shorts and careless when emptying his bladder. All his trousers were so stained, but nothing else distracted our eyes from his beauty, and he was indeed the embodiment of all that is now implied by the cliché Brideshead. He was mysterious in the sense that we knew of him as 'protected' by an older man with whom he lived in Italy. Evidence of the protection lay in everything about him, his London lodgings within short walking distance, his clothes, the smart little Fiat in which he commuted between the Courtauld and Florence, his command of half a dozen European languages and his careless arrogance towards, not only his fellow students, but the grandees of the Institute at whose feet he had come to sit. Among the dowdy sparrows of the student body this peacock did not long perch – 'a spell,' as he later put it without definition. To put the record straight, in his mid forties he fell in love with a young woman at the British Institute, married her and fathered five children, Bacchus, Athene, Artemis, Aphrodite and Demeter. I treasure his memory, not only for his beauty, but for his active interest in curtailing the wholesale slaughter of birds migrating over Italy, the annual mindless pleasure of Italian hunters – the last care to be expected of him when he was a student.

The long summer vacation brought me an extraordinarily well

paid job. Several of us depended on vacation jobs to supplement our grants and I had already worked in factories making condoms and sanitary towels, and as a night watchman in Covent Garden Market, then still in the neighbourhood of the opera house. Compared with the mockery and mimicry I suffered from the women in the factories, vicious in their sour humour, the marketeers were genial and much like old hands in the army when confronted with raw subalterns; they treated me to more mugs of tea than I could ever drink. This new job, however, was not one in which old clothes, clumsy sandwiches and ribaldry played any part, for it was the task of conducting a very small group of American tourists round almost every museum, gallery and distinguished country house between Aberdeen and Arundel, round London, Paris and Rouen. They were four wealthy women who had answered an advertisement in a magazine devoted to antiques; the magazine had expected many more and sought to cancel the expedition, but these women had paid their deposits and were threatening to sue. They were to have been accompanied from New York by a Mr Fixit (their term) and an American expert on antiques, but instead, through Charles Clare, whom the magazine regarded as the Mr Fixit of the Courtauld Institute, got me, on Charles's instructions masquerading as a junior member of staff.

In some ways a year spent studying English art and architecture was the perfect preparation for such a jaunt, but these women were serious collectors of silver, porcelain and furniture – subjects of which I knew little – who wanted to be taken to public collections and to centres where they might add to their own; these they believed to be Aberdeen, Bath, Leamington Spa, London and Paris, and they also, and particularly, wished to visit the factories of Stoke-on-Trent. All this had been arranged from New York and my duties were to follow the schedule, check them in and out of their hotels, solve any problems that might arise there or in purchasing antiques from dealers, and conduct them round the houses and museums. For me this meant a crash course in hallmarks and factory marks, for the only expertise I could reasonably claim was recognising the difference between the blue and white porcelains of Caughley and Worcester, my mother's mild enthusiasm. Days spent in the silver collections of the Victoria and Albert Museum gave me some grounding in that field, and to the collection of china there, formed by Charlotte Schreiber, I owe knowledge enough to mask my ignorance. Even so, I expected my four charges to be formidably knowledgeable and to unmask me sooner or later. As for the country houses, thank God for Margaret Whinney and all the architecture from Inigo Jones to John Soane that she had crammed into my head, was my thought.

I went to Southampton to collect them from the France, a ship that was to make several journeys to and from America before I put them back on her in Le Havre some six weeks later. On the train to London I got something of the measure of them. The leader of this pack of widows was Renata Buchanan Cameron Duncan, Magna Carta Dame and Daughter of the Revolution, constantly reiterating her claim of ancestry from 'one of the barons who wrested the Charter from wicked King John,' from all the Scots that ever were and from the early English colonists. Majestic in gait and proportion, all her dresses were made with what she called 'a window-box front' so that she could clip a slim wedge-shaped vase of water between her breasts for which one of my many unofficial duties was, every morning, to find posy flowers (not easy in Stoke-on-Trent). Profoundly deaf, she had brought with her another Daughter of the Revolution, Mrs Renshaw, very much her side-kick and as mute as Mrs Duncan was voluble, but accustomed, it seemed, to tuning the hearing-aids that Mrs Duncan wore in both her ears. Mary Sowell, a sweet woman from Alabama with neither quite their wealth or social standing, was also deaf; her only minus point was her insistence that, in spite of the different spelling of our surnames, we must in some sense be related. Fourth, youngest and most vigorous was Peg Heller from Charleston, South Carolina, whose husband's fortune lay in the lowly manufacture of screws and files and other engineering bits and bobs, and whose amused contempt for the pretensions of the Daughters was already well-developed.

We were in the last carriage of a long train, with a stack of heavy luggage for which, when we reached London, I needed a porter with a cart. My instruction to 'Stay where you are while I fetch help,' too softly spoken, was neither heard nor heeded. I felt Mrs Duncan immediately behind me as I dismounted and, turning to warn her of the considerable gap, was dismayed to see her about to transfer her weight onto a foot that was poised midway between carriage step and platform edge. Daughters of the Revolution survey the world with their noses in the air, taking no account of what is at their feet. Flinging myself forward I was just in time to get my forearms under her armpits, but I could not hold her weight and we were nose to nose as I sank to my knees and she slid into the gap until her feet were on the track. She screamed mightily. Mrs Renshaw joined the screaming but could not leave the carriage without standing on Mrs Duncan's head. Other First Class passengers gathered round us, the train's guard blew an alarm call on his whistle, porters came running, and Mrs Duncan, cut off at the level of her window-box, the flowers and water of the silver vase tipped about her bosom, a surreal and potentially ghastly phenomenon, became astonishingly calm. She also proved to be immovable. When a bedizened station master arrived, she had exactly the right words with which to put an end to the confusion – she simply bellowed 'Who do I sue.'

Men got down onto the track and heaved her from below while others hauled her from above; retrieved, she was carried off on a stretcher to a waiting ambulance. Only at that point did the other women leave the carriage, Mrs Renshaw to run after her; Mrs Heller, who had seen enough over Mrs Renshaw's shoulder to know that she should tread warily, dismounted safely enough, but then there was another scream and we all turned to see that meek, mild and stone deaf Mrs Sowell had replaced Mrs Duncan in the gap, without the benefit of my slowing her descent. Taken away in another ambulance, she proved to be much more bruised, scraped and shaken than Mrs Duncan, whose clothes had borne the brunt of her misadventure. For the magazine employing me I had to write a detailed report of the calamity, and the compensation claim initiated by Mrs Duncan, in which I was included as in some sense responsible, dragged on for months.

Their tour began the following morning, but when I reported to their hotel, the women were in no mood for the scheduled antique hunt. Feeling that I ought to do something easy and nearby, I took them to the National Gallery where my party of four grew to forty or so as strangers became hangers-on, one of whom, when we had finished, approached Mrs Duncan who all the time had hung on my arm, and asked 'Tell me madam, where did you get your guide?' Mrs Duncan's immediate response was the clearest possible warning of what was to come – 'Get him? We bought him.'

With the rape of Portobello Market done, every shop in Church Street Kensington inspected, Chrichton's (specialists in silver) stripped of every trifle made by Hester Bateman or Paul Storr, with Syon, Osterley and Kenwood explored and with envious homage paid to the silver and ceramic treasures of the V&A – with a wink from me to Charlotte Schreiber – we took an overnight train to Aberdeen, were met by a Humber Pullman limousine, and began the tour in earnest. We had tickets for the Braemar Games, of which I recall only brawny men in kilts tossing cabers of increasing weight; was there, I wondered, some element of phallic boasting in this ridiculous competition? I wondered too why we were there at all, but the answer to that riddle came when the leader of the pack found shops in which to buy plaids in the three tartans whose names she bore. Our hotel there was the bleak and turretted Scottish Baronial Castle, Craigievar, where we were entertained to dinner by its boastful, libidinous and Gaelic-speaking Laird, William Francis Forbes-

Sempill (Forbes to be pronounced Forbiz, he insisted), the 19th Baron Sempill. Penniless, he was reduced to entertaining rich Americans for cash, but it amused him too; my rich widows he drove up the narrow winding stairs of every turret, not to see the changing view, but with the purpose of pinching whichever of their bottoms was before him and within reach, though all were in their sixties. He gave them exactly what they had paid for – to be treated as old friends in an ancestral setting; he had a piper on hand, wore a kilt in the Forbiz tartan, broke into Gaelic, Lallans and Old Scots, and switched unnervingly from *dix-huitième* courtesy to medieval boorishness. At me he winked as to his conspirator.

And a conspirator he perhaps was in a quite different sense. One of the most distinguished long-distance solo aviators of his day, internationally as much honoured for his pranks as for the high seriousness of his prowess (he was the kind of man who could, and did, park his seaplane on the Thames when asked to lunch at the Savoy), he had been responsible for the development of the Japanese Air Force in the mid 1920s. Loyalties engendered then were to bring him suspicion and opprobrium when Japan entered World War II. To get and keep this high-ranking officer in the Naval Air Services out of trouble, he was deprived of his post in the Admiralty and transferred to one in Canada for the rest of the war. If, indeed, he had spied for the Japanese, he was not paid for it and, always short of money, his paying guests were what kept the roof on Craigievar.

As we drifted south I began to realise how little my four charges knew; their seeming indifference to Kenwood and Syon I had attributed to the uncertainties of an unfamiliar country, its food, water and strange customs (they never did become accustomed to driving on the left), but at Mellerstain Castle, on our way south from Edinburgh, a house by Robert Adam with some claim to be among the richest of his interiors, I saw a truth revealed. They were indifferent. They knew nothing of architecture and could not respond to it even with simple awe. They knew something of their small enthusiasms but did not want to learn anything of the wider culture to which these scraps belonged, and if they could not buy it, saw no point in looking at it. Their curiosity was limited to the age of a church, the height of a tower, the name of house and its occupants as the Humber ambled past, and to such unanswerable questions I learned that any answer served me better than a hapless 'I don't know,' for Mrs Duncan's response to 'Don't know' was a spiteful 'Why don't you know? – knowing's what I pay for.' The women grew fractious. There was a wearying sameness about their days – breakfasts that none of them wished to eat, coffee that if available at all was never to their liking, loading the Humber, the 'Oh, you're in my seat' squabbles, another country house of little interest and another provincial museum of even less, a prim country hotel for lunch, village antique shops to be inspected and another railway hotel in which to dine and stay the night. The Revolutionary Daughters always left me to get their luggage to the car, while they settled into the wide and deep rear seat, leaving the jump-seats for the others; at first I sat with the chauffeur, but Peg Heller soon usurped me, preferring his male company; in a jump-seat, Mrs Duncan could jab her finger in my back.

In Stoke-on-Trent we stayed in a red brick hotel designed for more prosperous times and yet again there were complaints about the rooms and having to share with unknown men the bathrooms and lavatories at the ends of gloomy corridors; I had to console the motherly receptionist accustomed to commercial travellers who might bathe once a week, with whom Mrs Duncan had been viciously cantankerous. I dreaded dinner, dreaded having to see her again so soon, and was last to reach our table in the otherwise empty dining room. Mrs Duncan's mood had changed; she was, as usual, holding court but her tone was affable. I later discovered that she had returned to the reception desk with an offer that could not be refused – no other rooms on her corridor would house a man, and a 'Private' notice was hung on the bathroom door. The ancient waitress brought us lentil soup. Mrs Duncan, gesturing to make a point, caught her spoon in the cord of her right deaf-aid and ripped it from her ear; that it described a wild parabola and fell into her soup was enough to provoke a giggle that I might have been able to suppress had she not then used her spoon to retrieve it, popped it into her mouth, sucked it and plugged it back into her ear, hardly pausing in her narrative. The giggling then became the helpless laughter that no effort of will can stop and I was well and truly in disgrace.

By the time we reached Paris it was clear that the women had lost all interest in museums and great houses, flea-markets and *antiquaires* – they wanted to shop for clothes and perfumes. Diligently I saw them for dinner and outlined the programme for the morrow, but they wanted nothing to do with any of it; instead, as they spoke no word of French, Mrs Duncan and her side-kick demanded that I accompany them. This I refused on the grounds that Peg Heller and Mary Sowell, who had formed something of a bond, might want to stick to the schedule – but they did not and were happy to explore shops on their own. This left me to do my duty – as I saw it – alone, and without them I followed the programme for which, months before, they willingly had paid; the appointed Cadillac limousine drew up at the hotel door, I climbed in beside the driver, and off we swept to Versailles and Malmaison, Fontainebleau and Anet, a very useful preparation for my next year of study at the Courtauld. The driver taught me where and what to eat, where and how to find a prostitute *de cinq à sept*.

It was after one of these jaunts, spiritually and intellectually lifted, that I decided to skip dinner with my charges; instead, in the little streets behind what is now the Musée d'Orsay but was then our hotel, I bought a picnic – snails and salami, a custard tart, fruit, bread and wine – and took it to my attic room in the eves over the grand facade. It was a tiny room, fit only for the servant that I was, with a single chair, a table on which one might just have fitted a game of patience, and a dry bidet – that is one not connected to any plumbing; its one touch of luxury was a rouge marble fireplace.

I had just pulled the table and chair to the window so that I could sup in the setting sun, the picnic laid as best I could with only a penknife and a tooth glass, when Peg Heller knocked on the door, Mary Sowell behind her. 'What are you doing for dinner tonight?' 'Having a picnic,' I replied. 'Have you enough for three?' Her response to my firm negative was to call room service and order more things to eat and more things with which to eat them.

My scholar gipsy evening suddenly became rather jolly. Peg sat on the chair, Mary on the bidet, the basin of which we had stuffed with a folded eiderdown, and I sat on the bed; we drank too much and laughed too much, and Mary, rocking on the bidet, rocked a little too far, fell backwards from it and hit her head on the fireplace. For some moments unconscious, she groggily recovered when dowsed with water and slapped by Peg, who then took her off to be put to bed. I had just finished tidying my room – the snail shells made a gratifying clunk on the spreading glass canopy far below – when the door opened. I assumed that Peg had come to report on Mary's condition, but she had not; instead, she closed the door and stood with her back to it, her arms widespread, and froze me to the bone with 'I'm old enough to be your grandmother, but I'm going to bed with you.'

And so she did, after a fashion. I had no wish to tell her that I was queer, and it says something of the weakness of young man's will and the overwhelming strength of his sexual triggers, that she so easily had her way with me. I remember more clearly than all else the interruption of pleasure when her diamante spectacle frames occasionally plucked a pubic hair; as for the rest of it, what we did was entirely determined by Peg and she seemed well enough pleased by it. She stayed in touch for several years, sending cookies that are peculiar to South Carolina, accompanied by letters so explicitly pornographic, so minute in detail, so far – I believed – beyond the imagination of a woman, that I was appalled by them. These letters were, oddly enough, the first things ever to make me consider the possibility of death: what, I wondered, would my mother think were I to die young and she to find them? Decades later, during the Blunt Affair, another elderly woman, Elsie Crombie – a friend to both of us – used to conclude our telephone conversations with 'Do you think MI5 is listening?' With the preamble 'Then let's give them something worth hearing,' she could launch into the most extended and extraordinary phallocentric fantasies.

The last night for my American charges was spent in Rouen where they were foolish enough to think that they could experience Monet by watching the cathedral dissolve into successive brush-strokes of Impressionist colour; Mrs Duncan was particularly high-pitched in her disappointment and would not be hushed, but worse was to come. In the Grand Hotel de la Poste, grand in name but not in comforts, she outdid herself in shrill recrimination at the reception desk and in the dining room, there explaining to an incredulous waiter that ladies do not eat the dark meat of the chicken and she must have only breast. In the morning she called me to her room; a towel was draped over the bidet – 'Look,' she commanded, and I did. In it lay the emptyings of her bowels. It was perhaps her revenge for my (everything not to her liking about the tour had been my fault) having made her spend the night in yet another room with a distant lavatory. Quite what she expected of me I did not know and did not ask. I simply said 'Perhaps you should call the maid,' and walked away. At Cherbourg I saw the women to their cabins on the France and said my farewells – coldly to the Daughters of the Revolution, almost affectionately to Peg and Mary, and then, for the crossing to Southampton, climbed to the windy upper deck where they were unlikely to find me. For some years my attitude to all things American, particularly American politics, was coloured by my having been a slave to Mrs Renata Buchanan Cameron Duncan; I am still reminded of her every time I see posy flowers suitable for her window-box front, and every time I eat the leg of a chicken.

*   *   *

For my last year, the year of the seventeenth century, my dedicated subject, I saw even less of Jill, closeted with Christopher Hohler, a gothic expert of demonic quality with the appearance of a middle-ranking army officer disappointed not to be commanding a brigade. She was now married and set up in a gloomy rambling flat in Emperor's Gate and the morning coffees in the Gondola, reduced to an occasional pleasure in our second year, now fell away altogether. David Allibone was fiercely ambitious as a solicitor and Jill, on the rare occasions when time could be spared from her gothic duties, talked of her new interest in solicitory matters – she eventually became a formidable magistrate; she was, moreover, swiftly pregnant, heavily so when she sat Finals. For me, work was more intense than ever. My tutorial group was often of only two with a second year student, Francine Sorabji, having to endure my growing sense of urgency and pressure. Other students in her year had long since rechristened her Francina and pronounced it as though it were Italian; this she suffered well enough, but I have often wondered since whether I made life unbearable for her with my constantly driving on impatiently. Two or three years my senior and taking a second degree, she had every right to be impatient with me – moreover, she came from a distinguished academic family and Sorabji is a name that may still echo in the corridors of Oxford and Anglo-Indian history. Warm, enthusiastic, enquiring and old enough to be motherly (she was to marry another Courtauld student, David Irwin, a then emerging expert on Neo-Classicism – 'God knows what they see in each other' said Anthony Blunt), she seemed driven by an infuriating innocence, and wide-eyed with wonder, was too easily wounded by my occasional superiorities. We were the beneficiaries of an extraordinary level of teaching, not only from Wilde, Blunt and Kitson, but from such visiting luminaries as Gerson and Van Gelder, who inspired me to spend my last vacation before Finals in Holland, looking at Rembrandt, Hals, Vermeer and all the little masters – another exercise to prove of great significance when I joined Christie's a year later.

Within the Courtauld there was one more tutor, often forgotten, to whom I owe a great debt, Philip Troutman, who was responsible for opening my eyes not only to Zurburan, Ribera and Velazquez, but to a host of minor masters, and to seventeenth-century Spanish sculpture and architecture, tying it all to the economics and politics of the day. Desperately shy and inhibited by the worst of stammers, he sometimes fell into long silences and had to be coaxed out of them by our proposing hypotheses to which he could respond with nods or shakes of the head that then released his tongue. Sometimes we were compelled to suggest alternatives and ask for his silent assent to one of them; but if jollying him along like a car with a hiccupping carburettor was the price of access to his remarkable sensibility, shrewd eye and intuitive intellectual response, it was worth the stumbling effort that we had to make.

Small though the undergraduate student body was, by tradition it had to have a President from the third year and a Secretary from the second. My election was a case of giving it to the least unwilling of half a dozen survivors none of whom wanted to take on anything that might interfere with Finals nine months away. The secretary was Juliet Bareau, now international scourge of Goya scholarship, scrupulously competent and wonderfully unselfish in carrying out the chores. Neither post was burdensome – our only prescribed duties were, once a year, to wash Roger Fry's pots and organise a garden party for the staff, but there was some pressure from younger students to give them something of what they understood real university life to be, even for affiliation with the Students' Union at University College far away in Bloomsbury. I thought the Courtauld Institute no place for beer and skittles. Instead, in Laytons, a newly-opened (and short-lived) restaurant in nearby Manchester Square, its wine-shipping owner happy to quote a bargain price, a handful of us gave dinner to an eminent guest content to return with us to Home House and the other students and informally debate some peripheral aspect of art history, or simply talk about his life. The willingness of John Sparrow, Warden of All Souls, connoisseur, collector and lively homosexual, I can understand, but why Gombrich should have given us such a bonus beyond his lectures and tutorials, giving us glimpses of the Warburg Institute before it came to London, I cannot imagine, unless it was his passion to open intellectual doors. Among younger worthies we entertained Richard Wollheim and A.J. Ayer, philosophers less than a generation older than ourselves, peripherally interested in the visual arts; they seemed, then, whimsical, even foolish, and, in our field, not as intellectually disciplined as we. Decades later, Wollheim became something of a celebrated writer on art, but his ingenious thinking was never better than the cockerel brilliance of the clever Oxford undergraduate who cannot see. And then there was Vice-Admiral John Hughes-Hallett, Conservative MP and uncle of Richard Hughes-Hallett, one of the few survivors of my year; he proved contemptuous of the arts – 'no use to any man'; his own enthusiasm was for cycling at furious speed on a lightweight machine with dropped handlebars and sixteen gears. Richard also proposed that we should invite his cousin several times removed, Lord Raglan, author of *Jocasta's Crime,* to discuss incest and other anthropological aberrations, but to this the student body strenuously demurred. A decade or so later, when Richard told me that he was infatuated with a spotty adolescent boy, I wondered whether raising the question of incest had been a covert way of introducing the subject of his particular subsection of homosexuality – it was not a subject ever discussed in the Common Room and I doubt if anyone thought Richard queer, but by the time he and I were talking freely about it he was too far down the road of mania and melancholy ever to recover.

One significant external event disturbed our ivory tower. At more or less the same time as my personal crisis over the invasion of Suez threatened to disrupt my life, the Hungarian Revolution of October 1956 occurred. Of this, one consequence was that two of the some 190,000 refugees who fled into exile, knocked on the door of Home House. They were an unlikely pair – George, short, sturdy, hirsute and uncouth, and Ursula, pale, ethereal and blonde. The bare bones of their story was that, as students of art history, they knew of the Courtauld Institute and of Johannes Wilde as a fellow Hungarian, that in making for Vienna on foot, George had come upon an exhausted Ursula and had half dragged, half carried her to safety over the Austrian border, and that with some help from the British embassy, they had made their way to London. The Courtauld, though sympathetic, at first rebuffed them – it was late in the first term of an academic year, there was no measure of their academic level, they had no money on which to live and no means of paying fees, and their command of English was too wretched for them to understand any lecture or tutorial. Had their visit not coincided with the afternoon break at which the whole Institute halted for Mrs Winkle's tea and cake, in which a despairing Charles Clare dumped them in the Students' Common Room, we might never have known of them. Their sudden presence inflamed my anger over Suez and how this folly had utterly wrong-footed the British in the arguments we should have had with Russia over the invasion of Hungary, and I felt that the Courtauld, the beneficiary of so much middle European scholarship, should be the last place to turn away these refugees.

By the grace of God Jill was there and we went at once to Charles with the proposal that were the students to stump up enough money to feed, clothe and house the pair, the Institute might cover their fees. The decision lay with the Director, was his answer. I do not know how it was squared with the authorities of London University, but squared it was, and Jill, Joan Seddon – a brilliant student of conservation in the Technology Department – and I each contributed £75 to a fund administered by Charles. As most other students were as poor as mice we kept this largely to ourselves and refrained from rattling the begging-bowl in the Common Room.

Ursula did not long need our financial, or any other, assistance. George was inconspicuous – apart from flooding a bathroom and bringing down a ceiling in the house where Joan lodged in Pembridge Square – and must have left the Institute early, for his name does not appear in any list of graduates at the Institute. Ursula did not graduate until 1961, four and half years on, by then married to Kenelm Digby-Jones, briefly a fellow student who, of ancient lineage (with an ancestor at the Court of Charles I painted by Van Dyck) and considerable wealth, was for her a giant step on the ladder of English society that she had, from the very beginning, been determined to climb. The girls at the Courtauld were awed by what they saw as her strange beauty – for Francina Sorabji particularly, it was as though a Botticelli Venus had walked in – but the boys were less convinced that her lofty and wide brow, long and straight blonde hair, wide-set pale blue eyes and extraordinary pallor amounted to beauty and thought the combination weird. Coldly arrogant and boastful, she soon lost our sympathy, and if we remember her for anything other than her looks, it is for her repeated claim that this famous painting and that celebrated master-piece had once hung in her mother's bedroom in the huge castle on the vast estate that she, an only child, should soon inherit from her brutal drunken father – there was not a girl in the Institute who did not at some point mimic Ursula's throaty utterance – 'Zat voss in my muzzer's bedroom . . .'

Kenelm Digby-Jones was, as Robin Chanter before him, an adult student of twenty-seven putting in 'a spell' at the Courtauld, but in the hope that it would lend some gloss to his ambition to be an art dealer, not for the sake of scholarship. How old was Ursula? As old as Dracula, perhaps, and old enough to make a bee-line for a possible husband. To all other male students she responded with contempt, dismissing us both as poor and as wilting homosexuals – an accusation that she could neatly spit. After her death in 1981, her then brother-in-law, the painter Timothy Behrens, pieced together from her journals and other papers, a biography[12] the first years of

12   Timothy Behrens: *The Monument*, Jonathan Cape 1988 .

which, if not entirely fictional, are so embroidered and embellished, as well as simply wrong, as to be laughably preposterous. That Ursula became a student at the Courtauld through a chance encounter with Blunt in 'the History of Art Department at Oxford' (and where was that in 1956, I wonder), that he immediately 'put her through a searching test' and found her 'grasp of both artistic and historical concepts exceptionally mature,' was enchanted and whisked her away to Home House, there to become 'very fond of her . . . his favourite pupil,' with the expectation of an academic career for her, is the stuff of a romantic novel. The only fact of any interest among the fantasies of Ursula's life was the bloody manner of her death, messily self-inflicted in Khartoum in 1981, after a prolonged and painful infatuation for a Sudanese policeman for whom she was nothing more than a trophy blonde. As one of her contemporaries at the Courtauld put it when I told her the news – 'I can't feel sorry for her – she had such a marvellous time while it lasted.'

She haunts the Institute still. At a gathering of 'Early Courtauld Graduates' – crocks and crones still capable of reaching it in April 2009 – her name was on the lips even of many who had not been her contemporaries. Deborah Swallow, the Director, asked me if I had known her and what sort of girl she was. Half succubus, half siren, the creation of Edgar Allan Poe.

*   *   *

It may have been the arrival of George and Ursula, and the financial troubles of another student, an older post-graduate who had come late to the history of art and was very promising (indeed, eventually a professor), who could not, without help, have completed his studies, that enriched my simple pupil-professor relationship with Anthony far beyond the enthralling tutorials from which I learned an academic discipline of wide enquiry that suited me so well. The affairs of the Student Common Room had occasionally to be discussed with him, and I also had to confess the difficulty into which I had precipitated myself over the Suez Affair and the possibility of a Court Martial – just in case Military Policemen came knocking on the door.

One morning he came to my desk in the library. 'Oh good – you're wearing a jacket.' Why his surprise? I always did, and a tie. It demonstrated how little he saw if seeing was not essential, how distracted and unaware he generally was. 'I'm off to the Palace in ten minutes and thought you'd like to come.' And to Buck House we went to re-hang a painting just returned from restoration. What then happened was so akin to the action of Alan Bennett's play of 1986, *A Question of Attribution*, that I wondered if some palace worthy told him the tale thirty years after the event, suitably embroidered. The Queen did indeed come in and find us; I was up a ladder straightening the picture and Anthony was yards away directing me. She and he began a conversation and I stayed where I was, above them but with my back to them, my nose only inches from the canvas, wondering what the Devil I should do. I stood stock still for what seemed many minutes, though it was probably only seconds before Anthony told me to come down, but with my feet on the carpet and having turned to face the Queen, I still did not know what to do. Bow? – but to what degree between a nod and a Japanese kow-tow? Clasp my hands behind my back? Reach out to shake hers? Join in their conversation or be mute? Later in the day I had no recollection of what, in my confusion, I had done.

*   *   *

In the Easter break I went to Amsterdam with the one friend I had retained from school, Malcolm Tomkins. Never in any sense sexual partners, the subject never raised in conversation, our friendship was based on a common intellectual frivolity with matters that most boys then treated with reverence – the Bible and English literature among them. Far better at it than I, at sixteen he began to send pieces to *Punch*; the difference between us was that I would rather have been as good as Keats, attempted to be so with pastiches and failed, while Malcolm was content with polished witty mockery. The pity of it is that he came from a background that neither believed in what he did so well, nor would support him in his doing it, and taking the advice of the school's careers adviser, he sat the Civil Service examination for a job that drained the mischievous spirit from him. He married early and spent his honeymoon in my mother's house in Castle Hedingham; he died early too, oblivion the consequence for a modest genius who should have been remembered for his wit.

Not much interested in paintings, he was patient enough with me in the Rijksmuseum – even a literary man can stomach Rembrandt and Vermeer – but found other things to do when I took trains to Utrecht, Haarlem and other centres of Dutch art. For me this was the consolidation of insight and understanding that can only be stirred by photographs and reproductions. It was all very well for Johannes Wilde to suggest that I might, after graduation, work on Jan Steen, as he did after I had written a more than usually hard-won essay on the man, but not until I went to Holland and saw more of his paintings than I could in England, did I fully recognise their beauty, complexity and scale. It was all very well for Johannes to expound on Rembrandt and for me to know and love the paintings in the National Gallery, Dulwich and Kenwood, as well as to have spent so many hours with others in the great winter exhibition of 1952–53 in the Royal Academy, but to stand in front of *The Night Watch* was to see and understand a development in the history of art as explosive, disruptive, essential and revelatory as Leonardo's *Last Supper* or Signorelli's frescoes of *The Last Judgement* in Orvieto.

In the last weeks before Finals we were left to revise in anxious peace – no tutorials to attend, no essays to write. We sat our examinations scattered among a thousand strangers being examined in other disciplines, in a vast room in the old Imperial Institute, separated only by a corridor from the Warburg Institute where the accumulated wisdom of its staff would have answered all our questions of whatever period. Knowing that, after several retreats in the past year or so, my vocation as a priest had been recognised and that I should soon be a student of theology, I was in an utterly fatalistic mood. I said a short prayer – 'Dear Lord – let me get the degree that I deserve' – and did what I could with the first examination paper.

I wonder now what my examiners made of my handwriting; my essays I always typed because my broad-nibbed and heavy-pressed longhand was often impossible even for me to decipher, but without a typewriter and with haste and desperation playing their part, every page they had to read must have been a cat's cradle of unruly scribble. It has not much changed and recipients of my letters occasionally return them with the note 'Translation please.'

At the midday break we found Michael Kitson on the steps outside, there like an anxious parent waiting to sweep us off to lunch in a nearby restaurant – a gesture of extraordinary kindness that steadied us for the afternoon session and prepared us for the morrow in that he had shrewdly shown us where we could eat for a modest sum on any other full day of examinations. The last exam was in the morning and, farewells to the others done, I took myself to the cinema to clear my mind of all anxieties – two films in quick succession in neighbouring houses. *Boy on a Dolphin*, with Sophia Loren and Alan Ladd, was a pretty piece of highly coloured romantic nonsense that did nothing for my sudden sense of emptiness; nor did the unrelieved pessimism, the certainty of perdition, of Henri-Georges Clouzot's dark thriller *The Wages of Fear*, though it seemed enough of a masterpiece to be worth sitting through a second showing as, long ago, one could. Or was it that, as long as I stayed in a darkened cinema, I was not compelled to confront what had to be done next?

CHAPTER 10

A Second Intermezzo: 1957–1958

For three years I had been studying to become an art historian of sorts – much longer if my first two aborted years at the Courtauld and the two more of serious intention during National Service are taken into account – and these had been years of increasingly monkish devotion to this academic discipline. It was still June and there were only two certainties in my life, the Viva that was very soon to come and the theology to which I was to be devoted in October, an even more monkish discipline. I suffered what can best be described as withdrawal symptoms; the last weeks of term, revising for Finals, and Finals themselves, had masked the absence of the drug – but now I needed a lecture on Michelangelo, a tutorial on Rubens, an essay to write on Bernini, I needed to sit at the feet of Wilde and Blunt and to go on learning. I began to realise that with art history I had become addicted to a powerful drug with which Latin, Greek, Aramaic and theology could not compete; I wanted to consolidate what I already knew, not venture into disciplines in which I should be a neophyte.

This misgiving I could not confess even to my parish priest. Nor could I confess a second misgiving, released by the first. This, of course, was sex. With a seamless and immediate transition from art history to theology I might have kept the lid on this bubbling cauldron, but with three months between, sex seemed to rip into my mind and, let loose – for the time being – from obligations to my future priesthood, I experienced what I can only describe as intellectual rape by the idea of sex. Thought, desire, need – all were inescapable and ever-present in my mind, but I had become, in spite of adolescent experience, shy, secretive and inhibited – the vow of chastity that I had made to vanquish the demon had done a terrible damage that I could not easily undo. Because of it, over the next twelve months or so, a handful of small incidents that would have been trivial in the life of any normal man, assumed absurd importance in my sexual reconciliation with myself.

My way of dealing with withdrawal from student life could be described as funk, or, as I thought it, as weakening the addiction by diluting the drug. I asked the Professor of Technology at the Courtauld, Stephen Rees-Jones, to take me on as an unpaid dogsbody-cum-student for three months. The technology of paintings, their conservation and restoration, had been a basic weekly course in our first year. I had had it twice, but in my first incarnation the course had been under Helmuth Ruhemann in the room set up for him as a studio on the main floor of the National Gallery (then still recovering from the damage caused by the war, with more paintings on storage racks than hanging); Stephen's teaching was close to home in the Institute's Department of Technology established in every nook and cranny of the mews cottage that formed the north wall of the garden. They were very different teachers.

That there was a Department of Technology is one of the unsung master-strokes of those who founded and funded the Institute. The English tradition of restoration was wholly amateur and unscientific, the rare best of it done by failed painters with some capacity for subduing their own instincts in favour of those of the artists whose work they were employed to restore. Damaged edges were trimmed from canvases, with even whole sections cut off and discarded (Glasgow's Giorgione, *The Adulteress*) is an example, though this may have happened before the canvas came to Britain – a former owner, Christina of Sweden, was notorious for trimming pictures to fit spaces on her palace walls); what was left of the originals was then ironed with an unreliably hot iron onto a supporting canvas, the adherant the sort of animal-based glue used by makers of furniture, and lesser wear and tear to the flattened paint impressed with canvas grain, liberally overpainted. The cracked and parting panels of paintings on timber were often skimmed until wafer-thin and then they too were glued to canvas. These processes, in many cases, did irreversible damage. Much continental conservation was not much better; a number of paintings in the National Gallery that passed through the hands of esteemed Italian and German dealers in the nineteenth century have, through restoration, the aesthetic qualities of that period (at the risk of reopening old wounds I point to some lesser pictures in the Mond Bequest) – but it was, nevertheless, in Germany that science began to influence the business.

When Ruhemann, in the forefront of the debate and internationally known for his work in the Kaiser-Friedrich Museum in Berlin, fled Nazi Germany in 1933, within a year he found willing employment in both the Courtauld (with which he stayed until Home House closed in 1940) and the National Gallery. He believed that cleaning should be thorough and thrust small swabs of solvent into our hands, bidding us to swab and swab until we were through the accumulated dirt and varnish and the bright nakedness of the paint layer was revealed. If our swabs were eventually tinged with colour – as they were from Botticelli's *Adoration of the Kings* (the tondo version NG. 1033) – he was not in the least perturbed, for his view was that what came off could as easily be put on again. This he proved with Vermeer's *Lady seated at a Virginals*, to whose unconvincing forearms he added substantial touches of improving and more brightly coloured paint (removed in 1965).

Here was a man who talked to us of painters who subtly adjusted tone and colour with glazes so fine as to be fugitive at the first touch of solvent, of glazes that might post-date the first fine varnish, of scumbles of translucent delicacy, and yet it seemed not to trouble him that these he had, if not removed, disturbed and disrupted in his determination to reach unarguably original pigment – but then he also told us that if we scrubbed the most obstinately tenebrous Rembrandt long enough, colours as vivid as those of purblind

Monet would emerge. Ruhemann's work on a handful of National Gallery paintings during and after the war, when revealed to the general public in an exhibition in 1947, raised a controversy that has never since quite died away; his contract was nevertheless renewed by the Trustees in 1948, 1951 and 1953.

Stephen Rees-Jones, though only half a generation younger than Ruhemann (born in 1909, against the other's 1891), was so infinitely discreet in his treatment of paintings that I felt compelled to ignore (I could not forget) all that I had been taught in the National Gallery. He had been with the Institute since 1935, an unobtrusive, indeed almost invisible, presence until, appointed head of the department in 1951, he succeeded Ruhemann. He had come to the Institute as a scientist with an MSc in the application of X-rays and other forensic techniques, and his approach to conservation was that of the tender nurse rather than the bruising charwoman. His views on restoration were evidence of rare insight and sensibility, for he recognised that his science could never be enough in itself and must be the tool of feeling and perception. He put me in the care of Joan Seddon, one of his established students, a fine-boned, fragile-seeming beauty with a fine enquiring mind, two years my senior and long since an expert in relining canvases, stabilising panels, tinkering disconnected fragments of paint into position, making moulds of canvas grain, analysing paint and developing techniques for seeing the invisible. She went on to do great things, none greater than her restoration of Mantegna's *Triumphs of Caesar* in the Royal Collection; these nine canvases almost three metres square were so overpainted and dirty that they were all but impossible to read when, in 1962, she and the far more boastful John Brealey began their campaign of discovery – in both the current and obsolete senses of that word. It lasted twelve years and, as is the way of these things, to the woman fell the drudgery, the credit to the man.

Those who put their difficult pictures in Joan's hands will not be surprised to learn that the Mantegnas took so long. Strict scruple dictated that she should solve problems rather than, for convenience, bury them in haste, and that science and aesthetics should have primacy over the commercial concerns of any art dealer wise enough to trust her; private owners were often dismayed to find that her enquiring interest in an obstinately warping panel and its separating gesso ground outweighed any obligation they might suppose she had to finish and return their paintings – her record for treatment was fourteen years. Sensitive restorer, probing and pragmatic scientist, she was for a while president of the British branch of the International Institute of Conservation. As she was also, to her bones, a painter, her landscapes unconsciously akin to the private works of Degas, her nudes influenced by Coldstream, though she was not his pupil, to her restoration she brought a painter's sensibility – not her own, but in some inspired sense, that of the painter on whose work she was engaged. She could be a Quattrocento Florentine, she could be Rembrandt, and she was herself as often as she could be – but not often enough, for the wounded patients in her studio were always on her mind.

There were other siren calls – her related instincts as a collector and a gardener. As a student living in one room she nurtured Alpines, tiny glaucous little things on every ledge. As a young professional in a flat above the Moti Mahal restaurant in South Kensington, the fumes of curry blended with those of acetone and white spirit in her studio, but the Alpines flourished in her bathroom. With marriage to Gerald Griffith they moved to new quarters on Kew Green, and they were with her still at Wellbrook Manor in the last decades of her life. There gardening took over and her ambitions grew to rival Repton in the distances and Jekyll round the house, and the bantam hens that enlivened her tiny patch in Kew metamorphosed into sheep of rare breeds that played a Thomas Sidney Cooper role in the long view from her windows.

She had collecting in her blood. Her uncle, Dyson Perrins, was a celebrated collector of illuminated medieval manuscripts, but Joan was passionate about too many things ever to be so constrained.

She was a voracious magpie, accumulating with Gerald more drawings and paintings than they could ever hang. Their shared interests were Modern British – Gilman, Ginner, Clausen, Maitland, Lucien Pissarro – but Joan was far the broader in her taste and could be as thrilled with unattributable portraits and drawings by esoteric old masters if she discerned in them some peculiarly convincing quality.

She was a rescuer, a nurturer, a healer in her way; these abstractions embrace all her interests – in works of art damaged and discarded, in plants and trees (from nurseries she often bought the saddest specimens), in the cats she rescued, and in Titan, the gelding whom she rode, fearlessly, without a saddle. The long muscles of her thighs were iron hard and she was as proud of them as of her work on the Mantegnas.

'Can you afford to buy a damaged canvas?' Joan asked, 'if you can, then nothing is at risk and you can be let loose on it.' And so I did, for five shillings in Portobello Road – a sunset coastal scene with an elegantly wrecked ship and rescued figures in the foreground, in the manner of Vernet, with a big H-shaped rent in the centre, fragments of paint still clinging to the loose breakaway threads. It was a tough old thing and it survived my clumsy attempts to reline it, mend its wounds, clean and restore it, and a year or two later I sold it at Christie's for 300 guineas, gleeful in a profit that seemed a measure of my competence, but the real benefit of this crash course in conservation was not this profit, nor the skills that I could later (even more profitably) put to use, but the change from acquaintance with Joan as fellow student into an intense friendship that lasted exactly half a century, until her death in July 2007. I cared for her Alpines whenever obligation compelled her to leave them. I took her to dinner the night before her wedding and comforted her for the miseries and anxieties brought about by Gerald's sudden confession that he suffered from epilepsy. To comfort her mother, in hospital stilled and silenced by a stroke, I smuggled in my whippet, Hecate – and in her eyes never saw better evidence of the healing effect of animals. I helped, after their deaths, to empty her parents' house in Cheltenham of their extraordinary accumulations – her father had been an eminent aviator before and during the Great War. I was with her when, at dinner with Joe McCrindle, many of whose collection of paintings she had cleaned, a young American curator scoffed at her claim to have ridden bare-back – up came her skirt and there indeed were the long hard muscles of her thighs. With no other woman friend was my life so closely interwoven, not even Jill, whose ventures into multiple child-bearing, the mysteries of magistracy, lake-digging, viticulture and other virtuous pursuits suitable for the wife of an increasingly eminent solicitor, drove us apart for twenty years or so, though we lived within short walking distance of each other.

*   *   *

Working with Joan, an experience that chanced to be one of the most useful in preparation for what was to become my career, was a diversion from the preparatory studies in which I should have been engaged. When, immediately after my Viva, Anthony Blunt took me on one side and said that I must, not should, embark on a PhD and not (though he did not put it so crudely) waste my time with theology, I blurted out some of my misgivings about my intention to become a priest – and the first of many lunches in his attic kitchen was the consequence. Only a really wretched cook could over-grill lamb chops and under-boil potatoes. Only Anthony could blindly tolerate the subdued squalor achieved by the ancient Irishwoman who cleaned his flat, short, squat and moustached, her ten-to-two feet dragging in short shushes along the linoleum in sheepskin slippers, her voice a throaty growl in the accents of west Kerry, a trail of dropped cigarette ash from room to room proof of her hoovering presence there. Above the kitchen table hung a large coloured reproduction of Poussin's *Kingdom of Flora*, a painting that he had not seen since before World War II and that he thought he might never see again.

He asked for ideas. I said that I had not expected to continue with art history and had made no financial provision for it – in brief, I had not applied for a grant in the next financial year. He ignored this and returned to ideas. I said that I thought the activity and influence of Rubens in France still had to be explored – but that this would require money and long absences from England; an English subject might make life easier and I fancied resurrecting Alma-Tadema. At that, horrified, he said that no one at the Institute could supervise me (though I am certain that Michael Kitson could have done so) and that I would have to do it under Tom Boase, his predecessor and the only man he could think of with the requisite knowledge of late Victorian art. I drove to Oxford to see Boase and was the victim of a crushing interview; he assured me that nothing of any interest could be said of Alma-Tad, that nothing remained to be discovered and that I would waste my time – and then put forward the suggestion that Andrew Geddes (1783–1844) was a marvellous portrait painter well worth investigation, and that if I agreed to him as the subject of my PhD, he, Boase, would be happy to supervise me. At this point Boase had not quite finished the typescript of his English *Art 1800–1870*,[13] of which the preface is dated January 1958; in this, Alma-Tad appears in one sentence, Geddes in two.

If of Geddes I knew anything, it was his small sensitive portrait of David Wilkie painted in 1816 – and that only because Michael Kitson had shown us it in a tutorial on Wilkie – and his vague position as almost an amateur in English circles dominated by Lawrence and Scottish dominated by Raeburn, a portrait painter with ambitions to paint histories. In the various libraries of the Courtauld I could find nothing to confirm Boase's opinion that he was a worthy subject for a PhD and angrily refused his proposal, my anger pretty fierce because I remained convinced that Alma-Tad was a worthwhile subject. Geddes remained uninvestigated

13   Oxford University Press, 1959.

until 2001 and even then the diligent catalogue of an exhibition at the National Gallery of Scotland seemed the stuff only of an MA thesis.[14] That Boase was in error with Alma-Tad has since been made clear by several serious books (to one of which my contribution was not acknowledged), a major exhibition[15] and, particularly, by the serious interest in him developed by the London art market;[16] had he allowed me to write my thesis, I would have been the first in this field.

At much the same time I was offered a job by Peter Brieger, Professor of Art History at the University of Toronto, who had two years earlier completed his *English Art 1216–1307*, Volume IV of *The Oxford History of English Art*, edited by the ubiquitous Tom Boase, and was in England seeing it though the final stages of production. He sought me out because he needed someone to teach, particularly, the seventeenth century, but able to fill gaps in other fields. An immediate leg-up into academe, with a salary significantly higher than I could expect in England, was an almost overwhelmingly attractive proposition, and it forced me to confront the issue of my training to become a priest – with the curious consequence that I decided to delay the latter and refuse the former. I liked Brieger and felt very comfortable with him for, like Johannes Wilde, he was not only grounded in the severe academic disciplines of German art history, but had far wider interests than might be expected from a man whose English reputation was restricted to medieval English art and architecture; by chance he also knew and liked Joan Seddon's uncle Dyson Perrins, as much for himself as for his distinguished ancient manuscripts. But Canada seemed too remote – I knew no one there, no one even on the continent other than Peg Heller and the Magna Carta Dames, and it would

14   See Helen Smailes, *Andrew Geddes, a Man of Pure Taste*, 2001.
15   *The Van Gogh Museum*, Amsterdam and the Walker Art Gallery, Liverpool, 1997.
16   See the sale of the Allen Funt Collection of thirty-five important works by Alma-Tadema, Sotheby's Belgravia, 6 November 1973.

have meant deserting my dog, Penny, who had just re-entered my life. With the exception of the first, all my previous lives had been in ready-made societies – school, the army and the Courtauld – and among the values of these experiences lay the adjustments that had to be made if I was to be part of them. All had in their very different ways immediately offered the comforts of companionship (even if only in adversity); of Toronto, however, of which I knew nothing, I feared the probability of loneliness.

I also felt compelled to examine what I had thought my spiritual vocation. Examined and interviewed in retreats over a period of years, I had the comfort that others too had perceived a vocation, but my own certainty was weakening. To reinforce it I had taken to attending Mass in the middle of the week as well as Sunday, as though a double dose of piety might compensate for, or reverse, a decline in conviction. I wanted to believe the miracles and myths, particularly of the Transubstantiation of the Host, for I found them beautiful and I was so often emotionally touched by the evidently unquestioning beliefs of others (and am so still) that I doubted my own doubts. I had long taken refuge in observance, in ritual and custom, in the music of the church, its bells and whistles so to speak, but now, in stripping the great celebrations of Christianity of their pagan clutter and examining them as verifiable events, reducing them to the unembellished simplicity of a verdict that declared them true or not true, I discovered a scepticism that no will to believe could reverse. I felt impertinent, even blasphemous, and the improbability of what I had once fervently believed became impossibility – and that done, what was left? I felt that I should close my mind to such thoughts, pull down the shutters on this creeping agnosticism, and return to the comfort of unquestioning belief that I had enjoyed throughout my childhood and adolescence, but I could not make that leap, and until I could, I knew that I must not take the next step towards priesthood. Besides, what should I do as a priest? Would I be content with the Seven Works of Mercy? Was it not every man's duty, not just that of the priest, to feed the hungry, give drink to the thirsty, clothe the naked, harbour the stranger, visit the sick, minister to prisoners and bury the dead? Were these injunctions even peculiarly Christian rather than the common decencies of every civilised society? And if I turned from the Seven Corporal to the Seven Spiritual Works of Mercy, then praying for the living and the dead, forgiving injuries, bearing wrongs with patience and comforting the sorrowful seemed universal responsibilities, and this left converting the sinner and instructing the ignorant as the only possible priestly duties for me – an ignorant sinner – for the last work of mercy, counselling the doubtful, I could not even do for myself.

As if this were not enough, I had too to contend with the increasing pressure of sex and its conflict with piety. I could no longer persuade myself that masturbation was no more than an assisted bodily function, a purging as natural and necessary as the emptying of bowel and bladder – 'Think no more of it,' my parish priest once said, 'just as you think nothing of going to the lavatory' – for unlike these, it engaged my imagination in fantasies that could not be dismissed and which, in their focus on other men were in violent conflict with the state of grace that I profoundly believed essential to achieve before attending Mass. These fantasies made nonsense of ideals of chastity and purity. No amount of prayer banished them or reduced the frequency of their storming through my mind, and even the boys and young men who carried cross and thurible in procession were the subjects of speculation, encouraged by memories of the mutual masturbation I had so frequently enjoyed with other pubescent altar boys while our priest was preaching from the pulpit.

∗   ∗   ∗

Within a month of Peter Brieger's offer, running out of money, I was to reconsider Canada. In the 1950s there was a scheme for sending fit young men to remote camps there as lumberjacks for stints of a year, the pay ridiculously high to compensate for isolation and primitive conditions; with free accommodation and food part of the deal, I could return to London with enough in my pocket to live on comfortably for at least two years if I spent nothing in Canada on booze and wild women, so to speak. Surely a lumber camp could be nothing like as harsh as the conditions to which National Service had accustomed my generation? And then it occurred to me that this too was perhaps another indication of funk – that fleeing as a newcomer into yet another closed society was a way of avoiding responsibility for myself. Joining a lumber camp might seem brave and purposeful, but might it not unwittingly be just one more monkish thing to do after school, army and university, and an even more foolish choice than a seminary for a young man muddleheaded about sex.

Anthony introduced a hiatus to the confusion by offering me work at Windsor Castle, cataloguing the architectural drawings of Carlo Fontana and his workshop, kept in the Royal Library there. There was to be no payment, but the experience would be useful and prestigious and I would have the opportunity to browse at will through the rest of that mighty collection. There was some urgency. The catalogue had first been commissioned from Arnold Noach, Professor of Art History at Leeds, as one of a series of volumes in which all the important drawings at Windsor were to be published; many of these were begun, at Anthony's invitation, during the war, providing a serious purpose for many eminent scholars whose galleries and museums were shut and who had scant opportunity to teach, and at least two had been completed by the end of it, with others following in the late Forties and early Fifties. Noach, however, had been diverted by other responsibilities, had done pitifully little work and produced nothing that could be published, even with what Otto Kurz, the writer of another volume, described as Anthony's 'Socratic midwifery, patience and perseverance,' though some of his material was eventually incorporated in the final text.

The Windsor drawings by Fontana are a formidable cache of material by a long-lived (1638–1714) Roman architect and engineer (both structural and hydraulic) trained by Pietro da Cortona and Bernini, and in some sense their heir – it is a tragedy that his most ambitious and imaginative projects were not realised, particularly his new town plan for the Vatican with a piazza behind St Peter's. His plans and elevations throw light on many important seventeenth-century buildings, sacred and secular, functional and decorative, permanent and transitory, primarily in Rome but also in Urbino, Naples and Prague, ranging from St Peter's itself to a prison for young criminals. This last, a *Casa Correzionale* attached to the Ospizio di San Michele, pioneered the concept of single cells with individual sanitation. To me these drawings were a treasure trove, an extraordinary insight into the workings of a fertile and inventive mind. Excited by my first skirmish with the fifteen volumes in which they were bound, I went, as a matter of courtesy to see Noach, whose qualifications were far weightier than mine, hoping for his blessing. I was not given it. Instead, he proved spiteful and ungenerous; he broke the first appointment, leaving me an unapologetic note to read when I reached his home, and on the second, berated me as though I had engineered his usurpation and refused all help. He had not even done the basic chores of measuring and identifying the medium of each of the 783 drawings, nor had he grouped them by subject with an index to the volumes, but had been diverted by the problem of distinguishing the hand of Fontana himself from the hands of his two main assistants, Alessandro Specchi and Nicola Michetti – an almost pointless exercise when it is evident that they (and every other assistant) conformed to a common workshop style.

Windsor was, to put no fine point on it, fun. The writers of other catalogues, John Pope-Hennessy for example, wrote forewords that suggest it to have been what Hogarth might have described as 'a self-regulating community of equals' and a place of earnest industry; and so, no doubt, it was, but my two immediate bosses there, Sir Owen Morshead, Royal Librarian, and Aydua Scott-Elliot, Keeper of the Prints and Drawings, both had a mischievous sense of humour. Aydua, 48, bespectacled, iron grey hair drawn sternly back and long of skirt, was a bottomless pit of Royal Library gossip that reached far back into the nineteenth century. She should have written these tales herself, but as a royal servant could not, and I recall only a handful, of which the first was of pornographic drawings by Leonardo da Vinci.

There was once, it seems, in the 1870s, a plan to publish in facsimile every one of the Leonardo drawings in the Royal Collection of which there were hundreds, indeed far the largest single group, and many more lay undiscovered on the versos of sheets laid down. There was, however, a moral hiccup: a dozen or so were of what are now called homo-erotic subjects that could never be put into the public domain by the Royal Collection, yet, as these drawings were by a man esteemed as 'the most universal genius of all time' they could not be censored or suppressed from a publication that was to be declared complete, even to the slightest scrap. It was decided that as the drawings had not been documented in any way, not catalogued, not numbered and certainly not photographed, the offensive sheets could be discreetly lost or even stolen from the collection. A German visitor was then invited to examine the collection. Was this the Professor of anatomy whom we know was to assist in publication? Was he from the Berlin press chosen to print the facsimiles? – German printers were far ahead in this then new technology. Or was he, as Aydua averred, a Leonardo scholar as much suspected of homosexuality as celebrated for his scholarship? Whoever it was, after his visit, the then Royal Librarian found that the unpublishable drawings had conveniently disappeared.

The ambitious publication nevertheless fell by the wayside and when Edward VII succeeded Victoria in 1901 it was decided that every drawing should be stamped with his collector's mark – a discreet oval bearing a crown and the initials ER VII. This means that were the stolen drawings ever to reappear, on the market or in some other collection, they could never be identified as having once been in the Windsor group. One sheet is possible – I must argue probable because of its claim to an unbroken German provenance back to the 1860s (then a little vague) recently re-discovered in a private collection in Germany; it is of a young man posing as an angel or John the Baptist, with a substantial erection, foreskin drawn back, the large testicles hanging low in the scrotum, on blue paper identical with sheets in Windsor. It is not by Leonardo but by an immediate imitator – but that is true of many drawings in Windsor.[17]

There is no doubt that the intended publication reached an advanced stage, for Carl Ruland, a Royal Librarian who left the Royal Collection in 1870 to take up a post in Germany, wrote eight years later to enquire the fate of 'the Leonardo negatives or Stones'. An earlier letter refers to the half-dismantled state in 1869 of the volume in which the Leonardo drawings had been safe for centuries, with the remarkably prescient 'it might become dangerous too, to let so many hundreds of leaves and fragments of leaves remain quite loose; there it is lucky that nobody gets easily access to these treasures'.

Windsor became the rock on which I spent every day other than those few occupied by earning my living. I was grateful for odd jobs that offered payment, for the garage man who had passed me, as a student, the work that he could not handle as a chauffeur, had gone up-market, and my twenty year old Wolseley no longer suited him. The Arts Council asked me to translate the intro-ductions to catalogues of small exhibitions shipped in from France, of which the second – by René Huyghe, once one of the most distinguished (and, during World War II, gallant) curators of the Louvre, but by 1957 more all-purpose cod-philosopher, pseud and first holder of the Chair of the Psychology of the Visual Arts at the Collège de France – proved untranslatable. When I confessed that his elusive language and slippery ideas had utterly defeated my

---

17   This was published usefully and at length by Carlo Pedretti, *The Angel in the Flesh*, in Achademia Leonardo Vinci. Vol. IV, 1991, pl. 11.

attempts to render them into English, back came the response that
this was always so and I must write something of my own, but with
a high-flown touch that would pass as his. Years later, Jonathan
Griffin, poet, diplomat and Director of BBC intelligence during
World War II and a much superior linguist, confessed that he too
had much the same experience when commissioned to translate
Huyghe's psycho-spiritual ramblings. Lectures on Poussin at Senate
House interrupted Fontana for days – the lectures themselves were
short enough, but their preparation, as I was treading on Anthony's
territory and I assumed that the job came to me at his prompting,
had to be scrupulous; they were later repeated at Birmingham
University, doubling the fee. And then came God's gift, as it
were – work on the Royal Academy's Winter Exhibition, *The Age
of Louis XIV*, scheduled to open on 4 January 1958 but far behind
in the preparation of the catalogue – and yet again I had good
reason to be grateful to the army for teaching me to type.

Work on Fontana skidded to a halt. Aydua Scott-Elliot and I
drew dust sheets over the volumes on my desk, ordered my papers
and locked the door of my room so that nothing could be disturbed,
and for the next two months or so I abandoned the riches of Italian
baroque architecture for the pell-mell thrills of working on an
exhibition that brought me into the closest possible proximity
with, not only Poussin, Claude and Georges de la Tour, but with
dozens of seventeenth-century French painters of whose names I
knew, but whose work I had had no opportunity to see.

I was, however, deprived of a rich source of sexual speculation,
for at Windsor my concentration had often been disrupted by the
sight and sound of the young soldiers guarding the castle. At the
Courtauld there had been almost no such reminders of my
suppressed sexuality – almost, for Alton Jenkins had come near to
breaking my resolve in my first year, and in my last, Juliet Bareau,
on a day spent exploring Stourhead and its Claudian garden, had
brought with her an aristocratic Italian boy in his late teens of a
dark animal beauty that I found impossible to ignore – Saint

The climbing tree in the
garden of Cefn Bryntalch

The author's mother
aged thirty-four, after
banishment from Cefn
Bryntalch

My mother aged twenty-three, when working with Kate Coughtrie

My mother at the time of her involvement with Heseltine / Warlock, far the most beautiful of his mistresses, most of them dumpy little frumps

Philip Heseltine as Peter Warlock, 1926

Robert Sewell, the author's stepfather, sketched by Eric Kennington

The author, winter 1934

Haberdashers' 3rd XV,
autumn 1947: the author
fifth from left, back row

Haberdashers' 7-a-side
winning-team, 1948: the
author far right, back row.
Note the extravagant
contrapposto

The author at the Courtauld Institute, summer 1957, at the conclusion of his Finals

Johannes Wilde, Deputy
Director of the Courtauld
Institute and its greatest
professor

Joan Seddon in the summer
of 1957, when the author
was her 'pupil' in the
Technology Department of
the Courtauld Institute

The author at Christie's, May 1960, Peter Chance in the rostrum, Patrick Lindsay on the left

Above left: Anthony Blunt in 1962, with Velazquez's *Baltasar Carlos as Hunter* (Prado)

Above right: Claudio Corvaya, a lesser Lampedusa leopard in 1963

Left: David Carritt, William Mostyn-Owen and the author at Christie's

From the *Weekend Telegraph Magazine*, June 1966.
Experts were asked how they would spend £200 buying art.

David Carritt seated
with the Rubens
Modello, which was
sold at Christie's in
November 1966
and is now in the
Cincinati Museum

A story of deceit or

How a trusted
official at the
British Museum
bought a small
masterpiece for
£50 after first
rejecting it as an
appalling daub

**Brian
Sewell**

POLIDORO Caldara da Caravaggio is not exactly a household name, even among art historians, let alone among sane men on the Clapham omnibus. One must search lexicons, encyclopedias and indices under all three possibilities, Polidoro and Caldara and Caravaggio (taking care not to confuse him with his namesake, *Michelangelo Merisi da Caravaggio*, painter of dim shadows and bright boys), to find him worth only a column inch or two, or even altogether absent.

Short-lived and with most of his major works destroyed, total oblivion might by now have been inevitable had he not been so much admired by such great later masters as Annibale Carracci, Domenichino, Poussin, Rubens and Pietro da Cortona, his influence on them evident, and had he not left a large number of drawings made, not as preparatory stages in the development of paintings, but as entirely independent works in their own right. These indicate an unfettered and idiosyncratic mind, an imagination dark and never genial, in which borrowings from Raphael, Michelangelo and the dramatic traditions of Netherlandish and German art are blended and moved on into Polidoro's own independent territory. His work was, indeed, a vital link between the high Renaissance and the high Baroque, between the emotional extremes of mannerism and the restraints of 17th century classicism.

His working life was short. Born in c.1500, in the Lombard town of Caravaggio, near Bergamo, Polidoro was in Rome by 1518, working as a builder's labourer in the Vatican — as Giorgio Vasari, his almost contemporary biographer has it, carrying hods of lime for masons. When Raphael and his assistants began the decoration of the new loggias of the papal palace, young Polidoro attached himself to the most able of them, by imitation taught himself to draw and "learned the art of painting so divinely well that he was judged ... the most noble and most beautiful intellect among their number".

Vasari, born in 1511, did not know Polidoro, who died in 1543, but he knew at least three of his contemporaries under Raphael —

Giulio Romano, Perino del Vaga and Giovanni da Udine — all of whom must have given him information for his biography and we cannot therefore dismiss the tale he tells as romantic nonsense.

We must accept that a powerful genius lay dormant until he was 18, that he became a painter, "not by long training, but by Nature", and that in his peers' esteem he earned "an honoured place among the most exalted spirits". If further proof of the near immediacy of Vasari's biography is needed, we should turn to its end for the lively account of Polidoro's murder; he was stabbed and strangled in his sleep by an apprentice and accomplices who stole his money. The apprentice suffered the torment of having his flesh torn by red hot pincers and was dispatched by being quartered.

I raise the ghost of Polidoro, cut off in his prime, because the National Gallery has just acquired its first painting by him. The gallery has nothing by the associates with whom he worked under Raphael's direction and this picture throws light neither on them nor on his own early work, work that is all but lost. It is a later invention, sombre and tenebrous, painted in Sicily, whither he had fled when German troops sacked Rome in 1527, settling in Messina after a year in Naples.

His Roman work was almost entirely secular or mythological in subject, his Sicilian work religious — but religious with the fervour and intensity of a man who had undergone some sort of

revelatory experience under the influence of Spanish mysticism (Naples and Sicily were then a Spanish dominion). Of this, Vasari says nothing, but Polidoro's life and work in the Sicilian years, 1528-1543, were beyond his reach and he writes in detail of only one painting for all those years, but in such a way that we must assume he did not see it — "executed with much excellence and very pleasing colour" is not exactly an informed reaction to a major altarpiece that, though it was carried in triumph through the streets of Messina and was revered as thaumaturgical, is a dog's dinner of a picture and a Dutch dog's dinner at that, for it is more like a bad Scorel than The Road to Calvary by Raphael, of which the National Gallery's new picture is a recollection.

IT is a preparatory sketch, some 30in by 24in, for an altarpiece measuring 10ft by 8ft. Though the third of three attempts to resolve a complex composition and haunted by Raphael's treatment of the subject in an altarpiece of much the same size then hanging in a church in Palermo, 150 miles away, Polidoro's sketches and the altarpiece are very different in figure scale, lighting, perspective and, above all, finish.

The altarpiece could almost be mistaken for a bad painting by a bad Dutch painter, laboured, orderly and meticulous, but the sketch reveals the turbulence of Polidoro's mind, the haste with which he worked, the many alterations and re-thinkings, the inclu-

sion of almost too many subsidiary ideas, the brushwork clumsy in its hurry to reflect a change of mind, the paint clouded in its colour by a dirty palette, space and perspective (both linear and aerial) discarded. The tumbling composition is anchored to the red cloak of Christ, triangular beneath the weight of the massive cross, the only patch of colour in the procession of figures. On the right, an armoured soldier restrains a woman, one of the lesser Marys, perhaps, and on the left, the movement is halted by St Veronica holding the cloth with which she will wipe the blood and sweat from Christ's face. Behind Christ is a bald man blowing a trumpet into the Saviour's ear (a cruel motif completely changed in the final altar), and before him is a ragged executioner hauling on a rope about his neck (a motif later much reduced in violence). The traditional group of the Virgin fainting at the sight of Christ's torment is relegated to an afterthought in the middle distance.

The contrast with the half-remembered altarpiece by Raphael is telling: his is a work of didactic clarity, the violent figures statuesque and documentary; these characteristics are revived in Polidoro's altarpiece, but in his sketch we have a crowded confusion of responses, impetuous and urgent, headlong and capricious, a 16th century anticipation of Picasso's Guernica, which went through nine stages of similar development.

For this remarkable rarity, the National Gallery has just paid the

he road to Calvary

estate of Philip Pouncey, a former deputy keeper of prints and drawings at the British Museum and former assistant keeper at the National Gallery, the not inconsiderable sum of £500,000, of which £80,000 was contributed by the National Art Collections Fund.

For Pouncey's ownership I can offer some explanation. In 1959 the painting was sent for sale to Christie's, where I was the new boy at the bottom of the heap in the picture department. One of the rules of the house was that everything of Italian Renaissance interest must be shown to Pouncey, then, at 49, widely respected as an expert in the field and, by the firm, as its infallible consultant.

I catalogued the picture as an indubitable Polidoro, drawing attention to the altarpiece (then and now in Capodimonte, Naples) for which it is a sketch, though very different in mood and clarity. Pouncey disagreed, his immediate and very strong reaction that it was an appalling daub, grotesquely unrefined and with nothing of Polidoro's qualities to commend it; I was compelled to concede and, simply labelled Polidoro without reference to the altarpiece, the picture was lot 71 in the sale of 19 June 1959.

The bidding stopped at 48 guineas (£50.40) and the picture was bought by FT Dent, a dealer notorious for buying trifles unconsidered and disdained by other dealers. The sum was so much lower than I had expected — a tenth of my annual income — that I immediately asked him if he would sell it on to me. "Can't do that, my boy. I bought it on commission." Ten years later, by which time I had left Christie's and Pouncey had become a leading director of Sotheby's, he asked me to dinner and, as

Philip Pouncey: admired

'Pouncey stole from me some small credit as an art historian and, by deceit, stole from the painting's owner'

a pre-prandial treat, showed me his treasures. Of these the most astonishing, the most shocking, indeed, was the Polidoro over one of his many mantelpieces. I did not stay for dinner. I did not speak to him again. It was he for whom Dent had acted on commission.

After all these years I do not care that £50 has become £500,000, but I care with anger not one whit reduced that Pouncey stole from me some small credit as an art historian, stole credit from Christie's, a firm that trusted and, by deceit, stole from the owner, Christie's client. Of course someone from the National Gallery should have seen it on the walls at Christie's — Pouncey, indeed, its assistant keeper for 11 years, must at once have known what a valuable addition to the national collection it would be and should have gone, hotfoot, to Trafalgar Square and bruited it about, but he did not and kept it for himself.

It is now the centrepiece of another of the small exhibitions in Room 1 that the National Gallery sometimes does so well. Its companions are the two oil sketches that preceded it, a group of drawings that demonstrate his skill and imagination as a draughtsman, and a portrait belonging to the National Gallery since 1876, which has been catalogued as Italian School, Florentine School, Rosso Fiorentino and now as Polidoro and a self-portrait to boot. Alas, neither Raphael's Road to Calvary nor Polidoro's altarpiece lend logic to these smaller things.

● *National Gallery, Trafalgar Square, WC2. Daily 10am-6pm. Admission free. Until 7 December.*

Polidoro's Way to Calvary altarpiece in Naples: "a dog's dinner of a picture and a Dutch dog's dinner at that"

The author's art column in the *Evening Standard*, Friday, 12 September 2003

Arts & Reviews

POP **39** CRITICS **41** IN LONDON TONIGHT **42** BANK HOLIDAY TELEVISION **46-49** GAMES & QUIZZES **50** READERS' VIEWS **51** MOTORING **55**

Spot the difference: The Sleep of Arthur at Avalon, more than six metres wide and nearly three high, on which Burne-Jones was still working on the day before his death in 1898. It has not been exhibited in the UK since 1933

Can you see anything wrong with this picture?

Our critic reveals the secret history of Burne-Jones's huge last canvas, on temporary display at Tate Britain

PAINTINGS OF THE WEEK
BRIAN SEWELL

WHAT is in effect the National Gallery of Puerto Rico is closed for renovation. This startling information must be of little interest in London, but for the advantage taken of it by Tate Britain which, for some months, is to offer refuge to two of the gallery's most important British pictures, Lord Leighton's **Flaming June** and **The Sleep of Arthur at Avalon** by Edward Burne-Jones. Flaming June has some claim to be the picture that reversed public distaste for High Victorian art in the mid and later Sixties, and Arthur at Avalon has been described by the director of Tate Britain as its painter's "last and greatest work". Last it unarguably was, for Burne-Jones worked on it the day before his death on 17 June 1898, and the canvas still shows signs of unfinish, though his assistant, the loyal and attentive Thomas Rooke (never credited) must have tinkered it into saleable condition. The old boy's greatest work, it certainly was not: less of a composition than a stiff, stilted and staged tableau, it has nothing of the invention, energy and bravura of The Perseus Cycle with which it overlapped; nevertheless, it is worth more than a passing glance.

More than six metres wide and nearly three high, initiated in 1881 as a commission for the library of Haworth Castle, the home of the painter's friend, George Howard, this vast canvas was to be for Burne-Jones what Parsifal — which took twice as long to complete and was also a last work — was to Wagner: a too personal, spiritual and emotional exploration of himself and a romantic mythological past with which he identified himself to the extent of self-portraiture as Arthur. It is sentimental, anguished and morbid; it reeks with the odour of sanctity; and just as a recent critic described Parsifal as "a bit of a pill ... staggeringly pretentious", so the sane man might say of this picture. It underwent more significant re-composing than even Picasso's Guernica, and became the ageing painter's obsession so much so that Howard released him from the commission so that Burne-Jones could paint it for himself without constraint.

"I'm not in good spirits about Avalon," said the old boy to Rooke in 1897, exactly a year before his death, "it might turn out no more than a piece of decoration with no meaning in it at all, and what's the good of that? I shall have to ... go at it with more fury." But then, within weeks of the first brushstroke in 1881, he had asked himself: "Why did I begin

Flowery detail: by collaborative hands

it?" Two months before his fatal heart attack he complained that he must finish it without any expectation of a sale; and one month later he demanded larger brushes, "thumpers and whackers", so that he could paint faster. And still he did not finish it.

In the winter after his death, Arthur at Avalon was first seen by the public in a memorial exhibition. It was subsequently sold to Charles Goldman, a collector who in 1929 offered to sell it to the Tate; when the offer was refused, he lent it instead. There it was last exhibited in 1933, the centenary of the painter's birth. It remained on loan until April 1962, but at some point, probably in August 1939 when the Tate evacuated its paintings in preparation for the Second World War, it was removed from its stretcher, rolled, and put into a stout box some half-metre square and three metres long. In that it stayed undisturbed until 1963, when Goldman's heirs consigned it to Christie's, where I was then working, for inclusion in a sale by auction on Friday 26 April.

The box containing the canvas was not delivered until the previous Friday, 19 April. From a small black and white photograph I had to concoct a cata-

CONTINUED ON: PAGE 38 ▶

'Lying on cushions on the canvas Joan began work at the top, and I, on my knees, began at the bottom on the easier business of repairing the flowers'

CONTINUED FROM: PAGE 37 ►

logue entry for a picture that no one had seen for 30 years and played no part in the then available literature; it was thus with particular interest that I watched its arrival in the lofty anteroom, the unscrewing of the lid and the myriad spiders that scuttled from the box. The vast canvas was then gently unrolled on the floor, obstinate in its curvature, and the mass of webs and other arachnid detritus removed from it. How could we display so large a canvas without a stretcher? As a tapestry on a tapestry bar, I decided, but not one in the house was six metres long and another had to be procured. With the canvas tacked to it by the raw edge that had formerly folded over the original stretcher, it was hauled up the wall with a dozen of us supporting it to ensure that the inevitable inverted curvature was kept as open as possible. It worked. The canvas, however, was much weightier than any tapestry.

CHRISTIE'S chairman, Peter Chance, then came in to see the masterpiece. Demure, a pink and silver man, short, stout and erect, he strode to its very centre and within a pace of it; at that moment the weight of the canvas began to tear it from the bar. Poor Peter reached to press it against the wall, but the avalanche could not be stopped, the canvas ripped away, curled forward and enclosed him in its vastness. Instead of standing still, he panicked, fought his way out of the belly of this whale, dishevelled, and the canvas lay face down, a crumpled heap.

The one thing that must never be done with a painted canvas is to roll it face in, but that is more or less what happened in its fall. When we reversed it and flattened it we saw the consequences — flaked paint lay thickly on the floor, the whole width of the canvas where flowers fill the foreground, the area of heaviest initial impact, was extensively damaged, and the widespread random

damages elsewhere reflected the chairman's efforts to escape.

I called Joan Seddon, old friend and distinguished conservator of paintings then working on the restoration of Mantegna's Triumphs at Hampton Court. We had until 9am on Monday morning, when the picture was officially on view — some 30 working hours, we thought — in which to camouflage the damages. Lying on cushions on the canvas Joan began work at the top, and I, on my knees, began at the bottom on the easier business of repairing the crudely painted flowers. Thirty hours were not enough and we worked through the night on Sunday.

During the week of the sale not a word was said by anyone. Did no one notice how much of Arthur at Avalon had been damaged? And if they did, did they assume that the damages were old? When the painting was bought by

the museum in Puerto Rico, it was relined, cleaned and stretched before being framed and installed in a specially constructed room — did none of the experts responsible for these procedures not notice how much of the paint was new? Or were all the damages stripped and re-restored without a word to the new owner? Looking at the painting now, 45 years later almost to the day, under the uneven glister of a patchy varnish, I could identify very few of

Joan's interventions, but was appalled by the crude quality of the irises, bluebells and forget-me-nots — is any one of them by Burne-Jones himself, or are they all by one of the 20 assistants he once had, by Thomas Rooke, by me and subsequent restorers?

■ *Tate Britain (020 7887 8008; www.tate.org.uk) is open daily, 10am-5.50pm, and until 10pm on the first Friday of each month. Admission free.*

The author's art column in the *Evening Standard*, Friday, 2 May 2008 showing *The Sleep of Arthur at Avalon*, by Burne-Jones, 18 sq metres of unstretched canvas catastrophically damaged a week before its sale at Christie's in April 1963, restored over that weekend by Joan Seddon

The staff of Christie's. Patrick Lindsay, Peter Chance and Guy Hannen in the front and the author in the third row.

Patrick Lindsay auctioning *Turner's Dutch Boats in a Gale* (*The Bridgewater Sea Piece*)

A Second Intermezzo: 1957–1958

Augustine would have understood, even forgiven, the desire that he roused in me; but at Windsor the reminders were continuous. Then, on a late autumn evening, I received a jolt that was impossible to ignore. It was my custom to drive to the castle, but once, having travelled by train instead, waiting near Paddington station for a bus to take me home, a teddy-boy asked me for a light. It was my own fault for I had been covertly – though not quite covertly enough – looking at him and his codpiece prominence in skin-tight jeans. 'I don't smoke,' I said, and 'I don't want to,' he replied, 'I was just asking.' And then he made so blunt an invitation that my panicked brain stumbled into instinctive refusal. Later that night I called myself a fool.

Could I ever have settled down with a girl? It would have been easier, indeed easy, because expected and conventional, and occasionally I thought of it and the possibility of children. A life with Juliet Bareau would have been fun with a fiercely intellectual side to it, and she was slim and boyish enough in looks almost to bridge the sexual attraction gap, but I doubt if I could ever have matched her imperturbable aplomb, her command of every situation, her stern social grace, and I was pretty sure that she was shrewd and worldly enough to know the truth. Baby Helen was none of these things; the younger of two Helens among the students, she was warm, funny and affectionate, and on a trip to Waddesdon, picnicking, she had taught me how to roll downhill. She, I thought, was too sweet and unsophisticated to suspect my homosexuality and would far too easily be hurt if she discovered it. But I should have been wholly honest with myself, recognised the flaw and known that it could not be remedied with heterosexual deceit. I should have made a pass at Juliet's Italian boy, at a soldier in Windsor, or at the Paddington teddy-boy – but I was not yet ready for such undisguised adventures.

*   *   *

The Age of Louis XIV proved to be a full-time occupation in the sense that, until it opened to the public, I spent not a waking hour of any day on anything other than it and the quotidian essentials. I have always believed that this inspired and instructive exhibition was conceived by Michel Laclotte, a young art historian with the General Inspectorate of French Provincial Museums, rather than by any of the many older worthies thanked in the preface to the catalogue and happy to take the credit for it. Initially my task was only to translate Michel's catalogue, but I could not resist adding odd observations of my own and notes that I thought might help the general reader rather than the art historian. It was my first experience of compiling bibliographies and the histories of ownership and previous exhibitions – a chore that to this day I regard as essential if paintings and their variants and copies are not to be confused. That this detailed clerical information is now almost always omitted from exhibition catalogues results in the concealment of contrary opinion and disputed authenticity. Of this the Royal Academy's Winter Exhibition of 2004, *The Genius of Rome*, was a deplorable example: of the fifteen canvases included as by Caravaggio, seven were not, yet the visitor was left wholly unaware of the controversies surrounding them, and the reader of the catalogue had to dig very deep into dissembling texts to discover here and there the rare admission that even the curator had her doubts.

Working on the exhibition was not only an invaluable experience in terms of the practicalities of such an enterprise, its logistics too, but I learned that whenever credit is to be claimed, art historians and panjandrums descend like vultures. The British had no case for doing so – the idea was French, the scholarship was French and every loan was French – but still they came to poke their noses in, the august editors of *The Burlington Magazine* and *Apollo*, Benedict Nicolson and Denys Sutton, the considerable collector and maverick art historian Denis Mahon and every scholar with an axe to grind on any aspect of seventeenth-century painting, and particularly on Poussin. The French were worse by far. Michel's immediate boss (whom he adored), Jean Vergnet-Ruiz, had every right to be there as Inspector General of the *Musées de Province*, for they had both worked, separately, for years on forgotten paintings in neglected provincial museums until Michel was appointed to the same office. Sharing their research put them in a very powerful position when the time came to lend an over-arching national order to the country's heritage of paintings of all kinds, and that the museums and galleries of Dijon and Tours, Strasbourg and Toulouse, Lyons, Lille, Colmar and the rest of far provincial France are so fine and logical is entirely to their credit. The only other presence who deserved to be let loose in the Royal Academy was Jacques Dupont, the Inspector General of *Monuments Historiques* responsible for many loans – wonderfully suave, benign and mischievous; the sort of Frenchman who cherished English tailoring and bought his umbrellas at Briggs, he was amusingly contemptuous of his supposed peers, some of whom were merely on the bandwaggon, but others were vain, aggressive and consumed with amour-propre. René Varin, Cultural Counsellor to the French ambassador, to whom all French art historians felt compelled, it seemed, to be obsequious, was particularly odious.

Michel and I lived and breathed this exhibition. I was constantly astonished by his range and depth from the factual nuts and bolts of art history, to extraordinary leaps of perception, whether we were dealing with the matter in hand or drifting towards Trecento Italian primitives and nineteenth-century German Romantics. This was the practical application of art history, the purpose of the discipline, and of it I had had not the slightest glimpse as a student at the Courtauld. Barely two years my senior, the courage of his connoisseurship and his willingness to challenge received know-ledge were wonderful examples for me to follow. Born in 1929, a schoolboy in Paris throughout the German occupation of 1940–44, the Louvre emptied of its masterpieces by René Huyghe (then its chief curator of paintings), Michel had cut his teeth on the provincial museums that were later to be put in his charge, precociously planning their reorganisation. When, after the war, both Huyghe and the paintings returned to the Louvre, he thought Huyghe's quixotic new hang appalling and was bold and shrewd enough to say so and be noticed. Vergnet-Ruiz was utterly seduced by his scholarship, connoisseurship and enthusiasm, as well as by his practical abilities. Later, as successor to Huyghe, Michel virtually reinvented the Louvre, and later still it was he who lobbied for the conversion of the Gare d'Orsay into the astonishing gallery of nineteenth-century art that it has been since 1986. I too was utterly seduced. From Michel, more than from anyone at the Courtauld, I learned to respect the seemingly dry disciplines of cataloguing – so much more systematic and diligent than interpretation (which can be, and so often is, whimsical); without the basic structure of his draft catalogue entries I doubt, for example, that I would ever have become curious about Cardinal Fesch, the half-brother of Napoleon's mother who, profiting from his nephew's exalted position, amassed a collection of some 16,000 paintings, many of them masterpieces, including Leonardo's *St Jerome*, now in the Vatican. Alas, he also accumulated so much rubbish that at his death in 1839, grouped by size rather than by school or attribution, his pictures were hastily dispersed by auction at the rate of a hundred lots a day.

In embellishing Michel's catalogue there was no point in disrupting the literary flow by claiming credit, but in one observation on Georges de la Tour and Caravaggio suggesting the possibility of the Frenchman's presence in Rome, Michel, thinking it important, inserted the words 'Brian Sewell points out that . . . ' Anthony, reading the proofs, then told me that he had made precisely the same comment in the course of a lecture at the Courtauld in 1953, but when I reminded him that I was then in the army and could have no knowledge of that lecture, and, moreover, that in his book of the same year[18] he appeared to argue

18 Anthony Blunt: *Art and Architecture in France*, 1953, p. 177.

against La Tour's having journeyed to Rome, he generously agreed with Michel that I should be given the credit. Now, of course, I believe that he should have had it, and that had he published it, the idea of the Italian journey would be much more widely accepted. A further indication of this journey may lie in the similarities between La Tour's *Woman with a Flea* (Nancy) and Caravaggio's very late *Martyrdom of St Ursula* (Naples, Banca Intesa), which the Frenchman could only have seen in Genoa, where it was sent before the paint was dry, and where it remained until 1832. This is not the place for me to launch into the connections between the courts of Genoa and Lorraine that offer further support for this hypothesis.

As there were press and private views for which we had to prepare immediately before the exhibition opened to the public on 4 January 1958, work was unrelenting – we were, amongst other things, preparing a second edition of the catalogue while the first was being printed, and it is to this second edition that interested scholars should refer. Even so, we snatched a day to dash to Manchester to see the exhibition of paintings by old masters with which the city was celebrating the centenary of what has some claim to have been the greatest exhibition of art and artefacts ever mounted – altogether more than sixteen thousand of them – in the Manchester Art Treasures Exhibition of 1857, as it is now fondly known (its proper title is *The Art Treasures of the United Kingdom*). Otherwise ours was a daily slog, often of twelve hours, breaking only for quick snacks in the Kardomah Café on the other side of Piccadilly – neither of us had money for fine food and could not afford even the Academy's own restaurant, then run by Fortnum's. Kardomah was a chain of slightly superior caste, a significant step up from a Lyons tea-shop and further still above the tea-shops run by the ABC (the Aerated Bread Company) where tinned sardines on toast cost a penny less if the toast was not buttered; Kardomah coffee was almost good enough to be drunk by a Frenchman without complaint. The only other breaks were the interminable formal lunches that the Academy offered to French visitors who used them to berate Michel and me for our perceived incompetence and to further their own aggrandisement – with very few exceptions French art historians old enough to be my father were pernickety, bickering and boastful.

Exhibits reached the Academy over a period of days, the thrill of uncrating them almost erotic in the slow foreplay of unscrewing cases and stripping away the packing to see, at random, parts before we saw the whole. Last minute adjustments to some catalogue entries had to be made, canvases had to be inspected and given minor cosmetic attentions by a conservator from the Louvre (from whom I learned a good deal in terms of desperate camouflage), and when everything had been delivered it was clear that we must make changes to the proposed hanging plan. On this the Academicians had their own ideas: they propped the pictures against the walls of every gallery in hangs based on size, shape, proportion, colour, tone and balance. As interior decoration it looked fine, but in common art historical sense it was disastrous and made nonsense of Anthony's lucid introduction to the show in the first pages of the catalogue, a room by room account of the contents of each, with the reasons for their being there. This they had done on the day we spent in Manchester. We knew that this was their intention, but to our misgivings their response was of the 'there, there, now don't you worry your pretty little heads' kind, and the loftier 'we always do it' kind, and when pushed, the 'bugger off, it's our exhibition, not yours' kind. Anxious to see what they had done, though it was late in the evening when we returned to Euston, we took a cab straight to the Academy. Michel was appalled. Off came our jackets and the heaving to and fro began. I warned him that the Academicians might be furious, but he responded that they were more his paintings than theirs and he would hang them as he wanted. It was early morning before he went to his hotel and I to my bed, and early when we returned to the Academy next day, for he wished to be there before any Academician could undo our work and be ready, physically, to defend it.

It was also on this long day that I made a fool of myself with Michel. Small and spare and, with hair *en brosse*, very French, he was not immediately attractive in any physical sense, but working so closely and so intensively with him, talking in an increasingly fluent mixture of French and English (for each of us was at first equally hesitant and un-idiomatic in the other's language) that enabled us to reach far beyond art and the exhibition that had brought us together, I had grown fond. Washing our hands after re-arranging the paintings, exhausted, I sighed. I did not know that I had, but he asked directly 'Why a sigh so deep?' and, remembering the boy at the Paddington bus stop, I seized the opportunity, though only in words. Michel laughed, dismissed my longing as 'a craving for *chaleur* – you are like a puppy-dog – you will grow out of it.' Except for the *chaleur* he sounded like all the adults who had lectured and hectored my generation on matters masturbatory and sexual – grow out of it, indeed. Though we remained friends for some years before the intensity of our careers pulled us apart, there was never a further mention of the subject.

Once the exhibition had opened I returned to Windsor, intending to slave there until all the preliminary chores were done. There was more gossip from Aydua, including a tale about the princely Hanovers that, twenty-five years later, had a sequel. As relief from Fontana – who could be tedious – I worked my way through drawings by painters, accumulating knowledge from the writers of catalogues already published, training my eye and memorising images, ways of thinking and manners of drawing in the hope that I might recognise them as readily as handwriting, sometimes daring to argue against an attribution or even authenticity. When I expressed misgivings about Leonardo's *Masquerader on Horseback*, that was to question Kenneth Clark's authority and I was severely slapped down; yet after half a century I still hold these doubts, now even more strongly. Alone with the Windsor drawings, studying at as slow and as pensive a pace as I chose, holding them to the light to see the nature of the paper and acquaint myself with watermarks, turning them to see what might be on their versos, deciphering inscriptions and committing to memory a basic lexicon of collectors' marks, was a more intense experience, slower and therefore more instructive than, white-gloved and always watched, was to be had by working my way through the solander boxes of the British Museum, the Albertina or the Louvre. Valuable beyond measure, it turned interest into passion and established a firm foundation for what was to become expertise.

At precisely the point when – though the basic chores were still by no means finished – I was beginning to see how the catalogue of Fontana's drawings (to be published by Zwemmer) should, perhaps, take shape, work was again interrupted; the British Council asked me to catalogue the British loans to *Die Welt des Rokoko*, a Council of Europe exhibition opening in Munich on 15 June 1958. In this Anthony had no hand; it was, admittedly, the immediate consequence of my work on *The Age of Louis XIV*, but not at his prompting – the decision to ask me was made by John Hulton, then head of the Fine Arts Department of the Council. The British loans were, with the exception of two Venetian canvases by Canaletto, British, and they included silver and porcelain – how wonderful, I thought, be so soon rewarded for suffering the tedium of the Courtauld Institute's English year and my confrontations with Hogarth, Gainsborough and Reynolds, and never had I thought I would be grateful to have experienced my frantic preparations for, and experience of, my weeks of antique-hunting with the American grandmothers. Necessary discussions brought me into contact with all sorts of experts and museum grandees – the tyro confronted by the tyrant in the case of John Pope-Hennessy, then Keeper of Sculpture at the V&A, a monster to so many but kind enough to me, probably because I roused in him nothing of the sexual interest that governed so many of his contacts with budding scholars, young men now eminent art historians, particularly in American museums and universities, whose first step on the ladder of preferment was taken on their knees before him, facing one direction or the other.

Another grandee was Francis Watson, then Deputy Director of the Wallace Collection, who knew as much as any man about Rococo art and artefacts; a sometime Registrar at the Courtauld (1934–38), he was kindly inclined to all Courtauld students, though very few chose the eighteenth century as their special period (was Anita Brookner alone in this I wonder?), and with me he shared his knowledge with enthusiastic frivolity as well as depth – I loved him for his dottiness and for keeping (so it was said) eighty-seven cats. Charles Oman too, father of Julia, the stage-director, and father-in-law of Roy Strong, was kind, but in a lordly, lofty, distant way, as though he were a saint disturbed in contemplation; Keeper of Silver at the V&A, he prevented me from making an ass of myself in territory of which he was undoubtedly the king. Most of all, however, I enjoyed my brief contact with Roger Hinks, the now forgotten luminary of the Warburg Institute who, as blameless Assistant Keeper of Greek and Roman Antiquities at the British Museum, had been more or less driven into resignation by claims made, largely by the press, that the Elgin Marbles had been harshly overcleaned. I cannot now recall the matter on which I consulted him – he was never a *dix-huitième* specialist and Caravaggio was about as modern as he got – but he seemed to know something about everything and expressed his knowledge with wonderful clarity; an amiably ugly man, he made – though I did not recognise it at the time – what might be described as an intellectual pass.

Working on the Munich catalogue was another formidably useful experience. The formula of each entry was laid down by the editors in Munich and I had simply to follow it; my occasional attempts to add a little interest were savagely cut back and nothing distinguishes my entries – but that is, perhaps, because, as the Chairman of the Planning Committee, Eberhard Hanfstaengel, acknowledged in his Preface, I 'gave valuable assistance in correcting the English edition

. . . '. Behind this simple statement lies a tale of pure panic. When the proofs of my catalogue entries were sent me for correction, they bore not the slightest resemblance to my typescripts, but were nonsense in some German-flavoured pidgin-English of the kind used by Denis the Dachshund and Englishmen making tired anti-Nazi jokes. It transpired, after at first fruitless telephone calls to Munich and a sickening sense of disaster at having my name attached to such gibberish, that the editor, Arno Schoenberger, unable to read English, had been given rough translations by assistants who had then mislaid my typescripts and, rather than confess the loss, re-translated them. When I demanded that all evidence of my participation be removed from the catalogue, the Munich editors realised that the whole of the English version might be as flawed, agreed to reinstate my text (of which I had two carbon copies) and asked me to revise the various translations into English made by Germans from the French, Italian and German originals. What had begun at a leisurely pace giving me time to do ten times more research than necessary, ended uncomfortably at a frantic gallop, but the long-term benefit of looking at British art in the broader context of the Enlightenment, the Age of Reason, was that I experienced a quiet revelation and my scorn for English art as a student, reflecting the view of Roger Fry (a Courtauld panjandrum if ever there was such a thing) that 'ours is a minor school . . . not altogether worthy of (British) civilisation . . . ,' evaporated. Work on that exhibition sowed in me the seeds of a belief that Hogarth, Ramsay, Gains-borough, Reynolds and Wright of Derby, with young Lawrence at its end, are in their various ways the equals, even the betters, of the more esteemed European painters of the century.

I was still working on the Munich catalogue when William Martin – Bill, as he was always known – head of the picture department at Christie's, approached Anthony, whom he had known as a young lecturer at the Courtauld when he was taking a post-graduate diploma course there, to see if I would like to join the firm and work as his assistant. He had noticed the scrupulous diligence of the Royal Academy catalogue (more Michel's than mine) and thought that I could lift the quality of those produced by Christie's – the man who had since 1919 been responsible for the basic entries in the catalogues of sales was about to retire, and it was the perfect moment for the department to introduce new blood. Anthony, it seems, told him that he had never had a student interested in so wide a range of painters – thinking of Alma-Tadema, no doubt – and put us in touch. I had been slipping into Christie's since I was fifteen or so and was intrigued by the idea and the possibility of a regular income that would lend stability to my life – I had already learned that the free-lancer is flush with money one month and on his beam ends the next. 'You'll like Bill,' said Anthony, 'but you'll loathe Patrick Lindsay, the other director in the picture department.'

Bill took me to lunch at his club, the seedy and bedraggled Oxford and Cambridge. At the bar he ordered mild and bitter for both of us; not much at my ease, my heart sank at the demand, for mild and bitter was 'a man's drink' that I had suffered in the army and detested, but instead of beer we were given sherry, a blend of Bill's own devising, half cream, half amontillado. I saw the point of it neither then nor a thousand sherries later. He nodded to a painting hanging behind the bar, the subject almost impossible to discern beneath the coating of nicotine. 'What's that?' 'George Morland,' I replied, 'though in that state it's impossible to say if it's really by him – most are not.' After lunch at one of those beastly communal tables at which conversation must be had with strangers after introductions that cannot be heard, we spent an hour in his office, a rather grand room on the first floor looking onto King Street. 'What's that?' he said again, this time of a small bust length portrait propped on a chair. 'Caroselli,' I answered – which was right, but – as with the Morland – not particularly clever. 'Is it, by Jove? I knew it was a good picture.' That was typical of Bill – an unerring natural eye for quality and no scholarship to back it, 'Bloody good – we must look into it' so often his accurate but lame response. I learned not to know the answer sometimes so that he'd not look a fool in front of Patrick Lindsay (who really was a fool without an eye), but would tell him later in the privacy of his room. His course at the Courtauld had done him no good, and his only relic of the misspent year was his ability to mimic cruelly the high-flown voice and manner of his contemporary there, John Pope-Hennessy, talking about Domenichino to the barman of the local pub in an attempt to seduce a bit of rough – such a seduction might, just might, have been managed by another student talking of Michelangelo (of whom even a barman might have known), but not of Domenichino, a then deeply unfashionable painter of the seventeenth century unknown even to his fellow students, but not by the preposterous John.

Bill's practical art education had been in Christie's at the knee of his father, Sir Alec Martin, a formidable and ridiculous old fraud whose wilful ignorance over decades had done Christie's reputation great damage. This Bill knew, and now that Old Alec (as he was known) was about to retire, thought he might remedy, but Old Alec, a man of immediate attribution where paintings were concerned and intransigent refusal to consider even the possibility of an alternative, had a disciple in the form of Patrick Lindsay, second son of the Earl of Crawford and Balcarres who had for many decades been the friend and ally of Old Alec in many enterprises. Following Alec's example, Patrick believed aristocratic ownership to be proof of authenticity – a Reynolds the property of an Earl must be a Reynolds, a Gainsborough the property of a Duke a Gainsborough – and it never occurred to either of them, though Alec must have known of the substituting activities of Joseph Duveen (the most conspiring of dealers), that an ancestor impoverished by wagers and women might have bequeathed a later generation an inheritance of copies. Bill, the only one of the triumvirate with an eye yet always the last to be asked his opinion, might murmur his characteristic expression of doubt in these circumstances – 'I suppose (with emphasis on the second syllable) it's right' – but, only momentarily exasperated, they always ignored him. To witness the three of them in discussion was always a reminder of the Mad Hatter and the Mad March Hare with Bill inevitably the Dormouse.

Alec Martin had joined Christie's in 1896 as, in his own words, 'a lad about the house', when he was twelve. The eighteenth of twenty children living in a workman's cottage in Yeoman's Row (now a very smart South Kensington address), the son of a shopkeeper who sold oil for lamps, he was a very pretty boy, small (as he remained), with golden curls. As the lad at Christie's he caught the eye of both Hugh Lane, then building his formidable collection of Impressionist paintings (now in the National Galleries of Dublin and London), and Claude Phillips, art critic of the *Daily Telegraph* and first Keeper of the Wallace Collection (1897–1911), both notorious homosexuals attracted by what Francis Watson was later to describe, ingenuously, as Alec's 'natural sunniness of nature'. Bill, who never outgrew the prurience of adolescence (at Oxford he and his friends had conducted experiments – in the bath as well as bedroom – to test the flammability of farts), was fascinated by the notion that his father had been buggered by these men. It is certain only that they were profoundly influential in furthering his career and that what education he had was largely at their hands. Neither, alas, ever persuaded him to drop his cockney accent or adopt manners that were not ingratiatingly obsequious to the grandee and the bullying of the rough-tongued termagant to everyone else – even to his family. Bill was cowed by him and still called him 'Daddy', and to Claude Phillip Martin, his youngest son, Alec was so mercilessly cruel, both physically and mentally, that the boy spent most of his adult life in a nursing-home of sorts. The tipping point for his sanity occurred when he was fourteen, when, having disobeyed his father's instruction (as a punishment) not to ride his bicycle, Alec, in a terrifying tantrum, smashed it; a portrait of Claude Phillip (named after his godfather, his father's early patron), painted by Sickert at much the same time and inscribed 'To our dear Alec,' catches something of the boy's pathetic nature – it is in the Tate Gallery with equally telling contemporary Sickert portraits of his parents.

To his dying day Alec dropped his aitches. Our first words were exchanged after another lunch with Bill, this time in Overton's, St James's, where he was evidently well-known, again offering me no choice but simply ordering for both of us 'Jellied eels and the Widow'. I hated the tasteless eels and the widow turned out to be Veuve Cliquot. 'You have to meet my father – he's still in charge until the end of the season and has to decide.' Fortified by the Widow, Bill knocked on his door. Seconds passed before we were commanded to enter and even then Alec did not look up but continued to write a letter – he rarely used a secretary for anything other than a letter of acceptance or rejection, both of which began with 'We have now carefully examined your picture and . . . ' – these his secretary could write for herself, for the catalogue note of every rejected picture was scrawled with a huge N (for No), and those of accepted pictures concluded with a note of the proposed reserve. Eventually Alec paused; then Bill stepped forward and said 'Daddy, this is Brian Sewell.' Alec, still sitting, pen in hand, in preposterous wing collar and watch-chain, peered at me through his rimless spectacles and more seconds passed in silence until he broke the stillness of the tableau with 'We know you've no social connections, but if Willy wants you, 'e can 'ave you.' Nothing else was said, no wishing well, no handshake. He resumed his letter and we crept from the room.

My last sight of Alec in Christie's was late on a Friday afternoon, descending the main stair to go home just as some poor soul had reached the reception desk – always known as the Front Counter – with a painting he thought by Hogarth. Ridley Cromwell Leadbeater, the silver-haired, pink-cheeked and carnationed panjandrum of the Front Counter, scuttled to the bottom of the stairs holding the picture high for Alec to see – 'Gentleman says it's by Hogarth . . . ' Alec, with not the slightest slowing of his step, immediately replied 'T'aint 'ogarth. I'm off to Ro'ampton.' The 'gentleman', an unrecognised lord, was none too pleased and his painting proved to be a decent variant of *The Rake's Progress*.

Back in Bill's room, he sent for Patrick, who took a good ten minutes to appear. The job Bill had offered me was as his personal assistant, and though this description was to some extent to shield me from Patrick's bullying, it meant, nevertheless, that I would be much in contact with him and, in hierarchical terms, his inferior, for he was a partner in the firm and for me ever to be his equal would take at least a decade and involve an impossible level of investment. There were, Bill explained, a hundred shares in the business, all held by partners who were not necessarily directors or auctioneers, though the latter were all partners. Were a new partner to join the board, others would have to be persuaded to relinquish, for a price, a share or two, sometimes a half-share; power on the board was established by the percentage of shares held by each partner. Who owned what was never disclosed outside the partnership.

There had been, early in the year, the most formidable upheaval in the firm. The Chairman, Robert Wylie Lloyd, millionaire industrialist and collector – his Turner and other English water-colours, Swiss aquatints, Chinese lacquer and Japanese swords he bequeathed to the British Museum (the watercolours on condition that they should only be exhibited to the public for two weeks in February, when daylight in London is at its weakest) – had retired at the age of ninety and then, in April, died; and Alec, at seventy-four (but far older in his business attitudes), had been unseated as managing director and forced to agree to retire in July at the conclusion of the 1957–58 season (Christie's then adhered to the Court Seasons and closed from late July until well into October and from mid-December almost until St Valentine's Day). Lloyd and Alec had a weekly meeting every Friday afternoon in the former's limousine as it was driven to Alec's house in Roehampton and then on to Lloyd's weekend retreat. This, weirdly, continued in my day: I knew of it only because of my interest in cars and had noticed Alec being shown by the chauffeur into the rear of the very rare landaulet limousine body built by Grosvenor on a Vauxhall 25 chassis in 1937 or so, a huge car doubly obvious in the attention-seeking Art Deco combination of cream and coffee brown. A coachbuilt big Vauxhall seemed so eccentric a choice (unless the owner knew something of the marque's early history as a maker of great cars), that I remarked on it to Bill, and it was he who told me that Lloyd had left instructions for the car to be at Alec's service until the day that he retired. Did Alec, he wondered, tiny in the cavernous passenger compartment, commune with Lloyd's ghost, cursing the young Turks who had ousted him, confessing sins, perhaps?

There was one sin – of carelessness, if nothing more. Late in 1957 a tiny unframed painting on copper was taken by one of Christie's Front Counter staff to Alec's room for his opinion. He immediately recognised the composition as one popularly known as *The Small Tobias* by Adam Elsheimer, and asked for the owner, Mrs Margery Green, to be brought up. It was, she explained, a family heirloom, traceable back to Dutch ancestors who, in the seventeenth century, had settled in Norfolk as drainage engineers. Alec in turn explained that he too had a version of the painting[19] and would like to compare them; as he had also, until very recently, owned a major panel from Elsheimer's celebrated altar *The Finding and Exaltation of the True Cross* (The Frankfurt Tabernacle, Städel Museum) and this, in his opinion, was enough to elevate him to

19   Both were listed as copies by Keith Andrews, a respected authority, in his *Adam Elsheimer*, Aberdeen University Press 1977, p. 150, Cats. 20g and 20h, Alec's given the provenance as passing from Claude Phillips to Lady Martin. Andrews was unjust in describing the Green version as a copy for he had not seen it – even the best of the half dozen known versions he described as only a 'contestant' with some claim to be the prime original.

the rank of expert, to this Mrs Green agreed. She was given a receipt with the disappointing insurance value of £500 and watched Alec slip the little panel into the drawer of his desk with 'It will be quite safe there.' And so it should have been – and to be fair, Christie's porters, who never recognised the fragility of paintings, were the last people to be trusted with an unframed sheet of painted copper some 12 by 18 centimetres – but it was not. Mrs Green never again saw her Elsheimer, but still had the frame to remind her of her lost inheritance and, until her death in 1999, fought an obsessive but wholly justified campaign for its recovery. Alec could never explain its loss and was widely believed, even by Bill, to have pocketed it.

Alec was not in any serious sense a collector. The dreary brown interiors of his house were sparsely hung with prints and memorabilia rather than frame to frame with masterpieces and offered no evidence of an excited sensibility, yet, over decades, he bought paintings, certainly by the hundred and possibly in thousands. Enquirers into provenance who check Christie's records in the original books kept by the auctioneers and sales clerks will find an astonishing number of purchases by 'Whitehead' over so wide a range as to suggest a dealer rather than a collector. Whitehead, however, was Alec's *nom-de-vente* for himself, and Whitehead bought so much that he was privileged to have a room for his purchases below stairs at Christie's to which two loyal porters, Jock and Les, barred access even to Bill. The contents of this room were from time to time removed to a store thought by Bill to be somewhere in Shepherd's Bush and nothing more was seen of them. Even on Alec's death in 1971 they remained in obscurity, and Bill, who was eventually to fall on hard times, never succeeded in tracing them.

It was on this old man's implacable certitude that Patrick Lindsay modelled his behaviour – not on his treatment of his family, nor on what may have been dealing on the side not in the best interests of Christie's, nor on his foul language – the *fucking* this and *fucking* that of his abuse of junior staff and porters. He showed scant sign of being amused by Alec's juvenile humour – Titian's Latin signature was always pronounced Titty Anus and painters whose names were variants of Cock (and there were many) or could be wrestled into a resemblance of arse or arsehole, were greeted with ritual sniggering, and to the innocent question 'Where was this found?' the expected chorus of response was 'Up the back passage of (for example) the Duke of Devonshire.' But, like Alec, Patrick was resolute in his refusal to pronounce any foreign name with even the hint of a French, Italian or German accent, and though he knew from the upheaval that had unseated the old monster that Alec had been, commercially, a disastrous influence on Christie's fortunes, he chose to become, as it were, his master's continuing presence.

When Patrick, not easily biddable – least of all by someone he despised, as he did Bill – at last deigned to respond to his summons to come and meet me, it was with overwhelming presence. Bill was short and stout, I short and slim, and Patrick was magnificent, his considerable height and bulk enlarged by crutches and a leg in plaster – the consequence of a skiing accident at Klosters or Davos. That was Patrick in a nutshell – he did not just break a leg, he broke it where some Prinzessin von und zu was there to kiss it better. Again there was no welcoming hand, but for that the crutches may have been the reason. Startlingly erect of carriage, he dwarfed me, and my sense of being contemplated by a giant was enhanced by his short retroussé nose, the perfect instrument for expressing his disgust for everything beneath it. He knew what had to be known about me – school, army, Courtauld, Windsor and the Royal Academy exhibition – and within minutes had made me aware of his absolute supremacy. I already knew his father to be the eminent and, in the old art establishment, ubiquitous Lord Crawford, but now I learned that he had Eton, the Scots Guards and active service in Malaya, Oxford (Magdalen – where he failed to finish), and a brief apprenticeship to Bernard Berenson with which to trump all that I had to offer Christie's, and he had been a partner since 1955. This was the man who within four months of my joining the firm was to give me lunch at White's, making an absurd fuss over the colour of the legs of partridges – grey when they should have been pink, and it was the second day of September (the shooting season opens on the first). The purpose of his hospitality was not, however, to show off – as at first I thought (the fuss was Patrick's natural bullying behaviour) – but to attempt to poison my loyalty to (and increasing affection for) Bill Martin, whom he described as an 'ugly little toad,' How could the Honourable Patrick Lindsay put me in such an insufferable position?

* * *

There were things to do before I did my first day's work for Bill on Monday 5 May 1958. He knew of my obligation to complete the Fontana catalogue and had promised that I could work only a four-day week for him and spend one full day at Windsor – four days a week for £400 a year; if there were any unforeseen problems with the Munich catalogue (as there were), I could take leave to settle them. I argued for Mondays to be spent at Windsor, and Bill for Fridays; but Friday was traditionally Christie's day for selling pictures (Wednesday Sotheby's, Thursday Bonham's) and for everyone in the picture department it was the busiest day of the week, for there were always last minute crises over reserves and bids, or pictures damaged when taken down from the walls, stacked in the passage behind the 'Great Room,' removed from the stack to be held up by a porter at the moment of sale, re-stacked in another part of the passage, and roughly handled when a buyer known to tip wanted to collect a purchase during or immediately after the auction – and when all that was done, the remaining pictures were bundled down to the store-rooms below. In the process of being sold by Christie's a painting suffered more casual and careless handling than in all the putting-up and taking-down of a domestic life of several centuries. Moreover, as the pictures in one Friday's sale were removed, those for the following Friday were brought up and hung, some wrongly identified – some three hundred and fifty pictures moved by a handful of porters. Friday was never the day on which I could be absent, for the appalling rate of casualties – canvases scraped and punctured, panels split and the corners of carved and moulded frames shattered beyond repair – required the presence of someone who could apologise and offer remedy.

With my promised Fridays I had also offered Aydua Scott-Elliot alternate Saturdays at Windsor (the others to be spent at Hedingham mowing my mother's lawn) and we had worked out, if not a schedule for the completion of the typescript, a point at which to aim – some time in 1963, five years away. Over those years, however, my mother became increasingly frail (or so I thought and she pretended), my Windsor duties were neglected and by 1963 Fontana had all but fallen by the wayside. To my chagrin, Anthony, convinced that I could never finish the catalogue as long as I remained at Christie's, then transferred the commission to the (he thought) steadier hands of Allan Braham, an ex-Courtauld student working at the National Gallery, an altogether more lenient employer. Allan, working in collaboration with Hellmut Hager (later to become Professor of the History of Art at Pennsylvania State University), did indeed complete and publish the catalogue – but not until 1977, fourteen years later.

I had also to find somewhere to live. When my mother left London I had taken to living inconspicuously in the flat that my stepfather shared with Elizabeth, their friend, his mistress – an uncomfortable arrangement that with the promise of a monthly salary could be remedied. I answered half a dozen advertisements in the personal columns of *The Times* in which young men and women constantly sought others with whom to share flats that they could not afford, and thus it was that I spent the late spring and summer months of 1958 with Peter Hunt in Barons Court. I had his flat largely to myself, for he spent most of his nights in the bed of one or other of the two girls who shared the identical flat above – he came home, shared supper, played the same Brahms symphony every night and then disappeared upstairs – I can recall every bar of that symphony. On one of the rare occasions when he slept in his own bed, it was because the mother of one of the girls had come to stay – and she, of course, came down to sleep with Peter. Realising that their vigorous preliminaries must have wakened me, they asked me to join them, and in the spirit of enquiry, I did. If Peter realised that he, rather than Edie, was the object of my fondling, never a word was said.

The only friend from my army years with whom I had stayed in touch, came to spend a weekend. A rowing man, with what in the 1930s might have been described as conventional aquiline good looks, he had been at Brasenose, Oxford, while I was at the Courtauld, and we had seen each other often in a hearty sort of way, deceitfully on my part when it came to mutual confessions on matters sexual. Not very bright, on graduation he had secured a traineeship with Coates, a cotton manufacturer in Paisley, but it taught him nothing other than to hate Scotland and the cotton trade. His purpose in making the journey to London was to pour out his miseries, and I was easily led into pouring out my own, for my suppressed homosexuality had become so onerous that I too needed confession and the counsel of a friend. The visit had its consequences. Max encountered Edie, slept with her, made her pregnant, married her and found a job in London – and then I destroyed our friendship in a rage at what I took to be his betrayal of all that it should have meant. His marriage to Edie swiftly ran into difficulties that he thought insuperable. Early in January 1959 they came to dinner and quarrelled furiously, Max striving to draw me into the row as an ally; then he decided to attempt divorce, and as she was blameless he blithely told her that he was queer and wanted to spend his life with me. Only after they had separated did he tell me. I felt used, sullied by the lie. I was fond enough of Edie to value her trust in me and not to want her hurt, and on my own account was wounded to find that my confession, uniquely entrusted to a man I thought my friend and for whom I had never harboured even a speculative thought, had been exploited to his advantage. Worthy of Iago, it was my first experience of perfidy.

CHAPTER 11

Christie's in 1958

Of Christie's public face I knew the entrance hall, the slow-rising and welcoming stairs, the ante-rooms in which pictures were displayed and the great octagonal room in which they were sold. Of its private face I knew only the rooms occupied by Alec and Bill Martin, particularly Bill's with red damask on the walls and more of it for curtains, a huge desk and a handsome eighteenth-century bookcase with almost empty shelves; I cannot recall the carpet on which he and Alec's secretary, Beatrice West, were rumoured to have been discovered by his father in sexual embrace. Of Christie's workface I knew nothing when I entered the building on Monday 5 May 1958. Bill was not in his room, but as I turned away from the door I caught a glimpse of him, with Patrick, far away in the octagon; by the time I had sidled past the bulky furniture always displayed on the narrow galleries flanking the well of the stairs, he and Patrick were walking towards me across the central ante-room. 'Oh Brian, come and look at this,' he said, returning to the octagon. I followed his glance towards a large painting hanging above the bar on the west wall – 'What is it?' 'An El Greco,' I replied, 'a later version of the Dresden picture.' In this I was in error – it is much closer to a version in Parma, but of this I did not know. 'Oh Gawd . . . ' was Bill's response.

The painting had been hanging on view only since mid-afternoon on the previous Friday (the premises were closed to the public over the weekend) and yet, within half an hour of opening on Monday there was already a buzz of anticipation. Of this the porters were first aware – as always – and seeing dealers gathering like flies, they had reported the interest to Bill. Somehow the painting had slipped unrecognised past Bill and Patrick and been catalogued under an unconvincing and unconvinced attribution to Veronese – unconviction frankly indicated by the omission of that painter's Christian name, then an ancient shorthand in English auction houses for we don't know, we don't care, the painting is a poor thing but it vaguely resembles Veronese; the inclusion of the Christian name indicated authenticity, and an initial – P for Paolo – suggested that the attribution was uncertain but the painting had some merit. It transpired that Alec knew the owner, George Smith-Bosanquet, and had, as a favour, promised to catalogue the picture himself and see that it was swiftly sold; this he had done without reference to Bill who had meanwhile replaced him as head of the picture department and thus bore the brunt of the row that followed. I am certain that had Bill seen it, though he might not have recognised it as by El Greco, he would have gone into his 'Bloody good picture . . . we must look into it' routine – which meant, with old masters, that it would not have been included in a sale until Ellis Waterhouse had seen it.

Ellis was one of a small handful of art historians, museum curators and respected dealers on whom the picture department depended for expert opinion, some of them unreliable because the interests of the businesses or institutions they served were greater than any friendship they felt for Christie's – and all that Christie's ever offered for their knowledge was a word of thanks (and hardly even that from Patrick). Ellis Kirkham Waterhouse, however, born 1905, at Marlborough a friend of Anthony Blunt, two years his junior, was a man of independent means only interested in scholarship. He had worked at the National Gallery for three years from 1929, then becoming librarian at the British School in Rome until resigning in 1937 to work on the following year's Winter Exhibition at the Royal Academy, *Seventeenth Century Art in Europe*. World War II he spent first in the Macedonian and Greek campaigns, then with Military Intelligence from Cairo to the Caspian, and in 1945, in the last stages of the war, by then with the Monuments, Fine Arts and

Archives branch of Allied Military Government, he was responsible for culturally important buildings, museums and collections in Belgium and Holland. On crossing the Dutch border he ordered the arrest of Han van Meegeren, the notorious forger of paintings attributed to Vermeer, whose role as their painter he had suspected as early as 1937 (though given no credit for it). He had been a brilliant Director of the National Galleries of Scotland for three years but could not tolerate the, to him, insufferable social conventions of Edinburgh, and had returned to academic life as Professor of Fine Arts at Birmingham University, and Director of the Barber Institute there. An undemanding post, it offered him freedom enough to become himself.

The essential Ellis was the independent seeker after truth, the man to whom every scrap of information might contribute to the solution of a mystery, not only of attribution, but of the uncertain history of a painting as either the prime original or as a later variant, and he was as indefatigable in his investigation of the backs of canvases and their stretchers as of their painted surfaces, pushing his glasses over the crown of his skull and short-sightedly peering from a distance of three or four inches. Sometimes he would only hum and ha, offering no answers – this, I suspect, he did to reward Patrick's impatience – but on his return to Birmingham he sent me postcards in minute handwriting, not only identifying the pictures that Christie's had for sale, but drawing attention to variants seen before the war in Poznan and Plovdiv (he played a vital role, after the war, in the restitution of looted works of art across the whole of Europe), often supplying details of provenance that might have taken me months to discover. The wry twist is that he had a lifelong interest in El Greco and, in 1927, at the age of twenty-two, after months spent in Spain, began (and continued) work on a monumental monograph that was never completed; and it was he who brought to the Royal Academy exhibition in 1938 El Greco's forgotten masterpiece in the collection of the King of Roumania (now in the National Gallery, Bucharest), the enormous *Adoration of the Shepherds*. Ellis, of all English art historians, was the man to whom the 'Veronese' should immediately have been shown.

Bill should have ordered the El Greco's removal from the sale, but as its owner had consigned it more to Alec's care than to Christie's, the old monster had to be informed of events and he, eyeing me with evident malevolence as a trouble-making little busybody, obstinately resisted this sensible course. Instead, a note of the revised attribution was pinned next to this very distinguished painting hanging among comparatively worthless others – the sale so unimportant that its unillustrated catalogue could not have drawn foreign buyers to London – and on the following Friday Agnews paid 35,000 guineas for it at the auction. This then very substantial sum made headlines in newspapers, but the mishandling did Christie's memorable damage. It was soon reported that Agnews had sold the painting to the New York collector Charles Wrightsman for double their outlay plus another £100,000.

Later that morning Bill took me to see Christie's new chairman, Peter Chance. His real Christian names were Ivan Oswald, and the staff always spoke of him as IOC, but among his friends he was known as Peter, and he was indeed the rock on which the new, young, thrusting and successful Christie's was to be built – though each course of bricks rose very, very, slowly. Sturdily built, about my height, he was a pink and silver man, a middle-aged *Rosen-kavalier*, pink of complexion, silver of hair and often of suit, prinked, perfumed and immaculate, his bearing military, given to doffing his overcoat as he climbed the stairs each morning and handing it to Roy Davidge, the clerk in charge of reserves, commissions and the preparation of the catalogues that auctioneers used during the sales, who invariably 'happened' to be there to hang it for him. I warmed to Peter and to the very day on which I left the firm he was affectionate; never once did he undermine or bully me and, had he had his way, I would not, years later, have resigned. To my surprise he claimed that it was he who had asked Anthony to suggest a new recruit, instructed me to introduce whatever changes I thought would help to bring the picture department into line with current practice in the exhibition and museum world and to come to him if ideas for change were frustrated. Apart from Bill, he was the first director of the firm to offer me his hand and wish me well. 'Call me Peter' were the last words of the interview.

Bill next took me to what was to be my room – a small, dark, cramped box of a room, one of a pair on the west flank of the main entrance, convenient for those working on the Front Counter who might wish to show me a picture brought in by a client. Already occupying it was John Hancock, clerk to the picture department, in his mid-thirties, quiet of manner, wry of humour, and soon to play much the same supportive role in this new life as Corporal John had in the army. He was one of the small handful of men whom I have known to be of absolute honesty, reliability and scruple. He had developed an unscholarly instinct for nineteenth-century paintings and over the next few months acted as my cautionary guide through backwaters of markets I did not know existed, 'Are you sure you want to reject this?' his gentle way of suggesting that I might have made a mistake. He was also a shrewd judge of the dealers to whom we had in some measure to kow-tow, as clear-sighted over the great Agnews and their ilk as over the crooked little runners who too duped their clients and were themselves occasionally duped.

Behind a second desk sat Vic Heather, the man whom I was to replace but who was not to retire until the end of July, three months away. As much a dropper of aitches but not quite as old, he had been Alec's man since 1919, travelling with him to take dictation when an inventory or insurance valuation of paintings in a country house was required, yet in all but forty years he had learned nothing, had developed nothing of an eye and – it seemed to me – cared nothing for quality, beauty, rarity or the history of art. Paintings were a commodity as tedious as any other and, wearing a brown cotton overall, he catalogued them for four hours every morning and then, returning to our room, banished

John and me while he gulped doorstep sandwiches and a flask of tea and, that done, lay back in his chair, hands folded over belly, and fell into a snoring sleep that could be heard as far off as the Front Counter. The only thing for which I have to thank him was his valuable description of the working practices of Hercules Brabazon Brabazon, a prolific painter in watercolour and gouache much admired by John Singer Sargent, whose assistant he had been as a boy.

Brabazon was discovered at the age of seventy. Rich enough always to winter abroad, this friend of John Ruskin, Arthur Severn and James Holland – and much travelled with them (and other watercolourists) – held his first one man exhibition in 1892, when he was indeed seventy. A sell-out, it created a seemingly insatiable demand for more, and in his considerable house, Oaklands, near Sedlescombe in Sussex, he set up a painting room with trestle-tables in a ring against the walls. On these it was the job of Vic Heather, a local boy of twelve in 1900, to place, at random, sheets of coloured paper, blue, pink, beige and white, the rectangles vertical or horizontal and of different sizes – again at random; he then mixed paint in glass pots and laid out sticks of charcoal and a range of brushes. When HBB came in he first made a few indications of a composition in charcoal on several sheets, and then with a pot of colour in hand, wandered from one to another painting the skies, the trees or some other salient feature until, concurrently, a dozen compositions, landscapes and copies of old master paintings became recognisable, while Vic washed brushes and replenished pots. After a long break for lunch and a nap, HBB reappeared to sign and inscribe the day's work – HBB Ischia, HBB Tangier, HBB Hyderabad, HBB Velazquez, HBB Rembrandt . . . Vic then stored them alphabetically by place or original artist with hundreds of others in solander boxes. This Vic had done until 1905, the year of Brabazon's last exhibition and the year before his death at eighty-four. What Vic had done between 1905 and 1919, when he joined Christie's, I was never told, but he was profoundly deaf without a hearing-aid and I wondered if this had been caused by some hellish experience in the Great War.

It was Vic who introduced me to the picture warehouse and the art of cataloguing Christie-style. 'Why 'aven't you worked on the Front Counter?' he asked, 'Everybody works on the Front Counter before they join departments, even the directors . . . ' To this there was no answer that could please him. In the cavernous storerooms stacked with paintings yet to be catalogued or already sold, I was introduced to Jock and Les, the two porters in charge of paintings up to the point of sale – Jock old, frail and given to lunchtime drinks and afternoon confusions, Les younger, but as tiny as a boy of twelve. Between them they struggled to keep the stacks in order and not to damage frames, but I hated the sessions when Bill and Patrick came to check the latest intake and Vic's (and subsequently my) cataloguing, and Patrick, always impatient and far stronger, let them lift big pictures without offering a hand. Both, in their way, were patient and loyal saints.

Vic was far from a saint, though sorely tried; if he was bullied by Patrick, he bullied Jock and Les. I thought him belligerent, resentful and uncooperative, but I dare say he felt threatened by a young whipper-snapper in a suit suggesting other ways to do his job – 'Now look 'ere sonny, I've been doing this for forty years . . . ' But he scarcely looked for signatures, could not be bothered with inscriptions on stretchers or the backs of canvases, and to anything he saw but could not understand he omitted reference. I was, for the first week, expected to stand behind his shoulder and observe, but when I saw something that he did not want to see, he hurried on and would not hold the picture back to take a longer look at it; if I protested, he switched off his hearing aid. When, at last, I was allowed to catalogue, I tried to make some very simple changes – to group previous owners, literary references and exhibitions under the simple words provenance, bibliography and exhibitions, but provenance was a term that neither Patrick nor old Alec recognised and at bibliography they laughed. The suggestion that we should use metric measurements for sales important enough to attract dealers from the continent was also ridiculed. But to some small extent I got my way within weeks, for in the first sale of old master drawings over which I had limited control – the Skippe Collection – I was allowed to use the terms collections, literature and exhibited and even, in brackets, to introduce the metric measurements that are precisely accurate with small sheets of paper.

It did not occur to me that Vic's was a forlorn situation. Within the month I had made superfluous his dogged four-hour stints of cataloguing, and yet, every day he was in the office or the warehouse expecting to work out his time and to train me in the model that he had for so long followed, only to find that I was rebellious and wanted to overturn the rules by which he worked. I should have been more sympathetic, but I could not like the man. We were there to do exactly the same job and the overlap was intolerable; it was to produce a basic catalogue entry, based on supposedly thorough examination, for every one of the five hundred or so pictures that were delivered to Christie's every week, either in bulk at the back door or singly at the Front Counter. Pictures accepted at the Front Counter were always seen by me, Vic, Alec, Bill or Patrick, even by John Hancock and our initials noted on the receipt; for these to be rejected on further examination was very rare. The much larger intake at the back door was never inspected and sorted on arrival, and as rather more than half these bulk deliveries were of pictures too wretched to be sold by Christie's and were thus automatically passed on the Bonham's – 'Nil nisi Bonham' a frequent quip of Bill's – there seemed to me little point in spending half our time producing catalogue entries that could only be for Bonham's benefit. I wanted to apply an immediate vetting system to large deliveries, but this was refused by Patrick who insisted that he must see everything; even so, unofficially and by degrees, and with the connivance of Jock and Les, this is what I did.

It was not comfortable to know that I was trammelled by blind custom. Peter Chance had made this clear, but not quite clear enough to prepare me for the weight of opposition to any change that I might, on his instruction, try to introduce in order to improve the picture department's performance. A bruising encounter with Alec revealed the entrenched autocracy of the old guard. When Jock and Les drew from the stacks a rare and beautiful still life of glasses in a basket, I knew at once that it was by Sebastien Stoskopff, a Strasbourg painter of the first half of the seventeenth century, but the accompanying correspondence between its owner, Senator Maguire of Dublin, and Alec, suggested that it was by Jan van Huysum, a baroque Dutchman of the second half – an absurd attribution, quite inexcusable. I catalogued it with the enthusiasm of discovery – an almost physical pleasure – wrote a note on its relationship with other examples in date and style (Stoskopff was all but unknown beyond the walls of Strasbourg), and bounded up to Alec's room to tell him the great news. 'Stoskopff?' he said. 'Stoskopff?. Never 'eard of 'im. That picture is by Jan van 'Uysum. That is what I've told Senator Maguire and that is what 'e wants to 'ear from us. I will write and tell 'im.' And so, tossing my notes into the waste paper bin, he did; he also wrote a new catalogue entry that was later supported by Patrick and shrugged off by Bill with a 'Never mind, my boy'. I sent a photograph to Michel Laclotte and a copy of the catalogue so that there could be no confusion over the lot number. I also wrote to Philip Hendy, Director of the National Gallery, for I felt that so rare a thing should be on its walls, but it was outside his narrow range of interests (Renoir's grotesque women, clothed and naked) and he did not have the courtesy to reply. The painting eventually returned to France and recovered its identity. Years later, long, long after old Alec should have ceased to be his model, I was to have much the same experience with Patrick who had urged a friend to send for sale a handsome full length portrait of a young man. I catalogued it as by Lemuel Francis Abbott, even though Patrick's notes indicated that he had told the owner it was by Joshua Reynolds and would get her a Reynolds price. I also put it aside for Ellis to see, for unlike most Abbotts the sitter's anatomy did not much deteriorate below the waist and I thought it a better example of his work than any in the National Portrait Gallery. Patrick, however, was obdurate, adopting the stance that as he had said it was by Reynolds, then by Reynolds it must be, developing eventually into the 'I am the director of the picture department and you will do as you are told' stance. It wasn't worth a battle and he had his way – but to every enquiry about the painting I responded with the truth and it was, after its failure to sell, returned to its owner.

Even before the end of May there was another crisis of the El Greco kind in yet another undistinguished sale. It was perfectly reasonable for lot 111 on 30 May 1958 to have been catalogued by Vic Heather merely as an Italian painting by an anonymous painter, but it was beyond reason that its quality had not been recognised and that it had not been set aside for Ellis to see. The subject, *The Flight into Egypt*, composed of the Holy Family, its donkey and a playful putto, at evening in the last horizontal shaft of dying sunlight, dramatic in its chiaroscuro contrasts, is cramped within the dimensions of the canvas, its energy made explosive by the close containment, a steep diagonal running through the group. Caravaggio haunts it, but the colour and the sentiment are too sweet for him – even so, St Joseph's forearm, central to both the movement and the canvas, should have jolted the perceptions of all who vetted Vic's catalogue description. I was astonished when I saw it and went at once to Bill. 'I thought for a moment that it might be by Ribera,' he said, 'but it so obviously isn't that I didn't press the point.' 'It's Milanese,' I opined, 'by one of those tenebrous painters of the kind that were around when Caravaggio was a boy – but this one is later and the influence is reversed. Shouldn't we withdraw it and start again?' To this the answer was that its value was too low for such a bother, and Bill wandered off.

And so did I – or rather rushed off to the Courtauld Institute

where, in old Robert Witt's collection of photographs and reproductions I found enough to confirm my hunch that the painting
might be a late work by Cerano, the most important painter in
Milan in the first quarter of the seventeenth century – the similarities
were strong, but the painterly qualities of the Christie picture
seemed so infinitely superior to everything with which I could
compare it that I was not wholly convinced. The only explanations
for the difference were either that it was by another hand, powerfully influenced by Cerano, or that it was entirely autograph and all
the larger public works in churches against which I had tested it
had been executed by inferior assistants. Was this enough for me to
be insistent with Bill on Monday morning? I decided that it was
not and spoke instead to Philip Troutman who had just finished a
tutorial, running very late, as usual – but as he too was hesitant, I
did nothing to remedy the matter. The afternoon before the sale,
Denis Mahon, the distinguished independent art historian on whose
research, connoisseurship and wisdom almost all current scholarship
in seventeenth century art is founded, and a formidable collector,
came to see me, said it was by Cerano and asked me to bid for
him – up to 150 guineas.

At the sale bidding was so brisk that I did not even raise my
finger; Agnew's paid 1,700 guineas for the painting and within a
year had sold it to the City Art Gallery in Bristol for a rumoured
£7,000. When Mahon catalogued the *Seicento* paintings shown in
the Royal Academy's Winter Exhibition of January-March 1960,
he had the gall to claim that he had recognised the authenticity of
the Cerano at the time of the sale – true enough, but so had I and
so too, no doubt, had Agnew's and the underbidder who had
made them pay so much for it (the price, a trifle now, was not
unreasonable for half a century ago); I wonder if he recalled how
paltry his bid had been.

The following sale, on Friday 6 June 1958, was another disaster,
but for very different reasons. The trustees of the Lady Lever Art
Gallery, Port Sunlight, had instructed Christie's to sell 175 paintings

and drawings deemed no longer suitable for the collection. In many cases they were right – a public gallery is no place ever to exhibit watercolours by Yeend King or Wynne Apperley, or paintings by Fred Appleyard and Edmund Monson Wimperis, but in with works by such forgotten minor painters were others of serious interest by painters whom we now hold in high regard. Half a century ago most painters on the heights of the Victorian Olympus had so tumbled in fashion as to be worth very little money, but trustees should make decisions to discard – and acquire – only on the basis of quality, never on fashion. These trustees shed twenty-nine drawings and two oil paintings by Burne-Jones for less than £600, an important sketch by Leighton for his *Cimabue* for 110 guineas, a Waterhouse *Siren* for 28 guineas, and a minor Alma-Tadema for 230 guineas – this last passing into the Allen Funt Collection that in a single-owner, single-artist sale at Sotheby's Belgravia in 1973, only fifteen years later, sold for £3,600;[20] it must now be worth some £360,000 and thus, by the trustees' false criteria, well worth having in Port Sunlight.

Even old Alec had recognised that unless at least a handful of less unfashionable pictures were included in the consignment the sale would be embarrassing for both Christie's and the trustees; thus *The Violet's Message* by Millais at the tag end of his Pre-Raphaelite years, and *A Bowl of Flowers* by Fantin-Latour, at 800 and 9,000 guineas, accounted for more than half the sale's total. The importance of this auction has been the use made of it since 1988 (when the matter was first raised by government) as proof that for museums and galleries to de-accession works of art is to court disaster, for that was also the year in which the Fantin-Latour reappeared at Christie's and new trustees of the Lady Lever thought they should re-acquire it, only to be far outbid at £950,000, pretty well exactly a hundred times the sum given for it thirty years before.

---

20   This sale, of thirty-five paintings by Alma-Tadema for a total of £235,000 marked the re-establishment of his reputation as a serious painter.

At least the discards of the Lady Lever were given the chance to survive in private hands; on the first morning of his employment at the Victoria and Albert Museum in 1960, the junior curator Lionel Lambton was bidden by the museum's Board of Survey to light a bonfire in a dustbin in an inner courtyard, and up in smoke went Richard Redgrave's design for a mural in the House of Lords, forty copies of Raphael's Roman frescoes, an unrecorded number of designs to scale for stained glass windows and other decorations by Burne-Jones (too difficult to store) and an unspecified quantity of Victorian artefacts.

$$* \quad * \quad *$$

During the summer break, when there were no sales, the pace and pressure lessened and at last Vic Heather left – but the comparative serenity was shattered by Patrick's causing for me a crisis that was both moral and professional. Amongst a range of property accumulated by the Rolls family, the Barons Llangattock of The Hendre (an old house preposterously renovated in the mid nineteenth century as a mock Tudor mansion) and 6,000 acres of Monmouthshire, scheduled for sales in the winter, was a book known as *The Llangattock Hours of the Virgin*. In this property Patrick took a proprietorial interest, not through cousinage but cars, for the third son of the second Baron was the Charles Stewart Rolls of Rolls-Royce and something of an heroic model in his daredevil activities. He also had the interests of the picture department in mind, for he thought that were the fourteen full-page illuminations extracted from the book and sold as paintings, they would provide the core of an important sale. As a book it should automatically have been sold as a book, but Patrick physically nabbed it, brought it to my room, told me to cut out and catalogue the fourteen and then pass the carcass to the book department.

I had never had such a thing in my hands. The illuminations were obviously by several collaborating painters, all more or less derivative from Jan van Eyck and, in my critical view, of indifferent quality as paintings. To me, the value of the volume, still in its original mid-fifteenth century binding – distinguished enough in the binder's mind for him to have signed it LIUINUS STUUAERT ME LIGAVIT and inscribed it A GAND (thus giving it a binding date of 1448–1458, the illuminations a little earlier) – lay in its condition, undisturbed since then, and here was I, in the mid twentieth century, about to disturb it, indeed to wreck it. I bearded Patrick in his room upstairs and was appalled by his rage; reminding me that I was an inexperienced employee and he a partner in the firm, he ordered me to do as I was told – he even used the phrase 'I order you . . . ,' and clinched the argument with the threat that he, if I refused, would do the job himself.

Bill, to whom I immediately went, shrugged off my plea – Patrick, it seemed, had been responsible for securing the Llangattock property and he, Bill, had no idea what undertakings and agreements had been made. In the end I went to Peter Chance, told him that I thought that breaking the book would be bad for Christie's reputation, proposed that the proper thing to do was to offer it as a perfect book with the reserve that Patrick might think the total value of the illuminations if sold separately – even to offer it as one lot in a sale of paintings (not such a silly idea, for two of the three dealers who eventually formed a consortium to buy it were the art dealers Edward Speelman and Marlborough) – and think again if it failed to find a buyer. I even said that I would feel compelled to resign if the integrity of the book were to be destroyed, and were this to be the chosen course, I would, as a last resort to save it, report the matter to *The Times*. Peter thought Patrick's proposal butchery (his word), assured me that it would not happen and took the Hours from me. It did not happen, and on 8 December 1958, as a book, lot 191, the Hours were sold for the world record price of £32,000. Christie's held that record for two days, and then it was trounced at Sotheby's by another book of hours from the collection of Dyson Perrins, Joan Seddon's uncle. *The Llangattock Hours*, after languishing in the trade for some years, returned to Flanders and are now in the Bibliotheque Royale, Brussels.

The bruising encounter with Patrick, his determination to put me in my place as his inferior and employee, was gentled a little by an invitation to the Congress of Art Historians in Paris in September, a reassurance that my academic work over the last ten months or so had been recognised. Bill encouraged me to attend, arguing that though I was not so soon entitled to any leave my presence in Paris might be good for Christie's – and this was good for me as Christie's paid the bills. By chance encountering Jill whom I had not seen since we had left the Courtauld, I was within days both dismayed and disappointed to learn that she too had secured an invitation (so much for what I had assumed to be recognition of my scholarship) and wanted to arrange our travelling together. In retrospect I should not have been surprised – she was later to intrude (there is no kinder word for it) on journeys to Albania, Turkey and even Liverpool. We stayed in my mother's old hotel, walked everywhere, attended seminars on every aspect of French art – two, memorably tedious, on the influence of seventeenth-century French architects on the formal buildings of late nineteenth century Roumania and Canada – and went to formal dinners, first in Malmaison and then in the newly restored Versailles, where the flamboyant curator, Gérald van der Kemp, had been responsible for much restitution of furniture and other artefacts lost to it after the French Revolution. Most of this he did through the Versailles Foundation established in New York with the assistance of his rich American (second) wife, Florence Harris, attracting huge donations from Rockefellers, Huttons and Lauders, with Rothschilds and Wildensteins not far behind. I liked him in spite of his overwhelming ebullience and self-esteem, and knowing that Christie's were searching for a major European figure (with, of course, social connections at least as much as expertise and experience of the art Market) to represent the firm in Europe, on my return to

London I suggested that he might be a suitable candidate and negotiations did, indeed, begin. I was never told why they failed but I suspect that van der Kemp was so far from Christie's idea of a gentleman that Peter and Patrick could not stomach him; instead there was the far greater good of his taking on, in the later 1970s, the restoration of Monet's estate in Giverny.

For me the special pleasure of the jaunt to Paris lay in renewing my friendship with Michel Laclotte who took Jill to be a sure sign that my puppy-dog days were over; I did not disillusion him. Through him I met the vivacious and very useful Roseline Bacou, then curator of drawings at the Louvre, who later let me loose on everything in her cure. I also met Carlos van Hasselt, then a curator at the Fitzwilliam but soon to become head of the Netherlands Institute in Paris and, for the rest of our lives, a fine and affectionate friend. He in turn introduced me to John Woodward, Keeper of Paintings at Birmingham City Art Gallery when that was a post of international stature, a brilliant judge of paintings but too unassuming, companionable and on the tipping-point of his descent into alcoholism. Poor John, he later became an Ancient Mariner from whom all friends fled, for he told, repeatedly, the same tales of, misfortune to explain his downright pennilessness, tearing trousers and raincoat to prove that he'd been mugged and now needed just enough money to buy a ticket back to Birmingham 'and for a taxi to Euston too, if you can spare it.' He was my first encounter with the condition – it was later to overtake Bill – and for a while, believing him, I gave him money, but when one day, by then uncertain, I took him to Euston, just as I was about to buy another he showed me his return ticket and broke into miserable sobbing.

In October Bill went to America. In a letter to my mother I complained of so much work that not only had I not been to Windsor for some weeks, but had found it necessary to go into Christie's at weekends to keep up with the flow of pictures to be catalogued – a state of affairs that was to prove more or less permanent for years. In Bill's absence, Alec, by then retired but mistakenly retained as a consultant, had taken it upon himself to resume his old responsibilities; I observed that 'All would be well were it not that old Sir Alec is the most difficult and most dishonest old idiot, and I have to do as he tells me.' He disliked Jewish dealers; to the Leggatts and Agnews he kow-towed, but were the Herner family who owned the Hallsborough Gallery to bid successfully at auction he'd knock the lot down to 'Ballsborough' in crude allusion to their borrowed name; and when I suggested that we should show a Parmigianinesque painting to Lili Fröhlich, an expert in the field, whose full surname was Fröhlich-Bum (pronounced Boom), his scorn for all the middle-European art historians who had fled from Europe in the 1930s and become dealers because there was nothing else to do, was expressed in his near-screaming repetition of 'Bum, bum, bum – what can anyone called Bum tell me?'

We crossed swords too over a decent still life by William Somerville Shanks – of whom I had never heard and nor, I suspect, had he; bright in colour and briskly painted with evident panache, I wanted to include it in a sale, but Alec did not. Argument was terminated in his usual way – repetition in increasing volume. 'Somerville Shanks? Somerville Shanks? That's not a good selling name' – introducing me to a ludicrous means of establishing the market value of a painter's work. In our worst encounter there was an additional element to his hostility in that, as he put it, I had caused mortal offence to Freddy Turner. At first, as I had no idea who Freddy Turner was, Alec's tirade was incomprehensible, but as it wore on in language that I had not heard since my first weeks in the army, I realised that Turner was the stout little man I had found on Christie's doorstep an hour earlier when returning from lunch, sending away a man with a large painting. At a glance I knew that it had qualities to be found in Mola and Testa, near contemporaries of Poussin, and intervened – tactlessly no doubt, but I wanted to save the picture rather than the face of the idiot rejecting it with assertions that it was too large and too dark to be worth anything, suggesting that it might find a buyer at Bonham's 'but it ain't good enough for us.' The idiot, however, was Freddie Turner, and Freddie Turner, old Alec spat at me, was his brother-in-law and had been valuing pictures for Christie's for more than forty years – hot dinners and short trousers too came into the argument. When I told Bill of the episode, apologetically, for Freddie was his uncle, his response was that he had indeed been Christie's travelling valuer up and down the country and 'God knows what damage he has done.' The rejected picture did turn out to be by Testa.

At much the same time I had an offer from Robin Fedden of the National Trust offering me a post that covered Dorset, Somerset, Wiltshire and Gloucestershire, with a flat in Dyrham Park and a starting salary of between £800 and £1,000 a year. After an interview, Robin, who was later my next door neighbour and a friend, confirmed the offer in a letter and this – double my salary at Christie's and more with the flat – I took to Peter asking how I should resolve the difficulty. His response I took to be a promise: it was that he could not immediately match the offered salary, but would, in the new year, reach some way towards it (in the event he almost doubled my starting salary), and that if the firm prospered I should be made a director within four or five years.

For me the main event of the autumn was the sale of the Skippe Collection of Old Master Drawings, scheduled for 20 and 21 November 1958, a field of connoisseurship and collecting in which even Patrick realised I had the better of him and he did not interfere, though he may have had something to do with securing the sale much earlier in the year. John Skippe, 1742–1812, much travelled in Italy, was an amateur painter now best known for trying his hand at the rare skill of making woodblock prints in colour (chiaroscuro woodcuts), mostly after Parmigianino, in the manner of Antonio Maria Zanetti; but he also amassed some eight hundred drawings, mostly by Italian hands, varying so widely in quality that his judgement was evidently uncertain. In 1939 A. E. Popham (Arthur

Ewart – but Hugh to his friends), who had been Assistant Keeper of Prints and Drawings at the British Museum since 1912 (Keeper 1945–53) and was widely regarded as a scrupulous connoisseur and art historian, compiled a manuscript catalogue in exquisite writing small and clear. I had nothing to do but collate comments and corrections that were the consequence of another decade of scholarship and brooding, adjust this to a pattern that was a compromise between Christie's customs and my wish to reform them, and hope for his approval. Great man though he was and often gloomy of expression, nothing about him froze the impertinent tyro to his bones – as did the unbearably lofty manners of Pope-Hennessy and Kenneth Clark – and the thin and solemn face that seemed so fifteenth century and Eyckian could occasionally be persuaded into a slow smile. In 1958 it was difficult to believe that he had joined the Naval Air Service on the outbreak of the Great War and been shot down at Gallipoli, then to transfer to the Royal Flying Corps, in which he had known Joan Seddon's father. It was difficult too to imagine the tall, gaunt, slow-moving figure sailing and playing tennis, for at sixty-nine or so, scholarship had bent his back and bowed his head, and there was scant evidence of a muscled body within his tired old suits. But until his death in December 1970, whenever I knocked on his Islington door to show him some scrap that I thought might have relevance to the great corpus of Parmigianino's drawings[21] that were his last and longest preoccupation, I sensed a smile behind the seeming melancholy and warmth in his slow and drawling voice. Never impatient, he could nevertheless be remarkably wry, dry and ironic.

I also found myself in charge of prints – engravings, etchings, drypoints, woodcuts, mezzotints and aquatints. This I had not expected. Prints are not only an old man's field, for connoisseurship depends on decades of experience, but are better fitted to the mind

---

21 A. E. Popham: *Catalogue of the Drawings of Parmigianino*, 3 vols, New Haven and London 1971.

of the philatelist than to the spirit of the man who rejoices in colour and the brushstroke. The print man must know every detail of the beginning and the end of a print's development, the successive adjustments to the plate that make one pull minutely different from another (or occasionally, as in the case of Rembrandt, a sweeping change); he must know about the nationality and makes of paper, the width of margins from inches to mere thread, about too much and too little ink, and about all the other factors that make one print worth ten times the price of another, though the images are, to the sane man, identical. It was Christie's long-established custom to sell unframed prints, watercolours and drawings in whatever packaging they came, described as 'A parcel of . . . ' counting their number the only attempt at cataloguing. From this carelessness I had, as a schoolboy and as a Courtauld student, some benefit, occasionally bidding 3 guineas (and once 5 guineas) for parcels in which there were as many as a hundred sheets of paper, assuming from the price that nothing was of any individual value. Now, in charge and expected to make reforms, I inspected incoming parcels and put aside everything that I thought might reward investigation. Patrick dismissed the idea as a waste of time, but Bill allowed me to pursue it. But under whose tutelage? There was no one in Christie's to whom I could turn, but at Colnaghi's, the Bond Street dealers in prints and drawings from whom I had, when I was in the army, bought a Zanetti woodcut and a fine Castiglione etching, there was Arthur Driver who manifestly knew a thing or two, a moody bloke with a hefty working-class chip on his shoulder. When I put my problem to him he had the good grace to send me to Harold Wright who had recently, at seventy-three, retired from the firm after more than forty years as head of the print department. It was Wright who gave me the foundations of almost all that I know of prints and who opened my eyes to the post-Whistler generation of British printmakers – Strang, Cameron, Blampied, Smart – as well as knocking sense into Dürer and Rembrandt. He dined early – as old men do – and well into 1959 I spent many later evenings with him working our way through his orderly solander boxes, the annotated *catalogues raisonnés* on his shelves and his own unpublished manuscript catalogues, taking instruction from him. In his way he was as generous with his experience and scholarship as Blunt and Wilde, but where they revealed the spiritual best of things, he interpreted nothing, but acquainted me with the facts on which judgement could be made – this print is better than this because . . .

*   *   *

When the year came to its end it was time for summing-up. I had hardly set foot in Windsor and the promise of a four-day week so that I could, had been broken in such a way that I knew it to have been nothing better than a good intention. Another blow to possible scholarship had been a visit from Ben Nicolson, editor of the *Burlington Magazine*, specifically to tell me that as I had joined the trade, he could publish nothing more from me (nothing more? – one Shorter Notice and then nothing more?) – not even if it were connected with my work on Fontana which I knew would turn up all sorts of unpublished bits and pieces. This was a bitter blow, for I thought (and was right to think) that Christie's might be the source of all sorts of unknown paintings that for the sake of other art historians ought to be published in the *Burlington*, for Christie's catalogues were then not much seen beyond the trade and we very rarely published illustrations.

Christie's had become my world – yet not even the whole Christie's, but a picture department that was only part of it, riven between Bill and Patrick, held together by John Hancock; I had made little impression on it, my scholarship had been only haphazardly applied and I had become successor to Vic Heather, wasting my time putting together sales of ghastly and near worthless pictures when I should have been writing catalogue entries that drew attention to the rarity, beauty and particular or art historical interest of the better pictures that we sold. We were overwhelmed with bulk and should have taken much more care with paintings that had quality, but Patrick regarded Christie's as a clearing house for the trade at all its levels rather than an ally of museums, serious collectors and the nation's heritage, and any attempt I made to write the kind of note that I had written for the Stoskopff was at once deleted.

Of the rest of the firm I knew virtually nothing other than the bare bones that Jo Floyd was head of the furniture department, Guy Hannen was in charge of objects of Vertu – both by virtue of family relationship – and that Arthur Grimwade, brilliant silver expert, had no such connections and had achieved his worldwide eminence through enthusiasm and scrupulous hard work. With Patrick, these were the Young Turks of the board – and not nearly Turkish enough. The Old Guard was still represented – by Jo's cousin, Sir Harry Floyd, and Guy's father, Gordon Hannen, both of whom always carried neat leather cases but appeared to do no work; Sir Harry, rarely seen, was said to turn up in King Street once a month to collect his stipend in cash, but in his, Gordon carried bottles of gin and tonic – I once saw the case open and it was indeed neatly compartmented to prevent bottles and glasses from rattling. He tippled all day and when he set off for his homeward journey from Paddington was more or less plastered – his death on the concourse there, run down by a train of luggage trolleys, a Pooterish calamity, was the cause of grim and cynical laughter among Christie's lower employees.

My one friend was John Herbert, son of that colossus of the Thirties, A.P. Herbert, who had joined Christie's on the same day as I to invent and nurture a press office that could turn failure to advantage – as was his immediate task with the El Greco. John was surprisingly bumbling for a man of thirty-four, far too easily disconcerted by Christie's too frequent occasions for dismay. Constantly astonished by the uncomprehending arrogance of the directors, he was wily enough to become, through a fluke of circumstance, one of their number within a year. An absolutely honest man, he was incapable of what we now call 'spin,' and half a century later could never have been even an office boy in his now devious and unscrupulous profession. It was characteristic of him to drive a Citroën Six, a hopelessly old fashioned and under-powered but utterly engaging car of the Thirties – Patrick drove an Aston-Martin DB2, Jo a Jaguar 2.4, and Peter an R-type Bentley.

In asking myself if I really wanted to stay with Christie's, I realised that I had learned a phenomenal amount about painters of whose work I would otherwise never have heard, that there were periods and genres of painting in which the trade merrily traded – Style Maples, for example (to be pronounced as though it were French), the kind of paintings that went well with the 'Louis Quince' furniture sold by that once eminent emporium to devotees in St John's Wood – but of which the art historian knew nothing, and never would. Of these there were no monographs and the only reference books on Christie's shelves were an ancient set of Bénézit's eight-volume *Dictionnaire*[22] (they possessed neither Thieme-Becker nor the Vollmer Supplement)[23] and a broken-backed copy of Graves' *Dictionary*,[24] an alphabetical list of every painter who had ever exhibited in England, but as it was published in 1901, it was useless for the twentieth century. To learn anything of Benjamin Williams Leader and his crude imitator Dan Sherrin (the old drunk in the horse trough at Whitstable) one had to work at either Christie's or Sotheby's and piece together scraps of information randomly acquired – and those of us who took minor painters seriously made, by doing so, some contribution to the scholarly esteem in which some are now held – Atkinson Grimshaw and Albert Goodwin, Hercules Brabazon Brabazon and Alma-Tadema are all examples who have risen from nothing to being the subjects of monographs and exhibitions.

22 E. Bénézit: *Dictionnaire des Peintres . . .* , Librairie Gründ 1910.
23 U. Thieme und W. Becker: *Algemeines Lexikon der Bildenden Kunst . . .* , Leipzig 1907 and later.
24 Algernon Graves: *A Dictionary of Artists 1760 –1893*, London 1901.

But much of what I saw at an average rate of a hundred a day was irredeemable rubbish and offered so little intellectual and aesthetic nourishment that I harboured a Communist dream of appointment as a Commissar of the art market with absolute power to order the destruction of crotcheted landscapes by E. J. Niemann, glossy flower paintings by Cecil Kennedy and Davis Richter, pretty farmyard friends by Walter Hunt and the jolly carousing cardinals exquisitely achieved by Giuseppe Signorini and Alessandro Rinaldi that ought to have been wry and subversive, but were not. All these horrors were worth substantial money then (and far more substantial now) – good selling names, as Alec had it – but there was not a scrap of merit in them, yet there were dealers in decent premises in St James's who sold nothing else and would turn away a Titian were one ever offered them. Did I want to devote my life to these? Were they really a rewarding match for the Claudes and Poussins with which I had dealt at the Royal Academy or the Canalettos I had catalogued for Munich? With the unrelenting pace at which Christie's turned over the thousands of pictures delivered in a month, they depended on what I already knew in the important art historical fields that I had studied as a student and as I had been given scant opportunity to deepen my knowledge, it seemed inevitable that in this conveyor-belt world I too would sooner or later make mistakes to match the El Greco and Cerano.

It was, however, a much smaller thing that almost tipped me into resignation – a Christie's ritual. One of the benefits of employment was the Luncheon Voucher – a slip of paper entitling the bearer to food worth three shillings (fifteen pence, or seventy-five over the week) at any café that would take them – that is very few in St James's, the territory of the great and exclusive London club and of such restaurants as Wilton's, Overton's and Prunier's. In practical terms it meant scrambling for a seat in The Bonbonnière, an Italian café in Duke Street used by the slaves of the art market, the lowest forms of salesman life, the packers of parcels and collectors of purchases, the commission agents who never betrayed the skeletons in their employers' cupboards and every itinerant workman unfortunate enough to have employment in the neighbourhood. At the Bonbon the rule was to share tables and shuffle seats, order quickly, eat quickly, pay and go, for only by packing us in and throwing us out could the ever-smiling Italian family that ran it keep their prices down to a level that made the Luncheon Voucher a viable bill of exchange. I found this subsidy humiliating and would much rather have been paid a few more pounds a year. But even more humiliating was the Lady Bountiful business of the Christmas bird and bonus. The bonus was supposed to reflect, according to our status in the firm, the profits of the year, but these were so low – even dipping into loss, we were told – that the envelopes distributed by the company secretary, Charlie Puddifoot, on the eve of the Christmas break, contained so few banknotes as to be insulting, particularly as news was leaked that the cash came straight from the pockets of the poor suffering directors. And then – the final straw – there was Ridley Leadbeater's circus at the Front Counter, the distribution of Christmas birds to every member of staff.

Ridley had a stake in a smallholding or poultry farm near nether Basildon and had a contract with Christie's for the delivery of perhaps a hundred geese and turkeys labelled with our names, but in no discernible order, alphabetical or departmental. This disorder led to bad temper, even panic, and was not helped by Ridley's taking off for lunch at the Ritz – another ritual – with one of the many dealers to whom he gave favours, returning glassy-eyed. Frith could have painted *Christie's on Christmas Eve* as a pendant to *Paddington Station* or *Derby Day*, and the performance, thoroughly Victorian, perfectly encapsulated the hierarchy of the firm, the lordly directors on the stair looking down on the scramble as though the staff were terriers rat-catching in a barn. I wonder if any of them ever noticed Ridley snatching opportunities to grope the upturned bums presented on these occasions? He was an inveterate but butter-would-not-melt groper of both boys and girls behind his counter, his favourite trick the vicious jabbing of a pencil at the anus of a boy leaning forward to attend a visitor – an idiotic thing to do when most of them were the close relatives or godchildren of directors; even Charlie Allsopp, later Lord Hindlip, whom on his joining Christie's in 1962 I immediately (and rightly) identified as a future chairman of the firm, was the victim of Ridley's anal poke.

From these small things I learned exactly where in the hierarchy I stood. There had been other indications. With Vic Heather's departure, Frits Lugt, fastidious collector of old master drawings and scrupulous keeper of records, offered me half a crown to do what Vic had done for years – set aside for him a catalogue of every picture sale inscribed with prices, the names of buyers and any other information gleaned on the day. Dealers offered me a fiver to ensure that paintings were included in sales no matter what Patrick of Alec might think of them, another fiver to place a picture half way through the catalogue, another still to tweak the attribution, and I swiftly learned that behind Christie's grand facade ran two economies – the upstairs theatre of the saleroom with a suave director playing auctioneer, and downstairs the black economy of staff so poorly paid that they depended on the tips and bribes that so easily came their way. Was this why Vic Heather had for forty years endured the foul mouth of old Alec? – it explained why, until the very day of his retirement, he insisted on putting the catalogue entries in order, disrupting any logic that I had tried to introduce and determining in which sales pictures should be included; this, until his job was mine, I had attributed to some arcane wisdom of ages, but once I had his desk, the possibility of doubling my income was immediately apparent. In resisting that temptation I became unpopular with the many dealers whose regular delivery of paintings by the dozen provided background for the few from private sources that might revive the gloss of Christie's reputation. Bill, who continued his father's custom of being close to dealers of the old guard who had no premises but simply bought from country shops, auctioneers and old ladies on whose doors they knocked (hence the term 'knocker' for the itinerant dealer) and sent their accumulated bulk to Christie's to apply attributions and make profits, received many complaints of my arrogance.

Was it to please these that I had deserted not only the scholarship of art history but the theology that might have interrupted it? Was being something of a buffer for Bill when Patrick bullied him to be my career? Had I in eight months made anything of the mark I had been led to believe Christie's expected of me? To all these questions there was the same unarguable answer. Mulling over them with my stepfather, he counselled caution with the questions 'Have you learned anything?' and 'Is there more to learn?' – and to these the answer was equally unarguable, but opposite. 'In that case,' said Robert, 'stay with them until you are giving more than you gain from the experience.'

*   *   *

And what other life did I have in the later months of 1958? I went to Mass as regularly as ever, drove to Castle Hedingham frequently enough to mow my mother's lawn and take Penny for long walks through the Gainsborough landscapes that then lay between the village and Sudbury, seven walking miles away, though at thirteen she was getting old for such a distance. Mignon Frossard replaced my mother as companion at the opera; I saw a good deal of Baby Helen who had graduated in the summer and been appointed Philip Troutman's assistant as Keeper of the Courtauld Institute's collection, and began a long friendship with Richard Hughes-Hallett, one of my immediate contemporaries at the Courtauld, largely because I had moved to within three minutes walk of his family's house in Allen Street, Kensington. This move, to the basement of 16 Phillimore Place, the house in which Kenneth Grahame wrote *The Wind in the Willows*, brought me back to the heartland of my childhood, the churches of Our Lady of Victories and the Carmelites still familiar though rebuilt since the war, the High Street very much the same, the ground floor food department of John Barker's, where I had so often queued for rations during and after the war, quite unmodernised, some of the old staff still behind the counters – particularly the pink giant of a butcher who always gave me a tit-bit for Penny when she was with me, for dogs were then allowed in food shops.

The house belonged to Mrs Cecil Chesterton, the sister-in-law of G.K. Chesterton, who in 1927 had achieved admiring notoriety by establishing, with some advice from my stepfather, a hostel for homeless women (it still exists, as the Central and Cecil, in Waterloo Road). The basement was gloomy but the ceilings high, and white and ice-blue paint were my response. I asked John Critchley, my equivalent in Christie's furniture department, for advice and he told me to drive along the old road to Bath and haggle in the junk and antique shops, never paying the price asked. This I did, but instead of furniture found a painting that I could not afford – as Berenson once said, 'One look is enough if concentration is absolute.' The dealer, Frank Smith, whose wife kept a little china shop at the north end of Church Street Kensington, let me pay half the price with a promise to pay the rest within a year. It has lasted well. I have it still. As for furniture, friends gave me cast off chairs and an ottoman, Mignon gave me her spare piano, and I slept well enough on the floor for some months. Years later, long after his death, Frank Smith stared at me from the window of the Fine Art Society – a portrait painted by Maxwell Armfield – and I bought it, an act of purest sentiment.

Joyce Smith once told me a tale that I treasure. She had a tiny scrap of landscape acquired with a parcel of porcelain and put it in her window with a price tag of £3, just to get rid of it. Imagine her dismay when Graham Reynolds, author of the catalogue of all the Constables in the Victoria and Albert Museum, came into the shop and bought it without a word – had she, for nothing, let slip a masterpiece? Some days later he was back; 'I'm afraid I don't think this is by Constable,' he said, 'may I return it and have my money back?'

CHAPTER 12

Further Misgivings at Christie's

In one of the dead days between Christmas 1958 and the New Year break I was called to the Front Counter to talk to a young man who had brought nothing to show Christie's and who made little sense to Leadbeater, but who would not be sent away. To me he seemed in so emotional a state that he could hardly explain his errand, but slowly it emerged that he was offering the remaining contents of John Minton's studio, the proceeds of the sale to be given to the Artists' General Benevolent Fund. Prolific painter, illustrator and designer, melancholy Minton, compelled by a weight of miseries beyond relief, had committed suicide in January 1957, convinced that he was exhausted as an artist. He has since become a romantic hero, and his work is indeed burdened with romantic notions of anguish, haplessness and wistful longing. Consumed with tenderness when confronted by young men, his portraits have a telling truth about them, and it was the subject of one of these who stood before me; Minton was born on Christmas Day 1917 and we were talking of him and his work two days after what would have been his 41st birthday.

I met Minton only once, late in the Autumn Term of 1956, by the coincidence of our leaving a party at the Royal College of Art at the same moment, to which I had been invited by Keith Townend, an architecture student in whom I had found a kindred aesthetic spirit while we were training to be subalterns. I was stone cold sober, he very very drunk: I walked with the shambling, lanky, anguished man almost draped about my shoulders, to his home in Apollo Place, World's End, and, not knowing what to do with a famous artist almost old enough to be my father, would have left him on his doorstep had he not so obviously needed help beyond the door. I saw him to his bed, tugged off his clothes, turned him onto his side in a foetal position and drew up the blankets; his silent response was to indicate a card on the side table – 'Mr John Minton has removed from 5 Shaftesbury Villas W8 and is now installed at 9 Apollo Place SW10. Tel: FLA 0433.'

Like many of my generation of schoolboys, I had been compelled to read Alain-Fournier's *Le Grand Meaulnes*, slipped into the Higher Schools Certificate syllabus by some benign old queen, and had used as crib an English translation illustrated by Minton, conveniently published in 1947. To a romantic adolescent the sub-text of both the book and the illustrations was patently the puppy love of one boy for another, and this, of course, is the clue to much of Minton's work. He was an unrequited homosexual, the fifth former in love with the prefect, the boy in love with the man, the skinny with the muscular and stocky, the educated man with the never educable ignorant, the refined with the rough and tough, and, most miserable of all, the homo- with the heterosexual. 'What one paints and what one is are inescapably interwoven' said Minton in 1940 – as true of Leonardo da Vinci and his pretty boys, Rubens and his plump women, and of Lucian Freud whose paintbrush crawls into a woman's crutch with the insistence of a caterpillar into a cabbage heart, as it was of himself.

With the exception of the war years, Minton's adult life was spent in an atmosphere of sexual persecution, the trials of homosexual miscreants so notorious – Wildeblood, Montagu, Gielgud (for whom Minton had designed sets for *Macbeth*), Croft-Cooke and naughty old Ian Horabin among them, the judgements so prejudiced and the penalties so extreme that both the police and the law sank deep into disrepute, their very bigotry at last stimulating the liberal attitudes that brought about reform, though not until long after Minton's death. His sexual isolation, however, might not have mattered quite so much had he not felt even more isolated in his work. From the beginning he had been a painter of people and places, communicating an elegiac mood or romantic narrative, drawing on a peculiarly English thread that reached from Samuel Palmer's Shoreham to the Wales of Graham Sutherland. He was too graphic an artist ever, as a painter, to respond to the growing demand for abstract art, for bravura brushwork that when cold might or might not mean something, and had no patience for the contriving painters of St Ives. He tried his hand at it, even, under a false name, exhibiting abstracts as a jape, but this only confirmed his contempt for facile non-figurative art.

The material from his studio was delivered at the very beginning of 1959, accompanied by the same young man, who told me that a painting of a Michelangelesque male nude imposed on an abstract pattern was the canvas on Minton's easel when he died. I wanted to make a fuss of these sad remains, to publish in the catalogue a note on Minton explaining who he was and what he had done, even to hold a wake of sorts when the pictures went on view to which his students and fellow tutors at the Royal College would be invited – but nothing of this was to be. Patrick, probably recognising the homo-eroticism of the subjects was appalled – 'We don't do studio clearances' – and, having bullied me for committing Christie's to the sale, allowed it to take place only because the benefit to the AGBI could be seen as a justification for selling such contemporary rubbish. Without beat of drum or funeral note the paintings were hurried into a sale on 20 February 1959, tucked into a catalogue that was already prepared for the printers, and John Minton slipped into three decades of obscurity.

Had Patrick allowed me to treat the studio clearance as an exhibition we would have had not only, in art historical terms, a decent record of Minton's work in the months before his death, but almost certainly greater insight into his distressingly turbulent state of mind. The most significant indication of this was the painting on his easel at his death; bought by Lord Stanley of Alderley for 12 guineas, he paid for it but did not collect it and within weeks instructed Christie's to get rid of it. In the sale on Friday 17 July I gave myself a birthday present and bought it for 3 guineas. Half a century later it rewards me daily, hanging in my dining room, the first of a small collection of Minton's drawings and small paintings.

The Minton episode confirmed the haplessness of my situation in Christie's. Brought in to make changes and, above all, to raise the scholarly level of the catalogues, I was at every turn frustrated and I got little help from Bill who, never combative with Patrick, always let him have his way – over the Mintons his only contribution to the argument was 'Well, we've never sold contemporary art.' Sales were categorised as Important or Highly Important if paintings or their owners were thought to merit such terms, but the run-of-the-mill sales, the weekly attempts to clear the warehouses, were given the portmanteau title 'Ancient and Modern Pictures and Drawings,' and were a jumble of parcels of unframed prints and drawings on trestle tables and framed oils and watercolours on the walls, occasionally three rows of them reaching almost to the ceiling, with auctioneers competing to beat the record selling-rate of 120 lots an hour. As for the catalogues – these were no more than identification lists and offered no evidence of research, scholarship or expert opinion; if Ellis Waterhouse had thought a canvas quite certainly by a French follower of Caravaggio and just possibly by Trophime Bigot, this was regarded as perversely obscure and the simple listing as Caravaggio was preferred, with no note that he had looked at it with interest. Bigot was, in the 1950s, known only to a handful of scholars and years might have passed before I had proved or disproved Ellis's point, but simply by raising it another shred of evidence could have been brought into the open. Such shreds very rarely were.

Ancient and Modern was, to me, the title of a hymnal and seemed ridiculous in the context of a vigorous art market in the middle of the twentieth century. I suggested that we should dispense with both it and the haphazardly mixed sales that were the bulk of our turnover, by the very simple device of separating paintings into categories of period, nationality and type, colour-coding their covers and setting up independent sales devoted to watercolours, prints and old master drawings. When I proposed the term *genre* for nineteenth-century paintings of pretty children, immaculate farm animals and carousing cardinals, Patrick said 'I don't know the meaning of the word' and left the room. Bill was rather more receptive and, tentatively, the reform began and Ancient disappeared from our vocabulary. Genre was not a term ever used by Christie's for what Baudelaire described as 'oeuvres charmantes dans les regions moyennes du talent,' and we settled, for a while at least, on *Narrative*, for almost every nineteenth-century picture told some sort of story.

The one advantage of the old system was that if a consignment was a big mixed bag of paintings, drawings and watercolours of all ages, all were sold in one sale – one entry in the books, one sale catalogue to the owner, one cheque. With my meddling the department might now spread the consignment over half a dozen sales and the increased work caused administrative confusion and delay with which John Hancock and I could not keep pace – and it was thus that Ian Lowe joined the department in April 1959. Tall, erect, elegant, impossible to ruffle and slightly mysterious, Ian was utterly dependable. At Oxford he had been awarded the prize that honours Laurence Binyon, poet, playwright, translator of Dante, art historian, authority on the arts of China and Japan and slave in the British Museum for forty years; this was to encourage students to study works of art abroad and Ian's chosen subject, born of pan-European travels in long vacations as an undergraduate, was the baroque and rococo art and architecture of South Germany and Austria. This, studied for a year, brought him close contacts with the grandees of the Ashmolean and Victoria and Albert Museums, and with Brinsley Ford, the most eclectic gentleman scholar of his generation (he was born in 1908), the writer of some 300,000 words on the history of the

Grand Tour[25] and generous mentor to every young man who consulted him on the art and artefacts of the eighteenth century. At the V&A Ian had spent the six months from September 1958 editing the *Notes on Italian Monuments* bequeathed it by Margaret Longhurst, the formidable Keeper of Architecture and Sculpture who, in 1938, had been one of the two who were the first women to be given such high appointments there. It was the commendation of her successor, the ebullient Moley, Hender Delves Molesworth, an early enthusiast for the baroque of central Europe, that convinced Peter Chance that he should appoint Ian to the picture department; there Ian hoped to expand and consolidate his scholarship; as with me, his hopes were thwarted.

Ian relieved me of much of the basic chore of cataloguing. For this the tools provided were a spotlight on a long flex, white spirit in demijohns and rolls of cotton wool with which to swab it onto paintings obscured by varnish that had grown dark and opaque with age or, worse, that had 'chilled' – that is, turned greyish-white. Under the heat of the spotlight the white spirit evaporated fast and we had only seconds in which to discover signatures and dates carved in the bark of trees or hidden in the shadow of a dock leaf. With well over a hundred pictures the daily target unless I was present to thin them out on their arrival, we had at most four minutes in which to write a 'manuscript' – that is, on half a foolscap sheet, a record of ownership, correspondence and any information the vendor had supplied, notes of measurement and materials, the subject, signature and date, and if these last could not be found, a suggested attribution. Interruptions from the Front Counter, telephone enquiries and the visits of such necessary friends as Ellis Waterhouse, reduced the four minutes to three and two as we worked at breakneck speed. I could never keep my writing

25 Unpublished other than in short articles and the invaluable *A Dictionary of British and Irish Travellers in Italy 1701–1800*, compiled from his archive by John Ingamells, Yale 1997.

small and neat enough and so imported my typewriter – Ian's, however, was perfect for the task and wonderfully legible. That Christie's gave him no time to learn but merely turned him into a drudge, was in part my fault, for I should have seen, that as with me for the past year, all that was wanted by Bill and Patrick was another Vic Heather – and that I was determined not to be, but it was far from a suitable role for Ian.

He was far more disciplined than I and had nothing of my emotional involvement in the firm – he stuck to the hours of business, but I stayed late and sometimes returned after dinner knowing that in two uninterrupted hours I could achieve as much as in a working day; of these interruptions Ian was later to observe that with the public and other members of staff, I 'was not a master of the gentle word, nor of the encouraging gesture.' Ian disappeared for proper lunches, often collected by superior officials from the Ashmolean or Fitzwilliam who had announced themselves to Ridley at the Front Counter, unaware of the mock-grovelling charade that would then be performed in our office; never once was he seen where the humiliating vouchers were the currency. He spent weekends away, we knew not where, for he never boasted of the social connections that meant so much to the directors – Patrick always let it be known if he thought I'd be cowed by the, for me, unattainable grandeur of his. And fearlessly, he took holidays when he wished – fearlessly, because we were expected to fit in with Patrick's plan for absences to fly his Spitfire, race Remus, his famous Alfa-Romeo, and play with a fabled Napier that he claimed to have been (*pace* Rolls-Royce) the best car in the world (at times the most expensive, the marque – defunct by 1924 – was particularly popular with Maharajahs). I envied Ian's aplomb in these small confrontations; I always gave way, but he did not. One way and another we both took more than our allotted three weeks, but my breaks were always combined with work for Christie's and at random times, and in most years I took nothing that could be described as a conventional holiday. My only glimpse into Ian's private life was his purchase of a painting by Denis Wirth-Miller at a charity sale one evening; at the time this was bewildering, but now that Denis is perceived as a significant presence in Francis Bacon's life and art, I recognise the far-sightedness of it.

On 20 March 1961 Ian succumbed to glandular fever; early in April he flew to Rome to convalesce because Mary Howard, to whom he proposed on 30 April, was there; and early in May, returning to Christie's after a long excursion across northern Italy, he resigned. Glandular fever and the journey brought about this turning-point; with time to think he realised that work at Christie's was a useless grind and that work in a museum would better suit his temperament; he had learned little, and that little was in barren fields in which he had no interest, perfectly illustrated by the paintings of Alfred de Breanski, in the later nineteenth century and beyond a prolific exhibitor of anaemic sub-Barbizon (and worse) landscapes, the greens glaucous, the brushwork loose, the flamboyant signatures enormous, the Franco-Russian name his father's fraudulent invention. Within a year or so Ian was happily appointed an assistant keeper in the Ashmolean. We remained in touch, partly through Joan Seddon, more through Hecate, a whippet born to one of Mary's bitches – born to order, indeed, for I had said 'If ever you have a perfect blue bitch pup, call her Hecate on her pedigree papers and let me have her.' Ian and Mary brought her to me on 24 October 1967, a tiny creature to hold in one hand and keep warm peeping from my jumper.

With Ian's departure from Christie's, the height of the season upon us, I was in despair at the prospect of another bout of basic cataloguing in the airless cellar with Jock and Les for company. I was also ill with a malfunctioning kidney that required surgery and some time away for recovery. David Barclay, then a failing Courtauld student, was brought in. I had known him for some years as the friend of a girl student at the Courtauld, good-looking in a Young Conservative sort of way, a kind-hearted blameless boy, infuriatingly inhibited and proper, heir (it was said) to a grandfather's fortune made from the mass manufacture of sanitary towels, and rich enough to be among the first to have a Triumph TR2, the rare AC Aceca and the monstrous Facel-Vega. He had long wanted to work for Christie's, thinking it a suitable setting for a gentlemanly life, and to delay the day when he might seek my help in applying for a job, I had urged him first to learn something of art history by going to the Courtauld. To my astonishment he was accepted there. This had not been my intention; I had assumed that he'd be found wanting and, abashed, would then seek some other career, relieving me of the duty to tell him my harsh opinion that he'd not be fit for Christie's. David was not in any sense academic material and it became clear that there was no point in his sitting longer at Blunt's feet at precisely the moment of Ian's leaving Christie's. It was the worst possible coincidence. Through Ellis Waterhouse, Anthony knew that Ian was leaving and it has always been my belief that he saw the chance of easing David out of the Institute and into Christie's, the boy's declared ambition; without a word to me, they commended him to Patrick.

David was an early example of a Courtauld student who knew nothing of the Old Testament, nothing of the New, nothing of the legends of the saints, nothing of Greek and Roman myth and history; this is common now, the consequence of modern education systems that hold such background cultural foundations in contempt and see no use for them, but David was educated at a public school where these traditions had not quite faded – he, however, always incurious, had simply let them wash over him with no osmosis taking place. Looking at pictures, he recognised nothing, and correcting his catalogue manuscripts took more time than initiating them myself. The end came after six months or so when he described the subject of a seventeenth-century Dutch panel, not as Christ with the Pilgrims on the Road to Emmaus, but as Three men going for a Walk in a Wood. What happened then was described by John Herbert as a clash of personalities. It was nothing of the kind. It was an ill-tempered and abusive tantrum expressing feelings so intense that the words could never be withdrawn. Wholly justified, the manner of it was inexcusable.

John Morrish replaced David early in 1962. He too had a private income from a family business with which, in middle age, he had become disenchanted, and this enabled him to work for Christie's for a pittance. Quite how he joined the firm I can no longer recall, but his interest in art was in no way informed and his useful social contacts were even fewer than mine. Thin, spare, red-haired but greying, bearded and bespectacled, he looked both scholarly and shrewd – useful attributes. When one particularly dominant woman visitor to the Front Counter dismissed my arguments against the authenticity of her Rubens with 'Young man, I don't believe a word you've said; bring me someone older,' it was John I sent to her and he, instructed what to say and how to say it, sent her on her way, contented in the belief, not that she had a Rubens, but a painting so investment-worthy that she'd be foolish to sell it. I was to find John's dissemblings – 'Do you really need to sell it? It would be wiser to hang on until you have some pressing reason to let it go. Gosh, aren't you lucky to have this!' – much easier weapons to wield than the blunt truth.

John was also responsible for inventing Lawrence Bastard. Christie's had for many years sold old Dutch paintings of indifferent quality as by an unrecorded painter whose name had been suggested by Daan Cevaat, a friendly dealer from Holland whose advice old Alec Martin had occasionally sought, and I accepted this attribution when, often enough, it was suggested by Bill or Patrick for some kippered interior with drunken peasants, though my usual response to artists not recorded in Thieme-Becker was that they had never existed. But then Cevaat, kind to the new boy, dropped in to tell me to stop using it, for the name was not that of an artist, but Dutch slang for the penis. Lawrence Bastard, however, was not a trick but a necessity. A landscape some six feet wide was sent in by a solicitor closing an estate. Not signed but evidently English and from the 1930s, it was more than competent, but none of us recognised the hand, nor did any ancient Royal Academician or member of the New English Art Club. The solicitor grew impatient – the sale of the picture was delaying the settlement for which the heirs were clamouring. John and I looked at it yet again and still we were completely stumped. 'It's a bastard,' said I, to which John responded with 'That'll do – think of a Christian name.' And thus was Lawrence Bastard born. The painting was bought by Pulitzer, a small dealer in High Street, Kensington, who advertised it as the masterpiece of a genius too little known, and any who shared interest in it were given an entirely invented biography. We used his name again and again until we were in danger of constructing an oeuvre, and he spawned both Laurent Batard and Lorenzo Bastardo; soon David Carritt was to invent Van Esserbel for Netherlandish still lives of doubtful quality and innumerable variations on De Cock and De Haas.

Older than Patrick, John eventually found his bullying difficult to tolerate, exploding with futile incoherent rages. Increasingly restive, he thought first that he might leave to become an art dealer of some sort, for almost total ignorance was obviously never a barrier in that business, and then, to accumulate capital for it, there was his mad plan to dig for diamonds in West Africa for a year or two. He left early in 1964 and disappeared.

It was Ian who found his replacement, Noël Annesley, an Oxford undergraduate whom he had encountered in the Ashmolean; bearing in mind his own disappointment at Christie's, his commendation was diffident. I interviewed the boy over supper in Phillimore Place – a supper that he later described as a cruel test, for it consisted entirely of things eaten with the fingers. Though he had nothing to bring to Christie's and I realised that in the beginning it would be, for him, a crash course in distinguishing geographical origins and five centuries from each other if he were ever to be able to tell a Rembrandt from an Ingres, I liked his oddly hapless air, his modesty, enthusiasm and willingness. Interviews with Guy Hannen and Patrick followed (Patrick characteristically kept him waiting long after lunch at White's), and within ten days I was able, on Guy's instruction, to offer him the post, starting in September. He was a good choice: Christie's at first shaped him, but when, surprisingly early in his career, the imbalance reversed, he contributed much to its reshaping into what it now is some half century later.

*　　*　　*

On 1 May 1959, when I had been with Christie's for fifty-one weeks and Ian had for two, we witnessed an event that was to give Patrick absolute supremacy over us. It was a Friday, the day on which sales of paintings always took place, and this, as it included a consignment from the Marquess of Northampton, was a sale described as of Fine Pictures by Old and Modern Masters. Bill Martin was in the rostrum; liked by dealers, sympathetic to amateurs unused to the pace of the auction room, and above all, persuasive on behalf of private vendors when the bidding stalled at a point when the reserve could be reached with just another bid or two, he was a better auctioneer than most of his fellow partners, occasionally humorous, always well-tempered and, never tempted into a record-breaking pace, a little slower. At lot 149, twenty lots before the end, he slowed to a halt. His eyes unfocused, he seemed to gaze into a distance far beyond the opposite wall of the octagon, his mouth opening and closing in slow motion – and then he collapsed, more or less held in place by the confines of the rostrum, but falling backwards from it when the door was opened by the sales clerk. Within seconds, it seemed, Jo Floyd was in his place briskly concluding the sale while Bill, carried out of sight, deeply unconscious, the victim of a cerebral haemorrhage, lay waiting for an ambulance.

He was for weeks in the Middlesex Hospital, and for many evenings that early summer I walked from Christie's to Mortimer

Street to find at his bedside, not Margery his wife, nor Penny his daughter, nor Gregory his son (then a keeper at the National Gallery), but Beatrice West, his mistress, an uncomely woman broad of hip, her bespectacled face porcine, her possessive manner that of a practised termagant. Almost three months passed before, very tentatively, he returned to work; as he could make no decisions, bring in no business, remember no painter's name, I had to carry him and, as best I could, protect him from the manoeuvrings of Patrick who, during his absence, had unquestionably been the head of the department and was determined to remain so. Bill hung on at Christie's until forced by his partners to resign at the end of 1962, the worst year ever for the firm with so substantial a loss – for which Patrick was far more responsible than he – that he got very little for his shares and spent the rest of his life in near penury.

As he faded, there were some who still respected him, among them Paul Getty who, on a whim one Friday, spent 500 guineas on a large and handsome copy of a landscape by Hobbema. Bill and I had had some trouble with this painting, for it had been brought to us by Jack Harris, a dealer whose usual stock was would-be *dix-huitième* French furniture but who could never resist gambling on pictures; he drove a Mercedes 300SE when this was still a flashy and vulgar thing to do. He knew Bill well enough to insist on his seeing him at once, refused to accept his view that the picture was only a later nineteenth-century copy, rejected the same view from me, and insisted that we sell it with a reserve of 500 guineas, a figure we thought far beyond the realms of possibility. Bill, as usual, gave way.

It was this that Getty had bought without even knowing how it had been described in the sale catalogue; he had simply dropped in with nothing but curiosity in mind, had seen the picture from the back of the octagon and, hearing the bidding falter at what seemed an absurdly low figure for so handsome a thing, had joined in until he reached (unknowing) Harris's reserve. 'What have I bought?' he asked as his factotum followed him into Bill's room, carrying the landscape. 'Oh my Gawd!' was Bill's response. He then told Getty the whole tale. Getty turned to me: 'Do you think it's a copy?' And when I said that I did, the factotum, at some signal from his master that I neither saw nor heard, slammed the canvas down over the back of a chair. With a serene 'Good day,' Getty and his man then left the room, the farce so exquisitely executed that I wondered if they had performed it many times before.

*   *   *

Ian's dependability made it possible for me to take a long break in the early autumn of 1959. I had managed to spend enough weekends in Windsor to justify a jaunt to Rome to look at buildings by Fontana, and by chance — for neither Bill nor Patrick could read any European language (Patrick pronounced every foreign painter's name with such exaggerated Churchillian ignorance that I wondered how Berenson had endured his presence at I Tatti) and all foreign correspondence to the picture department fell to me to answer, letting me gather enough requests for visits to plot a route to Rome through France, returning through Switzerland and Germany. Hans Backer, Christie's representative in Rome, had also set aside some clients for me to see. Bill, indulgent as ever, sent me off for as long as the journey might take, instructing me to keep all bills and claim repayment on my return.

I took Baby Helen with me. We had seen a good deal of each other since her graduation and so flirtatious had we become that I had to tell her the truth about my sexuality — to which her response was of the 'never mind, it's not important' kind. I now had to raise the matter again, for thinking it immoral to charge Christie's for feeding and sheltering her on the journey, we planned to camp where we could and stay in the cheapest hotels, both of which might bring us into the sort of proximity that in normal circumstances might reasonably end in companionable conjugation. Thinking it folly to tax the reliability of my old Wolseley by driving it to Rome, I hired a Morris Minor Traveller — an oak-beamed thatched cottage kind of car – and into it we packed decent clothes for the inevitable formal occasions on the way (and certainly in Rome), my camping things and, I thought, the tent that Helen had agreed to bring.

Our route was dictated by my responsibilities to Christie's, but the pace was deliberately leisurely, and though it was the second week of September, the blazing sun as we crossed the Channel encouraged us to make for Le Touquet, swim and laze the rest of the day, spending the night in nearby camping-site on the edge of Meaulnes, a village too small for the map, where, to our delight, we found the school announced as the Lycée Alain Fournier. I erected my tent while Helen appeared to rummage in the car. 'Where's yours?' I asked when mine was up. 'I haven't brought it.' Her smile, demure, seraphic and direct, was enough to tell me that this had been deliberate and I was briefly furious. I could not pretend that my tent was too small for two – it had housed four on its last journey to Italy – nor could I compel Helen to sleep in so small a car as the Minor; it was a moment for very plain speaking. In a letter a week or so later I told my mother that 'Helen is a delightful and amusing companion: all the French call her Madame – I suppose they think her my wife.' And so, indeed, they did, in spite of our passports, and put us into double beds in which we lay like brother and sister, in perfect innocence; only in puritanical Switzerland, weeks later, did a Calvinist hotel clerk, examining our passports, question our relationship and object to our sharing a room.

We spent some days in Paris before driving south to beyond Clermont-Ferrand where, in a small hunting-lodge, I found a sketch by Rubens. Jubilant, we spent that night in an inn named Le Lion d'Or in the village of La Chaise Dieu, tucked up in the deepest of feather mattresses. Then there was a man in Avignon with a fake Simone Martini to be seen – and never have I been so badly bitten by mosquitoes; and after more things to inspect in Nîmes and Arles and Aix, we had freedom to laze and swim at Fos-sur-Mer and Rayol before setting off more purposefully for Rome.

There, Helen recalls, I kept on saying 'I've seen it all before' – but I had not and it was familiar only from closely-studied photographs. In the first days of October I made ecstatic notes on Tivoli, Frascati and other beauty spots in the Campagna – 'wonderful, wonderful, all so very close to Claude.' Rising early to see before breakfast churches that seemed accessible only during early Mass, I walked myself to a standstill; Helen, made of tougher stuff, did not quite collapse, but I did – every bone aching, every sinew so stiff that I could not, one morning in our pensione, put weight onto the first foot out of bed. There was too, the daily worsening attack of fresco neck, the failure of neck muscles to return, unaided by a helping hand, the head to its normal position after looking at painted domes and ceilings. Hans Backer required my services for several days, swanning about the city in the beautiful Lancia Aurelia coupé that he was far too small to drive, and far too timid too; most of this work was a waste of time, an exercise in diplomatic flattery, but one errand stopped me in my tracks, for as soon as the door of the apartment opened, I saw over the owner's shoulder, a beautiful Modigliani portrait of a young woman – reward enough and more for my journey, though not its objective, for what I was really there to assess was a wretched copy of a Caravaggio.

On our very first evening in Rome we bumped into Anthony Blunt, staying at a nearby albergo almost as humble as our pensione, and had the first of many dinners with him in a restaurant at which he was evidently known. Within spitting distance of the Pantheon, it was the haunt of local families and workmen, cheap and simple, and there – never having been in his company without professional reason – I saw an astonishingly different Anthony, warm, funny and engaging, for with the master-pupil relationship set aside he became an older brother or young uncle. Helen, by then contentedly established as Philip Troutman's assistant in his new post in charge of the Courtauld collections, he treated as an equal. Of course we talked about Fontana, but not even the constant frustrations of that project affected the new chemistry.

A month after leaving London we began the return journey, pausing in Arezzo, Bologna and Parma before the long haul over the Alps. Jubilant that I had found two important paintings for Christie's to sell, with the words 'I hope these are not too much,' I laid notes of my expenses on Puddifoot's desk. Within the hour he came, I thought to reject them as too high with 'I can't accept these.' 'Oh Puddy,' I said reproachfully, 'they are what I spent.' 'I know, but when the auditors see how long you've been away and how little you've charged, they'll start questioning the directors' expenses.' I do not know how he got the sum, adjusted to almost £1,000 unsupported by bills, past the auditors, but he assured me that it was still well short of what Patrick would have spent and that I must never undercut him by so much again. On a trip to Switzerland the following year I based myself in the Baur au Lac in Zürich.

I wrote to Monsieur Joly in whose hunting-lodge I had identified the Rubens, explained in detail my certainty that it was an autograph sketch, proposed that it was worth a considerable sum and asked him to send it to London for sale. When it arrived, Bill was uncertain and Patrick dismissive. I was instructed to show it to Michael Jaffé, then already well on his way to becoming the most published expert on Rubens and, by constant self-declaration far the most important. A prominent post-graduate student at the Courtauld Institute in my first incarnation, he then occasionally appeared in a black leather jacket and tight pale blue jeans, and it was said by Francis Hawcroft (one of his peers and later Principal Keeper of the Whitworth Gallery, Manchester) that he haunted Hyde Park at night in search of sadistic sex. Of this raffishness there was not the slightest hint – the professorial Jaffé was as exquisitely suited and overcoated as his city banker ancestors when he came to see the sketch hanging in the large and well-lit room that I had been newly given at the top of the main stairs. Now stout, his corset creaked as he bent to peer into its grisaille subtleties. Within seconds he turned to me with 'Why do you waste my time?' and went on to say that he could see in it nothing to support an attribution to Rubens, that it was not even by a pupil or close follower, and left. Blushing with chagrin, I told Bill. He suggested that I should say nothing to Patrick, who had probably forgotten the matter, but return the painting to Joly with an apology and an offer to pay all the charges involved in sending it to us.

A second blow swiftly followed. Hans Backer brought the Modigliani to London and showed it to Bill. It was, I suppose, not unreasonable to want an opinion more authoritative than mine – if wrong about Rubens, on whose work I still hankered to work for a PhD, I could be wrong about anything – though I doubt if he knew that forgeries of Modigliani had been made within five years of his death in 1920. He asked Oliver Brown to come and see it. Oliver was head of the Leicester Galleries, long established just off the south-east corner of Leicester Square, a firm that for more than half a century had dealt in contemporary French and British art – it had, for example, been first to exhibit a complete set of bronzes by Degas (in 1923) and landscapes by Kokoschka (in 1928). A Leicester Galleries label on the back of any painting is still regarded now, some forty years after the business closed, as a guarantee of quality, and I must argue that the firm, in constantly mounting exhibitions – the first one-man shows in Britain of Van Gogh, Cézanne, Matisse, Picasso (1921) and Klee – did more in its heyday for the education of the British public than the two absurdly celebrated exhibitions arranged by Roger Fry in 1910 and 1912, *Manet and the Post-Impressionists* and his *Second Post-Impressionist Exhibition*. Into his seventies, wobbly on his pins, profoundly deaf and given to uttering at the end of every sentence an interrogatory 'What?' in a throaty voice gurgling with accumulated spittle (inherited by his son, Nicholas), Oliver made an unconvincing show of expertise with the Roman Modigliani – 'I never met the man . . . I never gave him a one-man show . . . there are a lot of forgeries about . . . you must ask someone else . . . show it to Pfannstiel in Hamburg . . . '

Arthur Pfannstiel was, in 1929, the author of the first monograph on Modigliani and had ever since – though it was hardly an illuminating book – been regarded as an authority. Over a very wintry weekend in November I took the canvas to him. On the Friday evening he could not make up his mind, asked me to leave it with him and invited me to dinner the following day. On Saturday evening he still could not make up his mind; we had dinner, accompanied by his wife, and stayed late into the night in a telephone-table bar in the red light quarter. In such bars one sits at a numbered table either making calls to young women at other numbered tables or receiving them – my inexplicable discomfort caused the Pfannstiels much amusement. Back at their flat I was again asked to leave the Modigliani with them and, happy enough to spend another day prowling the museums of Hamburg, I agreed to pick it up on my way to the airport on Sunday evening. This I did, and still he would say neither yea or nay. I sensed that he wanted a fee and had earlier called Bill, but he told me not to offer payment and to refuse if asked for it – 'We never pay for expertise.' From Pfannstiel's obviously impoverished circumstances I could see that he needed to earn whatever he could, and when at last he suggested a fee, found it painful to repeat Bill's mantra; that he had not condemned it was of no help to me when reporting events to Patrick, who with some relish told Backer to take it back to Rome.

In fairness, I could see that the promise of a fee might well corrupt an expression of opinion and, by and large, it was sensible to ignore most certificates written on the backs of photographs, as was then the custom of the day. Max Friedländer, an ancient art historian whom I much admired and whose *Landscape, Portrait and Still Life* had consoled me as a subaltern, abjured almost all his late certificates; those written before 1933, he told me, were his true uninfluenced opinion, but after being forced by the Nazis to leave the Berlin Gemälde Museum of which he was Director and in which he had worked since 1896, he wrote certificates for cash. Lavish with praise, these were often for Jewish owners, the victims of forced sales, in the hope that Nazis would pay more for poor pictures with wonderful certificates; for Party Members, for whom he was compelled to write certificates for nothing, he wrote in such hyperbolic terms as might prompt the shrewd reader to realise the truth. I was soon to learn that American experts on Impressionist and Post-Impressionist painters, writing aesthetic or art historical assessments rather than certificates, expected to be paid as much as five per cent of the price realised if pictures were sold with their support.

In December 1962, among the Shorter Notices – those snippets of art historical information that are so valuable to other scholars but too slight to be the subject of a full-scale article – the *Burlington Magazine* published *An Ecce Homo by Rubens* and gave the painting a full page illustration. It was Monsieur Joly's sketch. As the writer of the note was only Marcel Röthlisberger, an art historian not known as an expert on Rubens, but on Claude, I assumed for a moment that in treading on an alien field he, like me three years before, had made a serious error of connoisseurship, but then I read the first line of his text: 'I am grateful to Professor Jaffé . . . for having most generously helped me with this note.' He went on to remark on its 'excellent, fresh preservation, the handling suggests that it is entirely by Rubens. It can be dated just before 1620 . . . it is not an engraver's model . . . Whether in painting this sketch Rubens was thinking of a large painting (which was never executed) remains an open question.' These were exactly the points I had made in my letter to Joly in 1959.

My stomach clenched at this proof of Jaffé's foul play. If Röthlisberger brought the sketch to his notice, he must have recognised it as the panel he had seen earlier in my room – he had a photograph and knew the owner's name – and should, with such a change of mind, have done the decent thing and ensured that I knew of it. My supposition is that he did change his mind but preferred to hand the discovery to Röthlisberger, 'most generously' helping to write the note with his own name prominent in the first line rather than relegated – as is customary – to a footnote in small print far below.

Within a year or so I saw the Modigliani again. The Italian owner, disappointed to the point of distaste, had sold it for nothing to an Italian dealer; he in turn had sold it to a Lebanese – the Lebanon was, in the 1960s, at peace and a centre of great wealth – and he had at once taken it to Pfannstiel; with his wholehearted confirmation of its authenticity, it returned to Christie's. I wrote him a reproachful note; his response was that he had not so much changed his mind as confirmed it – scant consolation for me.

There were experts in whom Christie's could absolutely trust; there were others whom we could not, knowing them to be rogues, but they were nevertheless acknowledged to be expert in particular fields and buyers expected us to consult them; and there were experts who fell into both categories, either concurrently or over time. Teddy Archibald, of the Maritime Museum at Greenwich, and David Piper, of the National Portrait Gallery, were indefatigable in their rounds of the London auction rooms early every Monday morning and could always be drawn into the warehouse to see paintings set aside for them, giving their opinions freely; Ben Nicolson, expert on Caravaggio and all his followers, was one of a number of scholars and academics with particular interests on whom I regularly called; and I kept notes of all Courtauld students working for higher degrees whose subjects and the market place were bound to coincide. All these gave us scrupulously honest help and advice, their quid pro quo the benefit of seeing things first and often of seeing them in the very short interval between their emerging from and returning to obscurity.

Of the known rogues, most were French. In Paris, Paul Pétridès held sway as sole agent over the uncannily prolific Maurice Utrillo, in his reclusive dotage a painter of increasingly wretched suburban views. For a full decade after the painter's death in 1955, his widow, Lucie, was involved with Pétridès in the certification of forgeries, many of which he included in the five-volume catalogue raisonné that he began to compile in 1959 (published in 1974). As an *Expert près la Douane* his certificates were legal documents, proof absolute that paintings were authentic, often supported by Lucie's 'recollections' of having seen her husband at work on them, but I was one of many put in the awkward position of feeling in our bones that we were dealing with forgeries, yet, certified as genuine, we could not refuse to sell them. Almost as often, it seemed, we dealt with this situation in reverse – that is, with genuine paintings that had a provenance reaching back to some respected German (and Jewish) dealer in the 1920s but could not be sold because Pétridès, though in charge of Utrillo only since 1937, refused to recognise them; one particularly sour example of this malpractice was the Utrillo belonging to Mrs Lisa Gurr (originally Goehr), the collector (by inheritance) whose generosity so enriched the Museum in Leicester with twentieth-century German paintings – this had an impeccable Flechtheim of Düsseldorf provenance even including the bill paid by her father, but this did not influence Pétridès.

Many years after my involvement in the art market had ended, after a case in 1979 in which he was found guilty of forging documents, Pétridès was sent to prison for three years; accused of issuing false certificates, dealing in fakes, misusing the title 'expert' and acquiring paintings from the Nazis during the Occupation, he was at last stripped of his right to issue certificates. All this, however, will be forgotten – if not already so – and his mendacious catalogue raisonné, seeming important in bulk and binding, will live on to support in perpetuity the hundreds of fakes commissioned by its author.

Alexandre Ananoff, less flamboyantly culpable, escaped with nothing worse than a damaged reputation. This silver-plated self-appointed expert on Boucher and Fragonard, much the same size and shape as Peter Chance and as immaculately presented, burst into my room one day and, having told me who and what he was, dumped on my desk a folder of drawings to be included in a sale. I leafed through them with misgiving, overwhelmed by the presence of the man. The papers were of the period, but the fringe damages seemed recent and deliberate; the images were possible for the eighteenth century but were, I thought, by a recent hand copying figures from paintings, and the drawing techniques, bold and crude, were of the twentieth century – one drawing, signed and dated 17FB22 (when Boucher, at 19, was employed as an engraver after Watteau) was absurdly coarse. But who was I to argue with the greatest expert in the field, who was I to refuse to sell a dozen drawings by these great *dix-huitième* masters, signed, dated and certified? I went to Bill, and at the mere mention of Ananoff he groaned. I went to Francis Watson and he uttered a strange high-pitched sound that was both snort and yelp. And when next I saw Ananoff, I was vigorously accused of ignorance, impertinence and malevolence.

With such downright dishonesty it was comparatively easy to deal, but with betrayal it was not. Philip Pouncey, Deputy Keeper of Prints and Drawings in the British Museum, was another regular visitor, as much interested in obscure and unattributable paintings as in the drawings I was supposed always to show him, but after hearing too often his quip that 'an attribution a day keeps depression away,' usually uttered when the artist proposed was too recondite ever to be checked, I began to lose my trust and think his cleverness one-upmanship. I lost trust altogether when a beautiful drawing by Jan Brueghel, the only decent thing in a wretched sale that I had had to pull together, flopped. Bumping into Hans Calmann, a dealer in old master drawings who would have been engaging had he not been quite so overbearing, wilful and dismissive, I asked why he and almost every other dealer in the field had sat on their hands and let it be bought for nothing. 'Ah,' he said, 'You didn't know? Pouncey wanted it, and he warned us off with the threat that he'd never again give us help if any of us thwarted him.'

There was a worse betrayal, more calculated, directly personal. Lot 71 in the sale of paintings on 19 June 1959 was a *Road to Calvary*,

attributed to Polidoro. I had catalogued it as indubitably by Polido
Caldara da Caravaggio, a short-lived labourer in the Vatican under
Raphael, an unfettered and idiosyncratic mind, an imagination dark
and never genial. This remarkable rarity I showed to Pouncey. He
disagreed. His immediate and very strong reaction was that this
appalling daub, grotesquely unrefined, had nothing of Polidoro's
qualities to commend it; I felt compelled to downgrade it to mere
attribution, and, as nothing but a fumbled copy, made no mention
of its obvious links with an altarpiece in Capodimonte.

The bidding stopped at 48 guineas (£50.40) and the picture
was bought by F. T. Dent, a dealer notorious for buying trifles
unconsidered and disdained by other dealers. The sum was so
much lower than I had expected – a tenth of my annual income –
that I immediately asked him if he would sell it on to me for a small
profit. 'Can't do that, my boy, I bought it on commission.' Ten
years later, by which time I had left Christie's and Pouncey had
become a leading director of Sotheby's, he asked me to dinner, and
as a pre-prandial treat showed me his treasures. Of these the most
astonishing, the most shocking indeed, was the Polidoro over one
of his many mantlepieces. I did not stay for dinner. I did not speak
to him again. It was he for whom Dent had acted on commission.
He stole from me some small credit as an art historian, stole credit
from Christie's, a firm that trusted and admired him, and in his
deceit, stole from the owner of the painting. After his death his
estate sold it to the National Gallery for £500,000; as Assistant
Keeper there for eleven years he must have known in 1959 what a
valuable addition to the national collection it would be, but instead
of going hot foot to Trafalgar Square to tell them what had been
discovered, he kept it to himself.

Buried in Christie's archives there is, I hope, a brief correspondence with Picasso that I should, perhaps, have kept. I sent him
a photograph of a drawing that had been greeted with suspicion,
for it was an isolated offering from a vendor of whom Christie's
knew nothing and who could supply no provenance, but I felt it

worth pursuing. The photograph was returned, the word FAUX scrawled large between diagonal lines across it, with a signature. This, from Picasso himself, should have been the last word, but I was still puzzled and spent hours leafing through material in the Courtauld Institute until I found it reproduced in, I think, a *Cahier d'Art* of 1934. I wrote again. I wish I could recall precisely Picasso's answer – it was a French equivalent of David Carritt's favourite apology 'Hey Ho! Silly me.'

*   *   *

David Carritt did not join Christie's until January 1963, but it was in 1959 that John Herbert began to campaign for the board to appoint an internationally known expert to join the picture department and David was their eventual choice. That there was such a campaign made it clear that no one on the board – not even John, whom I had thought my ally – thought of me as an expert in that sense, though it would have been easy enough to build on the scholarly connections I had made in France and Germany before I joined the firm and that I was keeping in good repair. Instead, I was the drudge who dealt with weekly sales, occasionally retrieved from the troglodytic conditions of the warehouse to perform clever parlour tricks. Peter Chance took me with him to Ireland to make a valuation of the paintings at Birr Castle, Offaly, the home of the Earl of Rosse, an old school friend (it was on many such old loyalties that the prosperity of Christie's had come to depend); Anne Rosse, his wife and earlier the mother of Anthony Armstrong-Jones, said of me to her husband when I was midway through the task, 'Oh darling, dear Mr Sewell is saying such darling things about our pictures,' but such esteem was not enough to make me seem, even in Peter's eyes, an expert. Nor was my saving a very different situation first thing another morning, when he whisked me off in his Bentley to placate a west country nobleman whose Van Dycks Patrick had just valued for insurance at enormous figures, sending the bill in a scale related to the total sum, not realising that the portraits were copies made when Duveen had bought the originals at the beginning of the century. It was my job to save Patrick's face and keep the client's business. This I did by praising the quality of the copies, by attributing them to Pierre Coulette, Duveen's most skilful forger (to put no fine point on it), by praising the original frames that lent such weight to the deception – themselves worth many thousands – even by saying that the household wear and tear of open fires and tobacco smoke had given them a patina of age that any expert might think dated back for centuries; but throughout this placatory dissimulation I was aware of an odd protocol – I was there, not to speak to his lordship, but to tell Peter what to say, which he did with an even more conciliatory gloss and a dozen Chinese whispers that I could not correct. Between us we left this heir to bogus family portraits with the impression that his copies were infinitely superior to the originals – Van Dyck, when all is said and done, I said, was only a fashionable hack – reduced the bill to nothing and saved the day, but I remained puzzled by the business of my being the oracle but somehow socially unfit to talk to noblemen. There were to be other valuations by Patrick to redeem, other noblemen to whom I was deemed unfit to speak, even occasions when Christie's partners were asked to lunch but their dogsbody sent off to the local pub to fend for himself.

I had, however, begun to find my independent feet in the field of drawings by old masters, an area of connoisseurship in which Patrick could not even pretend to have an eye. In this I depended very much on the help of a trade that was largely in the hands of dealers who had earlier been art historians or were, at least, trained in the discipline, scholars of Austrian and German-Jewish origin who traded from their homes and occasionally mounted small exhibitions at the Alpine Gallery in South Audley Street. A few of their more fortunate peers had joined the Warburg Institute or taught me at the Courtauld, and I was immediately at ease with them, their knowledge and their judgement; apart from the Old Bond Street firm of Colnaghi's, then under the saintly wing of James Byam-Shaw (their match in scholarship), they were the only dealers in any area of the art trade in whom the innocent might put his trust. All are now gone, and the few who remember them have left too late the worthy business of recording their brief presence in London in the decades between *c.*1935 and *c.*1975 when they exercised so civilising a presence on the trade.

Herbert Bier (1905–1981) was the quiet and unassuming grandee among them; with work at the Kaiser Friedrich Museum and the Alte Pinakotek behind him, he came to London in 1935 – earlier than many who fled the Nazis – and was able to establish museum contacts here and in America that bore fruit after the war when he dealt at the highest level. Incapable of deceit, he was a man whom both the inexperienced collector and the callow employee of an auction house could trust. Hans Calmann (1899–1992) was in every sense his opposite; tall, broad-shouldered, blustering, he was so often given to standing over me like a vulture, telling me that I was mistaken in an attribution when I knew absolutely that I was right, that I was confused – that is until I realised that this was nothing but a ploy to make me miscatalogue a drawing, not for his advantage, but for malicious fun. He bought many good drawings and made huge profits, but was deeply flawed in his obstinate belief in his own attributions; for these he had no foundation in scholarship but attempted to browbeat the relevant experts into supporting them – and woe betide any who offered him the slightest support out of politeness, for even the most grudging 'I suppose it might . . . ' would be used as wholehearted agreement. This manipulation brought him into many conflicts and at the end of his life few art historians, museum curators and fellow dealers had much respect for him, though they might like him as a man, enjoy his hospitality and feel for him over the death of his son John. It was a wry thing that he so frequently voiced contempt for homosexuals and accused all Englishmen with being tainted by the vice, yet it was John's promiscuous homosexual activity that brought about his violent death near Avignon in April 1980.

Of Lili Fröhlich (she at last dropped the hyphenated -Bum), at the pathetic other extreme of this group, my fond memories are oppressed by guilt. Older than the others – her magnum opus on Parmigianino was published in 1921, and in 1959 she may well have been eighty – tiny, bent, her notable nose enlarged with age, and her command of English (learned too late) slipping away from her, she tottered round sales with the help of a stick, encumbered by a huge handbag that made leafing through the folders and solander boxes hazardous for the drawings they contained. And there's another thing – Christie's, until I joined the firm, showed drawings in flimsy paper folders and I had to beg them to commission stout folders and solander boxes as a conservation measure. Lili never bought anything on the day of an auction, but took small shares of things bought by friends on her advice. When I first knew her, in her gloomy flat on Parliament Hill she held a small stock of intriguing drawings that I could take back to Christie's, but after a while everything she had was recently familiar and my visits became infrequent. After one long gap I telephoned Peter Claas, the dealer in drawings who had introduced us, and suggested that we go together. 'Oh. Didn't you know?' he said.

There were, perhaps, a dozen others eking a living on the fringes of this market, dependent on the vestiges of scholarship founded many years before, decent, civilised and sad. They were part of the overwhelming influx of Central European culture in the later Thirties that bore fruit during and after the war in chamber and orchestral music, opera, theatre, literature, philosophy, the visual arts and critical argument that so transformed, enriched and enlivened our native cultural activities – a cultural revolution now utterly forgotten by those who command the wilful mediocrities that are the BBC and the Arts Council, the very institutions in whose hands the arts then flourished, affecting and enhancing all our lives. With so much continuing emphasis on the horrors of the Holocaust, it has slipped from our minds that in this unintended consequence the Jews who escaped the Nazis and came here, gave us a second Enlightenment.

With new solander boxes in hand, as early as July 1959 I put together a sale built largely on my vigilant sorting of miscellaneous consignments, but it also contained the properties of three people whom I knew – so much for Alec Martin's jibe 'We know you've no social connections.' John Brophy, the father of Brigid Brophy and himself a writer, was an indefatigable collector of drawings, most of them worthless rubbish, but with careful dredging it had been possible to assemble a handful that shamed neither him nor me. Frida Brackley, the devoutly Christian granddaughter of Ludwig Mond, the industrialist whose bequest to the National Gallery ranged from undoubted masterpieces to irretrievable wrecks, had inherited part of his small collection of drawings. Sitting by her bedside – she was always in bed when I dashed up to Blakeney from Castle Hedingham to see her – I wondered if she had ever walked the short distance to Walsingham, for its nearness to this pilgrimage site had been her reason for buying so ordinary a house. I also found it difficult to believe that she needed the little money that her drawings would bring, for, like her grandfather's pictures, many were not what they had been thought to be – but she was in a constant state of anguish about her wealth (or lack of it – I never knew quite which) and seemed to relish the torment of betraying her grandfather by shedding the last scraps of his collection for more prayers and candles at the Shrine of our Lady to which, emotionally, she had become umbilically attached.

The third of my contributors to this humdrum sale was Dr William Crofton who owned a sketchbook by Domenico Becca-fumi to which I had been alerted by a note in the *Burlington Magazine* in December 1957. I bearded him in his huge house in Regent's Park, hoping that he might have other treasures. He did. The walls of hall, stairs, passages and every room were crowded cheek-by-jowl with canvases that pretended to be by Corot,

Constable and Turner. The Corots were uniformly glaucous, the Constables were impastose masses of dark green, and in every one of the supposed Turners a sunset shrieked in flaming agony. Not one was genuine and I dared not ask how one collector could have been so utterly seduced by three forgers – for all the Corots were by a single hand and the Constables and Turners by two others – and yet not be suspicious of the improbability. Amongst all this the intriguing sketchbook was a lost soul. It was also something of a disappointment (as Beccafumi so often is); incoherent in date and subject, the studies undoubtedly by Beccafumi interspersed with a few by other hands, I was not wholly convinced that it was even a sketchbook in the conventional sense and thought it a gathering of sheets bound, perhaps posthumously, by a pupil or workshop assistant – the binding pages offered no clue.

Crofton did not want to sell it – 'I'd rather sell a Constable or Turner.' I asked what he thought it might be worth and £1,500 was his answer – I had the impression that he had snatched this figure from the air as an absurdly demanding price that would put an end to the discussion. I accepted it as his reserve and then asked if I might separate the pages and sell each separately if everyone agreed that it was a compilation rather than a sketchbook once held in Beccafumi's hand. He was horrified, but I sensed that he was warming to the idea of selling it – 'Sell any of your paintings and you'll have to re-hang your walls,' I argued, 'sell this and no one will notice.' At last I came away with it, though I feared that he might change his mind – and he did, but only by raising his reserve at the last minute on the morning of the sale, to £2,000. In the event, Agnew's bought it for 4,800 guineas, a trifle over £5,000, and some years later broke it up for an exhibition from which they sold it page by page.

It was far from an important sale, though that term was used in the title of the catalogue; nevertheless, it was important for me, for in the wake of the Skippe sale it proved that Christie's could have an independent specialist department in old master drawings and, subsequently, in English drawings and watercolours, in nineteenth-century works on paper, and in prints. No one thanked me for it and Patrick was never to let go of his conviction that he was as much in charge of these as of every other aspect of the picture department. My Latinity is now frail; even so, I perhaps do Terence no injustice in translating a quip from his *Adelphoe* as 'never is anyone more unjust than the ignorant.'

CHAPTER 13

Abandoning God

There was in 1959 a change in my life far more important than any happening at Christie's – a change essential for my sanity. Deliberate observation of my religious duties had continued since my graduation in spite of my then immediate change of course, for I was by no means certain that the change was permanent, but it was as a dry discipline, scarcely spiritual and much troubled by my sexuality. One Sunday morning in the spring, however, on my way to Mass at the Carmelites in Church Street, a little early, I walked on and into Kensington Gardens by the passage through York Place, and there I challenged God. A sudden inspiration, there is no other word for it – I challenged him to give me a sign of some sort. In a one-sided conversation I told him that he had had my physical chastity (insofar as anyone else was involved) since I joined the army more than seven years before, that I had willingly given it in the expectation of becoming a priest, though I had found chastity of the imagination impossible to achieve, and that this, now more turbulent than ever, was separating me from the Church. I sat on a bench on the Broad Walk and let pass the hour of Mass. I wandered through the arched espaliered trees of the sunken garden, familiar from my earliest childhood, recalling lines from Francis Thompson's *Hound of Heaven*, a favourite poem as a boy, and compared his conviction that he could not escape the hound, with mine that the Dog of God had lost my scent. I returned to Phillimore Place with no further thought of Mass and have not since been a communicant.

Oddly disappointed not to have had a Pauline revelation, not even the staying hand of an angel vouchsafed Abraham, there was no obvious step to take. Homosexual activity of any kind was illegal and 'importuning male persons', a common offence much reported in newspapers, meant immediate social disgrace and, quite probably, loss of employment. I knew that there were pubs and drinking clubs with queer reputations, but not their names and whereabouts; and I also knew that there were the streets. That night I walked the length of Church Street idly inspecting the windows of antique shops. Exactly as I thought I might, with an exchange of glances I caught a man and took him home. Older by some years he was quickly efficient, but I doubt if it was much fun for him; for me the business was less erotic than mechanical and left me profoundly disappointed, asking myself if this could really be the alternative to chastity. By chance, a few days later, on the New Books shelf of the local library I found a novel by James Courage, *A Way of Love*. I can recall nothing of the plot, only that it was for its time a liberating tale suggesting that homosexuality could indeed be more than just the sexual acts. I wrote to him. He asked me to tea on Saturday, and to this mild man, elderly, precise, I said enough to make him think I wanted him to pimp for me – to which his response was 'Well, your golden years have passed you by.' He did, however, introduce me to a pretty youth whose golden years had not, but undressed, from his belly-button almost to his knees he was coal black, for the climax of his recent induction ceremony as an apprentice printer had been the dunking of his buttocks in a vat of ink. After all my years of abstinence, to have a willing boy in my hands should have been an explosive release, but I found the aesthetic disruption sexually unmanageable. Years later much the same thing happened when undressing a butch little toughie, only to find him clad in a woman's scarlet underclothes. Courage then introduced me to an Australian boy of my own age with whom I had some shared intellectual interests, but for whom my pent-up affection was far too demanding – unlike me, he was not wholly queer and eventually married and had children; we perfectly illustrated lines (slightly paraphrased) from Cavafy (Rae Dalven's translation was reissued yet again in 1959) – 'the consummation was lacking that must be intensely desired by both – we were not both equally given to deviant sensual pleasure. I alone it had utterly mastered.' I owe him something for his tolerance and much more for what he did for me beyond his bed, for he lived in Hampstead and his introducing me to his friends there led directly to lifelong friendship with the photographer John Vere Brown and, through the intersection of queer circles, to something approaching friendship with Keith Vaughan, the painter.

The most important instrument of my metamorphosis from celibate to whore was Eric Bewsey. Eric, a civil servant two or three years my senior, was wholly at ease with his sexuality and neither blazoned nor concealed it. Devoutly sensual, sex was for him as necessary as food and drink and he was as expert in finding casual partners as he was in preparing delicious simple suppers. I was one of his mistakes. After a few minutes on his bed he said 'You've got the flattest belly in the business, but you're hopeless.' He then undertook my sexual education: he would give me, he said, precisely three months to learn everything he could teach me of sex between men, every trick, every practice (though some of the more arcane now popular had not then been devised), disrupting every conventional notion of what is passive and what active, separating pleasure from love, distinguishing the satisfaction of sexual desire from emotion. Whatever I might think of these things I must learn that they are done and might one day be expected of me – that indeed, I too might expect them. This course of instruction was a roller-coaster of nights on which I reached from ecstasy to disgust, that taught me a great deal about my body and, by extension, the bodies of those with whom I might find myself; and I learned that sex ranges from tenderness to violence, from the short and sharp to the night long, from the security of the bedroom to the thrilling risky business of doing it while standing up in a canoe, and that the opportunist must make his opportunities. Eric was abashed by nothing; his preference was for the long, slow and tender at home with the body beautiful, but if a uniformed policeman in a dark alley was available, then this was a dish most fiercely spiced. Three months to the day the teaching ended and never again did I share a bed with Eric, but our friendship lasted until he fell in love – promiscuity is no bar to that – and he dropped us all to depart with his lover to New Zealand. His London friends were largely literary and, as is the way of these things, I subsequently slept on many a bed of letters before moving on to freedom.

Letters intersected with the arts and parties given by both offered opportunities to intersect with the men of pursuits and interests who were their friends and lovers, current and discarded, cutting across all barriers of class – indeed, the barriers were for some the erotic stimulus for sexual relationships. Three young men living in the rambling basement of Christabel Aberconway's house in North Audley Street held parties almost every Saturday of which she must have known, though perhaps, as a celebrated hostess between the wars and the mistress of Samuel Courtauld, she was amused to see how little had changed in this peripheral department of the demi-monde. Jack Harriman, one of Eric's friends, troubled about his sexuality and desperate to cast aside his doubts, was another regular party-giver in a mews cottage near Portman Square, miserably surrendering to alcohol when all his guests paired with each other and abandoned him. To these gatherings we were expected to take a bottle of wine for immediate consumption and a friend to exchange for the night. Much the same entry fee was charged at not quite so frequent orgies in Emperor's Gate and Little Venice. At these the sexual activity was immediate, common, multiple and public, and beginning at once, might last till morning; at one of them, in Little Venice, there was a posse of London Transport staff and for weeks after I had assignations with a bus driver on the 46 route that meant my waiting at a particular bus stop for him to whisk me off to the terminus in Wembley; at another there was a policeman based in Hyde Park who, infatuated, entertained me throughout the summer with theatre tickets given gratis to his station – never opera, always musicals or Saturday Night at the Palladium – until, with relief, I broke the contact by going to Rome with Helen.

In all this there was always considerable risk and yet not once was there a betrayal of which I am aware – though betrayals there must have been, for these circles reached across London and beyond (as any casual visitor to the old Turkish baths of Greenwich and Bermondsey must have known). There were too the contacts made in the open, effected with nothing more than a glance, a turn of the head and a pause in the stride – all so easy once one had the knack. The easiest place for this was the street, any street a happy hunting-ground, but it worked in a bus queue too, scanning the oncoming walkers, and in the Underground or walking the aisle to descend from the top deck of a bus. At weekends museums and galleries were the encountering points, none better, even on a fine Sunday afternoon, than the free-standing glass cases of the V&A. One exhibition there, of Italian Bronze Statuettes in 1961, produced a particularly rich crop of casual lovers, and I realise now that the exhibition catalogues that crowd my bookshelves are as much reminders of such episodes as records useful for the jobbing art historian. With so much sex so easily available, I wonder if Eric Bewsey was the God-given sign for which I asked. Meanwhile Helen, for three years so important in my life and wholly unaware of all this, though made miserable by my deliberate detachment, was offered a job at an American university that led to a jolly husband, three boisterous sons and half a lifetime in the Boston Museum of Fine Arts. We are still friends.

*   *   *

On 10 July 1959 the Arts Council's exhibition *The Romantic Movement* opened at the Tate Gallery – just short of a thousand exhibits (Arts Councillors now should look at such a great national and international event and compare what the Council achieved in the past with its current futile and transitory exhibitions). I recall it not only for its marvellous self, but for two episodes associated with it – the opening of the case in which Delacroix's *Massacre at Chios* had been sent from Paris, and my second encounter with John Vere Brown. I had been asked by the authorities at the Louvre to be present when the great Delacroix was delivered and to check its condition. To my surprise the painting had been taken off its stretcher, rolled, and slotted into a long coffin of a case, the lid of which had been nailed down, not screwed, as one might expect; as this was prised away it was clear that some of the nails had not been driven their full length into the sides of the box, but had curved inwards, in some cases perforating the canvas. Two days later I was again at the Tate when a restorer from the Louvre came to inspect the punctures and, if possible, execute a running repair; this he did with tiny pellets of malleable wax applied with a palette knife and moulded to comply with the surrounding textures, a temporarily effective method that I had not been taught in my brief weeks in the Courtauld Institute's technology department. When I saw the painting again a year later, I could discern no trace of these small damages.

I had a season ticket to the exhibition – ten shillings, fifty pence – and was there the day after first meeting John Vere Brown, for whom I had at once developed a powerful dislike at dinner with the Australian boy, and to whom I had been pretty abrupt before leaving early. John – a painter who wanted to be a portrait photographer and a photographer who wanted to be a landscape painter – was a slightly Quasimodo figure with the head of a late ancient Roman emperor and a voice that combined the pseudo-cockney affectations of the Edwardian beau with the mew of a cat and the shriek of a parrot, larding his language with fuck and its derivatives as often as any illiterate workman. It was this voice that I heard from many rooms away: he was with his elderly mother, tiny and profoundly deaf, to whom he was explaining paintings with such extraordinary sympathy that my dislike was overturned. I apologised for my misbehaviour, and that apology laid the foundation of a close and lasting friendship – not entirely unruffled, but always repaired after a spat – that enriched both our lives until his death in 2000.

It was indirectly through John – intersecting circles again – that I met Keith Vaughan, a distinguished painter whose innumerable lightly abstracted compositions of male nudes, singly and in various contiguities, were as lightly homo-erotic – so lightly indeed that most who purchased them hardly noticed the probabilities they deftly camouflaged. His small drawings in gouache particularly stated his sexual preference, their honesty gently pleading their cause without blatant propaganda. Many grew from the haunting imagery in his mind's eye as well as from studies of a younger lover for whom – unfairly – his affection turned to hate, Ramsay McClure, one of his students at the Central School in 1948, whose large rounded skull is instantly recognisable even if his puny body has been idealised to heroic proportions. Ramsay he made utterly miserable, but through mental cruelty rather than any putting into practice his sadistic fantasies, and I, over some months, had to comfort the weeping man (though I always saw him as a boy) with long-drawn hugs. For one of these episodes – in which it seemed they might destroy their strange and strained relationship and I had whisked Ramsay away for a chaste weekend – Keith gave me two prints by Picasso, the subjects ballet boys, that I believe were things of some early influence. I drifted out of their lives after I left Christie's and had little time for anything other than building a new life of my own; Keith, stricken with cancer, committed suicide in November 1977, and Ramsay died, as much of misery as anything, four years later, his life destroyed by love. I learned from them that love can be extraordinarily cruel and destructively submissive, that love of a sort can remain long after the sexual interest is extinguished, and that lovers can be lovers for years without ever understanding each the other's needs and wants – Keith was both a sadist and a masochist, tormenting himself with whip and thong while longing for a victim, but Ramsay was neither and did not know how to gratifyingly respond. Only in Keith's confession that he spent two thirds of his waking hours dwelling on sexual matters, did I find some reassurance.

In 1959 I launched into a life of such promiscuity as might suggest that I was making up for the golden years that had passed me by, for the opportunities lost in the arid years of denial, but it was sheer intoxication with the sudden ease of it and the abandonment of guilt. It was not unusual to pick up a companion on my way home – Cléo de cinq à sept, so to speak – to have had a fuck one way or the other and be home having a bath by seven, then to go and see my current lover (duration three days to three weeks, perhaps), and on the way home to pick up someone else with whom either to have a quickie before bed or take home for the night – which usually meant another perfunctory fuck first thing in the morning. Throw in a few Jack Rabbit weekends and all this might amount to a thousand fucks a year and easily a thousand sexual partners in a quinquennium. Now, when both times and I have changed, my first thought when seeming strangers begin a conversation with 'You won't remember me, but . . . ' is that half a century ago we had a sexual encounter that meant more to him than me – but the blankness of my mind is only another bout of the prosopagnosia with which all my life I have been cursed, the face-blindness, the near inability to distinguish one face from another when out of the context in which it is familiar.

It was at a party early in 1961 that I met Peter Norris, a young Canadian poet; tall, his skin so pale it was as though it had never seen the light, his eyes a startling dark blue, his curly hair a reddish gold well short of ginger, at twenty-four or so his beauty was androgynous, Pre-Raphaelite. He let slip that he had just parted from a much older man, a Greek racing driver named Embiricos of whom I knew, though only because in 1939 he had been the famous owner of a famous Bentley of that period, an astonishing aerodynamic Bentley by Pourtout, a great Parisian coachbuilder who in this car anticipated the post-war designs of Enzo Ferrari. It may seem odd, but there was a certain frisson in taking on the boyfriend of Embiricos. There was also risk – though not of some vengeful Aeschylean tragedy with me the victim; their parting had left Peter emotionally damaged, unstable, difficult, even inconsolable – and he was, too, a poet, given to unaccountable disappearances into himself – but his ethereal beauty was reward enough for me as he lay sated in the lamplight that drifted in from the street, for me he was Endymion. Our friendship did not end until his death in the 1990s, but our relationship as lovers came to a sudden and appalling halt when, late in 1961, at a party given by Richard Hughes-Hallett, he slashed his wrists. Richard's flat was a rambling basement round the light well of a small block in Palace Gate, and through the bathroom window two boys who had gone into the well to smoke saw Peter and the blood; gatecrashers, they did not know whose flat it was and rather than waste time it was they who broke down the door, they who, with me, knelt on the floor and tried to stem the blood until an ambulance arrived.

In St Stephen's hospital I stayed with him until I was sure that he would survive and then returned to Richard's flat, intending to deal with the mess, but other than the shattered door-frame there was no trace of it. The boys who had seen Peter's attempted suicide had sluiced and mopped the bathroom and were still there, for the party was still going strong.

One, Sicilian, spoke only very broken English, but fluent French and German, and after a helter-skelter conversation in any language in which we knew the words, I was, if not enchanted, then mightily amused. He was not handsome; tall and almost fair-haired, he did not even look Italian – an ancient Norman strain, perhaps. He came from Taormina and was the very last of a line that had governed the town for a thousand years before the unification of Italy and the new nobility of Victor Emmanuel II displaced the old in 1861. The Marchese Corvaya was then dispossessed, the Palazzo Corvaya became municipal offices, and the family moved to an unpreposessing villa on the city's edge and faded into bleak obscurity; that Marchese was Claudio Corvaya's great-grandfather, a lesser Lampedusa leopard.

When Peter Norris's physical wounds were sufficiently healed, he returned to Canada to fall into the hands of a good woman and write bad poetry. Claudio moved into his place. It was, at first, an almost casual relationship, its irregularity forced on us by his employment with CIT, the Italian state tourist agency, always dashing back to Italy or being shunted off to Spain and Switzerland (he spoke as perfectly as Hochdeutsch the Swiss guttural corruption, Schweizerdeutsch), leaving me to be promiscuous. Perhaps because of these partings, the enmeshing of our lives was so slow that we did not realise how strong our loyalties and longings were becoming. With Phillimore Place his pied-à-terre, it seemed quite rational to take him to Castle Hedingham to equally enchant my mother – 'Isn't he hateful,' they said to each other when I was difficult, laughing and hugging. For seven years we were to be content.

*   *   *

When my stepfather died in May 1962, leaving my mother penniless, I was determined that she should stay in her house in Castle Hedingham because I could not bear the thought of losing my freedom by bringing her back to London to live with me. I was, however, under notice to leave Phillimore Place because Mrs Chesterton had died in January and the house was to be sold, but this, after some months of misery and misfortune, brought me a stroke of luck. I found a small Pooterish house near Westbourne Grove for £7,000, which, with a mortgage and lodgers I could almost afford – the necessity for lodgers compelled the exclusion of my mother. An American PhD student at the Courtauld lodged in what he described as the *piano nobile* sitting room, an art student took the small back room on that floor, Claudio and I occupied two rooms on the first floor and John Morrish the third, finding his

Blackheath house inconvenient for working at Christie's; we all shared the bathroom and the kitchen. It was hell. In addition, in the long half year that we were there, burglars broke in three times, my car was vandalised as often, and the Westbourne River (the source of the Serpentine in Hyde Park), long buried in a crumbling conduit beneath the house, twice invaded it through the basement floor. I was in despair when luck came in the shape of a middle-aged couple who knocked on the door one Sunday afternoon and asked if I had just moved in, or might be leaving, so dishevelled looked the house. Whatever their reasons for offering me £14,500 on condition that I was out within a week, I did not question them and did exactly that, paid back the mortgage and returned to Phillimore Place when I learned that for the sake of Mrs Chesterton's housekeeper-companion the house had not been sold and might not be for some time.

I had profited by seven years of my salary in as many months and for the first time felt at ease in the worldly world of Christie's; moreover, I could afford to keep my mother in her house and thus retain my treasured independence from her. Pious, banal and silly things are said about the relative unimportance of money. To me my puny profit was a fortune; it freed me from penny-pinching and my total dependence on my income from Christie's; it let me buy books and catalogues and begin to establish the working library that was to become the essential tool of my career as an art critic; it allowed me to travel without always having to key my journeys to work for Christie's, to fly my car over the Channel and dash to exhibitions in France, Germany and the Low Countries, and it bought and maintained the succession of slightly flamboyant cars in which I then took foolish pleasure, Daimlers of some age and character. With most of it wisely invested, that ludicrously small sum of money changed my life. From the grim prospect that had confronted me on Robert's death I was, within a year, released.

CHAPTER 14

Christie's in the Doldrums

It could be argued that in the early months of 1960, with Bill's perhaps unexpected return to Christie's, the *status quo ante* should also have returned, but this was made impossible by the planned sale of a collection of seventeenth-century Dutch paintings consigned from Holland by the ageing Dr C. J. K. van Aalst. This was the only important sale on the firm's horizon and Patrick had assumed absolute command of it, effectively side-lining Bill who had neither the energy nor will to assert his position as head of the department. Among these paintings was one by Rembrandt of the goddess *Juno*, an allegorical portrait of a woman too handsome to be Dutch, dark-eyed and full-lipped enough to be Italian, an ermine cloak over her broad shoulders, held there by jewels too fabulous to be anything other than theatrical junk from the property boxes that we know he kept. For this Patrick instructed John Herbert to tell the press that the expected price was £100,000 or so – then still an astonishing sum. Though naive reporters were impressed, the mocking scepticism of the trade roused their misgivings and when they turned to Bill he characteristically expressed his honest doubt. Asked by an *Evening Standard* reporter what I thought of it, I said that it had been so crushingly relined that Rembrandt's distinctive impastose brushwork might be discerned more easily on the back of the relining canvas than in any surface that we could see, which resembled ancient and well-polished linoleum – true, but I should have remained silent.

In the event on April Fool's day, the bidding dried up at £50,000 with most of us convinced that Peter Chance – the head of the firm lending his lustre to what he had been told was a most important sale – had not received a single bid from anyone in the room. Though other paintings in the sale did well, the embarrassment caused by the failure of the *Juno* before the television cameras and reporters assembled by John Herbert was damagingly public; Patrick, of course, showed not the least sign of humiliation. My feeling was that he had rushed into the sale for Christie's short term benefit and had not given van Aalst the advice that he should. The *Juno* was in a condition widely thought acceptable between the wars but not a generation later; the flattening of brushwork caused by relining could not have been reversed, but the canvas should have been stripped of its glutinous varnish to remove a veil from Rembrandt's robust and daring handling of paint, to let the whites startle with their freshness and reveal the subtleties of colour lost in the darkened tonal gloom. Even in the hands of the most conscientious restorer this surface treatment would have delayed the sale only by two months, and there might well have been some benefit in scheduling it late in June, traditionally the high point of the saleroom season. There is another possible explanation for the flop, concealed from us by van Aalst but known in the trade – that *Juno* had already been offered to museums and art dealers in Holland as a national treasure and that no deal had been done, for in those days, when significant paintings were by no means rare, none was more tarnished than one that had been traded but not sold. Years later, cleaned more or less as I wish I had been able to suggest, it now hangs in Los Angeles, an undoubted treasure of the Hammer Museum, worth every penny of Patrick's estimate mutiplied two hundred times.

In May, Bill – still the boss I had to ask for leave – let me escape to Paris with Anthony Blunt for the opening of his great and unprecedented Poussin exhibition at the Louvre, a gathering of 120 paintings, 120 drawings and one sculpture in wax. I drove him to Paris. Earlier in the year I had blown the engine of my old Wolseley attempting to maintain 70 mph on the new M1 – conrods through the engine block, the most dramatic and catastrophic of failures –

and had replaced it with an eight year old Daimler Special Sports, a very pretty drop-head coupé built by Barker that waffled along quite happily at speeds mortal for the Wolseley. I was intrigued to notice that Anthony had no reaction to anything that I or any other driver did, nor any to the rare epicyclic gearchange and pre-selector lever on the steering column that invariably intrigued drivers aware only of synchromesh and crash gearboxes; this convinced me that he could not drive, yet in my first incarnation at the Courtauld we all knew the tale of his driving a yellow Railton – a car as fast as it was rare – to Rome, and abandoning it, boiling, in a traffic jam just within the Porta del Popolo. I observe in passing that in the Beaulieu Motor Museum there is a photograph of a yellow Railton mud-plugging in the 1938 Cambridge University Automobile Trial, with Donald Maclean at the wheel.

In mid afternoon we reached the Louvre and scampered upstairs to the exhibition of which the scholarly purpose was to establish a chronology of Poussin's work with which all interested scholars could broadly agree, the early years of his development long a matter of uncomprehending and often spiteful controversy. Miranda Carter, author of Anthony's one biography,[26] has it that he had for several weeks been in Paris supervising the hanging of paintings lent by museums in East Berlin, Dresden, Leningrad and Moscow, none of which he could have seen since 1939, and from Florida and California, perhaps never seen, as well as those familiar in western Europe and the less distant museums of America. I must argue the contrary; for Anthony to abandon the Courtauld Institute in weeks so close to Finals would have been a selfish dereliction of responsibility of which he was not capable. I have no doubt that he played some theoretical part in planning the hang, but am convinced that he saw it in its finished state for the first time when we arrived that afternoon. We had been there only for seconds when he muttered 'I was wrong' – and again and again he was to

26 Miranda Carter: *Anthony Blunt: His Lives*, 2001.

mutter it. Michel Laclotte was responsible for the final hang and we saw it in the company of Germain Bazin, Charles Sterling, René Varin and Jacques Dupont, worthies all and all well pleased with it, though Anthony was not. He was the victim, as are so many art historians, of hypotheses based on photographs and reproductions, notes and memories, when none of these can readily be checked against the original paintings – the Poussins from Russia, for example, he had seen only once, and briefly, in August 1935, a quarter of a century before. He had written so much, lectured so much, that even the French were prepared to surrender Poussin to him, Poussin their most intellectual painter, yet here in Paris he was confronted with the failure of his eye, the instrument of connoisseurship that can instantly demolish not only a hypothetical chronology, but one seemingly securely documented: I am not the first to believe that when connoisseurship is in conflict with a document, the sensible art historian believes his eye. The immediate necessity, however, was that Anthony should shrug off his anguish, for this was almost a French state occasion and a bold front was required for the speeches, lectures, toasting and formal dinners that would follow. It was my first experience of his ability to switch into another character, that of a man thoroughly at ease with the enthusiasm of others.

In spite of its flaws it was a great exhibition, the foundation of many leaps in Poussin scholarship of which Anthony should have been allowed to make the first. It was his intention to publish a revisionary commentary on the Louvre catalogue, but, returning to a Courtauld Institute on the brink of Finals, he had more immediate responsibilities. Denis Mahon, however, had none to prevent or delay his publishing his observations. Mahon, an art historian of independent means, was almost single-handedly responsible for reviving in England the reputations of seventeenth-century Bolognese and other Italian painters despised by Ruskin as 'art-weeds' and the 'scum of Titian,' and by Roger Fry as painters 'whose expression of sentimental and melodramatic emotion provides a slope down which the imagination glides without effort . . . '[27] He was not quite alone in this, though his admirers maintain that this is so; Ellis Waterhouse, John Pope-Hennessy, Blunt and Wittkower were in the vanguard too, but the difference between Mahon and these older peers, now all dead, was that he was a free spirit unencumbered by the obligations of employment in any museum, gallery or university with anxious students sitting at his feet. The other major distinction that set Mahon apart was the powerful instinct (and the funds to support it) that drove him to acquire paintings by any painter who became a new enthusiasm – in later life as true of Poussin as of his first love, Guercino, the painter with a squint – and it was in opening his collection to students that he influenced their taste and demonstrated the inadequacies of the National Gallery.

Mahon had gone to the Poussin exhibition in the spirit of enquiry, expecting to find that the arguments over the order of paintings executed in the early years – *c*.1624–*c*.1633 – had been resolved; instead, he found what he later described as 'a hotchpotch' so fundamentally and obviously flawed that he could not allow it to stand unchallenged. Though not at this stage recognised as an expert on Poussin, that is what he became, overnight, when his observations appeared in the July issue of the *Burlington Magazine*. That these were in print so soon was tragic in their consequences for Anthony, only a handful of whose friends knew that he was desperately anxious to publish his own new thoughts on the chronology but could not give them priority over his students at the end of their third year. Mahon, however, considered it a matter of great importance that the debate should begin before the exhibition closed and the paintings were dispersed. A kinder spirit would have waited.

The debate was increasingly unkind on Mahon's part and it was not pretty to see Anthony, whose life had been so occupied by Poussin, inexorably usurped by the persistent (some might say malignant) Mahon. For me, having heard that plaintive murmur 'I

27 Roger Fry: *Transformations*, 1926.

was wrong,' it was a wretched business, knowing that if only Mahon had waited for six months, giving Anthony time to deal first with his academic duties, they might never have been so seriously at odds in their conclusions, their guarded friendship destroyed. Things went from bad to worse and disputes over Poussin reached far beyond the exhibition. Mahon had been kind to me as a student and at Christie's I had sometimes been his errand boy; I liked him and his occasionally Puckish humour; worse, I thought him nearer the mark than Anthony, and Anthony too, I am convinced, in some respects thought so, but was, not surprisingly, grudging with the admission. This was unusual – but then the circumstances of the challenge had been acutely disagreeable; in the course of any normal argument Anthony would, if convinced, generously concede, even to a student.

Anthony's memory was not infallible – as was evident in a later squabble with Mahon who, in 1964, had bought a painting in a sale at Sotheby's that he believed to be an early Poussin. I was not privy to the row that developed over whether Anthony had seen the painting rather than only a photograph before doubting its authenticity, and more's the pity, for I know that he had and that his memory betrayed him. In the summer of 1963 the painting was in the window of a shop in Pimlico Road owned by Geoffrey Bennison, an outrageously camp interior decorator and dealer famous for his sharp eye. Edward Lucie-Smith, then more celebrated for his poetry than as an art historian, made me dash in a taxi to see it. Grubby and obscured by darkened varnish, I wondered, without conviction, if it might be by Andrea di Leone, Poussin's Neapolitan follower, but it was Poussinesque enough for me to drive Anthony to see it that same evening. We looked long at it in good late daylight and came to no definite conclusion. That a year later he had no recollection of our doing so is perhaps not altogether surprising, for in April 1964, convinced of his guilt as a spy for the Russians, the interrogations of MI5 began. Again Mahon was right; the painting is now accepted as an early work undoubtedly by Poussin, but I am inclined to dispute the date, c.1627, proposed for it; indeed, the dating of Poussin's paintings before 1624 when, at the age of thirty, he settled in Rome, and for the next decade, are to me still almost as much a matter for dispute as they were when Mahon and Blunt began their quarrel in 1960, for so many lost paintings have been rediscovered to give a shadowy idea of his work before he went to Rome and thus reshape our notions of the early Roman years.

With Anthony usurped from his position of primacy among Poussin scholars – for Mahon's assault achieved no less a consequence – the way was open for further erosive attacks in 1979 when he was exposed as a spy, attacks by the press whose false logic had it that he was flawed in all aspects of his life and work, attacks even by many in some way attached to the Courtauld Institute who could see some professional advantage in playing jackal. Miranda Carter (op. cit. p. 434) quotes just the kind of gleeful tale that was circulating in the Institute, in this case of a very small painting of *The Agony in the Garden* that he owned but had attributed to a follower or imitator, identified as autograph well after his death – I can still hear the exultant sniggering. The truth of that matter is that I bought that picture on his behalf and he knew unequivocally what it was. He knew too exactly what was under his nose when I brought back from Florence the fine preparatory sketch of *The Martyrdom of St Erasmus* for an altar in St Peter's, a canvas that, if not exactly lost, had by 1963 been quite forgotten. At Dover, Customs men had gone so far as to take the tyres off my car in their search for drugs (though why their suspicions were roused I could not fathom), but in the canvas under a blanket they showed not the slightest interest. For me, finding this Poussin was an exultant experience that, but for Claudio, would not have come about, for I had driven to Italy to see other pictures proposed for sale at Christie's and he had come for the ride. It was April and the spring was glorious after what, in the early months of 1963, had been a dreadful winter with temperatures so far below freezing-point that a burst water main had levelled the street outside the house under ice so thick that for weeks we could not distinguish the pavements from the road. In Switzerland, in Villeneuve, I had identified two wonderful bozzetti[28] by Piazzetta for altarpieces in Venetian churches – the consequence of an 'if you ever find yourself near Vevey, do drop in' conversation, and was in jubilant mood until I reached Milan; there, however, the collection that was my real objective proved to be of the sort of dregs that Christie's reserved for end-of-season sales when bargains were to be had by the bad Italian dealers who had contributed so much to this accumulation of rubbish. We escaped within hours rather than the projected days and, with time in hand, drove south to Florence where Claudio had cousins with whom we could stay. It was through these and a wearying round of lunches and drinks with a decaying nobility whose titles were as moribund as his, that we encountered the Poussin. In spite of its ghastly subject – St Erasmus tied down in agony while his intestines were wound onto a roller – I was enchanted by the vigour and freedom with which this large sketch was painted (it is a metre tall) and was at once convinced that it was by Poussin in an unusually easy mood. Significant but minor differences from the altarpiece for St Peter's proved its primacy over the larger work.

For some months it hung in my room at Christie's. Anthony's immediate response was absolute conviction; others were equally convinced; but when, at last, the time came to include it in an auction, I ran into difficulties. I could not catalogue it without quoting its full provenance and that would identify the owner who had no permit to export for sale what might well be regarded as an Italian national treasure – my driving it to London without the necessary papers had been quite outside Italian law. Christie's had thus to return the painting to Florence and trust the owner to initiate the proper process for export. He did not; instead, using my

28 A bozzetto or modello is a more or less final preparatory sketch in oils for a much larger painting; when the terms are used for sculpture the material is usually terracotta or plaster.

valuation, he saved himself the commission on the sale and all associated expenses by selling it to an Italian dealer who, in turn, sold it to one of the most eminent dealers in New York, and in 1972 the National Gallery of Canada announced its acquisition.

Later in 1963 Anthony identified another painting by Poussin, belonging to Duncan Grant who had bought it in Paris in the 1920s without quite knowing what it was. *A Landscape with a Man pursued by a Serpent* is related to a very much larger variation on the theme in the National Gallery. It is not absurd to say that Anthony fell in love with it – his desire to own it was as much emotional as intellectual; this he confessed to Duncan with 'everything I own I would exchange for it.' He was thus confronted by the moral problem of the man who is both the expert and the would-be purchaser, resolving it by asking for valuations from three experts in the market known to both Duncan and himself, deciding in advance that he would pay the highest estimate. Both Colnaghi's and I fitted this description and without collusion arrived at £12,000 as a fair figure between willing buyer and willing vendor if no commission or other expense came into play. I have no idea how Colnaghi's arrived at their figure – mine was based on the far larger sum I had suggested as a reserve for the *St Erasmus*, a painting almost twice the size. The third estimate came from Tomas Harris, a flamboyant dealer long retired to the comforts of Majorca but known to Anthony before the war – and perhaps not known at all to Duncan; his significantly lower figure can be attributed to his being out of touch and it was ignored. Duncan was pleased enough with his £12,000 (then enough to buy a decent house in middle Kensington) – but Heaven knows what he did with it, for Charleston, the house that he had shared with half the denizens of Bloomsbury, increasingly ragged and dilapidated year on year, remained as cold and damp as ever, often with so little evidence of food in it that I and Joseph McCrindle (a mutual friend and collector of Duncan's work) made a point of dropping in on him with assortments of smoked tit-bits and things in tins and jars that he need not cook, whenever we were weekending in Joe's cottage in Winchelsea – a custom from which, in the mid-seventies, we were sternly deterred by Paul Roche, Duncan's self-appointed guardian.

Joe I encountered in 1962. Checking the auctioneer's book of a sale of drawings in which all reserves and prior bids were recorded, I saw yet again the name McCrindle among the bidders, his bids wildly high and absurdly low. 'Who is this idiot?' I asked John Hancock – to which the answer was 'A nice American – but he knows nothing about drawings.' I took him to lunch at Prunier's and gently told him what I thought of his bids, suggesting that I might help him be nearer the mark; some days later he asked me to dinner at his house in Edwardes Square – a chaotic affair in which a hired cook produced and served everything in the wrong order, Bruce – a disorderly Labrador – settled on a weighty American lesbian for his sexual victim for the evening, and assorted aspiring writers, both hetero and homosexual, played games of vain one-upmanship beyond my understanding. It was, nevertheless, the beginning of almost half a century of friendship.

As an American, Joe lived in London as much as the taxation authorities allowed, his friends as conscious of his absences as of his presences, for the emptiness of the first was as noticeable as the fullness of the second. He belonged to a generation of old money and the Social Register, a New Yorker whose grandmother – a profound influence – lived in a whole house on Fifth Avenue and saw to it that, through private tutors, he spoke French, German and Italian as idiomatically as English, and learned to box, dance and play the violin – for none of which disciplines had he any talent. She owned an ocean-going steam yacht and in the long summers of the Thirties Joe sailed alone – but for the crew and his tutor, Lanning Roper (later a great gardener) – to fashionable Europe and once to the Near East; what can it have meant to a boy of eight to be on the wilder shores of the old Ottoman Empire? At eighteen Grandmama gave him a Duesenberg, the very best of American cars, as his runabout at Harvard, and there he studied law.

This he had neither the wish nor the need to practice. His loves were literature and art. He conceived, and for two decades subsidised and edited, *The Transatlantic Review*, a magazine in which the early strivings of scribblers were published, stepping-stones to fame. For more than twice as long he supported the careers of young painters and collected paintings and drawings by old masters, for which he had an instinctive rather than an educated eye; only Eric Hebborn, the notorious forger, abused his trust and fell into both categories. Never vain, as his collections grew in importance, he could not see that the friendship of museum curators was often nothing but mainchance flattery – as, indeed, was the interest of so many of the elegant young men who dined with him.

At dinners with Joe the American novelist rubbed shoulders with the English academic, the literary agent with the art dealer, and staunch friends with the latest favourite boy. Joe was a romantic giver, successive boys unromantic takers who left him with unhealing hurts. In friendships not disturbed by sex he was formidably loyal and generous.

Strokes eventually disabled his stout form, restricting him to New York. His last visit to London was in a wheelchair; he could neither speak nor feed himself, but nevertheless we lunched in what had long been a customary restaurant, another fond friend feeding him as might a mother a big baby. Between us, conversation with Joe was by proxy, so to speak, widening eyes his only contribution. When we parted, having juggled the wheelchair into a taxi, there was a long and telling pause, a holding of the gaze, for we both knew that we'd not meet again. What can a man do in a circumstance for which there are no words? A fumbled hug. A graceless kiss. In July 2008 he was altogether gone, his absence his permanent memorial.

*   *   *

By far the most important matter in which I was briefly involved in 1962 was the Royal Academy's sale of *The Virgin and Child with*

Saints Anne and John the Baptist, by Leonardo da Vinci, known as *The Leonardo Cartoon* or simply 'the cartoon' – cartoon used in the sense of a full size final preparatory drawing for a painting – now in the National Gallery. Late in January, Humphrey Brooke, secretary to the Academy, who had become something of a paternal friend during and since my work on *The Age of Louis XIV*, gave me a furtive lunch in one of his clubs, after which he asked a question that explained his attempted *sotto voce*. A big man, often noisily exuberant and always voluble, his was the whisper and furtiveness of the stage farce, and when I got the gist of it so did every other man in his long earshot. He wanted to know what I thought Christie's might get for the cartoon if we were given it to auction. This it was impossible to answer. Few drawings by Leonardo are not in the captivity of impregnable collections and this cartoon, the last stage in the planning of a major painting (never executed) before the first stroke of the brush swept onto the panel or the canvas, must surely count more as an unfinished painting than as a drawing, and be priceless – Humphrey, however, was at that stage thinking of it as a drawing and had thus approached me rather than Bill or Patrick, both of whom he had known rather longer. I hazarded a guess that £1,000,000 might be a starting figure for debate, stressing the importance of a shrewdly judged reserve in case major museums might agree to pool resources or not compete; I also said that if the cartoon were to be sure of a foreign buyer, it would have to be at such a price as to make refusing an export license quite impossible. Humphrey then swore me to secrecy – no sure decision had been reached, it might not happen, and no one at Christie's was yet to learn of it. Feeling slightly sick and at the same time intoxicated – to sell so wonderful a thing would be a mighty coup – I returned to work. Should I tell Bill, who always found discretion difficult? Should I tell Patrick, who was likely to dismiss the possibility as absurd or at once storm the Academy? I did neither; instead, after two days of brooding I telephoned Jacob Bean in New York, the wonderfully urbane and gentlemanly

Curator of Drawings recently appointed at the Metropolitan Museum, less than a decade my senior in age but a lifetime in Jamesian sophistication, whom at that stage I knew only through Michel Laclotte and Roseline Bacou at the Louvre, where Jacob had been a voluntary assistant in the Cabinet des Dessins. I asked him – hedged about with ifs, buts and supposes – Humphrey's hypothetical question; and his response – 'Two million dollars and beyond' – I relayed at once to Humphrey, whom I knew in my bones had probably asked half a dozen others in the market.

I do not quite know the subsequent course of events in what was to become a fractious and distasteful squabble between the Academy, the government, the fundraisers who came into play and a population that did not care a hoot about something called a cartoon – about which newspaper cartoonists were making pretty fierce fun. These developments, traumatic for Humphrey, triggered another bout of the manic depression from which he suffered – in the end he only wanted a conclusion, any conclusion, to a decision that had brought him and the Academy only opprobrium, scorn and notoriety. That decision had been to sell the cartoon. When I learned that there had been written valuations from James Byam Shaw of Colnaghi's at £750,000, from Geoffrey Agnew of £500,000 to £600,000, and from Peter Wilson of Sotheby's the assurance of a reserve price of £850,000, I knew the secret was out – and must have been out for some time – and needing no longer to hold my tongue, I told Bill and Patrick of my small part so far. My preliminary estimate of £1,000,000 had been tempered by Jacob Bean's 2,000,000 dollars – then just over £700,000 – and I felt that a firm estimate of £1,000,000 should be confirmed, vaguely supported by the gloss of Jacob's 'and beyond'. Bill was dismayed by the unprecedented figure; Patrick, on the other hand, was more dismayed that I, not he, had been consulted by Humphrey and at once, exactly as I thought he might, rushed off in a rage to beard him in the Academy with a higher bid than Sotheby's. In the bearding he was right, but the rage, I suspect, undid him. Humphrey was at least as large as Patrick and well able to rage back. Patrick, on his return, forbade me to have any further conversations with Humphrey. A sale through Sotheby's was then announced.

This was greeted by an outcry from the great and good and the Academy backed down, agreeing to sell the cartoon to the nation at what to all sane men was by then the bargain figure of £800,000 – that sum to be raised by an appeal to the public; if the appeal failed, then selling it at Sotheby's – where Peter Wilson had raised the proposed reserve to £1,000,000 – became inevitable, as did the certainty of a foreign buyer. Patrick's father, Lord Crawford, the public face of the National Art Collections Fund and thus of the campaign and public appeal, was unrelentingly bitter and disparaging in his expressed view of the Academicians and their folly; would he have been more amicable, I wondered, had the sale been scheduled at Christie's, the firm at which, through his influence, his son had become a partner?

On 16 March the great and good gathered to initiate the public appeal and determined that the cartoon should go to the National Gallery as a painting not yet begun, rather than to the British Museum where the nation's drawings are housed. Two weeks later it was taken to Trafalgar Square so that the public could more easily understand and respond to the rattling of begging-bowls. Response was slow and grudging; on the last day of the appeal, 31 July, after four full months only a very little over half the sum had been donated, but the government then contributed £350,000 and the NACF the rest, and the cartoon remained in the National Gallery. No one came out of it well; the Academy was damned for greed and blackmail and the government for failing yet again to establish a reasonable means of protecting the heritage – as is still the case. The only consolation for Christie's was that Sotheby's was not given the sale.

Within a year, however, on 26 March 1963, I did have a drawing by Leonardo in a sale. Captain John Noel, descended from the

Earls of Gainsborough, Noel their family name, still using his military rank forty years after his resignation from the army, came into Christie's with Mary, his unlikely wife-cum-housekeeper as fat as he was thin and every ounce a peasant. I knew him very slightly through a much younger officer in his regiment, recently disgraced, who, when keeping an occasional eye on his ancient aunt (and hoped-for inheritance) declining in the cathedral precinct of Canterbury, looked in on him in his Kent cottage not far off. As Nigel was certainly queer (hence the disgrace – something about being buggered over the barrel of an antique cannon) and John Noel, though born in 1890, in his early seventies seemed to be still consumed by a romantic passion for George Mallory, the lost hero of the 1924 Everest Expedition, I assumed that he too was queer and Mary merely a convenience. I was wrong; Noel was twice married and had a daughter by Mary, but whenever he spoke of Mallory – which was often – his eyes filled with tears that I mistook for those of a sometime lover (and Mallory, often said to have been the most beautiful of men, is now thought by many to have been at least bi-sexual). He was quite the last man I expected to ask for me at the Front Counter, shabby of dress, with a drip from his nose and any passing thought that he might once have been a gentleman, banished by the even shabbier bulk of Mary, yet he had with him two small drawings some 110 by 80 mm, one on a mount inscribed *Leonardo da Vinci*, the subject a grotesque caricature of a bald old man in profile, the other so benign an observation of a nutcracker male profile that the old man seemed quite beautiful.

The provenance of both reached back to the collection of the Earl of Arundel early in the seventeenth century, from which the Leonardo drawings in the Royal Collection came, but when I took them to Popham – so much regarded as the expert that I was bound to be asked by every serious enquirer 'And what did Popham say?' – his opinion was that only the grotesque was genuine, dismissing the other as by an imitator; he had a point, for the direction of the shading lines indicated beyond argument that the draughtsman was right-handed – but it was, nevertheless, the more beautiful scrap and I advised him not to sell it. But he did, two years later, at Sotheby's, for £750. For the grotesque Christie's got him 14,000 guineas, a sum quite large enough to relieve the impression of penury and discomfort given by the circumstances in which he lived – but whatever benefits the drawings brought, they must have expired long before his death in 1989, just short of his centenary.

*   *   *

At much the same time as the Leonardo Cartoon became our focus of interest, Christie's were called in to arrange a sale from the remaining contents of the studios of Augustus John, forced on his family by death duties. As a student I had taken to what became the lifelong habit of falling asleep with the wireless on, to be wakened in the morning by the early news bulletin. On Tuesday 31 October 1961 a voice announced John's death, two months short of his eighty-fourth birthday, and the President of the Royal Academy, Charles Wheeler, delivered a touching eulogy that ended with the phrase 'Truly, he could draw like a God.' I could not explain then, and cannot now, why I felt such an emotional wrench – bumping into him in Bertorelli's as a student in search of a cheap supper (soused herring and boiled potatoes) was not enough to call acquaintance and yet the news had for me something of the sense of loss felt by half the nation on the death of Princess Diana. A few months later, nothing (other than securing the Leonardo Cartoon) could have pleased me more than being despatched to Fryern Court, the John family house at Fordingbridge, in which he had lived and worked since 1927, late in the decade during which genius slipped away from him.

It was, as so often with life at Christie's, a job to be rushed; the sale was an important stage in settling the estate and perhaps an even more important event in our increasingly meagre calendar, but choosing what was to be included in it was far from straight-forward, for wonderful drawings had been eaten away by extra-ordinary moulds in black and brilliant pink, hundreds of canvases scattered between three studios were filthy with the ingrained dirt of decades and hung about with the webs of spiders whose crumpled corpses nestled behind the stretchers, and panels from his very early years were scuffed and scratched. Some paintings were as good as any of their various periods; others, unfinished, he had halted at a stage acceptable enough to the aesthetics of the Sixties; to others still he had returned after decades of wondering how to continue and had ruined them with revisions in a wholly different style. One particularly beautiful full-length portrait of a young woman, three-quarter life-size, almost completed in 1900 or so, he had very recently attacked with altogether cruder brushes and cheap paint, inspired to do so by a postcard of a painting by El Greco pinned through the canvas to the stretcher. To sell paintings and drawings in such conditions would have suited the trade well enough, for dealers can always see through dirt and damage and, as a rule, profit greatly from their remedying and improvement by uninhibited restorers – Kahnweiler's exploitation of Cézanne's studio leavings a warning to us all – but most private buyers are deterred by flawed condition, and it was to these and particularly to John's diminishing generation of admirers whom I thought this sale would have immediate appeal. I discussed the problem with Sir Caspar John, eldest son of Augustus, a relaxed and rather jolly Admiral of the Fleet and First Sea Lord who had inherited his father's libido, and we agreed on a crash programme of cleaning and repair; we also agreed that he should put this to Patrick so that he, in turn, could put it to me – 'What a splendid idea – why didn't I think of it?' to be my spontaneous response.

The drawings I took to Doreen Lewisohn, the most modest and most scrupulous of restorers specialising in works on paper, a tiny, bird-like, bicycle-riding wit, living and working in the smallest cottage in St John's Wood. Though born in London in 1916 she was, through her wider family, in many ways thoroughly Viennese, after the *Anschluss* a neighbour briefly familiar with Freud and witness of his departure, even assisting the formidable housekeeper of Berggasse 19 who kept inquisitive Nazis at bay while she packed the master's treasures for transport to Hampstead – if only Doreen had kept a diary . . . Her first venture was into the design of furniture and that her only comfortable chair was often mistaken for one by Breuer gave her constant pleasure. She then became the world's only expert in the repair and conservation of antique globes, but for this arcane skill there was scant demand and she drifted into the related field of works on paper, with which she was so sensitive and deft that her interventions could rarely be identified. Of her one rival in London this could not be said and by the adjective 'Drescherised' we all knew exactly what was meant – a ruined drawing on bleached paper into which the faded ink had sunk and from which much chalk, charcoal or pastel had been flushed away. Once Doreen's skills had been enlisted by the Fitzwilliam Museum, she became so involved there that she moved to Cambridge and was appointed conservator for works on paper. I adored her for daring to attempt the seemingly impossible, her gossip, and for her diligent kindness to my mother with whom she had some kindred spirit, never neglecting to see her on her not infrequent visits to London. Of her work on the 115 drawings included in the first Augustus John sale there was not a trace and, though some had lost their freshness from exposure, most were as fresh as on the day they were executed.

The paintings were dusted down by Joan Seddon. I had selected 68 that were both fair to his reputation and required least work to prepare – except for a vast unfinished canvas, some four by twelve metres, neither stretched nor framed, intended as a Canadian War Memorial, potentially magnificent but halted in 1919 (though Lord Beaverbrook was still angling for it as late as 1959), that we hoped might be bought by a Canadian museum (in the event it went to a private collector in Chile who, it was later rumoured, commissioned its adaptation to celebrate the victory of Bernardo O'Higgins over Spanish forces at Chacabuco in 1817, establishing a new republic). Joan had a year before dealt with an emergency repair to an extraordinary still life of flowers that we had catalogued as by Francesco Guardi. I thought it a fake, but this was a period when Guardi had been expanded far beyond the painter of Venetian views by the recent discovery of huge rococo illustrations to Tasso's *Gerusalemme Liberata* and by Antonio Morassi's publication of a batch of similar still lives as genuine early works. Our example fell from the west wall of the octagon – the wall that always spelt misfortune – late on a Friday afternoon and was raggedly pierced by the back of a chair; scheduled to be on view first thing on Monday morning, something had to be done. Joan, then new to Christie's, came at once – the brutal hacks in service to the art trade, to whom Bill and Patrick always turned for help with our not infrequent accidents, turned them down. The proper course was to reline the canvas but for that there was no time; instead, we closed the tears with discreet stitches and joined the broken threads of an improbably coarse canvas with an invisible adhesive, masking these repairs with paint to match the broad brushing of white pigment that appeared to 'dust' the reverse of the canvas (for which there was no obvious genuine reason). On the following day Joan restored the damaged flowers in tempera and when the picture was returned to the wall no one could see that it had been the victim of a very recent accident. Some fool paid 11,000 guineas for it. Over the next few years so many Guardi flower pieces increasingly inferior in quality appeared that Christie's were compelled to refuse such obvious fakes; they migrated to the lesser auction rooms, Phillips, Bonhams and Knight, Frank and Rutley, and when there the prices eventually dropped to £100 a pair, the fakers turned to mock-Montgolfier ballooning pictures. There was at the same time a flood of mock-Guardi drawings, hundreds of them, small and unambitious, given the suggestion of age with spots of mould immediately recognisable to any housewife (though not to art historians) as the dust of Nescafé blown onto damp paper.

Taking into account the amount of work to be done by Doreen and Joan the date of the John sale had been scheduled as late as we dared, 20 July 1962, for by tradition the last Friday of July was the end-of-season sale in which we cleared the warehouse rooms of paintings that had failed to reach reserves, been forgotten, or were too embarrassingly bad to show unless hung at least three deep on every wall – a bargain-hunter's paradise. The room was crowded and inexperienced amateurs were slow in bidding, but the total slowly mounted to £99,645 – rather more than we had expected when we considered the steep decline that the old boy's reputation had suffered for almost forty years. I produced a rotten catalogue; it had no note on Augustus as once the white hope of British painting, but by 1962 neglected, even forgotten, by the old establishment of his day, and unknown to the new; it had no notes on sitters, friends, family, time, place or meaning; nor did it recognise what an important document such a catalogue should be, a record, a memorial, a work of reference. But that was how Christie's was at that time – a catalogue entry was mainly for identification purposes so that Jock, Les and the other porters were quite sure that they were putting the right number on each lot. There was too the long-drawn business of my stepfather's dying; he had held his own until the beginning of the year, but then the cancer accelerated and I took to dashing to Castle Hedingham on weekday evenings, and the repercussions of his death at the end of May coincided with the final preparation of the catalogue for the printer.

With Peter Chance in the rostrum, performing with his usual élan and warmth, it was the most successful sale of the season. Perhaps relieved that so unpredictable an event had exceeded all expectations, he celebrated after lunch by giving a job to a boy who wanted one – no ordinary boy, but a boy tall, loose-limbed, flopsy and passably handsome in a very English way. At £6 a week (and Luncheon Vouchers), the Hon. Charlie Allsopp joined the

Front Counter to endure Ridley Leadbeater's pokes and prods for a trial period of a year. I took one look at him and predicted that this dyslexic, shambling, trustful and innocent golden retriever of a boy would one day be Christie's chairman – and was right; to see him in Peter's company was to see the older man in love – not the lustful physical love with which I was now familiar, but pure unquestioning adoration.

Eleven months after the first John sale there was a second. On 21 June 1963, 110 drawings and 63 paintings made the wretched sum of only £33,405, clear evidence that the market had been flooded, yet this, in terms of diversity and invention, as well as decline, was far the more interesting sale, particularly among the drawings, revealing moments of improbable achievement; lot 117, for example, a life-size study of a *French Peasant Youth* from the first decade of the twentieth century, would not be shamed in the company of a Blue Period painting by Picasso, John's very near contemporary. The catalogue was designed to match the first, but was a marginal improvement. The choice this time was far more difficult. Twenty-one wonderfully handsome academic nudes, male and female, from John's years at the Slade, had been eaten away by mould, losing their feet, and had to be stabilised and patched by Doreen – restoration was impossible; and for the paintings we established a studio for Joan in one of the few warehouse rooms with a rooflight. Hers was an Augean task but she carried it out with great sensibility and I dogsbodied for her as much as I could. On a day that I had wholly set aside for her, John Maxon, Director of the Art Institute of Chicago, came to see if by chance I was free for lunch; never less than dapper, he expressed surprise to find me in a porter's apron, sleeves rolled up, arms black with dust, surprise changing to dismay when I introduced Joan with 'This is Joan Seddon, here to clean the Johns' – in American slang Johns are lavatories.

On the afternoon of Friday, 19 April 1963, it was just as well that Joan was on the premises. A vast painting by Edward Burne-Jones,

The Sleep of Arthur at Avalon, was delivered to Christie's for sale the following Friday. I had had to catalogue it blind, so to speak, from drawings, bibliographical references and ancient photographs, and was anxious to know how much in error I might be. More than six metres wide and nearly three high, this enormous composition was a too personal, spiritual and emotional exploration of himself and a romantic mythological past with which he identified so closely that one may well see it as his *Parsifal*, which occupied Wagner twice the seventeen years that Burne-Jones spent on Arthur. Sentimental, anguished and morbid, reeking with the odour of sanctity, it underwent more significant re-composing than even Picasso's *Guernica*. No one had seen it since 1933, the centenary of the painter's birth, other than, on the outbreak of World War II, to remove it from its frame and stretcher, to roll it, and put it in a stout box some half-metre square and three metres long (much as Delacroix's *Massacre* had been twenty years later); in that box it stayed, unseen, until it reached Christie's.

The lid unscrewed, a myriad spiders scuttled from the box; gently we unrolled the heavy canvas on the floor of the lofty anteroom where it was to hang and dusted away the mass of webs and other arachnid detritus that obscured it. How could we display so large a canvas without a stretcher? As a tapestry on a tapestry bar, I decided, but none we had was long enough and all we could do was procure a six-metre length of timber; with the canvas tacked to it by the raw edge that had formerly folded over the original stretcher, it was hauled up the wall with a dozen of us supporting it to ensure that the inevitable inverted curvature was kept as open as possible. It worked, and for the first time for thirty years, eyes feasted on the masterpiece. The canvas, however, was much weightier than any tapestry.

Peter Chance strode in to see it, pink, silver and immaculate; he strode to its very centre and within a pace of it, and at that moment the weight of the canvas began to tear it from the bar. Poor Peter reached to press it against the wall, but the avalanche could not be halted, the canvas ripped away, curled forward and enclosed him in its vastness. Instead of standing still, he panicked, fought his way out of the belly of this whale more dishevelled than his wife had ever seen him first thing in the morning, and the canvas lay face down, a crumpled heap. When we reversed it (no mean feat) and flattened it, we saw the consequences – flaked paint lay thickly on the floor, the whole width of the canvas where flowers fill the foreground, the area of heaviest initial impact, was extensively damaged, and widespread random damages elsewhere reflected Peter's efforts to escape.

Joan and I had until Monday morning, when the picture officially went on view – at most some thirty working hours we thought – in which to camouflage the injuries. Lying on cushions on the canvas, Joan began work at the top, and I, on my knees, began at the bottom on the easier business of repairing the more or less crudely painted flowers. Thirty hours were not enough and we worked through the night on Sunday.

During the week of the sale not a word was said by anyone. Did no one notice how much of *Arthur at Avalon* had been damaged? And if they did, did they assume that the damages were old? When, on the following Friday, the painting was bought by the museum in Puerto Rico, it was relined, cleaned and stretched before being framed and installed in a specially constructed room – did none of the experts responsible for these procedures not notice how much of the paint was new? Forty-five years later when the painting returned to England to spend a year in the Tate Gallery, I could identify very few of Joan's interventions, but was appalled by the crude quality of the irises, bluebells and forget-me-nots in which I had a hand.

*   *   *

Even though the second John sale was a disappointment, there was still more to do for Caspar, for there remained at Fryern Court over a thousand drawings and some four hundred canvases, all of which had to be valued for further discussions over tax. Many of the drawings were early, small, irregular in shape and dirty, but in their inventive and intriguing subjects they were precursors of major paintings and thus of value to future art historians, were there ever to be any attracted to study so minor a figure (for that is what Augustus had become), but in commercial terms worth nothing in so saturated a market. Other drawings, later, sketchier, scrappier or evidently discarded (even scribbled over), were not only worth nothing, but would always be virtually worthless in commercial and art historical terms. As for the canvases, a handful – of which the figure on the easel with the El Greco postcard was an example – were worth preserving as art historical documents, but the rest, the bulk of them failed portraits, were fit only for scraping and re-use; this I proposed for the benefit of students at the Slade, but this was deemed impossible (it was not – as I later proved with more than fifty of my own paintings, between heart attacks in 1995); I then suggested that they should be destroyed rather than expose John's reputation to further ridicule. The tax men disagreed; pointing to the sales, they took the view that every canvas and scrap of paper had a value and must be taxed. I argued that to preserve the value of works already sold, those remaining at Fryern must never escape onto the open market – a view as incomprehensible to tax men as the ludicrous idea that one of our duties was to preserve John's reputation by not preserving works that he, by retaining them for decades, had ensured should never be seen by the public. I spent many days at Fryern Court and grew fond of Dorelia, devoted mistress, muse, wife and widow to Augustus, at 81 more truly beautiful than any portrait he had painted of her in her sensual twenties. Setting aside drawings that I was sure were not by Augustus, but muddled with his, I asked her opinion. 'I'll ask him,' she replied, took the drawings from me and left the room. Some minutes later she returned with 'No, they're not.' When I told Caspar what had happened he chuckled – 'She asked her wedding ring – on a thread, you know.'

Matters were not finally settled until Dorelia's death in July 1969, aged eighty-six and still wistfully enchanting. Caspar, still the Admiral, wrote me an oddly nautical note – 'She managed it very well and had a peaceful passage out . . . the end of an era and a generation.' On her estate yet more tax had to be paid – £25,115 – and what was left in the studio was again a matter of dispute with the authorities, resolved by a block sale of over a thousand drawings to the National Museum of Wales; the museum bought the remaining paintings too, but of these there were only 110, 'nearly all unfinished or rejected portraits, mostly later than 1920,' according to the Keeper there, A. D. Fraser Jenkins, in 1978. So many decades later it is now safe to say that Caspar took my advice and burned some three hundred canvases. To Joan he gave a wonderful small early painting on panel of the highest quality, the very best of Johns, and to me a random handful of drawings, among them some mould-rotted academies that had lost their feet – more work for Doreen Lewisohn.

*   *   *

Of Charlie Allsopp I had no fear, for his obvious destiny was remote from my ambition – I simply wanted to head a department of prints and drawings without losing my toe-hold among the better paintings, no matter what their date and school, and in this Charlie had no hope of treading on my heels. David Carritt was an entirely different matter, ushered in to do what I had never been given time to do and likely to deprive me of the only thrilling aspect of my job, the identification of masterpieces. He was charming, generous and witty, his quips as deadly as stilettos, his broader humour crude, lewd and often bluntly homosexual – after his corruption of Sir Geoffrey Agnew (notoriously vain and boastful) and his mournful crew to 'Geoff and the Agonies, the Bond Street Pop Group,' we none of us could take those bullies seriously, and his having to explain to an uncomprehending Patrick what he meant by a 'pork injection' (his euphemism for the act of sodomy) was a moment of pure farce. Nor could Patrick chuckle with the rest of us at David's Monday morning gossip of obliging frustrated heterosexual young men picked up outside the Hammersmith Palais late on Saturday night and whisked back to 120 Mount Street – though Patrick himself, reputed to have seduced most of the secretary girls in the directors' flat in Christie's attic (intended only for emergencies) was not above letting slip hints of his own sexual prowess; David, I suspect, told some of his stories simply to provoke Patrick's puritanical distaste for everything sexually divergent. Often David's nonchalant audacity in divulging not only his own escapades but those of others in the art world, was the only thing that could break the oppressive mood imposed by Patrick when, as a group, we were inspecting the latest batch of paintings. As an aside it is worth recording that sex in Christie's was as much downstairs as up; in the carpet warehouse there was regular brothel business at lunchtime, with the senior porter in the department guarding the door and taking the entrance fee from below-stairs staff wishing to conjugate with a working girl or two on the heaped treasures of the Silk Route. And how, in this context, can I omit Bill Spowers, 'The Major', the dapper, dashing and diminutive Australian, at some time of the Grenadier Guards and the Parachute Regiment, who joined the book department in 1960, presumably for what must have been to him mere pocket money? Apparently Croesus rich, when offered the car registration plates WS1 to WS6, Bill bought the lot, and then bought cars to match them, among them a silver Gullwing Mercedes, a pale blue Rolls-Royce Silver Cloud drop-head coupé and an open Bentley Continental. He also bought a flat above Prunier's, ostensibly to use after working late (he lived in far off Windlesham, minutes away in any of these cars), but its principal purpose was as an afternoon bolt-hole to which to repair with whichever Christie's girl he had in tow as his *Cléo de trois à cinq*. According to gossip, his penis was wondrously disproportionate.

David Carritt joined Christie's in January 1963 at seven times my salary with expenses and privileges accorded only to the partners – of which he was soon to become another. To the wider public he was a man who had for four years been the art critic of the *Evening Standard*. To Christie's partners he was the man who, as a private dealer – that is one working without a gallery or other business premises – had made a remarkable series of discoveries, among them paintings by Caravaggio, Dürer, and Guardi. To the art trade he was tainted as a partner in a leading auction house (as John Herbert, his chief advocate, should have known would be the case) and wary dealers were suspicious of him – leopards and spots, they thought. To Peter Wilson of Sotheby's, an almost equal wit, he was 'a rat *joining* a sinking ship.' Scholars too were suspicious; Francis Watson, who had for so long known the whereabouts of the great Tiepolo discovery that David was to make in 1964, had not thought the paintings missing, and fizzed with rage – a matter of different generations, I suppose – and the Dürer, now in the National Gallery, was and still is, disputed, increasingly to boot. As for the Guardis – four huge canvases (the largest 2.5 × 4.5 metres) and four narrow upright filler panels – these were the illustrations to *Gerusalemme Liberata* that he, with Patrick O'Connor, Curator of the then moribund Hugh Lane Gallery in Dublin, but more widely known as a thoroughly unscrupulous dealer-cum-restorer, had identified, lending authority to the recently forged flower paintings and precipitating the fierce argument as to whether all these sudden extensions to our knowledge were by the celebrated Francesco Guardi, his elder brother Antonio, or both combining in the family workshop. Of this discovery we shall never know the whole truth; the bare facts are that these paintings had been part of the decoration of a once great house overlooking Bantry Bay, near Cork, and that in 1956 O'Connor had paid a mere £12,000 for them, had rolled them face in (a dreadful thing to do – it cracks the paint and abrades the cracks), and to make them look like nothing more than rolls of old canvas found in a barn, covered them with some foul adhesive, stable straw and dung that might deter customs officers from their curiosity, and sent them to London. The point at which David came into play is uncertain; Mrs Clodagh Shelswell-White, descendant of the 2nd Earl of Bantry, who brought them from Venice in the early nineteenth century, might well have been foolish enough to let him into Bantry House, but I doubt if the big, blustering and boorish O'Connor would have been given that courtesy for knocking on the door.

Patrick was the son of Andrew O'Connor (1874–1941), a not undistinguished sculptor born in Massachusetts and trained in Paris, who had settled in Ireland in 1932; unlike his father he underwent no formal training – indeed, no perceptible education of any kind – and his conservation and restoration methods were not short of brutal. Anne O'Connor, his American wife and my engaging friend, never wavered from her version of the tale that David saw the paintings in situ in the house and said nothing to the owner, but went to O'Connor to see if he would do the dirty work of paying as little as he could and exporting them to London. They should, as part of independent Ireland's Georgian heritage, have remained in the house of which they were a significant embellishment; as a public servant of sorts threatened with the possibility of imprisonment in Ireland for his part in the deceit, O'Connor fled to Palm Beach and set up his studio as a restorer to the local millionaires who adored the sight and sound of him. The four large paintings and one upright were bought by Geoffrey Merton and, in 1960, exhibited at the Royal Academy;[29] the last sentence in the catalogue entry offers no more information than 'The identification of the series was made by Mr David Carritt.' Seeing them as tainted, Merton subsequently sold them and they, together with the remaining three upright panels (at first retained by O'Connor) are now dispersed at points between Copenhagen and California – but Dublin is not one of them.

29   *Italian Art and Britain*, Royal Academy 1960, Nos 457, 460, 462, 465 and 466.

My first encounter with David had been much earlier, and by proxy, in my first incarnation at the Courtauld Institute. In the attic room in which I then chose to read and write there hung a marvellous painting by Caravaggio, a temporary loan to the Institute's collection, to be removed at a moment's notice and thus to be greedily and urgently absorbed. Facing the window, it caught the long warm rays of the autumn sun and sang of things languid and sensual of which I knew nothing but sensed much, for it seemed to touch part of my nature, then half recognised. When I should have been writing essays on Filippo Lippi and Tino da Camaino, instead I sat and gazed, enthralled, enchanted, transported, at the four indolent boys who inhabit Caravaggio's *Una Musica*, making the music of the love song rather than in praise of God – very different putti from those of Donatello and Luca della Robbia. One day the wall was bare, the canvas packed and flying to New York, the Metropolitan Museum having paid for it the then enormous sum of £20,000. Years later, driving David from Chatsworth to spend the weekend with Lord Faringdon, he told me the circumstances in which he had discovered and identified the Caravaggio that had for so many weeks occupied my mind and eye. As a small boy, at Rugby, he had become insatiably enquiring about paintings by old masters and, when the opportunity occurred, had used his intuition, wit and charm to knock on the doors of likely houses; with success, this impertinence became habitual. In such a house, in remote Cumbria, in the hamlet of Maulds Meaburn, midway between Barnard Castle and Carlisle, the property of Surgeon Captain W. G. Thwaytes, he found himself – though no longer a boy but a young man of twenty-four – in the captain's bed, the subject of ancient naval custom and, looking back through the arches formed by two pairs of thighs, glimpsed, upside-down from this angle, the four boys making music. I cannot recall whether David kept his counsel until the captain's energies were spent or whether he brought the proceedings to a sudden halt with the disconcerting cry 'Look! Look! A Caravaggio!'

David did more than sing for his supper; he brought the painting to the attention of Denis Mahon, who published it in *Paragone* and the *Burlington Magazine* in January 1952. In 1953 Bernard Berenson and Roger Hinks included it in books, and Roberto Longhi too acknowledged it, followed by Walter Friedlaender in his catalogue raisonné of 1955 – thus did David not only draw the attention of the great and good among art historians to a wonderful unknown painting, but establish himself as a new and very clever eye. For my part I owe him the particular debt that my few weeks in the company of *The Musicians* (the title given it by the Metropolitan Museum since 1953) resulted in a treasured awakening, an undimmed passion roused.

David in his first few weeks at Christie's showed – quite rightly – every sign of impatient boredom with the bread and butter paintings inflicted on all of us in the almost daily catalogue-checking sessions in the warehouse, but his presence did not result in the expected sudden influx of masterpieces, and the financial years of 1962–63 and 1963–64 ended with a loss of £6,000 and a puny profit of only £11,000 – not even enough to pay David's salary and expenses; in surveying the later year Peter Chance tersely observed that paintings by old masters had been in noticeably short supply. From a weekend in Milan David returned with a supposed Raphael in his overnight bag, confronting us with the irreconcilables of public auction and illegal export from a very prickly country of origin. I said I thought it a fake; David pointed to obvious recent restoration as an indication of authenticity – 'Oh that old trick,' I replied, having too often seen the deliberately clumsy repair of a deliberately damaged forgery. We went together to the technology department of the Courtauld Institute where Stephen Rees-Jones without hesitation damned it as a dud. David then had to spend another weekend in Milan, running the gauntlet of customs officers (the painting was later the subject of a fierce Italo-American squabble). He was often away; he had only to begin telephone conversations (quite knowingly) with 'David here . . . ' for the wealthy and noble of all Europe to offer him a bed – he said it was his 'little trick,' for 'David here . . . ' were always the opening words of the Duke of Windsor when he telephoned and David could pitch the timbre precisely – 'Imagine their surprise when little me turns up.' From his overcoat pocket one morning he drew the Dürer that he had identified in 1956, *St Jerome in the Wilderness,* and we discussed its possible sale; as I doubted the attribution then, and do so still,[30] and he himself had become less convinced, he returned it to its owner. In 1996, long after I had left Christie's and twelve years after David's death, quite unaware of our doubts, Christie's sold it by private treaty to the National Gallery for £10 million; in recent monographs on Dürer it has had intriguing treatment – acceptance, illustration without comment in the text, omission without explanation and, most recently, well-argued rejection.[31]

David could not even claim a part in securing for sale five important paintings from what little was left of the Cook Collection – a great nineteenth-century accumulation of old masters that in the curatorial care of old Maurice Brockwell had remained intact until 1939. In 1940 – a year in which the National Gallery, the National Art Collections Fund and the government were hardly in a position to object to the third baronet's decision to sell what was once one of the greatest treasures in the land, *The Three Marys at the Sepulchre* by either Hubert or Jan Van Eyck (without the divination of a medium the painter's identity will be for ever a matter of dispute), left for Rotterdam and the Van Beuningen collection; this was the first of the dribs and drabs that during and after the war eroded the collection to pay death duties and settle the demands of disgruntled wives, the prices invariably wretched. As Sotheby's in June 1958 had sold 156 paintings by

30 See *National Gallery Report 1996–97,* p. 14, note 1, where, curiously, my rejection is recorded.
31 Katherine Crawford Luber, *Dürer and the Venetian Renaissance,* Cambridge University Press 2005.

old masters for the insignificant sum of £64,668, it is not surprising that when Sir Francis Cook and his seventh wife decided to sell a handful of the remaining fifty, they called Peter Chance to their tax exile in Jersey – and with him went Patrick to hold his hand and David to lend a little gaiety to the occasion. The great prize was Rembrandt's *Portrait of Titus* as a child of perhaps seven, an enchanting and affectionate study, the handling of paint wonderfully broad for less that four square feet of canvas, and for this alone we expected to raise ten times the total of the Sotheby sale seven years before.

When it went on view on the afternoon of Friday 12 March 1965, I saw that not only had the gilt frame been chipped, leaving a white scar, but that the canvas had been punctured. Careless handling was a constant problem at Christie's; old Jock and Les were as tender as they could be, but once the pictures left their domain downstairs, any fool could handle them – there was no training of any kind (and woe betide any whippersnapper like me who dared to tell an upstairs porter how to carry precious fretted frames or support the fragile paper of unmounted drawings) and more porters were instinctively careless than were careful. Joan Seddon was nowhere to be found, nor was Ivor Jones, an able restorer for the Fitzwilliam Museum whom I trusted and always used when Joan was not available. As none of the partners was about – they had all seen the Cook pictures hanging in the directors' flat, by then converted into a private viewing room – young *Titus* was removed to my room while I tore home in a taxi to collect what tools I needed, Barbola paste, dull brown stains and gold wax for the frame, and for the painting, a patching material in case I could not persuade the broken threads of canvas to rejoin, my smallest spoon-shaped palette knife and, in the hope of a perfect match with Rembrandt's impastose paint, my cherished tins of brown shoe polish, evaporated, stiff and cracked, that when applied with the palette knife would have the dull gleam of old varnish.

Barbola paste and shoe polish survived unobserved their week of intense scrutiny, and when, the following Friday, as lot 105, *Titus* ended the sale, it was to the American collector Norton Simon for 760,000 guineas (2,234,400 US Dollars) – but it is less for this record price that the event is remembered than for the confusion over the bidding that resulted in its first being knocked down to a rival bidder, Marlborough Fine Art. Norton Simon was entirely responsible; a cautious man, he wished to be present at the sale but did not want to be seen bidding; nor did he trust anyone to bid for him; he therefore gave Patrick, though Peter was to be in the rostrum, written instructions that in the heat of the moment it might be impossible to recall. Minutes before the sale these were verbally simplified to 'When I'm sitting, I'm bidding; when I stand up, I've stopped.' In the event, from 300,000 to 650,000 guineas he bid openly and ostentatiously by calling out his bids, then dropped out of the bidding and made as though to leave the room while others took the bidding further; he then returned to his seat. Bidding faltered at 740,000 guineas, but Simon did not respond, and only when Marlborough was declared the buyer did he leap to his feet and invoke the original nonsensical instruction to Patrick which ended with, in the case of his having resumed his seat and raised his finger 'he is continuing to bid until he stands up again.' There was uproar – the press and television crews could not understand what was happening and though we were all on our feet, few of us on the ground could see. I seized one of the tiny gilt chairs brought in for great occasions and stood on it – and still could not see; but when I stood on my toes and could, the cane seat gave way and I dropped through to the floor, shackled about the knees, keeled over against my neighbour and toppled him and half a dozen others, adding farce and helpless laughter to the mayhem.

Perhaps the best thing David did for Christie's had nothing to do with discovering a masterpiece but, within months, to suggest that the firm's great weakness lay in the fields of Impressionism and later developments in painting, urging that a dedicated specialist should be brought in. This was undoubtedly true, and in spite of Sotheby's trouncing us again and again with such pictures, something of the old prejudice embodied in Alec Martin – 'this 'ere filth', as he once put it to Anthony Lousada, the firm's lawyer – still clogged the arteries of Christie's. In 1958, in Paris, at the Congress of Art Historians, I had been sought out by a mischievous old dealer named Paul Botte to see a painting bearing the inscription *Georges de la Tour*, we sat beneath it in his dining room while we ate white sausages, boudins blanc, and for the first time I heard the inevitable joke. I said I thought his picture a preposterous fake, quite new (in the 1980s it was to draw me into a disagreeable controversy), but was forgiven and we became friends. It was Botte who in 1962 called me to Paris to see Georges Renand and his collection on the Quai Bethune. This was one of the great thrills of my life, one that I recall every time that I go to the Courtauld Galleries now, for there, in a tiny room in which hang eight oil sketches on panel by Georges Seurat, I recall the long day spent in Renand's company as one of revelation, of my beginning to understand the workings of Seurat's aesthetic mind. My notes, if they survive, are buried deep in Christie's archive vaults and my recollection is now insecure, but it is that Renand had at least an equal number of such sketches, and it was the sale of these that he proposed. The panels – as was common for Seurat – were all within a fraction of 6 × 10 inches (or 10 × 6); most were horizontal landscapes, but at least one was a study of a standing female nude; all were steps towards a loose pointillism, in a touch that was lyrically free, before the freezing of the rigid formula. I was enchanted. He wanted a sum in francs that divided into an average of £9,000 each, and I agreed that this, with some flexibility to take into account connections with major finished paintings (or their absence), should be a running reserve. To Botte I promised, in my excitement, an introductory commission half a per cent above the customary two.

My exultation died within two minutes of my telling Patrick; nor, in these last few months as a partner, was there support from Bill. Both were appalled that I had agreed such a price. I pointed out that Sotheby's had sold a similar sketch for the Tate's great *Bathers at Asnières* for £12,000 four years before, but this they seemed to think had been achieved through evil genius – this was a period when rivalry with the ever more successful Sotheby's had become a manic loathing and mistrust that poisoned many decisions. They were intransigent. My arrangements were, to my humiliation, cancelled, the sale did not take place, and Renand's sketches began to dribble into the trade; the last left in the collection were finally dispersed through the Parisian auctioneers Drouot in 1987. All these years later I wonder why I did not plead with John Herbert for support, for he surely, as an advertising man, would have understood how this most distinguished private collection could have been promoted to bring the firm success – but then John was never brought into any departmental discussion, never informed of what made a painting or its collector important, but merely presented with very basic information and left to get on as best he could. Looking back on my years at Christie's, time and again I see what fools we were, how naive, how complacent and how blind.

Telling him my Renand tale may have lent strength to David's determination that someone should be brought in to cover this field, in which he had no strengths and I had very few, and he suggested David Bathurst, then working for the Marlborough Gallery. This second David, as the future Viscount Bledisloe, had all the social connections Christie's could desire – Eton, Magdalen, the 12th Royal Lancers, cricket and the Cresta Run – and I am inclined to argue that, hardly noticed by Patrick, he was, with the comfortable increase in Impressionist business that his presence brought, far the most important single force in Christie's revival at a time when the firm was all but moribund. He was fortunate in that the idea of departments within the picture department had already been established, though only mine – of drawings and prints – had a clear identity and independence, while the rest were not yet the subjects of specialists but areas in which we all had a hand, even, to begin with, David's Impressionist department. Poor soul, even he was the victim of the basic cataloguing system in which we all gathered to look at every picture – and perhaps just as well at that early stage; as a large and flashy watercolour was drawn from the stacks, David began read his catalogue note – 'Raoul Dufy, *Venus rising from the Waves* . . . ' a list of American dealers' labels providing a respectable provenance. 'It's a fake,' I said, 'It can't be,' the response. Telling Jock and Les to remove it from its frame without damaging the labels, I said that a bosh shot at the composition would be found on the reverse, smaller, less bold, and scribbled over with a brush loaded with blue wash, and, moreover the paper would be a full imperial sheet bearing an English watermark. I had recognised it as one that I had made for Alan Harverson in my last year at school – 'What would you like for your birthday?' I had asked, 'A painting by Dufy,' his answer. When Christie's were disinclined to sell a painting a reason was usually offered – the value too small, the market uncertain, the condition too poor – but of these for my Dufy none was plausible; what can David have written to the New York dealer who had confidently gone to the expense of consigning it to London?

Christopher Wood, who was to become widely acknowledged as an expert and dealer in Victorian art and artefacts, also joined Christie's in 1963 – not a boy for whom I much cared. After his death in 2009 a close mutual friend asked me the reason for my lifelong coldness towards a colleague who had done so much to revive respect for the nineteenth-century Olympians of English art and, having held my tongue at the time and ever since when accused of envy, I felt some relief in at last telling her the reason for it. It was well into 1964 before Christopher felt certain of his place in the picture department; his degree in art history at Cambridge under Michael Jaffé was not much of a recommendation and what we still needed was another Vic Heather to slave over the paintings in which neither David nor I were interested – and this, after some bullying by Patrick, was the mould in which Christopher seemed willing to be formed. I thought him admirably scrupulous – until his father gave me lunch and made a proposal. From Christopher he had learned that setting aside paintings for particular sales did not please clients whose need for a sale was urgent; how would it be, he asked, if he offered to buy such pictures and banked them for a year or two before selling them at Christie's who would lose nothing by the delay? It would mean setting up a business in which my partnership was essential. I think my refusal to have anything to do with it meant that this shoddy notion was still-born, but I was never certain that this was so; I was, moreover, angered by the assumption that I could be drawn into the deceit and my trust in Christopher was never recovered.

*   *   *

With Bill Martin's almost unnoticed departure and the arrival of the unruly Davids, it seemed to lesser hands in the picture depart-ment that there must have been a recriminatory upheaval among the partners of the board, Patrick its victim, for in the proper course of things he should have been acknowledged as our supreme Gauleiter, but was not. Perhaps Peter Chance and the others had seen through his ignorant bluster and had realised how useless he was, useless in exploiting his social connections, useless in what the army called 'man management,' and useless in almost every question of identification and attribution. Guy Hannen, who hardly knew the back of a picture from the front, suddenly announced himself to be the department's administrative head, its real authority, and at once we had to contend, not only with our own feelings in the matter, but with the evident animosity between our two directors, relieved only by the farce of their throwing open my door, often within minutes, to proclaim each his supremacy over the other – 'Yes, Patrick . . . Of course, Guy.' Had the board had the courage to rid themselves of Patrick, Guy's shrewd ability to respect and trust his employees, allied to his instinctive sense of order, would have made him the best head the department ever had.

CHAPTER 15

Dénouement

I should have recognised the threat embodied in David Carritt's joining Christie's, for he, like me almost five years before, had been invited to join the firm to improve the status of the picture department, and it was inevitable that the aspect of my work that I most enjoyed when I had time to do it adequately – research – would pass to him. It did; and when, eventually, he was disinclined to do it, he requested, and was given, as his assistant, his friend Willie Mostyn-Owen, a wealthy landed intellectual who for seven years had worked with Bernard Berenson and wonderfully resembled the loftier English Grand Tourists recorded in caricature by Thomas Patch; his salary immaterial, he can only have been persuaded into the job as a remedy for idleness, David's merry company his real reward.

I had last had a holiday in 1961 – a long haul round Spain and Portugal with John Croft, a painter of exquisitely judged hard-edged abstracts and a civil servant in the Home Office, whom I had met through Richard Hughes-Hallett (we all lived within spitting distance). 'What,' enquired Richard of him on the day he introduced us, 'are you working on at the moment?' in so very much a polite tea-time tone that I was absurdly surprised by the reply – 'Oh, an outbreak of sodomy in the approved schools of Wales.' Our weeks away were a test of stamina over appalling roads, thwarted by floods, burnt by the sun and twice the victim of road accidents when we were stationary – my pretty Daimler could hardly have been more rent and torn had it been in Guernica in 1937. I remember crossing the Bay of Biscay in a storm so wild that every inch of everything on the boat that could provide a perch was occupied by a migrating bird. I ate goat for the first time in Oviedo. With cold clarity I remember the nausea and anger induced by the bull fights that we saw in Seville, though determined, in the spirit of enquiry, to endure them to the end. Compostella sowed the seed of curiosity in its great pan-European pilgrimage. Cordoba and Granada put flesh on the work I had done with Professor Bargebuhr. And in Barcelona, where we stayed with Joe Baker, a devil-may-care American friend of John, there was the thrill of meeting an ancient warrior from the Civil War, El Campesino the name by which he went, riding out of the darkness on an antique motorbike, and back into it when he had done with us, his appearances as much a danger to us as to himself were the Guardia Civil to become aware of them. The first thing I did when I returned to London was to buy Hugh Thomas's book on the Spanish Civil War, published earlier that year to great acclaim, to find this of Valentin Gonzalez, El Campesino: 'Today he is in Brussels allegedly forming an army to invade Spain.'

There had been no break for me in 1962, a year too crowded with my domestic and financial problems to even think of taking a holiday, but the following summer, deposed by David Carritt, as it were, with every French museum celebrating Delacroix on the centenary of his death, I began a trawl on 4 July during which I saw more than three thousand of his paintings, drawings and watercolours, and concluded that never had a major painter done himself more mischief in the production of so many ill-considered minor works. I was back in London for no more than ten days before a real holiday began with the great exhibition of *Piedmontese Baroque*, an overwhelming accumulation of sculpture, painting, architecture and artefacts my prime objective. I set off with Robbert Gras, a Dutch psychologist of eventually considerable academic eminence, with whom I had had a foolishly fierce affair, though its burning-out had left us friends. Genoa, Naples and the far south were also our objectives and to some extent we achieved them, but by the time we reached Cape Palinuro, then a deserted beauty spot well south of Paestum, I was so troubled by the heat that we had to flee still further south and climb into the hills of La Sila, where I lay for several days like a gaffed haddock. There was, I suppose, some small point in seeing Cosenza and Catanzaro in impoverished decay, and Matera when most of the rock houses were still in use, and there was certainly much at which to wonder sadly in Lecce, a baroque Turin in small that had irreversibly crumbled since Ellis Waterhouse photographed it in the early Thirties (a gift of his photographs prompted this detour into Italy's heel). No memory is more deeply etched than our sleeping, just for the romantic heck of it, in the magnificent ruin of Castel del Monte, the architectural marvel of a hunting lodge built for the Hohenstaufen Emperor Frederick II, begun in 1240, thirty miles due west of Bari. I wish that we had slept in the temples of Paestum too, for they were then equally uncluttered with railings, souvenir stalls and hotels and seemed as wistfully Ozymandian as they were when first revealed to the Grand Tourists of the later eighteenth century.

Within a month of my return I was off on another crucial journey – one booked and paid for by Christie's while I had been in Italy, and the only move the firm ever made to improve my education and contacts. The Museums Association had organised a jaunt to east coast America so that interested members could meet their peers at all points between Boston and Washington, and I was to go with them. Roy Strong, then still in his infancy at the National Portrait Gallery, and I were far the youngest and kept each other company in evenings and situations that might otherwise have been deadly dull; together we lost something of our innocence in a bar in Baltimore where young women without knickers danced among our glasses while we gazed upward, aghast in my case, gloating in Roy's, at what we had never seen before. It was also my first real exposure to pornography – far beyond the smutty photographs of Paris and the army – readily available in both pictorial and literary forms among the newspapers of almost every bookstall on the streets. In addition, it was an invaluable experience to see, often out of hours, the astonishing riches gathered in what were essentially private, provincial and comparatively new museums densely packed over much the same distance as separates Edinburgh from London. I did not know it then, but this journey was the first foundation of the life that I was to lead when I left Christie's.

Back in England there was, almost immediately, a day in Paris – one of many mad jaunts demanded by Austin Bradfield-England, a strange emaciated little man whose few front teeth were so large and far apart that his mouth was a distraction in any conversation. Fascinated by paintings, he was frequently in Christie's to offer things that he had seen in Paris, where he lived, and on his travels in Switzerland and Italy, but both Bill and Patrick had ignored him; I, in my naivety, had not and swiftly had been woven into his web to discover that his contacts were by no means contemptible and that he should have been taken seriously. The trouble was that his appearance in old and grubby clothes that had never been of quality (least of all his hats) matched neither his double-barrelled name nor his talk of masterpieces – but the paintings and clients he introduced were almost always worth the journey. He lived in a succession of hotels with half a dozen telephones and made a fortune by buying and selling the cargo of oil tankers in transit, content to take a percentage profit too meagre for any ordinary broker. He had neither property nor car, ate frugally in back street restaurants, and his only extravagance was a string of boys from the less joyful pages of a Genet novel, one of whom, unknown, eventually murdered him. On this occasion I was to see a *bozzetto* for an altarpiece by El Greco; this involved an early morning flight from Heathrow, breakfast with Austin, lunch with two disagreeable Spaniards and tea with a young and astonishingly handsome Portuguese (though his legs were too short), who claimed ownership of the painting, an exquisitely impetuous sketch on panel. Try as I did, I could not bring the discussion to a close, but when I stood up and said that I must leave to catch my plane, not only was the reserve figure suddenly agreed but I was asked to take the panel with me. I asked for something in which to wrap it, but neither paper nor cloth was to be had and I set off with it under my arm, certain that I would be stopped by a customs officer. And I was. 'What's this?' he asked. 'An El Greco,' I replied – at which, with 'This idiot thinks he's got an El Greco,' he held it aloft for other officers to see; they laughed, and my inquisitor let me pass, shaking his head, with an expression of sad sympathy that said 'Poor sod. Poor deluded sod.'

At the very end of the year, recognising that for months I had not been to Windsor and that my work on Fontana had run into the sand, I surrendered him or had him taken from me by Anthony Blunt in a stern and unforgiving mood – both perhaps, though I am sure of nothing other than the blow to my hope of recognised scholarship. Fontana had been part of my life for six whole years, a leitmotiv through all my jaunts to Italy, but Christie's had never let me have my promised four day week and I had failed to complete my work by the end of 1963. I spent a sad day in Windsor with Anthony and Aydua, explained what I had done and not done, and have never since returned – to do so would be too painful.

*   *   *

Nineteen sixty-four began with yet another journey, first to Rome and then to Sicily, where Claudio had rediscovered a half-length portrait by Bronzino that had once belonged to his family. Though not quite by Bronzino, it was a perfectly decent portrait of his period and type and made the journey well worthwhile – which was more than could be said of the paintings accumulated in Rome by Hans Backer, Christie's resident representative there, a man with great expertise in porcelain but no eye at all for paint on canvas. The Bronzino's owner, a local countess (half the inhabitants of Taormina seemed claimants to a defunct title), drove me as far up Mount Etna as was possible with a Volkswagen Beetle in deep snow, our mad intention to have a picnic, but the Beetle jammed its nose into a snowdrift at a point where we could both see and hear red streams of lava sizzling all round us, a sight infinitely more frightening and beautiful against the snow than any Vesuvius has offered in my lifetime, and single-handedly manhandling the car through what seemed a thirty-three point turn with a hapless and hysterical Contessa at the wheel, was a strenuous matter of some urgency.

Above and behind the Roman theatre of Taormina I had a more melancholy encounter. Claudio took me to meet an old man living in a featureless shack with a marvellous and often painted view towards the sea; his skin saurian, his back and joints bent and broken, his worn clothes far from clean, he welcomed us in a form of Italian that I could hardly comprehend – a patois into which Claudio slipped easily and merrily. To my disagreeable 'What are we doing here?' his answer was a mysterious 'Wait and see – this will take time.' It was worth the wait. Until the old man passed me one, I did not notice the heaps of glass photographic plates that lay in a dark corner of the room – and when he did, I knew at once why we had come. I held to the light an image typical of Wilhelm von Gloedon, a German photographer born in 1851 who in his early twenties had settled in Taormina. There he photographed the local boys, sometimes merely naked, more often embellished as though they were the catamites of ancient Rome enacting mildly erotic *tableaux vivants*. As paintings, his compositions were very much of their time in academic circles, but of pubescent boys rather than the lower ranks of obscure female divinities and virgins; but these were photographs, with none of the subtleties that classical painters introduced, and their abundant penises were almost always on their way to or from tumescence. I thought of Oscar Wilde, Max Reinhardt, Richard Strauss and the notorious performance of *Salome* in which the enthroned Herodias stroked to erection the naked negro boys at either hand while Salome tossed aside her seven veils.

In 1939, eight years after von Gloeden's death at 75, Mussolini's police, on grounds of obscenity, destroyed what they could find of his work; during the German occupation, more still were destroyed in 1944; but this old man, now unrecognisable as one of the olive-skinned pubescent boys, had saved the residue. It is one of the most profound of my regrets that I did not do what I wanted to do if the old man agreed – that is, transport the plates to London for inclusion in a sale. Now it would be possible and I can imagine the razzmatazz that would be attached to it, for the blatantly homosexual imagery would be set aside for the sake of von Gloeden's place in the history of the photograph, and absurd prices would be paid by grave collectors and institutions of high seriousness for whom erotica of this kind is no more than an abstraction; but I knew in my bones that were I to propose it only David Carritt would support me and that I should not risk humiliation at the hands of a disgusted Patrick.

The most important event of the year was the death of 'Old Spencer-Churchill' (Captain Edward George Spencer-Churchill) who had long before inherited the remains of the some 1,500 pictures that, accumulated in the early nineteenth century, had formed the once celebrated Northwick Park Collection; an impression of its status is quickly gained in the National Gallery where Botticelli's *Portrait of a Young Man*, Raphael's *St Catherine* and Annibale Carracci's *Quo Vadis?* are all of Northwick provenance, but its status in my day was much diminished. I and every other young man in Christie's had from time to time stayed in that great ugly house, starved of food and frozen to the bone in winter, charming the old man into specifying in his will that his collections should be dispersed by Christie's on his death. This exercise in charm may have been easier for those interested in antiquities, furniture, books, manuscripts and the applied arts, but for me it was difficult, for old Spencer-Churchill was less interested in his inherited paintings by Guercino, Reni, Rosa, Jordaens, Gentileschi and the elder Brueghel's family than in what he called his 'rescues.' Seduced by the conviction that he had a discerning eye, for years he had haunted Christie's for paintings obscured by chilled varnish or damaged beyond reasonable repair, and had had them 'revealed' as masterpieces by restorers who without scruple were able to find precisely what he hoped to find. In truth, for paintings he had no eye at all – indeed, by the time I knew him, into his eighties, his eyes were so rheumy that he could hardly see, with discernment or without it.

To his dreadful death at eighty-eight on 24 June 1964 (caused by his inability to turn off the scalding hot water in his bath), Christie's reacted with indecent haste. Under Patrick's command we descended on the house, directors, experts, secretary girls and porters, catalogued everything as best we could – which was not well – and physically emptied it. It was a period of intense slavery, my sleep broken every night by the noise of rats scrabbling for soap in the adjoining bathroom. There was very little light relief. Bill Spowers tried water-skiing on the lake, Charlie so mis-managing his speedboat that it overturned and sank. I tried to demonstrate the pile-driver on Annabel Hoyer-Miller, one of the more substantial young women employed by Christie's; accusing me of being puny she had challenged me to this all-in wrestling manoeuvre in which, holding the ankles of one's adversary, his (in this case her) head is driven into the floor of the ring; I managed to turn her topsyturvy but could not lift her free of the floor to complete the exercise. A bout of rather more close-knit wrestling with Charlie ended with our tumbling in a tight bundle of limbs all the way down Northwick's grand staircase; and I also discovered the knack of tearing telephone directories in half. If all this seems absurdly irresponsible, our excuse was the tension brought on by the unrelenting pressure of our work there, at a time when television had introduced the whole nation to the gladiatorial pleasures of professional wrestling.

The Northwick sales did not begin until the following year, the first of the Old Masters on 28 May 1965, the second on 29 October, and the last on 26 February 1966. In spite of the time in hand, the catalogues, appallingly muddled in school and date, were a disgrace to anyone with a sense of order and a claim to scholarship, but the decisions were entirely Patrick's in the hope that the first sale might break, if not individual records, the record for a sale total (it did not). The tiny Fra Angelico, some eight inches square, of *The Dream of the Deacon Justinian*, was, for example, catalogued as unarguably by him, though I knew it to have been disputed since at least 1919 and felt that we should have included some discussion of the matter in the catalogue entry – as had been the case when I first saw the painting with Michel Laclotte (who knew more about Fra Angelico than any of us) in the Manchester exhibition of 1957;[32] Patrick, however, laid down the law and that was that – an opportunity in which David, Willy and I could have lifted our sale catalogues to an unprecedented level of honest scholarship was denied us, and old Vic Heather could have done what we did.

*   *   *

In 1957, Charles Merrill Mount, a young American, published a biography of John Singer Sargent, fifty years earlier the most fashionable portrait painter in London and New York. That the book was not a success should have surprised nobody, for with the Great Depression of 1929–33, followed by World War II, international art markets had collapsed and Sargent's swagger portraits were worth less than their ornate frames. By 1957 there were haphazard indications that the market for Impressionist painting was reviving, but this did not include Sargent and Mount's book on him was doomed to be remaindered.

Even so, it established him as something of an authority. In his preface Mount paid tribute to a long list of the institutions – the Royal Academy, the Imperial War Museum, the Metropolitan Museum and others – that had let him loose in their archives, and to the great and good of private patronage and the art market, establishing his credentials as a diligent enquirer; he let it be known

---

32 *Art Treasures Centenary*, Manchester Art Gallery 1957, p. 1, No. 1.

that he had had help from Sir Alec Martin, Sargent's friend who had prepared the contents of the painter's studio for posthumous dispersal; and the preface ends with 'I cannot forget . . . the kindness and help of the artist's sister, Violet Ormond, with whom I spent evenings plunged into a world known only to the two of us'. Here then was a man who knew all the right people, a man to whom the art market might look if ever it needed an expert on John Singer Sargent.

In 1964 Mount walked into my office at Christie's with a bundle of watercolours by Sargent. 'Gosh,' I said – or something of the kind – and 'Whoopee' too, no doubt. He had found them, he said, in the forgotten collection of an old lady in Dublin, now in need of money. They were of landscapes, mostly small, loose in handling, not quite of the quality one might expect, but in 1964 Sargent was still a dead and buried artist and no one of my generation had seen much with which to form a value judgement. Christie's sold them for prices between £200 and £1,100 – prices high enough to suggest, perhaps, a revival in the market. Mount came back with more – another gosh, another whoopee. But when he appeared a third time, the watercolours were so bad and smelled so fresh that I took them to Peter Chance, with whom Mount had struck up friendship, and demonstrated why I thought them slapdash forgeries.

We had what can only be described as a row; I was overruled and on 13 November 1966 Christie's sold nine more watercolours as by Sargent, authenticated by Mount, for £3,700 – the sort of money that would then have bought a decent mansion flat in Kensington. As Mount's watercolours were bought by Agnew's, Newman, Maas, the Fine Art Society, Charles Jerdein and other reputable London dealers, and sold by them to American dealers of equal reputation, it is not altogether surprising that Peter felt justified in ignoring my lone dissenting voice, but in 1967, when an American dealer cast doubt on those that he had bought, alarm became widespread. A panel of experts, one from Sotheby's, a keeper from the National Portrait Gallery, the librarian of the

Boston Athenaeum and a director from Christie's who had been glad enough to sell them, inspected as many of Mount's water-colours as could be recovered and, wisely after the event, condemned them all as 'dreadful' and 'awful' forgeries.

Mount not only defended his reputation against what, with some justification, he called 'these Johnny-come-latelys,' but asserted that he had, through his assiduous work, 'created the present interest in Sargent.' Of this there is no doubt and it is a wry thought that without Mount's putting his forgeries into Christie's, the revival of interest in Sargent might not have occurred until much later – it is to Mount's credit that for genuine Sargent watercolours we must now think in five and six figure sums, though there is now no doubt that Mount's discoveries were by Mount himself. Many of them survive, stashed away among the stock of the duped dealers, waiting for the moment when, Mount forgotten, they might more successfully be reintroduced to the market.

In the early stages of his deception I was completely gulled by Mount, yet at much the same time I came to the conclusion that Eric Hebborn, then not notorious as a forger of old master drawings, was a cheat and had deceived me with several that I had catalogued and put in sales. An able draughtsman and painter in outworn English academic traditions (so able indeed that as a student at the Royal Academy in the mid-fifties it was he who was trusted to restore the Leonardo *Cartoon* when it was damaged by scalding water spurting from the bleeding valve of a radiator – or so he claimed), in his two years of a scholarship at the British School in Rome he met Ellis Waterhouse and, infinitely more important, Anthony Blunt, through whom I met him, and whose flat in the Courtauld Institute was in later years to become his London *pied-à-terre*. As a student at the RA he, and others, were, in the lane leading from Burlington Gardens to the students' entrance, canvassed by George Aczel, the most blatant of restorers to the trade – and, incidentally, the restorer most employed by old Spencer-Churchill — to earn pocket money as his assistant. Aczel was one of several trade restorers used by Christie's until I joined the firm, and in turning nothing into something he was no exception — only in his flagrant openness about the old Dutch landscapes he produced (Wynants a specialty) did he differ from the others. Early in my first months at Christie's I witnessed Geoffrey Agnew — a man so arrogant that he did not care that he was heard — having a 'What can we make of it?' conversation with a restorer in Albemarle Street, and am sure that this rotten streak ran right through every level of the trade. Later, having discovered that the studio of Campbell Mellon — the most obscure of painters of the Norfolk scene — had remained untouched since his death in 1955, I brought its contents to Christie's, where his small plein-air sketches on panel fetched remarkably high prices; for years after, a Duke Street dealer who bought only a couple of pairs, was never out of stock, so adept was his restorer in imitating them.

It was from Aczel that Hebborn learned the basic business of restoration forgery and its camouflage. Turning to drawings — the field in which Eric most made his name — John Minton was his first victim (even to employing one of Minton's models) and Augustus John his second, and from these he moved to old masters as rare and eminent as Bellini and Mantegna, as big and generally desirable as Piranesi, and as improbable as Corot and Pissarro. Setting up a business as The Pannini Gallery, he issued an illustrated catalogue from which Joe McCrindle bought a large landscape by Pissarro, on which I expressed doubt, but eventually surrendered on the grounds that it was so improbable that such an attribution could never have been made unless supported by external evidence, now lost; then Anthony asked me to drop in one evening and I met the man himself, saturnine, dark, bearded and persuasive, and I was shown drawings that he wished to sell at Christie's.

In spite of Anthony's apparent backing, I was not convinced, yet on the other hand, without more than mere suspicion, how could I reasonably refuse? I cannot now remember what I agreed should be included in a sale, but the receipt given him by Christie's on 1 May 1963, reproduced in his autobiography[33] as evidence of my gullibility, is not in my handwriting, nor does it bear my initials – as would have been the case had I seen him or the drawings at the Front Counter. But then Eric was much given to errors of fact, as was demonstrated in detail in one scrupulously researched review:[34] according to 'an old memorandum' he claims that he saw me at Christie's on 2 June 1966 and for supper on 13 June 1966, but I was at Chatsworth on both dates, and had severed relations with him for ever in October 1964, for I was by then absolutely certain that he was forging both drawings and paintings.

Of this, proof lay in a portrait by Sickert. The sitter was Cicely Hey, a painter who acted as Sickert's model in the 1920s; it was recognisably of her but corresponded with none of the five known portraits; Eric had sold it to Joe for a *prix d'amitié* and I had thought it, though ugly, not a foolish acquisition – but then I caught Eric *in flagrente*. I had been in Malta for a few days, looking at Caravaggio's *Beheading of John the Baptist* in the Co-Cathedral of St John, talking to John Gauchi, the director of the museum in Valetta, and being stoned in the Governor-General's limousine – independence for the Maltese was then a matter of furious argument – and as it had been impossible to make contact with Eric by telephone, I simply turned up in the middle of the afternoon at his rambling apartment in the Piazza Paganica. There the door was opened by Eric's lover, Graham Smith, and over his shoulder, framed at the end of a long view through an enfilade of rooms, stood Eric at his easel, working on an identical portrait of Cicely Hey; when I reached his studio there was a third on another easel, possibly the original from which Joe's was copied – at least that is what I was led to believe when Eric said 'You can only really learn from copying,' adding that he

33 Eric Hebborn: *Drawn to Trouble*, Mainstream 1991, p. 155.
34 Gertrude Prescott Nuding: *Hebborn the Fake, The Art Newspaper*, December 1991, p. 16.

had been in love with Sickert since his earliest days at an art school, but only now could afford to buy one. He did not at that point know that I knew Joe. When I told him that I did and thus knew of three identical Cicely Heys, he did not argue or rebuff; I still do not know if any of them was by Sickert himself – certainly, if one is genuine, it does not appear in Wendy Baron's catalogue raisonné.

We parted on bad terms. I told him that there would be no point in his ever again consigning drawings or paintings to Christie's, for I would not hesitate to reject them even if, grudgingly, I thought them genuine – for he had, I believed, played the stale trick of mixing evidently old and genuine drawings of small value with his far more ambitiously attributed forgeries. He responded that he could manage well enough through Sotheby's and Colnaghi's. Within months, however, of my leaving Christie's in 1967, he consigned two drawings that caused something of a rumpus, one by Pontormo, the other by Castiglione,[35] each of which sold for 1,400 guineas – too much for duds, not enough for the real things. When the catalogue became available, Hans Calmann, who had bought dozens of drawings by Eric and sold them to the most eminent private collectors and museums (as had, Eric claimed, Agnew's and Colnaghi's), at last alerted by some common factor in them all no matter what the date or nationality, demanded that I 'do something.' 'I can't,' I replied, 'I no longer work at Christie's. I cannot interfere.' I had some sympathy with his outrage, but greed had blunted his perceptions and he had chosen to ignore the gossip that was running through the trade, of which I knew because while I was still at Christie's I had had conversations with a number of dealers – particularly with Regina Slatkin and Helene Seiferheld, of New York, the first to express their doubts to me – all of whom suspected or knew that they were Eric's dupes, and had been able to assure them that since October 1964 he had been warned off and nothing of his had since been accepted for sale.

35 Lots 139 and 140 on 26 March 1968.

I had, of course, to tell Anthony that he too had been gulled by Eric, if only in the careful indiscretion of his giving C/O Blunt, 20 Portman Square, as his London address. Aghast at the tale of three identical Sickerts, he told me that he had already begun to wonder how quite so many distinguished drawings had fallen into Eric's hands in quite so short a time, but he did not do what he should have done – cut short their association and forbid Eric's presence in Home House – he merely asked him to desist. I suppose the infatuation was too strong – the sentimental longing of an older man for a younger, never physical, is a much tougher thing to break than a sexual relationship. Anthony was then betrayed by his partner, John Gaskin, a shrewish kept woman of a man, greedy for money, who, carefully schooled by Eric, became his agent and delivery boy, taking drawings into Bond Street dealers, letting it be thought that the attributions had the blessing of Anthony, even that they belonged to Anthony, too shy to let it be known that he needed to sell his private collection. It was a wretched betrayal and it did Anthony great harm in 1979 when many supposedly expert dealers were happy to talk to the press about the part that Gaskin's bandying his name had played in countering their intuitive suspicion of drawings by then thought to be by Eric.

The events of the winter of 1979–80 brought Eric to the fore to such a degree that I was forced to defend him in the sense that he could not possibly have drawn all the doubtful drawings attributed to him, so great their number, their styles and mannerisms so diverse that there was nothing of the common character that, in retrospect, had in the 1960s, been so evident across the board. In 1981 we exchanged not unsympathetic letters on the effect that the exaggeration of the number of his forgeries was having on the reputation of the trade, but I refused to see him and renew what he called our friendship. In January 1996 Eric was murdered, his skull fractured by so brutal a blow that his death must have been intended. On this ugly crime the Roman police expended very little energy. His lover in the 1960s, Graham Smith, long since discarded, appeared on my doorstep some weeks later to pour vitriol on his memory. He too had written an autobiography[36] using the same obscure publisher – a nauseating book that perhaps corrects a few of Eric's lies and offers credible glimpses of Anthony's unhappy life with John Gaskin; those intrigued by this important and largely successful example of art forgery in the later twentieth century should read both lives in tandem, for together they offer an account that is neither wholly mendacious nor close to the whole truth.

*　　*　　*

In the spring of 1965 David Carritt returned from a weekend jaunt with an album of drawings in his pocket, found in an idle hour in Earl Beauchamp's library in Madresfield Court, Worcestershire. It contained 167 drawings by Giandomenico Tiepolo – enough to provide me with a whole sale if detached from the album and sold separately, as David had already arranged. The date of the sale was fixed on 15 June 1965, immediately putting me under pressure with the catalogue. The first step was to take a photograph of every sheet in the album so that we had a record of every drawing and inscription. The disbinding of the album was then entrusted to Doreen Lewisohn, so too the necessary minor restorations – she was later to claim this task, rather than the repairing and cleaning of the drawings by Augustus John in 1962–63, to have been 'her professional breakthrough;' and mounts had to be cut so that the chances of clumsy handling were reduced while the drawings were on view before the sale. As both these procedures involved the long absence of the drawings, I had to write the catalogue from the preliminary photographs – no bad thing, as it happened, for I developed German measles and was banished from the building by Guy who seemed to think half the secretary girls might be pregnant. I drove to Castle Hedingham and retired to my bed

---

36   Graham David Smith: *Celebration*, Mainstream 1996

with photographs all about me, grouping them by subject and making what notes I could from memory. As a matter of courtesy, when I recovered, I informed James Byam Shaw, of Colnaghi's, the only real authority on Giandomenico Tiepolo, that I had pillaged his book for guidance,[37] and showed him the photographs; he was the first outsider to see the drawings when they returned from the mount-cutter.

The last lot in the sale was the binding of the album – a sad little relic but of interest for the bookplate of Horace Walpole (a most distinguished previous owner) and the inscriptions, one of which is possibly by Francesco Guardi (Giandomenico's uncle) who seems to have had the drawings for sale individually at prices from 15 cechini (sic) to 22 lira, presumably to Grand Tourists. Now, of course, I regret the disbinding, for we could have learned from the original folds which two drawings were on the same sheets of paper and thus intellectually as well as physically connected, and whether the album was a random gathering or, as I now suspect, prepared for the removal and sale of individual sheets, and merely a convenient means of storing and display. A French inscription gives the number of drawings as 162, an English as 166 – but the number photographed and for which I wrote a catalogue entry was 167. The announcement of the sale roused overwhelming interest, particularly among Italian dealers, and it became necessary to arrange viewing facilities before the manuscript of the catalogue had been sent to the printers. Intended to be a substantial work of reference this was the fattest catalogue issued by the picture department in my time, and we made a particular effort to provide illustrations of a higher quality than ever before, using matt paper and a semi-photogravure technique that proved hopelessly unsubtle in distinguishing grey inks and washes from those in brown. As for the text – it was not bad for its time, but when I think what could and should have been made of it, the idea that a thing so

37 James Byam Shaw: *The Drawings of Domenico Tiepolo*, Faber 1962.

intellectually meagre could ever be a work of wider reference is laughable.

The course to the sale total of £87,260 – then a sum remarkable enough to figure in the records for the year – should have been direct and smooth; Doreen made an exquisite job of the disbinding, cleaning and repair, and newly separated in their mounts the sheets gained a high seriousness and presence that, crammed into the album, they had lacked; and Noël Annesley, who had had to hold the fort while I recovered from the debilitating attack of measles, had so much command of the logistics that I was content to let him stay in charge. The logistics, alas, included the early viewing arrangements, early in which one drawing was stolen – we thought, through process of elimination, by a pair of Italian dealers. Guy, administratively in charge of us, was furious, justifiably so, for it was far the most important of the drawings, not only in its subject, *The Apotheosis of San Giacomo Giustiniani*, in which it was directly associated with a painted ceiling in the Doge's Palaca, Genoa, of 1783 – from which we could perhaps assume a *terminus post quem* for binding the album (the *terminus ante quem* already established by Guardi's death in 1793) – but in its lending focus to six other drawings more loosely connected with that ceiling. In its detailed finish I thought it more likely a *ricordo* than a summary of pre-liminary ideas, but I hoped nevertheless that it would be bought by the Metropolitan Museum, New York, where there is a fine preparatory modello in oil on canvas – certainly it was the drawing for which I expected the highest price. There was panic when a count revealed that we had lost a drawing; as the binding recorded 166 drawings as its contents, Guy could not at first see that one was missing, but Doreen, the mount-cutter and the photographer had recorded 167, and I had written the longest entry on this drawing and in an index of subjects the other six had been grouped with it – a physical check left no doubt that it had been removed. Guy as good as accused Noël of taking it, so nearly reducing him to tears that in his defence I sparked a terrible row that, with Guy's logic of 'Well if it wasn't Noël it must be you,' diverted the accusation of theft to me. Never was there a darker, bleaker moment in my life at Christie's – seven years of loyal slavery rewarded with suspicion.

I could not afford to alienate Guy. In spite of his maddening habit of jingling change in his trouser pocket while he watched us vet incoming pictures, in spite of his total incomprehension of the ways in which our minds worked and the speed of their working when answering the unasked questions 'Who painted this and is it any good?', and in spite of our regarding him as superfluous, even an impediment, unlike Patrick he had the good sense or good grace to laugh at the puerile jokes that both relieved our boredom and restored our concentration – in that, at least, he understood us. I knew that I needed him as an ally, not an enemy, if the picture department was ever to escape Patrick's time-worn atavistic stronghold and if prints and drawings were to become a separate department under my direction. He could tell, he said, when I was nearing the end of my tether because my nostrils flared like those of a rearing horse, and I dare say they flared in the row over the stolen Tiepolo – of which the one reward had been Noël's stout loyalty to me (indeed, I felt that he would have sacrificed his job for me). It was too much to expect an apology from Guy but he made amends soon after by inviting me to spend a night at his house in Berkshire – and rather jolly it was, with hardly a word said about Christie's, but I felt that underlying the jollity and the domesticity of washing dishes was something in the nature of a War Office Selection Board. There was always something inscrutable about Guy, something of the cobra hissing before the strike, something of the school prefect sticking to the rules, something of the teddy bear – and I could never predict his reaction. Standing with him and Patrick at the bottom of Christie's main stairs late one morning, waiting to set off on an errand with David Carritt, we were all surprised to see him begin a slow descent with arms outstretched, one before and one behind, the palms of both hands upturned.

'What the hell do you think you're doing?' bellowed Patrick. 'Oh,' said David when he reached us, unperturbed, 'I just thought I'd come downstairs in the Egyptian style.' Guy was as much consumed as I with laughter.

My relationship with Patrick worsened in the autumn of 1965. I was called to New York by Robert Lehman, the banker, most of whose collection is now housed in its own wing in the Metropolitan Museum, though in constantly toying with the idea of selling things, he kept curators, dealers and auction houses alert and in attendance. On an earlier working journey he had allowed me to see his drawings and I knew that his was a summons for which I should drop everything in my diary and get onto a plane. I understood him to be, in New York, the client of Eugene Thaw, a powerful dealer of considerable physical presence, from whose character the gods had omitted modesty and candour. In London he was Hans Calmann's client and he, with indiscretion born of vanity, let it be known that Lehman thought nothing of spending £25,000 on a single drawing – indeed, I am inclined to think that he was at heart as much influenced in favour of a purchase by its outrageous price as its exceptional quality. He died in 1969 and was seventy-four or so when he made the telephone call to me. 'Young man,' he said, 'I am calling you because you are the only professional visitor to my collection who did not offer to be of service, did not leave me a card.' Unlike the others, whoever they were, I had simply looked at the drawings, envying them, learning from them, and my note of thanks, though written from Christie's, had been just that – thanks.

In one sense only was it an easy week – Lehman knew the market price of everything. He did not work on the stale principle still in force at Christie's that it was the auctioneer's business to establish a basic figure on which the dealer could make a handsome profit; to him the buying price at auction was exactly the same for the dealer, the collector and the museum, and it was the auctioneer's job to get that price, to establish at the moment of sale the highest price that could be paid, whether by a museum (the end of the line in any series of transactions), by a private collector who, by the nature of things, could only own his possessions for a comparatively short while, or by a dealer who could no longer expect to make an immediate and huge percentage profit. I had some sympathy with his view, for I too thought it foolish to hand dealers a hundred per cent profit on their auction bids, but at Christie's this was heresy. So Lehman and I worked on his heretical principle when we discussed the reserves to be placed on the drawings he had all but decided to sell. At the very end of our negotiation he asked 'Now what are your terms?' Terms for ordinary vendors were a ten per cent commission on the selling price and a charge for illustration in the catalogue; if the business had been introduced by a dealer, lawyer or other intermediary, two per cent went to him and Christie's did the work for eight. I sensed danger and offered a commission of eight per cent with no other charges. 'Not good enough,' he said, pointing out that he was offering the most important sale I had ever mounted, openly lending his name to it (pure gold in the influence that this might have on other vendors), and that, as a banker, he never settled on the first offer. To my response that I had conceded as much as I could and that any further reduction in our charges could only be negotiated by a partner in the firm, his retort was volcanic, beginning, if not with the monkey and the organ-grinder, something very like it, mounting in discourtesy until I found myself in the street. How much of it was theatre, I could not judge.

I returned to London on the first plane I could catch and went straight to Peter Chance – a mistake, but Patrick I thought would do no more than pick up the telephone and speak *de haut en bas* when humble pie was necessary, and Guy might just not understand what was at stake. Peter did understand, but what I wanted – that is Patrick's prompt despatch on a diplomatic mission to New York – did not come to pass. Instead, I was hauled into Patrick's room and roundly bollocked for having first spoken to Peter – and then the death knell – 'No old Jew in New York with a handful of drawings is going to tell me how Christie's should run its business.' Patrick did telephone Lehman, but the opportunity to sell his drawings was lost, leaving me angry, disappointed, bruised. It was not the first such mishap: almost exactly the same course of events had happened on a previous journey to New York when Judge Untermeyer, a supposed 'old friend of the firm,' had shown me paintings and drawings, but his were too unremarkable to merit hefty concessions from Christie's and his behaviour more measured; even so, I should have learned from it that in America, without the status of partner or director, worse trouble might confront me.

*   *   *

In January 1966 I bought my third old Daimler, built nine years earlier and cossetted by an owner who had his coat-of-arms blazoned on the rear doors. Big, beautiful and rare but at the bottom of the market (for new Daimlers were by then indistinguishable from Jaguars and the great old name on its way to oblivion), it was mechanically much the same as any Daimler built thirty years before, but it carried a very pretty close-coupled saloon body by Mulliner, of which it is said that only twelve were built. Under its long bonnet lay a lazy and whispering 4.5-litre six cylinder engine that settled down to cruise quite happily at 80 mph and was perfect for German Autobahns. I also bought a house, a large, ugly, late Victorian monstrosity in Barnes, fronting what proved to be the intolerably noisy Castelnau (once considered a good address, alas by then considerably run down), but with an open view at the back over a reservoir that is now a wetland for wild birds. It was a rash decision far from wise, compelled by the sudden sale, at last, of 16 Phillimore Place, but if needs be was large enough to house my mother too; meanwhile, it could pay for itself with lodgers.

Within a week of buying the Daimler I was off to Germany in it with Ulrich von Artus, the very bright, very shrewd and very German (blonde straight hair and a flawless skin the colour of a butter biscuit) apprentice at the Front Counter, working without pay for the experience, the son of a friendly art auctioneer in Frankfurt. His father had a string of contacts with whom he felt unqualified to deal. It was my first acquaintance with the under-world of the post-Nazi art market; two full decades after the end of World War II, paintings without provenance were creeping onto a market where questions were not asked. Occasionally, in London, paintings were brought to Christie's that I recognised from pre-war museum catalogues and these we always made every effort to restore to the institutions from which they had been removed, though sometimes they had been de-accessioned on the grounds of degeneracy, *Entartete Kunst* the great scandal of the Nazi art establishment in 1937,[38] and the new owners often had every right to them; with old masters and nineteenth-century paintings it was a very different matter and with this wave of material consigned to a small local auction house in Frankfurt – and, I later learned, to many others of its ilk – I sensed confusion between genuine ownership and the consequences of forced sales to Nazi collectors in the Thirties. After I left Christie's my link with Ulrich and his father was to bring me into direct contact with the most unpleasant, perhaps even evil, of men in the art market.

There was a second unpaid apprentice from Germany working on the Front Counter, Jens Wollesen, son of an antique dealer in Bad Oeynhausen, a big, tall hobbledehoy but intellectually a far more interesting boy than Ulrich, who eventually became a dis-tinguished specialist in Trecento art and a professor at Toronto University – an odd coincidence when I think how close I came to a post there in 1957. As he lodged with me in Castelnau I was a close observer when he fell into a dog-like infatuation for Yvonne tan Bunzl, the daughter of a wealthy Austrian family, who had just

---

38 See Peter Adam: *Arts in the Third Reich*, Thames and Hudson 1992.

begun to make her presence felt as an adventurous dealer in old master drawings. It was the only time that I have heard the moans and groans of unrequited adoration; he was eighteen, she I guessed to be in her mid-twenties, but the gap in sophistication was far greater. Eventually, without too clumsy an excuse, I introduced them and left him to get on with his fawning. The sighs continued until, at last, she let him take her to dinner; then, aware of her wealth, I made sure that he had cash enough wherever she might want to go. It was a salutary lesson; almost every penny of the cash consumed, and very late, he had to walk back to Barnes with not so much as a chaste kiss of encouragement. He burst into my bedroom to curse and swear at his expensive disappointment, and then made an unpolished offer to get into my bed. This I refused. It was not that I resented playing second fiddle to Yvonne; it was that I cared too much for him, patently heterosexual, to let him go through the anguish of guilt, denial and self-doubt that might well be the consequence of such a one-night stand when simple masturbation with Yvonne in mind was so evidently the wiser release of his frustration. Late in August, shortly before the end of his apprenticeship, we spent a riotous week in Landsberg-am-Lech and Munich looking at more old masters that might be sold at Christie's, our evenings spent in the manly pursuits of eating too much and getting very, very drunk.

Three whole weeks in June and July, as well as many odd days after, were spent at Chatsworth working on a valuation of the drawings collected, largely, by William Cavendish, the second Duke of Devonshire from 1707 until his death in 1729. In 1966 it was, and – in spite of major depletions through subsequent sales at Christie's – is still the most important British collection of old master drawings outside the Royal Collection and the British Museum, to which so many of its treasures have been transferred. Many drawings had been exhibited both singly and in large groups in this country and America, and these had been properly catalogued by A. E. Popham and James Byam Shaw; other scholars had noted their observations and attributions on the mounts, among them Johannes Wilde, Jacob Bean and Philip Pouncey, and to these David and I occasionally added ours; and with Tom Wragg on hand – Chatsworth's Librarian and Keeper – with not only the typescript catalogue written by his immediate predecessor, Francis Thompson, but his extraordinary recollection of what every worthy visitor in his time had said, though not written, we were not short of information. Tom was an unlikely Keeper in that he was a local Derbyshire lad of no conventional education as an art historian, with no command of foreign languages, and nothing about his dress or manner to suggest that he was anything other than a downtrodden collector of weekly sixpences for a Life Assurance Company, his raincoat perfect for the flasher. He was, however, greatly respected and much loved. I had known him since *The Age of Louis XIV*, as it were, and he had been much in evidence at Christie's in June 1958 when twenty-four paintings were sold from Chatsworth as part of the settlement of the 10th Duke's death duties (I am amused to find, scribbled in my copy of the sale catalogue, a list of art books bought that week – £45 spent on twenty-one, ranging from Denis Mahon's *Seicento Theory* at £3.10 to fifteen shillings for the catalogue of the Lotto exhibition in Venice in 1953, this last still with the bookseller's note, 'Pile. £45.' My salary then was £8 a week).

'D. Carritt & B. Sewell come back tomorrow to continue valuing the drawings and prints. It's a scream watching them work, I'll keep my imitation up my sleeve & will try & perfect it tomorrow. I love them both (rather) . . . ' So wrote Deborah (Debo), Duchess of Devonshire, to Nancy Mitford on 27 June 1966.[39] My weeks spent at Chatsworth, partly with David, partly with Noël Annesley, looking at drawings and cossetting whippets, were among the happiest of my life and full of laughter. We giggled helplessly as

---

39   Charlotte Mosley ed: *The Mitfords – Letters between Six Sisters*, Harper 2007.

Debo decided that she would entertain James Rorimer, Director of the Metropolitan Museum, to tea and give him tomato sandwiches made with fruit grown from seeds, not planted, but spontaneously growing in the Chatsworth sewage – and then let him know that this was so. We giggled helplessly a lot.

In the dead days of late July and August the support work for the Chatsworth valuation continued in London, the rummaging through exhibition and collection catalogues, books and photographs, to confirm or adjust attributions, the checking of auctions at Sotheby's and elsewhere, uncovering prices recently asked by dealers in a rapidly rising market. Others took holidays but my nose was to its grindstone, not only in this enjoyable chore but in the daily grind of the department and the preparation of sales for the autumn season. My week away in Bavaria with Jens only increased the pressure, but I knew that on Friday 16 September I should be off and away again – with nothing to do for Christie's – to Spain with Claudio, partly to fill gaps in my journey with John Croft five years before, and partly, having with him followed the pilgrimage route to Compostella across the north of the country, to rejoin it at Burgos and return to England along the route from Bordeaux to Paris.

Ten days or so before I left, urgently assembling manuscripts (as raw catalogue entries were impertinently called) for a sale catalogue while the printer and Guy hovered at my shoulders, a boy from the Front Counter came into my room holding part of a split panel in each hand, laughing as he told me that 'some woman' had insisted that it be seen by an expert. I simply said 'Don't let that woman leave the building – don't,' and continued shuffling manuscripts. 'What is it?' said Guy – to which, my nostrils no doubt flaring, my deliberately infuriating answer was 'Guy, you've ordered me to finish this catalogue, and finish it I will. Then I'll tell you what it is.'

It was a sketch by Rubens in preparation for his *Samson and Delilah*, now in the National Gallery but then, if known at all, thought lost. I knew it only from an engraving by Jacob Matham seen years before, but the picture itself had never been reproduced in any monograph and I had some reason to believe that it had been destroyed in British bombing raids on Hamburg. For this my source was Ludwig Burchard (1886–1960), a devoted scholar who had since 1922 been compiling a catalogue raisonné of paintings by Rubens, to whom I had been sent by Johannes Wilde when I first thought of Rubens as a subject for a PhD. His *Corpus Rubenianum* was then a vast amorphous mass of notes, papers, tentative publications, photographs and memories – and remained so at his death (even now it is still in course of publication); no one ever knew more of Rubens, but overwhelmed by what he knew, he could organise almost nothing for publication.

It was thus with great excitement and enthusiasm that I told 'some woman' what she had brought in. I learned later that she had already been to Sotheby's and to the National Gallery which used, on Wednesdays, to hold an open day for enquiries and often shed persistent nuisances by sending them on to nearby Christie's for second opinions and valuations. 'I've just been to the National Gallery and they said this is a Rubens (or Raphael, or Rembrandt)' was always a bad beginning to a consultation, but on this occasion it was I who began the conversation with no ifs, buts and caveats about the attribution.

I left for Spain with Claudio, and in my absence John Herbert released to the press an announcement that David Carritt had made another astonishing discovery – the preparatory *modello* for a great painting by Rubens long believed lost, *Samson and Delilah*. David was photographed holding it. I dare say he was blameless. The press release was concocted by Patrick and his naive intention was to publicise David's thaumaturgical abilities in the hope of invitations hither and yon to discover other masterpieces long unrecognised – a break from the firm's tradition that it, rather than any individual within it, made discoveries. The *Daily Telegraph* made most fuss, so much indeed that someone in Christie's sent the editor an anonymous note asserting that his report of the affair was nonsense and that it was I who had identified the Rubens. When, on 17 October, I returned from Spain, it was to a raging accusation of disloyalty from Patrick who had assumed me to be the author of the note. I had no idea what he was shouting about and did not know how to respond. The note could have been sent by anyone in the department, indeed by almost anyone in the firm, for the tale of how I had driven the grin from the face of the boy on the Front Counter and kept Guy fretting in anticipation for a quarter of an hour was the gossip of the day, but it could not have been sent by me, driving long and fast to Cordoba. I suspected Patrick's secretary, Julia Lucas, who had earlier been mine; we were fond of each other and both resented the way in which, recognising her ability, intelligence and the perception that enabled her to compose letters as though I had written them myself, he had broken our partnership.

I had been away for four full weeks – time enough to brood, and between the delights of Granada, Toledo, Madrid, the Escorial, Segovia, Burgos and points between and north, I had contemplated leaving Christie's. It had become too rarely a happy place to work. My initial role had been scuppered by the ghost of Vic Heather and the department's dependence on a workhorse, blind, ignorant and unambitious; what connoisseurship and scholarship I had been able to add had now been usurped by David – not his fault and my resentment was never directed at him, but at Guy and Patrick who were puppet-masters to us both; the difference was that I had been asked to join the firm before they had defined what I was to do and be, and that their having later discovered the definition, they applied it instead to David. My second role, discovered by me for myself, the builder of a department of prints and drawings independent of the picture department, had been frustrated for fully five years since I had proved that it could be done. And now, this melancholy much in mind, I was confronted by Patrick in a poisonous rage that he had sustained and nurtured the full length of my absence.

I had a busy week. There was a month's correspondence to read and a month's cataloguing to check – though Noël had proved to be a shrewd and sensibilitous pupil. There was, too, a mad dash to Wales in my diary – a journey promising a Van Eyck that in the event proved to be a worthless copy of Van Dyck's portrait of *Thomas Wentworth with his Secretary* (one of hundreds). Driving gave me yet more time to think about Patrick and work at Christie's that was now turning me into little better than a travelling salesman; it was a time when few people had access to a camera, before the invention of the polaroid and when owners wrote descriptions of their paintings, the words of this Welshman so lyrically poetic that his Eyck-Dyck became a late medieval masterpiece. I did not expect another *Arnolfini Portrait* – that was too far beyond the bounds of chance – but the description of a man holding a letter, seated before a rich cloth-of-honour, could have been of a portrait by Memling later in the fifteenth century, or even by a sixteenth century German hand, and 'the family tradition that it is by Van Eyck' was tempting. There were no other pictures of note in the house and I returned to London empty-handed.

Was this to be my life? – a life of largely fruitless journeys in hope of a discovery or two with which David would be credited? Was I to be not even the replacement for Vic Heather now, but the new Freddy Turner (old Alec's ignorant brother-in-law), always on the move, always alone at night in cheap hotels or at the mercy of bed-and-breakfast keepers? Still brooding, I spent the weekend at Castle Hedingham, saying nothing of my mood – easily managed with so much to say of Spain and pilgrimage. The following week I drove to Hull to advise on the insurance value of paintings in a proposed loan exhibition, and then on to Newcastle to inspect the stock of two dealers who regularly consigned paintings in bulk to Christie's. One of the paintings I saw in Hull was by Kate Coughtrie, *Remembrance*, and I telephoned my mother to ask if she had any recollection of it or had played some part in it. It was on the long slog back to London in the dark that I decided to talk to Peter Chance.

Dénouement

In the first week of November I asked Peter to give me a few uninterrupted minutes. I told him that working under Patrick had from the very start been difficult, but that with Guy too in charge of the department matters had worsened in the sense that I had to contend with the competition between them. I recalled my difficulties in America and our loss of the Lehman sale. I explained that the market for old master drawings was driven by American collectors and dealers, and expressed the opinion that without a dedicated director we could never play any part in it other than second fiddle to Sotheby's where, even though they had the year before taken Philip Pouncey from the British Museum to add expertise to that department, Richard Day, its workhorse, younger than me and far less experienced, had been made a partner and director. I reminded him that on the three occasions when I had been approached by the National Trust, the British Council and an American university collection with offers of a post, he had urged me not to go, reiterating and reinforcing the promise made at my first interview with him in 1958 that I would eventually be appointed a director. Those offers should have reassured him that I was worth having in his employment. 'This time I have not been offered another job. I am not being tempted to leave by any outside prospect. But I am no longer happy here, and for this the only remedy is my being able to talk to Patrick on equal terms.'

'Give me three days,' he said, 'I'll talk to the others.' He took a little longer. In mid afternoon on Wednesday 9 November 1966 he called me to his room. 'I'm afraid it's no. It's Patrick.' I had no alternative but to resign; I had, perhaps, been too frank and talked myself into a corner – certainly that is how I felt – but to retreat from what had been something of an ultimatum would not only have been humiliating but would have put me in an abject relationship with Patrick. I had long said to myself that I should be settled in a career by the time I reached thirty-five and I expected to spend the rest of my working life at Christie's, but the extraordinary peak of happiness and contentment in the first part of the year had been wiped out by the affair of the Rubens sketch, which I had not even been allowed to catalogue, and I felt that I had been eliminated as effectively as a dissident Russian general from a photograph of Stalin.

I told Peter that I would leave in three months or on completion of the Chatsworth valuation, whichever was the sooner, and returned to my room wretchedly downcast – a mood that turned to hurt, anger and absolute resolve when David Carritt came to see me. He told me of the meeting of his fellow directors at which my joining them had been discussed. All but one had been in favour, but the decision had to be unanimous. Patrick had objected, and objected in such terms as had humiliated David – 'We've got one homosexual on the board; we don't need another . . . ' Other directors, when confronted, confirmed that this was so. So there it was; my knowledge, experience and dogged devotion counted for nothing because I was queer; even, illogically, my uncomplaining exploitation when knowingly packed off to spend a night or two with any titled Old Etonian who had a picture he might sell if enchanted by a pretty boy, counted for nothing; in Patrick's view I was contemptible – and that was to be the lurking elephant with us for the next three months or so.

As Chatsworth, like refurbishing the Forth Bridge, proved to be a matter that dragged on for decades, resulting in spectacular sales under Noël Annesley and acutely embarrassing misjudgements by the British Museum, 9 February 1967 was officially the day of my departure. In the event, my life at Christie's both fizzled out and fizzled on. While completing that part of the Chatsworth valuation for which I was responsible, I took on nothing new that could not be completed within a day or two and inexorably became what in my army days was dubbed the spare prick at the wedding. Half a dozen times, both before and after Christmas, Peter took me to lunch and tried to persuade me not to leave, 'You don't have to go' always his refrain. His charm and sincerity were persuasive – but how could I weaken when I knew that he had concealed from me Patrick's 'We've got one homosexual on the board . . . ' My only misgiving was for Noël; for a year or so I left him my reference books on the prints of Dürer and Rembrandt – the essential keys to any that he might have to catalogue – and from time to time slipped back to look at drawings with him, but towards the end of 1967 this no longer seemed necessary, so much had his confidence grown, and my occasional visits dwindled away.

In spite of Patrick, leaving Christie's was painful. The longest episode of my life – longer than school, the army or the Courtauld Institute, it had been a period of continual growth in knowledge and experience, of constant opportunity, though I felt that I had given the firm as much as it had given me. And I was leaving it, not because I had exhausted its resources, nor because it had exhausted mine, not for any professional advancement, but because I was damned for being queer.

Coda

If a man's life is indeed the biblical term of three score years and ten, then mine was half done, but, far from Dante's predicament when writing of that midway stage - 'Nel mezzo del cammin di nostra vita' - I was neither lost nor terrified. I had told very few within and without the firm that I was about to leave Christie's, I had made no plans, I had not even done what afterwards I learned that 'everybody did' – that is take a copy of the client list and of subscribers to the relevant catalogues – and my future was uncertain. I was, however, overwhelmingly aware of a sense of freedom. All my life I had been under the control of others, parents, priests and mentors, or at school and in the army one of many in a large group with a common and disciplined aim, but now I had the opportunity to do, if not entirely what I pleased, then at least to find work that I enjoyed and to pursue it at any pace I chose. There were false starts and the discovery that avenues were closed, but I had more friends that I had realised; America and Europe became happy hunting grounds and in my travels I saw not only great museums and galleries, but many forgotten, obscure and rarely visited by Englishmen, constantly widening and complementing my know-ledge. Dali was for some years my friend, Warhol an occasional acquaintance across a smoke-filled room, Bacon a sometimes petulant and demanding neighbour. I rode the moors of Derbyshire on a docile gelding and was nourished by the solitude; I took my skis to Norway and was delighted by the flight of ptarmigan; I learned, if not to climb them, to clamber about in mountains and cherish isolation; and for fifteen years or so, summer and winter, I quartered Turkey in pursuit of Greek, Roman, Christian and, particularly, Armenian monuments. No scholar gypsy could have been happier.

Now well beyond my second half I ought, at eighty, like old

King Cole, to be a merry old soul content with Burgundy and 'baccy. Instead, I chose to write this book, partly because so many friends have begged me to record such matters as the working methods of Hercules Brabazon Brabazon, and the survival into the mid-sixties of Baron von Gloeden's photographic plates, but more because it may reassure readers not remotely interested in art, particularly young men in times far more enlightened than mine, that it is not quite the end of the world to be a bastard or queer. At eighty I have felt far more able to be candid than at sixty, and even what-the-hellish about matters in which candour may still shock, in the hope that my survival may help others to survive.

I have had one small difficulty with language: buggery was the common word for sodomy when I was young and, as the Oxford English Dictionary has it, 'in decent use only as a legal term;' now used quite comfortably in almost all the exclamatory and idiomatic senses listed by the great Eric Partridge in his *Dictionary of Slang*, to today's ear the word seems blunt and brutal in its sexual sense. Those as intrigued as I by etymology will understand my clinging to the word for the sake of its period feel when writing of my early years; if there is a sequel to this book I shall, no doubt, as the transition is now absolute in vulgar parlance, use the verb *to fuck* for the very same activity.

OUTSIDER II

One friend more than any other has, in caring for my dogs, enabled me to write this book. 'I hate dogs,' he has said a thousand times when removing the evidence of loose bowels and revolting stomachs (as must all who share their lives with animals), and yet he has affectionately and diligently fed, watered and walked them, and on their deaths has felt as much distress as I and in tears seen them to their graves.

Acknowledgements

Such a book as this must begin, as a rule it seems, with acknowledgements for help and information. I have only one to make – to my mother, whose keeping of diaries was indefatigable until, during the later Eighties, dementia eroded both her sharp mind and what was engaging in her personality; then her records declined into notes of the cost of milk delivered to the house and the frequency of burglar alarms that disrupted sleep. These diaries I had not read until, occasionally uncertain of a date in my own, less scrupulously kept, I turned to them and found, not only the information I sought, but her comments on my life. I had no idea of the extent to which she had invaded my privacy, had timed the coming and going of men casually encountered as bedmates for an hour and had commented, always adversely, on the motives of others who lasted a little longer and might, briefly, qualify as lovers; her vilification of others still, who graduated to staunch friend from random fuck, was the pure bile of jealousy. Of one she was particularly envious, seeing him as a constant and lasting threat to her supremacy in my affections. She was mistaken; a man's love for a lover, male or female, does not impinge on or clash with his love for his mother – only the mother herself can affect that unique emotional bond, and mine, consumed with irrelevant hatred, poisoned ours, destroyed it. I am, nevertheless, deeply grateful to her for her diaries.

I am also grateful for my own, but wish that I had been more persistent with them, for often their keeping fell away for months, the thought of writing in my hours of leisure, when writing is my work, almost repellant. On the other hand, my journals of journeys are sedulous in their detail, recording not only what I saw and did, but even my dreams and the wanderings of my mind – how odd, during a sleepless night in Istanbul, to ponder the implications of an

inscription on a drawing by Dürer in the British Museum –
occasionally enlivened by elementary drawings and the groundplans
of fallen buildings – but then all these were written for the benefit
of the books that were to follow (always almost, never quite).
Knowing now that they will not, that they belong to an activity
and period of my life to which there can be no return, I shall read
them once more, reduce them to a set of notes that to another
traveller might be useful on, for example, the early churches of
Cappadocia and Turkish Armenia, and destroy the private jottings.
All the diaries too, my mother's as well as my own, will be
consigned to a bonfire (to keep for an unknown posterity too
many papers is an insidious vanity).

CHAPTER I

Introduction

I have three times in a long life experienced some significant understanding of myself – epiphany, in its modern and shallow sense of any sudden realisation, now the fashionable term for such enlightenment – at twelve, twenty-one and in my eightieth summer.

At twelve, in the deep midwinter of 1943–44, the earth of the school's playing fields so frozen that the fierce rough and tumble of rugby football was quite out of the question, we were sent on a cross-country run of three miles or so, an endurance test for scrawny little boys ill-nourished on the meagre food rations that reached London at the height of the Second World War. I had no experience of long-distance running; mine was the quick sprint baulked by a tackle, rarely more than twenty yards, perhaps embellished by a swerve or two, breathless only when thumped to the ground by an opponent, the stitch, that deep disabling pain in the side induced by long continuous exercise, no part of it. Running across country, however, was – at least in part – precisely that long continuous exercise, the pace and stride regular, sometimes for hundreds of yards, the stitch and the nausea that accompanied it, the enemy lurking within my body, with only a hedge or ditch or gate to break the rhythm with a leap. On that first freezing day I ran – and ran. I leaped all obstacles. I discovered that the further I ran and leaped, the easier it became, and was aware of something beyond the physical experience – elation. This was something I could do alone; it was not a team sport, I had no other players to take into account, and whether I won or lost was entirely my own responsibility. I won that first race, and won it by such a margin that I was accused by the referee – who happened to be Mr Keevil, the art master – of cheating, and was sent off to run half the course again. That small injustice left no mark, but the sense of elation did and cross-country running became a secret pastime – secret because not shared – and still, so many years later, it haunts my unconscious and surfaces in dreams.

At twenty-one, in September 1952, I reported to Aldershot for my two years of National Service in the army – and my solitary running stood me in good stead. There, over rough heathland tracks, we ran in heavy army boots for seven miles, sometimes as an exercise, sometimes as a punishment. For me it was an escape from military drudgery, a time – the only time – when as a squaddy I could be alone, my body doing its pleasurable duty on the run but my brain let loose to contemplate the conflict between imposed (even unthinking) obedience to Queen and country and my chosen and educated obedience to a Christian and Catholic faith, the obligation to respect the Seven Virtues and to be generous with the Seven Works of Mercy. The issue of such obedience arose when we were trained to fire rifles and, screaming abuse, plunge bayonets into the bellies of the sacking and straw lay models that represented the enemy. I might, I thought, in the event choose not to fire a lethal shot, not to inflict a mortal wound with the stab of a bayonet that no soft tissue could resist (we were advised to strike low, avoiding the ribs from between which the bayonet might be difficult to withdraw, the image painted for us of a soldier dying at the end of a rifle violently shaken to, as it were, get him off the hook, quite vile), but being trained to do so was not only not the deed itself, but not the time to make a moral point to an uncomprehending sergeant. The real argument must wait until and if I found myself on active service in Korea, Malaya or any other theatre of war (as was quite possible) in which a young National Serviceman might be compelled to use his weapons in order to preserve himself or his companions. There, of course, lay the rub: why should I have the moral luxury of saving my soul if, in saving it, the young soldier to the left or right of me were to lose his life through my action or inaction? This epiphany was slow to mature but in the end was sudden; almost disconcertingly I learned that I had changed, that I had developed in my brain a place of ice-cold reason remote from religious belief, moral philosophy and an educated sense of right and wrong, and knew that, were it necessary, I would kill. Again I felt elation; I felt, indeed, that in commanding circumstances there was nothing that I would not do – and God, not I, must take responsibility for sorting out the moral mess.

In 2010, early in my eightieth summer, I completed an account of my early life, thinking (mistakenly) that I might celebrate its publication in July 2011 on my eightieth birthday. Very long, insofar as any autobiography can, it began at the beginning of my life and concluded on 9 February 1967 when, at thirty-five, I was halfway through my biblical allowance of three score years and ten. For two decades friends – one in particular – had urged me to write it, pleading that what I knew of the art world, its workings and its characters, should be recorded; but I wanted to deal with other aspects of my life as well and thought an autobiography at sixty premature and, since I hoped for more years of sound mind and physical activity, was not yet ready to reveal what I believe to be essential in such books – the truth, the whole truth and, if not quite nothing but the truth, unfettered honesty. I did not at that stage, writing journalism as well as art criticism, want to discuss my homosexuality, for queers are rare among the desks of Fleet Street and editors were (and still are) all too ready to exploit the old-fashioned sensation attached to any revelation that a man is sexually attracted to his kind. I did not, at that stage, want to discuss my illegitimacy, for my father had a legitimate son whose life might have been rocked by the sudden appearance of a half-brother. I did not want to discuss my childhood, fatherless, in the sole care of a gifted and intelligent mother still very much alive, and with the remnants of her beauty, who had brought me up in the Thirties, deeply impoverished at a time when illegitimacy was a terrible stigma for both the parent and the child.

These were, however, the facts and factors that formed my character as an Outsider, homosexuality a driving force that could be, and was, resisted, only for me to recognise, almost too late, how much damage that resistance had done, and the illegitimate birth that had to be kept secret, that made me dissemble throughout my schooldays and, particularly, my years in the army and at Christie's. There, where my final interview in 1958 was with Sir Alec Martin, a vile, arrogant and ignorant old martinet who had obscured his working-class origins and converted his cockney speech into a post-Edwardian affectation, his first words were more accurate and wounding than he knew – 'Well, we know you've no social connections, but . . . ' But I was a good enough art historian and judge of quality to catalogue paintings sent to the firm for sale and he was prepared to employ me.

I stayed with Christie's for nine years until, weary of the blindness and obstruction of my departmental head, the Honourable Patrick Lindsay, I asked for a department of my own, Prints and Drawings by Old Masters. I had created it and built substantial turnover. It was a category of which Patrick knew nothing; he knew very little of anything to do with art, had no eye for it and was much given to declaring that this picture must be catalogued as by Reynolds and that by Gainsborough for no better reason than that he had told the owners so; where drawings were concerned he had neither knowledge nor experience, nor even an instinctive eye for quality. Christie's was a partnership and to be the director of a department meant becoming a partner, involving some re-apportioning of shares (somehow to be paid for by the new partner) and the unanimous agreement of all on the existing board. Patrick argued against my appointment and in such terms that made the prospect of any long-term career at Christie's suddenly insufferable; I had two friends on the board of directors, one of them David Carritt, a now forgotten wayward genius in the tradition of Bernard Berenson, and it was he who immediately told me of Patrick's response to the proposal – 'We've got one homosexual on the board (David); we don't need another . . . ' I resigned.

In spite of Patrick, leaving Christie's was painful. The longest episode of my life – longer than school, the army or the Courtauld Institute, it had been a period of continual growth in knowledge and experience, of constant opportunity to explore great museums and collections and the dark places of the art market, though I felt that I had given the firm as much as it had given me. And I was leaving it, not because I had exhausted its resources, nor because it had exhausted mine, nor for any professional advancement elsewhere, but because I was damned for being queer.

Writing my scrupulously honest account of childhood, boyhood and early maturity often felt like self-administered psychoanalysis – deeply painful and disturbing – and, re-reading the typescript before it was sent to a publisher, I experienced my third epiphany, dispassionately examining myself and seeing, for the first time and with absolute clarity (though far too late to profit from the revelation) what had been amiss with my life and career, what had been my own fault and folly, and what had been brought about by circumstance. I saw too that I had achieved my objective with it, not just as a record of my experience in the art market and the handing-on of things known but not published, some dating back to the early decades of the twentieth century, but that I had dealt frankly with the business of being both a bastard and a bugger and how this came about. This last had not been easy: that I cast aside so many decades of deceit that became dissembling and dissembling that relaxed into an attitude of 'I don't care what they think as long as I don't have to talk about it' at last became a purpose – the good it might do, the reassurance it might offer to the many who, particularly in early adult life, suffer extraordinary anguish from being cut away from unknown parents, one or both, and those who, in these still quite unenlightened times, are for their homo-sexuality made to feel Outsiders.

CHAPTER 2

Scratching a Living

I had made no preparation for leaving Christie's; I had told very few outside the firm of my intention; I had made no overtures and had no inkling of another job; I had not done what most leavers did – taken a copy of the catalogue subscription list, an invaluable record of names, addresses, telephone numbers and interest all over Britain, America and Europe. A cleverer man than I would have prepared his ground and not left the firm so precipitately. I had no money, having recently bought a large, ugly and near derelict house in Barnes, inconveniently south of the narrowest and most fragile bridge over the Thames, had been defrauded by an incompetent builder who had set fire to it, and was burdened with mortgage repayments that must monthly be settled.

This was midwinter, the first months of 1967, and for the moment there was no means of heating the icily cold house. Wires dangled from square gaps in the plaster where sockets and switches should have been, and radiators lay propped against the walls, not yet connected to pipes that in the boiler room below were not connected to a boiler for which I had paid, but which had not been delivered by the dismissed builder. I could cook and boil water with which to shave, but bathing was the shivering business of showering in water cold enough to freeze – as it did, in a pipe embedded in a wall on the first floor which, when it thawed, brought down the plaster in that room and the ceilings of the floor below. To such an ice-well no sane man would bring a lover and the only comfort was my dog, Susie – or, more properly, Susannah, named so after a beautiful girl I knew, whose carelessly elegant body language the pup's so much resembled. Claudio – who today would have been my civil partner, but then had to be explained as 'my Sicilian cousin, two or three times removed' – was in Sicily, doing his Christmas and New Year duties by his family.

Claudio, who could so easily have been one of a thousand casual lovers, one-night stands or urgently furtive sexual encounters in Hyde Park, had replaced all these. It had been a slow business – seven years in all. At first he was just another boy who might last a day or two – and to the promiscuous me that was initially enough – but, eight years my junior, he was physically puppyish and intellectually little brotherish, and his haphazard English amused me, forcing both of us into an absurd polyglot vocabulary that sometimes, too often in quite unsuitable circumstances, overflowed, with helpless giggling the consequence. Amusement developed into the sort of affection one might have for another man's dog, and eventually one's own, and for a while he and Susie were neck and neck. Steadily he reduced my promiscuity to the point at which he could begin to demand my constancy: 'I will kill you if . . . ' were the first words of many such demands that ended 'with a stiletto, just behind the ear, a wound so small that no one will know why you are dead.'

He was not small, dark, hairy and tough – as one might suppose a Sicilian to be – but tall and languid, his hair blond and floppily straight and his eyes large and dark, with something about him that was Florentine and Quattrocento. His skin was flawless and pale biscuit in colour, hardly darkening in summer, and golden body hair grew only in his armpits and in as neatly defined a patch as is to be found in the groin of a classical nude. I grew to be faithful to him when he was in England – as he was for months on end – but when his employers, the Italian state tourist board, sent him to Italy in the summers, that was a loyalty too demanding for me to maintain, and I lapsed into the opportunities for promiscuity so abundant on the towpath by the Thames between Hammersmith Bridge and the boat sheds at Putney. There the thrill lay not only in the hunt but in the menace of darkness, for it was lit only by the moon and, until one's night vision kicked in, one could see nothing and perception was left to other senses – it is odd how much hearing is heightened in such circumstances; there was also the danger of the sudden presence of the river police patrolling in a boat with the engine shut down and all lights off, the fierce beam of its searchlight suddenly cutting through the night. Far from running, the safest thing to do then was to lie flat and still in what small cover there might be, with one's face turned away from the beam. Often there was no time to disengage and we lay like a brace of spoons waiting for boredom to move the boat on. There was never much conversation, but occasionally my trophy was an oarsman who preferred to be taken home; to my amusement, these were always sheepishly passive, uncooperative in any foreplay, just wanting to be fucked – something to do with the repetitive action of rowing, I suppose.

My relationship with Claudio, a thing by this time of adoring tenderness, had not the slightest connection with the animal business of the towpath and he was never aware of that coarsely physical side of my nature. His long summer absences heightened my need for him to satisfy its other side, the side that feasts on looking, hearing, touching with the fingertips his silken skin, entering his body the most discreet and unselfish climax to these preliminaries. Always a bond of autumn, winter and spring, even this hibernal period had to be broken in its depth by Claudio's return to his parents in Taormina as one year turned into another, but this time, with the house in cold chaos and my career at Christie's shattered, his absence was particularly telling. He always resisted the pressure to stay in Sicily, determined to spend his life with me – and indeed he did return to London late in February 1967, but twelve months later he did not. Instead, there was a letter. He was his father's only son, it said, the last of a Norman line reaching back a thousand years unbroken, the Corvaya name unchanged, and as the only heir to the defunct marquisate he must, his father had argued, marry and beget a son. He did neither. He could not confess that he was queer and, in growing misery, he stayed in touch, but we grew apart and, when his father died, it was too late. He sold what property there was, bought a very good cast of Rodin's *Thinker*, moved to an apartment in Madrid and revived the title for use there. From time to time, at whim, he came to see me, always with a butch guttersnipe in tow, the last of them under the delusion that he was required to fuck everyone in sight, until a decade or so ago, Umberto Marturana, his boyhood friend in Taormina, came instead, to tell me that Claudio had been murdered, his skull cracked (by the Rodin, I wondered?) and his apartment stripped. Rent boys were suspected, but none was ever charged.

*   *   *

In Claudio's absence I was hamstrung. Without the daily discipline of going to work at Christie's, I felt lost, and there was little I could do about the house until I had money enough to pay another builder. We had talked of dealing in antiques, and that we could manage, for in 1967 one could easily begin trading with as little as £100, buying from one shop and selling to another for immediate small profits; Claudio had the cheek for this as well as an instinctive eye for quality, a sound visual memory and – as it seemed all Italians in London had – contacts with the 'mafiosi' who played so significant a part in the London auction rooms. Without him, however, I could do nothing to turn our thinking aloud into a plan; I brooded, and the more I did so, the less I wanted to be another unctuous dealer in Church Street, Kensington, or bluff in Long Melford, pretending that my battered household furniture was genuinely Georgian. By the time Claudio returned, I was exploring other avenues.

What could I do? What did I want to do? I went to see my vet. It was, I thought, an opportunity to change my life, to escape the tyranny of paintings right and wrong, to abandon the art market, its thrills, disappointments and moral dilemmas, and instead do something that seemed right and good. Russell Williams – Rusty to his friends – vet and oarsman, thought not, but in the spirit of 'Don't take my word for it' sent me to consult an eminence in the Royal Veterinary College. 'You have no biology, no physics, no chemistry, no maths, no evidence of ability in any scientific discipline and within six months you will be thirty-six. Even with all the preparation that you need and supposing that you sail through all exams, you will be forty-three before you qualify and more probably forty-five if we make allowance for failures on the way, for your mind is not as receptive now as at normal student age. Then you will need money to set up or join a practice, and within twenty years or so you will retire. It makes no sense. Stick to what you know.'

This inspired the thought that I might return to my studies again, aiming at a Ph.D., Rubens still my first choice, selling the house to fund it. I turned to Anthony Blunt for advice. 'What will you do with it if you complete it?' he asked. When I suggested that I might teach, might even apply for a post in the Courtauld Institute, he laughed. 'You'll be forty, with luck, competing with people not much more than half your age for a job at the bottom of the heap. Don't. You've left it too late.' A note in my mother's diary records that the following Sunday I descended on her house at Castle Hedingham and burnt all my notes and essays from school and the Courtauld and then threw my army uniforms onto the pyre; it ends with: 'He certainly is not well. Coffee poisoning?'

In spite of Anthony's discouragement and this futile gesture of wiping out my past, I applied for a post as tutor in art history in an art school – now long gone – conveniently nearby in Hammersmith, just across the fragile bridge; a Ph.D. was not among the requirements. As evidence of experience I could offer only a handful of lectures at university level long ago and the weekly lessons I had for some five years been giving in Brixton Prison. From this I knew that I could control a class of adults, catch and keep their interest, could teach, indeed, for demand for my classes grew until they were so large that they could only be accommodated in the prison chapel. I had learned that even the least educated prisoners, provided that I treated them as my equal, did not patronise them and encouraged them to interrupt with questions, could be taught something of that most improbable of academic disciplines, the history of art and the how and why of looking at pictures. How much of a *tabula rasa* some of my prisoners were was perhaps made clear when one asked outright if I was queer. I countered the question with 'Why do you ask?' – and to this the answer was, 'Well, Sir, you've shown us nothing but naked men this evening.' A glance at my list of slides was enough to remind me that flagellations, crucifixions and entombments had figured largely in my argument. For a week or so I believed that among my pupils were prisoners who had so little education that they knew nothing of the life of Christ (true even of Courtauld students now) and had never seen such images, but I was later to wonder if the true purpose of the question was to discover where my sexual sympathies lay, for some prisoners took advantage of the darkness. To my 'What on earth . . . ?' enquiry when I first thought a scuffle of some kind was happening (no guards were ever present), the response of one of the older men – 'I don't think you ought to look, Sir' – encouraged me to do just that. It was an episode of sodomy. I am sure that there were others, less excitedly conducted.

At the Hammersmith art school I was one of only two applicants for this piffling part-time job, the other was Theo Melville, a rather younger ex-Courtauld student. The interview was before a band of worthies on the further side of a long table and it seemed to have gone well, their interest in my Brixton prisoners paramount, but when the Chairman asked if there were any more questions, a man at the end of the table, balding and in a formal black jacket with a hint of gold chain about his belly, carefully put his fingertips together and said in a high-pitched churchwarden tone, 'Tell me, Mr Sewell, what is the common factor of excellence shared by Leonardo da Vinci and Picasso?' To this I heard myself respond – too quickly and with no gentling embroidery – 'There isn't one.' I had the impression that he had perhaps spent hours formulating this exquisite question and my response, honest but too immediate, was taken for a dismissive, even humiliating, rebuke – I should have hedged it about with nonsense so as not to make him look the fool he surely was. The board gave the job to Theo.

I was left with no alternative but to use my knowledge of the art market and its workings, but without funds. It was at this point that Eliot Hodgkin, fine collector and painter of delicate and quirky still lives, offered to lend me, for two years and without interest, £2,000 – rather more than my final year's salary at Christie's. As I had known him for only four years, this was an astonishing gesture. In the summer of 1962 I had seen in the window of Mallet's, Bond Street dealers in fine furniture and giltwood thrones, a strange little painting of dry stalks, dead leaves and bursting seed pods, as magical as though Salvador Dali had revised one of Ehret's botanical studies, retaining an eighteenth-century draughtsman's accuracy of observation but adding an hallucinatory excitement that extended the image far beyond mere realism. *Mrs Riley's Milkweed* was by Eliot and was to be had for sixty guineas – and to put that sum into perspective, my salary then, at a thousand a year, was enough to rent a basement flat in Kensington and run a dashing open Daimler. Mallet's could tell me nothing of Hodgkin, nor of Mrs Riley, nor even of milkweed or the painting's provenance, but I did not care. I bought the painting, and I have it still.

That desiccated sow-thistle, that bursting brimstone-wort, proved an *open sesame*. I had had it for a year or so when, one high summer evening, Carlos van Hasselt, then newly late of the Fitzwilliam and just appointed to the Netherlands Institute in Paris, came to dinner, saw the milkweed, and asked if Eliot was a friend. I was in awe of Carlos, master of seven languages and deep-dyed art historian, who knew, as equal, famous men whose names I knew only from the spines of books, and whose expertise in my chosen field of old master drawings far exceeded anything that I might learn in a lifetime; that he knew Eliot told me at once that the man who had painted *Mrs Riley's Milkweed* was no nonentity, no country cottage bumpkin with a delicate touch. With a telephone call and a taxi I found myself whisked into the presence of a painter whose Chelsea flat was a treasury of marvellous paintings by Corot and Delacroix, and of drawings by the ilk of Ingres, Degas, Fragonard and Liotard that made me ill with envy. There was not the slightest hint of grandeur about these small masterpieces – they were a cherished part of Eliot's domestic scene, part of his daily life and nourishment, reticent and intimate in scale, some standing in their own right as finished works of art, others perfect art historical documents that added to our perceptions of some greater work elsewhere, and that were in turn informed by awareness of those works. My fumbling and confused instincts as a magpie acquirer of scraps immediately recognised that this collection was the work of a clear eye and disciplined passion.

Not a Hodgkin painting was to be seen in this brilliant company, for Eliot was a man of modesty and claimed no place with older masters, but at last he was persuaded to open the doors of the cupboard that was his studio and show me the tiny pictures of fruit, flowers, eggs and feathers that he painted with such delight and diligence. Enchanted by two paintings of kohlrabis, purplish pink and acid green, gentled by a ground of greyish marble, I bought both. He chuckled, and told me that I had, in fact, bought one picture – he had painted five kohlrabis in a row, and when no one bought the long narrow frieze he had sawn it in two. In time I added parsnips, turnips, lemons and a lime, the lichened tombs of churchyards and a view in Switzerland; by a stroke of luck I found large early oil paintings that Eliot thought lost, one of which, a gaudy thing of a Christmas tree, he wished had stayed so. He thought me mad to buy so many, but they gave me a direct and simple pleasure that has never diminished.

He was a kind man. When he found me in despair amid the depredations of a dishonest builder in a house that had cost me every penny I possessed, he sent me his builder and a carpenter, who worked until the house was habitable, and whose bills he paid; he took only the repayment of the money, and would accept neither interest nor gift.

Five years later, when moving into my next (and almost final) house and I had carelessly left the side door open, he went into my dining room, put two roses into a celadon vase, broke away petals so that they fell at its foot, and put among them a curl of paper with his signature, exactly as though he had painted a characteristic still life for me. It is the only work by Eliot that I have owned but not been able to keep. Another I particularly regret not buying: it is the detailed study of the internal wall of a terrace house in Chelsea, revealed in 1976 by the demolition of its neighbour, a pattern of vile distempers made lovely by the artist's eye; sunlight fell on the wall only in the morning, giving the colours a peculiar intensity, and Eliot for a week or so rose early, slid between panels of corrugated iron that he had unbolted, painted amid the rubble of the site and left before the first builders arrived for work. He would not sell me the picture for he thought it suitable for the Royal Academy the following summer. He sent it, priced at £300, and it was rejected. Still he would not sell it – 'No. I shall send it in again.' And so he did, a year later, with the price raised to £500, and it was accepted and sold at the private view.

Eliot had a certain pride in his work, but no vanity. The small still lives by which he is best known were, for the most part, painted in tempera with meticulous care, minute attention to detail and a high state of finish, but such fine work was eventually responsible for the decline of his sight and his decision in the autumn of 1982 that he would paint no more. The saddest work that I have ever done was arranging the dispersal of his studio and the sale of all his preparatory studies for the elegant murals to which he turned his hand in the 1930s; it was characteristic of Eliot that he should make so clear-cut a decision and rid himself of the clutter of a life that he felt was past. The sale took place at Christie's in January 1983; his remaining tempera paints and brushes he sent to David Tindle, whom he did not know but whom he thought a good painter, and settled down to die. In spite of failing sight and the depredations of an ataxia that increasingly disordered his body, this he managed with good spiritual grace on 30 May 1987. Neil MacGregor, then newly Director of the National Gallery, read the lesson at the memorial service of our shrewd, generous, mischievous and Christian friend, and most of his collection was bequeathed for the benefit of charity.

With Eliot's £2,000 I trawled the many private dealers in old master drawings working from homes in Kensington, Hampstead, St John's Wood and even Golders Green, many of them of German and Austrian origin. These, fleeing penniless from the Nazis in the later 1930s would, had British universities as many faculties of the history of art as now, have found academic posts, but even the then unique Courtauld Institute was not much more than a finishing school and had nothing to offer them. Some had worked in major museums and universities, others had been independent scholars at a time when to be a scholar for the sake of scholarship was still possible on small means, and that there was a widening market in old master drawings was largely their responsibility. They were part of an extraordinary cultural influx from central Europe that during World War II began to have an influence here in all the arts, burgeoning with the BBC's wonderful Third Programme soon after the war, and that changed for ever our performance and understanding of all genres of classical music and the visual arts. The book recording their transformation of British culture and connoisseurship has never been written and now never will be, for it is too late – they are all long dead and my generation, the astonished witnesses first to benefit from their influence, is already following them.

With the help of these small dealers I was able within three months to mount an exhibition of drawings at the Alpine Gallery in South Audley Street (part of the Alpine Club, since removed to Wimbledon), long the traditional exhibition site for art dealers without premises. It was the suggestion of Peter Claas who, I now suspect, had already reserved the later weeks of May but had too little stock to fill the gallery. It was to be of fifty drawings each and some of mine I had to borrow from other dealers taking only a tiny commission if they sold, but, as Peter argued, with advertisements in art magazines and catalogues to distribute to his clients, it was an effective way of informing the Old Master Drawings world that I was no longer at Christie's but functioning as a dealer – and indeed, Peter's clients immediately became mine.

I learned a great deal from him, much of which I did not like. The most wretched of scraps can be made to seem important with a decorative mount and a good and obviously expensive frame; a client thus seduced, even a close friend in Peter's tight-knit homosexual circle, must be confirmed in his choice with weasel words – and one must always put the greatest effort into selling the drawing in which there is the highest profit, never revealing any uncertainty about an important-seeming attribution plucked, if not from the air, from a reproduction in a book with which it shares only the faintest resemblance. Friendly museum curators were to tell me that I had done myself no good with this transitory alliance, yet I was grateful for it, for if nothing else, it was an indication that I might be able to repay Eliot without difficulty. Besides, in many other ways Peter had become an engaging friend, outrageously and unashamedly queer, yet happy to flirt with my mother to the point where he could claim that they were engaged, and some of his friends thought him serious. My mother, however, though briefly amused to be his prop at the opera and other public places (her diary entry for 8 June 1967 records that it was Peter's sixtieth birthday, that she went to his cocktail party and then on to have dinner with the Swedish ambassador), wearied of the game and eventually refused to play it; I suspect that she was unsympathetic to his sexual preference for swarthy working men in their forties, slightly gone to seed.

It was this preference that drew him to retire to Malta when the lease on his elegant flat in Upper Brook Street had to be renewed. As no house on the island was quite what he wanted, he determined to build his fantasy, but bedding his builders led to inflated bills, his refusal to pay them and their blocking access to the site with a barrier topped with the legend 'Peter Claas – go back into the cunt of your mother' printed on a placard. He had no choice but to abandon Malta and, moving to Rome, was content there for some years until the persistent ailments of the old consumed his small income and compelled his return to London and the benefits of the NHS; his days ended in a dreary room in Ennismore Gardens – always the address of those who have abandoned hope. He left me a matched pair of drawings in red chalk, their subjects preposterously posed male nudes, their fussily decorated mounts elaborated with cartouches that, with characteristic enterprise, attribute them to Lagrenée.

Such drawings are known as Academies, the life classes of students in the eighteenth century perhaps their most common origin; many are fine drawings with some reasonable hope of attribution at least to the circle of an identifiable master, but more are bought for their mildly erotic nature – though this is always more the perception of the buyer than the intention of the artist. Among Peter's friends there was a steady market for such images and if they were too vague or too much covered at the crutch he was given to improving them with the help of a restorer employed to remove drapery and discover a full set of genitals. Size and angle therefore rarely disappointed and no one seemed to notice that the chalk (the most common medium for such studies), particularly when red, was often an imperfect match. One client who insisted on inspecting Peter's Academies but never bought one, eventually wrote a cheque for a nude who had been circumcised – most improbable in the eighteenth century (though Louis XVI was trimmed for ejaculatory reasons) but shrewd lateral thinking on Peter's part.

The exhibition had been a modest success but I needed sources of drawings other than my fellow dealers and the major auction rooms if I was ever to build the essential of every art dealer, a stock of material new to the market. I took to trawling the minor auction rooms in London, Bonham's in Montpelier Street, Bonham's in Chelsea (a most depressing dump), Phillips, Harrods, Knight Frank and Rutley, and others in the business of rapid clearance and never mind the unwitting mistakes of negligence. In these, prints and drawings, if not framed, were sold in unsorted and uncounted parcels, often almost too heavy to carry, just as they had been at Christie's before I insisted on being diligent there; these were sold for virtually nothing. This trawl was a deadly discipline, but if it was to be worth doing it must be done with scrupulous regularity and friends had to be made among the porters willing to bid in my absence (for my presence would betray my interest) and guard my purchases from predators. Among the worthless prints and amateur watercolours an etching by Picasso, two by Canaletto, a dozen by Charles Meryon (a great but forgotten etcher, colour-blind and, eventually, insane) and another dozen by Edmund Blampied (the Whistler of Jersey) were among my early rewards. Much later, to my surprise, I was outbid in a really dismal sale at Bonham's, for two huge folios of drawings, photographs and documents by and connected with Thomas Sidney Cooper, a long-lived painter of cows and sheep in pastures near his native Canterbury; nicknamed 'Cow Cooper' he spanned the nineteenth century. I was not interested in the handful of finished watercolours, nor in the sheets of sketches of figures and horses, in some cases several on a single sheet, every motif carefully initialled T.S.C., all in a remarkable dark brown ink, all with some resemblance to sketches by Géricault, though this did not occur to me at the time. I had pushed the price further than I wished to pay because I was intrigued by the photographs and related drawings, for these demonstrated a working process that it had never occurred to me that Cooper might have used. The photographs, all of his own paintings, were large, in sepia, and on very thin paper; many were whole, and to these were glued motifs cut from other paintings, then re-photographed as finished works. In these, and in pencil drawings on tracing paper, there was clear evidence that Cow Cooper used photography to plot the compositions of paintings in which the groups of animals in one landscape had simply been transferred and reproduced from others. There is, as far as I know, no record of his employing assistants, but in 1865 he established a school of art in Canterbury, where students, many of them women, followed the customary academic training of drawing plaster casts of antique sculptures; among these there were perhaps some willing to assist him with his landscapes while he secretly cheated with the cows and sheep. His output was prodigious.

The sale took place in the morning. Early in the afternoon I telephoned the young dealer who had staggered away with this heavy and unwieldy burden, to offer to buy the photographs and tracings. 'I've burned them,' he said. 'Already?' said I. 'Yes' came the answer and he cut the line. It was not long before the small drawings in that intense brown ink appeared on the London market, in the gallery of a small but reputable dealer who was something of a friend. With the initials T.S.C. removed he had bought them as by Géricault. I told him what I knew and left the rest to his conscience. I have since seen them in the most distinguished collections, public and private, in Europe and America. No one should buy drawings attributed to Géricault without a recorded provenance dating to before 1970.

Together with the photographic material destroyed were certificates of Cooper's attendance, as a student, at academies in Brussels and Antwerp; he is otherwise recorded only as a teacher there in the early 1820s. Thus that young dealer not only foisted false Géricaults onto the market, but corrupted what we know of Cooper.

A coup that gave my finances a tremendous boost and opened a new market for me was the discovery and purchase of a pair of bound volumes of late eighteenth-century Swiss landscape prints, in colour, in pristine condition within the battered bindings. Of these I knew, thanks to the catholicity of my interests as a student and my great good fortune in having been instructed in the byways of the print market by old Harold Knight after his retirement from Colnaghi's, the last English connoisseur in the field; but I also knew that though fashionable among print collectors early in the twentieth century, particularly among Alpinists (a sometime Chairman of Christie's, Robert Wylie Lloyd, had on his death at ninety in 1958, bequeathed a huge collection of them to the British Museum), they were in 1967 utterly forgotten and neglected in Britain. To find a buyer for them I must go to Switzerland.

And so I did, to Jürg Stuker, a dealer and auctioneer in Berne, who pressed into my hand the largest banknotes I had ever seen, in the highest denominations, making the largest sum of money I have ever physically held. Jürg, slightly preposterous, queer, given to wearing the jewelled and enamelled royal orders of Bessarabia, Roumelia and Pless that he collected for pleasure, their origin largely the satrapies of the Balkans and the minor principalities of central Europe, living in a castle, holding court, became something of a friend. I dare say he cheated me – it is what art dealers do when on their honour to pay a fair price – but I did well enough from our dealings and for years he provided an immediate buyer, not only for Swiss prints, but for the Swiss paintings that also occasionally appeared, as unremarked, on the parochial-minded London market. Plump, perspiring and unprepossessingly dapper, Jürg broke in terminal grief on the death – through the dread combination of BMW and tree – of his blond and beautiful lover, a perfect Aryan.

That friendly and hospitable dealers did indeed cheat, I was to have proof soon enough. One from New York, Helene Seiferheld, 'borrowed' one of the best of my finds – a large and dramatic on-the-spot study of the Colosseum by Vanvitelli – to show, on commission, to a client, and we agreed a price from which she was to take her cut. Over the next year or so I asked many times if her client was interested, her answer always that these things take time.

When, eventually, I asked for the return of the drawing, she said that it was with the Metropolitan Museum for consideration; this did not greatly please me, for I considered the Museum my own client, indeed every dealer's client. Then came news that the purchase was agreed, but that payment was delayed until the next financial year. When her cheque at last arrived it was with an apologetic 'let me make it up to you' invitation to stay in her gallery – an apartment in a brownstone house just off Third Avenue – when next I was in New York. This, some months later, I accepted, only to find among the journals left lying about with careless elegance to impress her clients, an old annual report from the Metropolitan recording the purchase of the Vanvitelli and the sum paid for it. The Museum had been her immediate client and had at once bought and paid for it; thus she had had the use of my money for two full years, and though she had doubled the agreed price, had still taken her cut from the figure that I had asked. I wrote a note of thanks for her brief hospitality, stapled it to the open page of the report, and early the following morning transferred to a small and cheap hotel in Columbus Avenue so riddled with cockroaches that they fell from the ceiling onto my nakedness in the rusty bath, but it was run by a friendly family from Prague with European ways.

That I had carefully laid down the terms under which the Vanvitelli was to be sold – the price to be asked, the percentage of the dealer's cut, and the offer only to be made to a private client unknown to me – was because I had earlier been on too vague a footing with Agnew's when effecting a substantial transaction for their benefit; most dealers offered a ten per cent commission for the successful introduction of a client, the deal unspoken but settled with a cheque in the post. John Wyndham, Lord Egremont, Conservative politician under Macmillan, Trustee of the Wallace Collection and, above all things, hereditary custodian of Petworth (which he too enthusiastically described as 'the finest house in Europe'), asked me to inspect a portrait of a boy, attributed to

Bronzino, that he had seen in Agnew's, the firm so long established in Bond Street that it had become the *pars pro toto* of the art trade. Geoffrey Agnew, the booming, bullying monster then in charge, showed me the painting; it was neither better nor worse than a number of similar paintings attributed to Bronzino, but lacked, I thought, the spark that distinguishes the portraits of boys of the Medici family in the Ashmolean and the Uffizi. To Lord Egremont I was frank; I told him that the portrait was of the period and place, and in good condition, but that the attribution to Bronzino would never be without questioners; as for the price, this was by no means a bargain. He seemed to be in thrall to the painting and, not as worried as he should have been by my lack of enthusiasm, told me what he was prepared to pay for it, modestly below the asking price. Geoffrey leaped at the offer and the deal was done. For me, however, there was no cheque from Agnew's and, bumping into Geoffrey some long weeks later, I asked him when I might expect it – to be met with the pretence of surprise, followed by blunt refusal: a lofty man, he put his arm round my shoulders, told me that I should have assumed nothing but made my expectations clear when we were bargaining. The books, he said, were now closed and could not be reopened. I was furious that he had cheated me so, but loathed him more for the avuncular intimacy of his gesture and his patronising implication that I might benefit from such a useful experience.

There was straighter dealing at the very bottom of the trade. Ernest Pepper in Newcastle, for example, who maintained what can only be described as a bulk supply business with art dealers in Scandinavia, needing more bulk than could be found locally, asked my help. It was easily given, though hard physical work: I sat through truly awful sales at Bonham's every Thursday, buying for very small sums paintings of landscapes, still lives and, particularly, children, twenty or so from every sale; these, on alternate Saturdays, I drove to Newcastle and sold to Pepper, returning to London the same night. The regular profit this provided was ploughed back into more and more drawings, but it was not a trade I much enjoyed.

*   *   *

Much of my last full year at Christie's had been devoted to an inventory of the old master drawings at Chatsworth – one of the world's greatest collections – and those who have since leafed through them must have seen among many scholarly notes and suggested changes of attribution some with my initials and those of David Carritt too. Noël Annesley, then my assistant, soon to be my successor (though neither knew this at the time) and, eventually, a high panjandrum in the firm, was with us. Together we greatly amused the Duchess, Debo, who was, as it were, in charge of us – never was there a merrier summer or serious work so pleasurable. When I left Christie's she asked me to undertake a similar inventory of the neglected old master prints at Chatsworth, but a couple of weeks of preliminary sorting in August (when the art market is pretty well dead) convinced me that to do this properly would entail months of concentrated work with much travelling to compare the most rare examples with those in other major print collections. It is not good enough, for example, simply to record the presence of landscape prints in colour by Hercules Segers, an early contemporary of Rembrandt (who owned eight of his paintings), for each of these very rare things is in some way unique and the apparatus of print scholarship requires precise observation of every technical difference – of the one hundred and eighty-three currently known impressions from the fifty-four currently known plates, no two are identical. In my then circumstances I could do no more than sort, identify and list the most important prints and, with lasting regret, bow out.

There was, however, one lateral benefit – the development of my friendship with Tom Wragg, curator of all the Chatsworth collections, whom I had known since 1958 when Christie's offered twenty-four paintings from the house, including two by La Hyre and Le Sueur that in the light of my contribution to the Royal Academy's exhibition earlier that year (The Age of Louis XIV) had been of particular interest to me. He was the most approachable of men, with a local touch to his speech, entirely without vanity in appearance, dress or manner, yet gravely respected by the lofty Londoners with whom he had so often to deal, and the guru of the north in that it was to him the art dealers of Derbyshire and thereabouts turned when they acquired something out of the ordinary; if he did not know the answers, he brought these things to Christie's when next on a jaunt to London. This little bit of business he transferred to me and it became an occasional source of decent drawings and paintings entirely new to the London market. Should I have had qualms of conscience in this diversion? I gave exactly the advice that I would have given had I still been with Christie's, offering to deliver the goods there, or, if the inevitable delay in selling at auction (often of months) was not acceptable, offering to buy outright; I doubt if Christie's lost a penny, for those in urgent need of a sale would certainly have sold elsewhere.

My only other crossover from Christie's was Captain Arthur Simmons, a florid thick-skinned man who tanned his face with almond oil until it looked like pork crackling, with whom I had often had to contend at Christie's. He drove Rolls-Royces because he dealt in them, but they also opened doors for him – literally – the front doors of decent houses whose owners, short of cash, were to be persuaded into swapping pictures for a splendid car. What was it about an old but well presented Rolls, the cellulose paint gleaming, the enormous headlamps blinding in their shining chrome, the classic architecture of the radiator proclaiming imperial status, that released the Toad in sane and gentle men? The Devil failed to tempt St Anthony with naked women, but Arthur Simmons would have succeeded with a Rolls. He drove to the door in a machine worth a thousand pounds, and drove away in a taxi with a painting worth ten times that sum, in a carved giltwood frame worth another thousand. Would it, I wondered, have worked with an Alvis or Lagonda? Probably not.

Making more money from the swaps than ever from straight purchases, he began to advertise for pictures in the personal columns of *The Times*, and once, when overwhelmed with offers, paid me to accompany him on a long trawl to Gloucestershire and back, eliminating paintings that were of no serious value; for those that were, he would return later with a suitable motor (men like Simmons always spoke, not of cars but 'motors'). By the end of the first day I loathed the man, so sharp had been his dealing and so loud his behaviour in the pub in which we spent the night, so loud his shouting for a better Burgundy, so loud his ghastly tweeds, and even doubted the genuineness of his captaincy. Our last stop on the second day was at the house of a woman with one quite decent painting, whose instinct, clearly, was to have nothing to do with him. He bullied and cajoled to a point that sickened me and weakened her resolve; in capitals I wrote in my notebook 'Don't sell. Throw us out,' and held it so that she could read it over his shoulder. And throw us out, she did. Simmons, for all the distinction endowed by his captaincy and splendid cars, was nothing but a 'knocker', an ignorant cheat of whom few house-holders could be rid without parting from their silver teapots for a sixpence.

That I became known in the London trade as a dealer who never deals pleased me well enough; of course I dealt – how else was I to earn my living? – and I bought from and occasionally sold to dealers, but I chose never to work with them, never to enter into agreements not to bid against them, never to join the ring or any form of syndicate. In this I was greatly helped by the independence of most dealers in the field of old master drawings, their preference, like mine, to work alone, and by collectors to whom, at Christie's, I had given sound advice from time to time. These, finding me no longer there, sought me out, and though some were not queer, it was evident that most were and that some sort of queer support mechanism had come into play. I sensed something fraternal that had little to do with collecting drawings but in which homosexuality was the shibboleth. In some cases there was a cosiness for which I did not much care, as though simply to be queer made me a member of some sort of brotherhood or sect. With others there was no obvious hint of knowing or sharing, only a relaxation of formality. Herbert List, for example, *Jugendbewegung* photographer of beautiful boys in the 1930s and the Joachim Lenz of Stephen Spender's autobiographical novel, *The Temple*, knocked on my door within days of my leaving Christie's; he talked about the range of drawings he had bought ever since his student days at Heidelberg, looked askance at the scatterbrained things I had, and told me how his taste had slowly narrowed to concentrate only on Italian examples. Over the few years until his death in 1975 he was a faithful client, always drinking coffee (on which he was an expert – it had been his family's business) while he made up his mind, picking my brains about drawings seen elsewhere, never gossiping about his earlier life and his work with the camera, yet seeming at ease as though nothing between us need be revealed or concealed. On his very last visit, however, something was concealed; he seemed disquieted and oddly shabby too, shrunken within his old raincoat; he found a drawing that he wanted, but his mind seemed on some more distant matter when he scurried off with it. No one told me when he died.*

Ulrich von Artus was not queer. Thirty years too late he was the perfect German boy for Herbert List, blonde of hair, biscuit of skin, lithe and athletic, but not queer. An apprentice at Christie's

---

* I later learned that Herbert had, in 1972, sold his Italian drawings en bloc to Adolf Ratjen (1910–1989), a collector who, generously, did not take possession until after his death and whose payment allowed Herbert to continue to buy at the highest level in an increasingly rare and expensive market. The Ratjen Collection is now in the National Gallery, Washington.

for some months in the summer of 1966, he was the son of
Friedrich von Artus, an art auctioneer in Frankfurt. We became
friends; he lodged in my house, got drunk (he was addicted to Pils
and Fernet Branca) and set fire to his bed, destroying my best
blanket, an expensive thing of camel hair embellished with (and
in this there was a Wagnerian irony) a broad band of Swastika
decoration at each end. I last saw him in the winter of 1970 when,
as captain of the Frankfurt Rugby Club, he telephoned to say that
he was short of a hooker for an important match on Saturday and
would I play for him. At thirty-nine and not having played for
well over a decade, I was a fool to agree, but it proved a rip-
roaring match and I enjoyed every moment of it. Ending the day
in a Spanish restaurant, consuming gargantuan quantities of paella
and rioja, every member of the team performed that ancient act
of manliness and unity, the corporate vomit, when, from the
overheated bodega, we stepped into the cold night air. I have not
since been drunk. Within months Ulrich was dead, seized by
some galloping cancer.

What Friedrich von Artus wanted of me in 1967 was advice
that prevented him from letting slip a masterpiece. The art market
in Germany had still not recovered from the tragedies of World
War II. Before that war there had been many eminent and reliable
art dealers in almost every city, most of them Jewish; these and
their Jewish clients were largely victims of Nazi anti-semitism in
the Thirties, and the German art they did so much to foster –
Expressionism and Neue Sachlichkeit – was damned, destroyed
and sold abroad in Switzerland by Hitler's henchmen. These dealers
lost their stocks and the collectors their collections through forced
sales and expropriation. Well into another century this is still an
emotional and inflammatory matter, now often one of very high
value too, but in the 1930s the effects of the Great Depression had
all but destroyed the art market in Europe, and in London old
Oliver Brown, who ran the Leicester Galleries (just off Leicester
Square), had throughout the decade a variant of *Van Gogh's Chair*

(Tate)* without his pipe, on consignment from a client at only £800, yet it remained unsold (and is now untraced and *hors de catalogue*); Brown also had almost forty landscapes by Kokoschka for which there were no takers at £200 apiece, and as many paintings by Max Liebermann in which no client showed interest at any price. Auction records demonstrate that the demand for Old Masters was just as weak – a double page in one Christie catalogue of 1933 lists only four paintings, of long provenance, two by Poussin, two by Claude, for which the total sum paid was less than 1,000 guineas. Sir Denis Mahon's collection of great paintings by Guercino, Reni and other seventeenth-century masters was founded on that sort of sum. These facts should perhaps be borne in mind when paintings, said to have been the subject of forced sale under the Nazis, are claimed by the descendants of former owners who, had they brought their paintings to England and sold them, would have got as little as they did from the Nazis.

Such claims were tentative in the 1960s and still uncommon, but von Artus was anxious not to be drawn into disputes that were profoundly uncomfortable for innocent parties; nevertheless he involved me in two other matters that were far from innocent, the second closely connected to Nazi expropriation. The first was the valuation of a collection outside Munich of paintings attributed to Titian, Velazquez, Veronese, Rubens, Rembrandt and others of first rank. I was to fly to Munich, take a taxi to the Drei Könige Hotel and breakfast there with someone who would drive to the Schloss in which the pictures were; my contact was persuasive – it is the only time that I have breakfasted on the brains of a lamb. The drive was aggressive and confusing, as though I was not to know precisely where I was taken (as I did not), and the Schloss more a rich man's villa of the late nineteenth century than some turreted castle of the

---

* The Tate's acquisition was through the Courtauld Fund in 1924, direct from Van Gogh's family via the Leicester Galleries as agent; Oliver Brown maintained his tie with the family at least until 1938.

Wittelsbachs. I was introduced to some eight or ten elderly men the cut of whose hair and evidence of old wounds reminded me at once of drawings by Georg Grosz of army officers after the Great War. That is what I think they were – though after World War II – and I feared that they might be Nazis rather than Junkers grown old. They explained that the paintings were an old family collection concealed during the war, not for sale, but to be valued as security for a loan. I had encountered this before, at Christie's, but it was usually the lending bank that commissioned the valuation to protect its interests. So far I had not seen a single picture, nothing in the spacious entrance hall, nothing in the room in which we were; when I asked to see them we moved to another room, once a ballroom, perhaps, where some seventy paintings by old masters stood on the floor, leaning against the panelling. The light was appalling and time and again I had to carry pictures to the windows to make any sense of them – and they made very clear sense indeed.

This was not an ancient family collection. This was a hotch-potch very recently acquired. If some were familiar it was because I had myself catalogued them at Christie's, and on the backs of all were the characteristic inventory numbers, dates of sale and lot numbers of Christie's, Sotheby's and Bonham's. Not one canvas was by the painter to whom it was attributed on the list given me, and I knew at once that I was being drawn into a fraud. I sensed too the unwisdom of blurting out the truth. Instead, I laboured over the list noting on it the information I had gleaned and estimating the real value in code, adding extra noughts for the benefit of the man at my shoulder who, thinking that I understood no German and having asked if they were pounds or Deutschmarks, told his fellow conspirators that I was putting satisfactory five-figure valuations on the wretched things. They pressed me for a gross figure – I refused, arguing that I had much research to do before that would be possible, shook hands with all the old rogues and was driven back to the Drei Könige for an early supper before catching my plane. With ghoulish humour the driver ordered brains again, insisting that I had so much enjoyed them for breakfast that he must repeat the treat. I told von Artus of the fraud and that I would send him neither the valuation nor the bill for my flight and services; unlike Geoffrey Agnew, he was apologetic and did not tell me that I would profit from the experience.

The more disturbing matter was Friedrich's introduction of Baruch, the only name by which anyone knew this shabby figure in the art market. 'Hier ist Baruch' was his greeting on the telephone, 'Hier ist Baruch' his salutation on the doorstep. He spoke only German, he sought only inexpensive paintings and he paid in cash; he divulged no means of making contact, gave no warning of impending presence and disappeared as swiftly as a wary cat. We met in Frankfurt, but once he had my address I could never shake him off and, to my distaste, our association lasted for some years until its fruitlessness exhausted him. Of him I learned two intriguing things, the first of which he evidently regretted; it was that though a Jew he had survived in Germany not only throughout the Thirties but through the war itself, surviving because he revealed the whereabouts of works of art that might otherwise have remained unknown to the Nazis, Jew betraying Jew. Not a dealer, and certainly not a scholar, I suspect that he had been an insurance broker or something of the kind with access to inventories. After the war his knowledge could, perhaps, have been invaluable in the recovery of works of art, and in a sense it was, for he chose to work for Ante Topic Mimara, who became a millionaire art collector and close confidant of General Tito, President of Yugoslavia. Quite when these two rogues came together we shall never know, but my hunch is that it was before or early in the war, rather than in the pan-European chaos after it, and that Mimara's few good paintings (not one of which has any known provenance) were acquired as a consequence of Baruch's betrayals.

Few, anywhere, knew anything of Topic Mimara, though he claimed to have begun collecting when a child and to have bought his first important antiquity in his very early twenties, until 1963, when Thomas Hoving, then curator of the Cloisters in New York, a department of the Metropolitan Museum, and later Director of the museum itself, brought Mimara out of the shadows by purchasing from him *The Bury St Edmunds Cross*, a medieval masterpiece that had no recent provenance. Rumour and insinuation multiplied, boosted by Mimara's boast that he had been the art adviser and friend of Hermann Goering, the rapacious Nazi leader whose collection of paintings and objects he had helped to form before and during the war. Of this there is no proof, though Mimara was in Berlin at the outbreak of war and spent most of it in Lörrach in Oberrhein, a few kilometres from Basel where Swiss safety lay if suddenly he needed it; it may have been mistaken vanity – my own belief is that in claiming this he adopted what had been Baruch's role as servant of Alfred Rosenberg, Goering's chief instrument in the sequestration of works of art from Jewish collectors. In the confusions of 1946 Mimara was appointed to the Yugoslav Military Mission in Berlin to supervise matters of cultural restitution, was given a diplomatic passport that enabled him to travel anywhere he wished in the vast range of ravished Europe, and was subsequently accused of transferring to Yugoslavia works that had been pillaged from Italy, France, Czechoslovakia and other central European countries. By the mid 1950s he had accumulated a huge collection for himself, of which he presented a substantial part to the then Socialist Republic of Croatia in October 1973, and had promoted himself to an ancient title of the Austro-Hungarian Empire.

When, early in 1983, I learned that in September Mimara's gift was at last to be accessible to the public and that a catalogue had been published boasting paintings by Raphael, Michelangelo, Parmigianino, Castagno, Caravaggio, Giorgione, Titian, El Greco, Velazquez, Rembrandt, Rubens, Van Gogh and most of the Impressionists, I went to see the collection. Housed in the Villa Zagorje, some distance from the centre of the Croatian capital, it proved to be, not the boasted Louvre of Zagreb, but an embarrassing assembly of travesties and misattributions, though the outright fakes were outnumbered by canvases to which pre-posterous signatures had been applied and by portraits and other subjects that had been heavily reworked. In anticipation I had mistakenly paid Mimara the compliment of supposing that among his pictures might be found the missing *Portrait of a Young Man* by Raphael, a masterpiece removed in the last months of the war from the Czartoryski Museum in Cracow for the benefit of Hans Frank, Gauleiter of Poland, never again seen, but of which there had been faint whispers from behind the Iron Curtain. It was not, of course, in Mimara's collection, in which not one painting in the selection on view suggested that he possessed a jot or tittle of the informed scholarship or instinctive eye of the true connoisseur, and everything conformed with what I knew of Baruch's pur-chases through von Artus. My notes on Mimara's paintings are despairing – 'Entirely repainted . . . fake . . . feeble imitation . . . very damaged . . . crude copy . . . ruined fragment . . . laughable . . . feeble . . . grotesque . . . ' The collection is now housed in the largest and most palatial eponymous museum premises in Zagreb, inviting ridicule. When, in 2009, in an essay on 'The Museums of Zagreb' (see Jadranka Beresford-Peirse, ed., *Croatia: Aspects of Art* . . . pp. 194–207), I first let slip some of this material, I caused outrage and was briefly *persona non grata* in Croatia.

*   *   *

The British art market today is very different from the art market of the later 1960s. At the top of the tree were the Bond Street Boys who thought they knew everything but, in fact, knew very little (except for Colnaghi's, and even that firm was soon to be stripped of its worthy reputation). To these the history of art and its associated connoisseurship was a mysterious academic discipline beyond their comprehension, attribution was a matter of the wild surmise and quality was measured in terms of distinguished (or otherwise) provenance. At the bottom of the tree were the dozens of dealers who dealt from the back of a van and, in the case of Raymond de Romare, from a caravan; this, badly parked in Duke Street, St James's, narrowing an already narrow street, was ripped to shreds one day by a passing army lorry, leaving his stock of ghastly paintings lying in the road among the splintered timbers. One of them, on a quite large sheet of copper, was badly bent; unwilling to pay the cost of a restorer's attempting to flatten it, he gave five shillings to the driver of a steamroller to drive slowly and ever so gently over it – of which the consequence was a much larger and much thinner sheet of copper with not a flake of paint adhering to it.

Between the top and the bottom were dealers who specialised in some particular aspect or genre – lap dogs and carousing cardinals, paintings of ships, horses, fox hunts and Montgolfier balloons, nineteenth-century Dutch landscapes – some of whom were respected as experts in their fields; and there were a handful who, like old Oliver Brown, had dealt, often face to face, with artists who were becoming a new generation of old masters, among them Sickert, Soutine, Kisling, Klee, Kokoschka and even Monet. How extraordinary to have been able to record in his journal, as Oliver did, 'John Sargent called with Claude Monet to introduce him and arrange an exhibition.'

Such respected old boys as he set the best practical example for young dealers moving into the trade and there was never a more revered reputation. Usurping them, the young revived interest in British artists of the earlier twentieth century – an interest that had sunk so far that many were surprised to find, for example, Duncan Grant still alive. Anthony d'Offay, who had made a fortune selling the dismal but indubitably genuine scraps retrieved from the floors of great artists' studios, cornered the market in Gwen John, Robert Bevan, Roger Fry, the Omega Workshop and the Bloomsbury Group, and was overjoyed when his rediscovery of Duncan Grant and hundreds of paintings and drawings of male nudes (some quite obscene) turned the old dear into a gay icon. An early move into contemporary art was his becoming Lucian Freud's dealer, but this collaboration ended abruptly and in tears with Lucian writing, by night, on Anthony's windows in Dering Street, an expression of opinion too extreme ever to retract; it did Anthony no harm (nothing ever did) and he moved on to become a high-end dealer with Warhol, Basquiat, Richter and Koons in his stable, and, with astonishing sleight-of-hand on his retirement, a benefactor to the nation. I must argue that I too, at Christie's, in setting up sales devoted to twentieth-century British art, had played a not in-significant part in its revival and was for decades regarded as an expert on Augustus John and Charles Ginner; now, at a time when both are being distorted by the addition of forged signatures to inadequate canvases, my reputation in this field is largely forgotten.

Charles Ginner (1878–1952) is, indeed, the perfect example of my many failures to achieve. One of the circle of English painters who, with Gilman, Gore and Bevan, both overlapped with and succeeded Sickert, Ginner's work is distinguished by his almost mechanical application of evenly impastose strokes of paint so thick that they rarely indicate the use of brushes – Van Gogh tamed and neutered, as it were. 'I shall paint as thick as I damn well please,' he responded in 1914 to Sickert's accusation in his mischievously punning essay *The Thickest Painters in London*, that Ginner attached 'a somewhat doctrinaire importance to the value of impasto itself.' It was, however, the impasto that in the end undid me; once formulated and then unvarying for almost half a century, this deliberate laying-on of paint lent a dread sameness to his hundreds of paintings to which, ultimately, boredom was my reaction. Alone, a painting by Ginner can be exciting; in a company of two or three that excitement is enhanced and one begins to understand the man; but with twenty or thirty this response is hard to maintain and, with more, it ebbs away. Malcolm Easton, of Hull University, was first to wave a banner for him, but even he, privileged owner of Ginner's scrupulously kept notebooks, lost his enthusiasm for the proposed catalogue raisonné; he gave me copies of the notebooks and passed the task to me. There were, at first, enough of Ginner's old friends and acquaintances to interview to make the task seem interesting, but my enthusiasm waned when no publisher offered encouragement, and an introductory essay in a catalogue for the Fine Art Society in October 1985 is the only evidence of an enthusiasm that ran into the sand.

CHAPTER 3

Return to Kensington

By January 1968 the full year of unrelenting activity and travelling that I had inflicted on myself had exhausted me. The collapse was sudden, brought on, I later learned, by eating infected bratwurst in Aachen, where I had spent a melancholy day searching for the ghost of Charlemagne. It was meant to be a day of aesthetic and intellectual renewal before doing some work for Friedrich von Artus and, that done, driving on to Munich, where I was to deliver some drawings bought blind by a collector. On the autobahn, two hours or so south of Frankfurt, a mild sense of unease accelerated into the certainty that I was about to faint and should not be driving – that I should, indeed, stop at once. And so I did; I staggered to the shelter of trees above the snowy bank, wrapped my duffel coat close about me and lost consciousness. It was still light when I recovered and, feeling ghastly but no longer faint, I drove on to Munich, stopping at the first hotel encountered in its dreary outskirts, the Hotel Carmen, there to drowse for three days and nights, eating nothing, drinking only water. When, at last, I felt, if not well, less ill and fit enough to shave, I was puzzled to find the mirror strongly tinted yellow. There was another mirror in the dining room where I struggled to eat a little breakfast. It was not until, having delivered the drawings and driven on to the Alte Pinakothek that, again feeling faint, I went to the loo there to splash my face with water, and realised that it was not the mirrors of Munich that were yellow, but me. I was so jaundiced that my eyeballs looked like pickled onions. I have no idea how many days it took, but slowly I nursed the car back to London, making first for France where I knew it would be easier to find both overnight accommodation and roadside places where

I could rest flat on my back for a while to ease the dull but pressing pain.

I did indeed have jaundice – the comparatively mild form of hepatitis that is not sexual in origin but is pretty serious in its effect – and weeks later emerged from a dreary hospital in south London very shaken by the experience, not only cripplingly debilitated but aware of how insecure a solitary life can be. It was, I thought, time to renounce my hectic ways, but I did not, indeed could not, so heavily I felt the pressure to get out of debt. The hepatitis recurred and, my liver grossly enlarged and hardly functioning, there was a second long stint in hospital; for weeks on end I could not drive, could not carry heavy pictures, could not sit through auctions, indeed, could not even sit for any length of time so painful was my liver in any position other than prone with my arms by my sides. It was in many ways a wasted year, but even so, the little work I did enabled me both to repay Eliot on the very day two years since his £2,000 had propelled me into becoming an art dealer, and to accumulate enough of a stock of drawings for me to think of myself as the specialist I wished to be. I could afford to slow down; I could even afford to stop for a while.

It was at this point that Bill Martin came back into my life, Bill who had been my first boss at Christie's and, as the then head of the picture department (the most important for the firm), the prime target of Patrick Lindsay's enmity and envy. To put no fine point on it, Patrick thought him an 'ugly little toad' (his very words at a lunch of which the purpose was to make clear to me where my loyalty should lie), and was immediately instrumental in ousting him from the firm when stricken by a cerebral haemorrhage. Bill had then gone into partnership with Harry Sutch, an elderly dealer with a small gallery in Bury Street (in the same block as Christie's), and there they spent their days drinking sherry and closing for lunch, which meant that either they were asleep behind the drawn curtains or eating jellied eels in Overton's. They carried no stock other than the old master drawings that Bill put in the window when he was short of ready cash, and had no clients other than the few who relied on Harry to update their insurance valuations, but they enjoyed smoking and drinking all day with no one likely to disturb them. The only cloud over this vale of Lethe was that Harry wished to retire altogether, but the once long and very cheap lease was by then menacingly short and renewal would undoubtedly be more than Bill could afford unless the business became more energetic.

Bill proposed a partnership. My jaundiced brain suggested caution and after much doubt, prevarication and delay, I proposed a joint exhibition of drawings as a trial. Bill agreed and we fixed dates for it in the first half of May. Only then did I discover that over the past two years I had bought every drawing he possessed and he now had nothing to contribute. Our joint exercise was joint only in that he provided the premises and I the fifty-five drawings that could be accommodated. Nevertheless it worked well enough and I discovered the great usefulness of having an accessible foothold in St James's in which to do business, instead of a house in far away Barnes; and even if Bill's drinking and smoking were irksome, his presence gave me freedom to cover the salerooms and go about other aspects of my business. The exhibition brought clients new to both of us.

This slower pace suited my miserably slow recovery from jaundice, the loss of energy, the often overwhelming sense of fatigue, and six months passed before we again did anything active – a 'Christmas Exhibition' of English drawings and watercolours, almost all of them again mine. These were exhibitions only in the sense of revealing stock; with no common thread of origin or scholarship they were not didactic and to call them exhibitions was impertinent, but they were the custom of the day at all levels of the trade and they drew in the collectors. Bill and I agreed that ours had augured well and that we should enter into formal partnership. Harry, who to my great annoyance had been taking ten per cent of our profits, quietly withdrew, the names over the door were changed from Sutch and Martin to Martin and Sewell, and it was under that heading that in May 1970 we mounted another exhibition of drawings, all bought by me, that included seriously good examples that I was a fool to let go, for the market was showing the first signs of short supply and steepening prices. This I had predicted but had not expected so soon; there were, however, everywhere many more dealers in the field, more collectors too, and American museums had greatly increased their rate of acquisition.

Logistically it could be a very easy trade, for drawings, unlike paintings, need no frames and are not necessarily enhanced by them – many collectors keep them in solander boxes.* Rarely do they attract public interest enough to rouse demands to keep them as the nation's heritage, and any possible difficulty with export restrictions can be avoided by casually carrying them between the pages of a magazine. This is exactly how an American dealer, Stephen Spector, carried two important drawings by Watteau from London to New York. Very young, ignorant, insufferably brash, noisily queer, and rich with his middle-aged lover's money, Stephen declared himself a dealer in old master drawings by buying the best of what London's most eminent dealers had in stock, none more eminent than Wildenstein's, the source of the Watteaus at, he told me, £15,000 apiece, then a whopping price. I wondered how he could make a profit, but Stephen cultivated a market as influenced as himself by price, working on the assumption that the more punishing it was, the better the quality must be. His camouflage copy of *Vanity Fair* he carried nonchalantly onto the plane home to JFK and, tucked into the pocket of the seat ahead, forgot it. Passing through customs he was reminded that he might

---

* Shallow boxes of standard paper size for keeping safe maps, charts, drawings and pressed specimens, devised by Daniel Solander, a pupil of Linnaeus, who accompanied Joseph Banks and Captain Cook on their first exploration of the Pacific Ocean.

have something to declare, and there followed an episode of pure black comedy. The Watteaus were never seen again.

When travelling across Europe my disguise was as a working painter, the car crammed with palette, paints and apparently blank canvases, though of these a number were half-finished Alpine views that could be brought to the top on the return journey. Never once, at a time when no European border could be crossed without a fuss, did the ruse fail.

Bill and I, happy with our May exhibitions of 1969 and 1970, hoped that they might be an annual event, but in 1971 we could muster only half the number of drawings needed. Prices across the market were rising and we had far too little capital, all of which I supplied. Bill's only contribution to our still informal arrangements was the little left of the lease of the gallery. I had long since asked that this should be renewed, making its extension a condition of the partnership. Nothing was done – or so I thought – and only when I could contain my unease no longer did I learn from our joint solicitor that the landlords, at first sympathetically prepared to accommodate us with a new lease of twenty years for £20,000 (a bargain), had eventually cut matters short with a refusal to renew on any terms. For this Beatrice was responsible – Beatrice, Bill's ever-present mistress, his 'bringer of joy' if the name's Latin root is to be trusted; this stout, plain, bespectacled termagant had quibbled too aggressively with the landlords and all we had to show for it was the dying end of the existing lease, a year or so.

That this brought our uneven arrangement to an immediate end was perhaps for the best – there would never have been equal capital and equal work and Bill's old-fashioned responses to certain situations would never have been mine. He tended to judge unknown visitors to the gallery by their shoes; he had once been so appallingly abrupt to a young man in trainers that I had followed him onto the street to apologise, there to discover that not only was he seriously interested in drawings but, with an American newspaper magnate for a father, was well able to afford them. Bill also kow-towed to the great; when Edward Heath came in to inspect a pair of political cartoons by Henry Tonks, Bill gave him them – not 'I'll knock off ten percent,' not 'You can have them at cost price,' but 'We are happy and honoured to give them to you.' Happy and honoured, my foot. On the days when he was on his own Bill reverted to his old 'Out to lunch' routine and either snoozed behind the locked door or toddled on his own to Overton's, once running up such a whacking bill – £800 – that they sent a man round to sit in the gallery until he got the money; as Bill and Beatrice were away on holiday, it was I who had to pay. As for their affair, to this, if it suited them – as often it did – they gave sexual expression behind the drawn curtains of the gallery. Once, having lunched with Peter Langan, I took him and his wife, Susan, to see a Sickert in the gallery and found the curtains drawn but the door unlocked; inside was Bill, in shirtsleeves, braces down, his hair dishevelled, struggling to move the heavy 'picture chair' that unaccountably now stood, not in its customary corner, but in the middle of the room; not a chair, but a velvet-covered prop designed to support pictures when clients wished to engage in close contemplation, it had been used for a less aesthetic purpose. We caught a glimpse of Beatrice scuttling down the winding stair to the basement, leaving, widespread on the floor, her elasticated gripper-knickers. Peter, at once recognising these signs (for he too had a taste for cunnilingus), chuckled, said 'I might as well still look at the Sickert, now I've spoiled your fun', did so for about ten seconds, and then we left.

Without me poor Bill bumbled on with Beatrice for a while, but there was no business to support his cravings for tobacco, sherry, champagne and eels, and when he had not only to close the shop but leave his comfortable mansion flat in Westminster after falling asleep on a sofa with a lighted cigarette (a vigilant policeman saved his life), she deserted him for the husband she had never left. Bill then ended his days with his ancient mother in Roehampton, a house of very unhappy memories as a child, occasionally pleasured by a Soho prostitute and then, taking a taxi home, on the way calling on me for a sub to pay the fare. He once arrived without shoes and jacket; he had not had cash enough to pay the whore and she had packed him off without them to get the money and ensure his return.

I had to reorganise my life. I recognised first that I had not enjoyed, indeed disliked, being tied to premises that must be open five full days a week – impossible if I had neither partner nor employee. I knew too that in my way I was as tactless as Bill with visitors – I should not, in answer to 'How much is that?' have answered 'Oh that's far too good for you.' The enquirer was a manufacturer of shoes from Leicester who collected paintings of children; he had come to see a seriously good Victorian picture of children playing in a wood, the rare Henry Mark Anthony its painter, had spent almost an hour of my time talking about the paintings he already had, and then rejected mine on the grounds that the children were barefoot – a thing unacceptable to a man of his trade (I would now suspect him of being a paedophile with a shoe fetish); then, glancing at a seventeenth-century painting of a modest feast, he asked the question that elicited my inexcusable response. Many years later I saw the Mark Anthony in the window of a Duke Street dealer and was astonished to see that the children now wore shoes – but then this was a dealer who had earlier bought from me an important landscape by John Linnell of which the principal dramatic feature was a great dead oak, and in his restorer's hands the oak sprang into spring leaf. I had also begun to question my future as a dealer: I liked buying because I liked the disciplines of looking, questioning, arguing, researching and identifying, for these were close to the disciplines of the art historian and the curator, and above all I enjoyed discovering things of art historical interest, but though I was happy to sell at auction, I had no instinct for adding a margin of profit and selling face to face. When Kenny Thomson, now Lord Thomson of Fleet and then Chairman of Times Newspapers, offered me £800 for a still life by Jan Vonck for which I had paid £900 and was asking only £1,100, I refused it with 'And shall I pay fourpence for your sixpenny *Times* tomorrow?' – another potential client lost. The third problem, working from a house in remote Barnes, was, however, easy to resolve – I exchanged it for one in middle Kensington that I had known since my toddling childhood.

Number 19 Eldon Road had an intriguing history. The first house of an intended terrace speculatively constructed in the 1840s on the southern edge of what was then the kitchen garden of Kensington Palace, it had been much extended in 1929 to accommodate Chester Beatty and his growing collection of Impressionist paintings, of which more than eighty were bequeathed to the National Gallery of Dublin. In spite of covering the entire garden with a lofty and very grand studio, his rate of acquisition exceeded the rate of expansion and neither he nor his pictures moved into it or any other part of the house which, despite its very good and pretty fireplaces, remained a typical London terrace house with two decent rooms on each floor and tiny rooms for servants in the attic, windows onto the staircase landings here and there making it light and airy; the roof of the studio was paved with York stone, and ivy, honeysuckle and wistaria clambered about high fences that offered considerable privacy. Beatty moved into a suitably larger house in Belgravia and, unable to sell Eldon Road in the great slump of the Thirties, lent it to his peripatetic, penniless and irascible friend, the painter C.R.W. Nevinson, for whom it was a reliable address until his death in 1946. Beatty then sold it to Arpad Elfer, an Hungarian photographer with (at least among my new neighbours) a reputation for soft pornography.

The studio was perfect for housing books and paintings (even for painting pictures myself – as I occasionally did in idle moments), and, exceeded in size only by Agnew's vast first-floor gallery, was a wonderful exhibition space for a private dealer; unlike Barnes, it was only a short taxi ride from central London. Working from it I would need no business partnership and be completely independent, and no dealer or collector from abroad could complain (as they did of Barnes) that it was too far from his hotel. The main house offered the additional advantage of splitting easily into two halves so that I could comfortably accommodate my mother and, in her doctor's parlance, 'keep an eye on her'. This was a terrible mistake far worse than leaving Christie's or the partnership with Bill. As old as the century, she played the game of being physically too frail to remain alone in her house in Castle Hedingham and I was weary of the need to go there, cut grass, prune roses, lop trees and fill the refrigerator; it would be altogether easier, we persuaded ourselves, if we lived independently in the same house – but there is no such thing as a bachelor's independence from his mother, for inexorably the relationship reverses and the ageing mother becomes his child without, however, relinquishing anything of her original authority.

Of my mad life after leaving Christie's and the failure of my venture with Bill, Anthony Blunt had been a constant observer, amused, benign and ever helpful, prompting friends and public art galleries over which he had some influence to buy drawings from me. Seeing that my career (for want of a better word) was again tottering, he first persuaded Toronto University again to offer me a teaching post – 'You don't have to ask for it, you have only to say yes.' But fifteen years on from the first offer and for all the old misgivings, yes I could not say; so late, I could neither leave my mother nor carry her there as baggage. Then he suggested to Jacob Rothschild (with whom his role was distinctly avuncular) who had just bought Colnaghi's, the only art dealers in London of never questioned respectability, that I had experience enough to run the firm for him. We met over drinks in Anthony's flat in the attic of the Courtauld Institute. When asked by Jacob how I would change things at Colnaghi's, I answered that I might change nothing, that James Byam Shaw (1903–92), its retiring head, was universally recognised as an honest scholar at least as much as an honest dealer, and that in buying the firm Jacob had bought that most precious of commodities, a long unblemished reputation, difficult to achieve, arduous to maintain, impossible to restore once sullied. Thus I dowsed any interest he had in me. I was not given the job; instead, there was a good deal of shifting and shunting among the bright young men of Christie's and Sotheby's, and for a day or two my former assistant, Noël Annesley, seemed to have been appointed, but in the event remained at Christie's. Slowly, in the hands of the unqualified and inexperienced young coxcombs whom Jacob eventually chose, Colnaghi's reputation faded away, and the great name became, as it is now, nothing more than the identification of premises in Bond Street.

Doors had opened and I, always my own worst enemy, had closed them. I reconciled myself to life as a solitary dealer and bought a bicycle. 'Oh,' said Renée Fedden, my new neighbour, wife of Robin Fedden who had years earlier offered me a job with the National Trust, 'a bicycle' – as though it were the most extraordinary thing in Kensington; and then she followed it with, 'We're off to Leningrad.'

*   *   *

Almost to the day it took two years to settle into Eldon Road, so much had to be done to the house to accommodate my mother, the contents of her house and of my own, and not quite all my books – for some of these, mostly from my schoolboy years, I shed; what extraordinary pleasure there has since been in finding other copies in old bookshops, even as far afield as Dresden and Oslo, and replacing them, for as sure as eggs is eggs, once a man has had a book he will again return to it, even after decades. I read Kinglake's *Eöthen* when I was twelve at the command of an enlightened schoolmaster; returning from my first journey to Turkey more than thirty years later, it was the first book I sought on my shelves – and then I remembered that I'd sold it for tuppence in a tea-chest with a hundred others.

I was right to buy the house, but in error to install my mother in it. She had, to some extent, moved into the house in Barnes, but half-heartedly, still clinging to her own house in Castle Hedingham; but this, with the return to Kensington, which we both thought of as our native village (as it certainly was in my case), she sold, and our coming together became irrevocable. She at once sought to tame my freedom. She watched, and recorded what she saw. She must have responded to every creak of the heavy iron gate, every click of the front door lock when turned by the key, every greeting of a joyful dog, and may well have hung for hours over the bannisters to catch a glimpse of my nocturnal visitors – 'Past midnight and another man brought to the house – where will it all end?' a typical wail in her diary.

Until I began to write about my life and turned to her diaries to supplement my own, I had no idea how vigilant she had been, how disapproving, commenting on every friend who came to stay and almost every casual bed-mate I brought back. Occasionally she attempted to make trouble – 'You're not the only one,' she said to a Danish friend, a museum curator, not a bed-mate. 'He's got a little Scottish boy, you ought to know.' The Scot, a six-footer and far from a boy, was another professional visitor.

Gloucester Road, nearby, had nothing of the sense of danger that so heightened the experience of sodomy on the Thames towpath, but it was a very happy hunting-ground for bodies, many of them American servicemen in a local hostel, in transit or on leave. Susie, one of my dogs, half-Hungarian pointer, brown coat, brown nose, brown toe-nails, offered them their opening – 'Taking your dog for a walk?' Why else would a man be out with his dog in the hour approaching midnight? But one night, without Susie, walking home from the High Street Underground, I was propositioned by an English bloke in his mid thirties or so, rather too old for me, but tall, very well put together, and with the animal magnetism that is occasionally immediately obvious in a man. 'Yours or mine?' was his presumptuous opening line. 'Mine,' I said, 'It's near.' His response – 'Mine's nearer, it's in Church Street' – clinched it. Crossing the road, within a hundred yards, with a nod to the guards and to my dismay, we entered the Barracks (demolished 1987). My companion was a sergeant in the Royal Military Police there. He took me to the room he shared with another sergeant, already a-bed, and without much in the way of introduction, fucked me; there was no alternative. Finished, but holding me down, he woke his mate with 'Do you want to take over? I've got to piss,' and off to piss he went, once his mate was comfortably ensconced. And so they changed and changed about until near four in the morning when, sated, my sergeant dressed to take me, I thought to the gate, but instead it was to the Mess where other sergeants were still drinking and, holding me by the ear, as it were, he offered me with 'Anyone want him before I let him go? – he's a bloody good fuck.'

Every man who risks a sexual encounter with another must expect, occasionally, to find the roles determined by the physically stronger. I felt not the least humiliated – the very reverse, released of inhibitions indeed, exhilarated by the pornography of an experience to which, once begun, I had abandoned myself, and that had been a match, not only for any of the experiences of officer cadets recorded by young Simon Raven,* but for the fantasies of porno magazines and films that I had seen in New York. My grudging willingness lent pleasure to what, long before and unwilling, had happened to me as a National Serviceman. Is it unreasonable to assume that these pleasures were perhaps nightly pursued, not only in this small barracks, but in others, and that to the vaunted heterosexuality of the armed forces there a constant homosexual undercurrent?

It is, perhaps, to many a mystery beyond understanding that sodomy can offer pleasure to the sodomised, but to some - by no means all – it does. 'You haven't lived ,' said Edward Montagu to Petter Kolrud during lunch at Beaulieu some summers ago, 'until you've been fucked up the arse.' He was being mischievous and wished, I think, to move the conversation on from poetry and

---

* Simon Raven: *Sound the Retreat*, 1971.

ballet, the preoccupations of two other guests, and Petter, every inch the brawny Nordic blond, was sitting next to him, munching away in silence. It was a sudden leap, the consequences quite uncertain, but Petter took the assertion in his stride and it was I who spluttered with surprise, amusement and anxiety. Petter is a skiing friend, a tennis friend, a clambering and climbing friend, twice married, a father, whose only flaw in our enthusiastic days of fierce activity was the frequency with which he attempted to telephone home for a sentimental chat when we were in places far away and international communications were fragmentary and unpredictable – I, when travelling, have always had the cold capability to leave my home behind. Petter, an analyst aware of all the sexual aberrations to which men are subject, said only, 'Yes, of course,' and went on munching and conversation remained in the control of the poet and the dancer, unaware of the interruption. The assertion was, nevertheless, worthy of debate - though perhaps not over lunch – for it is to some extent true that anal coition with a man (but not a woman) can involve, for the recipient, sexual stimulation and climax so intense that it is addictive – Lawrence of Arabia gave an honest and oddly innocent account of it in *The Seven Pillars of Wisdom*. Now, of course, this anal stimulation is no longer exclusive to the homosexual – heterosexual men are now aware of it and turn to female prostitutes for 'fisting'.

In the summer of my fortieth birthday I juggled three more or less steady lovers – an Indian student at the London College of Fashion who became tedious and irascible when drunk (too frequently), a young American art historian who was to desert me for John Pope-Hennessy (far more influential), and Angel, a Spanish waiter of such erotic allure that I had to share him with a dozen others; to these comparatively gentler souls my Military Policemen lent fierce variey. There was another soldier, a Horse Guard, equally determined, and he, capable of conversation even if mostly about the notes with condoms that tourists tucked into his boots and the chocolate bars that melted into his socks, lasted several months, as did a footman from Buckingham Palace, but most encounters were of the moment only, and that is how most wished them to be – an extended, more thrilling and often wonderfully enriched form of masturbation, with the huge advantage over the heterosexual fuck in that it had no consequences, no obligations.

These encounters, wholly consensual, were no longer illegal if both parties were twenty-one – that much, and only that much, had been achieved by the long fought for Sexual Offences Act of 1967. As the armed forces were excluded from this new freedom and it applied only to two men in private, my Military Policemen broke the law on both counts, and so too did the Lotharios of the Putney towpath, but this judgement of Portia, this pound of flesh but not a drop of blood, was better than nothing and something of a defeat for the Gwyneth Dunwoodys of this world. Mrs Dunwoody, a Member of Parliament of ancient Labour caste and childbearing hips, contributed to the debate both within and beyond the House in such flogging and castration terms that even I, who had no wish to suffer again from being labelled queer, wrote to her in protest. In the consequent correspondence she was so crudely unrepentant that I felt I had to do something: I joined the Campaign for Homosexual Equality (CHE). This I found to have its headquarters in Manchester (then, and still, another country), and to be run by the kind of men who are always dubbed 'old women'; a pro-London coup engineered by a handful of members of whom I was one, more or less succeeded in achieving independence, but then it too succumbed to what we unkindly called 'the couch parties' – the uncomely middle-aged and middle-sexed, turgid of mind and body, who wanted every word of every meeting addressed to the chair, and who could never reach agreement without setting up a working party. I and the other revolutionaries left and CHE eventually died of self-inflicted suffocation.

CHAPTER 4

Salvador Dali in Cadaques

It was to recurrent attacks of jaundice that I owe a brief, extra-ordinary and enriching friendship that ended as suddenly as it began. Although the type of the virus was identified as mild and fairly harmless, further bouts of jaundice were, for well over a decade, triggered by butter, oily fish, all forms of animal fat and alcohol, and sometimes, I thought, by anxiety and overwork. For a while, bread and salt were all that I could eat without reaction, and bouts of exhaustion unpredictably interrupted work. After several incomplete recoveries, and with Bill Martin able to hold the fort for a while, in September I left, exhausted, with three acquaintances rather than friends, for the south of France, the unfashionable coast of Hérault and Aude. It was an impulse prompted by gossip at a dinner party, four near strangers feeling sorry for themselves for having had no time to plan holidays with more familiar companions – and one of us had seen advertised in that day's *Times* a flat for four near a *plage* between Montpellier and Perpignan.

We booked it for two weeks but stayed one night. It was filthy, and so too was the featureless, bleak and shadeless *plage*. Cutting our losses we drove into Spain in search of a more friendly place in which to take an autumn holiday, to swim, eat, read and do nothing. We were bound further south, but the signpost to Cadaques triggered some more than half-forgotten memory and without another thought I turned the car onto the winding track that led down towards the sea. In the Sixties it was just that kind of Catalan coastal village – no crowds, no fashionable shops, no smart hotels, and one family restaurant for peasant and plutocrat alike, serviced by and serving the local fishermen. The cactuses in every garden were heavy with their prickly fruit, but within their armament of spines – the very devil to extract from fingertips and lips – lay flesh irresistibly sweet and succulent, free to anyone brave enough to pick them. Sand edged the deep bay, wild rocks enclosed it, and some welcoming spirit whispered, 'This is it.'

Simple rooms were to be had in the dilapidated Villa Tortuga and within hours I had been adopted by two beach dogs, Scipio and Hannibal; it was they who got me from my bed each morning, and with them at my heels I walked the length of what passed for the main street to the butcher's shop. Every day he found something unspeakable for the dogs, and the three of us then returned to the restaurant where, while drinking coffee, I fed them bloody morsels sliced with the knife that has travelled everywhere with me since National Service. And that is how I encountered Salvador Dali.

On that particular morning the butcher gave me the windpipe and lungs of a sheep, complete, intact and very bloody – and there it was, bloodying the wooden café table and my hands, the dogs slavering at my knees as I sliced it for them. I was scarcely conscious of the great green pre-war Cadillac as it whispered to a stop, car nerd though I am, and took no notice of the two people who'd got out of it, a tiny woman and a much taller man, both dressed from top to toe in velvet of a dark green to match the car. They sat in the sun a little way away and watched. Then the man came over. 'Do you know who I am?' he asked, his attitude imperious. 'Of course. You're Dali,' I replied – and to this day I do not know whether he was flattered that I knew, or disappointed that he had been denied another opportunity to announce to all in earshot, 'I am Dali.' 'And you've been waiting for me' – half question, half accusation. He seemed surprised when I said that I had not. To me, but not apparently to him, it was a preposterous notion that anyone would lie in wait for him with the dogs, the blood, the knife, the windpipe and the lungs as an elaborate ruse to draw him into conversation, but that is indeed what he supposed.

The encounter ended with an invitation to his house that

evening, but when I asked for the address I was given no more than a wave to the north-east. Then I recalled why it was that Cadaques was in some unknown sense familiar – in my work at Christie's, the best part of a decade earlier, I had damned a painting signed *Dali* as a fake and had, after a very long delay, received a note agreeing from his secretary in Cadaques.

Cadaques was not the place of Dali's birth – that was Figueras, twenty miles inland – but it was the spiritual and instinctive home to which he returned every summer, but for those of his absence in America, as driven there as the swallows and the swifts. As a boy the village and the wild coast flanking it were imprinted on his visual imagination, nourishing it with light and colour, form and fantasy. It faces east, the easternmost point of Spain, a place of thrilling dawns, and in the evening, looking out across the perfect symmetry of the deep bay, the compensation for never seeing the sun set behind the shoulders of the hills that shelter Cadaques from the west, is the eerie and compelling tranquillity of the skies so high and distances so gold and blue that are caught forever in so many of his paintings.

If Cadaques offered Dali the serenity of perfect natural balance, Cape Creus gave him the chaos of rocks once molten and erupting, stilled in their dying energy for the past billion years, eroded by the elements into age-old forms so animal, so human, so monstrous and so hallucinatory, that they engendered in him and embodied for him fantasies beyond our comprehension.

And it was at Port Lligat – no port, but a poor place of half-a-dozen fishermen's cottages tumbled together – that Dali put down his roots when, at twenty-five, with cash from his first commission, he bought one of these shacks. Piecemeal he bought the others, and piecemeal they grew into a single house, an organic thing leaning into the low cliff behind, a labyrinth of corridors and stairs, of rooms and spaces that lost their functions and became the repositories of would-be Surrealist objects, most of which remained obdurately kitsch. The moment the door opens, the twists and turns within the house mirror the erratic complexitiies of Dali's mind, the unexpected intuition, the fortuitous banality, the paradox of high intelligence and quite appalling taste.

These, not Figueras, were the real places of his birth, the womb from which he sprang, the womb to which he consistently returned. Here, if the exhibitionism did not quite go into abeyance, he was prepared to see the truth about himself, and occasionally to speak of it. Long after he had ceased to be a practising Catholic, Cadaques was his confessional.

A servant opened the door. The house was like a Schwitters *Merzhaus* leaning into the cliffside, climbing, a few stairs here, a wayward passage there, with glimpses into rooms and, through windows, repeated views of another, more complex, bay, more a long inlet of the sea, subtly changed as we gained height. As we emerged onto the roof, less a terrace than the clifftop, Dali seemed to be lurking in wait and not at ease; he mispronounced my Christian name – Brrreon – the *r* absurdly rolled. 'What shall I call you?' I asked, thinking Salvador impertinent and Dali even worse.

'What would you like to call me?'

'Majesty,' I suggested with a questioning lift to the last syllable. And Majesty it occasionally was, wryly, when he had been particularly lofty or absurd.

He ushered me to a giant eggshell, broken open as though boiled for breakfast, indicated that I should duck through a low hatch and sit inside. Of these there were three; Gala was already installed in one, Dali ducked into the third, and there we sat, at such a distance as to make conversation difficult; from mine in the middle I had to lob prattle over the jagged serrations of white cement at either Gala or Dali, knowing that the other could not hear it. Gala never responded; at that stage I did not know that she was deaf and thus thought her staring straight ahead, never uttering a word, a stratagem to make me go. Never have I been more uncomfortable.

Dali at last said, 'Let me show you my Christ.' Scrambling out of our respective eggs we set off, not back into the house to see a painting – as I expected – but away from it, past garden ornaments so kitsch that not even the nouveaux riches of Billericay would have bought them, and into an arid olive grove, to discover a gigantic figure lying on its back, arms outstretched as though crucified, its ribcage an old fisherman's boat, its curling pain-wracked fingers hacked from car tyres, its long limbs heaped earth and rubble, broken bricks and tiles, with fragments of glazed drainpipes that were, disconcertingly, the colour and texture of old medical prostheses.

I had not worked for Christie's for a decade without learning the ambiguous words of astonishment that to the gullible easily pass for praise. I uttered them, thinking myself a hypocrite, a shit.

This *Debris Christ* is perhaps Dali's least regarded work. It was fully finished in the autumn of 1968, but most authorities put it in 1969. In its use of materials it anticipated Italian Arte Povera by a full decade and Joseph Beuys by rather less, and I must argue that as Dali had made it in a mood of high seriousness and regarded his making it as an unconscious and ecstatic act, we should take it more seriously, not, as he thought it, as a work of ultimate Surrealism.

'Let me photograph you with my Christ,' said Dali.

'Yes, of course,' said I.

'There in the left armpit.' I obeyed. 'No, no, not standing; curled up as though asleep.'

Wearing my only decent trousers, I demurred.

'Take them off. Be naked. It will make a better photograph.'

And 'What the hell,' I thought, a little drunk, bemused and, I admit, awed.

'Lie down,' he ordered, and lie down I did, with grit and rubble biting into my skin as, responding to more commands, I turned this way and that in foetal positions and listened to the clicking camera.

'Now masturbate' (again the excessive rolling of the *r*) – and

'What the hell,' I thought again, but did, wondering where all this might lead.

Starting from scratch and in so un-erotic a situation, this took some time, Dali all the while clicking the camera and fumbling in his trousers.

When I'd done, I had to brush the grit from my skin, grimly thinking that masturbation can be remarkably unrewarding and mechanical. We went straight back to Gala, who was still sitting in her egg.

Dinner, an hour or two later, was in the village restaurant where we had met that morning, not in the house – and, indeed, I cannot recall ever eating in the house, or ever seeing the kitchen used for anything more than making coffee and producing ice cubes – both kitchen and dining room were, like most other rooms in Port Lligat, no more than theatre sets in which Gala and Dali put on their show.

In the restaurant they were treated as something between old and expected friends and feudal nobility; food and drink were brought, we consumed them, and then left. Neither Gala nor Dali asked for a bill and no payment was offered – they arrived and left as though food was their due. Next morning, there again for coffee and the dogs' breakfast, I asked if I might pay for what we had had, and was refused with the explanation that bills were totted up for a while and then paid by Dali's secretary. Perhaps this was the case in Paris and New York too, for not once did I see either of them pay for anything.

I was mightily pleased with myself when at last I went to my bed, for Gala, who had warmed a little over dinner, had asked me to come again the following day. But lying on the sand with Scipio and Hannibal, what did I see in the distance but the great green Cadillac sweeping into town and Dali gathering the hippy flotsam of the night – it was the weekend and there was plenty of it. I went to the house, as asked, and so did twenty others, and when most of the boys were taken off to see the *Debris Christ*, I stayed with Gala.

They were away far longer than I had been and the terrace was in darkness when they returned in dribs and drabs. Which of them, I wondered, had been in which armpit, which had masturbated for him, and which, perhaps, had done for Dali what Florentine boys had done for the last real Medici, and buggered each other for his delight?

If there was ever film in his camera – which now I doubt, for I think it was a camouflage for a voyeur who, though brazenly addicted to the habit, was still, at his age, both embarrassed by residual shame and unwilling to admit to homosexuality – then in his archive there must be thousands of photographs of unidentifiable young men in much the same situation as he put me.

I realised then that Dali, for all the fawning interest of strangers, was alone and could not bear his loneliness – Gala, his anchor in Cadaques since 1930, was not enough. Used as a child to the indulgent approbation of his family, as a young man to the profound affection, even lust, of Lorca, as a precocious Surrealist to the envy and curiosity of the older founders of the movement, and used above all, as a celebrity painter, to the patronage and adulation of the rich, powerful and equally celebrated, he could not, in his dotage, live without a daily dose of hero-worship – and if it did not come, then he was quite prepared to go out onto the streets to get it. Again and again I heard him go through the 'Do you know who I am?' routine and, whatever the answer, invite strangers to the house.

Dali at the end of the Sixties was perhaps not quite six feet in height; at sixty-four he had begun to stoop a little and, conscious of it, had the habit of often straightening his spine, squaring his shoulders and puffing out his chest. His hair was thinning, receding and, I think dyed, for there was no hint of grey or white; it was by no means fastidiously clean. His face had sagged enough to blur the once emphatic line of his chin, and only the moustache with its ridiculous waxed spikes remained as vigorous as in his prime. The moustache was, I think, important as some sort of delusory monument to an equally delusory virility. He could still widen his eyes to show a startling white all round their irises.

His breath was always foul, sometimes so foul that I wished he farted more and breathed much less – not that I ever heard him fart, but the subject fascinated him and he *claimed* to fart a lot, his farts as sweet as the perfumes of Arabia. He knew his breath was foul and claimed that it was foul enough to keep flies from perching on the wings of his moustache; when one once did it was made immortal in a photograph.

Dali spoke English with perfect ease, often with a dramatic sense of interval and emphasis, but sometimes, in public, he spoke very slowly and affected a heavy Spanish accent, elaborating diphthongs into syllables. In spite of eight continuous years in the United States, his Americanisms were few – but then he rarely spoke of anything that had happened there and seemed to have blanked out what had quite certainly been his most flamboyant and commercially successful period.

Dali must have had a dozen velvet suits in his favoured green, for he was always immaculate when out early in the day, the velvet never crushed or crumpled, the jacket never greasy round the neck, the trousers never discoloured by the urine dribble of the elderly man in boxer shorts. I wish he had been as fastidious with food, but he ate greedily, shovelling as though he had only seconds to empty his plate into his mouth, and this strain on his digestion may well have been the cause of his mephitic breath. He was one of only two men I have known capable of sputtering, not only on himself with a napkin tucked below his chin, but over every neighbour at a table for four with napkins on their laps. The other man was Bernard Crick, founder of the Orwell Prize for political journalism, who, on the occasion of awarding it to me, ruined a favourite tie in plain green silk, bought because it perfectly matched (or so I thought) the green of Dali's velvet. I now know never to wear a plain tie to lunch or dinner – only one that is heavily patterned can survive a gravy stain. At Port Lligat, not putting on the style (or rather, putting on another – that of the rich and ancient hippy), the velvet suits were never seen late in the day; then he took to jackets that were either marginally ethnic or operatic military, with cotton trousers and immaculate white shirts of loose Byronic elegance, and went barefoot or wore the classic sandals of the ancient Greek.

There was not much to do in Cadaques forty-odd years ago. In the village there was no exploitation of Dali's nearby presence – no museum, no kitsch souvenirs at which to giggle. Nor was there much to do at Port Lligat, for the phallic swimming pool had not been dug and many of the kitsch features of the garden had not been installed. Gala still swam just below the house and sunbathed on the terrace, but Dali did neither. Fully clothed he sat in the sun like an old lizard. Nor did he paint. Others claim to have seen him painting in these lean years, but I did not. It was as though his mind had emptied.

We occasionally walked a little on the beach, but his steps were the sandal-dragging slither of an aged Japanese. He must once have been lithe and careless enough to clamber those uncomfortable rocks with ease, but not in my day. The beach, however, had an astonishing effect on him – as though he had never been on it before; I was at first dismayed by this Alzheimer effect but I think now that he was overwhelmed by so dense a palimpsest of memories that he could not speak. Any other man would have given me a time and place to childhood recollections, and have said that here he saw a woman empty her bladder, that there Lorca had first buggered him, and on that rock Gala in his arms had talked of death, but Dali kept these things to himself.

I once suggested drawing a bead on the house and walking back in a straight line – perhaps a kilometre – instead of following a track. Taking no account of his flimsy sandals, off we set, but however much he thought that he belonged to that wild landscape, he knew nothing of it and was helpless among the thorny shrubs that tore at his trousers. Like a child, he had a tantrum and we returned to the track, he in a furious sulk and me in disgrace.

The swimming pool was a calculated attempt to extend the social life denied him in Cadaques. The more serious of his friends in his early years had seen the point of being there with him – but that was long ago and his coterie in the late Sixties were neither serious nor sincere, and few of them were prepared to be his courtiers anywhere but in Paris or New York. But it was naive of him to think that a pool in the shape of an erect penis would make Cadaques another Babylon. It seemed to me a kind of madness when the sea was within spitting distance of the terrace – though it was sometimes clogged with weed – and the village had long since outgrown its natural water supply and ran dry when the water tanker that steamed into the bay every few days was delayed – but Dali was nothing if not utterly selfish. I did not see it finished, but the Hollywood embellishment of the garden with hideous objects had begun in my time, and they all made the point that not even Dali could make an actuality of Surrealism, that this genre of fantasy wore very thin very quickly unless, filtered through his hand and eye, his wit and imagination – all of which he still had in abundance – they were translated into a painting.

Dali had read the works of Freud long before meeting him, but when that meeting at last took place in London in 1938, he was obsessed by the skull of the old and ailing analyst; he likened it to the shell of a snail, to be winkled out with a needle. But he had already winkled out as much as he needed; thus the inspiration of his Surrealism became the active process of cultivating fantasy and grafting it onto reality. Dali proclaimed that his art grew from hallucinatory energy, and that he must paint like a madman, documenting the functions of his subconscious mind and, again using his own words, 'completely discredit the world of reality'.

Through the obsessive contemplation of objects it was possible for him to enter another plane. By painting them the subconscious was liberated and the object freed from conventional associations – and at that point it became possible to introduce distortion, decomposition and putrefaction, and take the object so far from its original state and meaning that it must mean something new. This is where shock and horror may disturb the viewer, but if he is to share anything of Dali's private eye, he must engage in Dali's experience of obsession and transmutation. This is visionary experience, fantasy imposed on the world of natural appearances, psychological derangement, sexuality and metamorphosis, all in an infinite space recognisable from our own dreams and from Dali's 'hand-made photographs' of Cadaques. Everything that Freud knew, Dali knew better – and from his own experience.

Perhaps the most important thing that Dali did – apart from becoming the supreme Surrealist – was to confront the taboo that made masturbation quite unmentionable; but the polite society that was the art world in Britain and America seemed not to notice. In 1929, to call a painting *The Great Masturbator* was to provoke outrage – but outrage came there none, probably because so few who saw the picture, if any, understood the imagery and could not discern in its complexities any action resembling self-abuse, as was then the euphemism for it.

Self-abuse was widely recognised as 'impure'; psychiatrists advised anxious parents to tie their sons' hands to their bedsteads, or fit the strange preventative contraptions that could be bought in shops that sold rupture trusses, artificial limbs and condoms. It was a practice that could devastate the mind and debilitate the body; the boy who masturbated would go blind, become so enfeebled that he might not reach adulthood, and almost certainly not have children if he did; he must 'save' himself, all adults (who, lying, had abused themselves without these consequences) said, for the night following his marriage.

Dali would have none of this, but the picture was too obscure to become the great masturbator's manifesto, polite society ignored its implications, and the impolite society of the Surrealists, who knew all about fellatio and sodomy (Gala, they discovered, could not, because of some deformity, be fucked and buggered simultaneously), took masturbation in their stride. Had Dali been a member of the

New English Art Club or the Royal Academy in 1929, he'd have been drummed out of their premises with hypocritical bellows of disgust.

Did Gala and Dali ever have the straightforward sex life of a married couple? I doubt it. When they met in 1929 he, in hetero-sexual terms, was still a virgin, terrified of the vagina, disgusted by menstrual blood; she, on the other hand, was the sexually voracious wife of Paul Éluard from whom no orifice was safe; he found her 'the most intense incarnation of love, desire, and erotic pleasure', but was content to share her with other men to heighten the experience. Éluard was a French poet who, with André Breton, led the Surrealists in Paris.

What could Gala see in timorous Dali, at twenty-four a decade younger than herself and manifestly uncertain of his sexuality? Was she remarkably more prescient than all the Surrealists put together in recognising Dali's oncoming superiority? Can she really have thought in 1929 that he would make her rich beyond her greed and avarice? Can she really have gambled on his celebrity becoming the flame to which myriad moths might be attracted so that she could take her pick? That was certainly what happened and went on happening, and there must have been hundreds of young men who briefly bedded Gala and masturbated for Dali, thousands even, wondering which they might please more and from whom they might milk something of a fortune, only to find themselves milked for a day or two, then to be utterly discarded – but for Gala it was a hell of a gamble.

Some young men lasted longer. Gala had infatuations that cost tens of thousands of dollars to initiate and maintain, and if Dali never suffered the same hopeless sexual passions, there was always a legion of freaks and misfits that cost fortunes to amuse, the hunchback, the dwarf, the identical twin, those who surgically changed sex when this was rare and strange, the boyish girl and the effeminate boy. Had he discovered the ladyboys of south-east Asia he might well have been in his element, for to him the ideal body and the ideal state were those of the hermaphrodite, able in every way possible to be simultaneously hetero and homosexual. It was a fantasy: I asked him if he had ever encountered an hermaphrodite and he had not.

There is every indication that he disliked, even feared, the genitals of women and harboured some primeval distaste for menstrual bleeding. Excrement, however, fascinated him. He examined his stools for form and consistency and admitted to a profound sense of loss when flushing them away. This interest was, perhaps, the one lasting stimulus to his imagination engendered by his hated father, for this feared monster of a man had once returned home far later than expected, unashamedly announcing as he dismounted from the taxi, that he had crapped in his trousers; Dali, ten or twelve at the time, felt humiliated and ashamed, claiming later that this had been the turning point in his relationship with his father. Faeces became so much an open obsession that by the time Dali reached Paris a decade or so later, the established Surrealists suspected him of eating shit. 'Are you a coprophage?' they quizzed him, compelling Gala to ask the question; he was not, but in asking, the Surrealists succeeded in expanding Dali's deep-rooted but naive preoccupation with the business of his bowels into more sophisticated fields.

Dali was, however, fastidious to the point of squeamishness. Not for one moment would he have *touched* a stool, let alone eaten it. I doubt if he even touched semen, another product of his body and therefore a subject of fascination; and I know that he would not touch blood, though he could watch it flow with pleasure from a wounded bull at bullfights, the perfect combination of blood and homoerotic beauty.

I once saw Dali paralysed by the sight of blood. We were wandering on the deserted shore to the north-east of the house when a boy emerged from the sea – Dali's slim-hipped, brown-skinned ideal, twenty or so – and if that were not enough, he was bleeding heavily from one foot, staining the sea. The cut was deep across the sole, the pumping loss of blood considerable but almost stemmed if I held the foot firmly in both hands. It was then that I saw Dali utterly still, just staring. Staring was the one thing that he did more intently even than masturbation – and often they were the same thing, for he claimed that he could ejaculate merely by looking (that is when he wasn't claiming to be impotent).

'Bloody man's coming in his trousers again,' I thought, and shouted at him. This was not an occasion for addressing him as Majesty. Breaking into his trance took every word of abuse that I could muster, every obscenity, and at last I could offer him the choice of holding the foot and getting blood on his fine linen trousers, or running for help; he chose to trot off with a little more urgency than his customary shuffle. I have seen men paralysed with fright, but never before or since have I seen a man rendered insensible by sheer aesthetic pleasure; any normal homosexual would have taken hold of the bleeding foot and let me, much younger and much fitter, run for help.

By the time I knew him he claimed almost daily to be impotent and yet there was the almost daily fumbling in his trousers by his *Debris Christ*, and the not infrequent invitation to young women to withdraw into some other part of the garden and watch him masturbate. He preferred to watch men and be watched by women, and in 1929, in Paris, wild with excitement at having been embraced by the Surrealists, he wrote a vivid account of watching himself masturbate in the mirror of his hotel bedroom. It is something that most boys have done by the time they are fifteen, but immature Dali left it till he was twenty-five – a 'rhythmic and solitary sacrifice' that he prolonged for fifteen minutes before 'wrenching out the ultimate pleasure with all the animal force of my clenched hand'. Forty years later, impotent or not, the sperm and blood of other men still excited him as much as the abattoirs and butcher's shops that had by then been the sources of so much luscious imagery, of severed heads and viscera, of flies and putrefaction. His first interest in me had sprung, I was often to remind myself, from the lungs and windpipe of a sheep.

Dali was fascinated by the *idea* of sodomy. He knew how it was done, and believed that a harder erection was required, but never in any active sense had he been a partner in it. His penis was small, and cruelly mocked for it at school, he was embarrassed by it as an adult; he was, moreover, subject all his life to premature ejaculation. As is so often the case, the child Dali was father to the man in that at his first school he developed an affectionate obsession with the buttocks of another boy compacted into 'pants that were excruciatingly tight ... an invincible curiosity compelled me to look at these tight pants each time a violent movement threatened to split them open'.

As the recipient, he had found sodomy impossible, he claimed. His friend in early manhood, the poet and playwright Federico Garcia Lorca, Dali's 'twin soul', dazzling physically and intellectually and probably his only true friend in a long lifetime, attempted it in 1925. Openly homosexual and unembarrassed by the taboo that in Spain in the 1920s made this virtually unmentionable, Lorca tried twice to bugger Dali, and failed – or so, for years, Dali maintained, asserting that he himself was not and had never been homosexual, and, significantly, that the attempts hurt. Forty years on, and less guarded about it in the more relaxed atmosphere of the late Sixties, when Spain was notorious for the willingness of men to be casually homosexual, he felt able to admit that pain rather than absence of desire had been the deterrent. If it hurt, then Lorca had at the very least begun to penetrate him, and Dali had permitted it.

Lorca left only one observation on the matter: when in 1930 he heard that Dali had found in Gala a woman with whom to spend the rest of his life, he exclaimed, 'It's impossible – he can only get an erection when a man has stuck a finger up his arse.'

I observed that as some arseholes are tight enough to make emptying the bowels almost impossible, proper medical remedies had been devised, and the following year took him the very instrument, gift-wrapped as it were, from John Bell and Croyden in Wigmore Street. But I was forty years too late with this formidable piece of polished steel machinery; Dali chuckled over it and then showed me a drawer full of rubber phalluses – not an academic collection like those held in the Thorwaldsen and British Museums, but a sorry little band of working tools to be employed by one boy on another in the more exciting preliminaries in the armpits of the *Debris Christ*, as I then learned. Did he use them on himself? Who knows? – he had such a phobia about being casually touched that intimate sexual touching by anyone other than himself had become impossible, and anal masturbation with a dildo may well have been all that he had left if he was indeed impotent by then. The lifelong trouble with Dali is that so much was fantasy and so little the whole unvarnished truth.

Of all the painters of whom Dali spoke at length and frequently, Velazquez I am certain was to him far the most important. He even toyed with the idea that he might be the great man's reincarnation and was delighted when I told him that I knew a woman who claimed to be Delacroix re-born and painted watercolours to prove it. 'She is also,' I said, 'the head of a coven of witches in West-minster' – and that really did get him going. But beyond their both cultivating particular moustaches, both wearing their hair in styles sufficiently close for Dali, when his grew thin, to commission a wig modelled on Velazquez, their both having fathers who were notaries and both craving to be identified as of noble lineage, Dali could find too few parallels even to convince himself.

Even so, were he to be in the Prado at the unlikely moment of its bursting into flames, Velazquez's *Las Meninas* would be the one picture that he'd rescue. I considered him, frail and shuffling, struggling with all nine square metres of the famous canvas, and as everything that Dali thought or did was tainted with ambiguity, I wondered whether rescuing this greatest of all Spanish masterpieces would have suited him better than dying in the attempt – what a grand *Götterdämmerung* it would be if, shrouded in the great canvas, he and it were engulfed in the inferno, leaving not a shred of either to posterity. Would that not ensure his lasting fame?

Why did I stop seeing Dali? After four long visits to Cadaques I felt that we had exchanged as much as we could and that the friendship – if that is what it was – had run into the sands. It was clear that he had recovered sufficient energy and impulse to revive much of the international life that had been his before what I perceived as a doldrum had set in in the later Sixties, and was impatient to return to it, plans already made. It was as though he had stepped off a merry-go-round and now felt compelled to get onto it again, to recover the earlier pace and serendipity.

In 1980, when the Tate Gallery mounted an encyclopedic retrospective exhibition of Dali's work, it seemed an attempt to justify everything that he had ever done, to sanitise the man and his imagination, to be a Dali-can-do-no-wrong piece of propaganda, to counter the critical dismissal that had been the informed view of him for, by then, a generation. I wanted to shout that I knew another Dali, a dirty Dali so to speak, a Dali who had always since a boy had a filthier imagination than any army sergeant humiliating raw recruits. I wanted everyone to know of the hundreds of drawings that could never be published or exhibited, revealing the depths that he had plumbed.

I wrote the necessary note when Gala died, but when he followed her – and I am certain that he thought of it as following, for he had followed her every day since their first meeting, there was no one to whom I could express my grief – except myself – and I did genuinely grieve. For once the wider public had been right – and is right still: Dali deserves his reputation with them as the last of the great old masters.

CHAPTER 5

Joseph McCrindle

This was the point at which Joseph McCrindle began to play a major part in my life. Eight years my senior, but seeming much more, very rich and very lonely, though rarely solitary, we had drifted into friendship through the frequency of his visits to Christie's and his wayward enthusiasm for drawings by old masters. His father, Ronald, a British flying ace who had – as had my stepfather – fought with Allenby in the Mesopotamian and Jerusalem campaigns of the Great War, had married Joe's mother, Odette Feder, an American socialite, her wealthy family very jealous of their status in the Social Register, the American equivalent of Debrett's and the Almanach de Gotha. Divorce was swift; Odette immediately married a French Count, Guy du Bourg de Bozas, departed for Paris and the south of France, and little Joe became the charge of his maternal grandfather, Joseph Feder, and, particularly, of his formidable grandmother, Edith Mosler Feder, growing up in their Stanford White mansion on Fifth Avenue, privately tutored in boxing and the violin (for neither had he any aptitude), precociously collecting rare books and manuscripts with his pocket money. As measures of the Feder wealth (much of it subsequently his) it is worth recording that to entertain him on a long vacation when he was eight, they despatched him on their yacht to the eastern Mediterranean with Lanning Roper (later to be a distinguished expert on gardens) as his tutor and the crew for company as they explored the Aegean coast of Turkey; at eighteen he set off for Yale in a Duesenberg, the very grandest of American cars, with a chauffeur at the wheel and a footman to handle his luggage.

Joe was thus very much part of the American establishment, and

411

yet an escapee from it, living in both London and New York in untidy circumstances that seemed less obviously wealthy than donnish and scholarly, oddly down-at-heel. His passionate interest in the visual arts may have stemmed from his grandmother's genes, for she was the daughter of Henry Mosler, in his day a fashionable American Salon painter of portraits, landscapes and genre. Joe spoke and read French, German and Italian, and when travelling in Europe was never without the local newspaper. He ate very well but dressed appallingly, not because he bought his clothes in charity shops (though that is how they looked), but because his perspiring bulk – he was built as robustly as a Doric portico – and the spilling of food and drink combined to camouflage their much loftier origin; he was a tailor's nightmare. Repeatedly he fell in love with young men, his ideal the flannelled fool of the Ivy League, though he settled for many far less glamorous and far less suitable. Never predatory, he could be reckless – his cry of 'Don't stop, don't stop' at one of his own dinner parties when he had locked himself in the bathroom with Ted Pillsbury, the archetypal flannelled fool who was later Jacob Rothschild's grotesquely unsuitable nomination as Director of the National Gallery, still echoes in the ears of all who heard it. To his dying day he was driven by infatuation, and when it ended in wretched disappointment, as it always did, the few faithful friends, female and male, with whom he had never been in love and who played the dependable Nicklausse to his Hoffmann, were always there to console him and haul him to his feet.

His less formal dinners were notorious. At these, the mismatch of young men acquired through his literary interests as editor, owner and publisher for twenty years of *The Transatlantic Review* (a magazine of short stories, poetry and criticism) with those, fewer, discovered through the visual arts, seemed wanton. I might find myself with Mario Amaya, a clever young critic of the day, Mario Dubsky, Keith Milow and Mark Lancaster, all more or less forgotten bright young painters of the Sixties, or with Nikos Stangos, Brian Johnson, David Plante and other equally forgotten writers, and with strangers who came from neither camp; Brian Epstein, for example, of whose miserable affection for John Lennon Joe knew more than most – as did I through my tiresome compulsion to comfort the miserable (the Seven Works of Mercy, once dinned into a boy, become impossible to neglect).* Joe simply could not recognise that we were all sorts of oil and water and that our interests would not mix, and, smiling benignly, eating more than most of us, happy with second helpings as large as the first, was always puzzled that we did not clamber into bed with each other or, occasionally, with him. Joe was for more than forty years my very close friend, but whether in London or New York, his dinner parties were always the same, always bathetic for his guests and himself.

All this, everyone in his other world, the grandees of American museums, galleries and universities, knew very well and, in spite of gossip, they embraced him on their various boards, positions for which he did not greatly care – 'I never say anything at these meetings,' he despairingly confessed of the American Academy in Rome, nevertheless admitting that they were the perfect excuse for jaunts to a city in which he felt almost at home and where the Sestieri family (dealers, discoverers and, alas, restorers) found him something to add to his ever-increasing collection. To all these panjandrums he was known for his impulsive yet always inconspicuous generosity, and it was to their world that he introduced me so discreetly that I did not realise how subtly he

* Brian Epstein, the Beatles' manager (1961–67), haplessly attracted to John Lennon and tormented by his flirting, was eventually – when they were alone on holiday in Barcelona in the spring of 1963 – allowed to fellate him, with the usual heterosexual excuse 'just to see what it is like'. Brian took this as a sign of promise; Lennon, on the other hand, married, his wife Cynthia in hospital recovering from childbirth, soured the relationship, not only by refusing further performances, but by mocking Brian for his homosexuality. It was from Joe that Brian got his 'houseman', Lonnie Trimble, the very tall and handsome black man who served him in the years 1964–66.

was steering me away from the direct dealing that I had grown to dislike. His *Transatlantic Review* was a vehicle for promoting writers whose early promise was invisible to other publishers, and that talent he now applied to me. I became, as it were, the curator of his collection, three times responsible for hanging it as three times he moved to larger apartments in New York, and three more times in London, responsible for guarding its condition, responsible for maintaining its inventory; as there was never time to catalogue it properly, the task that I might most have enjoyed fell to the constantly disgruntled Fred den Broeder, another of Joe's shorn lambs. I was never able to slow his rate of acquisition; an obsessive traveller, he could go nowhere without attempting to buy paintings and drawings, and in their absence, such objects as Pre-Columbian sculpture and Tanagra figures, returning with as many embarrassments as successes. Nor could I ever persuade him to rid himself of the many things that he should not have bought; these were crammed into the servants' rooms of his Central Park West apartment, never to be seen by him again.

I already knew a number of American directors and curators, but Joe ensured that I knew many more, and for some of them I drifted into the intellectually and morally much more comfortable position of becoming their London and European errand boy. I was already in that role for museums in South Africa, reinforcing collections there of twentieth-century British art, paid small annual stipends rather than working on commission, and with similar stipends from American museums I eventually had an income that relieved me from all that I most disliked about being an art dealer, while retaining the extraordinary pleasure of having – at least in some small part – ensured that museums had been properly and suitably enriched. Freedom from the commission system on which most advisers worked meant that my advice on price or auction bid could never be interpreted as for my own benefit. It also meant that when negotiating with a dealer he could reduce his figure not only by the then widely acknowledged 'museum price' some ten or fifteen per cent below the asking price, but also by the percentage that he would normally set aside for an agent introducing a buyer (I had indeed learned my lesson from Geoffrey Agnew). For a small museum that extra percentage reduction often meant the difference between buying and not buying. This was a very different pattern of practice from that current now, when agents have been known to take commissions from both seller and buyer and even to add ten or twenty per cent to the initial asking price, pocketing the difference as well as the commissions.

I relished this combination of freedom and responsibility, hunting through auction rooms and the stock of dealers for my particular quarry, the ability to work almost like a curator filling gaps in a collection or opening new fields for a museum. Decades later I still experience a thrill when coming upon a painting or drawing in the acquisition of which I had a hand. I felt that no part of my experience as a student art historian with some practical knowledge of cleaning, restoration and forgery, as a precocious cataloguer of international exhibitions and a dogsbody for so long at Christie's, had been wasted and that all were now being applied in a wholly worthwhile way.

Four or five times a year I flew to New York, stayed with Joe to recover from jet lag and then moved on, if not inland to Chicago or Minneapolis or Cleveland, then up or down the eastern sea-board, even to Key West, its southernmost tip. There Joe had arranged for me to advise the redoubtable Mrs Frances Mitchell Wolfson who intended to found a museum devoted to John James Audubon (1785–1851), the celebrated French Creole naturalist and draughtsman who spent most of his life in America recording birds. As he had passed 1831 researching in the Florida Keys there was some justification for her ambition, and before I met her I foolishly hoped that this almost *tabula rasa* project might be to some extent mine as well as hers. In London I had known, briefly, her son Mitchell II (Micky), a collector of Eric Gill material and similarly stylish erotica, and should have been warned by his mercurial behaviour that his mother might be dominant and difficult. She was.

The Wolfsons were Florida aristocracy engaged in politics and philanthropy, and in 1958 had saved from demolition the mid nineteenth-century Classical Revival house that Frances intended to convert into her museum; talking to local builders and the local architect, considering the compromises compelled by her very proper wish to preserve the outward appearance while providing internally all that even a very small museum must prepare for its visitors, she was imperious and much less agreeable than the Marschallin at her levée in *Der Rosenkavalier*, with which her morning inspections of the site had much in common. We seemed to resolve nothing. After a week or so she invited me to dinner, letting it be known that I must be properly dressed – in levels of temperature and humidity that cook the pale-skinned Englishman – and sent the Cadillac. Did she own, I wondered, the hotel in which she appeared to live? For perhaps half an hour we got on well enough on the verandah and then went to her table. 'The usual?' enquired the waiter (whose hand she required me to shake), to which she assented, obviously for both of us. 'What is the usual?' I asked while he was still shuffling our chairs, 'Turtle' the answer.

'I won't eat turtle.'

'Why not?'

'Turtles are endangered.'

'This turtle is dead.'

So were my chances. 'Give him anything he wants,' she said to the waiter, which meant having to read the menu while she glowered in silence. My subsequent attempts to make conversation were blocked by her monosyllabic checkmates, and the letter that was delivered to my hotel early the following morning, she must have written before she went to bed. She had had second thoughts, she wrote, no longer considered her choice of building to be suitable, and was now uncertain that she would continue with the project. Nothing of this was true but it served her purpose in getting rid of me; the project was eventually completed on a rather larger scale than first intended and very neatly too, but on a considerably increased budget. Considering that I had paid for my flights to Miami, the hired car and the hotel, she enclosed with her letter a wretchedly ungenerous cheque.

I paid my hotel bill and drove the monotonous and often dead straight line that is the road to Miami and the flight to New York. I was now at a loose end and could have stayed, swimming in the warm Atlantic among the diving pelicans, or in the disconcertingly cooler Gulf of Mexico, but I did not care much for the hotel and even less for keeping my own or any other company there, for, booked by Joe in a moment of mischief, it was an hotel of particular reputation, not just queer but where the then still infant Fist Fuckers of America held gatherings. It was out of season, but with the handful of other guests shaven-headed, black-leathered, studded, belted, harnessed and chained with Harley-Davidsons between their thighs, it was no place for me to idle.

I could hardly reproach Joe; I could have upped sticks and gone to another hotel but was too indolent – yet I did wonder if Frances Wolfson had known of its reputation and let this colour her opinion of me, for the turtle tiff seemed a thin reason for my sacking. Back in New York and with time to waste I could explore the then much sleepier museums, the Metropolitan a Vale of Lethe, Brooklyn fallen into desuetude and selling its duplicates and trivia in the souvenir shop, fifty people in the Cloisters, none in the Hispanic Society. I trawled the dealers and bookshops and found drawings; I trawled the baths and discovered sex beyond my wild imaginings. New York in the late Sixties and throughout the Seventies was a blatantly sexual city. Live sex shows and printed pornography were everywhere; one might have to search a little for the queer variety, but it was hardly hidden, and even between lunch and tea it was possible to see a live burlesque show of boy strippers as a preliminary to astonishingly queer films.

There were too the time-honoured and occasionally menacing places for immediate sex in Central Park and the derelict docks, and there were steam baths the length of the town, in which, for the price of hiring a thin old towel, sex could be had with a chosen partner or an entirely random half-dozen, standing, lying and in positions studied by Michelangelo for his *Last Judgement*. All these, long-established, once served an honest purpose for a physically hard-working population living in tenements, but with widespread improvements in domestic hygiene had become superfluous, surviving on the sexual appetite of men for men; some had particular populations – younger, older, tougher, rougher or inclined to S and M – and all but one were seedy.

The Continental Baths were smart. In the basement of the Ansonia Hotel, they were the bright idea of an entrepreneur who saw that the sleazy older baths offered scant discretion or security; his, much more expensive, maintained the air of fashionable public rooms into which the passer-by might casually drop for drinks and cabaret – Bette Midler its most celebrated performer (once with Barry Manilow). Women as well as men went there to see who was about and it was not uncommon to see couples in evening dress after a do sharing a table with an old friend in a towel. I was surprised, even a little dismayed (for he had always seemed so much in coy denial about his sexuality that I and many others had long assumed him to be still pre-pubertally innocent), to encounter at a junction of corridors the length of which he could easily be seen, Bruce Chatwin on his knees alternately fellating two equally beautiful young men – but this was, after all, a place designed for the delight of aesthetes, one way and another.

Recourse to the baths – any of them – was hardly necessary unless in search of the particular thrill that accompanies leisurely sex with anonymous strangers to which no obligation is attached. Men in New York seemed everywhere to flaunt their sexual heat, and if it was not always easy to identify their sexual direction, this, bewilderingly, often did not matter, for it seemed that sex was sex,

required no classification by gender, could be had urgently anywhere at any time, and orgasm was all. I had experienced something
of this in Italy and was to see more of it among South African
whites, but in New York it was rampant and straight men seemed
as much on the hunt for it as queer. The Seventies were, however, not only my second decade of fervid, impetuous, careless,
abandoned and perhaps dangerous sex, the appetite only ever briefly
sated, but my cannabis years – and the effect of this on me was
sometimes sexually debilitating, pitching me lower if my mood
was depressed. In New York we not only smoked it but ate it as a
salad vegetable, chopped it into goulash and baked it in cakes and
cookies, its effect on tempers and tensions wonderfully soothing,
but on my libido quite disastrous. When a young curator from
Princeton took me to Andy Warhol's Factory for the first time it
was in anticipation of finding beautiful boys from among whom to
identify a sexual partner for the night, but the cannabis on offer
there was of sublimely powerful quality – and though the boys
were there in number and were indeed quite beautiful, there was
nothing to be done but, embraced with them, lie euphoric and
incapable like Arcadian shepherds on the banks of Lethe, smoking,
stroking, murmuring mindless gibberish.

Andy himself made very little sense at night. The Factory was his
court but he made scant effort to hold it in any sense that Charles II
might have recognised, though there were courtiers with minds as
bawdy and depraved as Rochester's. He was not much more
sensible by day and, apart from his notorious and much quoted
quips, was largely inarticulate. My abiding impression of him at
work on his now ludicrously expensive screenprints is that he was
so indecisive as to how they should proceed that adjustments,
interventions and colours were far more often determined by his
assistants than by him, and that the finished works are more theirs
than his – 'You decide,' his only instruction after fifteen minutes
pondering; this, however, was in the Seventies – of his practice
earlier I was never a witness, and never after 1979.

I cannot recall taking LSD at the Factory, but it was very much part of life in the Seventies, best taken in very small doses on cubes of sugar or tabs of, I think, blotting paper laid on the tongue like the Host at Communion, and certainly best taken in reliable company in case the effect was dangerously strong – though I doubt if there was ever an antidote. I had been introduced to it in London by a boy at Christie's, Ricky Daniel, who had been extraordinarily sensible in controlling the dose so that the visual effects were as good as Kandinsky's abstract paintings in the years immediately before the outbreak of war in 1914 (his earliest and best). Whether in London or New York these sessions lasted for six hours or so, during which one was not much good for anything, and always ended with a rabid hunger for food and sex – effects quite contrary to those of cannabis. There were tales of takers leaping out of windows convinced that they could fly, and of madness following drips of LSD into the eyes, but I saw neither and suspect that both are urban myths. I was once persuaded to take it in an eye – the right – on the grounds that the effects were more immediate than through ingestion, but it wrecked my focus for some days without in any way improving on the Kandinsky effect and was not tried again.

CHAPTER 6

The Seventies

I was in New York twice in the bitter winter of 1973–74 when the Arab-Israeli War and the oil crisis brought about by a quadruple increase in oil prices unsteadied the economies of the West. The art market was astonishingly slow to react and remained buoyant throughout the late autumn, but collapse, when at last it came, was sudden and devastating, destroying confidence. Prices at auction fell; no one, unless compelled by misfortune, sent fine things to market; dealers pulled in their horns and derived their cash flow from selling old stock at a loss; museums, their patrons directly affected by alarming inflation and rates of exchange at which only the Deutschmark and Swiss Franc held steady, bought virtually nothing.

This slump lasted until Sotheby's mounted the week-long Mentmore sale of May 1977. This dispersal of one of the world's most outstanding nineteenth-century collections, formed by a Rothschild and extended by a Rosebery, sumptuous pomp and circumstance their aim, unseen by art historians and untouched by the grubby fingers of the trade, could only be irresistible to both and it helped bring the art and antiques trades back to active life. That recovery, however, was more than three years away and I had to find something to do with my life. I resumed painting – a rusty business at first but, recovering the hang of it, I enjoyed myself enough; when the chance was offered – usually prompted by a valuation – I repaired and restored paintings that involved no greater difficulty than light cleaning, retouching here and there, and finishing with a sympathetic varnish.

On Friday 13 September 1974 my idleness was interrupted by John Hulton, Director of Arts at the British Council, who had in

1958 asked me to catalogue the British contributions to Europäisches Rokoko, the Council of Europe exhibition in Munich that year; he asked me to work for him again. The exhibition this time was Pittura Inglese 1660–1840. As it was the City of Birmingham's exchange for paintings lent it by Milan the year before, Lombard Painting 1595–1630, I was surprised, for the curator of paintings there was Peter Cannon-Brookes who, since he knew from our very first encounter in 1960 or so that I thought him a pompous ass, was very unlikely to agree to my cataloguing an exhibition that was essentially his; that I did so was at John's insistence, for he knew that I could work to a tight deadline without skimping scholarship. Peter had selected one hundred and fifty-three paintings to be borrowed from many sources and I had barely three months in which to complete my work; most I knew, some that I did not could easily be visited,* but others, in private collections, I was compelled to catalogue unseen, working from photographs – something no art historian should do. I never did see them: this was Birmingham's affair and though the Mayor and all his worthies were, in January 1975, invited to the celebrations in the Palazzo Reale, all expenses paid, I was not among them and times were far too lean for me to spend my fee on the vanity of such a jaunt.

I have just read some of that catalogue and am astonished by how good it is – my present sense that the essentials of all writing on art should be clarity and thoroughness was obviously well-established long before it became my sole occupation. My brief essay on the Grand Tour, written thirty years before I made a

---

* A small group, stored in the roof spaces of the Victoria and Albert Museum, where I had noticed here and there gaps through which the sky could be seen, were, later in the very day that I went to catalogue them, damaged by torrential rain that drenched me to the skin as I walked home and forced open the heavy iron drain covers in the streets. In some cases irreparable, the loss was never made public and is now forgotten and unknown. There was too little time to repair the less damaged paintings for the exhibition.

television film on the subject, is evidence of a grasp of the history of Italian influence on all English arts that I would now be hard put to summon, and on every page there are observations and facts that I no longer know, but know that I once knew. It is a melancholy reminder of a wasted life that should have been spent looking, thinking and writing – though that is, of course, exactly what I have done for the past thirty years, but for a daily newspaper in which interest lasts not even the twenty-four hours of its date and to which there can be no posthumous reference. Was there ever a more futile vehicle for perception, scholarship and sensibility?

There was one other exercise in curatorial respectability for me before the Mentmore sale; it was a commission from the National Theatre in the spring of 1976 to prepare for exhibition the theatrical paintings and drawings bequeathed to it by Somerset Maugham in 1965. Prompted by Hugh Lane, the perceptive collector of French Impressionist paintings who was drowned when a German U-boat sank the *Lusitania* in 1915, Maugham bought Zoffany's *Garrick with Mrs Cibber in Venice Preserv'd*, swiftly followed by Samuel de Wilde's *Bannister and Suett in Sylvester Daggerwood*, and began to haunt all the salerooms of London. Thus was born his idea of furnishing the walls of the National Theatre with portraits of great actors of the past. The Theatre itself, throughout his lifetime never more than a hope, was first conceived by David Garrick, but not until 1908 was it taken seriously, a committee formed, a site found in Gower Street, a foundation stone laid and substantial funds (to which Hugh Lane was a contributor) raised in the hope of building it by 1916, the tercentenary of Shakespeare's death; but the outbreak of the Great War in 1914 thwarted a proposal not revived until the closure of another war.

On his death Maugham's pictures were put in store and, as when the store was flooded no one noticed, they stood in an inch or two of water for some years, rotting; fine carved and gilded frames of the eighteenth century rotted; original stretchers rotted; the paper of watercolours rotted; and worst of all, the canvases of considerable paintings rotted. This was not discovered until January 1976; by then Denys Lasdun's National Theatre on the South Bank was nearing completion, its Lyttleton stage almost ready to open, its Olivier stage scheduled for a grand opening by the Queen on 25 October, and the authorities on suddenly recalling the existence and purpose of Maugham's gift 'to adorn the bare walls of the theatre and give it a pleasant intimacy', went to inspect the paintings and were horrified. I cannot imagine that I was the first 'expert' to be consulted, but the decision to give me the task of repair and restoration was made on 11 February after (I was told by Geoffrey Ashton, the theatre historian) a fiercely acrimonious meeting of the board.

I was, of course, sworn to secrecy. No one connected with the theatre or the bequest wished the evidence of its neglect to be exposed, and so, with one exception, no one in the team that I assembled knew to whom the paintings belonged or why there was such urgency for their repair. Ivor Jones was the exception; he I had first encountered through friends at the Fitzwilliam Museum, Cambridge, where, on returning from years of training in Rome, he had begun to establish a reputation for skilled and sensitive under-cleaning – that is never going too far with swabs and solvent, never removing even a smidgeon of original paint – and while I was at Christie's he had performed near miracles for us on fragile early German panels. Unlike my close friend Joan Seddon, he would not be diverted by the science of the task, nor be tempted to try new solutions, but would slog on until it was done; there were forty-one oil paintings on which to work and, at most, thirty-five weeks in which Ivor and I must get them ready. The forty watercolours were not a problem – all I had to do was get them to Cambridge where Doreen Lewisohn was ensconced at the Fitzwilliam as a conservator of works on paper and leave the decisions to her; no other restorer of drawings and watercolours was as capable and sensitive as she, nor as reliable in working to a delivery date.

My studio was suddenly more a war zone hospital for the wounded than a comfortable repository of books and paintings; almost all Maugham's pictures had first to be relined and the flaking paint secured before we could consider cleaning them and restoring the extensive losses. As for the frames, most of them of the same period as the paintings they contained, what parts that had been immersed in water had either lost their gilding and all embellishments in moulded plaster, or rotted away altogether, and what had not rotted was infested with active woodworm. Replacing them was virtually impossible, for sod's law is that no antique frame is ever the same size as the canvas one wishes to put in it, and there was, moreover, neither time nor budget for such perfection. Even so, the impossible was in eleven cases achieved and fine period frames replaced the wrecks. Two staunch friends, both expert assistants of Gibello (then perhaps the most celebrated frame maker in London) came to my rescue – Christina Leder, who is still gilding and framing in London, and Johann Peter Riemensberger, a Swiss boy, who could be trusted to restore a carving by Grinling Gibbons, and was as expert as a caster of moulds. Between them they worked miracles and the restored frames looked as though they had, for two centuries, been affectionately dusted by tender parlour maids – discreetly worn.

By the beginning of April Ivor and I had done much more than we thought possible – all the relining, that is the laying down of old canvases on new, was complete, and old stretchers had been repaired or replaced, so that all the paintings were ready for restoration. Of this we kept a scrupulous photographic record, for in some cases the damage and the loss of paint was so extensive that we had to invent solutions. We broke for ten days at Easter because, earlier in the year, the British Museum had been invited to send a party of twenty scholars to Albania, then intensely proud of what it had achieved by its archaeologists and historians in illuminating the Illyria of antiquity. Among its own experts the museum could find too few who wished to go, and even with others from the Courtauld Institute and Birmingham University, the party was short in number until I was asked to tag along, and then Jill Allibone, my contemporary as a student, tagged on too, though neither of us had any classical qualifications other than Latin enough to read inscriptions. On my return, Ivor and I set to work methodically and with total concentration until, at the very end of August, every one of the Maugham paintings and drawings was back in its frame and ready to be hung in the National Theatre.

Displayed in my studio, a posse of panjandrums, including Denys Lasdun, the architect of the Theatre, came to see them. It was not, for me, a happy experience. The panjandrums seemed bemused, as though paintings were alien objects of which they knew nothing (nor did they). Lasdun hated them and said, 'Of course, you'll have to remove all these ghastly frames – if these pictures are to hang on my walls, they must be in simple aluminium strips.' He and I subsequently had a blazing row and I feared for what might become of my children. In the event, and in their original frames, the paintings were hung in the theatre's restaurant and rooms reserved for VIPs, and looked very well, giving exactly 'the pleasant intimacy' for which Maugham had hoped – but not for long. Seven days before the official opening on 25 October, one of the Portuguese waiters in the restaurant threw a raw egg at another; it missed him, but hit a painting, and they had then attempted to wipe away the egg as it dribbled down the canvas. Raw egg and young varnish do not go well together and should not be mixed – their molecular structures change and, emulsified, they become opaque and very hard. By the time the picture was returned to me its disastrous condition had become impossible to remedy before the opening. This mishap and the almost immediate theft of the smallest things in the collection, lent strength to Lasdun's arguments against hanging paintings in his architecture and, on the grounds of their safety and security, all were removed from the theatre and have not been seen there since. They were first shuffled off to Mottisfont Abbey, supposedly on public view there, but the circumstances were impossible, then to the Theatre Museum, but when that shut down, neither the Victoria and Albert Museum nor the National Portrait Gallery would take responsibility for them, and they are now wretchedly divided between the Theatre Royal, Bath, and the Holbourne Museum there, the frames now fudged to make them look like modern fakes. I nourish a seething anger that Maugham's bequest should have been so betrayed by its supposed Trustees. There was a further, almost amusing deceit: a catalogue of the collection, written by the theatre historians Raymond Mander and Joe Mitchenson (engaging old rogues with a collection of their own, much inferior), was so long in preparation that by 1980, the year of its publication as a 'National Theatre Paperback' recording the 'remarkable collection of theatrical paintings, now on permanent display in the National Theatre's foyers' (as claimed on the cover) was long gone; this catalogue is now a rarity – the National Theatre, to prevent curious enquiry, ordered its destruction and very few copies escaped.

*   *   *

Life as a dealer did not entirely shut down during this doldrum; Joe McCrindle still bought drawings and so did Ted Pillsbury, then at Yale, though for himself rather than the University collection; there was, too, an importer of cheap Russian watches who seemed suspiciously anxious to spend money on paintings by Sickert and his ilk – rather good investments in the long term. And there was Peter Langan, the considerable restaurateur, confidant and friend: Susan, his wife, was later to describe me as a 'friend of long standing, though much tried and tested in his friendship, Peter's tutor in art appreciation and artistic merit, his guide through saleroom viewing and his adviser on what to buy, the friend . . . who was in at the beginning. He remained as a friend'.

We met through Nicholas Vilag, whose so-called Fine Art Gallery at 25 Devonshire Street in Marylebone was next to Peter's first restaurant, Odin's Bistro. He was an Hungarian Jew whose career as a photographer for *Picture Post* (the great magazine of the 1930s) had been interrupted by Horthy and Hitler, and broken by internment in England. After the war he settled in rooms over a shop in Croydon, the dreariest of boroughs in the distant south of London, and began to scratch a living by buying and selling topographical prints; willy-nilly he became an art dealer of sorts and opened the gallery – far less gallery than junk shop. It was hung to the ceiling with pictures of appalling quality, and racked and stacked with unframed prints and drawings obscured by filthy polythene that kept them clean but dirtied the hands of curious customers. Downstairs, where no visitor was allowed, the basement store was in part a dark impenetrable confusion of frames, canvases and bulky folders of yet more prints and drawings, labelled London, Paris, Prague, Fruit and Flowers, and Erotica, and it was on these, in the one lit part of this Hades, that Muriel Kay and other women worked, turning penny plain into tuppence coloured, tinting back into new life any watercolour that had faded in the sun, and making gay with gouache any simple outline print of European cities, Italian peasants dancing the Tarantella, and every sort of souvenir brought back by tourists before the invention of the camera. It was in rescuing from their attentions a fine and very valuable Canaletto etching of Padua, and paying Nicholas a proper price for it, that our affectionate friendship was established.

When Muriel became Nicholas's mistress and the urgency of their affection required immediate satisfaction – to be achieved only in the basement – the others had to go. Muriel blossomed; she became more and more the hostess of the semi-picnic lunches that Nicholas gave in the back office to his fellow expatriate Hungarians, his Mafia, and, as an improver of his prints, more ambitious, more characteristic of herself as a sometime graduate of the Croydon Art School – sweeping blue skies overwhelmed the faded greens and browns of distant forests and meadow foregrounds, Paris was roofed with bright red tiles rather than black slates, ancient Rome became a riot of rouge and yellow marbles, and from Dresden to Madrid no city was safe from her irrational enchantments. Even the gullible great doctors of Harley Street who were the regular customers, spending their untaxed Arabian cash-in-hand, began to express doubt and, eventually, Muriel had to go, banished to her home in Putney, never to be seen again.

There was, however, an overlap in her role as mistress. Muriel was small and neat and mouse-like, her replacement twice her size, ample and overflowing, useless as a watercolourist but smothering when it came to accommodating Nicholas. She came in to buy a print and stayed to inherit the business, and to the onlooker, the way in which, like a cuckoo, she edged Muriel out of the nest, was a fascinating performance, brutal and brief.

He had another friend who contributed mightily to the gallery's success, Robert Dumont-Smith, a one-eyed grandee of the Croydon Contemporary Art Group, piratically black-patched, an occasional exhibitor at the Royal Academy who, for a small fee, added signatures to oil paintings or replaced signatures with others more ambitious, occasionally so often that, after much wiping away, the final name stood proud upon a bald patch. All were culled from a dictionary of signatures that Nicholas cunningly pressed on any customer who asked for confirmation that the signature was genuine. When Peter Langan, who had bought a number of these masterpieces, asked me what I thought of them, I felt compelled, miserably, to tell the truth; some days later, with the excuse that a knowledgeable diner had doubted its authenticity, he returned one of the pictures to Nicholas and was so charmed by his immediate willingness to take it back, that he exchanged it for another at twice the price and just as much a forgery.

Peter's refusal to let rancour taint his relationship with Nicholas, who was always happy to take in early deliveries of food and wine, led to a topsy-turvy trust between them. Both were libidinous – Peter openly boastful, speculative, enquiring, Nicholas grunting and secretive – and there were times when one of the amateur watercolourists played amateur in another sense, making both of them happy among the frames and parcels in the basement, though not at the same time. Peter's 'I'm just going next door for a quickie', said in Odin's to anyone who cared to catch the phrase, meant that he would return to the kitchen in ten minutes with a strangely intense expression and a sheen of sweat.

The tale of our unlikely friendship, fierce, loyal and generous on both our parts, I recorded in a memoir written for Susan, his widow, to supplement the fragments of an autobiography on which Peter had worked from time to time as the Leitmotiv of a book of recipes.* On re-reading it I feel inclined to think it not only a fair account of a rumbustious and often roistering relationship in the course of which I learned enough of food and drink to qualify as a restaurant critic, but one that offers wry insights on David Hockney, Patrick Procktor and Ron Kitaj, all of whom were his customers, all of whom exchanged their wares for his and contributed mightily to the collection of paintings hanging in Peter's first two restaurants; moreover, it corrects assertions made by other writers, particularly those in Hockney's camp. My contribution was, yet again, to play a Nicklausse to a Hoffmann, to find what could not be found, to mend what should never have been broken, even to play waiter when, as was so in the early weeks of the larger Odin's, he had no money with which to pay professionals; but I could do nothing to remove the twin demons always at his elbow. That he drank wine in every waking hour of the day, I could do nothing to influence – he could not function without it; I could do nothing to restrain his insatiable speculation, voiced loud and unmistakeable, over the sexuality of the women he encountered, no matter how casual the occasion – even across a street – nor what their role or status, nor, so promiscuous myself, could I curb the prodigious sexual drive that compelled him, without a moment's notice, to turn to the nearest prostitute – wherever we were in London, he seemed always to know of one

---

* See Peter Langan, *A Life with Food*, Bloomsbury 1990.

nearby, and when he bought the old Coq d'Or and turned it into Langan's Brasserie, there was rejoicing, open-mouthed, among the whores of Shepherd Market.

Without Peter's introduction, would I ever have known David Hockney the little that I do, would I have known Kitaj and his wife (steadily overtaking him as a good figurative painter), would I have had Patrick Procktor as a confessional friend? It was my friendship for Patrick that prevented me from writing the biography that was looking for an author; I was his choice, but I knew that I would tell the truth as bluntly as in any review of an exhibition, or, indeed, as of myself in this autobiography, and that in doing so I would risk destroying our friendship. I valued it far more than the vanity of critical opinion and never once reviewed his work, for I felt so strongly that the robust promise of his early years had swiftly declined into a mannered delicacy from which he seemed unable to escape. It was through Peter that the formality of acquaintanceship with Lucian Freud was relaxed – the effect of my witnessing their competition for a girl from Fortnum's looking for a lover for the night. We were in Beth Coventry's bar, just south of Piccadilly, when in she came; within minutes Peter was telling Lucian what his pudgy hand could feel up the girl's skirt, and when they took to a tonguing kiss it seemed that both were in some sense challenging the older Lucian, already saurian – indeed, I suspected that she knew him and that what she did with Peter was done solely to arouse Lucian's libido, for it was he who effortlessly got her simply by opening his arms in welcome. I imagine that it was the fingering rather than the kiss that did it, together with Peter's commentary, for what his fat fingers found was as lubricious as a ripe persimmon, his word for it the blunt Teutonic radical that for centuries no polite literary man has dared to use. Lucian observed it often enough, always with deliberate scrutiny as though he were a kitchen-boy looking for slugs in a lettuce; he drew and painted it too, and let such studies leave the privacy of his studio to decorate the bedrooms of rich men – but, as art, even the crudest erotic fantasies of Keith Vaughan and David Hockney have more merit.

With the Fortnum's girl on Lucian's knee and not to be got off it, Peter raged obscenely and got drunk — but then he always opened his arms in welcome to whichever of the Deadly Sins was appropriate. His Sloth was indeed the spiritual torpor that undoes the active man, the Black Dog of depression that walked at Winston Churchill's heel — it had nothing to do with God, but it effectively excluded Him. His Envy was of prestige and popularity and the power they might have brought him in his field; and he was covetous of fine things finer than his own, vain enough to drive a coachbuilt Bentley. With Rage his face suffused with blood, shouting at cooks and, occasionally, customers; and serving Gluttony was his career, however delicately dressed in quality. As for Lust, night and day she jogged the elbow of this unquiet soul. A decade after his death, in a chance encounter with Lucian, I confessed how much I missed Peter. 'You must be mad,' he said, and I could see in his eyes that he meant it.

I once thought that in recollections of such small events as these lay an immortality of sorts, that in our chuckling over them Peter's bulky presence might be revived, but that was soon after his death in December 1988 — foul temper, alcohol, fire, self-immolation, *Götterdämmerung*; now, a quarter of a century on, I wonder, for I hear no one speak of him and, as with Simon Raven (considerable novelist), when I raise his ghost I must explain the who and what of him to provoke the response: 'Oh I remember . . . wasn't he the man with the bloody chopper wandering round Odin's?'

*　　*　　*

For me, 1979 was a very crowded year. At the end of January I was asked to give evidence for Tom Keating, the to-be celebrated forger, in his trial at the Old Bailey. I gave it willingly, for since February 1970, when I had first encountered one of his pastiches of Samuel Palmer in a modest auction room in Woodbridge, Suffolk,

I had been astonished by the behaviour of the art market and curators who should never have been duped. Half the trade was at the Woodbridge sale, £9,400 was paid for it, and at the end of the year it was exhibited by the Leger Gallery with a price tag of £15,000. That Leger accepted it as genuine was heavily significant, for the firm had dealt with Palmer until his death in 1881, and subsequently with his son Alfred Herbert, who continued to live in their Kensington house (6 Douro Place) until 1940 or so, constantly supplying Leger with original Palmers never before offered in the market. The gap of thirty years mattered not at all, for the head of Leger (a boastful man whose Rolls-Royce bore the number plate ART I) bridged it, and that was enough to lend his firm a reputation for peculiar and particular expertise with which they quelled the nay-sayers. As Tom's expert witness I argued that his pastiches had been given authenticity by the specialist art dealers and museum curators who had acquired them, and had they the expertise they claimed, they would at once have rejected Tom's imitations as impertinence – as did most experts at the British Museum. It takes two to make a fake – the faker and the grandee who declares it to be genuine – and in one early case, *A Barn at Shoreham*, Edward Croft-Murray, no less than Keeper of Prints and Drawings at the British Museum, supported a drawing bought by John Baskett, grandee of Colnaghi's, and saw that it passed into the collections of the Cecil Higgins Museum, Bedford, of which he was a trustee.

Tom in the dock was a pathetic figure: the flushed complexion suggested problems with heart and blood pressure, and he sat hunched and bleary-eyed, seeming to ignore the goings-on around him. He had the bladder of a mouse (sans sphincter), and had with miserable frequency to ask to be excused – recall the wretchedness of childhood disasters at school and then transpose them to the majesty of the Old Bailey; it irritated the judge, who did not care to be interrupted midstream. In the early stages he sketched in a palm-sized notebook – as did Sickert at the theatre – until authority discovered the reason for his downcast head: defendants are supposed to pay attention and not distract themselves with irrelevances, but the sketches were not irrelevant; they were of Christ's trial and trudge to Calvary inspired by recollections of Rembrandt and Tiepolo, and were quite beautiful.

In the end Tom was not crucified: there were delays because he had bronchitis and then, one morning, side-swiped from his Vespa on the way to court, the case came to an inconclusive end. I suspect that the judge had little sympathy with the prosecution and was grateful that a *deus ex machina* had relieved him of the embarrassment of sentencing a frail old man – there was, indeed, a general feeling that the wrong man had been brought to court. He returned to Dedham, penniless, to the comfort of four thousand letters of sympathy from strangers, and one from the Inland Revenue that spelled total, inescapable, ruin. Their demand was based on the assumption that all his fakes – of Rembrandt, Constable, Renoir, Degas et al – were worth the £15,000 paid for one of the many pseudo-Palmers in a sale at Sotheby's (27 June 1973, lot 68). This hammering for income tax reduced him to living in an unheated shed and more bouts of bronchitis interrupted the burst of activity through which he hoped to respond to the demand. I thought it would kill him, but a kindly soul in Dedham lent him a cottage for a while – though the ceilings were so low that he had to work on his knees to finish the foreground of a new Constable six-footer.

We became friends of a sort, though I preferred to take a picnic to the cottage rather than experience yet another garrulous per-formance from Tom in the Marlborough Head; all Dedham must by then have known what he thought of Bridget Riley: 'All talk and watered vino – she works out the rhythms and migraine-stricken assistants do the job.' He claimed to have once been one of them, but when his hand wavered she excluded him from her canvases and made him paint the stairs instead – all white; that done, she sacked him. He grew in celebrity; on Independent Television he taught us the techniques of the old masters and complained about cleaning in the National Gallery, but when a young man from the BBC made an approach with 'I am a Jew and a socialist . . . ' Tom's response, 'The one is obvious, the other you must prove,' caused such offence that, whatever the project was, it was not pursued. In the summer of 1982 we were both enlisted by Winsor and Newton to celebrate their one hundred and fiftieth year in the production of artists' materials, and in a pair of marquees on the lawns of the original Tate Gallery, I lectured on panels, canvas, copper, paints, brushes and all the other things that painters use, while Tom set up a still life of flowers and taught amateur ladies how to paint. His was far the more popular marquee, but by lunchtime, drunk, he was no longer capable of holding a brush and the Winsor and Newton men were blushing at his vocabulary; I had to take over and let the materials look after themselves.

On his death in 1984, a partial clearance of his studio gave rise to an outpouring of respect by the art market in the only way it knows – it paid absurd prices at an auction. Christie's had already held one sale, presumably to settle taxes, the year before, and this second sale was thought to be the last chance to buy a Keating. It was not – sales continued until at last the penny dropped and the salerooms recognised that there must now be a forger of Keatings: the forgery of forgeries in the case of Elmyr de Hory, very recently exposed, should have warned the market of the possibility with Keating.

*   *   *

The following months of 1979 were filled with journeys to museums, collectors and dealers in France, Germany, Switzerland and the Netherlands, and on 1 May I left for a long stint in America – my last (though I did not know it would be so) and far and away most ambitious in terms of work to be done as a consequence. On my return there was one of those jolts to memory and sensibility that are felt hard by the too sensitive soul – an invitation to the memorial service for Michael Jessett. I had not seen Michael since he left school and we had not parted on good terms. We had had schoolboy sex a hundred times before my sixteenth birthday, the night on which he, a few months the elder, fucked me for the first time; losing my virginity so painfully I interpreted as love (as indeed it was, of a kind, on my part, but not on his, and I was emotionally bruised by our swift drifting apart). More than thirty years had passed; I had later come to terms with my homosexuality and had recklessly enjoyed, at one extreme, its passionate engagements and, at the other, its madcap carelessness, its risks, its thrilling folly – indeed, one of the compensations for having to work in New York, Frankfurt, Geneva or anywhere else was that sex with new partners was everywhere available and became a matter of course. I had for some years been in love with a younger man, conveniently abroad and conveniently married, with whom I could indulge my occasional bouts of broody paternalism without the curse of having a family and with little risk of the relationship growing stale, the bedevilling characteristic of all homosexual relationships. I was therefore content with what seemed the best of both worlds and the disadvantages of neither. Michael's death was, nevertheless, a footstep on my own grave, not only in that, at forty-eight, it had come so soon, but in that he had become a distinguished musician (once my ambition too), his life celebrated in death by musicians in the church of the Royal College of Music, Holy Trinity, Prince Consort Road, a service to which I received an invitation. As our paths had never crossed again, who knew that I had known him and known him well enough to perhaps need to know of his death? That he left a wife and family reminded me that the homosexual pleasures of the boy are, for most of them, the transitory convenience of the heterosexual. Before the glorious Bach came to an end, I slipped away; were the tears that I wanted no one to see for Michael, for me, or for something indefinable that I still felt, even still feel?

In 1979 I did not go to Turkey.

CHAPTER 7

Turkey

If, 'In 1979 I did not go to Turkey' seems an odd conclusion to my recollections of the Seventies, it is not so, for the land beyond the Bosporus had developed, willy-nilly, into an obsession and was to become a Leitmotiv of my life for fully fifteen years. To go there for the first time in the doldrum summer of 1975 had been a whim prompted by a sudden sense of the familiarity of Europe and a weariness with the discipline of trudging round art galleries; what I did for a living had become, if not quite a Dantesque circle of purgatory, an inevitable drudgery – what, I wondered, had happened to my sense of adventure, to plans once made to drive round the Mediterranean, to explore Ethiopia, Persia or the Spice Islands that once belonged to the adventurous Dutch (this last a madness when I was eight)? Paintings had become, and are, a drug, and without them I suffer withdrawal symptoms; as my skiing companions know only too well, the question 'How far is it to Vienna?' – or Munich, or Geneva, or Turin – murmured at breakfast on the third day of a planned fortnight in a ski resort, was a clear signal that I had already had enough of piste and schuss and needed a quick fix of paint on canvas; so too would it be were I lying on a beach somewhere. Of Turkey, however, I thought that if, for paintings, classical ruins and Ottoman architecture could be substituted, then we might have a solution to my addiction and we might satisfy my longing for adventure. The lurking recollection of a book read while in the Lower School at Haberdashers' – Kinglake's *Eöthen*, a now forgotten young man's travels in the Ottoman Empire, published in 1844 – though I could not find my copy, put flesh on the bones of the idea. I have often damned that school for its not being Eton, as it were, for its low church bias and

437

dull-mindedness, but the English master who, in the grim and bitter winter and so-called Little or Second Blitz of 1943–44, set cold and hungry boys of twelve on a journey through the Balkans to the Grand Porte, was, without knowing it, a man of lasting inspiration. How many boys at Eton then read Kinglake? How many boys anywhere now?

From this first unprepared journey I returned with a jumble of impressions and the conviction that I must go again, but with serious intent. Relics of the Ottoman occupation of the Balkans – five centuries of it – increased in number the further south we went in what was then Yugoslavia, competing with those of Byzantium, and across the water into Asia, Byzantium gave way to ancient Greece and Rome, the Aegean coast and hinterland a wondrous palimpsest of cultures. No sooner back in London than the serious reading began – or so I thought it, but it was largely the chatty books of such travellers as Freya Stark that informed me until I discovered those of George Bean, a great man of Greek, Latin and archaeology at the University of Istanbul. His four introductions to south-western Turkey* were to be my *vade mecum* on all subsequent journeys; they opened my eyes not only to the subject but to a manner of writing that informs the reader of the present while bringing to life the distant past, functioning, not as a guide book, but as a guide, the writer – having seen and done everything himself and thus immune from the errors of the copycat – a lively and informed presence always at hand or in one's knapsack. Respected by the guardians of sites, many of whom had laboured for him on his excavations, to carry a Bean book in its bright orange wrapper was to carry a welcomed passport, 'Ah, Bin Bey,' their greeting. Some might reach high above their heads, palm down, to indicate his gangling height, so memorable to stocky Turks, and all would show me more recently excavated finds.

---

* George Bean, *Aegean Turkey*, 1966; *Turkey's Southern Shore*, 1968, *Turkey beyond the Maeander*, 1971, and *Lycian Turkey*, 1978.

Turkey

All that I know of the eastern spread of Greek and Roman influence is founded on Bean's scholarship; when, a decade later, I wrote a brief and slightly frivolous memoir of my, by then, many journeys in south-western Turkey,* the serious parts of it were in homage to his imagined tutelage. My intention was not to replace Bean but to bridge the gap between his scholarship and an ignorance (mine) that was then typical of most British travellers in Turkey; it was not that Bean's books were in any way difficult – they are far from stern in their approach, but they require a level of background classical knowledge that is no longer what 'every schoolboy knows', so much have the old essentials of education withered away. In the event – many events – the book fell between every possible stool and was not kindly reviewed; even so, it has been twice reprinted. I turn to it still when I need to recall such arcane matters as the customs of the gladiator, the extinction of the Caspian tiger, the Boy Bishop, the Mass of the Ass and the Wandering Jew.

My new enthusiasm I was foolish enough to disclose to Jill Allibone, who lived five minutes' walk away and was a constant borrower of books (always returning them). Before the year was out she had taken charge of my plans, was coming with me (or rather, I with her, for her husband's Range-Rover, not my Peugeot 404, was to be our vehicle), and we were to extend the journey far to the east, for she had spent her girlhood in Persia and wanted to see how Persian eastern Turkey might be.

In April 1976 I had a taste of what might be to come for Jill attached herself to the Albanian jaunt that briefly interrupted my work on Somerset Maugham's paintings. Even as a student she had been a little too dependent on alcohol (she came from drinking parents), and as a neighbour I had often seen her amiably sozzled, but one evening in Tirana she was in a foul temper and during dinner her response to my arguing some point was an almighty

* Brian Sewell, *South from Ephesus*, 1988, reissued 2012.

439

under-the-table kick that skinned my shin and bloodied my trouser leg. I should have taken it as a warning that the determined and purposeful girl whom I admired years before had, perhaps, become something of a shrew – but I did not.

We flew to Ochrid, a town of wonderful Byzantine churches then in southern Yugoslavia and on Albania's eastern border. This we crossed on foot over a stretch of no-man's-land, to be greeted at the barrier with a cry of 'Welcome to Shqiperia' from Rexhep, the English-speaking schoolmaster who was to be our *cicerone*. 'Abandon hope, all ye who enter here' might have been more suitable, for customs officers deprived us of all books, even our notebooks, a recording machine, binoculars and anything that roused suspicion. The procedures of formal welcome ended with a beckoning finger addressed to me; I was taken into a large room in the centre of which was a single chair with whatever it was that dangled on a wire from the light socket above, held in the hand of the guard who stood behind its back. Ordered to sit, I sat, a guard behind me, a guard on either side, and thus held down, the buzzing began and the clipper, cold on my neck, set off on its business of cutting rough swathes through my hair. Not even on my first day as a National Serviceman called to Aldershot had I been so crudely shorn. Thick and curly, but by no means long, my hair was, it seemed to the border guards of Shqiperia, evidence of moral turpitude.

Ten days in Albania in the inescapable company of scholars (we were allowed no freedom and were always in Rexhep's sight) provided enough experience to fill a book. By the oldest member of the party, a man who had spent his youth repairing the mosaics of Hagia Sophia, I was instructed, while waiting to board our plane at Heathrow, never to touch a Balkan door handle if I wished to avoid sickness. 'It is pointless to wash your hands in a lavatory,' he said, 'if you then open a door.' I learned from one expert how to read a wall and was astonished by the amount of information that can be gleaned from a stretch of re-used material converted into a defence; all that I knew of Byzantium was consolidated and extended by the amiable knock-about of professors from Birmingham and the Courtauld who knew the streets of Trebizond better than the Bullring and Piccadilly Circus; and by a youngster from the British Museum my eye was swiftly tutored into distinguishing the centuries of provincial Roman sculpture. All the while there lurked the violent Albania of the Dark and Middle Ages under the Serbs, Bulgarians and Normans to be elucidated with lubricious pleasure by historians, and half a millennium within the Ottoman Empire, to which even I could contribute a little; and all the while there was too the present of the present day, with three blue-clad Chinese under every Judas tree and the admonitions of the Communist tyrant Enver Hoxha writ 'HOLLYWOOD' large across the landscape that we should 'praise the labours of the freedom-loving people of Shqiperia'.

These freedom-loving people turned mute to the nearest wall if we approached them and, at Butrint, the most beautiful of archaeological sites, a place for Turner and Lear to paint, a palimpsest of cultures, where peasants were retrieving what they could from the beached jetsam, our Party Member drove them into the sea, thigh deep, so that we could not speak to them. We spoke to no one; archaeological sites were emptied of their archaeologists, museums of their curators, and even hotel staff fled if our presence coincided with their duties. Our Party Member drove us on dusty unmade roads past primitive oil wells, the air heavy with their stink, the land sodden with it, grazing sheep mired in it; but we also travelled through an Alpine hinterland where valleys were dense with Judas trees, their bark as sooty black as the stockings of Toulouse-Lautrec's can-can dancers, their blossoms as bright as their frilly underskirts. We saw meadows of wild flowers and upland fields so steep that their ploughed furrows could only be broken by ox-drawn wicker harrows weighed down with laughing women and children. And we encountered gun emplacements, always facing the enemy to the west.

This Albanian journey, coming so soon after the confusions of my first Turkish jaunt and a winter of making a nuisance of myself in the bowels of the British Museum, was Confirmation after Baptism; it lent sense to so much of what I had seen blundering about in Aphrodisias and Pergamon, Side and Termessos, and to have spent ten days so alert in the company of devoted and generous scholars had been an astonishingly educative experience. I was not arrogant fool enough to think myself their peer, but I was confident that my second Turkish journey, if researched and planned, would be far more intellectually revealing than the first.

It was not. Jill's husband, David, accompanied us on the outward leg, intending to return by air — as he did — from wherever we were at the end of the third week, while we drove on for another month or so. The Range-Rover was a pig to drive, nose up and down-at-heel with the weight of their whisky and claret, its steering light and vague, not helped by the case of Pedigree Chum on which I insisted, knowing that I would need to allay my misery whenever we encountered a starving dog — a futile gesture, I know, made more for my benefit than theirs, for all the tinned dog food in the world could not feed the feral dogs of Asia. We planned to drive fast, but the Range-Rover was unmanageable beyond sixty; we planned to be up with the lark, but stayed in proper hotels, ate proper dinner and proper breakfast, and eleven every morning was time for the first whisky of the day, David and Jill keeping each other tippling as they drove; it was on our picnic lunches that they downed their claret. On subsequent journeys, driving alone, sleeping and showering in camping sites, my Peugeot could be in Istanbul by mid afternoon on the third day, but in the sluggish Range-Rover we covered as little as two hundred miles a day and a full week passed before we crossed the Dardanelles. Diligence was at once abandoned: my plan had been to visit all the sites that I had not seen the year before, and revisit all that I had, but Jill and David soon declared themselves exhausted and decided that we should press on to Side, to an hotel that I had scheduled as a break before setting off for the east. I surrendered without argument for I was by then convinced that the expedition was doomed.

There had been two disconcerting incidents. We had been close friends for more than twenty years, but one evening, when we were alone, David had suddenly remarked, 'Even if I didn't know, I could tell that you're queer – you never look at women walking past.' The observation seemed charged with notes of deprecation and superiority, even aggression, and had nothing about it of the well-meaning but blokeish clumsiness of a womanising friend – I did, do indeed, have such friends, kindly in their attitude to my sexuality, if occasionally given to unseemly curiosity about the mechanics of the business. I wondered if David resented the ease with which Jill and I slipped into prattle of art history, felt excluded from it and blamed me for it; did he know that immediately after his proposal to her she had asked me my intention? Worse was to come: in Güllük, a pretty place on the wide bay north of Bodrum, Jill made what I interpreted as a clumsy attempt at seduction while David was away hunting for whisky. She called me to their room, and there she lay, flat on her back, in the tired pink of underwear much washed, the material broderie-anglaise, her pubic hair curling through its apertures. She offered no seemly reason for her call and I, determined not to enquire, left after some empty conversation. Perhaps I did her an injustice, but I have known other women suffering the conviction that with very little effort they can reorient a man's errant sexuality. Years later, persuaded to attempt a novel, I based the central character on Jill and enhanced this episode, but the more I wrote, the more monstrous and real the fictional character became – so much so that, preferring the Jill I knew rather than the Jill I had invented, I felt compelled to destroy the manuscript and retain the friendship.

The Turtel, in Side, was an hotel of high European standards, run with old Ottoman courtesy by Mardin Bey and Prussian efficiency by his German wife; to Jill and David it promised as much whisky as they could drink, and to me it offered respite from their bickering. There we found, with his entourage of staff from London, Bernard Breslauer, a notable antiquarian bookseller who occasionally picked my brains about old master drawings and the only man courageous enough to destroy a portrait by Lucian Freud. This he had commissioned, but Lucian had made the worst of his Fagin nose, his glasses (thick lenses in a hefty frame of horn), and the thin hair, dyed black, grown long and combed over his bald skull; I thought that such pure cruelty betrayed a commission that Lucian should have refused; Bernard loathed it and, reassured by friends that it was not a masterpiece of Goyesque mockery but a spiteful caricature that by any other portrait painter would have been damned as anti-semitic, he turned it face to the wall and would not hang it. I thought it an act of kindness to say that if he hated it so much that he could not bear to live with it, could not bear even to give it to either of his two devoted assistants, then he must do what Clementine did for Winston Churchill in the affair of the Sutherland portrait. Very carefully he cut the canvas into tiny rectangles that would not block his lavatory.

Imagine this procedure. Bernard was not a man to know or understand the physical structure of a canvas, the fabric stretched taut on a wooden support that is invisible once the picture is in its frame; this support, the stretcher, makes it rigid only when two triangular slivers of wood (pegs) are driven into slots in its four corners; nor was he a man to have in the house a pair of pliers with which to remove these pegs and collapse the stretcher so that the canvas could easily be removed from it. He must have cut the strained canvas with a knife; did he trace the blade along the edges of the image or slash it across the centre and tug at it with his delicate pale hands? Did he confront his image as he destroyed it, or attack it from behind? Had he by then stopped dying his hair and, reconciled to the grey of it and the shiny pate, had it cut *en brosse*? Had the portrait thus become the image of a man he no longer wished to be, no longer was? Only one thing is certain – that he cared not a damn what he'd paid for it.

Bernard was a disaster for my relationship with David. His noisy greeting and the hug were bad enough, but in Side he was as unrelentingly flamboyant as in London he was grave, the scholarly bibliophile to his bones. His hair suddenly grey and cut *en brosse*, narrow of shoulder, pot-bellied, the withered buttocks scarcely proud of his spindle shanks, the pouch of his tiny Parisian bathing slip far too loose for what little it contained, he can hardly have roused the appetite of the hotel boys, but I suppose he paid them well enough to do their duty on the deserted beach to the west where the straggly edge of the forest almost reached the sea and the village boys idly buggered each other in the heat of the afternoon. We saw him go and we saw him return, the perfunctory conjugation apparently enough to satisfy – but it was rarely with the same boy; having been with him and taken his money, each tended to avoid him, discreetly disappearing as only the Turk can. One, older and more a man than a boy, unfortunate enough to be put immediately on bar duty on his return, did his damnedest to avoid eye contact with Bernard who, weary of snapping his fingers for attention, shouted without shame: 'You fucked my arse ten minutes ago – now do me the courtesy of bringing me a drink.' Jill, for days in a bloody-minded mood, broke into helpless giggling; David, silent, walked off with his whisky and gazed at the sea.

Male travellers beyond the boundaries of Anglo-Saxony and the Austro-Hungarian Empire should, if homosexual, be monkish, celibate and chaste if any Islamic country is their goal. Whatever the prohibitions of the Prophet and his acolytes, the actuality is that though homosexuality may not be prevalent, homosexual activity particularly with western strangers is found all round the Mediterranean and in Pakistan (I have been no further east) – it may even be, or have become, culturally traditional. Where European men are part of the occasion it is largely opportunist, mercenary or even triumphalist in the sense that he who fucks a European despises him as a mere trophy. On every outward journey, once across the Turkish border, I had been advised by a now renowned venereologist and historian of sexual behaviour, Michael Waugh, to make myself asexual, to make no signals and show no interest that could be misinterpreted, and this sound counsel I had the will to follow; on the return journey, a busy night spent in the stews of Frankfurt or Cologne could assuage the released hunger. Young heterosexual men too can be vulnerable; in the course of my Turkish studies I have encountered several cases where misread signals led to extreme embarrassment, and two where the acceptance of hospitality at home led to gang rape. Bernard, of course, might have enjoyed that, but one boy in question certainly did not and, psychologically, seemed to have been permanently infected by hatred of both Turks and homosexuals, utterly failing to understand that homosexuality played no part in what was probably no more than common sexual opportunism by men in a family where casual sex with girls and women is forbidden by both society and religion.

Journeys to Turkey in 1977 and 1978 were made alone and possibly at risks that I did not recognise. Away for months, I planned to cover in detail quite small areas, all dealt with by George Bean, and do so thoroughly, adapting the car so that I could sleep in it if necessary, and learning a smattering of Turkish with which I might initiate a conversation, if not maintain it (it is not an easy language). I can recall no misadventures of any kind — only the pleasurable drudgery of wandering in ruins and occasionally sleeping in them, and the ease with which I adapted to activity by daylight hours and sleep as soon as it was dark. I had long known the importance of well chosen books to transport me, in adversity, elsewhere, and I learned that a portable chess set provokes conversation in the most improbable of places.

In 1977 the long journey back to London was punctuated by halts at every art gallery celebrating the fourth centenary of the birth of Rubens — wonderfully instructive; and the following year, north of the Greco-Yugoslav border, I paused to offer a lift to a hitch-hiker who would, I knew, if not picked up, find nowhere to spend the night. Joseph his name, Croatian his nationality, his parental home was some way off my route to Zagreb and Ljubljana, but I had time in hand and was rewarded, not only with bed and bath when we reached his home, but by his father's suggestion that we should take off into the hills to explore churches, monasteries and mansions within reasonable reach. For five days we hiked and I was introduced to the enchanting periphery of Austrian baroque architecture and painting, much of it, having survived the German occupation in World War II, soon to be damaged and destroyed in the Serbo-Croat war of the 1990s.

*　　*　　*

The strong revival of the art market prevented my going to Turkey in 1979, and Anthony Blunt's exposure at the end of that year had such repercussions that I felt in 1980 bound to stay within his reach, at least by telephone and within a day's journey. In March skiing took me to Norway with Colin Darracott (an established custom), and in August we walked for ten days along the great fence that then divided Germany – an episode of great pleasure and relaxation, though feasting on blueberries close to the wire provoked East German guards into an hilariously exaggerated response with armoured troop-carriers. In 1981 I noted in my diary that my income had fallen to a point at which I could no longer afford to run the house in Eldon Road and must consider leaving London for the country, and did indeed look at houses within reach of Bath and Marlborough, only to find the prospect utterly depressing – I am, I think, a Londoner to my bones and essentially a Kensington villager. In 1982 I had recovered enough to return to Turkey, but not for another deliberate exploration of a limited area; instead, with Michael Waugh, my useful doctor friend, our objective was the far south-east, the furthest point of the journey that Jill and I had thought to make.

It was plain idiocy. We failed to take into account the then two-year-old Iran-Iraq war, the floods of refugees, particularly of Kurdish origin, that crossed the mountains into Turkey, and the response of the Turkish army (then more or less the government), which was to make that corner of the country a military zone. We flew to Erzerum, intending to travel by bus to Van and south to Hakkari, where Robin Fedden had climbed as a young man before World War II and recalled wonders to behold – Robin had, indeed, given me all his large-scale maps of eastern Turkey, including those of the border with Russia, all printed in Germany in the 1930s and perfect for military purposes. Bus schedules were in chaos and only by sitting for hours in the bus station could we be sure of leaving Erzerum, though with no certainty of reaching Van; halted by soldiers at checkpoints, passports inspected, luggage unloaded, these delays repeated and repeated, we reached Van at two in the morning, after a twenty-hour journey. We fell into the filthy Hotel Kent because a light was on and we could see someone sleeping at the desk.

Two in the morning is no time to discover that the contents of one's knapsack are sticky with ginger marmalade. All my life I have suffered from travel sickness, particularly in buses (I have even managed to be sick on skis among the moguls), and it was Robin who advised a spoonful of ginger marmalade as a sovereign pre-ventative; foreseeing the breakage of glass jars, I had transferred two pounds of it to a stout plastic container – alas, not stout enough to withstand the rough handling of my knapsack by Turkish baggage handlers, and marmalade had seeped into everything about it. Michael mocked me for a fool, only then to find that his luggage was as soaked in a kaolin and morphine remedy for diarrhoea.

We saw something of Van, but as a garrison city we were much restricted. We were allowed to go by bus to Aghtamar, the best known of Armenian churches (though far from the best in quality), but our return transport was a lorry driven by a man almost blind with conjunctivitis. Hakkari too we reached by bus, only to be trapped for days by a military clampdown, staying in an hotel full of refugees in which there was no water and use of the lavatories was inhibited by the stalagmite of shit accumulated in the tray. We saw what we could – the landscape is spectacular – and waited; I had with me John Pearson's *Facades*, five hundred wonderfully distracting pages on the Sitwells to divert me from the dust, delay and Michael's temper. Eventually the departure of a bus to Diyarbakir was announced and we began another nightmare journey, this time with mechanical breakdowns between the military checkpoints and, over some wild stretches of road, armed soldiers ready to do battle. With the army constantly in evidence, Diyarbakir was not a comfortable place to be and a sequence of day-long bus journeys slowly took us back to the south-west.

Michael, moustached and gravely saturnine in emergency, attracted no attention from the Turks (indeed, he was often taken to be Turkish), and at one checkpoint stood watching a soldier butt me with his rifle when he found Robin's maps in my luggage – only the arrival of another bus laden with Kurds diverted him. To my protests that he might have come to my assistance, Michael responded that had I been arrested he could then have done something through diplomatic channels, but if we were both in a concrete cell, that might be the end of us. I was reminded of this on a later journey when unwittingly I crossed the porous and unmarked border with Iraq and did indeed spend some hours in a concrete box wondering what the hell might happen to me. The sheer funk that I then experienced brought my solitary adventures to an end, and Petter Kolrud, my other redoubtable and constant skiing companion, became the stalwart prop of all but one of my later Turkish follies.

*   *   *

It was with Petter that I tied the loose ends and filled the gaps of south-western Turkey; without him my one book on that country would never have been written (though mean publishers, worried about length, forced the elision of several chapters), and with him I

449

set out to write two more, of which only the skeletons were developed. In 1984 we made an inventory of all the rock churches in Cappadocia that we could find. These, excavated from the soft volcanic deposits of an overwhelming pre-historic eruption, are ingenious conventional church interiors, cruciform, arched, vaulted and domed, but windowless, and many have paintings or wholly painted surfaces, ranging from the crude and primitive to the sophisticated, the style uniformly Byzantine pre- and post- the iconoclastic controversy of the Eastern church that began with the first destruction in AD 726 and fizzled out in the middle of the following century. Some are no more than isolated hermit churches and burial sites; a handful are extensive enough to deserve identific-ation as monasteries (Christianity in Cappadocia reaches back to the second century AD). Harsh winters, with snow as deep as four metres, induce rock falls that bury some churches and reveal others, so that no inventory can be perfect; their gross number has been estimated at five hundred, but the number accessible in any summer is far fewer. Those most visited, usually by accompanied groups of tourists, are at risk from sudden changes of humidity brought about by their perspiring presence, the brushing shoulder and caressing finger.

One of the long-buried churches, revealed in the 1960s at Tağar, south-east of Ürgüp, devoted to Theodore Tyro, a local soldier saint, hideously tortured, led to our being invited to witness a village circumcision. The boy, Ahmed, six, was in the uniform of an army general, pinned about with banknotes, the gifts of family and friends; we pinned more on him. His mother came to talk to us; enormously stout, in baggy breeches of green velvet and a cardigan that spoke of Marks and Spencer, she chattered in broken German; home for a month from Berlin, her answer to my questioning was a melancholy, 'Was machen muss.' We were given ayran (a thin yoghurt) and Turkish delight; young men brought us cigarettes and were, as usual, amazed to see Petter roll his own (another useful knack for making contact); a band arrived –

violin, clarinet, guitar and drum – and teenage boys began to dance, slow, graceful, statuesque, intense, remote, pair by pair as though Nicholas Poussin was their choreographer. They were swept aside by young men in a dance that jostled shoulders in a forward-thrusting shimmy of aggression, the prelude to a single dancer, his first movements slow and spiritual, his eyes unfocused, but as the musicians increased their pace, his turns became a whirl that ended with his spinning on his knees in the dust.

Another ring of dancers replaced him, a boy in their centre seeming to adopt a feminine role with mischievous hip-wriggling and knowing glances – he would provoke them all and then concentrate on one who would eventually replace him. Both clowning and provocative, it was not without humour, but one particularly lithe boy could bend back so far that his face was upward at the crutch of his choice, continuing to dance until kissed by his victim. He it was who drew Petter from the painted farm-cart on which we stood for a better view, grasping his hand so that to refuse would have been churlish; Petter joined the ring and all was unremarkable until the wily boy once more got into the middle and bent his back until his face was at Petter's crutch and danced, it seemed interminably, while Petter gazed down at the upturned face too embarrassed to give the required kiss.

We ate yoghurt soup and macaroni, crunchy beans in crushed tomato, vine-leaves stuffed with rice, and crisp red water melon, the quantities enormous and not a sheep's eyeball to be seen; dancing was replaced by song and the musicians' clamour struck a softer note until cut short by a sudden silence in the crowd – the man with the knife had arrived, a doctor, not the Imam who had been present most of the day, who would do the deed. Ahmed's father insisted that we go with him to the upper room where the family elders gathered; he sat on an upright chair and the wary child in pyjama trousers was passed to him. The father loosed the cord and settled the boy on his knees, looped his forearms under and between the child's thighs and gripped his wrists so that, his bottom hanging low, knees wide apart, his crutch was thrust forward. The doctor swabbed behind the foreskin, pulled it over the corona and teased the little penis to tumescence; with the foreskin now painfully stretched forward by an instrument resembling pliers, a swift sweep of the knife removed it.

An astonishing quantity of blood spurted from the wound, much of it over my white trousers. Ahmed screamed and men called his name and snapped their fingers to distract him, but he screamed the more. Then the stitching began, a cat's cradle of a business with the tiny bloody penis tugged here and there as the stitches tightened and the profuse bleeding was reduced to a welling ooze; we watched in silence as the last drops of blood gathered and fell away. The penis, straight before this surgery, now veered to the left. The offending foreskin was tipped into the lavatory. That may well have been the fate of our inventory of churches: sent to the Ministry of Culture, I was thanked for it, and Cappadocia became a holiday resort.

*   *   *

Our report on the state of early Armenian churches in the northeast was probably as pointless. 'Armenia' is an unutterable word in many Turkish circles, but a century ago Armenians were a significant element of the population in eastern Anatolia, probably indigenous but certainly rooted there five centuries before Alexander the Great made his way across their lands on his way to Persia – that is some two millennia before the Ottoman Turks arrived. Now much reduced and land-locked in the southern Caucasus, its ancestral territory once reached far further to the west, to the Pontic Alps on the Black Sea and the mountains of Cilicia on the Mediterranean coast. Among the earliest Christians, they declared Christianity the state religion in c.314 and the Church has ever since lain at the core of their national identity and culture. The classical period of their art was from the fourth to the seventh century, then abruptly halted by Arab invasions within a decade of Mohammed's death in AD 632.

With the establishment of a Christian dynasty, the Bagratid, in AD 884, there was a brilliant cultural recovery, particularly in architecture, until the invasion of the Seljuk Turks in the 1060s. The cultural heart of the people then moved west to Cilicia, the kingdom of Lesser Armenia that played so important a role in the Crusades and built such impregnable castles.

Any boy of my generation, and particularly one brought up by as educated and enquiring a parent as my mother, was likely to have known something of the Armenian diaspora and the great tragedy of 1915 that was its climax, when far more than a million of all ages were driven from their homes to die of starvation and exposure in the desert of northern Syria. My long dormant interest was roused by a modest book given me by Robin Fedden much worn in the re-reading.* By Denis Hills, an old-fashioned traveller without objective, but for whom travelling itself, together with curiosity and the surrendering to impulse that enlivens everything, were enough, it is not a polemic, but to his continuous narrative he added eight appendices, of which one was on the Nestorians (Christians of whom I had hoped to find some evidence in my two attempts to explore Hakkari), and another, rather longer, *The Georgian Churches of Turkey* (as one is required to call these considerable monuments of the Armenians) – and it was with this that the seed was sown.

Hills himself, by the time I met him to compare notes, was seventy and still travelling, but only in Europe – Poland mostly – and long past his Turkish wanderings. He was a quiet shadow of the man who had been brave enough to dub Idi Amin a 'Black Nero' ten years or so before – the one thing for which writers of history may recall him. Teaching at Makerere University in Kampala in the early Seventies he had been appalled by the dictator's butcheries, and when the typescript of a critical book was leaked to the authorities he was, without formal trial but after

---

* Denis Cecil Hills, *My Travels in Turkey*, 1964.

a confrontation with Amin himself, holding his ground, condemned to be shot. After Harold Wilson and the Queen became humiliatingly involved, James Callaghan (then Foreign Secretary) was sent to bring him back to London. He died, aged ninety, in 2004, fretting at the penury that forced on him the institutional life of the Star and Garter Home for indigent old soldiers – he had been an officer in the King's Own Royal Regiment for most of World War II, his adventures as derring-do and humorous as any. Few men deserve less to be so forgotten.

It was not easy to expand Hills' notes, so many village names had changed beyond recognition and association – Keleşot to Filizli and Arkunis to Ilikaynak, and all Robin Fedden's maps had the former Armenian names – and it is an area not much written about in any language, but we set off for Trabzon (Trebizond) armed with notes garnered from all sorts of sources and were, we found, far better informed about the churches that we sought than any of the local 'guides'. It was a melancholy journey, for we found too many churches that, left neglected, might have centuries of survival left in them so soundly built were they, so accurately cut, trimmed and decorated their masonry, but, carelessly quarried (always from the bottom) for hearthstones and doorsteps, tumbling had been the consequence. At Dörtkilise (which means, literally, four churches) we found the fourth that other travellers have supposed not to exist; the main church was dilapidated and overgrown in the same sad beauty that obtains in many a Piranesi print, with two smaller churches close by, but the fourth is below it and across the valley, invisible so heavy is the overgrowth, but from it the main church can be seen. A fifth church, Bayirkilise (which means ascent or hill church), is two hours' climb to just below the summer snow line at ten thousand feet or so, a breathless finger and toe clamber with a local shepherd; at one point I felt the nausea that signals altitude sickness and clung for minutes with my face pressed to the rock, thinking this a beautiful place to die and not be recovered. Too far from any village, transporting a doorstep quite impossible, the tiny chapel, a thousand years old and still in perfect structural condition, must have been built for the loneliest of anchorites.

Penek, once a circular church of sophisticated magnificence, had long ago been used as an armoury or magazine and an explosion had destroyed its dome and upper walls, but the lower were still stout and beautiful and it was still possible to imagine a procession in the ambulatory, still possible to be as in awe of it as of S. Vitale in Ravenna. In Nikoma, where Denis Hills recorded nine well-preserved murals of saints between the windows of a chapel abutting a cowshed, we found the arches and the roof fallen and only three weather-worn figures left, the shell occupied by shepherds brewing the tea that was our only reward for a march of twenty kilometres. As stewed and bitter as any tea that I drank as a National Service-man, they demonstrated how to drink it while holding a small slab of sugar between our teeth; I noted that not one of them still had the central teeth of either register. At Barhal, because used as a mosque, the church was in fine condition, the masonry as crisp as on the day it was cut, the arcaded outer walls as mathematically perfect and proportional as any of Bach's *Goldberg Variations*, but close to the apse two poplar saplings had rooted and must by now have brought about its fall; I tried to convince the not unfriendly Imam that they should be dug out and that simply cutting them down would only delay calamity, but his response was very much 'what the devil has it to do with you?' and that the church's fall would enable him to build a proper mosque. In the north we followed part of Rose Macaulay's supposedly fictional journey to Lake Çildir – at six thousand feet the highest stretch of water in all Turkey, swarming with mosquitoes, teeming with seagulls, a place of six-month winters, Russia within sight. Reviewers damned her novel of 1956, *The Towers of Trebizond*, for its landscapes of fantasy, but every word of her descriptions was true and I was filled with admiration for her intrepidity thirty years before.

We strode, thigh-deep, through the meadow flowers that were the joy of the English countryside when I was a boy. Offered a lift in his trailer by a tractor driver, we found our feet in the grave soil of one Haydar Öz, his gravestone identifying the projecting bones. In Olur, where for some days we lodged in the fire station (no locks to the lavatories, no doors to the showers, the custodian part Quasimodo and part Argus fascinated by the blond nakedness of Petter), the Deputy Governor lent us his fluorescent peacock-blue Land Rover to shorten what would otherwise have been a two-day trek over the mountains, and insisted that a local man with a shotgun go with us. 'Why the gun?' I asked, 'To shoot bears' the answer – to which my response was to buy a large plastic container of honey and insist on leading the expedition. My trust in the gratitude of bears for gifts of honey, no doubt ridiculous, was quite beyond their comprehension (and Petter's), but A.A. Milne's Pooh Bear, my contemporary as a child, was pathetically lurking. There were no bears, but at one point I disturbed an eagle on a ledge – and perhaps have seen nothing more beautiful than the one lazy flap of its wings that set it on a seemingly effortless vertical flight up the sun-warmed cliff behind it.

It was in Olur too that I encountered a handsome young bitch, part Alsatian perhaps, but lighter, taller, rangier, her dugs heavy with milk. She sheared away from me, as do all feral dogs at first, and I had nothing to offer her. An hour later I found her again, dead, garrotted by thick wire; kneeling to remove it, she was still warm; rage kept back the tears and I did not believe the excuse 'rabies', offered by an uncomprehending passer-by trying to be helpful; I could think only of her desperate struggle (had I witnessed it, what would I have done?) and her pups slowly starving to death.

*   *   *

Dogs are the fiercest memories of other journeys. Walking round the Sea of Marmora – a drab and rubbish-strewn experience with scarcely a hint remaining of the marbled past from which its name is derived – Petter and I were in one dreary little town reputed to have a Roman ruin enthusiastically greeted by a small white terrier;

we found the wretched ruin and then returned to the town centre in the hope of lunch, just in time to encounter him again, this time a corpse chucked in the back of a rubbish truck. With Polly Hope, painter, sculptor, theatre designer (far better known in Germany than here) and others, wandering the Aegean shores of Turkey in a gulet (a timber sailing-boat with an engine), we came upon a dog chained to the roof of its bleak shelter by so short a chain that only its hind paws touched the ground, a great fly-blown wound on his brow; I swam back to the gulet for ointment, but the only food I could find was bread and milk; these we gave him and dressed the wound as best we could, but were unable to remove the chain – Polly and I were for desperate measures, but the gulet's Turkish captain would not allow the dog on board and we had to leave him. Did he starve to death? Did the infected wound eventually kill him?

We found an old donkey, alone on a deserted island with no obvious source of water – he trotted to us as though we were his friends and would not leave us as we searched for the antique fragments reported to be there; he must have been transported there to die, and we could do nothing for him. We did, however, rescue two full-grown turtles from the shallow, stagnant garden pool of an hotel where we had a drink while the gulet took on fuel one evening before mooring off-shore. I was so appalled by their condition, their shells shaggy with green weed, the larger a metre long, the water only half a metre deep, dead fish floating on its surface, that I begged the others on board help me to release them. At the first glimmering of light, four or so, we took the dinghy to within fifty metres of the hotel, abducted the turtles and returned to the gulet; the captain, thinking that we had stolen them to eat, could not understand the urgency with which we asked him to up-anchor (always a time-consuming business that involved his wife's swimming down to dislodge it), but eventually we sailed some miles from the coast and let the turtles drop into clear deep water; to see them dive at forty-five degrees, down, down, down until invisible, was our reward.

One dog I did bring back to London. In 1987, mystified that Freya Stark, in her book *Alexander's Path*, thirty years before (extolled by the *New Statesman* as 'as near perfect as such a narrative can be'), had written what seemed nonsense, I set out to prove her either wrong or right. I liked her, admired and envied her, but late in life she came into the category of 'dear old thing' and often fell asleep over lunch and oftener still in mid conversation in her unconventional house in Asolo – always to be forgiven, for she was, in my time, approaching her centenary. She was the last and latest of the heroic English women travellers in the Near East, a generation younger than Gertrude Bell, and her many books on Turkey are invaluable records of how things were there before the country became a holiday destination, but *Alexander's Path* did not live up to its title and served neither its subject nor Freya well. Armed with her account and those of Arrian and Quintus Curtius Rufus as correctives, David George, considerable photographer, my companion, we attempted to follow Alexander's leisurely meandering marches along and across Asia Minor to the site of the great battle of Issus and the defeat of Darius of Persia.

I had travelled before with David, in Denmark from the windy tip of Jutland where, at Skagen, Danish painters set up their easels and recorded the raw life of fisherfolk, imagined history and were seduced by light, to its far south bordering the territory of Schleswig-Holstein, that bane of history lessons long ago, where Sickert was born a Dane before being compelled to become an Englishman. Who now recalls, I wonder, the Eastern Roumelian Question? We had also been to Tunisia, concerned much more with Carthage and ancient Rome than anything Tunisian, and I knew that we would work well together in Turkey, for his eye was very much in tune with mine (and mine with his, as a photographer) and he had a wonderful capacity for being interested. The journey, which ended in chaos at Heathrow and across London, for we returned on the night of the great tree-felling and light-extinguishing storm of October 1997, so cemented our friendship and so educated us both – it was David who saw so clearly where the Battle of Issus must have been, to the south of Toprakkale, for only from that hill could Darius have commanded a view of the plain, the coast and the flanking hills, and have been sure of his line of retreat – that I think we could have walked the Silk Route together. He was subsequently my lodger for a while in Eldon Road, and often came into my study to say that he was off to do some shopping and ask if he could bring anything for me. Milk, I might ask, or bread, or oranges – but to no point, for often days might pass before his return. To my 'Where *have* you been? his answer was always 'I met such a pretty girl . . . such legs . . . such hair . . . such eyes . . . ' I could never say how much I wanted him myself.

I could have written a book on Alexander in Anatolia as long as Freya's, but did not, and all that remains of that aspiration is the grave, under a black pine in my garden, of Mop, the pup we found in the ruins of Mopsuestia, an ancient site in Turkey's armpit. Her right foreleg was broken, the shoulder dislocated, and she was so dehydrated that death was not far off. I should have broken her neck: instead, I emptied my knapsack enough to carry her with ease and, eventually, returned to London with her. She stands, *pars pro toto*, for all the dogs and donkeys whom I failed.

*   *   *

As only an enquiring amateur I have no academic root in any of this enthusiasm for Turkey centuries before the invading Turks arrived in Anatolia, but one small practical experience of digging, identifying and cataloguing in the field I owe to the late Dr Kenan Erim, Professor of Classics at New York University, who for years (and not without envious opposition) led the excavations at Aphrodisias, the site in western Turkey that supplied much marble and sculpture for Augustan Rome. He it was who, in 1979, uncovered the remains of the Sebasteion, an unique (so far) ceremonial approach to a temple, in this case that of the Julio-Claudian emperors, and a treasure of such narrative reliefs as Claudius seizing Britannia and

Nero annexing Armenia. After hearing him lecture on the subject in May 1983 at The Anatolian Civilisations, a vast and astonishing encyclopedic exhibition mounted in Istanbul by the Council of Europe, I asked him if I might join him as a neophyte later in the year. He set me to work on the defensive wall erected by the Byzantines round the old heart of the city, a higgledy-piggledy structure of fragmentary sculpture and masonry dragged from tumbled buildings. There was something about him that spoke of gentlemanly Ottoman Turks at ease with a dozen languages, alive and dead, with European culture, philosophy and politics; we slaved all day and in the evenings sat at his feet, much as did the students of Xenocrates in the olive groves of ancient academe, astonished by the polymathic range of interests demonstrated by this vigorous and autocratic aesthete who could not suffer fools.

Working with him that autumn was the remarkable Professor Juliette de la Genière, taking time off from the marine archaeology that she was pursuing on ancient vessels shipwrecked off the coast near Reggio, Calabria. She entertained us with a tale of interference by the Mafia and their having to be bought off with a share of the antiquities retrieved (a daily bargaining), and then let loose the notion that they were in possession of Caravaggio's *Nativity with Saints Francis and Lawrence*, stolen from the Oratory of St Lawrence in Palermo in October 1969 and subsequently housed in a church known as Santa Maria della Mafia in the hills of Aspromonte, to the east of Montalto (Monte Cocuzza); the large-scale map that she subsequently sent me identified the village as Sant di Polsi. Rodolfo Siviero, the honest Italian policeman most interested in such matters, had died only two weeks before and as there was no one else with whom I could discuss such a dangerous matter, I had to let it pass.

Two small things at Aphrodisias remain with me – the true taste of pomegranates bursting on the tree after a day in the sun, and, living in one of the ramshackle showers erected in the garden of the site, the family of toads that crowded onto my feet when water streamed down my body.

CHAPTER 8

The Blunt Affair

In 1979 I did not go to Turkey. Two years earlier, with the sensational Mentmore sale mounted in a marquee at the house, Sotheby's had confirmed the recovery of the depressed art market – indeed, had I not been asked to go to the USA for a month or so in January 1977 to discuss the wants of several museums, and to Paris in February, I might argue that the Mentmore sale had been the trigger of that recovery, so outstanding were the prices, so huge the crowds, but I now realise that it was the first major beneficiary of a new certainty that the slump was over. With my working life back on track after three bleak years, it seemed that I was spending more time abroad – mostly in the USA – than at home, and after a particularly intense stint in New York and the East Coast in May 1979, I was not in the mind to plan and execute another Turkish journey, and certainly not one that would break new ground, for I had by then learned the value of scrupulous preparation. Instead, with an old friend, Colin Darracott, and two of my dogs, Schubert and Gamage, at the end of August and for the first eight days of September, I walked first on Dartmoor and then along the shoreline to the south of it – at more than twenty miles a day, as exhausting an exercise as any trek in search of Greek and Roman ruins. Back in London on the evening of Sunday 9 September, I found messages from Anthony Blunt, more than anxious to talk to me – but not on the phone. I went at once to see him, and that, for me, was the beginning of the Blunt Affair.

At this point I must turn back to May 1970 when I sold a drawing by Constant Troyon, sight unseen, to Andrew Gow, an elderly Cambridge don of whom I knew nothing other than that he was Anthony's friend – and that I knew only because it was Anthony who told me of his wish to buy it and, further, that I was commanded to deliver it to Gow in Cambridge. He struck me as the coldest man I had ever encountered, a man of calculated silences, intimidating, and, beginning with 'Anthony wishes you to know . . . ' he told me the tale of Communism and espionage that now everybody knows; he offered no other reason for doing so. His account of the business was as dry, succinct, orderly and clinical as that of a pathologist recording the condition of a corpse, but I sensed that not only did he know more, but that he had eliminated from the recital any part that he had played, and took him to be mentor rather than confessor. I was not required to respond – nor did I quite know how to – but as it lent an armature to old Courtauld Institute gossip and mythology, I was not surprised. I sensed too, precaution against events unspecified and unpredictable but could see no particular point in the timing, and Gow's telling me rather than Anthony himself, I interpreted as Anthony's unwillingness to discuss the matter (though, surely, he must have been certain of my loyalty) or involve me more deeply. Were it ever to be raised, perhaps in some emergency, he had had the foresight to cut out the need for explanations. Now I wonder if this was Gow's laying-on of hands, telling me a truth that after his death and Anthony's disgrace might, if untold, be impossible to disentangle from rumour, blame and spite.

I said nothing of our encounter; Anthony asked nothing and everything he knew of it he knew from Gow. The only change in our relationship was, throughout the Seventies, an increasing warmth and, on his part, a relaxation in his essential privacy – his long relationship with John Gaskin, for example, though now in steep decline, affection reduced to the iron shackles of duty and responsibility, was something about which he felt able to talk freely. John, once handsome in the conventions of Thirties cinema, did not age well; as his body thickened and his skin grew coarse and red, the rich post-menopausal women who bought jewellery from Armour and Winston, the shop in the Burlington Arcade where he worked, found him less attractive and his well-paid occasional work as a *cicerone* on their Mediterranean travels fell away. So did his work for the shop and his last role there was more an act of kindness than employment – they let him act as a runner with unfashionable things taken in exchange, and these he pressed on scarcely willing friends until they had no more elderly relatives to whom such expensive trinkets could be given. Sinking into boredom and inactivity, he could spend hours slicing carrots very thin and whining on the telephone in the vile slang of the malevolent queen, often vicious about Anthony. He was not interested in any cultural pursuit – music was a mystery to him, he found it impossible to read a book, and what little curiosity he showed in art was only in the profit that might be made from it. When Armour and Winston's jewellery died away as a source of pocket money, it was replaced by Eric Hebborn's old master drawings, and John became a familiar figure in Old Bond Street and its environs, touting fakes that, by association, were eventually to menace Anthony's reputation. Anthony dreaded retirement: as long as he had the attic flat in Portman Square, with constant access to the library and his study, he could escape from John and ignore the great and growing gulf between them, but in the sort of flat he could afford when no longer Director of the Institute, life would undoubtedly be unbearable. How, he asked, could he get rid of him and live on his own?

It was I, not John, who ferried Anthony into hospital in August 1972 for surgery to remedy bowel cancer. Though serious enough for the Cabinet Secretary and MI5 to prepare themselves for what disclosures might follow on his death, he made a strong recovery – brave, even, for so fastidious a man – but the lurking menace of cancer made him think more purposefully of retirement. He had no savings, owned no property, and his pension was to be so small that he could hardly live on it. Completely out of touch with the realities of life in London, he was appalled to find the price of property so high and realised that one of his precious Poussins must be sold. As the then Director of the Cleveland Museum of Art had repeatedly told him of his serious interest in the larger, *Eliezer and Rebecca*, worth, he thought, much more than the smaller and likely both to buy him a larger flat and establish some investment income, the decision was easily made.

It was at this point that John Brealey caused havoc. Brealey was then a young restorer of the modern scientific school, by whom Anthony was charmed and to whom he had entrusted, with Joan Seddon, the conservation of Mantegna's *Triumphs* in the Royal Collection, which, though extensively and deeply damaged, have some claim to be one of the two most important works of Renaissance art in Britain (the other the cartoons for tapestries by Raphael, in the Victoria and Albert Museum). When, sitting below the *Rebecca* in Anthony's flat, Brealey learned that it was likely to be sold, he offered to lightly clean its surface, removing perhaps more than a century of the nicotine and household grubbiness that dulled its brilliance – a simple and straightforward job perhaps requiring no more than distilled water and cotton wool swabs – arguing that this might increase the price.

It did the very opposite: it wrecked the sale – as any old hand in the market might have guessed. A grubby picture is one that has hung undisturbed for decades, perhaps never touched by restorers, perhaps in perfect condition under the grime, its grubbiness an indication of long ownership, a denial of recent trafficking in the trade, and most museums, buying such a picture under the old rule *caveat emptor*, prefer to clean and conserve their purchases them-selves. This painting had hung for years in an obscure house in Cheshire until bought by the London dealer Duits in 1933, from whom it was immediately bought for Anthony by his close friend Victor Rothschild for a very few hundred pounds (the amount, variously recalled, was either £200 or £300), and in his ownership it remained in its seemingly sound and undisturbed condition, growing only a little more dimmed by yellowing varnish and the air we breathe – not even when he lent it to the great Poussin exhibition in the Louvre in 1960 had it occurred to Anthony to have it cleaned.

When Brealey phoned Anthony to tell him that the painting was now clean and that he wanted to discuss the next step, Anthony phoned me and said that he feared something was wrong – no next step should have been necessary. Together we went to Brealey's studio in Hamilton Terrace. 'My God' was Anthony's immediate and almost only response. Brealey had gone far further than remove the surface dirt, and for the first time I had an inkling of the difficulties that Joan Seddon had experienced with him as a collaborator on the delicate Mantegnas. This was not achieved through delicate swabbing with pure water; this was an acetone job with a Brillo pad. He had cleaned the surface radically, revealing every crack, bruise and other ancient damage, of which the worst were massive losses of original paint from the central subject of the canvas. After a long silence in which Anthony seemed physically bowed by the blow – for blow it was – without a word of reproach he asked Brealey to make the best that he could of it. On the way back to Portman Square he said, 'I can't possibly sell it to Cleveland now: in fact, I can't sell it to anybody, knowing what I now know.'

This painting was his prize possession, his ownership not only an earnest of his devoted scholarship, but of his lifelong homage to Poussin the intellectual and affection for Poussin the man. In having discerned nothing of its true condition he was not alone; in 1960 every Poussin scholar in the world had pored over it and seen nothing amiss – not even Denis Mahon, for whom this picture's date had been a matter of crucial argument, had doubted its condition. For Anthony this was no consolation and the sudden disclosure of such a major flaw was the cause of great distress. His protégé had turned what seemed a kindness into a betrayal that wrecked the hope of a comfortable retirement; worse, it made him doubt his eye, and in this he could not be consoled. Later, installed in far too small a flat, where it dominated the room, he confessed that he sometimes felt the same hatred for the picture as he felt for John Gaskin, and that in being compelled to live his last years at close quarters with the possession and the man he had once most loved, but for which and whom he now felt only profound distaste, was a circle of hell of which Dante had never thought.

Brealey effected a restoration that to me seemed obvious, his reconstruction of the draperies less defined than they had been, as though – in tune with the restoration philosophies of the time – he did not want his work to be mistaken for original and yet recognised that the camouflage of tonal hatching then practised by Italian restorers would disrupt the spectator's reading of the composition and divert him from the narrative. I could never understand how so many art historians, and particularly Denis Mahon who was responsible for the erosion of Anthony's status as the oracle of Poussin studies, when they saw the painting after restoration, failed to recognise that significant changes had occurred, evident even in photographs. When, after Anthony's death, I spoke out about the painting's condition, this was put down to disloyalty – an oddly critical and negative note, as his biographer, Miranda Carter, put it some years later; but I did so for the sake of John Gaskin when the probate value of Anthony's estate was published as £800,000 or so, the *Rebecca* valued, on the assumption that it was in sound original condition, at a far higher figure than it should have been. I hoped for John's sake – he was in considerable distress over the sum of death duties to be paid – that the valuation would, in fairness, be revised; it was not and I was scorned for denigrating Anthony.

Instead of the *Rebecca*, to fund his retirement in 1974, Anthony was compelled to sell the small Poussin landscape that for £12,000 he had bought from Duncan Grant only a decade earlier. That he made a profit of almost £100,000 gave spiteful gossips the opportunity to run to Duncan and make mischief; but he – whom Joe McCrindle and I were then regularly visiting with food parcels – was at eighty-nine in amiable dotage and beyond their manipulation;

it was, nevertheless, the first inkling I had that some in Anthony's wider academic field were inspired by malevolence.

Anthony did not know that he owned a third painting by Poussin. His confidence was so much sapped by the persistent undermining of Denis Mahon in the early Sixties that when he identified a to some extent uncharacteristically small, dark and highly emotional *Agony in the Garden* on copper as possibly by Poussin, he could not bring himself to believe it, anticipating another destructive attack on his connoisseurship if he published it. I had bought it for him for very little money but could hardly reassure him – he, in spite of all the Mahon artillery, was still the expert in my loyal view. After poring over it in the good light of his study in the Institute, he took it up to his flat and hung it in the dark corner by the door of the dining room that was so little used, almost ensuring that no visitor should even glance at it. He refused to let me give its filthy surface the lightest possible cleaning, refused to let the technology department examine it, did very little work on it himself and in his catalogue of Poussin's paintings* dismissed it as 'a Poussinesque composition in the writer's possession', perhaps connected with a painting now lost but known from records. I have not seen it since his death, but in 2001 it was, I understand, cleaned and found to have an inscription on the reverse that proved its authenticity as by Poussin.

The sale of Duncan Grant's Poussin brought not enough for Anthony to do what he most fervently wished – to discharge the responsibility that he felt for John, and live alone. Without John the small flat he found in Portsea Hall, a block within easy walking distance of the Institute, would have been comfortable, but with John, the disruptive enemy of the work he wished to continue, comfort of any kind was out of the question. The attic of 20 Portman Square, its servants' quarters, was nobly proportioned in

---

* Anthony Blunt, *The Paintings of Nicolas Poussin*, 1966, Critical Catalogue, p. 160, L 30.

comparison with the rooms in Portsea Hall, and the two men were inescapably on top of each other; moving there was the most serious of many measures of Anthony's long detachment from the practicalities of life. That in June 1974 he himself found the flat was almost astonishing, but having found it, he did not know how to buy it and I commended as solicitor to deal with the business, David, husband of Jill Allibone, and of David he became fond enough to appoint him his executor. I found him a carpenter to build bookshelves and sent him John Buttle, a gentle giant of absolute honesty, to remove his furniture, books and paintings. The beautiful big desk on which, for more than a quarter of a century, he had spread his books and papers to think and teach, was a Courtauld piece and belonged to the Institute and he had urgently to replace it with one much, and uncomfortably, smaller to fit in the new quarters; I found one, a plain English piece, early nine-teenth century, with practical extensions to pull out, almost doubling its size, should he wish to spread a hundred photographs; it was hardly Hepplewhite. In all the preparations for the move John played no part, but for the move itself Anthony planned, well in advance, to be in Peru, leaving everything for John to do so as 'to avoid disagreements – it's a job better done by one'. As is always the case, things long settled in old circumstances did not fit in new, and on the morning of the move, John made, from Portsea Hall, the first distress call of the day. On Anthony's return the flat was still in chaos and John's mood poisonous; I know no other man who could for so long sustain a bitter sulk and by the end of the year, exhausted with stress, Anthony was in hospital again.

They eventually made what they could of their new quarters, but, so close together, the gulf between them widened. Anthony went often to the Institute to telephone his miseries; John used a call-box round the corner from Portsea Hall; neither, unless on some trivial matter, called from home, wanting not to be overheard; John foolishly mistook me for his ally. Occasionally all three of us dined with Anthony's old friend, Moore Crosthwaite, in Crescent

Grove, one of those patches of Clapham that pretends to be Kensington, but John was always petulant in his boredom, his only interest there not Moore's collections of ancient Roman glass and other small antiquities (he had long been ambassador to Lebanon), but his boyfriend, Dick Spalding, a stocky American ex-sailor in the US Navy, an able seaman so to speak, of such abundant sexuality that neither woman nor man could have resisted him – he was, as it were, a Tom of Finland figure in small, without seeming the least queer; and if how Moore, querulous, secretive, ashamed and terrified of being identified as homosexual, first got him into his bed is a mystery, how he kept him is more mysterious still. To be bedded by Dick was to experience an irresistible exploratory force – and he preferred his subject territories not to have been bathed or showered for at least twenty-four hours.

John was by then given, even without alcohol, to humourless outbursts, tediously long, of queer bitchery about everyone whom he perceived as crossing him and Dick was always the trigger for these – Dick, who made his own choice of the body with which he might have a sexual adventure, but whose staunch, dumb loyalty to Moore John could never breach. John seemed incapable of recognising that he was further and further alienated from Anthony's friends (he had none of his own) by the unloveable behaviour into which he too easily slipped. His looks long gone, his spirit ugly, he had become an incubus.

Anthony used every excuse to get away. I drove him often to Waddesdon where he was not only much loved by the Rothschilds, but for ever working on the catalogues of the collections there; and on Thursday 12 May 1977, with Neil MacGregor (then very much his favourite student) huddled in the back (perhaps not quite the right word, but he seemed slightly scared by both of us and folded very small), we drove to Mentmore and spent a very happy day viewing the sale, breaking off for a picnic. Only two weeks earlier he had had his first cataract operation and was unsteady enough to need me as a prop, but that gave me the benefit of looking at everything with his deliberate diligence. At the astonishing gouaches of Blarenberghe he remarked that he had forgotten how blue they were (years later my response to light and sky after the removal of cataracts) and with some amusement corrected Sotheby's identification of a pretty hunting lodge as a view of Fontainebleau. It was one of those rare days when Anthony put up no sort of guard, but was funny, mischievous and boyish, much more of my age than his own. On 1 November 1977, five weeks after the event, he would allow no greater celebration of his seventieth birthday than a quiet dinner to which his friends John Golding (art historian, painter and teacher at the Royal College of Art) and James Joll (Professor of International History at London University) should be invited, together with John Gaskin; this went as he wished, without a disagreeable performance from the latter, though I had a disaster with an over-poached salmon. At nine in the morning of 28 December, Anthony telephoned to tell me that John, whose unremarkable birthday it was, was in a rage that I had arranged no matching celebration for him.

At the end of January 1978 both Anthony and I were in Düsseldorf for another Poussin exhibition to which he had lent his *Rebecca* and to the catalogue of which he had contributed two essays; the specific catalogue entry was by Pierre Rosenbourg, who repeated a remark made by Anthony himself very soon after Brealey's restoration – 'About my own *Eliezer and Rebecca*, I would say that recent cleaning has confirmed . . . that it is a very late work, dating from the Sixties.' What wry thoughts, I wondered, had passed through Anthony's mind as he considered the phrase 'a very late work.'* No one remarked on the new state of the painting, not Rosenbourg, the most eagle-eyed of French art historians, not even Michael Kitson who was there to support Anthony and who had as good an eye as any man I knew. Had any other scholar thought to

---

* See *Burlington Magazine*, 1974, p.761 for Anthony's review of Jacques Thuillier's *L'Opera Completa di Poussin*.

raise controversy over this, Anthony would not have fought, for increasing weariness made him gently indulgent here, accepting all, arguing with nothing. One little episode particularly amused Michael – in search of a restaurant we passed a McDonald's and Anthony murmured, 'How strange to find a Scottish restaurant in Düsseldorf.'

The years 1978 and 1979 too (at least until September) passed in a pattern of early morning calls from Anthony and late morning calls from John, each letting off steam about the other. We often had lunch in an Italian restaurant in Connaught Street, sometimes with Joe McCrindle, whose familiarity with Christie's and Sotheby's and the ease with which interesting things could still be bought for absurdly little, encouraged Anthony almost to haunt these auction houses. Sometimes, almost always unsuccessfully, he asked me to bid for him, and eventually it became clear that, having seen us together, too canny dealers supposed that every time I joined the bidding it was either for Anthony or for myself with his blessing. Proof that this was so came when Anthony identified an oil sketch for a banner hung in Notre-Dame, now lost, but known from a print; not by Poussin, but sufficiently close for Sotheby's to sell it under that portmanteau attribution, it was, though pretty enough, valuable only as an art historical document – even so, Anthony gave me a bid that he could ill afford. I asked him if he would mind my continuing to bid on my own behalf if I failed to get it within his margin – and that is what happened on the day. I dropped out at £5,000, far beyond Anthony's bid, but the bidding continued to £15,000 as two Italian dealers fought for it. Then I left the room, but was followed by the buyer with the question, 'What have I bought?' I replied that whatever it was he had paid far too much for it, for it was certainly not by Poussin, as I supposed he thought. 'But Blunt . . . ' he said, tailing off, crestfallen, as I shook my head.

In some ways 1978 was a terrible year for Anthony. On 2 February Andrew Gow, his mentor (my word for him) for half a century, died. From time to time I had driven Anthony to

Cambridge to see him while I spent time in the Fitzwilliam where friends told me that, into his nineties and restricted to a wheelchair and walking frame (both bequeathed to the sick bay of Trinity College), Gow had slowly exchanged his essential gravity for stingy bloodymindedness; on our return journeys we drove largely in silence, Anthony morose in mood and seeming physically shrunken. The net value of Gow's will was £357,736, then an enviably substantial sum; most of it went to the Fitzwilliam, and to Anthony he bequeathed only two Faenza vases, three small rugs and the £100 that was his trifling memento to several old friends. I found it impossible to reconcile so mean a bequest with so long and intellectually intimate a friendship, and was even more puzzled by our contrived encounter in May 1970, though confirmed in my then assessment of the man; with his death, had I become the only holder of the secret outside that secret world?

Worse, perhaps, was the death in the early hours of 6 July 1978, of Antoine Seilern, the greatest of benefactors to the Courtauld Institute – greater, I must argue, than Samuel Courtauld himself, so extensive, yet so severely art historical, were his collections. Any American university receiving them would at once have built new premises to house them, but the Courtauld has treated them shabbily in spite of knowing for decades that it was Antoine's heir.

Antoine, Count Seilern, born in London in 1901, holder of Austrian and British passports, was as discreet and retiring as he was rich and aristocratic. His mother, Antoinette Woerishoffer, who died five days after his birth, was the source of his Christian name and his American fortune. His childhood spent in England and New York, he settled in Vienna in 1910 and his years as a young man were spent there in a whirl of Straussian balls, horse-racing, great cars and private aeroplanes, and on African safaris of which the trophy heads and horns hung in what seemed hundreds on the stairs of his Kensington house as a reproachful reminder of his misspent youth. At the age of thirty-two, encouraged by his father to study the history of art, he enrolled at the University of Vienna, his courses there supplemented with private tuition from Johannes Wilde, ten years his senior, the great Hungarian art historian who was then curator of paintings in Vienna's Kunsthistorisches Museum and was later to be Deputy Director of the Courtauld Institute; it was he who steered Antoine towards his eventual doctorate on the ceiling paintings of Rubens, the painter who remained Antoine's passion for the rest of his life. This doctorate achieved in 1939, a year after the Nazi absorption of Austria, he engineered the flight of Wilde and his wife to London (and of other friends), and came himself with only weeks to spare before the outbreak of World War II in September. He volunteered to serve as a private in the Pioneer Corps but was eventually attached to the Intelligence Corps and given a commission.

He brought from Vienna his 'little collection' already important enough to send for safety to Aberystwyth to be stored in the National Library of Wales. Even during the war it grew, and it continued to grow until his death – thirty-two paintings by Rubens, a dozen by Giambattista Tiepolo, two by Parmigianino, two by Pieter Brueghel, fourteen by Teniers, and others by Van Dyck, Fetti, Crespi, Guardi, Ricci, Magnasco . . . and others still, by Cézanne, Degas, Manet, Morisot, Pissarro and Renoir that complement Sam Courtauld's pictures. Among old master drawings there were thirty by Rembrandt, nine by Watteau, six by Michelangelo, three by Dürer and one each by Bellini, Mantegna and Leonardo. 'A private collection,' he once said, 'is formed for no other purpose than the enjoyment of it.' In the foreword to his catalogue, scrupulously researched and written by himself, of Johannes Wilde he wrote of his 'deeply felt gratitude for many years of unfailing friendship, and for all that he has done for me . . . I have relied with the utmost faith – always rewarded – on his guidance . . . I have sought his opinion before acquiring every work of art, and have never regretted it. What merit there is in the collection is due to his counsel. So it is with the greatest sincerity that I say, Thank you'. It was typical of Antoine's modesty that he published his collection without his name, and that it is now known only by the address of his old home in Princes Gate, but in his quest for anonymity, Johannes too is lost.

Antoine was heavily built, with a booming voice and what seemed an overwhelming presence, but timid students he welcomed with unfailing kindly courtesy, young art historians too, leaving even the most raw and insignificant of them alone to contemplate his pictures, then comforting them with an elaborate old-fashioned tea. With one exception, art dealers and auctioneers were never allowed into the house, much to their annoyance – but James Byam Shaw was a dealer only by force of circumstance and much more a scholar whose role in forming the collection was significant. Antoine's connoisseurship was informed and passionate, considered and well judged, coherent and purposeful, never impulsive; his was an art historian's taste, educated and severe, yet enlivened by his response to emotion and sensuality – those who thought him a man more of head than heart were wrong. He railed against the misleading brightness of coloured reproductions, and for the over-cleaning and restoration of pictures in the National Gallery he had nothing but despairing contempt.

To some extent he remained a student all his life, attending many lectures at the Courtauld Institute, never missing those by Wilde on Michelangelo, Leonardo, Rubens and Titian. Sometimes he arrived on the heavy old BSA motorbike that in fine weather he used for tootling round London (replaced by a Vespa in his later years), and sometimes he came from his farm in Buckinghamshire in a wooden-bodied Austin Hereford shooting brake, a favourite pig sitting upright in the passenger seat beside him – the pair of them resembling a demonstration diagram from some eighteenth-century tome on physiognomy and expression. Long weekends on the farm gave him repose for reading and research, but from pig-breeding and orchids he derived great and simple earthly pleasure, and in his orchard he grew more fruit than he could give away.

The Blunt Affair

Was there ever another art historian of quite such varied interests? Was there ever another connoisseur so intent on his privacy that his collection does not even bear his name? In his lifetime he gave the National Gallery its finest painting by Van Dyck and some one thousand, two hundred and fifty old master drawings to the British Museum; on his death his bequest to his beloved Courtauld Institute was given a probate valuation of £30 million, a figure that today seems utterly derisory; but he received no honours for his generosity, nor has the Lottery spent a bean on housing his collection as it deserves, and his modesty has been rewarded with oblivion.

Anthony, distraught – for Antoine had been the last live link with Johannes (who had died in September 1970) and what was undoubtedly the brief Golden Age of the Courtauld Institute – composed the most drab and unfeeling of obituaries for *The Times*, with not a hint of the emotion that he felt. I too was distraught. When I joined Christie's in 1958, Antoine warned me that I could not come to his house again – I was not surprised, for I knew of the general prohibition against all in the trade and, whatever the partners in the firm might think themselves, Antoine viewed them as no more than one step up from Bond Street dealers. Nevertheless, he came to me for information and occasionally asked me to bid for him; that he was particularly cross not to have bought the Fra Angelico in the Northwick sale,* in which the doctor saints Cosmas and Damian replace the diseased leg of a deacon with one taken from corpse of a dead Ethiopian, caused me, in the light of his own death, some wry retrospective (but unsuitable) amusement. In my dealing years he bought things from me and, I think, trusted me, for when he learned from Anthony that I had turned into museum runner, dogsbody, errand boy or what you will, I was let into the house again.

Since the beginning of the year I had been working for him on a valuation of possessions *not* to be included in his bequest to the

* Christie's 28 May 1965, lot 14.

Courtauld. His tax affairs were in confusion and the Inland Revenue would, he was certain, pounce as soon as he was dead; he was worried on two counts – that there would be some catastrophic interference with the bequest in favour of death duties, and that his handful of relatives in Vienna might be deprived of the modest inheritances on which he had decided. My task was to identify easily portable works not listed in any inventory of which the Inland Revenue might be aware, and then get them to Vienna without involving any formal export process. Looking now at the schedules I am appalled to be reminded that we considered fragile ancient Greek and Chinese antiquities as well as more manageable prints, drawings and watercolours by comparatively modern Austrian and German artists as well as by old masters. All these were to be packed into my unassuming Peugeot 404 and driven to Vienna, camouflaged by my pretence to be a landscape painter. That under a number of blank canvases, paintboxes, palettes, bundles of brushes and other painter's paraphernalia, should lurk unseen solander boxes crammed with treasures worthy of the British Museum was not that much of a risk (a hitchhiker would add further distraction) and Antoine was boyishly amused by the conspiracy.

Here I must stress how much Antoine meant to Anthony as a friend as well as a benefactor of the Institute, and how close they were. Anthony was among the first to know, late on 10 June, that Antoine's condition – he had for months been recovering from heart trouble and the amputation of a leg – had suddenly worsened and that he was again in hospital, threatened with the amputation of the other leg; and the early morning call on Sunday 11 June was about that, not about some tiresome spitefulness of John. When Antoine returned to Princes Gate, still in possession of his leg, he was again capable of roaring like a lion, to be heard in the basement from his bedroom, and he was every bit as clear in his mind about the business on which I was engaged, but this was not to last and, again in hospital, he died. At 8.55 am on 6 July, Anthony's morning call was bleak. Within twenty-four hours it was my duty to take him into hospital for his second cataract operation; it would camouflage his tears.

*   *   *

On the evening of Sunday 9 September 1979 Anthony told me, less as a friend, I thought, than formally, as his executor perhaps, that he might soon, in a book, be exposed as part of the Burgess-Maclean-Philby business. What should he do? 'You must have signed the Official Secrets Act?' I asked, and he confirmed that he had. This seemed to me to offer him some protection, at the very least allowing him to neither confirm nor deny any accusation or rumour. I reminded him that as many older students at the Courtauld had known of the suspicions roused by the flight of Burgess and Maclean and had taken them in their stride, others too, outside the Institute, must have heard the rumours and not responded to them, and suggested that he should, if anyone now approached him, simply say that there had been much gossip over many years and that now, as then, he was constrained by the Official Secrets Act. Pretend world-weariness was my advice, say nothing and do nothing that might draw attention to his interest in the matter. He asked David Allibone's advice and he said much the same, but another friend sent Anthony to the eminent Michael Rubinstein, a powerful lawyer altogether more practised in such matters. That I have no idea who this friend was, was typical of Anthony: apart from Moore Crosthwaite and John Golding, I knew almost nothing of his personal and private friends, nothing of old loyalties, encountered none beside his hospital beds, none when he was recuperating, and as he kept us all in separate boxes it is reasonable to assume that they knew nothing of me. Of his lovers I knew only of Peter Montgomery, so often staying at the flat in Portman Square, with whom in the late twenties he had had an affair at Cambridge, and the amiable 'bloke', married, with children, who had for perhaps twenty years coolly fucked him once a week. Montgomery came from a wealthy landed family in

Ulster and was something of a big-wig there; in the late Sixties he was a tall, bluff, amiable man, conventionally handsome, prinked and perfumed in a way that did not wholly conceal the boy who had, forty years before, enchanted Anthony; garrulous and given to heavy drinking, within a decade he was showing signs of senility and I thought he had become an unsafe friend for the Anthony I knew I might one day have to protect. As for the 'bloke', he and I were on no better than nodding terms, for on our very first encounter he had, I thought, betrayed Anthony by offering for a not insubstantial fee to perform the same service for me, and I had tartly cut him short with: 'I give as good as I get and I don't have to pay for it.' I realise now, of course, that we all pay for it one way or another, and that Anthony's sex life, uncluttered by affection, was very easily put away in its box once the fiver had changed hands.

In theory, Rubinstein was a well-chosen solicitor for Anthony: the present menace was a forthcoming book and, as he had fought for half-a-dozen major publishers in libel cases, and for Penguin when, for issuing an unexpurgated text of *Lady Chatterley's Lover*, the firm was prosecuted for obscenity in 1960, there could be nothing that he did not know about counteracting literary accusations. It was not so: he was far too eager to take the battle to the foe without quite knowing the complex nature of the enemy – a doggedly enquiring writer who could not quite prove what he supposed, a press informed by rumour, innuendo and the malice of all sorts of minor figures anxious to pull Anthony down in revenge for imagined slights, an MI5 and MI6 thrilling to the renewal of a long-frustrated chase, and a naive Prime Minister inspired, not by spite but by such aggressive provincial patriotism that she could neither ask nor answer the question 'Why?' These forces were far beyond Rubinstein's power to control and, once unleashed, they swept him aside. It was he who, as a preliminary to quashing it, asked the publishers of Andrew Boyle's *The Climate of Treason* to let him see the text. As Anthony was not named in it, Rubinstein's asking to see it was promptly interpreted as an admission of sorts (had he been fool enough to name Anthony as his client?) and the publishers leaked the request to *Private Eye*; on 28 September the tumbrils of the press prepared to roll. With the publication of extracts from Boyle's book in the *Observer* on Sunday 4 November, I had the first telephone calls – from Stewart Tendler at *The Times* and Chris White at the *Daily Mail* – but all that I, an unknown nobody wondering, alarmed, how the hell these journalists knew of our connection, could say was that I knew nothing. I was in genuine ignorance of the situation, for I had not heard from Anthony for days and he had not answered the telephone when, troubled by his silence, I had called him.

On the morning of Thursday 15 November Anthony at last telephoned, whispering, as for some days he and John had been pretending not to be at home, had not turned on the lights, not opened the curtains, not even flushed the lavatory in case the sound betrayed their presence. Michael Rubinstein had just been informed by the Cabinet Office that the Prime Minister Mrs Thatcher was that afternoon to make a statement in the House of Commons that would confirm the rumours of espionage and treachery. Anthony, with the consideration for others that was habitual, thought that the life of every resident in Portsea Hall would be disrupted by the mob of journalists bound to lay siege, and asked me to take him, with John Gaskin, to stay with John Golding and James Joll in Ravenscourt Park; but he could think of no way of leaving Portsea Hall unobserved, for a handful of reporters were already clustered at the door of the block, prevented by the hall porter there from entering. I took a suitcase with an old loose overcoat that had belonged to my stepfather, mufflers and a broad-brimmed stitched tweed hat that I wore when walking dogs in the rain. Leaving the car unlocked in the road, I went into Portsea Hall and, without hesitation, up the stairs to the sixth floor, suggesting, I hoped, to anyone who might be looking, that I was on my way only to the first. Anthony let me in. John I instructed to take their bags, walk down the stairs and, as unhurriedly as he could manage, put them in the boot of the car and then sit behind the driver's seat – the front passenger seat was already far back on its runners so as to accommodate Anthony's long legs. Squinting through a crack in the curtains I could see that he had attracted no attention. That much achieved I, with Anthony muffled as an invalid and leaning heavily on me, took the lift to the ground floor, tottered past the hall porter (who knew perfectly well who we were) and, deep in conversation, made our slow way across the forecourt to the car. There was an awkward moment with his long legs as I got him into his seat, but not once did I look back at the reporters and it was only when I started the engine that one of them began to run.

On the way to Ravenscourt Park Anthony gave me very clear instructions. He presumed that the running reporter had a note of the car's registration plate and that I would soon be besieged. I was to keep the press occupied and him informed if they lit on anything particularly ghastly – as the *Sunday Telegraph* immediately did with the claim that Anthony, in betraying them to the Nazis, had been responsible for the deaths of forty-nine British secret agents in occupied Holland. Colin Simpson of the *Sunday Times* – to whom I had been useful long before in his exposure of auction rings in the art market – was kind enough to tell me that my telephone was being tapped and that I should not use it for any call I did not want the authorities to hear, by which I supposed him to mean MI5 and MI6; thus I made my calls to Anthony from Joe McCrindle's flat in Kensington Court, nearby. Reporters and photographers massed in my front garden day and night, followed me to Kensington Gardens in the early morning when I walked my dogs, watched me shop in Gloucester Road, and one of them even brought a bicycle when I took to riding mine in an effort to evade them, discovering my use of Joe's telephone (he was away in New York) and bribing the porter of his block; nothing I did went unobserved.

In retrospect it would have been wiser to disobey Anthony, say nothing and do nothing, for every scrap of rebuttal to a mob of journalists determined on obloquy and odium served only to reinforce their savagery. It has been said that Anthony was displeased by much of what I said and did, but he said nothing at the time, offered no change of instruction and the exhausting pantomime continued. John Golding or James Joll could easily have told me of Anthony's displeasure – if any – but did not, and when, with the publication of Miranda Carter's book in 2001* I first learned of it, I sensed the voice of Golding, always more possessive of Anthony's friendship than I ever was, more exclusive – and by the time he talked to Miss Carter he had been the victim of my comments on him as a painter. At the time, I could not understand how Anthony's presence in the Golding-Joll house had been discovered – to be followed by a mad dash back to Portsea Hall and the televised press conference arranged by Rubinstein – and it was only from Miss Carter's book that I learned the reason: James Joll, in responding to a radio 'phone-in' programme, had revealed it. That I should be reviled by the Golding faction when it was itself responsible for betraying Anthony's whereabouts, seems particularly wry.

John Gaskin too could with one word have stilled and silenced me, but from him I heard nothing; from Anthony's brothers, on the other hand, Christopher and Wilfrid, there was a deal of encouragement to continue the diversion – Christopher wrote: 'The purpose of this letter is to express the greatest appreciation from both of us for the defence of Anthony you put up – something neither Wilfrid nor I is qualified to do. We want you to know how deeply grateful we are.' There was even more reassurance from Michael Rubinstein from whom, at the time, I had support almost amounting to instruction, with direct telephone numbers to his office desk and home. Years later, long after Anthony's death, when an odd sort of 'clearing the decks' friendship had developed

* Miranda Carter, *Anthony Blunt, His Lives*, Macmillan 2001.

between us, Michael confessed that his initial advice, based on the conviction that he could scupper Boyle's book, had been in error, that everything that followed had been an *ad hoc* response, and that the press conference he had arranged at *The Times*, far from settling the matter, had inflamed it. When I asked if the statement then read by Anthony, so uncharacteristic in style and temper, had been written, not by him but (as I suspected) by the Cabinet Secretary Sir Robert Armstrong, he deflected the question at some length, leaving it unanswered.

Anthony too left a question unanswered. Three of many letters of support for him were published by *The Times* on 17 November; they were from former students, loyal to Anthony as a generous teacher and great art historian, from Michael Jacobs, one of his last post-graduate students and subsequently a distinguished travel writer, Mark Jones, later an enlightened servant of the British and Victoria and Albert Museums and now Master of St Cross College, Oxford University, and from me. Mine concluded with a declaration that 'the Fifth Man is dead', for the press, having labelled Anthony the Fourth Man after Burgess, Maclean and Philby, were already busily hunting for the fifth. It was disingenuous of Anthony to tell the press that he had no idea who was in my mind – it was, of course, Andrew Gow, to whom he himself had sent me all those years before – and yet, in a tricky way it was true, for we had never discussed that burdensome interview at which I had formed the not unreasonable assumption that as Gow had clearly played Father Confessor to Anthony, he might well have been his puppet-master too – and possibly for others. Later, when the press had hounded Leo Long (again I saw Anthony weep), John Cairncross and others, it became evident that the process was not unlike paring away the layers of an onion and that each revelation exposed another, but the sleuths eventually lost interest and never exposed the onion's core. When, very shortly before his death, Anthony asked who my Fifth Man was, he did not demur when I said 'Andrew Gow', but broke eye contact and stared out of the window.

On their return to Portsea Hall after the televised interview, Anthony and John were virtually imprisoned by the continuing attendance of journalists and photographers. Anthony could have braved them, but John could not and instead insisted on reverting to the regime of the days before their flight to John Golding's house, refusing to switch on the lights or pull the lavatory chain, pointless deprivations that deceived no one, and ended when Anthony could stand the stink no longer. Michael Kitson, Anthony's one loyal supporter in the Courtauld Institute, Anita Brookner, Joe McCrindle and I (and, no doubt, others too) took them food and drink until Anthony felt able to brave a local supermarket; Joe and I, having prepared the ground by telling the staff what we proposed to do, walked him to lunch in the familiar Italian restaurant and the welcome was wonderfully emotional. There were, he told me, episodes of jostling and shouting in the street that unnerved him, but when these died away he managed well enough. The cruellest blow was struck by the Courtauld, suddenly forbidden to him – but Anita Brookner broke the sanction and ferried library books to and fro. The Courtauld library was closed to me too, brusquely and publicly by the librarian; years earlier, before Anthony's retirement, I had made a will in favour of the Institute – a life interest for my mother, and then the whole lot, house, books, pictures to be kept or disposed of for its benefit – and for this my small reward was to be able to use the library. Banned, humiliatingly, a book snatched from my hand, David Allibone drew up a new will for me the following day, eliminating the Institute, but the wound it inflicted that day still suppurates.

John Gaskin's attempted suicide – if it was that, for he could well have been drunk – on 12 February 1980, caused some confusion in that it was widely reported as 'Blunt's friend' who had fallen six floors from the flat, and many in the press (and not in it), thought at first that it was I, not John; as I had gone to Germany and could not be produced, the misunderstanding was not immediately quashed. My mother attempted to phone Anthony but could get no reply –

but then no one could, for he had deserted Portsea Hall; he rang her two days later, full of apologies, and explained that he was moving from friend to friend and could not be contacted. John, he said, he had seen, a broken collar bone and damaged feet his only injuries, but (I quote her diary), 'This happening has brought him to his senses.' With John away for months recuperating in a convalescent home and, later, with his sister in the north, Anthony went to Rome to work on his *Guide to Baroque Rome*, described as 'the greatest architectural guidebook ever written' when it was published in 1982. On leaving, he passed through Heathrow without comment or obvious recognition, but on his return on 11 August there was some unpleasantness, the more shocking after months in Rome that had been entirely uneventful.

John had not been brought to his senses; he was, indeed, worse – wholly self-centred, whimpering and reproachful when sober, abusive when drunk, and tediously camp between. Both he and Anthony fell back into their routine of telephone calls, and when I was away they confided in my mother instead – and if ever there was a recording angel it was she. They had fewer friends now. Moore Crosthwaite, close friend and sexual confidant for half a century, could not bear even to speak of Anthony and was so shifty and furtive when he encountered me that I could only laugh at a man who had been an ambassador but seemed to have lost all his aplomb and social graces; Dick Spalding, however, remained loyal, and after Anthony's death was a stalwart help to me in managing John. Shrugged off by the Courtauld hierarchy and unable to use any of its resources, his successor as director, the useless Peter Lasko, did his best to suggest that Anthony's directorship had been no more than a trifling episode in its history, and the deputy director, George Zarnecki, frustrated in his ambition to succeed Anthony and blaming him for his failure, poured bile and vitriol on his academic achievements, matching those writers in the press who were determined to destroy him utterly. When the Institute moved to Somerset House and Anthony's manuscript notes (part of his bequest) were put out for the dustmen – some brought to me by dismayed students as proof of what the authorities there were doing – any hope that my once passionate affection for the Courtauld might recover, altogether died.

All this is ancient history to Courtauld students now, and there are, no doubt, new gods, just as art history itself is so much changed since Anthony's day that it is a different discipline. According to a recent prospectus first year students, knowing nothing of the European Renaissance art of which students of my generation were first made aware, took a course in 'Getting to Grips with Rembrandt', second year students, extending the 'detailed knowledge of art historical periods' acquired in three short terms, could devote themselves to American Art 1945–72, and in their third year study the representation of race in British art 1730–1860. The lacunae are larger than the fabric. In my young day the fabric was densely woven and there were no holes; then art history was the history of painting, sculpture, architecture and associated skills, from the birthpangs of the Italian Renaissance (with nods to ancient Athens, Rome and Byzantium) to the present day; it was the history of those who worked in these fields; it was the history of patronage from the Church, the state and individuals; it was also the history of nations, dynasties, the middle classes and the poor, the history of political ambitions and the conflicts of religion – it was, indeed, the history of history itself. We recognised art's connections with literature and music, theology and heresy, philosophy and theory. Art history was the key to connoisseurship, to our ability to distinguish the real from the fake and the painting that is wholly by Rubens (for example) from the painting that is partly by him or wholly by his students. Art history gave us a sense of period and nationality so that we could distinguish Italian painting from French, and a seventeenth-century painting from one earlier or later, and it taught us the importance of drawing as the first stage in the development of ideas, as document and record. Art history taught us to analyse and understand art, and gave us visual literacy far beyond the familiars of the *Mona Lisa*, the *Last Supper* and the *Night Watch*. It proved to be the most inclusive and wide-ranging of cultural disciplines, and that it was so was entirely due to Anthony's academic rigour in devising the syllabus, for exposing us to the grandees of every field within it (and occasionally outside it), for appointing Johannes Wilde to distil the mysteries of Michelangelo and Titian, Rubens and Rembrandt, Leonardo and Brueghel, and for teaching Mansart and Poussin himself. This was what Lasko and Zarnecki and their successors scorned.

*   *   *

Anthony aged, lost weight and became frail. By Michael Rubinstein he was unwillingly persuaded to write an apologia explaining, if nothing more, how he had become a Communist sympathiser and involved in espionage. He began it, but stickler for accuracy that he was, he too often found himself frustrated when he went to libraries or record offices to check his facts and, neither able to afford the luxury of taxis nor willing to risk the insults offered by their drivers, he wearied of the always time-consuming and often fruitless journeys that he had to make by bus, travel sick if he tried to read, conspicuous if he did not. One, in particular, to the National Newspaper Archive in Colindale, he found irksome, for there, after an hour's stop-start journey north through Kilburn and Cricklewood, the staff were ingeniously obstructive, balked his errands and wasted his time. He was, moreover, convinced that however innocent his research in such public offices, it was as noted and reported as it would have been in a totalitarian police state and might well, though wrongly, implicate in his skulduggery, men and women with whom his connections were entirely peripheral. There was another difficulty: though a practised writer with a stream of publications over half a century, divorced from the academic subjects that had been their constant, his writing, in terms of style, composition, wit, pace and narrative, became as deadly dull as any schoolboy's essay on how he spent a summer holiday. This, he said, was not how he wished to spend his dying days and, numbed by the chore, at some twenty-five thousand words he abandoned the uninspired memoir.

He should, of course, have burned or buried it, but it is the way of writers to hang on to the evidence of work and he could not commit the sacrifice. He allowed Michael Rubinstein and a handful of others to read it; they had thought that his written life might reflect his spoken warmth, wit, enthusiasm and evident humanity, but dismayed to find that his approach had been that of the tedious schedule, a supporting document rather than the life, they agreed that he should drop it. What had they expected of Anthony? Private man that he was, writing of his affections, relationships and sexual longings would have been impossible, and writing of his work as an art historian or for the Royal Collection would have seemed to him boastful, to his friends uncharacteristic, and to the general reader tedious. As for telling the truth, the whole truth and nothing but the truth – can any man do that and would his baying critics have believed him?

After Anthony's death, John Gaskin behaved as though the manuscript was in some sense a demon – hysterically he wanted it removed from the flat, but would neither touch it himself nor let anyone collect it; Anthony's brothers wanted nothing to do with it it – 'It's a desperate situation,' said Wilfrid in a letter of April 1984. Dick could hardly take it to Moore's house, and I refused to take care of it, suspecting that if I did, the news would be leaked and life made hell again. John Golding eventually took charge of it (I would like to have been a fly on the wall that day) and deposited it in the British Library with an embargo that kept it from the public for a quarter of a century; this was not enough, and when the embargo ended in July 2009, there was a flurry of interest from the press, but, as Anthony had warned, it proved to be deadly dull and empty of revelation.

His seventy-fifth birthday in 1982 we celebrated in the usual

Italian restaurant with Joe McCrindle, but without John Gaskin, who was spending more and more time with his sister in the north, and there was a faint glimmer of pleasure in the event that John's presence would have dowsed. When he was in London, though physically recovered, he pretended that he was not, compelling Anthony to be the household slave – not his natural role and one irksome to a man aware of his frailty and anxious to complete the art historical work he had in hand. He had six months or so. On 24 March 1983 I spent most of the day with Anthony poring over photographs of landscape drawings by Poussin, his brother-in-law Gaspard, and by other hands long confused with them. In spite of publishing a general clarification of his ideas as recently as 1979* he was convinced that he needed to reconsider their attribution and adjust their order, and as these were matters not only of style and intellectual approach but the certainty of distinct but as yet not definitely identified hands, he needed, he said, another eye. We reached no publishable conclusion, but I had the consolation of a day with him that perfectly recalled the enthusiasm, the lively enquiry and the willingness to consider ideas conflicting with his own that had enlivened tutorials with him when I was his under-graduate student. Thirty-six hours later he was dead and all hell broke loose again. I flew to Cyprus to escape.

Miranda Carter has it that he died sitting at his desk, after breakfast, about to make a telephone call. John Gaskin told me that it was in crossing the room to answer a call that he died – it is an unimportant detail, but it might as well be right, and John saw it happen (Miss Carter was too late to interview him). It was the right death for him, quick and clean, with nothing of the long-drawn business of the hospital bed and its humiliations, nothing of the last-ditch interrogation that MI5 or MI6 might have tried. As I had long since asked Anthony to release me from acting as his executor – the *Sunday Times* had taken to employing me, largely to investigate

---

* Anthony Blunt, *The Drawings of Poussin*, Yale 1979.

488

art scandals, but I suspected that this was that paper's way of having me on board should any further revelations about Anthony's past occur – his death could easily have ended this chapter of my life, but it did not. John Gaskin was beyond all comforting, but it was for himself that he grieved, not Anthony. He could not be persuaded to leave the flat in pursuit of any of his old pleasures – not even for the equestrian competitions that were the only interest we had in common (though much more his than mine); he had no interest in exhibitions, art galleries, theatres, music or even novels – I saw no evidence that he could read. If asked if he had money enough while Anthony's affairs were settled, he always said that he had plenty and that there were many things to sell if he ran low – whether these things were stock accumulated in his Armour and Winston days, Eric Hebborn's forgeries or Anthony's few paintings and drawings, he did not let slip. Dick Spalding and I did our best for him until, late in 1987, he decided to leave London for Dundee to be near the remnants of his family – a great relief to us both, weary as we were of the relentlessly self-pitying and reproachful daily telephone calls and, worse, encounters in the now utterly depressing flat in Portsea Hall; he told neither of us of his intention and it was only from the abeyance of abuse, recrimination and reproach that we realised that he had severed what little was left of the relationship. There were months of silence until the telephone calls began again, still peevish, morose and even hostile – Scotland, it seemed, he hated as much as London; Dick too he treated to the same long calls and we compared notes. One humid evening in July 1988, after a particularly long and vituperative conversation in which, yet again, he threatened suicide unless I, in London, came promptly to Dundee to prevent it, I lost patience and told him to get on with it. Conscience-stricken, I called Dick, only to find that he had done much the same and we commiserated with each other. Three days later John rose early from his bed, dressed, walked to the railway line along the north bank of the Firth of Tay, on which there is at least one level crossing every mile, and stood in front of a train. I was told that there was very little of him to retrieve.

*   *   *

I refused to be interviewed by Miranda Carter for her book on Anthony. My grounds were that she was too young to know anything of the political atmosphere in England in the 1930s and the pan-European poverty that followed the Great Depression; what could she know, other than at second hand, of brutal Russian Communism then, of Fascism, Nazism and the Iron Guard, of the Spanish Civil War and the creeping aggrandisement of Germany? I thought too that as a woman she could know nothing of the compelling force of male homosexuality and might care nothing for the predicament that then obtained, the activity, even the mildest approach to it, illegal, society's cruelly punitive responses scandal, prison and disgrace. This was to be her first book – I knew of her only as a journalist, and I had had a bellyfull of those.

I was to regret the decision, for I could have remedied the small handful of minor points that are in error and her five hundred pages will probably remain in perpetuity those to which future historians must refer. I do not come out of it well, but then those who poured poison into her ear were neither present at the time nor picking up the pieces afterwards. With an amused contempt for homosexuals and knowing nothing of art history, Miss Carter conjured perfectly the sense of drift in Anthony's life at Cambridge as post-graduate and don, his intellectual brilliance evident but without particular focus, his career heading nowhere in the mid Thirties until he came under the influence of Fritz Saxl and Rudi Wittkower at the Warburg Institute. Aby Warburg had, in Germany, widened the boundaries of art history to embrace all cultural enquiries that might illuminate its mysteries; his largely Jewish staff, brilliant scholars all, had recently fled the Nazis and brought his extraordinary library to London, and it was as their pupil and employee that Blunt grasped the essentials of art history as a rigorous academic discipline. As with many of his pupils at the Courtauld Institute, of which he was appointed Director in 1946, art history became his life and purpose, his conversion swift, certain and irrevocable as he metamorphosed into the Ignatius Loyola of art history in Britain; within five years of his appointment he had turned the Institute from a finishing school for witless girls into a seminary with a worldwide reputation.

The pity is that his political life was not subject to such a transformation. In this too he drifted, uncertain, influenced by friends and lovers until, trapped by affections and unwise private loyalties, he became a Communist spy of sorts. It is difficult to believe that he enjoyed the dangers and absurdities of this as an intellectual game, or that so intelligent a man could not see that, compelled to depend on obviously unreliable friends, he was sowing the seeds of his own destruction. At heart he had no politics and never voted in any general election; he was touched by Britain's evident poverty in the Thirties, touched by the tragedies of the Spanish Civil War, touched by the inevitability of conflict with Germany, but it is to be doubted that he had any profound interest in the political reasons or remedies for any of them. How then could so scrupulously scholarly a man, so dry, precise, considered and unemotional in everything he wrote of art and architecture, be such a fool as to put his scholarship at risk for a political philosophy in which he had virtually no belief? And to this the answer is Guy Burgess, with whom he perhaps never went to bed, but who won from him undying loyalty – Burgess, at first handsome, charming, witty and homosexually amoral, at last a scruffy drunken slob with the halitosis of a dragon. The obvious question to ask is why was Guy a Communist? Had he not been, nor would Anthony.

Perhaps the conclusion to draw is that had Anthony first dis-covered the pleasurable disciplines of art history, he would never have enmeshed himself in the doubtful loyalties of Communism.

CHAPTER 9

The Aftermath of the Affair

Of the Blunt Affair there were many unexpected consequences, some trivial, some not. The gaggle of reporters at my gate remained until Christmas, half convinced that Anthony was somewhere in the house, keeping a twenty-four-hour watch; the very last of them, no more than a boy not clad for winter, late on a bitter night I hauled into my kitchen, fried eggs and bacon for him, walked him round the house to prove that Anthony was not there, made him telephone his editor and packed him off to Gloucester Road before the last train to the far East End sped through. Elsie Crombie, wife of Theodore Crombie, long-serving critic with *Apollo*, art historian and expert on Spanish art, took to telephoning every day, always ending with 'now let's give MI5 something worth hearing', at which she launched into extraordinary sexual fantasies, reinforcing my notion that elderly women are far more sexually unbuttoned than old men. She it was who, bored by Royal Academy Summer Exhibition Dinners, once took with her a tape recorder and a tape of farts compiled and sold by *Private Eye*, bribed a waiter to set it off under a table and sat back to enjoy the general discomfiture. Another *Private Eye* commercial venture, the Willy Warmer, she bought in quantity and gave to male guests at a dinner party according to imagined size, insulting some and pleasing others. Another old dame, one I did not know, invited me to a weekend in the country at the behest, she informed me, of Princess Margaret; not even Stephen Sondheim foresaw all the miseries possible in such a purgatorial occasion. The Princess arrived an hour before midnight for a ruined dinner scheduled for eight; by then the servants hired from the village had gone home to bed and the rest of us, some half dozen, absolutely plastered, had to buckle-to, carry and carve the baked meats of sacrifice; she then kept us up until four in the morning, kippering us with her cigarettes. Long after the crack of dawn, with not a sniff of coffee nor sign of a servant in the kitchen to clear the mess left from the night, I wandered into the village, called a friend and arranged for a late morning death-and-doomsday telephone message requiring my immediate return home. And a young woman with a Mini-Moke (the tiny Meccano-like jeep version of the Mini) and bristling with pubic hair (as I was to discover on the first day of 1980 warm enough for her to wear very brief crotch-clenching shorts) became my stalker.

The first disturbing incident was what seemed a determined effort by the police to connect me with the forgery of a major painting by a then forgotten leader of the School of Paris in the Fifties. Friedrich von Artus had sent it to me to sell in a London saleroom as no one in Germany cared tuppence for post-war French painting, and I had sent it to Bonham's, the only firm able to sell it before the end of the year. No one had any reason to suspect that it was not genuine; it was certainly of its supposed period (there is no convincing means of falsely ageing the reverse of a canvas with heavy jute content – only time does that), but as, after the sale, the painter himself declared it false, the sale had to be cancelled. The painter demanded a police enquiry. When two hefty detectives came unannounced to my house one evening, gave me the impression that they were members of Special Branch and drank my whisky, I felt it necessary to protect not only myself but Friedrich and Anthony, for I divined that they were fishing only because they hoped that Anthony, whose reputation had been menacingly smirched by association with Eric Hebborn (notorious forger, emotional seducer), might be involved. For the first time since the Affair began in September, I was scared – scared that I should unwittingly be the agent of some further erosion of his reputation. I lied, but the lie was so preposterous a dead end that the investigation withered and came to nothing.

The second incident took place in Kensington Gardens, early on a Saturday morning when the otherwise daily dog-walkers were few and the cyclists fewer. Apart from a distant figure at an angle to my right, I was alone, yet in all those acres he chose a path and walked it at such a pace that we must inevitably meet, and when we did he said, barely breaking his stride, 'I thought you should know that MI6 is still watching you' – and walked on. If a joke, it required planning according to precise knowledge of my dog-walking habit and perfect timing; if not a joke, what was the purpose? I had ceased to care that my telephone was being monitored (as journalists at the *Sunday Times* insisted), and had learned that my face was so widely familiar that I could not buy a loaf of bread in Harrods without winsome recognition by the boy behind the counter. Indeed, Harrods had to stop being a haunt for casual sodomy in the third floor lavatories, where it was from a Harrods boy in the men's department that I learned the trick of camouflaging the feet of the recipient in carrier bags so that any suspicious guardian of morals glancing under the door would see only the feet of a heavily-laden customer.

After being reported in a gossip column as 'Blunt's little friend lunching at The Ivy' (I had been making an insurance inventory of the beastly pictures there – for which my bill was not paid: they suggested that I 'eat it down', as David Hockney did at Odin's when Peter Langan bought a painting, but, in the event, there was never a table when I needed one), I had also to realise that whatever I did, no matter how innocent, might be used as a peg on which could be hung some snide anti-Anthony jibe and yet again the accusations 'spy' and 'traitor'. To risk a sexual folly would be particularly silly. 'What on earth can I do?' I asked Michael, my expert on outbreaks of syphilis among Russian sailors in Murmansk. 'Nothing here,' he said, 'and when abstinence becomes insupportable, go to the baths in Amsterdam.'

For the few years before AIDS became an ever-present threat, those baths were a constant of every European trip; whenever I did my duty earning a fee or seeing a major exhibition in Paris,

The author in 1967 – at the beginning of the book. *Below*: Claudio Corvaya in 1967

My mother in 1972,
the year in which we
both moved to
19 Eldon Road in
Kensington (facing)
with its vast studio
(below)

Top: Mentmore Towers with the marquees of Sotheby's sale, May 1977
Below: Eliot Hodgkin: *Mrs Riley's Milkweed*

The painting attributed to Georges de la Tour hanging in Paul Botte's kitchen in October 1958

Below: Henry Sutch (*left*) and Bill Martin (*right*) in the Big Room at Christie's

Rüdiger Joppien, Hampstead, 1971

Below: Joe McCrindle

Zoffany, Charles Macklin in *The Merchant of Venice. Below left*: De Wilde, Thomas Collins in *The Merry Wives of Windsor. Below right*: De Wilde, Maria Theresa Bland, Ursula Booth and John Bannister in *The Children in the Wood*

Anthony Blunt in Italy after his exposure
Below: Anthony Blunt shortly before his exposure

Antoine, Count Seilern, in the Sixties (passport photograph)

Below: Johannes Wilde in his Dulwich garden

Anthony d'Offay 9 and 23 Dering Street New Bond Street London W1 01-499 4695

3rd June, 1982

Terry Murphy Esq
175 Junction Road
London N19

RENOIR   Head of a girl   (sanguine)

Received from Anthony d'Offay Ltd the sum of
£20,000 (twenty thousand pounds) in cash

Terry Murphy

VSH 1696

Anthony d'Offay 9 and 23 Dering Street New Bond Street London W1 01-499 4695

23rd August, 1982

C B Turner Esq
137c St George's Road
Lambeth
London SE1

and

Terry Murphy Esq
178 Junction Road
London N19

PURCHASE NOTE

Lawrence ATKINSON   Abstract Composition

£6,000

Acting on instructions of Mr Norman Dunne

I confirm that I am the vendor
of the above at the price shown
signed:

26-37

I confirm that I am the buyer
of the above at the price shown
signed:

—- be claimed by me in

30-13-74

Hill Samuel & Co

23 August 1982

Pay M.J. Murphy

£ 6000

or Order

ANTHONY D'OFFAY LTD

Andy Warhol, the photograph a gift

Below: David Hockney: Peter Langan, October 1969. Peter is in the kitchen of the original Odin's. His Löwenbrau, always drunk from a large brandy glass, stands in the right foreground

Above: Jill Allibone

Mary Debane in a wild moment in
Hyde Park

Above: Martin Shortis: the open plan office of the *Evening Standard*, 1990, the news desk in the foreground (*detail*)

Michael Leonard: portrait of the author as he might have looked as a Grand Tourist – one of the title shots later used in the television programme *Grand Tour*

Above: Fifty miles from Santiago de Compostela on what should have been the final stage of the pilgrimage

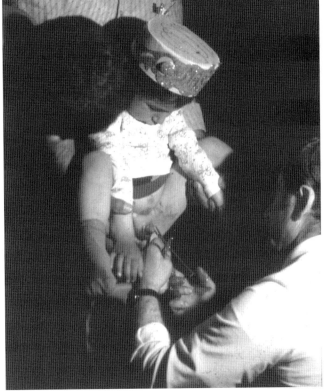

Circumcision in the wilds of Cappadocia

The author now, photographed by Zsuzsi Roboz shortly before her death in 2012

Frankfurt or Cologne, I then drove to Amsterdam, booked into a sleazy cheap hotel and took off for the nearby baths where one could spend both day and night, breaking off only for food and a few hours sleep, and continue the regime until sated. Oh to be in an orgy room again, inhibitions abandoned until all passion spent.

On a perhaps more serious note, the *Sunday Times* drew me into its web of further enquiry, but this was of some benefit to Anthony in that its investigative journalists Colin Simpson, Barrie Penrose and Simon Freeman, were all convinced that I knew much more than I did and, in betraying their confidences to Anthony, I was able to keep him informed of the directions of their research. These I could occasionally divert or even stall, steering them away from him and others. It also meant that I learned a great deal about Philby, Burgess and Maclean, Goronwy Rees and others – indeed, many others, for some of Anthony's old friends burdened me with names and notions, and retired officers of MI5 and MI6 fed me with information as well as lunch and dinner. With these it was difficult to tell whether they were confessing their own parts in various early aspects of Anthony's life, or ingeniously debriefing me to see if I knew anything that they did not – or so I thought until one of them gave me a bundle of ancient and faint carbon copies of what were obviously official reports written between 1930 and 1950 on worthies both Fascist and Communist suspected of sympathies, disloyalty or espionage. Many of their names I knew and I was left wondering how such institutions as the British Museum, the Victoria and Albert and London University could have been such hotbeds of political perfidy; some were still alive, some had family, some had overlapped with Anthony. I considered burning the parcel but instead lodged it with a much younger friend abroad, with instructions to send it to the British Library on my death; it may by then have some residual historic interest without doing harm to anyone.

Far the most important personal consequence of the Blunt Affair for me was the withdrawal of my American visa. By the end of

January 1980 I had received calls or letters from most of my American museum contacts suggesting that I should withdraw from my work as errand-boy, at least until the ballyhoo had died away; most blamed the prejudice of trustees and donors and the certain loss of funds and other patronage if my advice or activity was involved in any acquisition. I still had, however, a handful of significant American private collectors who had been sympathetic during the Affair, of whom some, including Joe McCrindle, were themselves the trustees of museums and well able to explain how things worked in their exalted circles – but these too, with the exception of Joe, I lost when, without a visa, I could no longer travel to New York and Washington. When my passport expired in 1983 I applied for a new visa; it was refused – but I had almost ceased to care, for by then it would have been difficult to revive my working contacts with museums as though there had been no hiatus, for curators die, retire or rise to greater galleries, and in many cases I knew that other dogsbodies had taken on my duties, and these I could not, with a clear conscience, seek to unseat; I had, moreover, begun to earn a frugal living as a scribbler.

That this was so was due entirely to Tina Brown, wife of Harold Evans, then editor of the *Sunday Times*. Early in January 1980 she, as fresh young editor compelling resurrection on the moribund *Tatler*, asked me to do a particularly Tatlerish thing – to give, at the magazine's expense, lunch to a dozen friends in my favourite restaurant, with a *Tatler* journalist recording our conversation. I had no favourite fashionable restaurant, nor had I fashionable friends, and in that grim winter, I learned that my professional friends were, at least for the time being, strongly inclined to shy away from me. I refused – but my note of refusal amused her enough to suggest that I might instead become *Tatler*'s art critic at £100 for a thousand words ten times a year. That this post as a critic was a contemptibly small acorn was made obvious at my first press view of an exhibition. This was at the old Tate Gallery (now Tate Britain) and was the Dali retrospective of May-

June 1980; with neither press card nor official invitation, I was not exactly welcomed and, though grudgingly admitted, the expensive catalogue normally given gratis to critics was refused on the grounds that *Tatler* was not an established journal. As well as with the milling mass of people whom I took to be critics (they were, and still are, only the Uncle Tom Cobleighs of the press), the gallery was crowded with radio and television crews and it was more difficult to see the exhibits than on a day when open to the public. I thought how odd it was to be almost certainly the only man in this assembly of hundreds who had hobnobbed with Dali himself over a period of years, and yet be an outsider. Only one man spoke to me – Angus Stewart who, though a man of magnificently Bohemian presence and later President of AICA (a useless international body of art critics incapable of criticism), seemed then to share my insignificance. To my chagrin, *Tatler* captioned my comments with the phrase 'blunt views on fine art'. There was no B for Blunt, but I thought the pun diminished me and for the first and only time in my life resented Anthony's shadow.

I remained *Tatler*'s art critic until June 1990, still then at £100 a column, but that mattered less than loyalty based on gratitude to the magazine that had given me my first toehold in the field. Tina Brown moved on to far higher things and Libby Purves, the most amiable of broadcasters on BBC radio, arrived in March 1983; she, however, was so scorned by all the pretty girls in *Tatler*'s offices that I took her to lunch at the nearby Westbury (where she insisted on nothing more than a tiny sandwich with which to toy), betrayed the treacherous doxies on whom she depended, and urged her – for *Tatler*'s sake, either to sack them or herself resign. The problem was that Libby, an ample frump, was in her way as wholly unsuitable to be the editor of a journal dedicated to celebrities and fashion, as I was as its art critic. I was not much thanked for what I said (and we have since not exchanged one single word), but in October, after only half-a-dozen issues, she departed and the office reverted to the gossipy frivolity that was *Tatler*'s *raison d'être*.

She was succeeded by Mark Boxer who made life more than a little difficult for me, almost forcing my resignation, but in 1983 work as a writer, mostly for short-lived or moribund art magazines, was very much hand-to-mouth and so poorly paid (largely at the rate of £30 for a thousand words) that I could not afford to surrender my steady £1,000 a year from *Tatler*. Unlike Tina Brown, who had asked of me only informed comment on the most important exhibition of the month, Mark wanted a more tittle-tattle approach with the focus on curators and directors and the artists themselves if still alive; when I did not give him what he wanted — gossip about the wretched speculative art dealers who attempted to turn Portobello Road into a hotbed of contemporary art, or flattering nonsense about artists with whom he had some acquaintance — he spiked (that is, rejected) my copy. I could have resigned; he could have sacked me and would have been perfectly right to do so. That he did not, I thought and think so still, lay some twenty years in our past, in 1963 or so when, as the creator and first editor of the first colour supplement to any British news-paper, the *Sunday Times*, he chose to publish the first of many behind-the-scenes articles on Christie's. As one of the experts there on paintings by old masters, then the most dramatic and important sector of the art market, I was appointed his guide. Tall and wonderfully beautiful, he did not rebuff the pass I made and amused dalliance may be the proper description for what followed, for he was of that not uncommon category of heterosexual men for whom experience with another man is, on his part, merely sexual, not homosexual, particularly if he does little more than let it happen. With his announcement that he was married and 'this must stop', stop it did. Even among the hundreds of sexual encounters that I had experienced, I had not forgotten ours; nor had he forgotten what may well have been a rare or even single adventure for so uxorious a man. Across his desk at *Tatler* neither of us uttered a hint of it, but the awkwardness of our first professional encounter was palpable, the *de-haut-en-bas* of it on his part calculatedly cold. I remembered; he remembered; it made him deeply uncomfortable and he wished me out. I did not go. After some sparring we established a *modus vivendi* that involved our never meeting and he left me in control of my reviews. On Mark's death in 1988 he was succeeded by Emma Soames who knew everyone ever likely to appear in *Tatler's* pages but was, as editor, an unloved termagant; overheard to remark that I thought her as sexually attractive as a saucepan of boiled socks, it was at last time for me to leave.

The *Sunday Times* I had deserted long before. Colin Simpson, its senior investigative journalist, was obsessed by the art market and, convinced that it was a nest of vipers (he was not mistaken), had in the mid Sixties exposed the 'Ring' – the mechanism that enabled a loose consortium of dealers to buy a work of art cheaply at auction (simply by not bidding against each other and, occasionally, by threat) and then auctioning it among themselves, one of them left in possession of it at a far higher price, the others all making money without the risk of ownership. Simpson then moved on to forgery, believing it to be rampant in the trade, even at its highest levels. In 1980 he lit upon a painting bought twenty years before from Wildenstein by the Metropolitan Museum, New York, *The Fortune Teller*, attributed to Georges de la Tour, a rare and enthralling seventeenth-century painter whose chronology and authenticity were in utter confusion and dispute (and are so still). Wildenstein was then and had long been the most formidable of French dealers and the painting, if genuine, should never have left France; that it had, suggested to Simpson that it must be a forgery and in this he was supported by Christopher Wright, a diligent young art historian who had contributed substantially to an authoritative monograph in 1974.* I had seen either it or an identical picture in September 1958, in the possession of a small and private Parisian dealer, Paul Botte, and had thought it not by La Tour but by an imitator, a

---

* Benedict Nicolson and Christopher Wright, *Georges de la Tour*, Phaidon 1974.

pasticheur, even a modern forger and, when consulted by Simpson, had told him so. I wish that I had not, partly because it brought me into conflict with Michael Kitson, whom I venerated as my tutor and who had been loyal to Anthony throughout the Affair and its immediate consequences, and partly because as it was a painting on which Anthony had commented at length as genuine,* there would inevitably be an accusation from some ill-informed source that he had been involved in passing it off – *Private Eye* on 7 November 1980 published *Fake's Progress* with a photograph of Anthony. Of two television programmes, one, American, was merely scandalous, the other, earnestly one-sided on the BBC, failed to prove the painting's authenticity; and Simpson's reports in the *Sunday Times*, as earnestly other-sided, could not conclusively prove it a forgery.

My problem was one of connoisseurship; no matter what the documentation suddenly produced, I simply could not make *The Fortune Teller* fit comfortably with what was known for certain (or even uncertainly) of La Tour's chronology and stylistic development. It is like, yet at the same time disturbingly unlike the other paintings with which it must be grouped; the so-called signature, ridiculously elaborate and prominent, is not a signature but an inscription (but when was it added?); and the scientific evidence provided by John Brealey (Anthony's adviser on how to clean a Poussin and by then working for the Metropolitan Museum) was selective, almost disingenuous. Stephen Rees-Jones, my sometime Professor of Technology at the Courtauld Institute, with whom I discussed Brealey's evidence in October 1980, observed that it was neither impartial nor reassuring and, when the controversy had rumbled on for a year, wrote to *The Times* in February 1982, confirming this view, criticising particularly the Metropolitan Museum's reliance on questionable tests of lead isotopes and

---

* Anthony Blunt, 'Georges de la Tour at the Orangerie', *Burlington Magazine*, August 1972, pp. 516–26.

linseed oil. My contribution was to argue that these isotopes give different readings according to the place of origin of the lead, and that only if the lead in *The Fortune Teller* and in La Tour's authentic paintings could be proved to have come from Lorraine or the Vosges, within carting distance of La Tour's workplace, could the dissenters be almost certainly mistaken. I still think this so, but in June 1982 a long (private) letter from Michael Kitson accused me of 'disingenuous twaddle', but ended with the conciliatory note that he would 'admit the possibility (though no more than that) that the picture, together with the two versions of *The Cheat*, is not by La Tour but by a clever pupil . . . ' Anthony had earlier (op. cit.) said, 'They do not fit anywhere in the main development . . . ' and, 'Generally speaking the borderline between originals and copies is quite clear, but in one or two cases some doubts may arise.'

Simpson was bold enough to go straight to Wildenstein and in spite of their Byzantine grandeur, cunning and reserve, they were at first sufficiently off-guard to reveal the name of their chief restorer for many years, long retired to Corsica and probably dead; at the mention of Paul Botte's painting they admitted to knowing of it – a copy, they said, one of several, and brought the interview to a close. If they knew of several copies of a painting wholly unknown until discovered during World War II, why did they not disclose this when selling the 'original'? The restorer, Emile Delobre, the favourite pupil of Gustave Moreau, was born in 1873, and is recorded as primarily a painter of copies after old masters, often of astonishing quality, worked for Wildenstein from 1910 until 1944 and, we were to discover, occasionally until his death in 1957. That he was dead was, to Simpson, of no account – his nephew, Albert Dion-Delobre, succeeded him at Wildenstein's and he too had retired to Corsica. Thither we flew on a small plane from Nice, by night and in a thunderstorm; not far short of the island the plane was struck by lightning and the left engine set on fire. Warned that we might be ditched, I took off my shoes and clothes. 'What the hell are you doing?' asked the man in the next seat (not Simpson), 'Getting ready for a long swim,' my reply. We were then told that we would reach the airport but, as the plane might burst into flames when we landed, we must descend the emergency chutes as swiftly as possible. We did, but into pelting rain, and clutching my bundle of clothes I sprinted barefoot to the terminal. Within ten minutes I was dry and dressed, but no one in authority would believe that I had been on the flight and I was put in custody for a couple of hours.

Albert Dion-Delobre told us that his uncle had painted *The Fortune Teller*, that the young man in it was Henri, Albert's son, and that he, Albert, had lightly cleaned the painting in 1958 in Wildenstein's premises in New York, that he had lightly retouched the paint surrounding the inscription to lend it greater strength, and that within the lace shawl of the gypsy pickpocket he had incorporated the word '*merde*' in capital letters so that he could shrug off any accusation of forgery, adding the extraordinary sentence: 'Unlike De Hory and Legros, we are not members of the gay freemasonry and have no one to protect us.' By chance, De Hory and Legros were to be the subject of an immediately following investigation, though not prompted by Dion-Delobre, who also told us that the canvas had been relined in New York by Loewy (a specialist firm) so that the original canvas was concealed. Was any scrap of this information true? Patrick O'Connor, an Irish painter, restorer, dealer and disgraced but amiable rogue, working in America, claimed to have seen Dion painting *The Fortune Teller* as a joke – but Patrick would board any bandwagon to revive his notoriety. Brealey promptly removed the *merde*, new paint between two coats of varnish, he told me – but this supported Dion-Delobre's account. Without a visa I could not go to New York and ask to see the technical evidence of the two layers of canvas and their age, nor see X-rays that might reveal changes in the composition, nor look scientifically at other evidence; those who could have gone, did not. Informed opinion ranged from the 'It is gloriously right', of John Brealey, to Christopher Wright's 'It is a squalid modern forgery', and there I think it stands, the dissenters in the minority. John Pope-Hennessy, high English panjandrum at the Metropolitan, damned all who questioned *The Fortune Teller* as upstarts and jackanapes and yet, simultaneously, in his *Study and Criticism of Italian Sculpture*, made a plea for connoisseurship – ' . . . art history is a looser, more speculative science than some of its practitioners suppose, and the technique of connoisseurship must be inculcated and encouraged if art history is significantly to advance.' Hear, Hear: connoisseurship had been, above all, the premise of my misgivings in the case of the La Tour.

On the return journey, we flew to Nice to spend the night in a squalid back street hotel called the Ritz, where every man's fart was audible. Colin paid rather more than the sum required and in return was given a handsomely engraved receipt for ten times the figure. On the flight to London he passed me a sheet of paper – 'These are the expenses you will claim from the paper.' As they bore no resemblance to reality and I was attached to the *Sunday Times* by no more than a thread, I demurred. 'Don't rock the boat,' he said. 'You'll spoil it for the rest of us. No one passes through Nice without spending a fortune at the Ritz.' As Colin had paid all the bills, I gained a cool £347.65 in addition to the much smaller writer's fee that I was later paid.

*   *   *

'Unlike de Hory and Legros, we are not members of the gay freemasonry and have no one to protect us,' Dion-Delobre had said; both were quite certainly queer and both may well have gained what advantage they could from it, but I doubt if they were as 'protected' as the Irish, Jewish, Armenian and Hungarian Mafias about which we occasionally dare to joke – indeed, I am inclined to say that their homosexuality made them vulnerable to the most dangerous exploitation by heterosexual rogues capable of murder. Elmyr de Hory, Hungarian by birth, Parisian by choice, a notorious pasticheur of Modigliani, Matisse and the Impressionists, 'the greatest art forger of our time' (a claim made for every briefly successful crook in the field), 'famous and legendary', had at seventy died in mysterious circumstances in 1976. Fernand Legros, some twenty-five years younger, his parents French, his birthplace Egypt, his passport eventually American, his base as an art dealer Paris, long Elmyr's Spalanzano or Svengali, had died in 1980 from throat cancer – from which no freemasonry or mafia could have protected him. I had known Legros in the early Sixties when he frequently dropped in on Christie's with a taxi full of paintings, straight from Heathrow, so immaculately dressed that he could not, himself, unload them, but required assistance from the commissionaire and all the staff of the reception desk. Among unimportant but good pictures by Daubigny, Harpignies and their ilk, worth Christie's while to sell but of small value, were always a couple by such second rank more modern painters as Derain, Vlaminck or Van Dongen, borrowing their honesty; these had diplomatically to be refused. It was a simple ruse, this genuineness of the true colouring reaction to the false, and when he by-passed me and asked straight for the chairman, it worked; it must have worked in other auction houses too. How these rogues came together, duped so many would-be connoisseurs, fell out and became the subjects of international police enquiry, is a tale first incoherently told in a wretched novelettish book by the American novelist Clifford Irving in 1970 when both subjects were still alive, later dissemblingly revised and brought up-to-date by one Kenrick Talbot* promoting himself as de Hory's kindly guardian and protector from himself.

De Hory's notoriety was enough for him to be much interviewed by newspapers and magazines, for Orson Welles to make a film of his life, *Question Mark*, and on his death (was it murder, was it suicide?) for the art market to show serious interest in his paintings. By then, scared by close shaves with the police, he had

---

* Kenrick Talbot, *Enigma!*, 1991.

become the genuine pasticheur rather than the forger, all his canvases flamboyantly inscribed on the reverse to assure buyers that they were the inventions of Elmyr himself and the police that there was no intention to pass them on as Fauve or Post-Impressionist. Christie's, at their secondary rooms in Kensington, had a remarkably successful auction, emptying the studio we were to understand; but how could it have been emptied when, for a year or two, so many more paintings followed in theirs and other London salerooms? Early in 1982, intrigued by the conviction that the forger was himself now being forged, I suggested to Colin Simpson that we might investigate, but he thought my notion too improbable and the sums of money involved (a few hundred pounds for each canvas, only) far too small. In April 1983, however, Simon Freeman, another investigative journalist attached to the *Sunday Times*, saw an advertisement in the *International Herald Tribune* offering for sale paintings by de Hory. I went to see the advertiser at his home near Regent's Park; he was Kenrick Talbot, claiming to have befriended de Hory from 1969 until his death, and to have bought some four thousand of his paintings in these seven years; some were hanging, many more were stacked in an upper room; a few were in oil paint, but most were in acrylic, a medium that de Hory loathed; and the canvases were all of Imperial measurements, not metric. Our guarded conversation was interrupted by the arrival of a gold Ford Cortina laden with many more – hastily dismissed, but not before I had noted its registration number. I left, convinced that all were forgeries and that I had seen the forger.

It was the beginning of a long and, at times, tedious pursuit with many ramifications, of which, in August 1983, I made a fourteen-page statement to the Fine Art Squad at Scotland Yard, depositing with them all my supporting evidence, never returned. It led first to Colin Turner – he of the car full of de Horys; he worked for Roberson's, a firm of artists' suppliers in Camden Town, had some pretty foul things to say of Kenrick Talbot and claimed that he was involved in de Hory's murder. From Turner it led to Mark Lewis, a tough little cockney living in Leytonstone, who claimed to be the illegitimate grandson of Wyndham Lewis and inheritor of a large number of his paintings and drawings that, for some time, he had been feeding onto the London art market; and to Dick Emmett, also in Leytonstone, a sweaty little tyke of sixty or so, who claimed to have bought paintings by Modigliani, Van Gogh, Renoir, Braque and others of the ilk from Talbot, their having been vetted by experts at Christie's, whom Talbot 'had in his pocket'. These daubs were appalling; they entirely lacked the occasional insight and sympathy that redeemed some of de Hory's pastiches and excused the innocents who bought them, and were instead brutally unintelligent in invention and inept in the handling of paint, the Cubist Braque an insult to both the painter and any viewer accustomed to looking at paintings of any period or mannerism. As for Mark Lewis's descent from the loins of the great Wyndham, this could only have been possible through random conjugation with a slut – far from improbable for a man who seemed to need a fiercely active but emotionally detached sex life, once so urgently that he fucked his landlady's daughter on the floor immediately within the front door of her house, only to be interrupted by the postman pushing letters through the letterbox to fall on his bared bum; that he would reward so casual a lover with a cache of drawings and paintings is, however, improbable, for none of his many known lovers and mistresses drawn from the artistic and intellectual circles in which he moved ever proved to be a source of lost or forgotten work.

In the course of several interviews Emmett involved not only Christie's but Sotheby's, Colnaghi's and the Courtauld Institute – all of whom he said had vouched for his wretched paintings; Colin Turner had restored them, he claimed, and had introduced him to Talbot. He modified his story so that his purchase of paintings was from Mark Lewis, introduced by Talbot, and his confusions and contradictions were so many that I concluded that nothing could be believed; the last straw was to be told that the paintings came from the collection of an old lady living in Winterton-on-Sea who happened to be Lewis's mother. Lewis, far the cleverer, maintained his simple story of descent. Both men, sensing danger in the enquiry, sought to divert my concentration; I was directed to Terry Murphy, a dealer in 'antiques' in the unlikely purlieus of Junction Road, Holloway, to an East End garage owner, George Clark, who owned some of Talbot's de Horys, thinking that he had invested in genuine paintings by Matisse et al, and to another garagiste, financially involved (but with whom I did not discover) who was, for a few days, physically the most frightening man I ever encountered; he was, however, supplanted by a demolition contractor in Bethnal Green who consented to a meeting in the open on a street corner of Cambridge Heath Road and threatened interment in the contents of his skips if I ever divulged his name. With such a Hercules this Antaeus could not compete.

For these rogues there was some compensation in Louis William Koolman-Darnley, of Rochester Terrace, Camden Town (now perhaps a good address but then a pretty slum), posing as a gentleman fallen on hard times, desperate to sell to Anthony d'Offay, the leading dealer in the field, his collection of works by Vorticists, Bloomsbury painters and toilers in the Omega Workshops. He was a garrulous old thing, a former music hall entertainer whose act had been a ballet of fountain jets that danced to coloured lights and the music of Swan Lake and the Sugar Plum Fairy. Never the top of the bill, this had not survived the war and he had then become 'an artist', and it was as an artist that he had first encountered Colin Turner at Roberson's. After a traffic accident in which his head and leg were injured, he had attempted to sue for loss of earnings; for this Turner, using Roberson's headed paper, had offered proof with letters withdrawing a non-existent contract for decorative paintings that, because of the injuries, could not be produced in time. With this deceit Koolman-Darnley was indebted to Turner and drawn into his plot.

Louis – I saw so much of him that we had to drop formality –

was to lend his name and person to a collection acquired in the Thirties, largely in exchange for cash and loans to other music-hall entertainers; these paintings, drawings and sculptures he kept in a wooden trunk, never opened, and having forgotten what it might contain, and at seventy-nine too frail to lift the lid, he had asked Turner to help. Turner had recognised many fine things and had turned immediately to d'Offay who, between the Augusts of 1981 and 1982, bought the following:

> *Henri Gaudier-Brzeska: an album of 68 drawings. £25,000, 28*
> *August 1981*
> *Jacob Epstein: an album of 56 drawings. £27,000,*
> *30 October 1981*
> *Ilya Gregorovich Tchachnik: Composition 1924. £12,000,*
> *20 May 1982*
> *An Omega Screen: £8,000, 22 July 1982*

At much the same time d'Offay bought from Terry Murphy and Colin Turner acting on behalf of Koolman-Darnley:

> *Lawrence Atkinson: Abstract Composition. £6,000,*
> *23 August 1982*

and on their own account, independent of Koolman-Darnley:

> *Wyndham Lewis: a book of drawings. £11,000, 4 March 1982*

From Terry Murphy alone, he bought:

> *Renoir: Head of a Little Girl (red chalk). £20,000, 3 June 1982*

These are the completed transactions of which I have indisputable records; there may well have been others; certainly others were contemplated, and of some of these too I have records.

Very little of this money, some £5,500 only, reached Louis. Cheques for cash and cheques in his name were countersigned by Turner and diverted.

Had d'Offay had the sense, at the beginning of the negotiation with Turner, who in appearance, manner and speech was hardly a convincing emissary for a distinguished old gentleman with a great collection, to visit the old gentleman himself (for the very first Purchase Note makes it clear that Turner made no attempt to conceal him), he would have found Louis' bell to be one of half-a-dozen at the door, and the name-tag 'Louis William Koolman-Darnley, Artist' to have been indelibly embellished, in an un-educated hand, with a capital F – presumably expressing the esteem in which his neighbours held him. The improbability of finding treasure-trove in such a house was manifest, but it was not until early in September 1982 that d'Offay began to have misgivings; then he invited Louis to dinner at the Garrick and asked him to come to the gallery in Dering Street and comment on the things said to have come from his collection. He recognised none.

It was at this point that Louis discovered the extent to which he had been gulled by Turner; suspicions six months earlier had led to his threatening Turner with a demand for cash within 'forty-eight hours; then I ring Dering Street. You should be ashamed of yourself to so abuse the use of my name'. Though then bought off with a paltry sum, suspicion rankled and after the Garrick dinner Louis began to confuse reality with the conviction that he really had had a collection, that there really was a wooden trunk crammed with masterpieces on rolled canvas, albums, artefacts and sculptures – and in truth he did own a wooden trunk, but one far too small to contain what Turner had told d'Offay was to be the next phase of their bargaining. D'Offay, still unwilling to admit to himself that he had been duped, encouraged Louis to turn to his eminent solicitors, Kingsley, Napley and Co. who, canny enough to recognise that Louis might not be able to pay their bill, passed him on to Payne, Hicks, Beach and Co., who listed the works in question and, in the High Court of Justice, Queen's Bench Division, before the Honourable Mr Justice McCullough, on 17 September 1982, required Colin Turner to reveal the whereabouts of the following works of art and by no means to dispose of them:

a: An abstract sculpture of a bird, attributed to Jacob Epstein, 3 feet by 2 by 1½ feet.

b: An oil painting, *Kermesse*, by Wyndham Lewis, 9 by 9 feet.

c: An oil painting, *Plan of War*, by Wyndham Lewis, 5 by 8 feet.

d: A portrait of *Ezra Pound*, by Wyndham Lewis, 6 by 9 feet.

e: A book of drawings by Wyndham Lewis.

f: A pastel drawing attributed to Degas, 2 by 2 feet.

Thus, to Louis, these inventions, these forgeries that he had never owned or seen, had become his property and he wanted their full value, not another poxy five and half thousand quid; the reality was that he had been paid that sum for, from a distance, never directly, fronting the sting that defrauded d'Offay, and had taken no risk until, absurdly, he had involved the law. From the measurements of the canvases and the weight of the would-be Epstein sculpture any clear-minded lawyer would have realised that the trunk from which they came must be of wholly improbable proportions and the whole business a farrago of nonsense. Later, in July 1983, Louis said that d'Offay had more or less compelled him to take to the law because he 'feared that Turner might sell the paintings, not to d'Offay, but to foreign buyers, and this would be a great cultural loss to the nation'.

The one benefit of taking this course was that the solicitors' Outdoor Clerk, Simon Knowles, was extremely diligent in his attempt to serve to Colin Turner a copy of the Order and as a consequence two new actors joined the cast, a Miss Lawrenson, said to be Turner's girlfriend, and George Weissbort, a painter living in West Hampstead, said to be restoring the paintings by Wyndham Lewis. But Mark Lewis had also been said to be restoring them, in Leytonstone, in a workshop under a railway arch, and with d'Offay's wife driving, Louis and an employee of the gallery known to him only as Marie-Louise, had made a frantic search of every railway arch they could find in what might be defined as Leytonstone, because d'Offay 'had the wind up'.

They found neither Lewis nor the paintings. Then they turned to George Weissbort, but could not find them there.

I grew to like George, born in Belgium in 1928, resident in London from 1933, and a thoroughly English painter in the best traditions of the New English Art Club – still lives, portraits, landscapes all gently observed, the soft style always consistent in its unobtrusive brushwork and discreet tone. Apart from an unfinished Renoir on his easel when I first went to his house in a seedy West Hampstead terrace, I saw nothing suspicious. Turner, he said, was always asking his opinion of photographs, but never brought the paintings, and the only work that he had ever done for him was to begin cleaning a screen covered in rough cloth primed in white, on which were painted nude male figures prancing and dancing, but this, before he could do anything much to it, Anthony d'Offay had taken away in a great hurry. Was this the Omega screen said to have come from Louis' box?

The High Court move made by Louis forced Turner to find a solicitor, and to him the story was that he, Turner, had acquired all these treasures years before and that, having no confidence in his own appearance, he had enlisted Louis' help as a front to provide these works of art with 'an acceptable provenance'. For this, Louis was to be paid a commission; at approximately five per cent of the sums so far involved, £5,500 was a not unreasonable percentage. Most of this, however, was wiped out by the fees he had to pay his solicitor.

Of all this there was no consequence. D'Offay wanted no publicity and the pathetic boobies of the Fine Art Squad at Scotland Yard utterly failed to understand what was at stake even when it had been demystified for them. The only excuse for their inaction was that the affair had as many suckers and side-shoots as a briar rose and that by leaving them be, even more art market crooks might be discovered, even more grandees might be involved.

On 25 May 1983 Sotheby's had for sale two drawings in black chalk, Lots 103 and 104, catalogued as by Frederick Etchells, a minor but original Vorticist, his surviving work very rare, the estimates £4,000 to £7,000; these I had thought poor in quality in terms of drawing and hopelessly incoherent in terms of Vorticism or Cubism (to which they seemed closer), but it had not occurred to me that they were fakes until they were withdrawn from the sale on the advice of Sotheby's restorer, brought in to effect some minor repairs, only to observe that the paper was much later in date than the 1913 of the identifying inscriptions. Sotheby's had consulted Ronald Alley, of the Modern Collection at the Tate Gallery, who thought them genuine, and had then given the woman who wished to sell them an advance of £5,000. The woman was later identified as the Miss Lawrenson living with Colin Turner. At much the same time Christie's announced a forthcoming sale entirely of Vorticist paintings, drawings and watercolours, to be held on 30 June 1983, but this was cancelled, possibly because Sotheby's had had the decency to inform them of the Etchells catastrophe.

Christie's were naturally unwilling to discuss the matter with anyone and, without information or explanation, no one could comment and, without gossip, no harm was done. Francis Farmar, however, then an expert there, agreed to talk to me and showed me what he could. His description of the vendor fitted Mark Lewis perfectly, and the address in Winterton-on-Sea tallied with Emmett's story that Lewis's mother lived there. Further, he told me that the first approach with the collection had been made to Christie's secondary saleroom in Kensington by a Mr Mason, moon-faced and sweating, with a complicated tale about their being security for a loan made to Lewis and his need to recover it. This was hardly significant, but it indicates that even after I had begun to ask awkward questions in April – perhaps because of them – they had shunted a huge consignment of forgeries onto the open market. Christie's too had consulted Ronald Alley and after his inspection he had proclaimed himself 'perfectly happy' with it; as the expert dealer in the field and likely to be among the heaviest buyers, Anthony d'Offay too had been invited to examine the consignment, but, quoting Francis Farmar, 'He said nothing, and I mean nothing.' Mason was, of course, Emmett.

I asked particularly to be shown a painting attributed to Cuthbert Hamilton, of whom I knew as an original Vorticist, but of whose work I had never seen an example other than a drawing in the Tate. Enormous, it was virtually a bolt of canvas, the painted surface rolled face inward – something that should never be done; the raw side of the canvas did not look the seventy years that it should and, slowly unrolled on the floor, its painted side resembled nothing to be expected of a Vorticist intelligence, the subject a seated woman conceived in black outline and flat planes of pink, yellow, brown and dark green, entirely on the surface with not the slightest hint of Vorticist depth; worse, it stank of fresh paint, not of oil paint but of Alkyd, a synthetic resin introduced only in 1976, new and bright and plastic. There was no trace of the insect life that abounds and multiplies inside rolled canvases, not a wisp of the spiders' webs that are so difficult to detach. Dirt proved to be water-based black paint washed on and then washed off, leaving pigment in the interstices of the canvas, still soluble in spit, the always available cleaning agent. If, when Christie's feels less pained by this failure of connoisseurship, a researcher wishes to pursue the case, the whole collection can be found under the Stock Number DP 309.

Looking back through my 'Fake File' – a haphazard record begun with the exposure of Han van Meegeren when I was still a schoolboy – a Sotheby catalogue of 10 June 1981 came to hand, in which I had noted that Lot 149, *A Dazzle Ship at Sea* by Edward Wadsworth, sold for £11,000, was a fake – 'inconceivable . . . a pastiche . . . utterly flat . . . borrowings reversed . . . ' I said nothing at the time, for I had been insultingly abused for my opinion when, the year before, in a sale at Christie's on 22 February 1980 (a time when, as a consequence of the Blunt affair, I was much insulted without reason or excuse and wondered if opprobrium would ever end), I had doubted the authenticity of Lot 80, a

Vorticist Composition attributed to Wadsworth, bought for £110,000 by Baron Thyssen. Both were in oil, the Thyssen picture said by Richard Cork (eximious expert!) to be unique in this; neither had a secure provenance – they had taradiddle enough to seem a provenance but nothing that withstood examination, and the immediate untraceability of both vendors was gravely suspicious. In retrospect, I concluded that both paintings, though not by the same hand, had come from the same Lewis, Turner, Talbot background and Mark Lewis was later to claim that it was his – but then he also claimed that it was genuine.

*   *   *

Now we must turn to Modigliani. Investigation had moved far beyond the mass forgery of paintings by de Hory, a matter of little aesthetic importance and small sums of money – though the total of those sums ran well into six figures. Probing had uncovered forgeries in quantity of works by Wyndham Lewis and some of his fellow Vorticists, by Gaudier-Brzeska, Nevinson, Wadsworth and the Omega Workshop, and to these must be added odd attempts to produce work by Braque, Degas, Renoir et al. Christie's, Sotheby's, experts at the Tate and, particularly, Anthony d'Offay (though there may well have been other art dealers too), had been misled. To give them their due, some at the Tate had, very early, expressed their misgiving, but been overruled, as in the case of drawings by Modigliani, an artist whose name had been raised at the very beginning of the enquiry when I thought that the de Hory fraud was central to it; as this proved not to be the case and Modigliani played no part in the Vorticist fraud, the whispers that there was, in addition, a Modigliani fraud, had been set aside and almost forgotten, yet it was certainly the earlier by a year or two.

The whispers had been persistent, and on 6 July 1983, Richard Humphreys, a junior curator at the Tate, unwisely but honestly confirmed that the gallery had been given a drawing by Modigliani that was considered genuine until rumours of the Vorticist fraud reached Millbank, and it had then been handed to the police. Why, I wondered, had the Vorticist fraud thrown doubt on a Modigliani unless the dullards at the Tate knew of some connection? But my immediate response was to ask why the acquisition was not listed in the Tate's Yearbook for 1980–82: had something triggered suspicion and consigned the drawing to limbo until research proved the case one way or the other? Another young curator, on seeing a photograph of Colin Turner in the *Sunday Times* of 10 July 1983, recognised him and promptly told me a tale confirming that it was he, Turner, who had brought the Modigliani drawing to the Tate very early in 1981. He had come, without appointment, with a young woman giving her name as Miss Ryder, who was the owner of an album containing some thirty drawings by Modigliani. On being told that they were genuine and of some substantial value (impossible for the Tate to define) as well as of great art historical importance, she became highly emotional and made the dramatic gesture of tearing, without much care, one of the drawings from the album to present to the Tate as an expression of her great gratitude.

Miss Ryder was, of course, Miss Lawrenson, Turner's girlfriend, and the dramatic gesture coolly calculated, for it enabled him to ask for a photograph of the given sheet and its roughly torn edge, for this, matching the edge in the album, was proof of the drawing's presence in the Tate as a genuine Modigliani, thus authenticating all the remaining drawings when he passed them on. This he did by first ensuring that Joseph Lanthemann, an acknowledged expert on Modigliani,[*] knowing of the presentation to the Tate, wrote certificates of authenticity for every sheet in the album before it was disbound. Speaking neither French nor German, Turner's telephone conversations with Lanthemann were conducted by George Weissbort, who kept records. On 13 February 1981

---

[*] Joseph Lanthemann, *Modigliani 1884–1920 Catalogue Raisonné*, 3 vols., Condal, Barcelona 1970.

Lanthemann asked Turner to bring the drawings to him in Nice – 'Bring them under your arm – there may be difficulties about re-export if you bring them in with all the proper documentation.' He added, significantly, that as an official expert he could ask no fee, but suggested selling them through the Zürich auctioneer Walther Germann at Galerie Koller, with an introduction to the sale catalogue stressing their art historical importance, to be written by Lanthemann for a substantial fee. Alternatively they should be sold through Giulio Urbinati of Galerie Le Point in Monte Carlo, who would give him a commission for introducing Turner. On 10 March Turner told Lanthemann that he had not received his certificates, nor had Germann, and that if they were not sent very soon the Zürich sale, scheduled for May, would have to be delayed. On 7 May Turner still had no certificates and Lanthemann refused them unless given an understanding that he could catalogue every sheet and write a prefatory essay that would be a lasting work of scholarship.

The Zürich sale eventually took place on 28 October 1981, but it was of only four drawings, Lots 59, 61, 62 and 67; a second sale, on 7 November 1981, included two more, Lots 434 and 435. The total reached was £45,000. Lanthemann had, presumably, given up the struggle to secure publication of the collection as a work of scholarship; it is doubtful that he received payment for certificates – Weissbort opined that, his having received a letter from Lanthemann, Turner had the headed paper copied in London and wrote the certificates himself; as Turner's was an illiterate hand and he had no German, it seemed probable that Weissbort had been of some assistance (I could never fathom their relationship, but was, and still am, convinced of Weissbort's fundamental decency).

Most of the remaining drawings were sold to Galerie Le Point, almost certainly the purchaser of those sold in Zürich, for some from both sources were included in a major exhibition mounted by the gallery in Barcelona and Madrid in 1983 – an exhibition funded by the Spanish Government and including indubitably authentic works from public galleries in Berne, Milan, Geneva, Düsseldorf and New York. As supervising expert, Lanthemann at last had the opportunity to write an introductory essay in the catalogue. Of the ninety-eight exhibits Urbinati listed his gallery as owning thirteen and having a further seven for sale; he let slip both that Lanthemann had guaranteed all these as genuine, and that he had for many years been dealing on the side and had contributed some drawings of his own that were for sale and others that belonged to clients and were for sale through his agency. When Colin Turner made a list of those for which he was responsible, it became clear that a third of the exhibits were fraudulent. This list and the copy of the Barcelona catalogue with which it tallied were among the papers that I passed to Scotland Yard.

Colin Turner was also responsible for fake paintings by Modigliani. A cache of these he claimed to have bought from the sister of Kenneth Clark, sometime Director of the National Gallery and, later, Lord Clark of *Civilisation*; K – as Clark's familars knew him – was, alas, an only child. 'Cache' is such a useful term – it can be applied to two or three or expanded to ten times that number if required by the stratagem's success. The first of these canvases so convinced Lanthemann in 1981 that he asked for the rest to be sent to him in Nice, where he showed them to Peter Wilson, retired head of Sotheby's, who might have supposed them to have come from a local collection; he did not; to Lanthemann's fury he damned them as forgeries. Turner, meanwhile, had sold £10,000 shares in them to Kenrick Talbot (he of the de Hory fraud) and J.L. Bendien, a businessman with a West End *pied-à-terre* (he lived in improbable suburban splendour in Crowhurst, Sussex) smart enough to convince other buyers that any paintings he might show them must be genuine. Lodged there, the paintings were security for his loan, which was for one month only at ten per cent, forcing Turner to act quickly. Klaus Perls, a New York art dealer who claimed to be 'the world's leading authority on Modigliani' (a title with which he often introduced himself to strangers), bought one painting for

£30,000, paid into an account held by Turner in a New York bank (Barclay's) in December 1981; the five that remained, Bendien kept and consigned to the London dealer Richard Nathanson who, Bendien complained, 'screwed' him for an enormous sum for insurance and then returned them as 'not kosher'. Asserting that there was yet more Modigliani material, Bendien then played me a tape on which Turner boasted of other paintings in the cache as well as seven large and three small drawings, not part of the album that had so excited Lanthemann.

Perls, before he realised the purpose of my enquiry, told me that he had sold his Turner-Modigliani to an American client and was absolutely sure that it was genuine. Bendien, blustering that he had been cheated by Turner and knew nothing of the ramifications of the business, released the five unsold 'not kosher' canvases to the police. Lanthemann died of cancer in April 1983, his reputation for scholarship in tatters, his great book worthless, his position as expert usurped by Osvaldo Patani, subsequently author of another substantial reference book.* When Patani reviewed the Barcelona-Madrid exhibition of June 1983 for the *Corriere della Sera* he claimed that of the two thousand or so works considered by Lanthemann (and others) to be genuine, at least fourteen hundred were fakes.

*   *   *

Of all this scrupulous investigative work there was no consequence. the *Sunday Times* published several reports over a period of months in the summer of 1983, always premature, ragged in argument, sensational in tone, and worse, inconclusive, entirely written by Colin Simpson while juggling this with other investigations and always slightly the worse for alcohol. They bore my name as second string, but from the very beginning I had argued for first finishing the research, and then, as straightforwardly as possible, presenting it in a single two-page article. Reconsidering it now, I

---

* Osvaldo Patani, *Amadeo Modigliani Catalago Generale*, Milan 1991–4.

see the difficulty. Dribbling the revelations had one advantage – that it stimulated a flow of information from largely disgruntled sources connected with Turner, from lesser employees of Christie's, Sotheby's and the Tate Gallery, and anonymous letters that mostly confirmed what we already knew, though one of them was the first indication that Bendien was involved. Important solicitors wrote convoluted and often silly letters to the editor, Harold Evans; these he passed to his features editor, Magnus Linklater, who, not much interested in art, took fright; he was also bored by the never-ending stream of information that he could not comprehend and, unable to see Colin Simpson's reports as usefully connected and inexorably constructing an important international case, he cut us short. Independently and unpaid, I tied as many knots as I could, wrote a day-by-day account of all that Simpson and I had done, submitted it to the Fine Art Squad at Scotland Yard on 23 August 1983, sorted my notes and evidence and filed it away in case, one day, it might be useful. It never was.

For reasons known only to themselves the Fine Art Squad, having all the information that we had uncovered and having themselves put considerable energy and resources into tracking down Colin Turner – even to having him in a police cell for some hours, releasing him on the grounds that the complaints made by Koolman-Darnley were a civil matter – lost interest. I felt at the time that the complexities of the affair defeated them and that, wholly unqualified in any technical sense, connoisseurship a word they could not even spell, they lacked the intellectual ability to present a clear case to the Director of Public Prosecutions, and the sceptic in me was inclined to aver that the distinguished legal minds in that great office were equally incapable and, perhaps as bored as Linklater and as befuddled as Simpson, were deeply uncertain of successful prosecution. Louis Koolman-Darnley, who was looking forward to cross-examination in the witness box as his unexpected final performance on a public stage, was convinced that money had changed hands, that either by Colin Turner who was, considering the figures of which we are certain, at least £150,000 in pocket, or by one of the dealers he had gulled, anxious to hold on to his reputation for reliability, the palm of Policeman Plod had been well greased. Poor Louis was bitter about the business, for even the paltry few thousands that Turner had given him were wiped out by the fees of the lawyer and the hearing in the High Court, and he was as penniless as ever.

We know that many of the drawings and paintings involved in this enquiry ended in the hands of the police, including the fifty-two Vorticist works that were to have been a whole sale at Christie's, but others did not and may still be in circulation, the drawings from the Modigliani album an indisputable example; but what of the four thousand paintings by de Hory, what of the fifty-four Epstein drawings, the sixty-nine by Gaudier-Brzeska, the unknown number by Wyndham Lewis and all the other things supposed to have emerged from Koolman-Darnley's magic box? Of these Ronald Alley, Keeper at the Tate, adviser to Anthony d'Offay, Christie's, Sotheby's and the Fine Art Squad made a laundering statement on 16 June 1983, worthy of a politician: 'It is a matter of great concern to everyone in the art market that forgers should now be taking advantage of current interest in these un-charted areas.' Note the weasel phrase 'these uncharted areas' – so uncharted that in April 1983, the very month in which this investigation began with the almost irrelevant Elmyr de Hory and Kenrick Talbot, Anthony d'Offay opened an exhibition of twenty-six drawings by Wyndham Lewis, supported by half-a-dozen notables claiming expertise. These waters, in my lifetime, have never been uncharted. The total asking price for d'Offay's drawings was £336,500; a discreet leak suggested that before the show opened, the British Museum had bought a twenty-seventh – for £42,500.

The difficulty for the future is that none of this material, whether it dates from the end or the beginning of the century, is sufficiently separated in age for most scientific tests to distinguish old original from modern fake, and only if the forger has been fool enough to use a recognisably modern paper or medium can we be certain on technical grounds; and the older they become, the less certain, technically, shall we be. Connoisseurship is then the only answer, and the chances are that forgeries of the 1980s will have an Eighties character, imperceptible when new but increasingly obvious with age – and that and intellectual misunderstanding by the forger will be his work's undoing. The great enemy of connoisseurship is, however, profit.

And what of Colin Turner, Mark Lewis, Kenrick Talbot and the rest? Where are they now? What have they forged since? Were they responsible for the neat little still lives that passed for Flegel and van Kessel in the old master sales of the later Eighties, for the paintings of birds so obviously not quite by Marmaduke Cradock? Were the gluts of whaling ships at sea, Montgolfier balloons, clipper ships off Boston and Shanghai, and other fashionable decorative trifles of the past thirty years or so, all theirs? Having blighted the market for late doodles by Lowry, will they turn to foul words on blank canvases by Tracey Emin and to the spots and spins of Damien Hirst? They cannot, surely, have been sitting on their hands since 1983.

When it became clear that there were to be no prosecutions, I asked the Fine Art Squad to return the evidence that I had accumulated, in case another use for it occurred. I was invited to collect it from Scotland Yard, followed by – as a reward – lunch and a visit to the Black Museum that is so notorious. Lunch began with drinks at the bar (a wretched ritual for me as alcohol and I do not work well together at any time of day and least at the halfway mark), and it was soon obvious that my visit was an excuse for a bit of a binge. At last in the dining room, where it seemed that hundreds of lordly senior officers were (every day, one must presume) able to eat at a most leisurely pace enough to feed an ordinary mortal for a week and drink far more, I was astonished to discover that Scotland Yard had its own French vineyard, and an abattoir too to judge by the steak that my hosts wished on me. For them, ruddy, perspiring and increasingly incoherent, it was such a merry occasion that lunch lasted until four, by which time the Black Museum was no longer accessible and I could not be shown either the amusements of sadism, torture and death that justify its name, nor the Modigliani, Vorticist and Omega Workshop forgeries expropriated over the past year or so – I had particularly hoped to see the rest of the sale announced by Christie's for 30 June 1983 in which the Cuthbert Hamilton was the extraordinary star. Sensing that the occasion was over, I reminded my hosts that I had come to lunch only to collect my evidence. 'You must come again,' they said, pressing two bottles of gift-wrapped Château Plod into my hands – but the second invitation never came, my hosts were moved on to higher things (for fear, it was said, that art might corrupt the incorruptible), the Fine Art Squad was reduced to one man and his dog, and the reputation of the art market and its marketeers as a phenomenon of impeccable expertise and absolute probity was perfectly maintained.

*   *   *

Late in the year Magnus Linklater called me to his office to investigate another rumour said to be about to rock the art world. Too trifling to interest Colin Simpson, to me too it seemed insubstantial and, after two days, proved to be so; Magnus nevertheless took my notes and worked them into a scrap of nonsense, published the following Sunday. I was furious – such rubbish did me no good and might well have done me harm in a world in which I had only the most precarious toehold. We had a row – I have always been rashly intemperate – and my link with the paper was severed. Once again I was without work, contacts or prospects, and more than a little desperate.

CHAPTER 10

The Evening Standard

It was the second time in the year that my pride – though I preferred to see it as scruple – had cut short a promising relationship with a newspaper. Towards the end of 1982 Stewart Steven, editor of the *Mail on Sunday*, had suggested that I become that paper's television critic at £200 a week – whoopee! Salvation and something approaching £10,000 a year. I wrote trial pieces for a month, not to be published but for Stewart to see whether I might fit his bill, and there was much 'splendid, my boy' (though he was six years my junior) as I reported to him with my pieces, much as a hesitant schoolboy with an essay for his English master. On 8 January 1983 my comments as the paper's new critic were, for the first time, published. 'Crucified' is the word in my diary, though some reference to the bed of Procrustes would have been more apposite, for my sentences were abbreviated, my paragraphs ripped apart, my punctuation reduced to the comma and full stop. What was printed could have been written by a boy of fifteen at a comprehensive school in Liverpool. To my anguished letter of resignation, delivered by hand that very day, Stewart's response was immediate and mollifying – 'Next Sunday I shall edit it myself and you shall read it before it goes to press – let's call it an agreed text.'

And so we did. He broke one sentence and split one paragraph, just to assert his position; to so little I could not object, but when it appeared in print, it had been much further deconstructed for idiots and I yelped and squawked again. Stewart explained that in his absence his sub-editors had 'got at it', and that this would not happen a third time; but it did and, resolute, I resigned. I know now, of course, but did not realise then, that all newspapers have a house style, that all writers suffer its imposition on their carefully honed texts and that the fee paid is the rarely substantial consolation for the damage done to the scribbler's reason, argument and language. How could I have been so dim-witted? I already knew from disappointing experience that the publishers of art books are not interested in art, nor in its history, but only in the profits to be made from books of scant distinction that fit their preconceptions and do not disrupt their uniformity. John Calmann, whose sister Marianne I had known for years, and whose father, Hans, was one of the most powerful of London dealers in old master drawings, had asked me as early as January 1973 if I would write a book for him on Hieronymus Bosch, the chronology of whose arcane paintings had intrigued me since my student days and to the sequence of which I thought I had the key (based to some extent on colour and the different figure scales that he employed). I should have realised that John wanted nothing more than another cheap picture book yet again repeating what every schoolboy knows and contributing nothing new to scholarship; had he wanted more, why should he come to me? I wrote a synopsis almost as long as the text he required, and when he called me to his office was treated to a performance of contempt and foul temper that far exceeded any I had experienced from Patrick Lindsay, my commanding officer at Christie's. He threw my synopsis on the floor and his whole telephone at me, the reach of the cord to its cradle mercifully short. On the basis of an edition of 10,000 he compared the costings of the book that I proposed with his, said that as I had 'no reputation as an art historian' mine was an impertinence, and mockingly suggested that I should not only write it without an advance, but pay him £1,000 for new photography and a further subsidy for its production – 'If we print a thousand, eight hundred will be remaindered.' Even if I agreed, he would consider publication only after his 'advisers' had considered it.

I have just re-read the synopsis only to realise how much I once knew and how intense and clear my looking was; were I today given it as the work of another art historian, I would enthusiastically commend it as a way out of the labyrinth; I also see that it might well have taken years to write and would have involved much travelling. Had John briefed me clearly instead of flatteringly, I could have compiled his picture-book within a week (such wearisomely inadequate things are the commonplace of art book scribblers and publishers), but he did not and his insulting tantrum made reversal and further overtures impossible.

Phaidon Press, in May 1979, did, except in one respect, brief me properly. They wanted a history of Victorian painting written round thirty full-page illustrations, with a wider introduction of five thousand words or so – a task scarcely more difficult than writing an essay as a student. Weeks of amusement lay in the preparatory elimination of the too familiar and the finding of the unfamiliar that would serve the purpose as well or better – and it was fun until I sent Phaidon a sample of the illustrations that I proposed together with the extended catalogue entries paired with them. I was asked to lunch – for which I had to drive to a pretentious restaurant in Oxford where the then current affectation was making pasta to order, of which the only benefit was much more time for conversation. In our case it was no benefit at all, for glum silence overwhelmed us even before the wretched linguini rolled from the mangle that produced it. Phaidon, I learned, had entered into an arrangement with Christie's to reproduce, without copyright fees, any painting that passed through an auction there, and my book must therefore be constructed round paintings that had been sold there in recent years. I could, off-hand, think of not one that could be described as a key work, and a visit to the *photothèque* in St James's revealed nothing that could be used to stretch the definition. This book too died the death, but a sensible writer would have taken Phaidon's paltry fee and scribbled them what they wanted – exactly what their stable of hacks invariably did.

After these disappointments I talked to Nikos Stangos whom I thought my friend – we were never close but when seriously penniless in the mid Sixties he had briefly lived under my roof and

I had given him money with an airy 'pay it back if and when you can'. As an editor at Thames and Hudson I thought he might encourage me with a commission, but I was of no interest – he could get as many books as he wanted from American professors on sabbaticals whose universities would offer subsidies for photography; me he would have to pay and that put me out of the running.

The next proposal for a book came from Lawrence King, an agent or fixer of some sort, very soon after I had cut short my attachment to the *Mail on Sunday*. It was for a history of art from cave painting to the present day, designed for first year students at American universities as both basic text book and *vade mecum*. There had been such a book for the past quarter century, but it was felt to be stale, stodgy and out-of-date – something fresher, brisker and not downright wrong was now required. As the last one had sold in tens of thousands over decades, the next was pretty well guaranteed to do the same – an income for life, so to speak (as I knew from a pair of ancient dog-walking women friends who had written an English Grammar fifty years before). I was only in part qualified and sample chapters were required; playing to my strengths, I wrote on Quattrocento Florence, Caravaggio and the Carracci, the Enlightenment and Impressionism. Perhaps, of the forty chapters proposed in my synopsis, I should have covered a wider spread, but at this early stage I did not want to reveal that I knew almost nothing about primitive pre-historic painting, nor of Japanese, Egyptian and African art, and that my grasp of the glories and grandeurs of Greek and Roman art was patchy and insecure.

It was not until 16 April 1984, almost a year later, that I had a response. The American publisher gave me lunch in a noisy Italian restaurant in Sicilian Avenue, the covered arcade that lies on the direct route from Holborn Underground station to the British Museum and resembles nothing to be found in Palermo or Catania. Lunch seems so often to have been the prelude to disappointment or disaster, and how should we account for this unholy tie of publishers to pasta? In mid April it was too cold to sit outside, but sit outside we did, talking against the echo of the crowd within and of the heavy traffic at both ends of the arcade. It was not for me to steer the conversation away from generalities, but when we had drunk our coffee and should be parting, I felt compelled to ask what he had thought of my draft chapters. The pause was so long that I laughed. 'Your silence tells me that they will not do,' I said, and still the pause continued. At last, abandoning the distance into which he had retreated, he leaned forward and uttered what seemed a carefully considered, even oracular, response: 'You will have to learn to write a less intelligent book.'

'You will have to write' would have offered hope; but to 'have to learn to write' offered no hope at all, for how can a man who is intelligent learn to abandon his intelligence?

This rejection mattered less than it might. I thought myself back on the treadmill of a thousand words for thirty quid for *Art and Artists*, a slowly dying little magazine in which one could at least be critical as long as this was never of the advertisers, or rather more (and very occasionally) for *World of Interiors*, for which, in its early years, one had always to be benign. Min Hogg, its founder-editor, sent me to Paris in the chill February of 1983 to write on an apartment of the night designed by Geoffrey Bennison, the cold formality of Style Rothschild made warm and comfortable by excluding the bleak north light. Geoffrey was a dab hand with such transformations; nothing looked new, rich things were used only if softened by age and use, value and importance were understated, rarity teased into knick-knackery and the knick-knack magicked into the curiosity; he conjured a sense of the nineteenth century with an inheritance from the eighteenth, lived-in and worn by generations of family, yet this marriage of Portobello Road and Bond Street (so to speak) was entirely new.

Geoffrey was also a dab hand at making buggers of men who had never thought of it. If his taste as a decorator was subtle and understated, his presentation of himself was the extreme reverse.

Plump, his gestures extravagant, his unremarkable ordinary speech lapsing into the bitchy repertoire of camp without embarrassment, his prize trick was to wear black fishnet stockings of the most flamboyant pattern under dowdy trousers, and when he thought he'd caught the attention of a suitable bloke – and blokes were his taste, the rougher and tougher the better – he'd draw the trouser leg higher and higher (never too quickly) until the bloke was in no doubt about what was being offered. In Paris this attracted no attention, for the ladyboys there were slimmer and prettier and younger and the blokes are rare, but at a large transport café on the fringe of London his better luck was notorious – he had only to catch an eye (or ear), reveal a stocking, tantalise and mince to the door to achieve a lightning stand-up fuck in the lavatory or, longer and safer, have it in the lorry driver's cab. This, the very bottom rung of the sexual ladder without the menace of attachment was all that he wanted.

This separation of the act of sex from the sentimental affections formed by homosexuals is a fairly common phenomenon; Geoffrey was, perhaps, an extreme example, but it was true too of Peter Claas, David Carritt and half a dozen art historians of more or less my generation, all of whom had affectionate relationships that were platonic; it was to some extent true of Anthony and, in my sexual opportunism, true of me. The most preposterous of my acquaintances was Tom Skeffington-Lodge – but then he was preposterous in everything by the time I first knew him, in the Sixties. He collected paintings by the then neglected Benjamin Williams Leader, winter landscapes rooted in mud draped in post-sunset gloom, always buying poor examples because they were even cheaper than the good. Born in 1905, his family wealthy (two thousand acres of west Yorkshire farmland), academic, liberal and actively Christian, his own high-minded and benevolent Christian Socialism was inspired by the plight of local miners. After a modestly heroic World War II in the Navy, mostly on Atlantic convoy duty (the most perilous of all), he was elected

Labour MP for Bedford but, far from the sort of original old Labour MP who would piss in the sink, his fussy upper-crust arrogance offended the party leaders Attlee, Morrison and Bevan and, never given the front bench seat that he thought his right, his political career was cut short at the next general election. Then he expected to be sent to the Lords as Baron Swillington of Yorkshire, a dormant barony to which he had some very slight claim and of which he never quite relinquished hope. If he is remembered at all it is only for Francis King's caricature of him as Dame Winifred Harcourt in his novel *A Domestic Animal* (1970); in the Dame he recognised himself and sued, winning the case and ruining Francis. A more spiteful defendant than Francis would have allowed the whole truth to be known – it might not have saved the case but it would have made Tom ridiculous; that the truth was already known to the Conservative Party was clear in 1969 when, in the course of another attempt to return to Parliament, he was dubbed 'the bed-and-breakfast candidate' by his rival, Julian Amery. Tom, by then a pot-bellied bag of bones with thinning hair and the speech of a churchwarden, was indeed the owner of a bed-and-breakfast house in Luton, where Vauxhall manufactured trucks and the drivers who collected and delivered were in need of beds, even prepared to share them if cheap enough; and when the Devil drove him, off Tom went to Luton to satisfy his sexual appetite.

*   *   *

On 30 April 1984 I had just returned from Kensington Gardens with the dogs when I had a telephone call from Bert Hardy, of whom I had never heard but later learned that he was 'a Fleet Street legend'. He asked, as though in command of the *Evening Standard*, 'Can you recommend anyone to be our art critic? We sacked Richard Cork three months ago – neither we nor the readers understood anything he wrote – and we've managed without until now but there is pressure from our readers to replace him.' I thought the question framed in such a way as to condition my response; it implied that they did not want me but thought that I might know someone who would do. My pause was for only a second or two but it felt an age, my mind racing, and then, contrary to the genteel social mores instilled by my mother – to be summed up as, 'Don't shake the tree, wait till the ripe plum falls' – I heard myself say, 'No. But I'd quite like the job myself.' To this the response was, 'We were hoping you'd say that; come to the office at midday.'

Why was it Bert Hardy who made the call? He was neither editor of the paper nor part of its team – though he was to become its Chairman in 1989 – and it was not he whom I saw a few hours later. The interview was with Louis Kirby and Roy Wright, the editor and his deputy. It took about two minutes: I was to write, not weekly, but only when there was a major exhibition in a major public place; I was not to write about poxy little shows in back street commercial galleries furthering the careers of unknown artists. I was to submit my texts to Roy, agree alterations and the final versions, and these would be printed; length was to be eight hundred words. Fretting that these were so few and sometimes fewer when advertisements took more space than planned, the consequent cuts in length quite arbitrary, I took to going to the office to read proofs and do my own cutting, for the usual procedure was to dock as much as necessary from the final paragraph, leaving an argument, even a sentence abruptly unfinished. This I have done ever since. When Roy raised an eyebrow at words beyond the range of Winston Churchill's recommended six hundred, I began to wonder whether I should use the commonplaces of the newspaper, but Roy sternly gave me advice that I treasure. I began a paragraph with 'Make no mistake . . . ' 'You are not a journalist,' he said, 'don't write like one,' and crossed it out. I owe a great deal to him. He let me have more words, argued that my increasingly long essays should not be crowded and reduced by advertisements and occasionally let mine be the only words on the page. He did not regard reviews as news and let me brood on exhibitions until my opinion had matured – and for this some institutions, particularly the Royal Academy and Dulwich, were grateful, happy to be the subject when visitor numbers had begun to flag. I was grateful too, for I believed that reviewing should be a considered process of seeing, thinking, writing, seeing again and then re-writing, never a creature of hastily formed (but ill-informed) opinion scribbled to a deadline. I was very much at ease and began to feel that I had become part of the paper.

Louis Kirby I never again encountered; his successor in 1986, John Leese, I did – a really decent man who asked me, if not riddles, wry questions that suggested an amused and sceptical eye on the art world, as though he felt compelled to acknowledge its existence but could not quite believe in anything it said or did. With his five years as editor the paper changed, became more various and less predictable; he supported well-argued difference and contradiction, and he liked words as much as I, liked the sight and sound of them and enjoyed the pinpoint accuracy of some as much as the lubricity of others. When cancer stalked and struck him, I asked Martin Shortis, then recently graduated from the Royal Academy Schools and an impressive draughtsman, to draw the paper's vast open plan office – a big drawing with the News Desk in the foreground, the Arts Desk and Londoner's Diary in the far corner, the perspective ingeniously curved to mask the necessary double viewpoint – to hang at the end of his bed in the Cromwell Hospital. A little recovered – enough to write a thank you and farewell – he took it home with him, but then he died. Even in death he did a charming thing – instead of flowers for his funeral he saw to it that I and others were sent growing roses for remembrance, roots to plant, cherish and enjoy. Mine still flourishes.

His successor was Paul Dacre, now High Panjandrum of the Mails and all they spawn – not a sympathetic boss, perhaps respected but not much loved. I was at once informed that I must never begin a paragraph, and preferably not a sentence, with the letter I. It was, and is, the custom of the paper to break up the mass of text with large and emphatic capitals; this is done only for the appearance of the page and signifies, not a new thread of argument, but nothing, nothing at all; this irrelevant whimsy of balance and composition is mere embellishment and as such an I is meagre and inadequate – an M or W is much preferred. How, I asked, shall I quote the first sentence of St John's Gospel – 'In the beginning was the Word . . . ?' 'You do not,' the answer.

He was editor for a year or so and we spoke only once. One of my contemporaries at school, not seen since then, appeared on my doorstep with a tale to tell, with which, as a minor diplomat in the Near East, he must not be identified. It was that the release of Terry Waite, foolish adviser to the Archbishop of Canterbury and then a hostage in captivity in Lebanon, had been offered to the British authorities, but in a state of raving lunacy. The offer had been refused, the British view apparently that to have him returned in that condition would rouse great public anger and make further diplomacy impossible; besides, the other hostages, still sane, were to remain in captivity. My schoolfriend – a mutual masturbating mate rather than a friend (a recollection that, while listening, I could not entirely banish from my mind) – thought the British agreement with the captors that all the hostages should stay in captivity until Terry Waite had recovered (on which matter they offered advice) appallingly inhumane and wished to leak it. 'Why to me?' I asked. 'Because you are only an art critic, you have nothing to do with foreign affairs, nor with the Near East (so much for all my Turkish travels), and you won't be the writer – nobody knows that we were at school together and nothing can be traced to me.'

I took him seriously, telephoned Dacre, asked to see him and within fifteen minutes was in his office. A minute or two into the tale, I halted, for something about his expression signalled weary familiarity with it. 'But you know this already?' It was more statement than question and his nod confirmed it. I made no note of anything he said – not much I think, 'D. Notice,' perhaps, and confused by the suddenness of deflation, went home with my tail between my legs, knowing that if the *Standard* could not use the story, no other paper could. I had no means of telling my informant of this outcome, for he had not defined the part of the Near East to which he was attached, and I was not best pleased with him for with half an ounce of sense he should have known that the matter was already common knowledge among editors. Months later, when Waite and the other hostages returned to England, we glimpsed him briefly as he left the plane and was then hustled away beyond the approaches of the press. Was this because he was still mad, I wondered?

When Stewart Steven succeeded Dacre in 1992 it was as though a menacing cloud had been removed. Jewish, and German by birth, Stefan Gustav Cohn (born 1935) was too young to be of the generation of European immigrants who, during and after World War II, so invigorated English culture and drastically changed the course of its development, but he was well aware of that influence and together he and I used occasionally to pay homage to Gustav Delbanco in his dotage – a sometime Cork Street art dealer (Roland, Browse and Delbanco, now Browse and Darby) who had in a small way been part of it. Old Gustav chuckled a lot, repeated familiar old stories, and slowly sank into the same urine-soaked senility as my mother; I gave up – one so stricken and so close is quite enough – but Stewart was made of stronger stuff; he needed to be, for his wife, Inka Sobien, a painter once imprisoned in a Russian gulag, was disabled by multiple sclerosis.

For me he was a good editor; he brought nothing from the *Mail on Sunday*, though it had been a failing paper diverted into resounding success entirely through his shrewd handling, but let the *Standard* be itself as a paper pitched at Londoners and Parliament, with an eye on Paris and New York. Never did he mention our disagreement over the television reviews ten years before, but he did bother to take an interest in what I wrote for him and often commented before it was in print (I had, on the other hand, arts editors who never read a word before my reviews appeared in the paper, and, perhaps, not even then). When, on 5 January 1994, thirty-five worthies of the art world, claiming to represent it (whatever it is), combined to write a letter to the *Evening Standard*'s editor, taking 'the greatest exception to Brian Sewell's writing', accusing me of homophobia and misogyny, insult and scurrility, and of a 'dire mix of sexual and class hypocrisy, posturing and prejudice', Stewart rubbed his hands together and turned their folly into a campaign for my support. Among the signatories were my erstwhile friend Nikos Stangos (what had I done to wound him? – never bear gifts to Greeks, I am inclined to say), Anthony's friend John Golding (by then not altogether a surprise), and Sandy Nairne (long the servile lackey of the Tate, the Arts Council or any other public body with which he could find employment, and now the unctuous Director of the National Portrait Gallery), who should have known better.

There was the most astonishing brouhaha. Nikos was fool enough to write another letter to the editor waspishly suggesting that I should write about cars instead of art, but the burden of correspondence and comment in a wide range of papers was in my support and Paul Johnson's essay in the *Spectator*, the cover headline 'God save Brian Sewell', just about summed up the public mood – never were there so many references to the Emperor's New Clothes. The most level-headed response was from Edward Lucie-Smith in *Art Review* under the headline *Out to Lynch*, cogently refuting the charges, recalling my enthusiasm for contemporary artists as various as Joseph Beuys, Michael Leonard and 'even Damien Hirst', and suggesting that, for the signatories, my real crime was that I ought to be one of their art world clique but had refused membership. Even so, I felt like a hunted animal and, on one television programme, confronted by a pair of shrill and vicious lesbians playing Diana to my Actaeon, I looked like one. I wondered how I should behave when next I encountered any of the signatories – as was inevitable. Norman Rosenthal, organiser of exhibitions at the Royal Academy, spat at me within its purlieus and twice, long after I had forgotten the row, used the excuse of a hostile review to thump me on the chest – but both these blows were after cardiac surgery and I was in no condition to hit back (one was hard enough to unravel a titanium stitch holding my ribs together). All three episodes were witnessed by members of the Academy's staff and I was thanked for my restraint – they did not know how much, had I been fit, I would have enjoyed a rough and tumble with that ill-mannered idiot. Almost to the day of his retirement he made a point of being present when I was in the Academy to prepare a review, circling like a rabid dog, murmuring, mumbling and even shouting to wreck my concentration – 'I know exactly what you're going to say . . . I could write your bloody reviews for you . . . you don't know anything . . . you've no right to be a critic . . . I don't know why we let you in . . . ' I had eventually to ask the staff never to let him know that I was in the building.

As for the other signatories, I developed the knack of not seeing them – except for Sarah Kent, the silly woman who was the despised critic of *Time Out* (I have a letter from its editor telling me just that); she had a fit of the vapours in the old Tate – 'I can't bear to be in the same room,' she cried, making no attempt to leave it; to save her dignity I turned on my heel and waited until she had moved on. A few apologised, saying that they had not seen the text of the letter but had been given its gist over the telephone; but this I doubted, for I had had warning of the letter from Leslie Waddington, the grandest of Cork Street dealers, who had been asked to sign one much more virulent but had told the writer that not only had he no wish to sign it but had warned her that it was actionable. I was grateful for his call but I wish that he had not mentioned libel, for the published text was considerably toned down; had the original been sent to the editor I would certainly have sued. Stewart damned the lot of them for fools: 'If they wanted me to get rid of you, writing that letter was idiocy – no editor could be seen to obey it.'

Stewart had much earlier, while still editor of the *Mail on Sunday*, made clear his attitude to the extremes of contemporary art when – perhaps as recompense for the miscarriage of my television criticism – he gave me the unusual commission to find for him a group of students still at art schools, good enough to earn their livings as professional painters. He recognised the common folly of enthusiastically predicting another Freud or Bacon at so immature a stage and set me a less hazardous and far more interesting task. 'I am not looking for the household names of the future,' he said, 'if we are lucky those will be a bonus, but they are too often the consequence of chance and hype rather than any quality. I want artists with whose work sensible people will want to live, rather than the mystifying sort always promoted by the Arts Council.'

I found a handful of promising artists, but it meant a slog through art schools as far afield as Manchester and Birmingham, Belfast and Newcastle (for some reason those in Scotland were left out), and their names and paintings were published in the paper's magazine, but, as Philip Solomon, a buccaneering art dealer much given to adventure, pointed out, newspapers last no longer than a day and if these youngsters were to be given a professional push worth having, their work should be exhibited in a London gallery – by which he meant the gallery that he had just opened in Bruton Place, then one of the arteries of the art market. At an extravagant lunch – at which I was as innocent as a child at a world chess tournament – I watched Stewart and Philip seek advantage in the deal, not because either needed it, but because it was custom deeply engrained in them. Stewart eventually agreed and Philip became an essential element in the exercise for all the years that the paper maintained its interest; when it withdrew after 1987, Stewart no longer seeing the project as energetic enough for his brisk dynamic *Mail*, Philip persevered and throughout the decades until his death in 2011, consistently supported young painters at the start of their careers.

We shared a love of dogs. He had three middling poodles to

which other occupants of the block of flats in which he lived decided to object; the fiercely argued compromise was that he could keep them but not replace them when they died. When the eldest gave up the ghost, in great distress he called me; I called a friend at the Mayhew Home for Animals and a young substitute was found; again and again we played the trick. At Philip's funeral there were no flowers, only donations to the Mayhew.

Stewart left the *Standard* in the autumn of 1995, his successor Max Hastings, who had for some weeks overlapped him as a lurking presence, observing in silence and determining our fates. His first morning as editor began what we called the week of the long knives, a series of interviews from which the paper's old soldiers, incompetents and skivers emerged ashen-faced to empty their desks and disappear into oblivion, a handful undeservedly. I, mere art critic and only a contributor, not an employee, was called in on Friday afternoon, the last scraping of the barrel. 'I'm not going to sack you,' he said, 'my mother would never forgive me.' 'Thank God for Anne Scott-James,' I murmured to myself, a critic I had admired since I was a boy. The best of editors, he brought his appointees with him and trusted them to make the paper what he wanted, to give it influence, to ensure that every member of Parliament read it and was frightened of its wrath, while he lunched and dined in lofty places with the loftiest in the land in the hunt for news, whispers, plots, intrigues and machinations, returning to Derry Street wagging his tail like a hound with a fat white truffle. Never in my years with the paper was it so sure-footed with news, anticipating the broadsheets of the following morning; never was I more certain that I had been right to refuse the blandishments of other papers. For this there were several reasons: to my bones I am a Londoner and this is the London *Evening Standard*; to my bones I am loyal, and this was the first paper to offer me the kind of employment I needed and for which I was perfectly qualified; and I knew that it was read by pretty well every member of Parliament, the Lords as well as Commons, all the denizens of Westminster and even Buckingham Palace, and that no morning paper had quite so concentrated and influential (and to be influenced) a readership.

Dominic Lawson, then editor of the *Sunday Telegraph*, suggested in the spring of 1996 that I might write an opinion column for him; this was permitted by my contract provided that the subject was not art and that I did not write as an art critic or art historian. An untamed political animal since the debates at school in the course of the post-war election of 1945 (I was then thirteen), I thought, as a man virtually disenfranchised by the voting system and who had only ever been able to vote for the least of evils since the Suez Affair of 1956, that I might enjoy this and agreed to a three-month trial. My very first piece was on a new method of abortion practised in the United States and destined here, in which the child is hauled out feet first and, while the head is still in the cervix, a suction-pump is inserted in the base of the skull to remove the brain, the legitimacy of this procedure a triumph of medical casuistry worthy of a medieval disputation. Max read it and on Monday morning commanded me to write no more, but I told him that I was committed for three months and could not go back on my word; moreover, I pointed out, I was not employed by the *Standard* but was merely a contributor with a contract that permitted me to write for other papers. This he did not know. Within minutes I was no longer a contributor, but on the staff as art critic and columnist, with a decent salary instead of casual payments, six weeks paid holiday, private medical insurance, an expenses allowance and the offer of a Vauxhall car. The Vauxhall I refused – I had nothing against the marque but had promised myself something out of the ordinary before I was too old to enjoy it and, short of finding a pre-war 25 with a coachbuilt body, Vauxhall could not fit that bill.

I told Dominic of my changed status and promised him his three months – time enough to find another writer. It was a useful experience both in finding every week a topic worth a thousand words of argument, and in dealing with the correspondence that it engendered. I had no idea how prejudiced, narrow-minded and mean-spirited the readers of the *Sunday Telegraph* could be – whatever I wrote about, they responded as though from the joyless, embittered, puritanical low church gloom of the later eighteenth century. These were people for whom I did not wish to write, whose rare support I did not trust, and I said my farewell to them in these terms:

'This is my final column for the *Sunday Review* – a weekly contribution that has given me great pleasure these few months past, though the correspondence engendered compels me to acknowledge that I have trodden on many toes. Let me, as a valediction, tread on more.

I am a natural Conservative, with the benefits and privilege of education, class and property, resentful of any government that interferes too much, belligerent towards a state that too often tells me that I must eat my Brussels sprouts and lumpy custard. My Conservatism is rooted in the conviction that all men are *not* equal, and that were we all given an equal chance, we would achieve very different ends and again be unequal within a generation – Christ's *Parable of the Talents* is as true of men now as it was in the day he told it, and if I were given Linford Christie's running shoes and jock-strap, I very much doubt if I would match him to the winning post. My Conservatism is rooted in philanthropy, in the conviction that none should starve on the streets, live, sleep or die there, that we all have responsibility for those less able than ourselves, and that a compassionate welfare state addressed to the needs and ills of the deprived is the mark of a well-ordered society. My Conservatism is rooted in the passionate belief that it is through education, cultural, Classical and Christian, that men learn the ancient virtues and philosophical abstractions – justice, probity, generosity, nobility, gravity, forgiveness, prudence, fortitude, self-sacrifice, honour and the Seven Corporal Works of Mercy – and that these, not the politics of envy, nor the politics of self-advantage, are the tenets that should inform society and government.'

To write on the same variety of social and political subjects for the *Evening Standard* was to discover a readership prepared to engage sympathetically with my occasionally maverick views on politics, society and sex. When I offended his friends and peers Max was vigorous in my defence – a letter rebutting a complaint from the Chief of Staff to the Archbishop of Canterbury, the hectoring George Carey, demonstrates how unreservedly: 'Brian Sewell is indeed intemperate . . . In recent months I have dealt with outraged correspondence about his column from assorted Zionists, art dealers, Scots, Jews and so on. If there is any section of society he has so far failed to take on, I am sure that he will soon remedy the deficiency. It is probably fair to say that dogs are the only people for whom he feels unqualified enthusiasm . . . I am sure the Archbishop is quite grown-up enough to take the view that if the likes of Brian Sewell are capable of stoking up fires too hot for him to bear, then he is likely to find the going very tough in the afterlife.'

Max was also very generous; aware that the column and an exhibition review amounted to my working eight days in every week, with no freedom at weekends, he'd suddenly announce that it was time I had a 'jolly' and send me off on an extended break to Paris, Berlin, Munich or some other centre of the arts. Irked by my lack of adventure, 'You can go anywhere you like, short of Hawaii,' he said, and was doubly disappointed when I went to Naples.

Up and down the hills of Naples and in and out its alleys I drove a Lancia Delta Integrale, a thrilling little car of almost razor-edged distinction, designed without compromise, and fell in love with it. At the time, I was writing an eccentric motoring column for the *Evening Standard*'s weekly magazine, and the Lancia was not only exceptional in itself, but in that it was fashionable when most of the cars of which I wrote were unfashionable, old and a disgrace to the industry – the Ford 10 of 1934, the Wolseley 12 of 1946, the ghastly Vauxhall Victor of 1957 and the Austin Metropolitan of the same period. In some, as a boy, I had been driven – by schoolmasters, priests and, particularly by Hodgetts (he had, as far as I knew, only this surname), a bluff friend of my stepfather who took me hill-climbing (a now forgotten sport) up Shelsley Walsh in Worcestershire and other muddy slopes in old ACs, Allards, Dellows, Singers and HRGs. Others I had driven, begged, borrowed and owned; and others still I found advertised, told the owner that I wished to write about his car, gave him lunch (my introduction to the worst of wayside greasy spoons), and then test-drove a model that not in a thousand years would I ever have wished to own – indeed I could have compiled a book on the worst cars ever made in England. This I greatly enjoyed as an escape from the art world and a reversion to boyhood, but Max indirectly deprived me of it by adopting a high moral stance over some minor mis-demeanour committed by the magazine's editor, mood-changing in nature, replacing him with a woman who, without informing me, dropped what she dismissed as 'boys' toys'. I delivered my column and was greeted with a disdainful, 'Oh, I don't want that,' as though it were pornography. I complained, to Max, for the column had twice won a prize for motoring journalism, not because I expected him to overrule her, but because I wanted to go on writing about cars and needed his permission; without hesitation he gave it, but no replacement offer came.

We knew that Max had no wish to be editor for life, that he had an academic ambition to become an historian and that he would leave more or less when he did in 2002, but we shut our eyes and minds to it and were unhappy when he went. His successor was Veronica Wadley, intellectually (if that is the word for it) shaped by the *Daily Mail*. Like Max she brought her own team with her, and out went Max's infinitely more subtle, honest and intelligent lieutenants, among them my column editor, Bernice Davison, and my arts editor, Annabel Freyberg, both of whom I trusted and, indeed, adored. Bernice lasted a few months, but Annabel was replaced immediately and without even a day's overlap with Veronica, who knew nothing of her or her capabilities yet had, without warning her, weeks earlier appointed to her post Norman Lebrecht, former music critic of the *Daily Telegraph*. Him she was fool enough to elevate to the position of her right-hand man with power to decide not only how the paper covered all the arts, his immediate bailiwick – though of mine he knew absolutely nothing – but with influence over the whole paper. Never was a favourite so puffed-up with amour-propre, so arrogant and so thick-skinned; never was a man so loathed by those with whom he worked and sought to oversee. For the first time in my life I was told what I should write and what view I should hold. Veronica told me that I should be loyal to him, but to this my response was that loyalty had to be earned and was not to be bestowed at whim or order. After his extensive revision of a review we had so blazing a row that I said, 'If you want me out, then you must tell me to my face.' He lasted a year or so and then, like the Cheshire Cat (though his was the smile of Iago), he began to fade.

There was trouble with my column too. It had always expressed my opinion, not the editor's and not the paper's, but in the newly-imposed traditions of the *Daily Mail* this simply would not do and I was expected to become Veronica's instrument. At first this was a matter of style – Veronica read everything in proof and we had a brush or two about the length of paragraphs and sentences – 'Do you realise,' she said one day, holding a proof between finger and thumb as though she had just retrieved it from the privy, 'your first paragraph is five inches long?' She walked off without another word when I replied, 'The argument is five inches long and cannot be broken.' Prompted by a column critical of Israel that she, for once, had failed to check – 'You've lost me forty thousand readers in north London,' she cried across the open office – she eventually told me that she had left me in peace long enough and that she now intended to control the column. I must tell her in advance the subject and the view I took on it, and that only if she agreed to both should I write the piece. To counter any evasion on my part she gave me all the telephone numbers at which she might be found out of hours and at weekends, and even those of her secretary and deputy. That I often had no view and that this was usually formed in the thinking and writing, often requiring radical revision as I progressed, she was unable to comprehend.

We jogged along not too uneasily, my position strengthened by my being given the Orwell Prize in April 2002, until a formidable row over her wish to illustrate a column with an irrelevant photograph that had taken her fancy; this required my re-writing a paragraph to make it relevant and I refused; she proposed to have another scribbler re-cast the piece and that too I refused. That brought about the end of the column. I deeply regretted (and regret) its loss, for I much preferred its variety to what had become the dread sameness of the art world, and had I been compelled to abandon one or the other, would have chosen to keep the Tuesday column, as it had been known. In an interview with Roy Greenslade in the *Guardian* in June 2004, Veronica attributed her decision to snuff out the column to her concern for my health – 'I felt responsible about Brian working too hard,' she said, and went on to labour the point with my age, my pacemaker, my not-the-best-of-health and the assertion that reviewing art exhibitions took a lot out of me. I was sickened by this disingenuous deceit – her sacking me was nothing less than a foolish demonstration of her power.

So thought others on the *Standard*. No one liked her; worse, no one respected her. Unctuous at one moment, shrewish another, no one trusted her. Her entry into the open-plan office immediately caused a general hunching of shoulders and ducking behind computer screens. Bill Hagerty, another *Guardian* writer, commented that, interested only in the paper's features and 'unable to differentiate between the readership of the *Mail* and the more sophisticated *Standard*', her editing was the subject of scathing derision. My observation was that she was hopeless at managing her writers, editors and necessary lackeys, whether male or female, that she was in thrall to her favourites – notably Will Self and Tim Lott, neither of whom troubled himself to give her of his best – and that she occasionally behaved like a fishwife in the general office, a man her usual victim. But there she was, in her power suit, eroding the readership by tens of thousands year on year, profit turned to haemorrhaging loss, Paul Dacre, the paper's over-arching panjandrum, and Lord Rothermere, its owner (though rumoured to have been heard throughout the building with his cry: 'It's the product that's wrong'), both so blind to her misrule that when her quinquennium was over, they foolishly reappointed her for another. Poor Veronica, incapable of realising how incapable she was, held the post until January 2009, when Alexander Lebedev bought three-quarters of the ruined paper for a pound. Then she was immediately out.

And so in a sense was I. As an economy measure I was discarded from the staff with compensation enough to buy a Ford Mondeo and the invitation to return as a contributing critic at a quarter of what had been my salary. I could have had a huff and walked away but felt a tug of loyalty to readers who, for a quarter of a century, had so often expressed their support for views that had earned me the art world's enmity, and I asked myself what I would do with a life that did not entail the daily discipline of art criticism. Cultivate my garden? Having heartily and unforgivingly despised Norman Lebrecht for unseating Annabel Freyberg without a thought of the consequences for her, to which other paper or journal could I go (supposing that one might want me) without doing exactly that to another art critic? As to not one was the evident answer, I swallowed my pride (though not entirely my reproach and resentment) and behaved as though nothing had changed. But it had.

The new editor was Geordie Greig, seduced away from *Tatler*; affable, even amiable, under his deft and Tatlerish touch the paper began to recover its circulation, and with the abracadabra of giving it away it now has the largest readership in all the years of its existence. I doubt, however, that it has the slightest influence in the House of Commons or the Mayor's Parlour, for too much of its editorial matter is by lightweight writers of no broad, deep or long experience and whose opinions are worth no more than those of any twitterer – though in this they may be perfectly in tune with the shallow interests of today's society. I plod on as seriously as I ever did, conceding nothing to the despots and nabobs of the art world, mildly irked by occasional hints that I should be more respectful to them. When Norman Rosenthal, of whom the Royal Academy had at last rid itself, wrote to the *Standard* complaining that my review of the Academy's Hockney exhibition was ' . . . not only mendacious and venomous but reaches new depths of jealousy . . . ' and more of this kind, Geordie allowed it to be printed. I wrote him a note:

24.i.2012

Dear Geordie – 'Mendacious.' The other insults crowded into his letter by Norman Rosenthal (published yesterday in the ES) are just bad tempered nonsense, but mendacious is a nasty word, dangerous too. Why did you allow it? Removing it would not one whit have reduced Norman's malice, but letting it stand seems an odd disloyalty to me. I am not best pleased.

Yours ever, Brian

This he ignored. Many who loathed Rosenthal – including Royal Academicians – urged me to sue him, but this Geordie had scuppered by printing the letter, lending it his editorial weight; the *Standard*'s letters editor had argued for removing the word, but had been overridden. I sent another note:

26.i.2012

Dear Geordie – 'Mendacious.' The accusation is defamatory and requires public withdrawal and apology from Rosenthal. You, however, in publishing it, have put me in an impossible position. I must ask, too, why the *Evening Standard*'s lawyers did not prevent the publication of the word. I feel that I cannot let is pass. What is to be done?

Yours ever, Brian

And yet another:

Dear Geordie – 'Mendacious.' The wound suppurates. I have heard nothing from you of your proposed contact with the irksome Rosenthal, but perhaps you inspired the observation by Matthew Bell in the *Independent on Sunday* on 29 January.

I am intrigued by the idea of suing the *Evening Standard* – is there a precedent for the defamation of a contributor by his employer and a consequent suit?

Yours ever,   Brian

Only with this did Geordie take action. An exchange of emails with Rosenthal resulted in his agreement to 'withdraw' the word 'mendacious' – a pointless exercise, for though the word was published in print his withdrawal was not and floats somewhere in the ether where no one knows of it. To me there was no apology.

As I write, Geordie has left the *Evening Standard* to become the editor of the *Mail on Sunday*, a rung on the ladder that he may well climb to become the Dacre of his day. The appointment of Sarah Sands as his successor has just been confirmed on twitter: is such a matter really so trifling as to be worth no more than an informal tweet?

CHAPTER 11

The Venomous Critic

In my first term as a student at the Courtauld Institute (in 1954 and at the conclusion of my National Service), I was instructed that method was all, that the eye counted for nothing, that abject belief in tutors – one in particular, Dr John White of *The Birth and Rebirth of Pictorial Space*, scarcely older than his students – was an article of faith, and scepticism a mortal sin. We were expected to hold in awe all works of art, no matter how wretched, no matter how much endowed with false importance by the accident of survival. That kind of worthless awe, however, did not last more than a few weeks before a student revolution put an end to it and, graduating to the feet of Johannes Wilde, we became aware of an entirely different authority – the authority of the eye; here was an old saint who knew his dry documents in every detail, and yet in his tutorials, as opposed to those of lesser men, we were aware of a still questing sensibility and a still lively emotional response to paint and images – he was to Michelangelo and Titian what Klemperer was to Beethoven and Mozart, the guardian Sarastro who, from the antechamber known as Knowledge, opened the door to Wisdom and encouraged us to look beyond. His friend Antoine Seilern opened other doors and so did Denis Mahon, their passionate enthusiasm for possession utterly infectious, their knowledge of art history at least as well founded as that of our tutors, yet informed by connoisseurship and an indefinable excitement that was far from academic.

These were the doors that I sought to open with my criticism, for critics in general I held in contempt. Years before, in January 1958, at the Royal Academy's Winter Exhibition (as they were then called), The Age of Louis XIV, on which I had worked with

Michel Laclotte and Anthony Blunt, I had encountered a posse of them from Paris, caricatural figures in camel hair coats draped open over their shoulders, perfume and body odour blending as on an unbathed tart; they twittered, raucous as magpies, complaining of the choice of works, the word *affreux* (frightful) echoing through the galleries, their enmity for the distinguished fellow Frenchman who was the exhibition's genius, blatant, their disdain for me, his dogsbody, palpable. They were strutting windbags, gascons, fanfarons, their opinions worthless.

The English critics whose number I joined were far less well dressed, with not a malacca cane between them, but just as unpleasant. I thought at first that I might make friends but was soon disabused; instead I learned that the world of critics was small, exclusive and greedy, morally without scruple, and damned if it was going to let a new man in. The art world thirty years ago was a cosy coterie greedy for patronage, and no place for the independent spirit. Patronage may seem an odd word in this context, but the jam on a critic's gingerbread was then provided by, for example, various arms and dependencies of the Arts Council asking him to play some part in the organisation and cataloguing of exhibitions, paying him handsomely for doing so – but only if they had his uncritical support. Art dealers too might ask him to write an introduction to a one-man show, for which the fee was a few hundred pounds or perhaps one of the exhibits, but the critic was required to suspend his critical faculties and gush enthusiastic bilge (this is still the case). An editor might commission a contribution to a magazine, but only if the scribbler toed the editorial line – Peter Fuller, late and still much lamented (a hideous car crash for which he was in no part responsible put an end to him), as editor of *Modern Painters* always put me through my paces on an issue, and if my views did not conform with his, said 'Thanks very much' and gave the work to someone else. The BBC, source of more patronage than any other body, was particularly vindictive if criticised; my harsh words on the intellectual level of its fawning programmes on the visual arts – little more than advertising – and the largely execrable generalists who dominated them, immediately ensured my total exclusion from all its programmes (this is so still). I was far too maverick and subversive to be welcome in such bosom nookeries.

Other institutions were as spiteful; the Arts Council and the Hayward Gallery, though they invariably denied it, dropped me from their press lists as a response to savage comments and never invited me to any of the international junkets that, long ago, were in their gift (these blandishments have since fallen away to nothing). Not, after mocking its sometime chairman, the preposterous and endlessly quoting Lord Morris of Castle Morris (a Welsh academic), did I receive so much as a press release from the now mercifully defunct Museum and Galleries Commission. The Royal Academy occasionally let me know that I had incurred that body's august displeasure, and in November 1994 informed the committee of one of its supporting bodies that I was permanently blackballed and not to be invited to take part in a debate. The coin of patronage had, and still has, the image of censorship on its reverse.

I am one of the brave brotherhood of those who have been publicly insulted by Norman Rosenthal. By a Bond Street dealer who thought his stock and reputation impugned I have been beaten about the head and shoulders with a wet umbrella – clammily unpleasant but, unfurled, an ineffective weapon. I have been punched in the right eye by a young painter, the blow so heavy that it disrupted sight for several weeks and the bruise spread over my cheek and neck before it faded, pummelled by a lesbian clad from top to toe in black leather (for me an occasion of almost helpless laughter), and jostled from their exhibition by video artists who shut down their contraptions and turned off the lights as soon as I entered their room in the Camden Arts Centre. These small events, the screams of feminists and the low booing of billiards players in the Chelsea Arts Club, are expressions of rage easier to tolerate than the closing of ranks by those who run the art establishment, whose defensive refrain 'He's only an art critic' they believe excuses them from taking notice of anything I write or say. Even Nicholas Serota once felt it proper to terminate a discussion with 'I'm a museum director and you're only an art critic' when he thought he'd lost an argument. To compliant critics, however, serving their purposes, these panjandrums are quite prepared to drop to the low kowtow.

In the Eighties (but less so in the tight-fisted Nineties) it was scarcely necessary for a critic to have a kitchen or keep a cellar, for the Academy, the Barbican and countless commercial galleries plied him with food and drink at lunchtime press previews (the Barbican's sandwiches were marvellously substantial with a perfect note of squidginess to make a mould of the roof of the mouth); and at evening private views he could gorge on canapés. Bernard Denvir, a critic whose importance I failed to recognise at the time (it was obscured, perhaps, by his self-importance), took his wife to every possible press and private view and, finding so little use for his kitchen, converted it into a second bathroom. At the Royal Academy's *Painting in Naples* exhibition in the autumn of 1982, there was a major logistical mishap: the Italian Tourist Board, in its innocence, invited to lunch, not the critics but the press, apparently unaware that there is nothing to choose in bad manners between a herd of journalists and a horde of locusts; when the critics arrived neither food nor drink was to be had and littering the floors and propped against the walls of the Academy's elegant private rooms were a hundred swollen bodies of sated hacks, for all the world like the plague-stricken Naples of Luca Giordano. Among critics, those who took greatest advantage of such hospitality were not the regular contributors to major newspapers, but the even worse paid wretches writing for small circulation magazines and local rags, or who were merely members of the International Association of Art Critics and never wrote anything at all; I once met one of these in Bond Street – 'You're going in the wrong direction' was her greeting. 'There's food at Wildenstein's.'

The Venomous Critic

When the Tate Gallery mounted its Hockney Retrospective in 1988 I was asked by a dealer specialising in his work what it would cost him for me *not* to review it. Five years earlier I might have found this deeply shocking, but by then John George, editor of *Art and Artists*, the puny little magazine that had offered me most work, had long since declared that: 'There is no such thing as an honest critic,' following it with: 'Art criticism is drivel, unmitigated drivel' – but his magazine depended on it and the advertising revenue it generated, and he could not stop the rot. His associate editor, Edward Lucie-Smith, one of the busiest critics of the time, speechifying at an exhibition in honour of his fiftieth birthday, confessed: 'I once thought of having principles – then I decided that I was too old for them.' In this Edward neatly encapsulated the status of the critic – rather than principled and poor, the critic must be, if he is to succeed, an essential part of a symbiosis with the market place, curators, the Arts Council and all others who use the arts for self-aggrandisement – and if this means being intellectually dishonest and despised, so be it. Edward eventually, through the medium of photography, became an artist of sorts himself; John George, honest soul, resigned from *Art and Artists* and became a postman to support his wayward ambition to write a doctoral thesis on Czechoslovakian contributions to philosophy; and when their desuetudinous magazine then fell into the hands of Bernard Denvir, it promptly died.

Art criticism in England thirty years ago was thus at a low ebb, corrupt, fawning, swamped in meaningless jargon, distorted by political correctitudes, the flattery of curators and their institutions its only purpose. I thought it would stay so, and to some extent it has, but, against the odds, there are now perhaps half-a-dozen critics to whom no obligations matter more than intellectual probity and who tell the truth; critical jargon, the political correctitudes and intellectual dishonesty have become the bailiwick of the curator in the field of contemporary art – the very man who should enlighten, now obscures, anxiously addressing his jabberwocky, not to the far wider audience that now visits exhibitions, but to other curators and their ilk. Catalogues of contemporary art are now incomprehensible.

Between critics and the curators of old master exhibitions there is a different gulf – its name is Superiority and it is maintained by curators less than half my age and hardly a whit of my experience. To one of these at Tate Britain, after ten minutes of being pressed to listen to what he had to say about Charles Ginner (a contemporary of Sickert, the subject of his exhibition), I posed the question, 'Where do you think I have been this past half century?' He did not understand; I had to tell him that I had been looking at pictures, among them many by Ginner, and that I probably knew more about the man than he did. To his, 'Oh I'm so sorry, I had no idea . . . ' I had to counter that in his bibliography he listed an exhibition catalogue that I had written in 1985, but obviously had not read it, for though everything he had told me, and much more, was in that catalogue, he had given me no credit. Nor did he know that I had been largely responsible for the selection and cataloguing of pictures in the *New English Art Club Centenary Exhibition* of 1986 – a trifling achievement, I admit, but one that fitted precisely with his field. The point is, I suppose, that at a certain age one drops below the horizon and young men at the beginning of their careers hardly know of one's existence – for years I have wondered why, when I have been around for so long, no one ever asks me anything: I am probably the only person living who knew and listened to the recollections of Pierre Coulette, Duveen's forger for forty years, or witnessed Bomberg shoo away from his doorstep an importunate dealer, or watched the shrewish widow of Frank Dobson burn his erotic drawings and smash his small terracotta sculptures of sexual conjugation. When I am gone no one will know of these small things.

Apart from my misgiving about the authenticity of Dürer's *St Jerome* in the National Gallery, recorded in the Annual Report of 1996–97, no art historical observation I have ever made has been acknowledged; was not one of them of any interest or pertinence? I have asked questions that any responsible scholar or critic might ask, but now no longer do so, for they are never answered. What sort of questions? No curator now openly admits to failure of any kind in the presentation of an exhibition – at least, not to a critic. Let us consider hypothetically an exhibition devoted to the history of Cubism from which Picasso's great *Demoiselles d'Avignon* is absent. This is a seminal work; without it the exhibition is the Bible without the Book of Genesis. The critic who knows something of Cubism and the fundamental importance of this picture, has the right to know the reason for its absence. Is it in such fragile condition that it is unfit to travel? Is it so highly valued that no insurer will accept the risk? Is it subject to a loan restriction – not outside America, say, or to be lent not more than once in a quinquennium? Is it that the authorities of MOMA have no faith in the temperature and humidity conditions of the borrowing museum? Is it that they have no respect for the scholarship of the exhibition's curators and believe them to be frivolous? Is it that they are planning an exhibition of their own on the same theme?

I have asked such questions and have been adamantly refused answers as though I am some kind of enemy, though the enquiries were made in an intended defence of the curators. I have asked questions about the *inclusion* of pictures that seemed unworthy of exposure in exhibitions (as was the case in the National Gallery's 2003 Titian exhibition), and again been refused an answer. The questions were nevertheless legitimate and again asked in an intended defence, for if the critic knows that the first choice of a curator, the sublime picture in the Prado, was refused, that his second choice, the adequate picture in Palermo, was promised to another exhibition, and that there remained to him as his only choice the overcleaned and heavily repainted wreck in São Paolo if he were to make his point, then the critic understands the presence of the restorer's ruin, even if he himself would have dropped the point rather than lower the overall quality of the exhibits.

Outsider II

To some extent I understand why curators may wish to be protected from people calling themselves critics, for far too many claiming to be of that ilk are nothing of the kind, but mere journalists incapable of understanding connoisseurship and interested only in sensation that can be better divulged, whipped up and managed for an institution's benefit by its press officers, whose duty it is to proclaim every exhibition the biggest and the best, a blockbuster, beano and bonanza (who can forget old Titian's 'first ever one-man show' at the National Gallery?). Press officers are not employed to tell the truth, but to control information, turn it into propaganda and compose lengthy press releases that both act as bait for idiot journalists and relieve them of all responsibility for what they write – or say, for the worst examples of regurgitation are invariably performed by those who masquerade as critics on radio and television.

I quite understand, too, curatorial contempt for the legion of so-called freelance critics who enjoy no regular employment and write nothing but, as members of AICA, attend every press view in hope (now vain) of the refreshment that was once the generous commonplace of these events. But there remain a dozen or so of us who deserve to be treated as the equals of curators, at least in our ability to make art intelligible to those who hasten from the Clapham Omnibus into the National Gallery, and some critics even have knowledge and experience that curators should exploit.

For my own part, I no longer expect a curatorial response to any small contribution I make to the sum of knowledge – indeed, so lofty are curators now that I doubt if they care tuppence what the critics say; when a new curator is appointed in a national gallery or museum, no attempt is made to introduce him – he is just suddenly there, another minor deity beyond our reach.

I now ask only two things of galleries. The first, often granted, rarely offered, is to be let into exhibitions days before the cattle market of the press view so that I do not find myself obstructed by journalists who cannot tell a Titian from a Tracey Emin, nor excluded from rooms in which television presenters are at work, for these tin gods have absolute sway over access and presence and make as much noise and nuisance as they will. The second, rarely granted, is to be able to read the catalogue a week or two before the exhibition opens. It is beyond my comprehension that catalogues are often not available until hours before the opening of exhibitions that have been perhaps as many as five years in preparation. Catalogues are now of biblical proportions and page length, cost a fortune, weigh a ton and contain a dozen essays in which a dozen scholars expound a dozen views – and yet the responsible critic is given no opportunity to read them before he must put pen to paper to meet the deadline of his editor.

In my three decades as a critic, the visual arts have become news as never before and my old remedy for these dilemmas – to write a considered review two or three weeks into the life of an exhibition, the catalogue diligently read, my arguments for or against it and the show punctiliously checked – is no longer possible. The pace has so quickened that without the cooperation of the exhibiting institutions, art criticism must inevitably be shallower and less well informed – a self-fulfilling prophecy, as it were, that justifies the curatorial conclusion that critics are contemptible and need be given by their press officers only such information as the curators think fit (the blind leading the blind). Matters are not helped when in newspapers and magazines, television and radio, critics are replaced by novelists, biographers, hacks and celebrities who write and speak for fees quite undeserved, parading at best the uninformed opinions of the amateur, at worst their downright and misleading ignorance. Matters are not helped when institutions exploit the press for maximum publicity: long ago, Serota knew exactly what would happen when he hung a dead horse in the entrance of the old Tate, and exactly the response to the Emin bed, just as the Royal Academy exploited the Myra Hindley portrait at the Sensation show. One may argue that the press expressed genuine outrage and was right to do so, or that in these cases it was neatly suckered by these institutions into doing precisely what was wanted and expected of it; the proper response, impossible to achieve, is to ignore such manipulation. The press did not learn the lesson then and is still manipulated now.

These are melancholy ruminations. Have I achieved anything other than a certain notoriety for speaking my mind, tact and dissembling eschewed? I know that in the world of journalism art critics are at the bottom of the heap, rarely read even by their editors. I know that in the world of contemporary art, critics are expected to be unreservedly the compliant minions of White Cube, Victoria Miro and all other merchants in the field, the lickspittles of the Arts Council and the toadies of the various Tates. I know that even the world of ancestral art prefers arse-licking to honest argument. In the face of all this, however, I still believe that art criticism should be passionately engaged with art itself, that the critic should be morally and intellectually honest, and should bring to bear, not an often ill-informed opinion, but the knowledge and experience that are the grounds of judgement. The critic must treat his readers as his equal when he discusses complex ideas and layers of meaning in a work of art; he must never pretend to see what cannot be seen – for that way lies Hans Andersen's emperor with his new clothes; and he must not lazily and dutifully praise every lunatic phenomenon ever produced by any man who has dubbed himself an artist. This last is precisely what is wrong with so many critics – that for fear of being in error, for fear of offending those who have influence, and for fear of vexing those who have the power of patronage over his work, the critic indeed nods dutifully and attempts no judgement of quality, invention or achievement.

Picasso one week, Mondrian the next, from the sublimity of Leonardo to the banality of Hockney, from the dense opaque impasto of Freud to the descriptive precision of Zoffany – thus does the art critic perform his intellectual leaps and bounds, thus does he discover the inadequacy of language. A day to see an exhibition and think; a day to read the catalogue and think; a day to write and think; a day to rewrite and crystallise my thoughts – would that I had a month.

With the National Gallery's astonishing exhibition Leonardo: Painter at the Court of Milan, of November 2011 – astonishing because none of us dared dream that such an accumulation of his masterpieces could ever be achieved – I had two days over a weekend to write a review, informed by only an hour in the exhibition on the Friday evening, influenced by sixty years of received authority and my own random seeing, thinking and opining. But that was sixty years of seeing Leonardo's paintings scattered all over Europe, separated not only by distance but by occasion, not gathered under one London roof with those available in Britain – and one of the purposes of such a gathering must be to see if it provokes a change of mind. The other purpose is, of course, to please the crowds happy to stand in awe of a genius known even in his own day as 'the most outstanding painter . . . his works quite perfect', and known in ours as 'the most universal genius' or, more romantically, in the words of Michael Levey, Director of the National Gallery 1974–1986, as 'supernaturally beautiful in youth and supernaturally wise in old age'. Even critics, I among them, did precisely that, overwhelmed to be in the presence of the master's masterpieces, and only slowly (if at all) did we realise that this was an unprecedented opportunity for scepticism.

With so little time to write I put aside misgivings (other than my certainty that the *Salvator Mundi*, newly discovered, is so much a wreck smudged and fudged in its repair that it must be discarded as a mere curiosity; and would Leonardo, so inventive in every other painting, have been so enslaved by traditional iconography in this?), and wrote an enthusiastic review that, though observant, was not critical. As an introduction to the court of the Sforza family, to the industrial (and therefore international) city of Milan at the end of the Quattrocento, and to the reasons that compelled Leonardo, the most Florentine of painters, to desert Florence for so seemingly alien a culture, the review has some merit and I am not embarrassed by it, but the more I saw of the exhibition, the more discrepant seemed the paintings, and the more I changed my mind about their chronological order and their authenticity. By the time the exhibition closed I was convinced that *The Madonna of the Yarn-winder* is a workshop production in which Leonardo played a part only as inventor of the composition, that the *Madonna Litta*, from St Petersburg, must be excluded from the canon; that with it, though for different reasons, must go the *Portrait of a Musician* and, most controversially (for she was used as the exhibition's poster on every wall in London), the *Lady with an Ermine*, Cecilia Gallerani, from Krakow. These four paintings, long attributed to Leonardo, are by four different painters, none of them the master.

The Madonna from Leningrad was lent on condition that its authenticity was not questioned, and the catalogue entry (written by its Russian curator) repeats the assertion that it is 'the Hermitage's most valuable treasure', dismissing as illogical any suggestion that Leonardo had little, if any, hand in it. The painting would not have come to London without the National Gallery's agreement to this condition and that would have been a great loss, stifling debate, but of this the visiting public was not made aware and will, supported by the catalogue, always recall it as an authentic Leonardo.

I had accepted without reservation the authenticity of the *Lady with an Ermine*, which I had seen only once before, under uneasy circumstances while the Russians were still dominating Poland. Seeing it in the company of other paintings by Leonardo a niggling doubt took root. I could not find a sequence into which it com-fortably fits – it is in too many respects different. Then a zoologist informed me that the ermine is not an ermine, but an albino marten, a much larger animal, and if this is so, then the argument that it is a punning reference to the girl's surname in that the Greek for ermine sounds like the beginning of Gallerani, no longer holds; nor do the supposed symbolisms of virginity and fecundity embodied in that animal. If the painting is not by Leonardo, the master of proportion, then the assertive disproportion of the hand is perhaps explained.

The Venomous Critic

We have almost exterminated the marten, but it was once widespread in Europe and in demand as a household pet; if caught as a pup it was easily domesticated and from Roman times kept as an expert ratcatcher; unlike all members of the ferret family, including the ermine, it has no smell noticeable to the human nose and leaves no odour clinging to the hands and clothes – that a wealthy girl should have so embraced a ferret is beyond the bounds of possibility; that the marten was an albino would have greatly increased its value. In removing the ermine we remove the clutter of a hundred years of misinterpretation, and with it, possibly, the attribution to Leonardo and all the associated assumptions; we must start again. This is why we must have exhibitions. This is why we must have critics capable of judgement, not in hapless thrall to the reputations of paintings, painters or art historians, nor influenced by monetary value. The purpose of an exhibition is to expose its subject for better or worse, and the purpose of the critic is to question received opinion and worry what he sees as a terrier does a rat. To look, think and look again leads to critical seeing; seeing leads to truth; truth must be the prime objective of both the exhibition and the critic.

In the course of looking at Leonardo so intensely I have concluded that he had a hefty influence on Caravaggio who, as an apprentice in Milan, must have absorbed into his memory every gesture and grouping of Christ and the Apostles in *The Last Supper*.

*   *   *

It is a solitary business, this looking at pictures with concentration so intense as to be exhausting, even painful, and it must be done alone sans interruptions. Roger Fry, father of English art criticism, commended trance-like hanging about for fifteen minutes waiting for spiritual harmony to couple the critic to the work of art; I, on the other hand, gaze at it summoning everything I know or have thought about the artist and the work, and reconsider him and it in the light of the exhibition, its curatorial purposes and its display, for giving a work of art new neighbours can transform and reveal more immediately than any words.

Is this a great Picasso, I ask, or a piece of casual cookery? Is this Mondrian the beginning or the conclusion of a train of thought? Is this attribution to Leonardo to be sustained? What has happened to the genius that Hockney seemed to display in early middle age? I ask, and seek the answers. I make notes only of an elegant phrase if it floats into my mind – the process is otherwise only of the gaze. It is not contemplation; it is a savage analysis, a cruel dismantling of the thing seen, and memory is both summoned and seared by it. It is far more the rigorous academic discipline of the art historian and the informed intuition of the connoisseur, than the opinion of the common critic and the jargon of the curator.

Have I reached the sad end of a once promising career? Shall I hie me to a monastery? Shall I buy a coat of camel hair and a bottle of something expensively malodorous by Calvin Klein and start again? Or shall I plod on wearily, as the ploughman in the elegy, certain that I have been ploughing sand, frustration my horse, futility my ploughshare?

CHAPTER 12

Mother

It was on 20 August 1982 that my mother suffered what she recorded in her diary as her 'little fright'. But for a few days she had lived in my house for a decade, her quarters entirely separate from mine – though mine, as she had to pass through them, were not nearly separate enough from hers. Her sitting room was on the first floor facing the pretty painted terrace on the south side of Eldon Road, larger than any room of mine, her bedroom above it, balconied. My quarters were below and, of course, in the extraordinary north-facing studio that occupied every inch of what had been the garden, its coved ceiling twice the height of any room – uncharitably cold in winter, but so expensive to heat that I could never afford to keep its temperature much above freezing point. We lived our lives separately, I thought, but her diaries so often record that I had an unknown visitor for the night that she must have had the hearing of a wolf or spent hours hanging over the banisters. In theory it was a sensible arrangement – I could keep a watchful but unobtrusive eye on her in terms of diet, physical fitness and general wellbeing, and she, if I was away, could deal with any emergency that might occur; she enjoyed answering my telephone and kept useful records of calls, not only of the who and when of them, but of her derogatory and contemptuous opinions of the callers. It was in this way that she became something of a confidante for both Anthony Blunt and John Gaskin, hearing from each about the other, things that neither would ever have told me; celebrating her seventy-ninth birthday during the crisis of 1979, she proved a staunch ally and a dab hand at putting down with dry severity any journalist whom she considered intrusive and impertinent.

There were minor eccentricities to tolerate and minor squabbles to repair. She had a rooted objection to large cars parked in small front gardens with so long an overhang that she had to step into the gutter, and was sharp with any driver bold enough to swing across her path. The young manager of Waitrose in Gloucester Road (the original first shop of the firm) took me aside one day to tell me that with her insistence on paying the correct sum to the very penny, she caused queues to form at the check-out desks, and would I perhaps do her shopping for her. I thought at first that this might be, as it were, a euphemism for shoplifting (common enough among old ladies), but it came about through her capacity for running addition as she put things in her basket – but she always read the price above the goods instead of below so that, although her calculation was impeccable it was invariably wrong, and whether her figure was more or less than the sum required, she insisted on paying it. The manager opined that, swings and roundabouts, Waitrose probably gained as much as it lost and he had instructed the girls always to take whatever she proffered, but she was so sharp that she always saw the discrepancy between her arithmetic and the figure on the till and was inclined to argue; worse, he said, 'It buggers the accounts and stock-taking.'

As old as the century, she had worn very well and could have been mistaken for sixty, still erect in spite of the beginnings of a painful spinal affliction that was eventually to bend her into the form of a question mark. There was probably no connection between this compression of the spine and the 'little fright', but the one immediately followed the other. She had come to lunch, as she frequently did when I had a delicious left-over from a kitchen supper with friends, and it was at precisely two, when I had taken things to the scullery, that I heard a short faint whimper that was not a dog's. I was just in time to catch her as she began to slide between her chair and the table and transfer her, unconscious, to the settee in the window. Her doctor diagnosed a minor stroke and between us we got her upstairs and into bed, peace and quiet the recommended medicine.

Within three days she was up and about again, seemingly so unaffected by the episode that, with the agreement of her doctor, within the week I set off for eastern Turkey with Michael Waugh. I had not left her alone – Margaret Evans, a friend from Castle Hedingham, came to keep her company until my return. There was, however, another little fright before the end of the year, and then another and another until I lost count of them. The pattern was constant – a sudden loss of consciousness and a full recovery after a few days of rest; but it was never a full recovery – it was always a small percentage short and, added together, these small percentages began to amount to a significant change, less in her physical abilities than in her state of mind. This, at first, I did not realise; by the winter of 1984 when I again went to Turkey for some weeks, interested to see it in midwinter, and Margaret again came to stay with her, my mother was a very different woman. On my return I found Margaret dressed to leave at once, her cases packed, desperate to get out of the house. On our way to Liverpool Street for her train to Colchester, she told me how appallingly my mother had behaved and that she would never again agree to stay with her.

My mother had indeed changed; my longish absence had perhaps been something of a tipping-point, for though she looked the same, little was left of sweetness in her nature and she had become reproachful, shrewish and demanding, her moods veering within the same few minutes of conversation from whimpering self-pity to tantrums of rage and accusations of theft, cruelty and neglect. Her spine began to curve, even to corkscrew and I now know, but did not then, that she must have been in severe and constant pain, both chronic and acute – and if I have any recriminations to make against myself for my treatment of her for more than the decade until her death, it is that I failed to recognise the degree of pain that she endured. Injections every few months were at first a help, but as years wore on these ceased to ease her pain and her doctor gave up. When she fell and broke her right wrist the hospital X-rayed both it and her spine; the wrist could be mended but the spine was beyond any remedy. For three months she forced herself to write with her left hand and with her wrist repaired declared herself ambidextrous – however foul her temper had become, she had not lost her determination. With another fall she broke her hip and was again in hospital, but in one in which the nursing care was not care at all and, as no one bothered to feed her, I took to visits that coincided with the absurdly early times of lunch and dinner; one day she had fallen out of bed and I found her badly bruised about the face, as though from a heavy blow. Her recovery was very slow and when eventually she was sent home she was intellectually in a sadly diminished state; even so, she made me swear that never again would I allow her to be carried off to hospital.

I moved her bedroom down a floor so that it was immediately above mine and, if she fell out of bed, I would hear the thump and respond; the floor beside the bed I covered with thick padding and sheepskins so that if I failed to hear she would not be too uncomfortable and cold. She could no longer dress herself, could walk only with a Zimmer frame and in hospital had learned to be incontinent. She needed, every day, a morning bath, a fresh nightdress and dressing gown, and fresh linen on her bed; these she sometimes needed twice a day – and I needed help. Help – rarely the same nurse for more than five days – came from an agency specialising in such matters for which the day fee doubled for the night and both doubled again for Saturdays, Sundays and public holidays; to have daily attendance and deal with the nights myself, the sum totted up in the first year to £26,000, wiping out far more than my gross earnings, and on this sum the government, rubbing salt in the wound, demanded VAT. There was no other form of help – no claim to be made against the income tax I could not pay (and the consequent persecution), no grant of any kind for which I could apply, no service available from any public authority: I cursed my ownership of a house in Eldon Road and wished myself at the north end of Ladbroke Grove – with an address in that slum the local authority would have fallen over itself to help me.

Then Ingrid appeared. A widow struggling to pay her son's fees at Marlborough, she had asked our common doctor if he had any patients whom she might, for money, assist, and he had suggested my mother. She saved my sanity. With not a hint of squeamishness and the sort of practical capability that refuses to recognise the impossible, Ingrid appeared at eight every morning and in two hours accomplished everything that had taken the professional nurses a day, and then went off to do the same for another old lady. In a whirlwind of cooperation my mother was bathed, changed and breakfasted, while I put her soiled clothes and linen in the washing machine and hung them in the boiler room to dry. I then had perhaps three hours in which to see an exhibition before returning to see my mother to the loo and give her lunch, and then another four in which to think, research and write. That I wrote at all was entirely due to Ingrid, for at the time she came into my life I was in despair. Even she, however, could not prevent an accusation that I had abused my mother.

Frustrated with her restriction not only to the house but to one floor within it, my mother frequently expressed her rage in tantrums, never to Ingrid, always to me, the worst and most frequent of which occurred in the evening. Every night I prepared her dinner on a tray as pretty and colourful as I could make it, always in a dish rather than a plate so that it was easier for her to eat with only a fork. It was always at the moment of delivery that she picked a quarrel and, no matter how much I tried to deflate it, pursued it to the pitch at which she felt justified in lifting the tray as high from her knees as she could and throwing it on the floor. If nothing smashed I could let the dogs clear away the food while I recovered the crocks and cutlery, but with a breakage I had to do the whole job myself. I then had to prepare more food and try again. I took to drinking Madeira, at least half a bottle every evening, to lend me, not tolerance but resignation.

Outsider II

It was after such an episode that I finished a whole bottle before going upstairs to settle my mother for the night. On her way to the bathroom she seemed to be lifting her Zimmer frame unusually high, slowing her progress and throwing her dangerously far back in her narrow arc of balance. I suggested that she should lean forward a little and lift the frame much less. 'Oh you,' she said, screwing up her face in enmity, 'you know everything,' and in lifting her frame even higher, fell backwards, full length, striking the back of her head on the glass door of her sitting room. The glass shattered and blood poured from a long slash in her scalp. She lay, conscious but scared and still, among shards like sword blades. I had somehow, simultaneously, to stem the flow, call an ambulance and shut the excited dogs away.

The ambulance men were disconcerted when I refused to travel to hospital with them and my mother, saying that I would follow later (as I did), but that I must first clear away the glass and blood and settle the dogs; they told someone at the hospital that I stank of alcohol and opined that I cared more for the dogs than my mother and might have pushed her. Nurses then identified bruises on her arms as caused by shaking (they were caused by Ingrid's helping her in and out of her bath and by my levering her from the deep armchair in which she sat all day), and the police and social workers were informed. Eight hours later these appeared on my doorstep. Nothing came of it but never have I felt so unfairly menaced.

In all this there was only one moment of humour, so wry as to be black – a letter demanding her attendance to do jury service. Bitterly I responded:

The Jury Officer, Southwark
24.vii.1992

Sir – Something must be amiss with your computer. My mother, Jessica Sewell (as you address her, sans Miss, Mrs or even the irksome Ms) is well beyond her ninetieth year, paralysed by strokes, almost blind, hard of hearing, incontinent and incapable of rational judgement (though not irrational).

You are welcome to have her in your court, but you must send an ambulance and nurses; you must feed her by hand and put her on the potty; and you must learn to ignore her random yelps and exclamations.

Do let me know if you intend to insist on her attendance.

Yours faithfully,

Brian Sewell

To this there was no answer.

And so the wearying business continued, yet with the help of friends and Ingrid (the most unfailing friend of all) I managed from time to time to escape again to Turkey (and write the book), and break new ground in Algeria, Tunisia and Pakistan. It was indeed my journey to Pakistan in October 1994 that settled the matter of my mother. I had by then exhausted the charity of friends – they would willingly live in the house and care for the dogs, but not for my mother – but one of them knew someone who had some trusteeship connection with a nursing home and persuaded its manager to take her for two weeks or so. Off she went to South Kensington and I to Rawalpindi, Peshawar and the tribal territories into which Pakistan fades on her north-western Frontier with Afghanistan, idly hoping to find some trace of Alexander's furthest point in his great trek to the east. There, at altitudes of ten thousand feet and more I experienced several bouts of a perturbing and disabling nausea that I attributed to the altitude, but on returning to London another bout hit harder and became a full-blown heart attack. Force majeure, my mother remained in the nursing home and years of disabling cardiac trouble followed for me.

When, after some weeks in hospital, I went to see her, she had retreated into a world of nebulous recollection far away in time and did not recognise me. 'I cannot understand,' she said with absolute clarity, 'why my mother does not come to see me.' As her mother had died in 1934, the slip in time exactly sixty years, I did not quite know how to answer but chose not to remind her of the death and posed a question of my own: 'Who do you think I am?' 'I have no idea,' she answered with some petulance. On another visit, when I found her curled up, leaning back, feet on a footstool, eyes shut, her fingers rapidly running about the keys of an invisible piano, I pulled up another stool and sat at her knees wondering if it was Chopin or Debussy that she could hear until, after some minutes, I put a hand on her left knee. I was looking at her face and I'd swear that her eyes stayed tightly shut when she said, 'I've told you before. Never interrupt me when I'm practising.' She had told me before, when I was tiny, but then her fine cello was her instrument, and she did not own a piano until she went to live in Hedingham, by then in her mid fifties and I in my mid twenties.

After some months she fell into rapid decline. The Portuguese and Filipinos who nursed her were kind, gentle and affectionate in spite of her infantile provocations. Her physical strength fell away and even anger was beyond her. Almost unable to see or hear, the quality of her life was wretched – a never-ending round of rousing, bathing, changing, feeding, mopping and falling out of bed, deprived of conversation, books and music; and yet I am convinced that as those things that had made her life enjoyable slipped away from her, she became adjusted to their loss. She accustomed herself to each downward step in her condition and holding on to life became an end in itself, a test of endurance and stamina, and in the end, of instinct. For so many years she lived a life that I could scarcely bear to watch and tend, and yet what little there was of it was hers and she was driven by some ancient force to keep it.

On 1 June 1995 I had a call to say that she was dying. I spent the day and night with her and she did not depart; nor did she on the two following days; early in the morning of 4 June, at six or so, the nurse said that her heart seemed a little stronger – 'She'll not go yet,' she said. 'Why don't you go home and have a few hours sleep. I'll call you if there's a change.' The dogs were so wildly pleased to see me that I took them to Kensington Gardens before I thought of bed and we were there when the nurse tried to recall me, there when my mother died. How like her, I thought, to cheat me even of this small duty of respect. How sad, I thought, that she died without benefit of clergy, without the last rites of the Catholic (or any) Church.

I did not love her then. The clever, witty, funny, loving mother of my childhood, the shrewd big sister of my early manhood and the companionable woman at the opera and Royal Academy, had all been succeeded by a spiteful old harridan whose fervent wish had been to outlive me – as she very nearly did. Had she died at eighty, I could have forgiven her spying watchfulness, her loathing of my homosexuality, her disappointment in me, her reproach for my ingratitude – 'You will never know what I have sacrificed for you' almost a refrain – for then so many better memories of her at Whitstable, in the National Gallery, in Paris and of her extra-ordinary tenderness with my deceitful stepfather when he was dying, outbalanced them; but in great age she became an erratic tyrant, for thirteen years the ungrateful termagant around whose needs my life revolved, destroying me.

I did not weep. For two days I did not register her death but took to my bed and slept. Only then did I set about the bureaucratic business of the death certificate, the funeral and will. There was no will. In hunting for it I found all sorts of papers that proved her long association with Philip Heseltine and Peter Warlock, the split personality who had fathered me, and other lovers too, and I wondered where these had been in my peripatetic childhood when we seemed to own nothing but a suitcase, a cello and a violin. Without a will there were no instructions for her funeral but I had some recollection of her impatience with old friends who had wished to be buried rather than cremated. Arrangements were therefore made for cremation at Mortlake, the service to be con-ducted by a Catholic priest – but I had forgotten that Catholicism and cremation are not bedfellows. A day before the event the undertaker telephoned to ask if a Church of England cleric would do and I agreed – after all, my mother had often slipped into the little church at the end of Eldon Road to take Holy Communion, acknowledging no distinction between one Mass and another. Some misgiving prompted me to read the Order for the Burial of the Dead in the Book of Common Prayer in the Restoration English of 1662, and I took it with me to Mortlake in case the priest preferred a version in the ugly modern English to which so many churches are now wedded. It was just as well I did, for the cleric was not a proper priest but some kind of non-denominational stand-by for emergencies – deacon might be a decent term for him – who had never seen or read the Order of 1662 and found it beyond his comprehension.

The hearse and one black car drew up outside my house. Colin Darracott, the staunch friend who had done so much to keep me on an even keel when my mother had been impossible to manage, and who had eventually drawn from her the identity of my true father, was the only other mourner. To my distaste a man in a top hat led this cortège at a swaggering pace to the end of the road, then leaped into the passenger seat of the hearse without its pausing, and off we swept to Mortlake. I looked down at my feet and saw that I had forgotten to put on my shoes – socks I had not worn since the heart attack.

We were met by the deacon carrying a book. I took it from him, saw at a glance that it was exactly as I feared, and gave him mine, the various passages marked with coloured tabs identifying which he should read and which were the responses, the long chapter from Corinthians (I have never cared much for St Paul) cut very short at ' . . . so in Christ shall all be made alive'. We had the one prayer book between the three of us; the deacon read as far as ' . . . whosoever liveth and believeth in me shall never die . . . ' (the first paragraph), stumbled over it and stopped, complaining that he had never had to read such language. With 'I will read it then', I took it from him, for long ago it had been for some years my intention to become a priest – an intention unseated by steadily increasing unbelief, the history of art as a demanding discipline, and by the eventually overwhelming menace of my homo-sexuality. For a moment, my unbelief suspended, it seemed to me that with the grace of God, for me to assume this priestly duty for my mother was entirely suitable; but with 'I know that my Redeemer liveth . . . ' there came a catch in my throat, the tears began to well, and that was that – God was not prepared to sanction my impertinence and silenced me. Somehow Colin and the deacon found their way through the rest of it while I sat hunched in a pew, sobbing. Sobbing for whom? – for my mother as she was at ninety-five, whose humiliated servant I had been for thirteen years and for whom I had at times developed a despairing hatred? Or was it for myself, at last free of this dark emotion but so stricken by a failing heart that I could not renew the life I had led before the 'little fright'?

*   *   *

Throughout these thirteen years of slavery there had been the constant and generous comfort of another woman, the daily companionship every morning of Mary Debane, a near neighbour in Southwell Gardens, five years my senior. We used to walk our dogs together, in deep midwinter before dawn in the damp mists, in high summer in the cool clear light before the heat set in. We talked without reserve or barrier. We compared our burdens – hers a husband of whom she always spoke as 'the horizontal one', deprived of his voice by cancer and suffering clinical depression, mine a mother bitterly resentful of the senility that in her lucid moments she knew to be destroying her. As Mary had spent the immediately post-war years of her young womanhood in Paris and Alexandria, she knew a thing or two about the perverse realities of life and we talked much of sex and its tribulations – and again and again I was surprised by the amused and perceptive frankness with which women of an age beyond three score and ten can confront and tolerate the wayward sexuality of men (we wretched creatures have secrets from each other, but not them). Joe, her husband, increasingly demanded the services of prostitutes and, as he could not make himself understood on the telephone, it was she who had to book these visitors and explain that it was fellatio that he required. 'Why don't you do it for him?' one had asked. 'It will save you a lot of money.' She found the women by collecting their cards from the telephone box in Gloucester Road and was surprised to find that Young Swedish Model, Helga new from Berlin and big-busted Veronica from Venezuela were often the same woman.

We talked of euthanasia and how she wished it, not for her husband, but eventually for herself. I thought of it in the context of my mother, but she, I had observed, clung the more strenuously to life with every reduction in its quality and was very much the other side of Mary's coin. In the event the death of the 'horizontal one' came almost suddenly and with not much fuss; a dozen of us supported Mary as she saw him off with a service at the very high Anglican church across the road in Southwell Gardens – not quite the Greek Orthodox ceremony required by his absent family, but with enough in the way of bells, incense and fluttering altar boys to convince the angels that we wished him well. I looked about me but could see no strange woman with fellating lips mourning the loss of a regular client.

For Mary the death of her husband proved not to be the expected release into the bosom of old friends and the renewal of pleasures enjoyed before his illness, but was instead the loss of the dutiful purpose of her life. The effect was profound; it was as though she had lost her reason for being. Her energy diminished further and faster with the death of Charlie, her dog. Suddenly she had no compelling reason to leave the house and thenceforth almost never did. The sherry, cigarettes and coffee that were her sustenance were brought by the Toy Boy, the Ponytail, Merlin's father, Michael the Plumber, the medieval-seeming Elizabeth of

Woldingham, the Princess and Hortense – I never knew her sobriquet for me, but herself she called my Doting Elderly. Like the Lady of Shalott, she lived by proxy, the telephone her mirror. She talked more and more of death; she did not fear death itself, only the indignities that she had seen precede it. She persistently pursued information on euthanasia; she asked her doctor for advice and was refused; though professing disbelief in God and any possibility of afterlife, she discussed it with the parish priest and the nuns of a neighbouring convent, all of whom gave her the proper conventual response; none of the rest of us knew how to help and yet, in the end, her departure was accomplished with astonishing aplomb.

On a Friday afternoon her hairdresser paid his weekly visit and was alarmed to find her jaundiced. She bade him do her hair and call the doctor only when he had finished. Within hours she was both elegantly coifed and lying in a hospital bed, the colour of mustard and, dressed in dark pink, an inspiration to any passing artist of German Expressionist tendencies. Cancer of the pancreas had obstructed her bile duct, the doctors said; it is incurable, but a by-pass operation might give her two more months, they said; without it she would be dead within days, they said. Feeling no pain, she refused the operation and settled down to die, but, disconcertingly, began to look as though she were recovering. She was calmly matter-of-fact about it, her only sign of uncertainty her whispered 'don't let me die alone'. On the following Wednesday she ate yoghurt without once fumbling the spoon and behaved so sparklingly that death seemed quite remote. Tonight, I thought, is not the night for me to stay.

But it was. Near midnight she complained, for the first time, of pain and was given morphine; an hour later she asked for more; and in another hour she was dead. I was not with her. Nor was any other of her friends. Did we let her down, or did she snatch the opportunity to engineer her death with a white lie or two? Did she really feel pain so suddenly? Am I in error in fancying that she contrived death in the quiet dignity she craved and of which the promise of euthanasia would have been a comforting reassurance? If in some sense she managed it with a small and exquisite deceit that left no one shouldering the blame, then I am more in awe of her than ever.

Dylan Thomas would have had Mary 'rage against the dying of the light', but that was not her style. I knew her to be capable of rage – rage against cruelty to animals, against the gross inhumanity of men, and against belief in a god whose supreme indifference to his creation was so often and so magnificently proved by natural disasters – but I had never seen her rage for her own benefit. The only thing she asked of life in her last years was that she should choose the moment to relinquish it in a quiet and comfortable death of the kind once described by an old Etonian as 'slipping away into the next room'. When the now forgotten 'Doctor Assisted Dying Bill' of 1997 failed, Parliament, fearing too little bathwater and too many babies, denied this dignity to those who, unquestionably lucid and articulate, are capable of expressing an unequivocal and determined choice.

*   *   *

How long shall I remember Mary, born in 1926, the year of the General Strike and Eisenstein's *Battleship Potemkin*, her death one of the closest, most telling and most touching of departures from my life? She was my confidante, a sharer in the small adventures of an urban life, a voice of common sense, and her memory survives in recollections prompted by bottles of Tio Pepe on an Oddbins' shelf, in sniffing the smoke of a Gitane and the whiff of coffee roasting, in the placard informing us that Sainsbury's have a special offer on champagne. I have eaten the tiny tin of caviar that, too late, I bought to share with her, though for years, sitting in my fridge, it acted as her monument; and I no longer reach for the telephone every morning – as I did for years – in mutual reassurance that we were still alive; these small things tell me that my memory of her is fading. Is there, after seventeen years, daily recall of my mother? I was determined that there should not be, but I hear her voice in mine, there are too many paintings everywhere with which she is inescapably associated, and on the rare occasions when I see a real Daimler with a fluted radiator, fluid flywheel and epicyclic gearbox, I think of her crashing my 4.5 litre Sportsman through the iron railings of Richmond Park with six dogs on the back seat. And I have inherited her spine.

CHAPTER 13

Heart Attacks

The date of my first heart attack is not noted in my diary – nor is much else in late October 1994. It came early in the day: I had walked the dogs and had a shower and was sitting in a white towelling dressing gown sipping coffee and attempting to write, but feeling slightly out-of-sorts in a way that could be attributed to jet lag, for I had returned from Pakistan only the previous day. Out-of-sorts turned to nausea and I took to my bed; there, to nausea a dull constricting pain in my chest and a different pain in my left arm were added; I was alarmed enough to telephone my doctor. At just after nine he was already seeing other patients and would call back between noon and one. 'I might be dead by then,' I said, 'I think I'm having a heart attack.' Allowed to disturb him, his response to my symptoms was that I was indeed having a heart attack, that he would both call an ambulance and come himself, 'and if the ambulance gets there first, go with it'.

Alone in the house, I thought it sensible to open the front door while I still could, but when I got out of bed my feet were dead and my legs gave way. On hands and knees I crawled to the door, opened it an inch or two and retreated to the hall, closing the glass inner doors behind me; I then lay exhausted on the floor where I could at once be seen. One thought excluded all others, even anxiety and hope; it was that no one should die while experiencing such pain, for it was of a quality that obliterated all composure and the quiet business of the commendation of the soul. Many years have passed since I abandoned the beliefs and observances of Christianity, and yet I cherish the notion of dying easily and with my wits about me, hands folded as in a medieval effigy, my dogs about me on my bed, farewells done, sins remembered and

576

confessed, affairs in order, and the ritual comfort of prayers murmured in Latin as in the fading light my consciousness departs. Mop and Titian surged about me in silence until the ambulance men arrived and then put on such a show of raised hackles, growling and snarling that they would not come in. 'Call off your dogs' they shouted through the glass, but by then a stricture had developed in my throat and I could not speak. My dogs, I thought, are putting on such a brave defence not realising that they may be killing me. A passing policeman solved the problem; recognising that Mop was the leading dog, he took off his tunic and, holding it wide open, wrapped it round her head and shoulders and, pushing against her thrust, tossed her backwards down the stairs to the kitchen; when Titian meekly followed, he shut the door on them.

I remember nothing else until we reached the hospital, the then spanking new Chelsea and Westminster with its absurd collection of contemporary art. There I had the clearest vision, not of the conventional tunnels and lights of the near-death experience, but of my brain leaving its skull; it hovered just out of reach of my right hand and then slowly drifted away towards a door; 'For God's sake bring back my brain,' I shouted – at least I think I did – and again lost consciousness.

For a long week I lay in bed attached to instruments. People brought food but left it out of reach and, eating nothing but some peas that I could just touch with my fingertips, I lost half a stone in weight. The curatrix of the hospital's pointless paintings (sick or well, no one stops to look at them, but to decry them is politically incorrect), one of the art world's signatories to the notorious letter demanding my dismissal from the *Standard*, earned a shoddy shilling or two informing the gossip columnists. I wanted only to sleep but friends came, with the best intentions, to sap my energy. When the cardiologists decided that they needed only to open the arteries with a balloon (an angioplasty) rather than to operate – a procedure that they could not offer for some weeks and for which I might wait at home – I was released. A nurse I had not seen before came with instructions not to eat red meat, chocolate or oysters, not to drink coffee, not to have sex. 'What precisely do you mean with not to have sex?' 'Well, you know . . .' she replied. 'No I don't – sex comes in many guises. Am I allowed to masturbate?' To this she made the sort of whimper-cum-splutter that a maiden aunt might make and scuttled off puffing with affront.

I left the hospital in the clothes in which I had arrived – underpants and the white dressing gown, unshod, unshaven and with not a penny in my pocket. The first three taxi drivers would have nothing to do with me but the fourth recognised me as a writer for the *Standard*, took me home, saw me through the door and would not take payment. I went to bed and very warily, almost enquiringly, I masturbated. Why should this puerile and much mocked activity seem so important to a man in his sixties? I do not know: I know only that it was an indication that, in spite of the heart attack, my body was not in other aspects malfunctioning, that I was still a man and had not become a vegetable. Why is it not to be mentioned in polite society, unless by a stand-up comic whose audience will, at the mere mention of it, fall about with laughter? As a subject of serious discussion it is taboo; is this because it is far more common among adult men than we admit or suppose? As all my married friends confess to it but keep it from their supposedly disapproving wives, it is still a secret pleasure in which they must not be too absorbed for fear of the wife at the bathroom door with her, 'Darling, what are you doing in there?' Wives can demand privacy without rousing suspicion, but men cannot. Is masturbation the real reason for the garden shed?

When the widening of my arteries took place it was not quite the calm and insignificant procedure promised – 'You will feel nothing,' they said, 'just watch the screen above you and see it all.' The *Dies Irae* from Verdi's *Requiem* echoed through the operating theatre – not the most comforting of music in these circumstances – and I subsided into a private twilight gloom; but then I felt something deeply unpleasant and the violent shaking of surgical shock began, with nurses and my cardiologist leaning heavily on me to prevent me from falling from the table. Only when the anaesthetist deepened my twilight to unconsciousness could they continue. The heart is reached by way of an artery in the groin and the incision must clot closed when all is done; I emerged from my drowsing to find the most handsome of young doctors – head boy and captain of the first XV rolled into one – pressing hard on the small wound and shut my eyes again to prevent any reaction, not quite as successfully as I had hoped. 'You're enjoying this,' he said with a grin.

The angioplasty did not last and within a year I had another heart attack. Had Colin not been in the house to hear the thump of my collapse, I might well have died; it was eight in the morning and as the nearest ambulance was trapped in traffic, he lugged me out to his car and drove me to the hospital. I was only faintly aware of things as the doctors did what was necessary, but quite clearly heard a young man ask, 'Why are we doing all this? This man is sixty-five and whatever we do he won't have much quality of life when he recovers. Why don't we let him go?' 'Mr Sewell may be inert and not responding,' said an older voice, 'but he's not dead yet and I suspect that he can hear. What you've just said will not encourage him.' I saw that young doctor some months later and reminded him. Now that I am eighty I am grateful that his superior bade him continue whatever it was that he was doing to me.

The surgical response was, eventually, a quadruple bypass; at some point I was enough awake to feel frozen with cold and with an almighty effort summoned the words to ask why – or so I thought – but heard no answer and lapsed back into comfortable unconsciousness. The impression of that chill remained with me and later I asked again, 'Why was I so cold?' 'Because you were; you were in a bath of ice; we were lowering your temperature. Were you conscious? – we thought we heard you mumble something.'

Everything hurt. My ribcage had been ripped open and stitched together with titanium wire; every muscle, tendon and ligament along the spine had been uprooted, stretched or crunched; every pulse in my skull and neck was beating loud as a lead drummer in Led Zeppelin, the noise intolerable, the metal structure of the very bed on which I lay seeming to reverberate in time with them. In the recovery room I would have welcomed death to end such torments, but I had things to do – such absurdly unnecessary things as seeing a painting at Sotheby's and going to the opera. It was these that drove me to recover.

I did both. The opera was Sophia Larson's debut in *Turandot* at the ENO. I had not heard her before, nor have I heard her since – a mystery, for I found her the most dramatically convincing singer in the role, her fine rich soprano perfectly suited to a production that, for the first time in my experience, made sense of an improbable and rather silly plot; her natural body language too lent it conviction. The later of my two small ambitions, and far the less stressful, I have no doubt that it contributed to my recovery; not for one moment did I sense the discomforts of the Coliseum's seats. Discharged on the fifth day after the bypass, on the seventh I tottered on a stick into Sotheby's to see, perhaps for the last time, Orazio Gentileschi's *Finding of Moses*, to be sold on 6 December 1995, lot 61A, a masterpiece irrecoverable if bought by a foreign museum. Painted by Orazio while at the court of Charles I and hung in the Queen's House, Greenwich, it encapsulates a sublime moment in the history of British art and patronage, and I believe its distinctly unclassical landscape to have been inspired by the Thames. I gorged on every brushstroke. As I turned away, 'My God, you look ill,' said an Italian dealer I had known for thirty years, a friend of Claudio. To my 'Oh I've just had a heart bypass' his response was, 'That was a mistake – it was not your heart that needed to be bypassed, but your tongue.' I wished that I had that sort of command of any language but could only murmur the insulting: 'Vaffanculo.'

On my way home, over-confident, I stopped at the V&A on some foolish errand now forgotten and, on leaving, was stopped by a guard and accused of shop-lifting my substantial and glossy catalogue of the Gentileschi sale. I refused to accompany him – 'You've made an accusation in public. You will apologise in public. Fetch the manager of the bookshop.' This he could not do without leaving me, so took my arm. I furiously forbade him. And then the manager appeared, took one look at the catalogue and apologised. I was shaking and thought I might faint when I tottered down the steps to the street but, unsummoned, a taxi driver stopped and took me home – it was another reason to respect the intelligence and responsibility of London cabbies, and not the last. Years later, when somehow the leads of my first pacemaker broke and I had a blackout in Pimlico Road, it was again a taxi driver who picked me up, literally carrying me, and took me to the *Evening Standard*; the Brompton Hospital would have been a better destination, but he had assumed me to be drunk after too good a lunch.

Blackouts were frequent after the bypass, sometimes with just enough warning to find myself a tree in Kensington Gardens or a sheltering gatepost, and I learned not to stand on the kerbs of pavements or on a platform's edge. I became a guinea pig for Dr Richard Sutton's tilt-table, an instrument of torture to which one was tied prone and then, deeply relaxed, tilted into the vertical to induce a faint, the nauseating consequence of a drop in blood pressure. There were, too, all the usual effects of swollen ankles, fingers drained of blood and other circulatory problems, and there were days when my blood pressure was so low that I dared not leave the safety of the house. The bypass quite certainly saved my life, but it also changed it – I could no longer ski or play tennis, the regular annual breaks in the pattern of my life, never again could I scramble about in mountains or walk twenty miles every day for a week, and I found myself breathless – with anxiety, I suppose – when driving even short distances, yet I had been a driver who enjoyed the skill, planning and endurance involved in covering eight hundred miles in a long day. My life changed radically from irregularly active to regularly so sedentary that even walking the dogs any serious distance was out of the question. The point was rammed home to me when, on a trip to Venice with friends from the V&A, we went to Possagno to see Canova's museum and I could not walk up the long slow slope to the great church above the village, but sat at the bottom and miserably watched my companions meander into the unattainable distance half a kilometre away.

For a while I became something of a zealot about matters of the heart. We should all, I preached, know enough to recognise the warning signs, foolishly believing that had this been my case I might not have had the attacks nor needed the disabling surgery – for that is what it was, disabling. Now I am not so sure that I would have believed the preliminary messages from my body and nor am I sure that I would have acted on them – one must have the heart attack to know how much it hurts.

A slow change I would have borne more easily and without the anger and resentment. I had always been reliably fit, my stamina exceptional, but the sudden removal of my toys, as it were, occasioned nagging rancour that I could no longer do what I had done so easily. At the same time, to others I became more indulgent and less critical, not towards the art and artists of my work, but to the failings of more ordinary people, and I no longer particularly cared if things went wrong. I became, I think, an oddly softer, kinder and more generous-minded man after the heart attacks – except where television is concerned.

CHAPTER 14

Television

It was the Blunt Affair that first brought me into contact with television, its minions and exponents, all pushy, abrasive, arrogant, self-admiring and under no circumstances to be trusted. They look you straight in the eye and stab you in the back; they wheedle and cajole to lay their hands on your material, but once they have it, toss you aside; they pretend, if not friendship, amiability, but if it suits them, they mock and mimic, deride and ridicule; and in their editing they subvert, distort, corrupt and lie. There was a time when I thought that television in the hands of the educated could be the greatest force for education beyond the ancient groves of academe, for cultural breadth and critical debate, for connoisseurship in the arts and for the background that one can no longer gain from school, but it is now in the hands of the barbarian for whom the notion of cultural background is quite incomprehensible. Television is now devoted to the amusement of the masses, often by the masses, and if the arts appear at all they are as often as not in the hands of presenters who know nothing of them, who speak of Leonardo da Vinci with a girlish gush of ignorance, or of Damien Hirst with the pubertal adulation of the fourth former with a crush on the head boy.

It was never my intention or ambition to perform on television and that it came about was due entirely to a small company that made modest travelogues for Channel 4 – half-hour programmes that offered honest insights on foreign cities and their environs presented by people who were informed, interested and able to command only a low fee. I was offered Vienna in midwinter and it was there, in the Kunsthistorisches Museum, the exchequer limited to the close examination of only one of the dozen or so paintings by Pieter Brueghel, that, looking through the camera lens, I experienced a revelation. The selected painting was, not surprisingly, his bleak *Winter* of 1565 from his set of the *Four Seasons*, but my choice was the infinitely more complex *Christ Carrying the Cross*, for through the monocular camera – eliminating the wide peripheral vision of a pair of human eyes – the almost undiscoverable figure of Christ (though he is dead centre in the composition) and every detail on the road to Calvary could be isolated and examined in ways otherwise not possible; it was as though I had found a hundred other Brueghels within the broad sweep of movement from the distance on the left to the very different distance on the right. If only, I thought, I had been able to do this for the ten years that I was teaching prisoners in Brixton.

It was an innocent and inexpensive little programme: there was no money for a box at the opera, or even a back seat in the Gods, but we pretended by walking up the steps to the door with wealthier visitors; nor was there money for the Mozart Mass sung in the Cathedral for the benefit of presidents and princes, so we huddled outside in the wind-driven snowflakes and listened to the broadcast – 'Ora pro nobis,' I murmured to myself. We searched for Mozart's burial place – as unmarked as Moore's at Corunna (not a drum was heard, not a funeral note), bought *Stollen* from a stall in the Christmas Market and ate *Torte* at Herr Sacher's very expensive café. It was the first of four seasons for me as well as Brueghel.

In spring we went to Bavaria and followed in the footsteps of mad queer Ludwig and I was, I'd swear, haunted by him, for something uncomfortable and strange – the sense of possession – took hold of me when left alone in the throne room of Neuschwanstein; I had just looked from a window onto a view fit for Altdorfer to paint and a pall of melancholy engulfed me – I had felt it once before, in Heracleia-under-Latmos, in the sanctuary of Endymion, a beautiful youth loved by Zeus, Hera and Selene.*

---

* See *South from Ephesus*, p. 60.

When we reached Starnberg I sought the site of his drowning in the lake, marked by a great timber cross, and waded out to it to weave about it a wreath of wild flowers; it stands waist deep – not nearly deep enough to drown so tall and strong a man unless held down by murderers.

In summer we went to Istanbul and I sat outside the Harem slicing cucumbers, as men did for centuries to prevent the Sultan's many wives from pleasuring themselves, and stood in awe of emeralds and early Chinese porcelain; we sailed the Bosporus and imagined a Turkish army bursting through the doors of Hagia Sophia, a young celebrant clutching the Host to his bosom and miraculously stepping into a solid wall as though through a door, so that Catholics believe that somewhere in that building rests the body of Christ subverting its conversion into mosque and museum. And in the autumn off we went to Pakistan and I came home in a rage against the abject poverty of the poor and the blatant cruelty to animals – my memory is scarred by the tethered pelican outside the chemist's shop, pinioned and filthy, by puppies dying in the gutter, by a donkey fallen under such a load that its legs splayed and it could get no purchase, three men kicking it, and so on and so on. Give the production team their due, they let me say what I wished, and all hell broke loose. It may have been that outspoken programme that scuppered my chances of ever working for the BBC – far too uncontrollable, unequivocal and unsparing for that, in the arts, patronising, complacent, mealy-mouthed, cliché-ridden institution and its top-heavy bureaucracy.

In the summer of 1993 I was asked to make – or so I thought – a programme for *J'accuse*, an interesting series in which the reputations of the great were impugned. I chose Leonardo da Vinci as my victim and wrote a carefully constructed script based on recognised sources and the too few surviving works. I realise now that in my inexperience I may well have mistaken the term 'present' for 'make' – a presenter merely fronts a programme conceived, researched, produced and directed by other minds, to which he contributes nothing other than his smiling face (my smile had long since atrophied) and is responsible not even for his words. I was put into the hands of an unfriendly and uncomprehending Australian director, an ex-ballet dancer grown too muscular and burdened with feminist tendencies; she knew nothing of Leonardo and was intent on bringing into the programme as many as she could of her Australian friends and corybants – one of these last a very pretty youth to play Leonardo in frustrated tantrum; and to these she added Sarah Kent of *Time Out* and half-a-dozen others of the monstrous regiment masquerading as art critics and historians, not one of them of any reputation. The squabbles amused onlooking gossip columnists primed by Kent but the ultimately unscholarly and shoddy programme was to me a wretched disappointment, a perfect example of a good idea made shabby by a formula. Someone should have taken me on one side and explained that I was not making the programme, that what I thought was of neither interest nor consequence, and that if making was what I wanted, then I must get a degree in media studies and conform to the dire pattern of pitching a programme well below the intellectual ability of the audience, including every classic cliché and banality in its construction, bowing to every possible political correctitude of race and gender. 'You,' someone should have said, 'are only the presenter. Yours may be the face on the screen, but in the hierarchy of those who make programmes you are the shit at the bottom of the heap. You will do as you are told.' Had that position been made clear to me I would have resigned and the dreadful directrice could have made the programme entirely from the slop of her imagination.

Nine years passed before another offer came. It was from Kim Peat, then the commissioning editor of programmes on art and religion for Channel 5. Throughout this period Martin Durkin of Wag TV had repeatedly made approaches, flattering but without substance, and nothing had ever reached beyond the 'Hey – I've had an idea . . . ' stage. This time there was not even an idea, just the suggestion of lunch with Kim in Rules, a restaurant where ageing schoolboys perspire over steak and kidney pudding in July. Nothing of interest was said until, Kim having paid the bill, we were outside on the pavement performing the rituals of parting, when she said, 'How do you feel about the Pilgrimage to Compostela?' 'Oh that would be wonderful – I've done the Spanish half – I'd love to finish it. This time next year, I suppose?' 'No. If you want to do it you're off in four days' time.' It did not occur to me until much later that a more desirable candidate for presenter must have fallen by the wayside.

As the great feast of St James is on 25 July we flew to Compostela and did the pilgrimage backwards and without any kind of the intellectual or emotional preparation that I knew I needed. Nearly forty years had passed since my last exposure to Catholicism in all its ritual splendour and, privileged to be in the cathedral – access to which was denied to thousands of genuine pilgrims on the morning of the feast – I was overwhelmed, I think with grief. What I felt so powerfully was not exultation, ecstasy or rapture; it was pain, misery and guilt, my Catholic inheritance in reproach for my abandoning it. I was trapped with evidence of every belief that reason and my homosexuality had compelled me to relinquish. I could hardly draw breath and could not speak. I wept. I could not perform for the camera. For what seemed an age I could not even watch but stood, shaking, my back to this great Mass, my brow against the wall. First Aid attendants came but could not help and I could not explain. I do not know what the crew made of my behaviour, useless to them: I gave them no spontaneous commentary on the service, none of the excited looks expected, none of the bogus involvement in which presenters specialise.

As the deceitful exercise of the pilgrimage itself continued, I realised that I was profoundly affected by the faith of others, of all who had truly made the pilgrimage. French students told me of their final ritual after the cathedral celebrations and before their journey home – it was to go to the nearby coast, strip naked, burn the clothes in which they had walked so far, and swim; thus newly bathed and clothed the return hike could begin. I thought it a beautiful idea and much more than a symbolic practice, and the embrace of the warm sea on my nakedness as I swam out of sight into the Bay of Biscay seemed entirely spiritual. So too were my farewell kisses for three boys one morning in Burgos, two walking back to Germany, one to Switzerland, their boots worn very thin and second-hand, who told me of another custom – the exchange of boots; any pilgrim rich enough to buy new boots must leave his discards tied to a tree where they can be seen, for there is always another pilgrim on the road whose boots are in even worse condition. My young director, a man of occasionally prurient interests, instructed me to ask them if they masturbated on the pilgrimage, but when I refused, falteringly asked them himself – the word is common to both languages. I recall only my own appalled confusion, not their answers. My three kisses on our parting were those of ceremony, an old man much given to the sins of the flesh recognising in the young something devout and righteous that he too once had. And in Lourdes, that Benidorm, that Blackpool, that Disneyland of Catholicism, two comfortably adult women from the north of England rammed home the irrelevance of quotidian human behaviour and appetites with their absolute conviction that a miracle was possible for their companion, an old woman in a wheelchair, that if God chose to use them as the instrument of his intervention in her ills, he was not likely to be obstructed by the flaw of a random sin or two.

Why were we in Lourdes? It is on no route to Compostela and as a shrine post-dates the pilgrimage by far more than a thousand years. We were there because this was television, and as the researcher employed by our television company could see no distinction between one pilgrimage and another, any pilgrimage would do. We even went to Sacré-Coeur in Paris – the monstrous white elephant of Montmartre consecrated only in 1919, because some fool of a graduate from a polytechnic university thought it a place of ancient pilgrimage. Time and again I wailed, 'Why are we here?' in some wretched church once visited by Napoleon III or the Grand Duchess of Bessarabia when I knew that only an hour away there was a greater station or hazard on the road to Compostela. It was on this journey that I learned how inflexible television is and that however flawed the research, once a schedule has been constructed on it, no change can be made. I learned that it is complacently content with its devices, tricks and mannerisms, with visual clichés that are utterly irrelevant, that it will spend hours on a traffic roundabout setting up a shot that for its effect depends wholly on the absence of traffic, and that I might be compelled to cross a bridge in Blois a dozen times because it was suddenly shadowed by a cloud or a clattering Deux Chevaux came from behind and blocked the camera's view; there isn't a cameraman in its employ who cannot be distracted by the utterly irrelevant.

In churches, chapels and cathedrals I was appalled by the crew's downright disrespect for worshippers and unsuspecting clergy – the only way I could put an end to their clambering over altar rails to arrange their lights, microphones and camera angles was to walk out and refuse to return; as for pleading the significance of the Reserved Host, I might as well have attempted to explain a logarithm to a Hottentot. The director, having dug deeply into the how and what of my homosexuality, mistook my misery for sexual deprivation and, no doubt at vast expense, procured a blond American to join the crew and service me. There was no servicing. I would not have it. I was insulted by this trivialising of my spiritual turmoil. Loren was, nevertheless, companionable and we escaped from the others for dinner, which otherwise I would have chosen to eat alone or not at all; we shared an interest in music, and in other circumstances I might well have been drawn to take him to my bed, but the thought that he had been procured for me made that impossible.

When the ordeal was over I told the director that I would never attempt another programme of this kind – or perhaps of any kind –

that it had been intellectually insufferable to work to another man's research knowing it to be puerile, inadequate and in gross error, and that I thought the whole business so trapped in the aspic of custom as to be immutable − as indeed it is. No director is capable of making a programme that involves travel without making it a travelogue. For me the best thing about the pilgrimage had been my days distanced from the crew because I was on a horse, a sweet-natured mare who took in her stride all the noisy pagan celebrations in the streets of Compostela.

The programme, *The Naked Pilgrim*, won the Sanford St Martin Prize for religious broadcasting. If only you knew, I thought as Cardinal Cormac Murphy-O'Connor presented it. Some viewers shared my Catholic miseries; others enjoyed the show; the most extraordinary response came from a woman in Highgate:

22.vii.2003

Dear Mr Sewell − I have just seen you on television in *The Naked Pilgrim*.

You are so inspiring.

You know everything about art.

You are a god.

May I kiss your penis?

Yours sincerely,

Ianthe Pole

'Nice bum' said an elderly woman in Kensington High Street. Martin Durkin, whose idea the programme had been, was delighted with it and began campaigning for another.

*   *   *

For two years or so I resisted Martin's meagre blandishments and then, at last, promised that the 'Written and presented by . . . ' assertion of *The Naked Pilgrim*'s titles would be entirely true in any new case, suggested the Grand Tour, a subject that with a television programme in mind I had explored in a tour of my own in 1989. Uncluttered by the obligations of companionship this had been a concentratedly intense experience, built on and connecting all my earlier travels in Italy. Eliminating all the post-Classical and pre-Renaissance places, buildings and paintings in which the Grand Tourist showed no interest, I concentrated on the ancient Roman and the High Renaissance, and in a different frame of mind, on the Baroque and Neo-Classical that were the modern and contemporary art and architecture of their day – Turin, for example, the Italian equivalent of Bath as rebuilt in the eighteenth century. I proposed a programme to the BBC but, having neither agent nor other interested party to effect an introduction, received not even an acknowledgement of my synopsis, nor even its return. With no particular objective in mind I had continued to collect material, read diaries and journals, make notes and collect souvenirs; with all this in hand, I was well prepared.

My synopsis for Martin was not only of the places on the Tour – from the Alps to all the glories of Piedmont, Lombardy, Tuscany and Umbria, to Rome, Naples and Paestum, and thence to Padua, Venice, Vicenza and Mantua – but of the mundane logistics of travel in the eighteenth century, the damp sheets of it, the piss and shit of it, the fucking and the syphilis. I prepared notes on accommodation, carriages, food, clothes, medicine, sex and every other aspect of the young Grand Tourist's life, including even death and burial, and in this lay my undoing, for Martin saw in some such things the possibility of incorporating travelogue. In the travelogue the presenter must, if he sees one, mount a dromedary, drink a fermented mixture of the milk of moose and the spittle of seal, and eat with evident relish the smoked testicles of his host's enemies; thus I, on the Grand Tour, within the grounds of Stupinigi, hunt wild boar, pretend to buy dapper clothes from a fashionable Milanese store, within sniffing distance of the exhausts of Modena take the wheel of a Ferrari too rare and precious to be allowed to take the road, and in Rome I must have my portrait painted by the hapless Batoni of today. With every one of these irrelevances I proved uncomfortable and eventually uncooperative, for the hours spent on them were hours not spent on great monuments and works of art; they were not what I had expected to cover, not scholarship, not history – they were the trifles of a travelogue and I, I thought, was making a serious programme about education, connoisseurship and the origin of such cultural institutions as the Vatican and British Museums in the century of the Enlightenment. I was mistaken: Martin had instructed his team to make a travelogue and, just as on the pilgrimage they had set their camera on me as I emptied my bladder behind a tree, so they set it again when I had to stumble from the car in Naples to vomit in the street. In Florence, in the Protestant Cemetery, they took elaborate pains to surprise me with the graves of Sewells said to be the bastard sons of William IV, conveniently adopted by a friend. 'Why show me these?' I asked. 'Because we wanted to tell you that you may be related to the Queen.' 'Don't be bloody silly – Sewell is my stepfather's name.' Their researcher back in Islington, whose research in every point of conflict they preferred to mine, had exhumed this useless information and we wasted a whole day on it; yet in Rome, the high point and very purpose of the Grand Tour, I discovered that we had no permit to film in the Vatican and were to omit the overwhelmingly influential antique sculptures of Laocoön and the Apollo Belvedere, Michelangelo's illusionist ceiling of the Sistine Chapel, and Raphael's frescoes of *The School of Athens* and *The Fire in the Borgo*. I imagined what I would, as a critic, say of these omissions, what conclusions I would draw of the man whose name followed the 'Written and presented by . . . ' and was cold with rage.

The Grand Tour was an incompetent failure that ran wildly over time and over budget. It need have done neither. Had Martin made clear that it was to be a travelogue I could have chosen to collaborate in the hope of only a little embarrassment, or – more probably – to resign. Alternatively, had we adhered to my scrupulous scholarship and employed a cameraman who knew how to explore a work of art instead of wasting time on innumerable driving shots ('the audience needs to know how you got here'), men on bicycles, cats on walls, white lines in the road and other banalities, the programme could have been taut, dense and well paced. It had odd moments that informed, a few that were quite beautiful and many that amused, but it was not what it could and should have been. 'Let's break the mould, let's abandon the clichés,' I had said to the director before we set off for Venice (this programme too was made in reverse), and he had enthusiastically agreed, but when it came to the point the travelogue remained intact and I was the broken mould.

I have made no television since. In 2010 I was asked by Tabitha Jackson, commissioning editor of Channel 4, to submit a list of proposals. It was as follows:

An Art Quiz inserting knowledge and instruction between ribaldry and fun.

Francis Bacon: a serious assessment based on the handful of survivors who knew him (of whom I am one), removing him from the current generation of art historians who impose their own interpretations rather than his.

Solitary paintings: great works of art that are isolated from others – Grünewald's Isenheim Altar, Van Eyck's Ghent Altar, Piero della Francesca's Resurrection in Borgo San Sepolcro or his frescoes of the True Cross in Arezzo, Stanley Spencer's Chapel at Burghclere, Roger van der Weyden's Last Judgement in Beaune, the swathe of great altars that stretches across Central Europe from Colmar to Krakow, and so on . . .

The Northern Grand Tour: Paris, Brussels, Amsterdam, Berlin, Dresden, Vienna, the minor German courts, Strasburg and Geneva, following the footsteps of James Boswell and others of his time.

Mad Ludwig of Bavaria – fantasy castles, palaces and Wagner.

The most influential pictures ever painted: Michelangelo's Sistine Chapel, Raphael's frescoes in the Vatican, Leonardo's Last Supper, Caravaggio's Conversion of Matthew, Kandinsky's moves into abstraction before the First World War, Picasso's Guernica, and so on.

Outsider II

The symbolisms of Faith, Food and Sex in art.

The Definition of Terms: an attempt to give viewers a sure grasp of such lubricious and often meaningless portmanteau terms as Baroque and Rococo, Classical, Romanesque and Neo-Classical, and the several Gothics and Renaissances.

To this last Tabitha's specific and only response was a snorted 'and certainly not that', yet of them all it would have been my choice, for it and the influential pictures have the bones of academic severity in them. Aware of the inevitability of travelogue in art programmes I offered three in which travel was integral, but none intrigued her. I can only attribute this to ignorance and incuriosity – the enemies that years before I had encountered from the BBC when Tom Lubbock and I proposed a programme on the eighteenth-century art historian and connoisseur Johann Joachim Winckelmann; not even homosexuality, murder and its ghastly penalty could persuade that commissioning editor that Winckelmann was interesting – 'Never heard of him,' he said, and that was that. The only other recent contact with the panjandrums of television was made by one of them suggesting that I should pair with Noel Fielding, lunatic comedian and cult eccentric, to make programmes on the visual arts. I refused, point blank – that way another murder lay.

The field is thus held by Andrew Graham-Dixon with casual enthusiasm, and by Waldemar Januszczak who has the physical charms of a North Korean despot and a command of French that compels him to pronounce Seurat as Sewer Rat. Eheu, eheu . . .

CHAPTER 15

Loose Ends

Thus quite certainly at the very end of a once promising career, all other avenues closed, there was nothing left to do but reconcile myself to my role as a Cassandra bewailing the end of the ancestral arts that have served mankind so well since his beginning. An old dame dressed as gypsy fortune teller, reading my adolescent palm at a church fête in one of the sunny summers soon after the close of World War II, observed that if I survived the break in my life line at sixty or so, I might live to be a hundred. Was it a coincidence that my first heart attack struck at sixty-four? The life line after its pronounced break is very long and curls almost to the back of my hand before it fades (I note with amusement that the line of Venus cuts very deep and ends abruptly – were the hazards of HIV and AIDS imprinted there?); but do I, at eighty, wish to spend another twenty years crying into the wind unheard, unheard?

When my palm was read my death was to me an impossibility and the disappearance of my future unimaginable – Damien Hirst's *Physical Impossibility of Death in the Mind of Someone Living* is true only of and for the young. After the heart attacks, the surgery, the loss of physical activity, the nauseous slides into unconsciousness with every sudden drop in blood pressure, the idea of death became a preoccupation reinforced by that of Jill in February 1998. Hers was quite unforeseen – five days of mystifying illness and she was gone, and she was the younger of us, if only by nine months; and with her eminence as an expert on Victorian architecture she had made so much more of her life than I of mine. My immediate contemporary at the Courtauld Institute, my near neighbour, my most persistent borrower of books (always returned – a rare thing in borrowers), my companion on three significant journeys and many insignificant, her death was the first to strike home my own fragility. The emotional effects of the death of Elsie Crombie in 1992, as old as my mother and almost as intensely close (and another neighbour), I had managed with some control, but for this there were the practical reasons of so many things to do in seeing to her wishes beyond the business of her will.

She was a passionate espouser of animal causes, a rescuer of dogs, an able pianist, a friend of Brendel, the discreetly rich patroness of young musicians. As the wife of Theodore, gentle, scholarly and respected contributor to *Apollo*, she and he were very much of the Establishment, but with this her outspokenness and eccentricity often did not fit. She loathed smokers and, at great expense, had commissioned a contraption resembling a diver's costume, the helmet an enormous globe of glass equipped with whatever technology was needed to enable her to breathe, hear and be heard; it caused such a stir that she was dropped from almost every guest list, exactly as she wished. In pursuing her war against fur coats she was expelled from Harrods too. There an elegant woman in a fur coat, disturbed by a light touch on hip or thigh, would look down in alarm expecting a pickpocket, only to find frail Elsie in her wheelchair stroking the fur. 'Oh how beautiful it is,' Elsie might murmur, 'how silky. Extraordinary that they can make such reproductions now.' The trap thus set, the woman invariably responded with, 'Reproduction? No, no – of course not. This is real . . . ' At this Elsie withdrew her hand as though from ordure, screamed to all in earshot, 'It's real, her fur coat's real,' and turning directly to the woman wailed, 'How could you? How could you?' ending in a high-pitched caterwaul.

Chaos was the invariable consequence. Fur-coated customers fled, deals were not done, crowds gathered about the mayhem, security men were called and Elsie was expelled – but she had made her point and, holder of an account in the bewildered shop, returned to make it again and again. I once witnessed it and it was wonderful. She left her emeralds to the cause. In her memory, without the wheelchair and the wailing, I sometimes ask of strangers, 'Is that a *real* fur?' Quietly and coldly done, it is marvellously dismaying to the wearer.

Harry Blacker, her near contemporary, was the Ancient Mariner of art exhibitions on the days reserved for critics, for he stoppeth one of three and often more, but though he firmly held one's arm he was never a greybeard loon. I first encountered him at an exhibition in my very early days as *Tatler's* man – he grasped my arm, bent my ear and told me a Yiddish joke, and that was the pattern, armature and flesh of our friendship. He had an instinctive eye for quality in paintings and the courage to say what he thought, which kept him low in the hierarchy of critics – the *North London Advertiser* is no match for the *Sunday Times* in curriculum vitae or obituary. He drew neat little cartoons signed 'Nero' that gently mocked the Jewish society that was so much the staple of his life and delivered little homilies, of which one has governed my reaction to beggars ever since. On Hungerford Bridge after some wretched show at the Hayward Gallery we came upon a young beggar, haggard, ill-kempt, the sockets of his eyes black with fatigue, and I emptied my pockets into his hand; later, when it transpired that the waif was an *Evening Standard* reporter investigating a claim that London beggars are Croesus-rich, Harry consoled me with the tale of a rabbi who, rebuked by one of his flock for giving money to a beggar with 'Don't you know he's a millionaire? replied, 'No, I do not, and if he is, let it be on his conscience, not on mine.'

Harry, born in Whitechapel in 1910, the son of Russian immigrants, with no education after fourteen, was something of a saint, and those of us who did not brush him off grieve less for his death (for that at eighty-nine may have been a mercy), than for ourselves, our loss. I took to missing press views, knowing that he'd not be there – an odd memorial, but my memory is all that I can offer him of immortality.

Preoccupation with one's death has odd little consequences; I bought no new clothes or shoes, convinced that I had no time to wear them out; knowing that I would never play them again I sold my violin and cello, but bought books without a thought of never reading them; I enjoyed a surfeit of opera and thought so much of buying a great car to remind me of the intimacy of machine and man that I had enjoyed when young, that I did not buy one, unable to make the choice; I funded three post-graduates in their pursuit of higher degrees; and four years after the first heart attack, still physically exhausted, I sold the house in which I had lived for thirty years or so. Tall and narrow, the first of a terrace built in 1840, typical of Kensington when it was still a modest urban village, its staircase steep, its condition neglected since modernised in 1929, the roof a constant anxiety, the basement occasionally inclined to flood, it was, my doctor observed, no place for a man with my cardiac condition. 'Find a flat,' he said, 'live on one floor. Make life easy for yourself.' Flats and dogs, however, do not fit well together. 'Get rid of the dogs,' said my doctor, as though they were useless ornaments to my life. A low-built house with a garden seemed to me a more practical solution, but such a house is very rare in Kensington and I was compelled to exchange all the comfortable familiarities of the borough in which I was born and still felt a villager, for the suburban unfamiliarities of Wimbledon, where I feel as much marooned as Robinson Crusoe. It is not that Wimbledon is a foreign country, for as a child it was a place to go on summer impulse on a Green Line bus from Kensington High Street, to lie in the long grass, have tea and return to Kensington as though the afternoon had been spent in *The Wind in the Willows*; and as soon as the war ended and I could have a dog, for the first and all subsequent dogs, seventeen of them, it has represented the wild alternative to Kensington Gardens, the long walk, the swim, the romp in the snow, a place of badgers, rabbits and foxes, herons, swans and wildfowl – but I know now that it is no place for townies.

The move to Wimbledon ended what had been an oddly contented period after the death of my mother. I had been warned not to live alone and young Valerian Freyberg came to keep me company while I searched for alternatives to Eldon Road. He brought me the pleasure of brotherhood – or what I imagined it to be. I lived my life, he lived his as a young political animal in the House of Lords (the amusements of Hansard were delivered every day) and we shared what we could in leisure and domestic matters – I will never forget the particular joy of hearing with him at the Albert Hall the concert performances of Wagner's *Ring* while Covent Garden was closed for refurbishment – for him his first exposure to it, though not to the Hall. He had a friend, the painter Zsuzsi Roboz, who had a box there, and after producing a portrait of me that disturbingly discerns something of my soul, she took to nourishing my musical life too. To own a box when the Proms are in season must be one of the richest aesthetic pleasures of London life and she, a survivor of years of hiding and deprivation when Admiral Horthy was in command of Hungary and of 1944 when he fell to the Nazis, perhaps found in it some small recompense. As a pupil of Annigoni, she was a survivor in another sense. A year or two ago I refused a concert if so-and-so was to be a fellow-guest. He was. 'Then are you free on such-and-such a date?' she asked without a pause. I was, and accepted her invitation knowing nothing of the programme but expecting it to be an evening of Schubert or Richard Strauss. It was not; it was an exquisite punishment knowingly inflicted – entirely of Sondheim unrelieved, I would rather have had a tooth drawn. There can be no more such punishments; for some days in July this year, tiny, delicate, fawn-like, Szuszi lay like a medieval effigy in surrender to the cancer that was draining away her life, and on the month's ninth day she died.

The nation does not know it but Valerian was a significant campaigner for free entry to museums and galleries (as too was I), acting as a conduit of information and asking questions that a member of the House of Lords might ask but a high museum official, prevented by his position as a civil servant of sorts, might not. It was an important campaign that has greatly increased the

number of visitors (though not entirely without unforeseen dis-
benefits), but in the beginning it was not wholly supported by the
then new Labour government – indeed, so much was it doubted
by so many Labour men that the cynic in me is amused to see that
its vociferous opponents have forgotten their original position and
have taken to claiming it as their own achievement, while those
who were really working for it, including one particular museum
director, have never been acknowledged.

I took Valerian to one of John Vere Brown's birthday parties
and halfway there, my feet suddenly cold, I confessed that John, an
old and close friend from whom I had no secrets, was not only
homosexual but what many might describe as a foul-mouthed old
queen – moreover, most of his guests were likely to be so too; but
my suggestion that we skip the party and go home, he refused. An
hour later I found him in the garden holding court with absolute
aplomb as though these were the most natural of circumstances
and, thinking of myself at his age (when I would have run a mile
from such company), I wondered how it was that one so young
had quite such poise. There were tiresome rumours that we were
lovers, spread by the high panjandrum of one of the country's great
museums disappointed that Valerian had shown no interest in his
daughter, his behaviour quite disgraceful but common enough
among heterosexuals, so many of whom deem the platonic friendship an impossibility for homosexuals. It is not; the friendship of a
homosexual for a heterosexual, uncluttered by a hint of sexual
interest, can be intense, generous and loyal – and last a lifetime.

There were two John Browns, the painter and the photographer,
and bound in one body they destroyed each other; much of his
work as a photographer is in the National Portrait Gallery, but his
paintings, hundreds of them, are to be found only in the homes of
friends. My friendship with him reached back to an encounter in
1959 in the shadow of Delacroix in the Tate Gallery, to Dartmoor
a year later among the standing stones of Grey Wethers, bleak
against grey skies, and later still to the desolate flat lands of the north

Kent coast in winter in icy greys and whites. In these and other windswept wastes I learned from him that colour is to be perceived in even the dullest light and that what to a mere townsman's eye must seem barren, cheerless, desolate and cold, can be persuaded by a painter into fields of warm brown and red and orpiment.

Early on a bright Sunday morning in May 2000, the eve of his seventy-fifth birthday, John and I had a merry conversation about this and that, as old friends do, until I cut it short with, 'We must stop gossiping or we shall have nothing to say tomorrow at your party.' The truth was that I wanted to go out with the dogs and get on with the day, and I hoped that impatience had not put an edge into my voice. Back from the Common I found a message that John had in mid word broken off a subsequent conversation, and that alarmed neighbours had found him dead in bed amid the wreckage of his modest breakfast. 'You must write an obituary,' said Max Hastings (John had photographed his mother).

It was then I realised how little I knew of John Vere Brown, JVB to me, Beige to others and John Very Brown to those friends who knew of this error made by some unfortunate girl in Harrods when John had an account there. I knew none of the staples of the conventional obituary, nothing of his father, nothing of school and very little of his life and work as a photographer of portraits and the theatre. I knew only his negligible parallel life as a painter, and his inheritances from his mother – the noble profile of a Roman emperor, the pitch of her voice, her tendency to strangle it with mews and hesitations and blurt startling political incorrectitudes no matter what the time or place or company. Her substantial house near Primrose Hill he sold and, one by one, he bought a dozen others, always losing money when impatiently he left them, for in almost every case his passion for removing walls and ceilings had induced collapse. The last house he owned was a stone barn in Derbyshire in which I, with Alan Bates and his brother, spent days stuffing the gaps between the stones with papier-mâché to keep out the wind; made of newspaper the papier was a perfect match for grey stones, but most of it was promptly eaten by the local mice. John died in poverty. At his funeral Alan Bates read *Lycidas*, Milton's elegy on the death of a friend of great promise.

I owe John other friendships – with Yonty Solomon, a gifted pianist, his near neighbour on Primrose Hill, an intellectual and aesthetic exchange, and a brief sexual fling with Samuel Menashe, the American poet, before his poetry was published by Gollancz. At that stage he wished to be known only by his surname and even his lovers had to address him thus – but like the Nusch of Nusch Éluard (another poet's wife) it was oddly sensual in pillow talk. He wrote a poem for me, impulsively pressing into my hand a lined sheet torn from a notebook as we walked through Cornwall Gardens –

> Running water, shining bright,
> Running water, shining bright

– and took amiss my foolish quip 'Oh Menashe, it is too long,' made before I knew that gnomic brevity was then the hallmark of his work.

John Brown's was not quite the first of the long close friendships that embellished my post-student life; of these the earliest was a John of another colour, John White, a clerk in the offices of Christie's when I joined the firm, eighteen in 1958 and pretty enough to stir the loins of any man with eyes to see, waiting to wed his childhood sweetheart – which he did, the marriage swiftly maturing beyond its once sweet simplicity. In the years between its end and the beginning of another, he lived with me and assorted tempestuous mistresses and we fell into the custom of an occasional oyster feast, reinforced after we had both had heart attacks, by the instruction of my cardiologist – 'If you must eat oysters, be gluttonous: two dozen twice a year will do you no harm, one every day will clog your arteries.' But in 2006 John, by then retired and living in far Herefordshire, began to die of cancer. He spoke cheerfully of coming to London before the end of April, after which, because there is no 'r' in the month, oysters are traditionally forbidden until September – 'Something to look forward to,' he said when April came and went. So too did September. I went with another contemporary from Christie's, Ray Perman, to see him. We took him to dinner in Abergavenny and lunch in Hay-on-Wye, but we had to lift him into the car; there were no oysters, and other food he could only poke and prod. When we left for London I hardly dared hold him in our customary hug, his ribs too apparent to my fingertips. 'I'm still coming,' he said, 'we've got to have those oysters.' Over his shoulder I caught but could not hold the sad eyes of his wife.

For the next six weeks or so we spoke almost every day, but oysters dropped out of our farewells. At our final conversation he seemed rather stronger and more confident; shades of *La Traviata*, I thought, and sure enough, early the following morning his daughter telephoned, and that was that. Had John held on for five more months our friendship would have lasted half a century, yet I, his oldest surviving friend, refused to give the valediction at his funeral – and just as well, for at it I was choked with tears. But I should have had the courage to stand before that congregation and speak of his steadfast friendship, I should have honoured with merry recollection the most honest, loyal and guileless man I ever knew.

What then of oysters? John left me money with which to continue our feasts and Ray Perman seemed the obvious companion. He had joined Christie's at seventeen or so as a 'boy' in the catalogue subscription office. Born in Lambeth in 1942, he has lost neither his south London accent nor his instinctive cheek and, in spite of becoming perhaps the most important business engineer that Christie's ever had, in both London and New York, the most shrewd and effective reformer of its hapless ways, is still, for me, a 'boy' – a boy who as a boy was so knowing that he can never have been innocent. In the fashionable tight trousers and bum-freezer jackets of the early Sixties he knew precisely the effect that he had on men (useful in the art trade), but it was with one Susie in the office, playing whore on a pile of carpets in the basement, that for ten shillings he lost his real virginity. What began for me as a tease in which neither of us was serious, has been a firm friendship for more than fifty years, and only in one small thing, the oyster feast, has Ray failed me – he has an allergy.

The last friendship formed in the late fifties was with Carlos van Hasselt, then an assistant keeper at the Fitzwilliam Museum in charge of drawings and watercolours, whom I met in Paris in 1958 at the Congress of Art Historians. A *bon vivant*, he was already stout, knew everyone who mattered both professionally and socially, and was known by them, and for years I revered him as a young uncle, discovering only very late in our friendship that he was two years my senior and not the two and twenty that I had assumed. In 1961 he was appointed curator-in-chief of the Fondation Custodia, the formidable collection of Dutch paintings, drawings and archival material formed by Frits Lugt, prodigious scholar and connoisseur (then in his late Seventies), housed in the Palais Turgot in Paris, which, combined with the Institut Néerlandais, was to be a major outstation of Dutch culture.* His apartment there became a home from home for many young men employed by Christie's and Sotheby's, as well as young curators from all over Europe and America.

Most of my memories of Carlos, apart from those of his generosity, are associated with his scholarship, his eye and his fund of gossip, but an exception is the sudden ability of this portly man to run, this man who would always take a taxi to travel half a mile. It was in May 1968. The perfect example of a man in a mid-life crisis and sick of working in the art market, I was in Paris idly renewing work on Rubens for the doctoral thesis that I still half hoped might get me into academe. It was a fine Saturday after-noon and in a restaurant on the Boulevard Saint Michel I had just

---

* For both Lugt and Carlos see J. F. Heijbroek, *Frits Lugt, Living for Art*, Fondation Custodia 2012.

had lunch with Carlos who was, for the moment, my mentor in all things to do with Rubens. Idling over coffee we became aware of something that disturbed our ease – a murmur from the street, no more. We should have stayed where we were but curiosity drew us out into a gathering turmoil – and then we heard the sirens, so loud that they must have been switched on by the police to announce their presence rather than their coming; then we found all side streets obstructed by their vans and we and a thousand others were trapped in the Boulevard.

With truncheons raised for the immediate blow, armed policemen launched themselves into the crowd. Incredulous, I stood my ground – this was Paris and de Gaulle, not some corrupt tribal tyrant, was on the throne. Carlos, however, seeing cracked heads, blood streaming and fallen bodies trampled, shouted 'Run' and grabbed my arm. Even at such a time it is astonishing to see a man who has acquired such dignity of position and the portliness of middle age, suddenly break into a sprint, but sprint he did, this way and that, with me in tow. At one point we were pursued, but Carlos knew where he was going and the *flics* did not – even so, not until we'd crossed the Quai des Augustins and ducked down to the footpath by the Seine, did he slacken.

Later I knew that I had witnessed one of the notorious student riots for which 1968 is most remembered. Alone, I saw the beginnings of another in the Place de la Concorde, and again I ran, for in the face of such blind brutality obviously enjoyed by those inflicting it, the sane man can do nothing and should fade away. Reports of these *événements* echoed round the world, not least in Britain where, within a month, students in a dozen universities, in colleges and even art schools, had confronted their authorities with sit-ins and demonstrations, but with far less intellectual authority for what they did.

By chance Kenneth Clark, Lord of *Civilisation*, was in Paris too in May 1968, towards the end of filming material for that celebrated television series, and it may be that the student riots there influenced his pessimistic conclusions, not only about the hopelessly damaging fragmentation of art, but of society through the demanded abolition of its institutions. He was right to compose a valedictory elegy for the vanishing past of the fine arts, but where society is concerned, it is not unreasonable to come to a contrary view and argue that when French students lent their intellectual weight to the inarticulate protests of the proletariat, they achieved what could have been, but for the police, a wholly bloodless revolution; the most sustained strike in French history gave both students and workers what they wanted, and sent de Gaulle to cultivate his garden.

Carlos retired in 1994; at sixty-five, though troubled by a worsening cardiac condition and the sort of weight that is so firm to the touch that one knows it will never diminish, he was not ready for retirement and, continuing as habit the duties of the past three decades, he travelled all Europe to see exhibitions of which he sent me criticisms on postcards in his small neat hand. Increasingly he felt, as I do, forgotten and ignored by curators much younger and less experienced than himself, and the changes that they wrought in their museums and galleries made them unfamiliar and unfriendly – one of the cruel truths of his profession is that once a curator has retired from his post, the successor generation brushes him aside, the accumulated wisdom born of long experience of no interest to the young. After six years of this disenchantment he suffered a paralysing stroke; the further five years vouchsafed him, speechless and incapable of responding to the gossip that had always been his only frivolous relief, were a terrible torment for so generously gregarious a man.

Of such ancient platonic relationships there is only one more of which I must write – it is with Rüdiger Joppien. In the autumn of 1968 we were both researching in the English rooms of the Witt Library of the Courtauld Institute in its original premises in Portman Square – not a library but a collection of photographs; we worked on opposite sides of the vast common table, he in absolute concentration, his face half concealed by the fall of his hair, and the hair the rare dark auburn that the English of my mother's generation always described as Titian red, though it was never to be found in the tresses of any Venetian Venus – indeed only in the sacks of henna sold in the souks of the East does this rich and wonderful colour exist. For several days we worked without so much as a friendly nod or the beginning of a smile, and not once did he look up until, at last, puzzled that I could get from him not the slightest form of acknowledgement, I willed him to look at me and when, suddenly, he did, it was to reveal a face that I felt I had seen a thousand times idealised by Pre-Raphaelites and Nazarenes.

What then? My diary is uninformative, but we became friends over Philippe James de Loutherbourg, the subject of his doctoral thesis and of an exhibition that he was to mount in Kenwood House in 1973.

I wove him into my professional friendships, particularly with Gert Schiff, the great authority on Fuseli, but ours was always to be a friendship constructed and maintained on the warp and weft of journeys, presences, absences, telephone calls and letters. I was often in Germany in its early days and when I could I stayed with Rüdiger in Cologne, where he changed addresses with astonishing frequency – one attic is for its freezing chill seared into my memory; later, after his marriage, in the apartment where he and Kathrin were joined by Charlotte, Johanna and a suicidal rabbit, conditions grew steadily more comfortable.

With Rüdiger it seems that no subject is excluded from his interest, ranging from the Panoramas popular in England in the eighteenth century to the voyages of Captain Cook and Joseph Banks and the artists who travelled with them, from the metalwork of Christopher Dresser to the glass of Dale Chihuly, from the doubtful authenticity of the latest Raphael at the National Gallery to the confusion of drawings by Franz and Ferdinand Kobell. This has meant, of course, that Rüdiger is not where he should be – that is in the first rank of historians of English art in the age of the Enlightenment and imperial expansion. For me this is a matter of great sadness, but not surprise, for in English art scholarship we have no place for the universal man; we must specialise; we must know a very small subject in very great depth, constantly publish trivial findings, and in this one field be considered expert. Rüdiger is too universal.

*   *   *

As an old man must, for in such memories he offers an oblique view of himself, I have written of a few old friends; there is a handful more – Baby Helen, a significant player in the first half of my life who, as hapless onlooker from the shores of Massachusetts, has devotedly and perhaps despairingly (so many have been my follies) watched its second, and Wendy Baron, the most important of all Sickert's women,* has been a constant since our student days – but most friends have come and gone, the friendships exhausted when too often we had nothing left to say other than 'Do you remember . . . ?' and stirring dead embers was how we spent our evenings.

I should, perhaps, have written of the few artists I have en-countered, as any mercenary critic might – Sewell on Bacon, Freud, Hockney or any other notable I could persuade to paint my portrait or engage in conversation – but I have kept my distance and my freedom as a critic. These three I knew in varying degrees long before I took to criticism and it never occurred to me that every word they uttered should be preserved by some devoted amanuensis. Hockney was first of this triumvirate and I was wise enough to buy one of his drab early townscapes and fool enough to refuse a more recognisable daub, *Help*, of 1962, when it was still wet, for £200 (probably now worth as much as my house). It is of

---

* See Wendy Baron, *Sickert Paintings and Drawings*, Yale 2006, the most towering of her many monuments to the old boy.

no significance that I did not much care for Lucian Freud and thought him cold and calculating, though I may know a little more than most of his dispute with Anthony d'Offay. That Francis Bacon, nearish neighbour, occasionally enlisted me as errand boy, woke me at dawn to play chauffeur to his still somnolent drunken lover, John Edwards, and ferry him to Long Melford for breakfast with his family, is hardly a contribution to the history of art, though that Francis deliberately cultivated the fart by drinking foul vegetable juices every morning, usually in Harrods' juice bar, possibly is. Should I dramatise my slightly frenzied acquaintance with Ruskin Spear in his later years into a claim that it was he who, overlapping with Francis Bacon at the Royal College, taught him how to paint? – the claim was certainly made. From an afternoon alone with Henry Moore at Perry Green, had it happened in my days as a critic rather than in 1978, before that transformation, a book could easily have been born, for in 1992, after a gap of fourteen years, I offered the Planning Inspectorate of the day a defence of Hoglands as he left it at his death in 1986, against its revision and development by the Henry Moore Foundation, as passionate as though I had eaten the great man's biscuits only the day before. The tale of my late friendship with Derek Hill, though I had known him since the early Sixties, I told in a foreword to Bruce Arnold's biography,* a formal note of affection and respect from which I felt compelled to exclude his obsessive, giggling and not particularly enlightening reminiscences of mutual masturbation when a boy.

When Michael Reynolds, founder of the annual Discerning Eye exhibitions, died in 2008, his deathbed admonition to a mutual friend was 'Tell Brian to protect my reputation' – a heavy burden for a man who knew how fragile that reputation was and had nothing to support it other than his recollection of sitting, or rather sagging, for his portrait a month after his quadruple bypass, a portrait for which we both ran out of time and energy, a failure.

---

* Bruce Arnold, *Derek Hill*, Quartet, 2010.

We were both outsiders and, a painter to his bones, his fiery contempt for the fashionable nostrums of contemporary art was expressed in foulest language – he is remembered more for his rancour and vituperation than any trenchant canvas that he painted.

Should I gossip about Patrick Procktor, distantly adorable, whose powerful early promise evaporated in frivolity, was fogged by drugs and drowned in alcohol? I was once asked to write a book on him, but I refused – too close, I thought, after a boozy lunch at Odin's and clambering over the railings at the back of his house (a short cut) to smoke a joint, I cannot hurt this man, I cannot tell the necessary truth.

What have I to add to the mythology of Derek Jarman, a scatterbrain, his creative instinct powerful but utterly undisciplined, flamboyantly queer? I knew him a little in his early days, for we had friends and acquaintances in common – Keith Milow, with whom he was in love (insofar as his short-lived fancies merit that description), John Vere Brown, Nikos Stangos, Heathcote Williams, Patrick Procktor, Mario Dubsky, Peter Langan and Joe McCrindle, whom I had persuaded to buy a taut small landscape. I thought Derek intriguing as a painter, technically more than competent, but quite unformed by the Slade School at which he had been a student between 1963 and 1967 and of which he left a disturbing account in his memoir *Dancing Ledge** – ' . . . the Renaissance had at last succumbed to the air-conditioned nightmare of Pop.' I am inclined to argue that this is one of the most revealing records of art and life in England at the end of the twentieth century. There was a long hiatus in our friendship; Derek had drifted from painting into cinema, theatre and high camp, but when, in the late Eighties, he settled in Prospect Cottage, Dungeness, more than a little mad, he was sometimes welcoming, at others anxious to preserve his deliberate loneliness. Of the old band only Joe McCrindle and John Vere Brown

---

* Derek Jarman, *Dancing Ledge*, Quartet, 1984.

survived, the others utterly forgotten. Joe and I trudged the shingle beach with him, hunching into the wind – there is nothing else to do at Dungeness; John took stark and subtle photographs of the cottage, the beginnings of its arid garden, its interior, the *objets trouvés* and of Derek himself, the very first to draw attention to the place that was, as an installation, his last mature work of art. He died in February 1994.

Tess Jaray, for whose paintings and pavements I twice expressed admiration long ago in the Eighties, wrote me a wry note in 2010 when I reviewed, with almost as much respect as I have for Anita Brookner's observations on art, her exquisite slim volume of essays on painting.* She thanked me for the phrase 'with much I disagree . . . ' for in this I had, it seems, ensured that she would not lose quite *all* her friends. I was reminded of the letter sent to the *Evening Standard* in 1994 by the 'art world', demanding my dismissal, for Tess, though not a signatory (she is incapable of any such spite), was closely associated with many of that self-appointed clique and its continued esteem is necessary to her professional wellbeing. I could see her point: my condemnation of a contemporary artist approved by the art world can easily be dismissed with 'Well, he would say that, wouldn't he?' but my praise causes a flutter of misgiving in the dovecot and might well prove toxic. I almost believe that in the present climate of Jesuitical orthodoxy my esteem is a thousand times more menacing than my obloquy, and am tempted to sing subversive praise of Chris Ofili and Anish Kapoor in hope of ridiculous reputations withered.

This absurd art world is oblivious of Michael Leonard, almost popular for his portrait of the Queen with a corgi. This most scrupulous observer of the nude, academic in the best ancestral sense of form in light and shadow, painted slowly and accurately, is perhaps the last surviving figurative painter whose imagery is not shallow and whose handling of paint is not slick – Freud came

* Tess Jaray, *Painting: Mysteries and Confessions*, Lenz, 2010.

nowhere near in such judgement. His painted athletes have a meditative air as though, in their activity, they are heirs to the Greek and Roman past of our cultural beginnings and perform a rite that reaches back millennia to athletic feats in old Aegean cities. Michael conjures the ghosts of Alexander, Hector and Achilles, not with Olympic triumphalism, but with the drudgery of the discipline that comes before and after it. His portrait drawings are elegant conceits mischievously removing his sitters to the historic period of which they remind him and then drawn as though by Van Dyck, or Rembrandt or Bronzino or whoever is most fitting; that done, he adds a further layer of meaning with the convincing illusion of broken glass, paper torn or crumpled, and the ingrained dust of ages; with these he implies that both image and sitter have been discarded, as though forlorn, forgotten and worthless – wealthy sitters perhaps do not see the point. Me he drew as a genial contemporary of Robespierre after a good day with the guillotine. All the disdain of an art world irremediably dedicated to the Serota tendency cannot diminish such an accomplished artist.

I have said much less of the friendship of my dogs than they deserve, and almost nothing of my cars. Both are a mystery to me. My intense need for the companionship of dogs, and particularly of bitches, I may perhaps attribute to some profound primeval dependence, but for cars, however, there is no such explanation. My interest was first stirred by the sight of a bare Rolls-Royce chassis being driven to a coachbuilder by a goggled driver muffled against the wind and rain, sans screen, sans roof, sans doors. This oddly heroic image of courage in adversity was the sort of thing that Biggles might have done, Biggles the literary model of derring-do for most boys of my generation.

Cars disappeared from the streets throughout World War II, but within months of its end in 1945 they emerged from their garages and the streets of Kensington became an exhibition site of wonders from the Twenties and Thirties, not only of the familiar grandees, Rolls-Royce, Bentley and Lagonda, but of such now long forgotten marques as Autovias and Packards, Salmsons, Railtons and Broughs, Hudsons, Cords and Auburns. I fell into the traps of longing, lust and love, drew them, redesigned them and, at sixteen, invented the hatchback. I still look at cars, but now that art has deserted them and surrendered their design to the computer, they are of little interest. Show me a Thirties Rover, however, and its absurd attempt at streamlining, and I will coo over it as over a friendly mongrel pup; show me a Lagonda V-12 of the Thirties and I will stand in awe as though of a Saluki of long pedigree.

I have had two whippets and an Alsatian of proper pedigree, mongrels and crossbreeds aplenty, dogs found and dogs from rescue homes. I have an affinity with dogs; I so easily attract the interest of other people's dogs that I could play Pied Piper and be off with them; and I know that, were I to up sticks and go to live in Spain, or Greece or Turkey, I would be overwhelmed by them and rendered penniless. Since the day on which World War II in Europe was declared to be at an end, I have had dogs; their companionship has kept me sane, their care has lent me daily discipline, and I cannot imagine my life stripped of their constant and unquestioning affection. That their lives are too short is my only complaint of them, and that their going is not made easier by its frequency. As I write, I know that my old Alsatian is dying and will soon be gone, but I am content to tolerate the consequence of her relaxing sphincters, to wake and put her to the garden in the middle of the night, to sponge the thick fur of her hind legs when the urine dribbles, for there is still light in her eyes and joy in her tail, still an appetite for food, and only when these things fade shall I see to it that what must be done, is done. There is, in the garden, a stone sarcophagus, made by Nicholas Moreton, a sculptor better known for variations on the human figure; it is engraved with one word - DOMINICANES - a monkish pun of which the meaning in this case is The Dogs of God, for if I do not believe in God for myself, I half believe in Him for them.

CHAPTER 16

Death

The old should cultivate the friendship of the young, if for no other reason than that the immortality of ordinary mortals – those for whom there can be no obituaries in national newspapers – lasts no longer than the lives of friends. As a child whose mother seemed only to have older friends, I am the bearer of received memories that reach far back, well into the nineteenth century; she took me to Paderewski's last London recital when I was perhaps eight, he nearing eighty and very very slow, but as a young man in 1890 he had sat to Burne-Jones, and Burne-Jones was born in 1833. My life has been much enriched by many such reaches and inherited awarenesses, but for most of my generation there will be, in the memories of our successors, no recollections of the who and what and how we were; thus, if we are old when we die and our friends are of our age and few, grief and mourning are bound to be short-lived before we and they are all swept away by the waters of oblivion.

The young, however, are carelessly unthinking and unkind. With age no part of their experience they know little of the wisdom of the old and nothing of their inevitable miseries, deprivations and frustrations, nothing of the lust and longing that lurk beneath the wrinkles, sagging skin and thinning hair. Were they to know of it, surely they could only be repelled by the old man of whom, despite the trips and stumbles, despite his uncertainties on stairs (he breathes as breathlessly in their descent as in their climbing), there is, in his mind if not in his mirror, enough of what years ago he was to make him think that he is still a sexually driven animal – a thought mightily provoked by a young man's languor, or his strut, by hair peeping from his chest, or the smooth lack of it, by the way in the underground he lounges in the fuck-me pose of the Barberini Faun, or reaches for support as though he were the Apollo Belvedere. But what is the point of such a thought? What would happen were an old man to let his fingers reach? Humiliation.

In recent years I have had such a young friend. With the visual arts a common interest we were brought together by his importuning – he grasped my forearm in Piccadilly, outside the Royal Academy. I was first taken by his boldness, then by his charm, and then by his imagined resemblance to Salai, the boy through whose curly hair Leonardo da Vinci used to run his fingers, a pickpocket, a thief, a street-boy prostitute. He wished to broaden his experience, expand his knowledge, sit at my feet; he wished to write, to be another pseudo-philosopher of art as unintelligible as the French Foucault, Lyotard and Derrida; and only I could help. I fell into the role of Higgins in *Pygmalion*, a man of Shavian discipline, and at first thought not at all of sexual possibilities, but then the recollection of kisses, licks and bites when I was his age became insidious and increasingly I realised how much I wanted him, wanted what Chesterfield called the ridiculous position, wanted his arse and the reciprocal clinging of the young.

One evening, after I had introduced him to Charles Saatchi, he plonked a kiss upon my mouth, but by then I knew him to be thoroughly heterosexual and deemed the kissing treacherous. Never once had I touched him or reached toward the fine brown skin so often glimpsed between his skimpy top and trousers, but he knew well enough what I felt. I felt as Zeus felt for young Ganymede, but in looks I knew I was Methuselah. 'Pay for my drugs,' he said, 'and you can watch me fuck my girl.' I toyed with the idea, but remembered my stepfather's old friend, Sir Ian Horobin, jailed for watching big boys buggering smaller while he masturbated, and considered the indignity of the spectator not worth the candle. He tried a better offer. 'Pay for my drugs and you can fuck me while I fuck her.' This mercenary response destroyed the very nature of our friendship.

As Methuselah I inhabit an increasingly discomfiting world of irrecoverable words, names forgotten, faces unrecognised in the blur of prosopagnosia, and the unconscious confusion of banana for umbrella and night storage heater for the microwave. My spine crumbles, my hips creak, and like most men of my age I have had the dreaded slippery finger of the urologist probing my prostate gland, with the accompanying threats of impotence and incontinence, the twin calamities that most men fear more than any other – though the onset of dementia terrifies me more. I have lost count of my days in hospital in recent years dealing with ischaemic heart disease, vasovagal syncope, uncontrollable drops in blood pressure already very low, the insertion of stents and pace-makers, the surgery of two mastectomies and efforts to remedy a corkscrewing spine, my trunk an old bag of scars and stitches, yet not one of these and their consequences, not even the possibility of sudden death, has seemed as wretched a malfunction as a leaking bladder and the abrupt reduction of one's penis to, as Eric Gill put it, a mere 'organ of drainage'. Drugs keep both in abeyance.

Who, young, girl or boy, would willingly conjugate with so patched and tattered an old man? Yet old men lust after the young, not once a week or once a day or hourly, but in response, if one is out and about, to almost constant stimulus. It is the young skin that does it; the conventions of beauty are a bonus, and all the old triggers of hair and eyes and lips are there, but when the skin of the young is flawless, it is what most makes the fingers reach, as though aching to caress. All the cosmetics of Paris and New York, all the nips and tucks, seams and gussets of plastic surgery, all the perfumes of the Arabian civet cat, all these together are no match for a skin poised in late adolescence or early adulthood. Inside his own skin, rough and wrinkled, pallid with approaching death, the old man feels the same sensual sensations as the young, but he may not touch. It is a terrible predicament. We laugh with sympathy at an old dog's sudden jauntiness when he sniffs a bitch in heat, but old men we mock, and despise as trull or catamite any submissive object of desire.

Death

And that is age, old age – an age of indecision, confusion and increasing disability, an age of shrunken shanks and shuffling pace, of grasp too feeble on the lid of marmalade, of eyes that sooner or later will not see and ears that will not hear, of padded underpants (not yet) and of a heart that from time to time palpitates like the single-cylinder diesel engine of a Turkish fishing boat. I embraced a girl the other day and quite without thought allowed my hand to stray a little lower than it should – 'He put his hand on my bum,' she cried, and shied away, not putting hers on mine. Our friends laughed. I blushed – the one thing that without hesitation I can still do as well as a teenage boy. Old men *are* sexual animals, but we make fools of ourselves when we lose our sense of the ridiculous. And in a sexual sense that is precisely what we are – ridiculous.

*   *   *

An eerie business, writing a will, dispassionate and coldly rational. It takes a man outside himself, detaches him from his possessions and makes him judge and jury of his friends, reward and revenge standing at his elbow ready to nudge his pen. It makes him make a judgement on himself, his life, his work, his character, not unlike writing an autobiography.

To make a proper will a man must think of himself as dead and gone, his house occupied by other men, his garden the demesne of developers who do not care for trees and ponds, his books as the stock of second-hand shops whose owners neither know nor care how thoughtfully he formed his library, his pictures as the possessions of the blind. Who of his friends will take his loving dogs? Who of his friends will see to his physical departure?

I have made several wills, the first as a young soldier, all of them the precautionary wills of those who do not think of death as immediately relevant. Even on the night before my ribcage was sawn open and my heart re-plumbed I was prepared to make a joke and bequeathed my eyes to Sarah Kent, the gushing art critic of *Time Out*, who is not blind but cannot see. Now, years later and of an age when almost every obituary page tells me of the deaths of old acquaintances, I no longer joke. Miss Kent is out of my will and my eyes and any other bits and pieces that could be useful are bequeathed to total strangers.

If no one wants them, then my cadaver is willed to any teaching hospital that has a use for bodies as material for aspiring anatomists. I quite like the idea of such absolute surrender to tactile intimacy, the hands that once played the violin reduced to bones and tendons, the brain that for so long thrilled in wonder at masterpieces of art and architecture, poked, prodded and perhaps preserved, like some old sheep or shark, in a jar of clear formaldehyde. As for the irreverent things that medical students are reputed to do with penises – so what? I too had my moments of adolescent ribaldry in the communal baths after playing rugger in my youth. And when the anatomists have done with me what George Stubbs and Leonardo did with the horse and criminal, what then? Ideally, what is left of me should be buried in the garden with the bones of the dozen dogs already there, nourishing the roots of yet another tree.

As for dying, I do not for one moment believe that death is 'the most beautiful adventure' or 'an awfully big adventure', or, indeed, an adventure of any kind; nor can I see it as an art. These are the romantic sentiments of poets and the brave. Death, in my experience, is a girl of twelve or so in the back of a crashed Peugeot 404, her skull cracked open like a box with a hinged lid. Death is the old man who had a heart attack in Kensington High Street a few months ago. Death is Lilian, an old friend, a sometime ballet dancer fallen on hard times, in a geriatric ward, her ascetic beauty hung about with tubes and drips, her spare body, even in its frailty, resisting the inevitable end; trained to endure, it instinctively resisted her intellectual command to let her go. Death is my mother, once of a beauty that stopped men in their stride, thirteen years a-dying, outliving all her friends, so that any who knew her at her death knew nothing of the former body and the former wit, but could recall only her senility; after those dreadful thirteen years even I struggle to leap the boundaries of memory to recover what I know to be another and a better truth.

'Men must endure their going hence,' said mad Lear in a sane moment. Endure; what a terrible prospect. Endure the crumbling memory. Endure the trembling hand of the octogenarian unsteady with the fork, unsteadier still with the lavatory paper. Endure the rheumy eyes that see hues differently, endure the creeping deafness that first denies conversation and then the music that might have made the loss of conversation tolerable. Endure the slackening sphincters and the stinks. What torment for the fastidious, lasting for years perhaps before the brain is addled and one is numbed to it. Imagine the slow erosion of pleasures, not of the flesh, though deprivation there induces madness in some men, but of the mind – no opera, no Schubert songs, no violin concertos, no theatre, no galleries, no books. Imagine not managing an oyster, the salt sea of it dripping from one's chin, the exquisite flesh of it running down one's shirt.

'A merciful release,' we say of death, and so it is when dying takes so long. Can we separate death from dying? The one is the inevitable consequence of the other but they seem two very different things, the dying often merciless, a prolonged torment as ingenious, excruciating and pitilessly cruel as any devised by Torquemada in the service of religion, death a sudden relaxation not only of the body, but the will. What virtue is there in such suffering? What virtue is there in the accompanying squalor? 'Who sweeps a room as for thy laws makes that and the action fine,' was all very well for George Herbert comfortably putting the seventeenth-century servant in her place, but does it really apply to bedpans and pisspots in modern hospitals where nurses vent their impatience on miserable males until they are gibbering with anguish and embarrassment? Death is not the great leveller – dying is. Dying reduces a man to leaking, dribbling and snivelling, to the helplessness of a baby, to impotent distress, to the long slow misery of being alive when he would rather be dead. That is levelling indeed.

I ask who of my friends will see to my physical departure? I think I know what natural death is like, having crept back from it; it too is a creeping thing, a slipping in and out of consciousness, the senses dwindling, waning, flagging and the will to resist falling away – and that is how I want to go, but swiftly. And if I cannot, if my body refuses when my brain commands, then I want some help. 'Do not go gentle into that good night . . . rage, rage against the dying of the light,' advised Dylan Thomas at thirty-eight, and at that age I too would probably have advocated rage, but most of us on reaching our allotted span would rather go gently, quietly, swiftly, cleanly, and some of us may need a push. I can think of no more loving act of friendship than that push. To me it seems a very cruel society that insists on my not determining the day and the manner of my going if death eludes me when I long for it.

Index

Agnew's 132, 200 –1, 207, 213, 254, 313, 317, 365–6, 387

Agnew, Geoffrey 279, 291, 315, 366, 374, 415

Albania 211, 425, 439, 440–2

Alley, Ronald 63, 512, 520

Allibone, David 133, 150, 468, 477, 483

Allibone, Jill 108–9, 123–8, 131–3, 139, 150, 153, 165, 211–12, 426, 439, 442–7, 468, 595

Alma-Tadema, Lawrence 111, 167, 185, 208, 219

Alpine Gallery 250, 359

Allsopp, Charles (Lord Hindlip) 222, 286, 291

Amaya, Mario 412

Ananoff, Alexandre 246–7

Annesley, Noël 235–6, 321–2, 328, 332, 334–5, 367, 389

Anthony, Henry Mark 386

Arnold, Bruce 609

Arts Council 121, 132, 173, 252, 260, 534, 536, 548–51, 556

Artus, Friedrich von 371–6, 380, 493

Artus, Ulrich von 326, 370

Ashton, Geoffrey 424

Atkinson, Lawrence 508

Audubon House Museum 415

Bacon, Francis 232, 337, 536, 593, 608–9

Barclay, David 232–4

Bareau, Juliet 140, 151, 174–5

Bargebuhr, Professor Frederick 134–6, 305

Baron, Wendy 140, 317, 608

Baruch 374–6

Baskett, John 433

Basquiat, Jean-Michel 378

Bates, Alan 601–2

BBC 37, 65, 68, 174, 252, 359, 435, 497, 500, 548, 585, 591, 594

Bean, George 438–9, 446

Beatty, Chester 387

Beccafumi, Domenico 253–4

Bendien, J.L. 517–19

Bennison, Geoffrey 272, 527

Beuys, Joseph 398, 534

Bevan, Robert 377–8, 529

Bewsey, Eric 258–60

Biddle, Eric 82–3

Bier, Herbert 251

Blacker, Harry 597

Blarenberghe, Louis-Nicolas 470

Blunt, Professor Anthony 45, 60, 61, 69, 110, 112, 115–18, 120, 121, 155, 165, 170, 178, 185, 233, 240, 268–75, 308, 314–19, 354, 388, 447, 467–501, 548, 561

Blunt, Christopher 481

Blunt, Wilfrid 481, 487

Boase, Professor Thomas 114, 115, 166–7

Bomberg, David 60, 136, 552

Bonham's 193, 204, 214, 285, 362, 366, 373, 493
Botte, Paul 300, 499, 501
Boucher (forgeries) 246–7
Boxer, Mark 498
Brabazon, Hercules Brabazon 202, 219, 338
Brackley, Frida (Mond) 253
Bradfield-England, Austin 307–8
Brealey, John 162, 464–6, 470, 500–3
Breslauer, Bernard 444
Brockwell, Maurice 79–81, 297
Bronzino 308, 366, 612
Brookner, Anita 118, 183, 483, 611
Brown, John Vere 258, 261–2, 600–2, 610–11
Brown, Oliver 242, 371–2, 377
Brown, Tina 496–8
Brueghel, Pieter 69, 117, 119, 129, 247, 310, 473, 486, 584
Burgess, Guy 69, 477, 482, 491, 495
Burne-Jones 208–9, 287–9, 614

Cairncross, John 482
Calmann, Hans 247, 251–2, 317, 323
Calmann, John 524
Canaletto 114, 182, 220, 362, 428
Cannon-Brookes, Peter 422
Caravaggio, Michelangelo 134, 176–9, 183, 206, 228, 240, 245, 248, 293, 295–6, 316, 375, 460, 526, 559, 593
Carey, George, Archbishop of Canterbury 540
Carter, Miranda 269, 273, 466, 481, 488–90
Carritt, David 235, 249, 291–9, 304, 319, 322–3, 328, 330, 334, 348, 367, 528

Cerano, Giovanni Battista (Crespi) 206–7
Cecil Higgins Museum 433
Chance, Peter (Ivan Oswald) 200–1, 205, 210, 214, 249–50, 267, 286, 288–9, 296, 298, 313, 324, 333
Chatsworth 327–9, 334, 367
Bruce Chatwin 418
Christie's 62, 125, 136, 137, 184, 193–4, 197–255, 267–338, 348–73, 378, 381, 388–9, 398, 411, 415, 420, 424, 435, 471, 475, 498, 504–6, 512–14, 519–25, 539, 602–4
Clare, Charles 62, 70, 112, 134–5, 141, 153
Claas, Peter 252, 359–61, 528
Clark, Kenneth Lord 6, 20, 115, 181, 517, 605
Coldstream, Sir William 9, 58–62
Colnaghi's 132, 216, 251, 275, 279, 317, 320, 364, 376, 388–9, 433, 506
Cook Collection (Doughty House) 297–9
Cooper, Thomas Sidney 163, 362–3
Cork, Richard 514, 529
Corvaya, Claudio 264–6, 273, 308, 330, 350–3, 580
Coulette, Pierre 250, 552
Courtauld Institute 21, 60, 62–4, 69, 99, 108–22, 131, 131–58, 160, 161, 166, 168, 174, 177–8, 182–6, 192, 206, 216, 223, 232–3, 240–1, 245, 249–50, 261, 265, 269–70, 273, 295–6, 300, 314, 335, 354–5, 359, 372, 388, 426, 441, 462, 472–7, 483–5, 491, 506, 547, 606

Index

Coughtrie, Kate 3, 4, 332
Craxton, John 56
Croft, John 304–5, 329
Croft-Murray, Edward 433
Crofton, Dr William 253–4
Crombie, Elsie 149, 492, 596
Crosthwaite, Moore 468, 477, 484

Dacre, Paul 531–3, 544
Dali, Salvador 337, 356, 394–411,
    496–7
Darracott, Colin 447, 461, 570
Davison, Bernice 541
Degas, Edgar 163, 242, 357, 434,
    473, 510, 514
Delbanco, Gustav 533
Delobre, Emile 501
Denvir, Bernard 550–1
Den Broeder, Fred 414
Devonshire, Deborah, Duchess of
    Devonshire 328
Dion-Delobre, Albert 501–3
Dobson, Frank 552
D'Offay, Anthony 377, 507–12, 520,
    609
Dubsky, Mario 412, 610
Dumont-Smith, Robert 429
Dunwoody, Gwyneth 393
Dürer, Albrecht 297, 473, 552
Durkin, Martin 586, 590
Duveen, Joseph 186, 250, 552

Easton, Malcolm 378
Elfer, Arpad 387
Éluard, Paul 405, 602
Emin, Tracey 521, 554–5
Emmett, Dick 506, 512–13
Epstein, Brian 413
Epstein, Jacob (forgeries) 508–10,
    520

Erim, Kenan 459
Etchells, Frederick 511–12

Fragonard (forgeries) 246–7, 357
Farmar, Francis 512–13
Fedden, Renée and Robin 214, 389,
    448, 453–4
Fielding, Noel 594
Fine Art Squad 505, 511, 519–22
Fitzwilliam Museum 212, 231, 284,
    298, 356, 424, 472, 604
Fontana, Carlo 170–1, 174, 181–2,
    194, 238, 240, 308
Frampton, George 3
Frank, Hans 376
Freeman, Simon 495, 505
Freud, Lucian 226, 378, 431, 444,
    556, 608–12
Freud, Sigmund 284, 403–4
Freyberg, Annabel 541, 544
Freyberg, Valerian 599–600, 698–9
Friedländer, Max 243–4
Fröhlich, Lili 213, 252
Fry, Roger 4, 85, 112, 151, 184, 242,
    270–1, 377, 559
Fuller, Peter 548

Gaskin, John 318–19, 462–3, 464,
    466–7, 470, 479–83, 487–9, 561
Gaudier-Brzeska, Henri (forgeries)
    508, 514, 520
Genière, Juliette de la 460
Gentileschi, Orazio 310, 580–1
George, David 458–9
George, John 551
Géricault, Théodore 362–3
Getty, Paul 237–8
Gill, Eric 415, 616
Ginner, Charles 16, 136, 164, 378–9,
    552

Index

Gloeden, Wilhelm von 309–10, 338

Golding, John 63, 470, 477–83, 487, 534

Gombrich, Sir Ernst 114, 116, 152

Gow, Andrew 461–2, 471–2, 482

Graham-Dixon, Andrew 594

Grant, Duncan 275, 377, 466–7

Green, Margery 190–1

Greig, Geordie 544–5

Guardi, Antonio and Francesco 293–4

Guardi (forgeries) 285

Haberdashers' School 17, 30, 36–56

Hamilton, Cuthbert 513, 522

Hannen, Guy 218, 236, 303, 319–22, 329, 331

Hardy, Bert 529–30

Harverson, Alan 32, 64–70, 302

Hasselt, Carlos van 212, 356, 604–6

Hastings, Max 537–41, 601

Heath, Edward 385

Heather, Vic 201–2, 206, 209, 217, 222, 312, 331–2

Hebborn, Eric 277, 314–19, 463, 489, 493

Helen, 'Baby' (Hall) 175, 223, 238–41, 260

Herbert, John 218, 234, 249, 268, 293, 301, 330

Heseltine, John Postle 23

Heseltine, Philip (alias Peter Warlock) 5, 17–23, 569

Hills, Denis 453–5

Hinks, Roger 183, 296

Hirst, Damien 521, 534, 583, 595

Hockney, David 79, 430–2, 494, 545, 551, 556, 560, 608

Hodgkin, Eliot 356–60, 381

Hogg, Min 527

Hope, Polly 457

Horobin, Sir Ian 32–3, 615

Hory, Elmyr de 435, 502–7, 514, 517, 520

Hoving, Thomas 375

Hulton, John 182, 421–2

Inness, Ivor 4

Irving, Clifford 504

Jackson, Tabitha 593–4

Jacobs, Michael 482

Jaffé, Michael 63, 241–4, 302

Januszczak, Waldemar 594

Jaray, Tess 611

Jarman, Derek 611–12

Jessett, Michael 48, 435–6

John, Augustus 16, 18, 22, 282–7, 289–91, 315, 319, 378

John, Dorelia 290–1

John, Gwen 377

Johnson, Brian 412

Johnson, Irene 37–8, 39

Johnson, Paul 534

Joll, James 470, 479, 481

Jones, Ivor 298, 424–6

Jones, Mark 482

Joppien, Rüdiger 606

Kay, Muriel 428–9

Keating, Tom 432–5

Kent, Sarah 535, 586, 617–18

King, Francis 529

King, Lawrence 526

Kirby, Louis 530–1

Kisling, Moïse 377

Kitaj, Ron 430–1

Kitson, Michael 63, 116, 118, 120, 121, 138–9, 158, 166, 470–1, 483, 500–1

Klee, Paul 242, 377

Knight, Harold 364

Index

Kokoschka, Oscar 242, 372, 377

Kolrud, Petter 21, 391–2, 449–51, 456

Koolman-Darnley, Louis William 507–9, 519–20

Koons, Jeff 378

Laclotte, Michel 176–81, 205, 212, 270, 279, 312, 548

Lagrenée, Louis 361

Lancaster, Mark 412

Langan, Peter and Susan 385, 427, 429–32, 494, 610

Lanthemann, Joseph 515–18

Larson, Sophia 580

Lasdun, Denys 424, 426

Lasko, Peter 484, 486

La Tour, Georges de 121, 174, 178–9, 300, 499–503

Lawrence, T. E. 392

Lawrenson, Miss 510, 512, 515

Lawson, Dominic 538

Leader, Benjamin Williams 219, 528

Lebrecht, Norman 542, 544

Leder, Christina 425

Legros, Fernand 502–4

Leighton, Lord Frederic 33

Leonardo da Vinci 172–3, 181, 278–80, 314, 355, 473–4, 486, 556–60, 583, 585–6, 593, 615

Levey, Michael 557

Lewis, Mark 505–14, 521

Lewisohn, Doreen 285–7, 291, 319–21, 424

Lindsay, The Hon. Patrick 185, 192, 205–6, 209–10, 216, 218, 227, 229, 231, 236, 241, 243, 249–50, 253, 267–8, 279, 300, 310, 323–5, 330–1, 333, 348–9, 381, 524

Linklater, Magnus 519, 522

Linnell, John 386

List, Herbert 370

Lloyd, Robert Wylie 189–90, 364

Long, Leo 482

Lorca, Frederico Garcia 400, 402, 408

Lowe, Ian 229–32

Lubbock, Tom 594

Lucie-Smith, Edward 272, 534, 551

Ludwig II of Bavaria 593

Lugt, Frits 222, 604

Macaulay, Rose 455

MacGregor, Neil 45, 118, 121–2, 359, 469

Mahon, Sir Denis 207, 270–3, 296, 328, 465–7, 547

Mander, Raymond 427

Mantegna, Andrea 23, 162, 164, 315, 464, 465, 473

Margaret, Princess 492–3

Martin, Sir Alec 186–92, 197–200, 205, 208, 212–14, 300, 313, 348

Martin, William 184–93, 197–200, 205, 208, 212–14, 300, 381, 394

McCrindle, Joseph 165, 275–7, 315, 411–20, 427, 466, 471, 480, 483, 487–8, 496, 610–11

Meegeren, Han van 199, 513

Melville, Theo 355

Menashe, Samuel 602

Meryon, Charles 362

Millar, Sir Oliver 63, 138

Milow, Keith 412, 610

Mimara. Ante Topic 374–6

Minton, John 225–7, 315

Mitchenson, Joe 427

Index

Modigliani, Amedeo 240, 242–3, 245, 504, 506, 514–18, 520, 522
Monet, Claude 149, 161–2, 212, 377
Montagu, Lord of Beaulieu 106–7, 226, 391
Montgomery, Peter 477–8
Moore, Henry 609
Moreau, Gustave 501
Moreton, Nicholas 613
Morrish, John 234–5, 265
Munnings, Sir Alfred 79–80
Murphy, Terry 507–8
Murray, Peter 63, 123

Nairne, Sandy 534
Nash, Paul 9, 16
Nathanson, Richard 518
Nevinson, C.R.W. 387, 514
Nicolson, Benedict 176, 217, 499
Noel, Captain John 280–1

O'Connor, Patrick 293–4, 502
Oman, Charles 183

Paderewski, Ignacy 614
Patani, Osvaldo 518
Peat, Kim 586–7
Pepper, Ernest 366–7
Perls, Klaus 517–18
Pétridès, Paul 245–6
Picasso, Pablo 61, 122, 242, 248–9, 262, 287, 355, 362, 556, 560
Pillsbury, Ted 412, 427
Plante, David 412–13
Pool, Phoebe 60–1
Pope-Hennessy, Sir John 116, 171, 182–3, 186, 215, 271, 392, 503
Popham, Arthur Ewart 214–15, 281–2, 327
Pouncey, Philip 247–8, 328, 333

Poussin, Nicolas 80, 118, 121, 134, 165, 174, 176, 213–14, 220, 268–75, 372, 451, 464–7, 470–1, 486, 488, 500
Procktor, Patrick 430–1, 610
Purves, Libby 497–8

Ranken, William Bruce Ellis 3
Raphael 117, 209, 248, 296, 310, 330, 375, 376, 464, 592, 607
Ratjen, Adolf 370
Raven, Simon 391, 432
Rees-Jones, Professor Stephen 160, 162, 296, 500–1
Rembrandt 14, 23, 119, 134, 150, 157, 161–2, 163, 202, 216, 235, 267, 330, 335, 367, 372, 375, 434, 473, 485–6, 612
Renoir, Pierre-Auguste 16, 112, 205, 434, 473, 506, 508, 511, 514
Reynolds. Michael 609–10
Reynolds, Joshua 136–7, 182, 184, 186, 206, 348
Richter, Gerhard 378
Riemensberger, Johann Peter 425
Riley, Bridget 434
Robbins, Professor Lionel 116
Roboz, Zsuzsi 599
Röthlisberger, Marcel 121, 244–5
Romare, Raymond de 377
Roper, Lanning 411
Rosenbourg, Pierre 470
Rosenthal, Norman 534–5, 545–6, 549
Rostal, Max 57–8, 62
Rothermere, Lord 544
Rothschild, Jacob (Lord) 388–9, 412
Rothschild, Victor (Lord) 464

Index

Rubens, Peter Paul 111, 119, 134, 136, 159, 166, 226, 234, 239, 241–2, 244, 329–31, 334, 354, 372, 375, 446, 473, 474, 485–6, 604–5
Rubinstein, Michael 477–82, 486–7
Ruhemann, Helmuth 160–2

Saatchi, Charles 615
Sands, Sarah 546
Sargent, John Singer, 136, 202, 312–14, 377
Saxl, Fritz 490
Schiff, Gert 607
Scott-Elliot, Aydua 171–2, 174, 181, 194, 308
Seddon, Joan 153–4, 162–5, 167, 210–11, 215, 232, 284–91, 298, 424, 464–5
Segers, Hercules 367
Seiferheld, Helene 317, 364–5
Seilern, Count Antoine 472–7, 547
Serota, Sir Nicholas 550, 555, 612
Sestieri family 413
Seurat, Georges 300–1, 594
Sewell, Jessica (mother) 1–16, 17–23, 24–35, 38–9, 45, 57–9, 61, 65–6, 69–70, 77, 78, 85, 98, 102–4, 124, 142, 149, 212, 194, 223, 239, 265–6, 284, 308, 325, 332
Sewell, Robert (stepfather) 24–35, 40, 58, 65–6, 70, 223, 266
Shaw, James Byam 251, 279, 320, 327–8, 388, 474
Shortis, Martin 531
Sherrin, Daniel 12, 219
Sickert, Walter 4, 16, 112, 136, 140, 187–8, 316–17, 377, 378, 385, 427, 433–4, 458, 552, 608

Simmons, Captain Arthur 368–9
Simpson, Colin 480, 495, 499–502, 505, 518–19, 522
Skeffington-Lodge, Tom 528–9
Skippe, John 204, 214, 254
Soames, Emma 499
Sobien, Inka 533
Solomon, Philip 536–7
Solomon, Yonty 602
Sorabji, Francina 150, 154
Soutine, Chaim 377
Spalding, Dick 469, 484, 489
Spear, Ruskin 609
Spector, Stephen 383–4
Spencer, Stanley 79–80, 593
Spencer-Churchill, Captain Edward George 310–11, 314–15
Stangos, Nikos 412–13, 525–6, 534, 610
Stark, Freya 438, 458–9
Steven, Stewart 523–8
Stewart, Angus 497
Strong, Sir Roy 183, 306
Stoskopff, Sebastian 121, 205, 218
Stuker, Jürg 364
Sutch, Harry 381–3

Talbot, Kenrick 504–7, 514, 517, 520, 521
Tchachnik, Ilya Gregorovitch 508
Thomson, Kenneth (Lord) 386–7
Thyssen, Hans Heinrich (Baron) 514
Tiepolo, Giandomenico 293, 319–20, 322, 434
Tindle, David 358–9
Titian 23, 27, 111, 117, 118–19, 192, 220, 270–1, 372, 375, 474, 486, 547, 553–5, 577, 607
Tonks, Henry 385

Index

Tour, Georges de la 121, 174, 178–9, 300, 499–501, 503

Troutman, Philip 151, 207, 223, 240

Turner, Colin 505–12, 515–18, 519–21

Urbinati, Giulio 516–17

Van Gogh, Vincent 167, 242, 371–2, 375, 378

Vanvitelli, Luigi 364–5

Vaughan, Keith 258, 262–3, 432

Vilag, Nicholas 427–30

Waddington, Leslie 535

Wadley, Veronica 541–4

Wadsworth, Edward 513–14

Waite, Terry 532–3

Warburg, Aby 114, 115, 490

Warhol, Andy 337, 378, 419–20

Waterhouse, Professor Ellis 137, 198–200, 228, 230, 233, 271, 306, 314

Watson, Sir Francis 183, 187, 247, 293

Watteau, Jean-Antoine 247, 383, 473

Waugh, Michael 446–9, 563

Weissbort, George 510–11, 515, 516

Whinney, Dr Margaret 111–12, 115, 137–8, 142

White, Chris 479

White, Professor John 118, 123–4, 131, 547

Wilde, Professor Johannes, 111, 118–20, 153, 157, 167, 328, 330, 473–4, 475, 486, 547

Williams, Heathcote 610

Wilson, Peter 279, 280, 293, 517

Winckelmann, Johann Joachim 594

Wittkower, Rudi 490

Wolfson, Frances Mitchell 416–17

Wolfson, Mitchell II 415

Wollesen, Professor 326–7

Wood, Christopher 302–3

Wragg, Tom 328, 367–8

Wright, Christopher 499, 503

Wright, Harold 216

Wright, Roy 530

Wyndham, John (Lord Egremont) 365–6

Zarnecki, George 484, 486